D0302979

The King, The Crown, and
The Duchy of Lancaster

The King, the Crown, and the Duchy of Lancaster

Public Authority and Private Power, 1399–1461

HELEN CASTOR

OXFORD
UNIVERSITY PRESS

OXFORD

UNIVERSITY PRESS

Great Clarendon Street, Oxford, OX2 6DP
Oxford University Press is a department of the University of Oxford.
It furthers the University's objective of excellence in research, scholarship,
and education by publishing worldwide in

Oxford New York

Athens Auckland Bangkok Bogotá Buenos Aires Calcutta
Cape Town Chennai Dar es Salaam Delhi Florence Hong Kong Istanbul
Karachi Kuala Lumpur Madrid Melbourne Mexico City Mumbai
Nairobi Paris São Paulo Singapore Taipei Tokyo Toronto Warsaw

and associated companies in Berlin Ibadan

Oxford is a registered trade mark of Oxford University Press
in the UK and certain other countries

Published in the United States
by Oxford University Press Inc., New York

British Library Cataloguing in Publication Data

Data available

Library of Congress Cataloging in Publication Data
Castor, Helen.
The king, the crown, and the Duchy of Lancaster : public authority and private power,
1399–1461 / Helen Castor.
p.cm.
Includes bibliographical references and index.
1. Great Britain—Politics and government—1399–1485. 2. Lancaster (England :
Duchy)—Politics and government. I. Title.

DA245.C37 2000   942.04—dc21   00-025746

ISBN 0-19-820622-4

1 3 5 7 9 10 8 6 4 2

Typeset by Regent Typesetting, London
Printed in Great Britain
on acid-free paper by
T.J. International Ltd.
Padstow, Cornwall

For G. *and* G.

Preface

There are a number of people whose expertise and encouragement have made the task of writing this book very much easier. First, I owe an immeasurable debt to Christine Carpenter, who supervised the research on which the book is based. Without her illuminating and challenging supervision, her commitment, and her warm encouragement, what follows could not have been written. I would like to thank Gerald Harriss and Barrie Dobson for their always constructive criticism and wise advice. Catherine Holmes, Rosemary Horrox, Ted Powell, and Simon Walker have been inspiring in discussion and generous with information. My thanks go particularly to John Watts, Benjamin Thompson, and Richard Partington: this book has benefited greatly from their learning and perception as historians; I have benefited greatly from their friendship. Needless to say, any mistakes and misjudgements which remain here are all my own.

I am very grateful to the Master and Fellows of Gonville and Caius College, Cambridge, the Master and Fellows of Jesus College, Cambridge, and the Master and Fellows of Sidney Sussex College, Cambridge, for the support which I have received as graduate student, research fellow, and fellow. I should also like to thank the staff of the various libraries and record offices that I have consulted, and particularly those of the Public Record Office, for their assistance. At OUP, first Tony Morris and then Ruth Parr have not only shown endless patience, but provided invaluable encouragement.

Julian Ferraro has contributed more than he knows to the writing of this book: thank you. Finally, I should like to thank my parents, an unfailing source of support and inspiration. The book is dedicated to them, with love.

H.R.C.

Contents

List of Maps   xi

List of Abbreviations   xii

Part I. Introduction   1

1. Public Authority and Private Power   3

2. The Duchy of Lancaster and the Lancastrian Kings   22
   1. The Lancastrian affinity to 1399   22
   2. The Duchy of Lancaster under Henry IV   25
   3. The Duchy of Lancaster under Henry V   32
   4. The Duchy of Lancaster under Henry VI   38

Part II. The Crown, the Duchy of Lancaster, and the Rule
         of the Localities: East Anglia, 1399–1461   51

3. 1399–1430: The Lancastrian Crown in East Anglian Politics   53
   1. Patterns of lordship in East Anglia to 1399   53
   2. 1399–1430: the establishment of a crown connection   59

4. 1430–1450: The Duke of Suffolk and the Rule of East
   Anglia   82
   1. 1430–1437: the rise of Suffolk's lordship   82
   2. 1437–1447: the de la Pole affinity   93
   3. 1437–1447: the challenge to Suffolk's lordship   100
   4. 1447–1450: the politics of confrontation   119
   5. East Anglia in the 1440s: the Paston evidence   128

5. 1450–1461: The Struggle for Control   156

Part III. The Crown, the Duchy of Lancaster, and the Rule
          of the Localities: Derbyshire and Staffordshire,
          1399–1461   191

6. 1399–1414: King and Duchy   193
   1. The Lancastrian affinity in the north midlands to 1399   193
   2. 1399–1414: the Lancastrian affinity and the Lancastrian
      crown   202

7. 1414–1440: Crown and Nobility   225
   1. 1414–1422: political assimilation and royal rule   225
   2. 1422–1440: the growth of noble lordship   234

8. 1437–1461: The Duke of Buckingham and the Rule of the
   North Midlands   253

9. Conclusion   306

Bibliography   313

Index   327

List of Maps

1. Duchy of Lancaster estates in East Anglia   54
2. The Pastons and their neighbours in northern Norfolk   132
3. Duchy of Lancaster estates in Derbyshire and Staffordshire   194

List of Abbreviations

BIHR	*Bulletin of the Institute of Historical Research*
BL	British Library
CAD	*A Descriptive Catalogue of Ancient Deeds . . .*
Cal. IPM	*Calendarium Inquisitionum Post Mortem*
CCR	*Calendar of the Close Rolls*
CChR	*Calendar of the Charter Rolls*
CFR	*Calendar of the Fine Rolls*
Complete Peerage	Cokayne, G. E., *The Complete Peerage*, ed. H. V. Gibbs *et al.*, 13 vols. (London, 1910–59)
CPR	*Calendar of the Patent Rolls*
DCL	Derby Central Library
DKR	*Reports of the Deputy Keeper of the Public Records*
DNB	Stephen, L., and Lee, S. (eds.), *Dictionary of National Biography*, 63 vols. (London, 1885–1900)
DRO	Derbyshire Record Office
Eg.	Egerton
EHR	*English Historical Review*
Harl.	Harley
HMC	*Historical Manuscripts Commission*
LRO	Leicestershire Record Office
NA	Nottinghamshire Archives
NLW	National Library of Wales
NRO	Norfolk Record Office
NUL	Nottingham University Library
PL Davis	Davis, N. (ed.), *Paston Letters and Papers of the Fifteenth Century*, 2 vols. (Oxford, 1971–6)
PL Gairdner	Gairdner, J. (ed.), *The Paston Letters*, 6 vols. (London, 1904)
POPC	Nicolas, N. H. (ed.), *Proceedings and Ordinances of the Privy Council*, 7 vols. (London, 1834–7)
Return of the Name	*Return of the Name of Every Member of the Lower House of the Parliament of England, 1213–1874*, Parliamentary Papers, lxii pts. i–iii (London, 1878), pt. i, 1213–1702
Rot. Parl.	*Rotuli Parliamentorum*
SRO	Staffordshire Record Office
Suff. RO	Suffolk Record Office
TRHS	*Transactions of the Royal Historical Society*
Wm Salt Lib.	William Salt Library, Stafford

In all quotations from manuscript sources, abbreviations have been expanded, the use of the letters 'u' and 'v' has been rationalized, and the letter 'thorn' has been rendered as 'th'. Wherever possible, reference has been made to both Gairdner's 1904 edition of the Paston Letters and Davis's edition of 1971–6; if only one reference is given, the document concerned appears only in that edition.

Part I

Introduction

Public Authority and Private Power

In the fourth year of the reign of Elizabeth I, the question of the relationship between the king, the crown, and the Duchy of Lancaster was addressed by crown lawyers. The fact that the Lancastrian kings had chosen to maintain the Duchy as a private possession, entirely separate from their tenure of the throne, meant that the question of the legal status of the Lancastrian estates had become a *cause célèbre*, which was being tried—not for the first time—in 1561 in relation to Duchy lands which had been leased out by Edward VI. The lawyers agreed that 'the King has in him two Bodies, *viz.*, a Body natural, and a Body politic. His Body natural (if it be considered in itself) is a Body mortal, subject to all Infirmities that come by Nature or Accident, to the Imbecility of Infancy or old Age, and to the like Defects that happen to the natural Bodies of other People. But his Body politic is a Body that cannot be seen or handled, consisting of Policy and Government, and constituted for the Direction of the People, and the Management of the public weal . . .'.[1] Because it belonged to the king as duke of Lancaster and not to the crown, the Duchy had therefore been held by the Lancastrian kings in their body natural, rather than their body politic.[2]

This was the most subtle and elaborate formulation yet recorded of the distinction between the private person of the monarch and the public persona which he embodied by virtue of his office; indeed, it forms the starting-point for Ernst Kantorowicz's classic study of the concept of the King's Two Bodies.[3] However, the significance of the distinction itself had been apparent from the earliest years of Lancastrian rule. By 1405, for example, royal judges were already differentiating clearly between those things 'que appertaine al corone' and those, such as 'son duchie de Lancaster', which the king held 'come auter person'.[4] By declaring in 1399 that his Duchy of Lancaster should

---

[1] E. Plowden, *Commentaries or Reports* (London, 1816), i. 212–12a; E. H. Kantorowicz, *The King's Two Bodies: A Study in Medieval Political Theology* (Princeton, 1957), 7.

[2] Though note the complexity of the 'mystic fiction' at which the jurists arrived: the body natural and the body politic remain distinct capacities, while at the same time being conjoined to form an indivisible unity: Kantorowicz, *The King's Two Bodies*, 3, 9–15, 20–3; Plowden, *Commentaries*, i. 212–22a.

[3] Kantorowicz, *The King's Two Bodies*, 7.

[4] S. B. Chrimes, *English Constitutional Ideas in the Fifteenth Century* (Cambridge, 1936), 352–3; Kantorowicz, *The King's Two Bodies*, 370.

continue to be treated exactly as it would have been 'if we had never assumed the ensign of royal dignity',[5] Henry IV was therefore ensuring that the private property which he held in his capacity as duke of Lancaster would remain separate from, and unaffected by, his public estate as king. This was a distinction in law which reflected and emphasized the difference in kind between the public authority of the crown—that which was 'constituted for the Direction of the People, and the Management of the public weal'—and the private power which the duke of Lancaster, like any other nobleman, enjoyed as a territorial magnate.

Private power of this kind, and the role within the polity of the nobility and gentry in particular, has formed the central focus of the resurgence of interest in the political history of late medieval England inspired by the intellectual legacy of K. B. McFarlane.[6] McFarlane's own work on the nobility, conceived as it was as a corrective to the institutional focus of the Whig tradition,[7] emphasized the role of individuals and of individual self-interest as a motivating force within politics, and suggested that the disposal of patronage played a key part in harnessing the interests of the various participants in the polity to form a coherent structure of power. Over the past three decades, this has become the dominant theme in the historiography of the period; medieval politics have been investigated largely in terms of personal relationships and private interests, and the issue of patronage has been placed at the heart of discussions of government.[8]

The influence of this approach has been such that, along with the abandonment of analysis of the institutions of government, the very concept of government as a public, national enterprise has all but disappeared. In so far as the nature of the king's 'Body politic' has been considered at all, it has usually been assumed that the concept of the

---

[5] W. Hardy (trans. and ed.), *The Charters of the Duchy of Lancaster* (London, 1845), 137–8.

[6] R. H. Britnell and A. J. Pollard (eds.), *The McFarlane Legacy* (Stroud, 1995), pp. xi–xii.

[7] See K. B. McFarlane, *The Nobility of Later Medieval England* (Oxford, 1973), 280; C. Carpenter, 'Political and Constitutional History: Before and After McFarlane', in Britnell and Pollard (eds.), *The McFarlane Legacy*, 185–6.

[8] J. R. Lander, for example, concluded that 'the king who administered his vast patronage wisely and fairly . . . could hope for enough co-operation from the aristocracy and their clients to make the system work. If the king was a minor, senile, or weak in resolution, control of patronage fell to a faction and the excluded revolted': J. R. Lander, *Conflict and Stability in Fifteenth-Century England* (London, 1969), 183. See also R. A. Griffiths, 'Patronage, Politics and the Principality of Wales, 1413–61', in H. Hearder and H. R. Loyn (eds.), *British Government and Administration: Studies Presented to S. B. Chrimes* (Cardiff, 1974), 69; R. A. Griffiths, introduction to Griffiths (ed.), *Patronage, the Crown and the Provinces* (Gloucester, 1981), 13; C. D. Ross, introduction to Ross (ed.), *Patronage, Pedigree and Power* (Gloucester, 1979), 9; and see comments on late medieval historiographical development in E. Powell, 'After "After McFarlane": The Poverty of Patronage and the Case for Constitutional History', in D. J. Clayton, R. G. Davies, and P. McNiven (eds.), *Trade, Devotion and Governance* (Stroud, 1994), 1–2, 8–10.

'public weal' was a rhetorical cloak in which private interests might conveniently be wrapped.[9] However, despite the self-consciously McFarlaneite framework within which this research has been pursued, the characterization of government as a whole in these terms sits uneasily with McFarlane's demonstration, particularly in his later work, that under normal circumstances there existed a community of interests between the king and the landed classes. The crown did not have to protect its position by purchasing the co-operation of a mercenary and limitlessly competitive nobility; rather, 'the area of possible conflict was extraordinarily small and any competent king had no difficulty in avoiding it'.[10] Some recent work has now begun to explore the king's role in underpinning this framework of shared interest, a process which has started to shift the focus of discussion back to the public functions of the crown, and indeed to raise questions about the interaction of public authority with private interests. This is making possible a new attempt to explore the late medieval constitution, not in Stubbs's institutional sense, but, as Christine Carpenter has recently described it, in the sense of 'political and governmental structures, and the beliefs of those who participate in them about how those structures should operate'.[11]

Of what did this community of interests at the heart of the late medieval constitution consist?[12] The support of the king's landed subjects, in a society lacking a permanent bureaucracy or military hierarchy independent of local power structures, underwrote royal authority, and allowed him to give that authority active expression. Equally, the supreme authority of the king underwrote the position of his subjects. The possession of land, the basis of private power, could only be guaranteed in a competitive society by universal acceptance of a consistent and binding authority—in effect, of royal law, which it was the king's duty to uphold. In theory, then, the king represented the absolute principles on which all individual rights depended. The universal application of the king's law protected the realm internally

---

[9] For discussion of this assumption and its limitations, see J. L. Watts, *Henry VI and the Politics of Kingship* (Cambridge, 1996), 6–7; J. L. Watts, 'Ideas, Principles and Politics', in A. J. Pollard (ed.), *The Wars of the Roses* (London, 1995), 111–20.

[10] McFarlane, *Nobility of Later Medieval England*, 121.

[11] As Carpenter notes, McFarlane's published work in fact gives little sustained attention to the public dimensions of government: Carpenter, 'Political and Constitutional History', 176, 193.

[12] For the argument that follows in this paragraph and the next, see C. Carpenter, *Locality and Polity: A Study of Warwickshire Landed Society, 1401–99* (Cambridge, 1992), 283–5, 347–8, 351–4, 621–5, 627–8, 631–2; C. Carpenter, *The Wars of the Roses: Politics and the Constitution in England, c.1437–1509* (Cambridge, 1997), chs. 2 and 3; E. Powell, *Kingship, Law, and Society: Criminal Justice in the Reign of Henry V* (Oxford, 1989), 29–37; G. L. Harriss, introduction to K. B. McFarlane, *England in the Fifteenth Century: Collected Essays* (London, 1981), pp. xxiii–xxv; Watts, *Henry VI*, 17–31.

through the maintenance of order; the king's right to call on the resources of all his subjects when necessary for defence protected the realm from external attack. It is a reflection of the public nature of this authority that by the fifteenth century the concept of the 'crown' in its broadest sense represented not the king alone, but the unity formed by the ruler and the ruled, the king and the realm.[13] The formal, official manifestations of royal rule—the increasingly sophisticated judicial machinery and central bureaucracy, and the developing role of parliament—therefore expressed and reflected the king's public authority; they did not in themselves constitute it.

Nor was it only through these formalized structures that the public authority of the crown was exercised. The absolute principles of royal law could not in practice be enforced absolutely because, on a theoretical level, they took no account of equitable justice, and because, on a practical one, landed society was itself responsible for implementing the legal constraints to which it was also subject. However, the king's authority was able to contain these limitations by its simultaneous embodiment of the concepts of justice and lordship. The king's duty to maintain the law was paralleled by his obligation to temper his judgement with mercy and with due regard to the requirements of equity. His authority was also responsive and representative, and as much a part of the informal hierarchies of lordship and service as it was of the formal structures of government. Like any other lord, the king was a 'means for the representation and realisation of interests'.[14] Unlike any other lord, the interests he represented were those of the 'common weal'—the realm as a whole—which, while inevitably failing to satisfy every individual interest, provided the foundations of a stable political structure within which individual interests could safely be pursued. In other words, inasmuch as self-interest determined the functioning of the late medieval polity, it was the mutual self-interest of the landed classes, which upheld royal authority as the public linchpin of a social order that provided the context for their individual ambitions. Moreover, the impulses of political pragmatism were submerged in the culture of a profoundly hierarchical society dominated by social and religious obligations which underlined the universal duty of obedience to the monarch.[15] At every level, the functioning of the complex combination of law and office, obligation and influence, as a viable

---

[13] Chrimes, *English Constitutional Ideas*, 14; Kantorowicz, *The King's Two Bodies*, 360–4; G. L. Harriss, *King, Parliament, and Public Finance in Medieval England to 1369* (Oxford, 1975), 510; Watts, *Henry VI*, 22.

[14] Watts, *Henry VI*, 67.

[15] Powell, *Kingship, Law, and Society*, 37–8; R. Horrox, *Richard III: A Study of Service* (Cambridge, 1989), 5; Harriss, introduction to McFarlane, *England in the Fifteenth Century*, p. xviii; Watts, *Henry VI*, 17–21, 35–8.

and co-ordinated social structure depended ultimately on the public authority of the crown.

However, the crown has not, for the most part, been the main focus of recent work on late medieval political society. Instead, research has once again followed the lead of McFarlane, who suggested that 'it is only by undertaking a large number of local surveys that a just understanding of political history can be obtained'.[16] A range of studies both of individual lords and their regional followings, and of local societies and the nobles with whom they were associated, have described the multifarious operation of lordship and service which permeated the social, political, judicial, and administrative relations between the nobility and gentry.[17] This focus on local power structures has brought many rewards, and some important recent work has used detailed regional analysis to shed new light on the wider workings of the constitution and the ties that bound the locality into the realm as a whole.[18] However, the widespread emphasis on private interest as the defining feature of politics, and the fact that some local studies have treated county societies as discrete political units in isolation from wider regional or national structures, have meant that the nature and functions of royal authority have been only marginal elements in the account of political society constructed by much of this research.

Perhaps with this in mind, some historians have now begun to extend analyses of the interplay of affinities and the workings of lordship directly into further exploration of late medieval kingship. Just as investigation of the operation of noble lordship has been accompanied by discussion of the lordship of the crown, so analysis of the functioning of magnate affinities has been paralleled by examination of 'the greatest of all these affinities, that of the king'.[19] It has been suggested

---

[16] McFarlane, *Nobility of Later Medieval England*, 296.

[17] See, for example, E. Acheson, *A Gentry Community: Leicestershire in the Fifteenth Century, c.1422–c.1485* (Cambridge, 1992); M. J. Bennett, *Community, Class and Careerism: Cheshire and Lancashire Society in the Age of 'Sir Gawain and the Green Knight'* (Cambridge, 1983); C. Carpenter, 'The Beauchamp Affinity: A Study of Bastard Feudalism at Work', *EHR* 95 (1980); Carpenter, *Locality and Polity*; S. J. Payling, *Political Society in Lancastrian England: The Greater Gentry of Nottinghamshire* (Oxford, 1991); A. J. Pollard, *North-Eastern England during the Wars of the Roses* (Oxford, 1990); C. Rawcliffe, *The Staffords, Earls of Stafford and Dukes of Buckingham, 1394–1521* (Cambridge, 1978); S. Walker, *The Lancastrian Affinity 1361–99* (Oxford, 1990); S. M. Wright, *The Derbyshire Gentry in the Fifteenth Century*, Derbyshire Record Society, 8 (Chesterfield, 1983); R. E. Archer, 'The Mowbrays: Earls of Nottingham and Dukes of Norfolk, to 1432', unpublished D.Phil. thesis (Oxford, 1984); I. D. Rowney, 'The Staffordshire Political Community, 1440–1500', unpublished Ph.D. thesis (Keele, 1981).

[18] See Carpenter, *Locality and Polity*; Powell, *Kingship, Law, and Society*.

[19] C. Given-Wilson, *The Royal Household and the King's Affinity: Service, Politics and Finance in England, 1360–1413* (New Haven, 1986), 203. See also D. A. L. Morgan, 'The King's Affinity in the Polity of Yorkist England', *TRHS* 5th series, 23 (1973); Payling, *Political Society*, ch. 5 ('Office-Holding and the King's Affinity').

that developments in the later fourteenth and early fifteenth centuries constituted a critical stage in the evolution of the 'royal affinity'—a political connection in the localities directly attached to the personal authority of the king. 'Like late medieval magnates', Chris Given-Wilson writes, '. . . the king traded money and good lordship for as widespread a network of local connections as he could afford. These men were the heart of the royal affinity.'[20] Given-Wilson traces this development back to the change during the reign of Edward III from royal retaining of household knights essentially for military service, to that of knights of the chamber, whose service, he argues, was more wide-ranging, including substantial involvement in the king's domestic government as well as his military campaigns. This paved the way for 'an even more significant change' under Richard II, 'that is, the establishment of a body of "king's knights" outwith the household, but attached to the king by indentures of retainer, and clearly employed by him not so much for their military value but for their local influence and authority'—a process made necessary by the growing importance of the gentry in both local and national politics, and 'the consequent need for the king to harness their skills and influence to his cause'.[21] Richard's retaining policy has been seen as the precursor of the significant role played in Henry IV's government by his Lancastrian affinity.[22] In turn, the growing importance of the royal household and retinue during the fifteenth century has been identified as the logical extension of these earlier developments; the centralizing tendencies of Yorkist government set the seal on increasing royal intervention in local affairs to pave the way for the emergence of a court-centred polity under the Tudors.[23]

However, although descriptions of the expression of 'royal lordship' in the formation of a 'king's affinity' merge seamlessly into the vocabulary used to describe other aspects of the late medieval polity, this apparent conceptual continuity should not be taken for granted. The application of the concept of a constantly evolving 'royal affinity' to all

[20] C. Given-Wilson, 'The King and the Gentry in Fourteenth-Century England', *TRHS* 5th series, 37 (1987), 99; see also Given-Wilson, *The Royal Household*, 203.

[21] Given-Wilson, 'The King and the Gentry', 89–92, 99. This argument has found substantial support in Nigel Saul's recent study of the reign of Richard II, though Saul stresses the novelty of Richard's policy rather more than Given-Wilson: N. Saul, *Richard II* (New Haven and London, 1997), 265–6, 440.

[22] Given-Wilson, *The Royal Household*, 226, 231–2, 262–6; Saul, *Richard II*, 440; A. L. Brown, 'The Reign of Henry IV: The Establishment of the Lancastrian Regime', in S. B. Chrimes, C. D. Ross, and R. A. Griffiths (eds.), *Fifteenth-Century England, 1399–1509* (Manchester, 1972), 19.

[23] Given-Wilson, *The Royal Household*, 264–5; Saul, *Richard II*, 440; D. Starkey, 'The Age of the Household: Politics, Society and the Arts, *c.*1350–*c.*1550', in S. Medcalf (ed.), *The Context of English Literature: The Later Middle Ages* (London, 1981), 268–71, 273–4; C. D. Ross, *Edward IV* (London, 1974), 312–13, 322–3; J. Guy, *Tudor England* (Oxford, 1988), 165–6; see also discussion in Carpenter, *Locality and Polity*, 633–4.

stages of this development obscures key issues raised by these profound changes in English political society. Royal retaining of lesser men for military service, for example, was a long-established method of gathering a fighting force.[24] Though the term 'knight of the chamber' does seem to have replaced that of 'knight of the household' by the end of the reign of Edward III, it is far less clear either that these were discrete terms, or that the change denoted a process of evolution from one set of distinct functions to another.[25] If Edward was throughout his reign prepared to entrust men of knightly status with a wider range of responsibilities than 'household knights' had previously enjoyed, this should perhaps be seen in the context of his consistent willingness to make creative and flexible use of all the resources of his realm, including the service of able lieutenants whether they were noble or gentle in origin.[26]

By contrast, royal retaining of members of the gentry in the localities by life indenture for general domestic service in peacetime—the policy which Richard II was actively pursuing in the 1390s[27]—was a radically new development. Moreover, its purpose was very different from

---

[24] K. B. McFarlane, ' "Bastard Feudalism" ', in McFarlane, *England in the Fifteenth Century*, 24–6; M. McKisack, *The Fourteenth Century* (Oxford, 1959), 234–6.

[25] The key determinant of the number of knights attached to the royal household (whether they are described as 'household' or 'chamber' knights) appears to be military activity in which the king was personally involved. The 57 knights within Edward's household in 1359–60, when the king led his last major expedition to France, for example, contrasts both with the total of 19 knights present in the household during 1353–4 (and therefore in the interval between the end of one campaign in the summer of 1352 and the resumption of war in Nov. 1355), and with the less than half-a-dozen knights identified in the majority of the wardrobe accounts examined by Chris Given-Wilson for the years between 1360 and 1377. Before 1360, Given-Wilson's evidence suggests, the distinction between knights of the household and those of the chamber was far from clear-cut, and the terms 'knight of the household', 'knight of the chamber', 'knight of the chamber and hall', and 'bachelor of the household' were used flexibly, and sometimes interchangeably, rather than categorically. The distinctive aspect of the period after 1360 seems to be that, for the first protracted period in the century, the royal household became primarily a domestic rather than a military organization. The decisive change in terminology from 'household' to 'chamber' knight may well reflect this change in the nature of the household—the retreat of the ageing king from active involvement in warfare—rather than the development of a new kind of service to the king and a new category of job description. Certainly, the very small number of 'chamber knights' identified between 1360 and 1377 makes any attempt to draw general conclusions about their political activities highly problematic. For Given-Wilson's discussion, see *The Royal Household*, 204–11, and appendices III and IV. I am very grateful to Richard Partington for discussing these issues with me in the context of his own research on the government of Edward III. His forthcoming Cambridge Ph.D. thesis, 'The Governance of Edward III, 1330–1369', will offer an important and wide-ranging reassessment both of Edward's rule and of the nature of the 14th-cent. polity.

[26] It should be noted in this context that Edward I's household knights had also filled a wide variety of roles, including service as commissioners and diplomats (see Given-Wilson, *The Royal Household*, 206).

[27] Given-Wilson, *The Royal Household*, 211–16; J. A. Tuck, *Richard II and the English Nobility* (London, 1973), 180; Saul, *Richard II*, 265–8.

Edward III's deployment of the manpower at his disposal, in that it was a policy which seems to have stemmed from Richard's failure to recognize the public nature of his authority and the necessarily co-operative functioning of the constitution, and from his consequent desire to undermine rather than exploit the power of the nobility. From the beginning of his active rule, as he struggled to assert his authority independently of the magnates who had dominated the minority government,[28] Richard seems to have seen his nobles' power as a potential threat to his own position, rather than a potential support, and to have viewed the prospect of government through the co-operation of all the estates of the realm as an infringement of his personal authority, rather than the ideal of successful kingship. A consistent theme in his developing policies, therefore, was the attempt to use men whose personal connection with the king was formalized and explicit as agents of a direct royal presence in the shires which was partisan rather than public.

This was an attempt which was apparent from the very beginning of Richard's active rule. As the young king's minority had never been a formalized arrangement, there was no point at which he officially took over direction of the realm.[29] Since his uncles, and later the earl of Arundel, continued to exercise substantial authority in the early 1380s, Richard began to assert his personal control of government by administration through an expanded household establishment. He advanced his own curial magnates, and used grants of land and office to members of his household to challenge the role in local rule of nobles he distrusted.[30] Although the crisis of 1387–8 marked the failure of this relatively crude device of 'planting' household men at key points in the shires, Richard continued his efforts to establish a new form of direct royal authority in the localities, and it is in this context that the less inflammatory policy to which he turned from 1389—that of retaining a royal following among the local gentry[31]—must be considered. This geographically wide-ranging recruitment, primarily of the greater gentry, allowed the king to establish the beginnings of what could be seen as a 'royal affinity' in a sense more directly analogous to existing magnate affinities.[32] Since this policy no longer challenged local political hierarchies by interposing new and essentially alien elements, but instead exploited established power structures, it proved less destabilizing than Richard's methods during the earlier 1380s.[33]

[28] McKisack, *The Fourteenth Century*, 399–406.
[29] Tuck, *Richard II*, 33; Saul, *Richard II*, 109.
[30] McKisack, *The Fourteenth Century*, 427–44; Tuck, *Richard II*, 60–3, 73.
[31] Given-Wilson, 'The King and the Gentry', 94–5.
[32] See Tuck, *Richard II*, 180; Saul, *Richard II*, 262, 268.
[33] Given-Wilson, 'The King and the Gentry', 95; Saul, *Richard II*, 266–8.

From 1397, however, the king's attempts to create a fully fledged royal affinity again threatened the cohesion of the political establishment. At the highest political level, Richard finally revenged himself on the appellants of 1388 and gathered around himself his own aristocracy, with the creation of the 'duketti' and the concentration of influence in their hands.[34] In the localities, the king began to retain in more depth, recruiting esquires and gentlemen as well as the most prominent knights. The most significant aspect of this expanding affinity was its association with a territorial power bloc. In 1397, Richard annexed the earl of Arundel's estates in Shropshire and the northern marches of Wales to the palatinate of Chester, and elevated this area to the status of a principality to form 'the largest single concentration on the political map of England in the years 1397-9'.[35] It was here that royal retaining during these years was overwhelmingly based. Cheshiremen had been prominent in the service of Richard's father, and formed the core of the royalist army at Radcot Bridge in 1387.[36] These traditions of loyalty now gave way to a far more specific and systematic association. The core of the Chester retinue was the king's personal bodyguard of 311 archers; by Michaelmas 1398 750 men, including 10 knights and 97 esquires, had been permanently retained by the king.[37] It seems likely that this concentration of royal influence in the north-west was intended to constitute not simply a 'king's affinity', but effectively a marcher lordship in the possession of the crown, characterized by exclusive, monolithic landholding, extensive privileges and immunities, and overt military significance—a development inspired by and intended to counter the almost unassailable territorial power which had allowed the marcher lords Arundel, Warwick, and Gloucester to challenge Richard's authority.[38]

The fact that the nature of Richard's retaining policy, and the purpose which it was apparently intended to serve, can be distinguished so sharply from the role played by the knights of the household and chamber under Edward III is an important indication that analysis of a 'royal affinity' within the late medieval polity demands precise definition of the political relationships which the term is being used to

---

[34] McKisack, *The Fourteenth Century*, 478–84; Given-Wilson, *The Royal Household*, 166; Saul, *Richard II*, 366, 381–3.

[35] R. R. Davies, 'Richard II and the Principality of Chester', in F. R. H. Du Boulay and C. M. Barron (eds.), *The Reign of Richard II* (London, 1971), 256–60.

[36] Bennett, *Community, Class and Careerism*, 168.

[37] By a proclamation of 1397 no archer of the county could serve another lord until 2,300 men had been chosen for the king's retinue. Richard's expenditure on wages and annuities alone in the principality exceeded £5,000 per year. Davies, 'Richard II and the Principality of Chester', 268–9; Bennett, *Community, Class and Careerism*, 168; Tuck, *Richard II*, 180, 192–3.

[38] S. Evans, 'The Earl of Arundel, Richard II and the March of Wales', unpublished BA dissertation (Cambridge, 1979).

describe, and indeed of the political structures which underpinned and informed those relationships. Most historians who have studied the rule of Richard II have assumed that the creation of a royal retinue in the localities would naturally strengthen the power of the crown. Nigel Saul, for example, argues that 'Richard's formation of a magnate-style affinity represented an intelligent and practical response to the problems raised by the exercise of royal authority in the later middle ages'.[39] Chris Given-Wilson attributes Richard's defeat at the hands of the appellants in 1388 to the fact that 'before 1387, [he] had made little attempt to recruit gentry to his cause'; he goes on to suggest that only a combination of bad fortune and bad management prevented the fledgling royal affinity from thwarting Bolingbroke's invasion in 1399.[40]

This conclusion has been sustained despite the fact that Richard's creation of his Cheshire retinue clearly proved divisive and destabilizing within the polity in the last two years of the reign. It is true that the deposition crisis of 1399 was immediately precipitated by the far more fundamental attack on law and property rights inherent in Richard's sequestration of the Lancastrian inheritance, and that the effectiveness of his new retinue as a bulwark of royal authority was not fully tested, since the king and the bulk of Chester's military forces were absent in Ireland when Bolingbroke landed.[41] However, if it is not possible to conclude that Richard's fall was a direct result of his radical innovations in royal retaining, it is evident that, as the influence and significance of the king's supporters in the north-west were increasing, his authority in the rest of the country was correspondingly becoming more equivocal. Richard's expressions of affection for the inhabitants of his principality were reinforced by the increasing amounts of time he spent in the region, and one chronicler reports the spread of rumours that he intended to exploit the resources of the realm to support a regime based exclusively in the west and in Ireland.[42] As Rees Davies concludes, by 1399 'Richard II was still acceptable as prince of Chester but no longer as king of England'.[43]

[39] Saul, *Richard II*, 268.

[40] Given-Wilson, *The Royal Household*, 223–6.

[41] C. M. Barron, 'The Tyranny of Richard II', *BIHR* 41 (1968), 1; Given-Wilson, *The Royal Household*, 226.

[42] Davies, 'Richard II and the Principality of Chester', 260–2, 272, 279; Bennett, *Community, Class and Careerism*, 211; McKisack, *The Fourteenth Century*, 491; Tuck, *Richard II*, 181; A. Steel, *Richard II* (Cambridge, 1941), 264; *Annales Ricardi Secundi et Henrici Quarti*, in J. de Trokelowe et Anon., *Chronica et Annales*, ed. H. T. Riley (Rolls Series, 1866), 239–40. In this context, Richard's antagonistic relationship with the city of London contrasts sharply with his evident fondness for the city of York, where he stayed for substantial periods in the 1390s: C. M. Barron, 'The Quarrel of Richard II with London 1392–7', in Du Boulay and Barron (eds.), *The Reign of Richard II*, 173–201; J. H. Harvey, 'Richard II and York', ibid. 202–17.

[43] Davies, 'Richard II and the Principality of Chester', 279.

These problems have not compromised the favourable assessment of the principles on which Richard's retaining policy was based because they have been seen as the result of specific areas of mismanagement on the king's part in the last two years of the reign, rather than as flaws in the idea of a royal retinue *per se*. For example, while Anthony Tuck concedes that Richard's creation of a royal power base in the north-west had 'many defects', he suggests that these essentially consisted of the king's over-emphasis on Cheshire rather than problems intrinsic to the 'impressive scheme' itself.[44] Nigel Saul approves of the king's retaining policy in the earlier 1390s, but argues that 'Richard's infatuation with Cheshire ultimately worked to his disadvantage', partly by narrowing too far the geographical base of his support, and partly because his indulgence of the arrogant and aggressive behaviour of his retainers caused resentment among the rest of his subjects.[45]

Certainly the chroniclers—whatever their attitude to Richard himself—are remarkably consistent in condemning the Cheshire retinue on this last count. Adam of Usk, for example, describes them as 'men of the utmost depravity who went about doing as they wished, assaulting, beating and plundering his subjects with impunity; wherever the king went, night and day, they stood guard over him, armed as if for war, committing adulteries, murders, and countless other crimes; yet so inordinately did the king favour them that he would not listen to anyone who complained about them, indeed he regarded such people with loathing'. Indeed, Usk goes so far as to suggest that 'this was the chief cause of his ruin'.[46] It is perhaps no surprise to find parallel passages in the pro-Lancastrian narratives of Thomas Walsingham[47] and the Monk of Evesham,[48] but it is striking that the Ricardian Dieulacres chronicler

---

[44] Tuck, *Richard II*, 193–4.

[45] Saul, *Richard II*, 444–5.

[46] C. Given-Wilson, *The Chronicle of Adam Usk, 1377–1421* (Oxford, 1997), 48–9.

[47] 'In order to facilitate further his evil designs, the king also commanded a great number of evildoers from the county of Chester to come and form his bodyguard, and committed himself entirely to their protection. By nature bestial, these Cheshiremen were ready to commit every sort of crime, and their shamelessness soon increased to the point where they regarded only the king as their equal, treating everybody else, however powerful or noble he was, with contempt . . . And so greatly did their unwarranted pride, disdain, and cruel insolence grow, that before long, when travelling through the realm with the king, either within the royal household or apart from it, they began to beat and wound with impunity the king's faithful subjects; some indeed, with extraordinary cruelty, they even killed. They also seized people's goods, paying nothing for their provisions, and raped and ravished both married and unmarried women, for no one dared to stand up to them . . .': from the *Annales Ricardi Secundi*, in C. Given-Wilson (trans. and ed.), *Chronicles of the Revolution, 1397–1400* (Manchester, 1993), 73–4.

[48] The *Vita Ricardi Secundi* talks of 'these iniquitous archers', 'in whom, above all others, [the king] had confidence, even entrusting the security of his person to them, whereby most of the kingdom was treated with disdain': Given-Wilson (trans. and ed.), *Chronicles of the Revolution*, 57.

should concur with these descriptions of the Cheshiremen: 'On their shoulders they wore the royal badge of the white hart resplendent, but among the common people there was much talk of the extortions practised by them. Because of this the innocent king was, through no fault of his own, held in fatal odium by his ordinary subjects.'[49]

This is a conclusion also echoed by the author of the early fifteenth-century poem *Richard the Redeless*, which offers advice to Henry IV on the basis of a critique of Richard's rule. The poet remarks on the emboldening effect which the king's badge had on those who wore it, while those who suffered at their hands became increasingly alienated from the king himself:

> For tho that had hertis on hie on her brestis,
> For the more partie I may well avowe,
> They bare hem the bolder for her gay broches,
> And busshid with her brestis and bare adoun the pouere
> Liages that loued you the lesse for her yuell dedis.
>
> (Passus Two, ll. 36–40)[50]

Playing on the 'harts' worn by the Cheshiremen and the 'hearts' of the king's loyal subjects, the poet concludes that for every retainer 'marked' with the former, Richard lost many more of the latter:

> For on that ye merkyd ye myssed ten schore
> Of homeliche hertis that the harme hente.
>
> (ll. 42–3)

However, the poet's analysis does not end there. The target of his criticism is not only the behaviour of the king's retainers, but the entire project of creating a royal retinue:

> Thane was it foly in feith, as me thynketh,
> To sette silver in signes that of nought serued.
>
> (ll. 44–5)

The poet professes bafflement at the actions of a king who had at the beginning of his reign enjoyed the allegiance of all his subjects; it was Richard himself who had introduced division through the giving of badges, with disastrous results:

> I not what you eylid but if it ese were:
> For frist at youre anoyntynge alle were youre owen,
> Bothe hertis and hyndis and helde of non other;
> No lede of youre lond but as a liege aughte,

---

[49] Given-Wilson (trans. and ed.), *Chronicles of the Revolution*, 154.
[50] All quotations from *Richard the Redeless* are taken from H. Barr (ed.), *The Piers Plowman Tradition* (London, 1993), 101–33.

> Tyl ye, of youre dulnesse deseueraunce made
> Thoru youre side signes that shente all the browet,
> And cast adoun the crokk the colys amyd.
>
> (ll. 46–52)

Why, the poet asks, should he have felt impelled to take this course, given that he could have commanded the loyal service of the realm as a whole?

> Yit am I lewde and litill good schewe
> To coueyte knowliche of kyngis wittis,
> Or wilne to witte [what] was the mevynge
> That [ladde] you to lykynge youre liegis to merke,
> That loued you full lelly or leuerez beg[a]nne . . .
>
> (ll. 53–7)

The only answer the poet can suggest is that Richard must have thought his retaining would make him more powerful:

> Yit I trowe youre entente at the frist tyme
> Was, as I wene, yif I well thenke in multitude of peple,
> That ye were the more myghtier for the many signes
> That ye and youre seruantis aboughte so thikke sowid;
>
> (ll. 99–102)

The king must have felt that his relationship with his new retainers gave him the assurance of their loyalty, even though the distribution of his livery was in fact undermining the wider allegiance of his subjects:

> And that they were more tristi and trewer than other
> To loue you for the leuere that legaunce stroied;
> Or ellis for a skylle [*reason*] that skathed youre-self,
> That comounes of contre in costis aboute
> Sholde knowe by hir quentise [*device*] that the kyng loued hem
> For her priuy prynte passinge another.
>
> (ll. 103–8)

As far as the poet is concerned, these were not calculations which made any sense:

> Yif that was youre purpos it passith my wittis
> To deme discrecion of youre well-doynge.
>
> (ll. 109–10)

To at least one contemporary observer, therefore, the problem lay not simply in Richard's handling of the men who wore his livery in the last two years of the reign, but in the very idea that the king should need to distribute livery to personal retainers rather than relying on the allegiance of all his subjects to the crown. This was a conclusion echoed in a petition addressed to 'the King and his Parliament', which was probably written in either 1388 or 1401 but was never formally entered on the rolls of parliament.[51] The petition observes that, in the past, all the people of the realm had been ruled 'come un comyn entier' under their king, 'saunz desseverance entre eux faitz par conisance du signes ou autre liveres'. However, this unity was now threatened by the fact that 'le Roy et autres seignurs du Roialme ount donez diverses signes entre la dite comyn a graunt desseverance de eux'. The petition concludes by requesting the abolition of all badges—and in doing so asks the king to remember that 'tout la poeple de vostre roialme sount vos lieges et entier comyn a vous come a lour Roy et seignour liege a vos leyes obeisauntz'.[52]

In the light of these contemporary comments, it is worth re-examining the suggestion that the second, less controversial phase of Richard's retaining in the earlier 1390s represented a 'sensible and successful strategy' which succeeded in reasserting and reinforcing royal authority in the wake of the traumatic events of 1386–8.[53] Chris Given-Wilson suggests that behind the king's retaining policy lay his overriding concern to secure 'a loyal base of support among the gentry of the kingdom in the event of a crisis'.[54] However, if the king could not call on loyal support from all his landowning subjects, and if his authority were now to rest on partisan force rather than on his leadership of the realm in the co-operative enterprise of government, then the workings of the late medieval constitution were already profoundly dislocated. The long-term success of this radical and rapid development of a 'royal affinity' directly subordinate to the personal authority of the king— especially a king with Richard's conceptions of the royal prerogative and the proper role of the nobility in government—would have necessitated a fundamental readjustment in the relationship between the crown and the political estates of the realm.

Indeed, when examined in the context of the public dimensions of royal rule, the very concept of a 'royal affinity' is fraught with constitutional ambiguities. The possession of extensive private estates was not an integral part of the authority of the English monarchy. Unlike his French counterpart, the English king had not acquired his sovereignty through a process of gradual expansion from a distinct royal demesne.[55]

---

[51] N. Saul, 'The Commons and the Abolition of Badges', *Parliamentary History*, 9 (1990), 303. I am very grateful to Dr John Watts for drawing my attention to this document.

[52] Saul, 'The Commons and the Abolition of Badges', 314. Note that, in his commentary on this petition, Nigel Saul takes a rather different, and much less positive, view of Richard's retaining policy than he does in his more recent biography of the king.

[53] Given-Wilson, *The Royal Household*, 222; see also Saul, *Richard II*, 268.

[54] Given-Wilson, *The Royal Household*, 223, and cf. 117; see also Saul, *Richard II*, 265–6.

[55] B. P. Wolffe, *The Royal Demesne in English History* (London, 1971), 34, 38–40.

The crown's authority was a public, national power, based on the universal application of royal law and royal justice, with the right to demand military and financial support from all its subjects.[56] When, during the thirteenth and fourteenth centuries, the crown did acquire a fairly substantial, permanent landed estate, it was used primarily to provide maintenance for the king's family, especially dower for the queen and an endowment which would allow the heir to the throne to take his place, until his accession, among the leading magnates of the realm. Under normal circumstances little remained in the hands of the king.[57] Richard II's possession of the earldom of Chester, the royal lordships of the principality of Wales, and the duchy of Cornwall was therefore highly unusual, and possible only because of his childlessness. The mere fact of his possession of these estates was, of course, not sufficient cause of a crisis in royal authority, but his decision to make active use of these private resources in support of his power as king played a significant part in creating one.

Even had Richard's conception of the role of the monarchy not been unusually combative and divisive, there are powerful reasons why the task he set himself of combining leadership of a regional affinity with his tenure of the crown should have proved so difficult. As has already been suggested, fundamental to both private and public aspects of political society and their co-ordination as a viable system of government was the role of the king. As guarantor of law and fount of justice, the monarch embodied the abstract principles which provided the framework for official administrative and judicial structures. As dispenser of grace and 'good lord of all good lords', he also represented the collective values of the 'common weal' which tempered the moral absolutism of the law, and underpinned the operation of the private hierarchies of lordship and service. In other words, the complex relationship between the many facets of the crown, both in terms of the formal and informal hierarchies of power and in terms of the distinction between the *persona privata* and the *persona publica* of the king, was already held in a fine balance. The most fundamental aspect of the polity was that the authority of the king—which was both universally representative of, and uniquely distinct from, the *communitas regni*—guaranteed all other forms of authority in the kingdom, and allowed government to function through a national public administration given flesh by the private power of the king's landed subjects.

If, however, the king were to use his possession of a landed estate to

[56] Ibid. 34–5; Harriss, *King, Parliament, and Public Finance*, 131.

[57] The county (later duchy) of Cornwall was acquired in 1227, the palatinate of Chester in 1246 (to which Flintshire was added in 1284), and the principality of Wales in 1284. Wolffe, *The Royal Demesne*, 52–8, 65, 72–3; Harriss, *King, Parliament, and Public Finance*, 149–50, 156–9; cf. J. R. Studd, 'The Lord Edward and King Henry III', *BIHR* 50 (1977), 4–5.

create a regional affinity just as his magnates did, this fine constitutional balance would be at risk. As a regional magnate, the king would have a responsibility to advance the interests of his own retainers and to protect his own sphere of interest from the local ambitions of other nobles; his retinue would require active support from their local lord in return for their local service. Tenure of the crown would, of course, give the king unparalleled resources with which to fulfil the requirements of regional lordship, most notably complete control of appointments to local office and an almost unlimited capacity to direct judicial process. However, these powers would have to be exercised with extreme restraint. Any lord who aspired to the undisputed rule of his 'country' had to take care that his maintenance of his affinity did not become too blatantly partisan nor too disruptive, since an important part of his authority was his claim to represent the 'common weal' of local society as a whole.[58] Nevertheless, if a magnate did mishandle his regional responsibilities, or if competition for local rule provoked serious instability, those who felt they were unrepresented in their locality could turn to the king, who alone represented the common interest of the entire realm. If, however, king and magnate were one and the same, the potential implications of any mismanagement of regional affairs were profound. Not only was there no superior authority which could intervene to restore order at a local level, but the risk was that regional instability could damage the crown in a national context. The unique authority of the monarchy was predicated on its unique claim to represent the whole realm, and, though the interests of some of the king's subjects would always have to be sacrificed in favour of the common good, such individual disappointments could be accommodated so long as confidence in the realization of national interests in the person of the king persisted.[59] If, on the other hand, the king were to demonstrate that he was a more specially good lord to one distinct, localized group of his servants than to his other subjects who had no specific connection with him other than the universal duty of allegiance and service, then—as Richard II discovered in 1399, and as the author of *Richard the Redeless* subsequently pointed out—his credibility as a national monarch would be significantly compromised.

Richard II tried in the 1390s to construct such a retinue for himself, and failed. Ironically, his deposition brought to the throne a man who already possessed what Richard had been trying to create: an affinity combining great military capability with substantial influence in local politics, developed from a position of exceptional authority and based on an extensive territorial power bloc. Henry IV did not simply 'adopt

[58] Carpenter, *Locality and Polity*, 358–9, 629; Watts, *Henry VI*, 63–7.
[59] Carpenter, *Locality and Polity*, 393, 628; Watts, *Henry VI*, 27–31, 74–80.

his predecessor's practice'[60] of royal retaining in the localities. The problems of combining the exercise of royal authority with partisan lordship, which Richard II had begun to create for himself, formed an intrinsic part of Henry IV's attempt to establish his rule. Where Richard's kingship was increasingly focusing on his personal lordship over one section of his subjects, Henry was seeking to develop his specific lordship into universal kingship, a distinction crucial to a proper understanding of the two reigns. The events of 1399 do not represent the culmination of the development of a 'king's affinity'. Rather, the crown was suddenly in the hands of a king who *also* commanded a lordly affinity, a circumstance which established profound tensions within the polity between the interests and responsibilities of the king and those of his *alter ego*, the duke of Lancaster.

The Duchy of Lancaster, and the peculiarities of its relation to the crown after 1399, have hitherto attracted remarkably little attention. For historians who have sought to trace the development of the 'king's affinity' during the fifteenth and sixteenth centuries, the innovative 'bastard feudal policy' of Richard II has been seen as the model which all of his successors attempted to pursue and which was eventually brought to fruition under Edward IV and Henry VII—a context in which Henry IV has attracted little more comment than that he 'followed Richard's example'.[61] For historians studying regions where Lancastrian estates formed a significant element within local power structures, the fact that the Duchy was held by the king after 1399 has tended to render its political role invisible, or at best indistinct, within analyses constructed in terms of relations between gentry communities, noble lordship, and central royal authority.[62] Those historians who have noted Henry's possession of the Duchy as a peculiarity of his kingship have assumed that control of a private affinity could only have enhanced the power of the Lancastrian monarchy. T. B. Pugh, for example, argues that 'after 1399 the crown was the centre of bastard feudalism because the king's own affinity was far greater and stronger than that of any subject', while A. L. Brown describes the Duchy

---

[60] Given-Wilson, *The Royal Household*, 226.

[61] Quotation from Guy, *Tudor England*, 165; see also Starkey, 'The Age of the Household', 269–71. Chris Given-Wilson has given sustained attention to Henry IV's retaining policy, but he too concludes that Henry 'attached knights and esquires to his person for broadly similar reasons as Richard II did': *The Royal Household*, 234 (and, more generally, 226–57).

[62] See, for example, Acheson, *A Gentry Community*, Payling, *Political Society*, and Wright, *The Derbyshire Gentry*. For detailed discussion of these issues in historiographical context, see C. Carpenter, 'Gentry and Community in Medieval England', *Journal of British Studies*, 33 (1994), esp. 361–3; and C. Carpenter, 'Who Ruled the Midlands in the Later Middle Ages?', *Midland History*, 19 (1994), 10–12. For a study of local politics which has taken account of the distinctive position of the Duchy of Lancaster under the Lancastrians, see Carpenter, *Locality and Polity*, pt. II.

retinue as a 'special advantage Henry enjoyed'.[63] The evidence in fact suggests that leadership of such a private connection was a sign not of authoritative kingship but of monarchy in crisis. Richard II's recruitment of a private and localized affinity helped to hasten the downfall of his regime, and reflected his wider misconceptions about the crown's authority and his own role in the polity. Henry IV's relationship with his Lancastrian affinity reflected the precarious nature of his position. As a usurper, he needed to exploit, and was bound to reward, the proven loyalty of the servants who had enabled him to win the throne. Nevertheless, in order to establish his kingship successfully, he had to broaden his lordship until he could plausibly claim the universally representative authority to which he aspired.

Investigation of the political role of the Duchy of Lancaster between 1399 and 1461 is therefore crucial both to analysis of the supposed development of a 'royal affinity' within fifteenth-century government, and to a proper understanding of the interaction between central and local rule in areas where the Duchy was a significant territorial presence. This book examines the way in which private Lancastrian lordship was accommodated within the public rule of the Lancastrian crown, and traces the effect on the polity at both a local and a national level of the interplay between these two facets of the Lancastrian kings' authority. An initial chapter presents an overview of the management of the Duchy as a whole; the remainder of the book examines the development of regional politics in two contrasting areas—East Anglia and the north midlands—where the Duchy estates made the king a substantial local landowner. Though these are regional studies, the explicit intention throughout is to explore the nature of royal authority, and the relationship between the locality and the centre, by focusing on the operation of Lancastrian kingship within government at a local level. The East Anglian estates of the Duchy were not used before 1399 as a basis for active regional lordship; from 1399 onwards, therefore, it is possible to trace the evolution of new structures of power in which the Lancastrian kings had a relatively free hand in attempting to manage the private resources of the Duchy in the context of their wider public responsibilities. The region also offers a particularly rich range of source material, given that the letters of the Paston family provide a

---

[63] T. B. Pugh, 'The Magnates, Knights and Gentry', in Chrimes *et al.* (eds.), *Fifteenth-Century England*, 108; Brown, 'The Reign of Henry IV', 19. Charles Ross argued—ironically, in the light of the arguments of David Starkey and John Guy about the development of the crown's 'bastard feudal policy' under the Yorkists—that it was a 'serious weakness' in Edward IV's management of his servants that he spent far less than Henry IV on retaining the services of gentry in the localities, a policy which meant that 'he did not command anything comparable with the great "Lancastrian connection"': Ross, *Edward IV*, 329–30. The phrase quoted by Ross is from Brown, 'The Reign of Henry IV', 18–19.

unique insight into local and national politics during the reign of Henry VI. The correspondence has played a key role in determining established views of the regimes of the 1440s and 1450s, but a re-examination of the Paston evidence in the context of the development of local power structures from the beginning of the century has made possible a re-evaluation not only of the Pastons' position within regional society, but also of the nature of the regimes as a whole. By contrast with East Anglia, the north midland counties of Staffordshire and Derbyshire had long been a centre of Duchy influence, and here the Lancastrian kings therefore faced the task of combining royal rule with the management of a highly significant role in pre-existing structures of private power.[64] The aim of these regional studies is to illuminate the complex relationship between the king, the crown, and the Duchy of Lancaster within the Lancastrian polity—and, in so doing, to shed new light on the nature and functioning of the late medieval English monarchy.

---

[64] These two north midland shires also provide an opportunity to investigate Lancastrian rule within a wider region which has already been the subject of influential research on various aspects of local society in recent years: see, for the later 14th cent., Walker, *The Lancastrian Affinity*, ch. 6 (2); for the 15th cent., Wright, *The Derbyshire Gentry*, Payling, *Political Society*, and Carpenter, *Locality and Polity*.

2

The Duchy of Lancaster and the Lancastrian Kings

1. THE LANCASTRIAN AFFINITY TO 1399

The Lancastrian connection was the greatest magnate affinity in late fourteenth-century England. It was exceptional in the extent of its territorial basis, in the size of its indentured retinue, and in the political pre-eminence of its lord. John of Gaunt, in right of his wife Blanche, held half of the vast estates of her father Henry, duke of Lancaster, from the latter's death in 1361, and in the following year, when Blanche's sister died without issue, Gaunt acquired the rest of the inheritance together with the title of duke of Lancaster.[1] In 1372 he exchanged his own earldom of Richmond for a range of estates which consolidated his Lancastrian holdings, and his heir's marriage in 1380 to Mary de Bohun brought to the Lancastrian line a share of the Bohun inheritance, including the earldoms of Hereford and Northampton.[2] At the heart of this range of territorial interests lay the county of Lancaster where, by a life grant of 1377, Gaunt enjoyed palatine powers.[3]

These estates and liberties formed the basis for an affinity of a scope unparalleled in the period. It has been estimated that a magnate retinue in the late middle ages might normally number between 60 and 80 men, but by the early 1390s there were over 150 members of Gaunt's household alone, and his indentured retinue, which numbered 173 men in 1382, apparently continued to expand thereafter.[4] At the head of this exceptional affinity was Gaunt himself, the king's uncle and himself a

[1] R. Somerville, *History of the Duchy of Lancaster*, i (London, 1953), 49–51.

[2] Ibid. 52–3, 67.

[3] In effect, royal jurisdiction in the county was exercised on the king's behalf by the duke of Lancaster, his authority limited only by the crown's right to correct errors of justice, and by the royal prerogative of pardon: S. Walker, *The Lancastrian Affinity* (Oxford, 1990), 142.

[4] C. Given-Wilson, *The Royal Household* (New Haven, 1986), 262; Walker, *The Lancastrian Affinity*, 11, 14. J. M. W. Bean suggests a figure of 200 to 220 knights and esquires retained for life by Feb. 1399: *From Lord to Patron: Lordship in Late Medieval England* (Manchester, 1989), 248. By the early 1390s, the duke was having to provide an annual sum of £5,000 for his household expenses, and nearly £3,500 in annuities: Walker, *The Lancastrian Affinity*, 18–20. See also S. Armitage-Smith (ed.), *John of Gaunt's Register, 1372–6*, 2 vols., Camden Society, 3rd series, 20–1 (1911), and E. C. Lodge and R. Somerville (eds.), *John of Gaunt's Register, 1379–83*, Camden Society, 3rd series, 56–7 (1937).

claimant to regal status as king of Castile. Though his career in the 1380s was dominated by discordant relations with his nephew and absences on campaign, he was an enormously influential figure in domestic politics after his return to England and reconciliation with the king in 1389.[5]

However, Simon Walker's analysis of the Lancastrian affinity in the 1390s highlights the danger of drawing conclusions too readily from the apparent state of national politics. It might be supposed, given the support which Gaunt provided for his nephew during the 1390s, that the split between Lancastrians and Ricardians in the localities was a late one, with Bolingbroke's determination to resist Richard's confiscation of his estates precipitating an enforced choice between two previously compatible loyalties. The picture of the harmonious involvement of the Lancastrian retinue in royal policy is apparently confirmed by Richard's dependence on Gaunt, whom he rewarded with substantial grants during the 1390s.[6] The king even bound his uncle into his plans for the principality of Chester by creating the duke and his heirs hereditary constables there.[7]

At a local level, however, a far more complex, and less harmonious, picture emerges. However close the alliance between Gaunt and the king in central government, the development of a powerful royal affinity based in Cheshire was always likely to qualify Gaunt's hegemony in neighbouring Lancashire, especially once Richard began to extend his local power beyond his principality to Gaunt's palatinate.[8] The scale of his recruitment began to appear threatening on two counts. First, he sought to win the loyalty of those who already served the duke. Thomas Holford, for example, a second-generation Lancastrian retainer, followed his father into the royal retinue and by 1399 was one of the seven esquire commanders of the Cheshire watch.[9] Secondly, he also recruited those who had secured no place in the Lancastrian affinity, and who therefore relished the opportunity to exploit a new source of local power with which to voice their resentment of Lancastrian domi-

---

[5] M. McKisack, *The Fourteenth Century* (Oxford, 1959), 426–42, 464–87.

[6] Gaunt's power in his palatinate, for example, was reinforced in 1396 by a grant of his liberties there in fee tail. These rights were also incorporated into a comprehensive 'Great Charter of the Duchy'. In 1398 the reversal of Thomas of Lancaster's forfeiture was completed by the king's release of any rights still vested in the crown, and by confirmation of Gaunt, Bolingbroke, and their heirs in their possessions. Bolingbroke was elevated to the dukedom of Hereford in 1397, despite his involvement as an appellant in 1388: Somerville, *History of the Duchy*, 65–7; McKisack, *The Fourteenth Century*, 454, 483.

[7] R. R. Davies, 'Richard II and the Principality of Chester', in F. R. H. Du Bouley and C. M. Barron (eds.), *The Reign of Richard II* (London, 1971), 266.

[8] On a single day in Mar. 1398, for example, he retained 5 knights and 22 esquires from Lancashire: Walker, *The Lancastrian Affinity*, 175–6; M. J. Bennett, *Community, Class and Careerism* (Cambridge, 1983), 168–9.

[9] Walker, *The Lancastrian Affinity*, 177.

nation. The same pattern is also evident in the strongly Lancastrian area of the north midlands.[10]

Simon Walker argues that the emergence of the crown as an alternative source of lordship in these regions meant that 'the inner logic of "bastard feudalism"—the perennial tendency of the gentry to search for patrons and patrons to acknowledge clients—drove the king and the duke towards opposite sides in the disputes and quarrels that animated the county community'.[11] Further, he points out that, in the course of confrontations between members of their affinities, Richard was apparently prepared to make few concessions to Gaunt, and from 1397 was making increasing use of the royal prerogative of pardon within the palatinate of Lancaster, effectively undermining his uncle's judicial authority there. He concludes that, though such tensions were of little practical significance while Gaunt continued to give an elder statesman's support to the monarchy, Richard was preparing eventually to unburden himself of the power of the Lancastrian affinity.[12]

Analysis of Gaunt's retaining during the 1390s supports the thesis that he was seeking some form of 'political insurance'[13] against potential threats to his heir's position. The primarily military criteria which had governed the composition of the Lancastrian affinity in the 1380s gave way in the following decade to greater concern with local power structures. Gaunt increased his retaining to spread over a broader geographical area and deeper down the social hierarchy, and especially after 1397 recruited young esquires as yet unconnected with the crown. He also began to reinforce his son's political position by granting supplementary annuities to the latter's retainers on condition that they remained in Henry's service after his own death.[14] As Walker concludes, 'the changing social composition of the Lancastrian affinity can be best explained as a positive response to a change in the duke's needs and expectations of service . . . that owed most to Gaunt's desire to lay the foundations of an adequate affinity for his eldest son'.[15]

---

[10] Walker, *The Lancastrian Affinity*, 176–7, 228–31; see below, Ch. 6.1.

[11] Walker, *The Lancastrian Affinity*, 229.

[12] Ibid. 176–9, 231; cf. Bennett, *Community, Class and Careerism*, 169.

[13] S. K. Walker, 'John of Gaunt and his Retainers, 1361–99', unpublished D.Phil. thesis (Oxford, 1986), 255.

[14] Walker, *The Lancastrian Affinity*, 32, 34–7, 177–8. An example is the esquire John Norbury, who served Henry throughout the 1390s and was granted a fee by Gaunt in 1398: M. Barber, 'John Norbury (c.1350–1414): An Esquire of Henry IV', *EHR* 68 (1953), 67; Walker, *The Lancastrian Affinity*, 37 n., 276.

[15] Walker, *The Lancastrian Affinity*, 36.

2. THE DUCHY OF LANCASTER UNDER HENRY IV

Richard's attempts to win men from Lancastrian loyalty to his own service while there was no question of incompatibility between the two allegiances at a national level raises the issue of what happened within the affinity when the conflict of interests became overt and irreconcilable in 1399. A month after Gaunt's death in February of that year, Richard confiscated the Lancastrian estates and distributed them among his supporters.[16] No trace of this remains in the administrative records of the Duchy, and it seems clear that the three months which elapsed between the sequestration and Henry's return to reclaim his inheritance were not enough to undermine established patterns of loyalty and service.[17]

However, assumptions about what those patterns were should perhaps not be made too readily. Bolingbroke was already in exile at the time of his father's death, so that his leadership of the Lancastrian connection on his return to England in 1399 was not a reassumption of established authority. His inheritance of the Duchy, and his first attempt at commanding his father's exceptional retinue, necessarily occurred at the same time as his attempt to assume the throne.[18] Henry had certainly been extensively involved with the Duchy throughout his life. His household was staffed by members of his father's retinue, and during Gaunt's absences abroad in 1378, 1386, and 1394 Henry was appointed warden of the palatinate, although he may not have played an active part in its administration.[19] Nevertheless, although his establishment as earl of Derby was closely connected with that of his father, it remained essentially independent, and was based not on possession of any substantial part of the Lancastrian estates, but on his wife's

---

[16] Somerville, *History of the Duchy*, 134–5.

[17] Indeed, it may not even have been enough to disturb the workings of Henry's administration. Revenues from the Lancastrian estates were still being paid to the receiver-general of the Duchy three months after the confiscation, and the money then transferred to Henry in France via Italian merchants: R. R. Davies, 'The Bohun and Lancaster Lordships in Wales in the Fourteenth and Early Fifteenth Centuries', unpublished D.Phil. thesis (Oxford, 1965), 329–30. See also the account of Simon Bache, 'receiver of Henry, duke of Lancaster', for the revenues of the Higham Ferrers receipt from the day of Gaunt's death until the end of the accounting year seven months later: Huntington Library HAM 49(1). Henry seems to have suffered few financial penalties during his exile; Richard granted him an annual sum of £2,000: J. H. Wylie, *History of England under Henry the Fourth*, 4 vols. (London, 1884–98), i. 7: A. Steel, *The Receipt of the Exchequer 1377–1485* (Cambridge, 1954), 81.

[18] K. B. McFarlane, *Lancastrian Kings and Lollard Knights* (Oxford, 1972), 14–15.

[19] The fact that Henry was first made warden at the age of 11 suggests that the appointment was largely honorific. By 1386 he would have been old enough to take an active interest in his father's affairs, but McFarlane points out that there is no evidence that he was consulted by Gaunt's officials, who remained closely in touch with the duke in Spain: Somerville, *History of the Duchy*, 120; McFarlane, *Lancastrian Kings and Lollard Knights*, 13, 28.

Bohun lands.[20] As has already been noted, the encroachment of Richard II's retaining on Gaunt's sphere of influence suggests that the king was seeking eventually to undermine the power of the Lancastrian affinity. The duke's reaction to this threat—the expansion of his own retinue and reinforcement of his son's—undoubtedly helped to draw the two threads of Lancastrian service closer.[21] Nevertheless, the very fact of Gaunt's concern for his heir's security emphasizes the complexity of Henry's situation in 1399.

Simon Walker has shown that Richard succeeded in winning some Lancastrians away from continued adherence to Gaunt's heir, and that, in areas where the Duchy interest was neither large nor active, the response of local men to the deposition varied considerably.[22] It is clear, however, that in the immediate crisis of 1399 the core of the Lancastrian affinity rallied to Henry's cause. His progress through the country after his invasion traced a relatively easy path via a chain of Lancastrian strongholds,[23] while Henry's own circle of intimate associates formed the backbone of his support in exile and on his return home.[24] Exact information about the extent and nature of Henry's support is limited, but it is clear from the names recorded in Duchy registers and accounts, totalling forty knights and esquires to whom wages were paid for their military service and that of their men during the crisis, that Henry's retinue was well supported by that of his father. Walter Blount, the duke's chamberlain, John Cokayn, chief steward of his northern lands, John Dabridgecourt, master forester of Duffield Frith—all three men executors of Gaunt's will—together with Thomas Wendesley, steward of the High Peak, John Curson, steward of Tutbury, Robert Waterton, steward of Pontefract, and Thomas Beek, steward of Newcastle-under-Lyme, were between themselves alone paid a total of

[20] Before his father's death, Henry held from the Duchy only a handful of scattered Lancastrian manors and an annuity of 2,000 marks: Somerville, *History of the Duchy*, 67–8; J. L. Kirby, *Henry IV of England* (London, 1970), 35.

[21] Walker argues that Gaunt's policy was 'concentrated principally upon safeguarding the continuity and integrity of the Lancastrian estates for his exiled son': Walker, *The Lancastrian Affinity*, 177.

[22] Ibid. 177, 206. Five of the 22 Lancastrian retainers at the Duchy lordship of Halton in Richard's principal recruiting-ground of Cheshire are recorded in the Duchy accounts as having joined the earls' rebellion in 1400: DL29/738/12097.

[23] He landed at the end of June in Yorkshire, one of the greatest centres of Duchy territorial interests outside the palatinate; by 1 July, the most northerly Lancastrian base at Dunstanburgh Castle had been secured; Henry then proceeded via the Duchy castles at Pickering, Knaresborough, Pontefract, Leicester, and Kenilworth, where a garrison had been championing his cause since as early as 2 June: Somerville, *History of the Duchy*, 137–8.

[24] His knights Thomas Erpingham, John Pelham, Peter Bukton, and Thomas Rempston and the esquire John Norbury accompanied him overseas, while John Leventhorp and Sir Hugh Waterton, Henry's attorney during his exile, were among the first to join him after his landing at Ravenspur: Somerville, *History of the Duchy*, 136–7; Given-Wilson, *The Royal Household*, 190; C. Given-Wilson (trans. and ed.), *Chronicles of the Revolution* (Manchester, 1993), 35–6.

£992 in wages. Their names appear alongside others with longstanding traditions of service to the Duchy—families such as the Foljambes and Montgomeries of Derbyshire, and the Swillingtons and Usfletes of Yorkshire.[25]

If immediate questions of loyalty had necessarily been put to a dramatic test in the summer of 1399, longer-term problems of the management of Duchy resources remained. Administration of the Duchy, now enlarged by the addition of Henry's Bohun lands, would have required skilled handling even had it been his sole concern, but he faced the additional problem of how best to combine this with his newly acquired royal responsibilities. Henry immediately demonstrated his commitment to the preservation of his inheritance intact, rather than its assimilation into the property of the crown. On 14 October 1399, the first day of his first parliament, the king declared his intention that 'our . . . heritage, with its rights and liberties aforesaid, in the same manner, state, form, and condition, in which it descended and came to us' should 'in all things be managed, governed, and treated, as they would have . . . been managed, governed, and treated, if we had never assumed the ensign of royal dignity'.[26] However, examination of the full series of Duchy accounts for Henry's reign suggests that it took some time for that 'state, form, and condition' and the manner in which it was 'managed, governed, and treated' to settle into a consistent pattern after the uncertainty of 1399.

Henry's attempt to create a Lancastrian royal administration involved, at least in part, the appointment of his father's officials to corresponding posts in the new government. Gaunt's former chancellor of the palatinate, John Scarle, thus became chancellor of England in September 1399; Thomas Tutbury, who had been treasurer of Gaunt's household, became treasurer of the new royal household; and John Legbourne, Gaunt's receiver-general, became receiver of the king's chamber and subsequently chamberlain in the exchequer of receipt.[27] This influx of senior Lancastrian officers was to have serious consequences for the royal administration,[28] but its immediate implications for the Duchy were that the Lancastrian estates were transferred into the hands of men who had either held lesser office under Gaunt, or had

---

[25] DL42/15 pt. 1 fos. 70–1; DL28/4/1–2; DL29/728/11987, 11988; Somerville, *History of the Duchy*, 67 n., 364, 367, 377–8, 381–2; Walker, *The Lancastrian Affinity*, 269, 275, 282–3.

[26] W. Hardy (trans. and ed.), *Charters of the Duchy of Lancaster* (London, 1845), 137–8.

[27] Scarle seems to have given up the chancellorship of the county palatine in 1394 when he became master of the rolls: Somerville, *History of the Duchy*, 365, 368, 475–6; A. Rogers, 'The Royal Household of Henry IV', unpublished Ph.D. thesis (Nottingham, 1966), 677–8; cf. A. L. Brown, 'Reign of Henry IV', in S. B. Chrimes *et al.* (eds.), *Fifteenth-Century England* (Manchester, 1972), 22.

[28] See below, p. 30.

served in Henry's establishment when he was earl of Derby.[29] This inexperience in administration may have combined with novelty of circumstance to produce the period of adjustment that is evident in the Duchy records.

The Lancastrian estates were divided into two circuits, the North and South Parts, each with its own auditor, but the place in one circuit or the other of some of the central lands, notably those in Lincolnshire and Northamptonshire, was not definitively settled until after the first couple of years of the reign.[30] The Duchy organization was focused around the many honours it held, but also incorporated individual estates which did not form part of a larger territorial bloc. After 1399 these individual landholdings were gradually drawn more and more firmly into the orbit of the honour to which they were most closely situated. The responsibility of the receiver of the honour of Leicester, for example, for the revenues of a group of lands outside the honour, including Castle Donington, became so established under Henry IV that by the beginning of the next reign the honour of Leicester was accounted as simply one part of a larger 'Leicester receipt', incorporating the neighbouring miscellanea of Lancastrian lands.[31]

This process was echoed on a larger scale by the emergence of dominant centres among the honours themselves. The largest and most valuable honours—notably Lancaster, Pontefract, and Tutbury, which alone accounted in the first year of the reign for a clear value of nearly £4,200 out of a total for the northern circuit of £5,700[32]—were naturally pre-eminent. However, since the structure of an affinity remained inextricably linked to tenurial patterns, these areas were pre-eminent not only territorially but also in terms of the Lancastrian retinue connected with them. The areas which produced the greatest revenue therefore also tended to be the most heavily charged with annuities, and so the most heavily overspent. In the years after 1399 smaller lordships, maintaining a more limited burden of annuities, became to some degree satellites of certain of these greater ones, as their revenues were routinely used to make up the deficit caused by the

---

[29] John Leventhorp, for example, who had been Henry's receiver-general since 1390, became receiver-general of the Duchy in 1399; the Duchy chancellorship went to William Burgoyne, who had served Gaunt during the 1380s and had moved into Henry's administration during the 1390s: Somerville, *History of the Duchy*, 155, 386, 388, 397.

[30] DL29/728/11987, 11988, 11991; DL29/729/11993–4. There is one subsequent anomaly in the accounts, when in 1410 the honours of Tutbury and Leicester were included in the audit of the southern circuit, rather than, as in every other year, being accounted with the North Parts. This exception is presumably related to the fact that at the time of the audits John Bonington, the auditor in the north since 1399, was exchanging responsibilities with his counterpart in the south, Thomas Somercotes: DL29/730/12014–15; Somerville, *History of the Duchy*, 433–4, 439.

[31] DL29/728/11988; DL29/729/11995–6, 12001, 12004; DL29/730/12006, 12008, 12011–12; DL29/731/12017, 12019A.   [32] DL29/728/11988.

granting of fees on a scale that even the extensive revenues of the major honours could not sustain. The consistent and substantial deficit at the Pontefract receipt, for example, was made up from the revenues of the lesser Yorkshire receipts at Pickering and Knaresborough.[33]

The scale of the charges on some of the Lancastrian estates brings into focus the question of the use which Henry made of the vast resources of the Duchy. From 1400, some revenue from the Duchy was paid each year into the king's chamber and wardrobe to assist with royal finances. These sums ranged from as little as £400 to over £2,000, but averaged about £1,120 a year.[34] Comparison of these figures with the scale of the Duchy's clear annual value, which was accounted at £12,500 in 1400, and of the annuities assigned on that revenue—nearly £8,000 in the same year—emphasizes that Henry saw the value of his Lancastrian inheritance clearly in terms of investment in service rather than as a source of additional revenue.[35] Somerville comments that by 1404 the Duchy with few exceptions paid for nothing that was not strictly Duchy expenditure, and that the balance of the revenues then passed to the king.[36] This is undoubtedly true, but perhaps fails to convey a fair sense of proportion, since Duchy expenditure was by this time vast, and the balance of the revenues almost negligible.

The scale of Duchy spending on annuities partly reflects Henry's attempt at a political 'balancing act' in the insecure years after 1399, as he not only sought to reward the loyalty of his own men, but also tried to reconcile both his opponents and the uncommitted through wide-ranging use of the patronage at his disposal.[37] It also, however, reflects his determination to maintain the Lancastrian affinity as an immediate and reliable source of servants whose loyalty was proven and personal. This service took several forms. The affinity retained its military functions, for example. The military summonses recorded in the Duchy registers refer almost exclusively to the retinue of the county palatine,[38] but military service apparently remained an accepted part of the duty

[33] DL29/728/11988; DL29/729/11995-6, 12001, 12004; DL29/730/12006, 12008, 12011, 12012, 12014. In 1413 Henry V extended this practice so that revenues from the lordship of Tickhill in south Yorkshire were also paid to the Pontefract receiver, and the Cheshire lands of the honour of Halton began to be used as some support for the massive charges on the neighbouring county palatine: DL29/731/12017, 12019A, 12021A, 12022, 12024, 12027, 12029.   [34] DL28/4/2-7.

[35] DL29/728/11988, 11993-4.

[36] Somerville, *History of the Duchy*, 164-5.

[37] J. B. Gillingham, 'Crisis or Continuity? The Structure of Royal Authority in England, 1369-1422', in R. Schneider (ed.), *Das Spätmittelalterliche Königtum Im Europäischen Vergleich* (Sigmaringen, 1987), 65; Brown, 'Reign of Henry IV', 20.

[38] The retinue in the palatinate was called to arms in 1405, 1406, and Feb. 1407 against the threat from France, in the summer of 1407 against Glyn Dŵr's rebellion, and in 1408 against the earl of Northumberland's revolt: DL42/16 pt. 2 fos. 35-35v; pt. 3 fos. 5, 85-85v, 90-90v, 94, 110v-111.

owed by all those in receipt of a Duchy annuity. A survey of the
accounts for the early years of the reign reveals at least seventeen
esquires from all parts of the Duchy who were refused payment of their
annuities because they had not served with the king against the Welsh
rebels or in the Scottish marches, an observation which bears out
Simon Payling's impression of the strength of Duchy representation in
Henry's forces at the battle of Shrewsbury in 1403.[39]

Vital as military service was, Henry clearly valued the Lancastrian
affinity for its peacetime service as well. The close personal connection
between the king and his retinue meant that Duchy service formed a
well-trodden path to high office in royal government. A. L. Brown has
outlined the problems which Henry faced because of the almost complete lack of a 'Lancastrian establishment' among the nobility, whose
ranks were much reduced by death and infirmity, and by the earls'
rebellion of 1400.[40] These circumstances forced the king to rely heavily
in government on lesser men, and naturally he turned especially to his
own knights and esquires. Henry used the offices of the household
extensively in government finance during the first two years of his reign,
and since his household was staffed mainly by Lancastrian officials
transferred from Gaunt's establishment, these Duchy men essentially
directed royal financial administration.[41]

The political crisis that Rogers has identified in 1401, which resulted
in the dismissal of Henry's chancellor, treasurer, steward, and controller and their replacement by men who had all been in office under
Richard II, appears to have been precipitated by two main issues. The
immediate circumstance of the change in personnel seems to have been
the inability of the Lancastrians to control crown finances adequately.
Just as Henry's own men were unused to the management of the Duchy
as a whole, so Gaunt's Duchy officers were relatively inexperienced in
royal administration.[42] Underlying this practical difficulty seems to have
been the wider problem of magnate resentment—meaning, in the context of a severely depleted nobility, essentially the resentment of the
Percies with the support of the Staffords—of Henry's decision to rule
largely through a personal following of non-noble associates.[43]

---

[39] Examples appear in the accounts for Lancashire, Pontefract, Tickhill, Leicester, Norfolk,
Sussex, and the 'south parts': DL29/738/12097, 12098, 12099, 12100; DL29/310/4981; S. J.
Payling, *Political Society in Lancastrian England* (Oxford, 1991), 136.

[40] Brown, 'Reign of Henry IV', 2–7.

[41] A. Rogers, 'The Political Crisis of 1401', *Nottingham Medieval Studies*, 12 (1968), 88–90;
see above, p. 27.

[42] Rogers, 'Political Crisis of 1401', 86–90. The previous experience in the royal administration of men such as the chancellor John Scarle had been at a somewhat lower level, in
Scarle's case as a chancery clerk and master of the rolls: Somerville, *History of the Duchy*, 475.

[43] Rogers, 'Political Crisis of 1401', 90–2; E. F. Jacob, *The Fifteenth Century* (Oxford, 1961),
30–1.

These difficulties, highlighted by this crisis but inherent in Henry's situation, continued to dog him throughout his reign. In the early years of his kingship his nobles were, with a few notable exceptions, too young or too old to take up their natural positions at the heart of government, and Henry relied instead on the unequivocal loyalty of his Lancastrian knights and esquires, who therefore achieved positions of unwonted eminence.[44] By the time some of the heirs of the major noble houses took possession of their inheritances, they had become natural allies of the prince of Wales in his attacks on the incompetence of his father's administration.[45] Henry's dependence on the support of his Lancastrian retinue was thereby redoubled. His response to the criticism of royal financial management and the attempts to curb crown expenditure that recurred throughout the reign re-emphasized the privileged position of his personal affinity. In July 1404, for example, financial crisis led to the ordering of a total stop on the payment of annuities, which seems to have lasted for two years.[46] In October 1405, however, Henry made a specific declaration that annuitants of the Duchy were not to be affected by this restriction, an exemption which seems particularly ironic in view of the king's expansive promise in 1399 that he would 'live of his own'.[47] It was the Duchy affinity which had enabled Henry to seize the throne, and his need to repay and to rely on the loyalty of his Lancastrian retainers meant that, although he took control of the Duchy and the kingdom at almost exactly the same time, he was not prepared to compromise his commitment to the former because of his new responsibilities to the latter. Indeed, it was a compromise he could not afford to make, given that, in the uncertain months and years following the deposition, and in the absence of a Lancastrian nobility, the support of the Duchy retinue was crucial to the survival of the regime.[48]

---

[44] Brown, 'Reign of Henry IV', 7, 14–18.

[45] McFarlane, *Lancastrian Kings and Lollard Knights*, 106–8; G. L. Harriss, 'The King and his Magnates', in G. L. Harriss (ed.), *Henry V: The Practice of Kingship* (Oxford, 1985), 32–3; G. L. Harriss, *Cardinal Beaufort: A Study of Lancastrian Ascendancy and Decline* (Oxford, 1988), 48.

[46] B. P. Wolffe, *The Royal Demesne in English History* (London, 1971), 81; Given-Wilson, *The Royal Household*, 136.

[47] DL42/15 pt. 2 fo. 73v; McFarlane, *Lancastrian Kings and Lollard Knights*, 49, 93.

[48] Brown, 'Reign of Henry IV', 5–19; A. L. Brown, 'The English Campaign in Scotland, 1400', in H. Hearder and H. R. Loyn (eds.), *British Government and Administration* (Cardiff, 1974), 48; T. B. Pugh, 'Magnates, Knights and Gentry', in Chrimes *et al.*, *Fifteenth-Century England*, 107.

3. THE DUCHY OF LANCASTER UNDER HENRY V

Prince Henry's contact with the Duchy and its affinity in the years before his accession in 1413 differed significantly from his father's experience. Henry IV had been brought up as heir to the Duchy of Lancaster. Before Gaunt's death he had used the latter's subsidiary title as earl of Derby; his establishment was founded on his possession of the Hereford heritage, which was later to be included within the Duchy administration, and his retinue was closely connected with the Lancastrian affinity.[49] Henry V, as heir to the throne, instead enjoyed the lands and regional influence which came to him as prince of Wales, earl of Chester, and duke of Cornwall. His involvement with the Lancastrian inheritance before 1413, despite the fact that his father had conferred on him the title of duke of Lancaster,[50] consisted only of a life grant from 1411 of Duchy lands in Lincolnshire valued at an annual total of £168.[51] Henry IV's establishment of his son as heir to the throne had resulted in an abrupt separation of the Lancastrian dynasty from traditions of Lancastrian service in its specific and partisan sense.

Many of Henry's associates as prince of Wales had in fact previously served his father, including Duchy officers and men from Lancastrian areas: Roger Leche of Derbyshire, for example, who was steward of the prince's household from 1407, served as steward of the High Peak from 1405 and of Tutbury from 1407.[52] Nevertheless, the 'special relationship'—the personal commitment which Henry IV had shown exclusively to his Duchy estates and retainers—began to break down because of the prince's experience of the Duchy as simply one part of a much wider responsibility. The political divisions of the years before 1413, and Henry's questioning of the financial and administrative competence of his father's government, helped to undermine further the survival of Lancastrian service in the form that had characterized the years from 1399. The prominence of Lancastrian knights and esquires in Henry IV's government, and the complete confidence he placed in them, meant that in some senses they embodied the regime which the prince was challenging. In these circumstances, the identification of Henry IV's personal authority with his Lancastrian servants can only

---

[49] Somerville, *History of the Duchy*, 67; see above, Ch. 2.2.

[50] On 10 Nov. 1399. The act of parliament declared that the king had bestowed the title on his son 'considerant coment luy Dieu tout-puissant de sa grande grace luy ad mys en l'onurable estat du Roy, et pourtant il ne poet mesmes pur certeine cause porter le noun de Duc de Lancastre en son estile': Hardy (trans. and ed.), *Charters of the Duchy*, 141–2.

[51] DL29/731/12016; DL42/16 pt. 2 fo. 61v.

[52] W. R. M. Griffiths, 'The Military Career and Affinity of Henry, Prince of Wales 1399–1413', unpublished M.Litt. dissertation (Oxford, 1980), 170–1; Somerville, *History of the Duchy*, 539, 551.

have reinforced the relative estrangement of his son from the Duchy affinity.

The Duchy's political significance to Henry V as king was conditioned by this markedly different perspective. His accession represents a watershed in the evolution of a new concept of 'Lancastrian' service, distinct from partisan involvement with the Duchy itself and embracing national allegiance to a new royal dynasty. Henry was not prepared to compromise the uniquely independent status of his Lancastrian possessions—indeed, he ensured that they would remain a distinct political entity by an act of 1414 confirming the independent establishment of the Duchy and annexing to it all lands which had come to his father by his right as duke since 1399.[53] However, a profound change is immediately evident in Henry's treatment of these lands and resources.

Even on a cursory reading of the most general administrative records of the Duchy, the vigour that was suddenly applied to a reappraisal of the management of the Lancastrian estates is everywhere apparent.[54] From 1413, the Duchy administration was subjected to a thorough overhaul, which rationalized and codified the procedures which had developed during the previous reign, as well as making their application more stringent. Henry instituted measures designed to maximize efficiency in financial administration and to stamp out what might previously have been seen as natural manipulation of the benefits of office, but was now clearly unacceptable to the crown. The new king ordered a survey of the Duchy estates so that rent values could be updated, and this process was repeated at regular intervals throughout the reign.[55] The attempt to increase Duchy revenue was reinforced by the establishment of direct royal interest in accounting procedures. In June 1414, the receivers of all Duchy honours were summoned before the king at Westminster to present a full account and to deliver the money that was in their keeping. This, too, became established practice; similar summonses were subsequently issued every two years.[56] These reforms culminated in February 1417 in a special meeting of the Duchy council, at which Henry was present, which produced a series of articles for the better governance of the Duchy.[57]

---

[53] The act also incorporated the estates of the Hereford heritage into the Duchy: Somerville, *History of the Duchy*, 177–8.

[54] This is perhaps unsurprising in view of Henry's effective management of the financial resources of his estates as prince of Wales, and the attempts of his conciliar regime in the latter part of his father's reign to restore the competence of royal financial administration: G. L. Harriss, 'Financial Policy', in Harriss (ed.), *Henry V*, 168–9; Harriss, *Cardinal Beaufort*, ch. 3.   [55] DL42/17 pt. 1 fo. 38; pt. 2 fos. 32, 103.

[56] Evidence of annuities allowable in the receivers' areas was to be presented at the same time, but annuitants were not to receive their fees until after this accounting process had been completed. DL42/17 pt. 2 fos. 12–12v, 63–63v, 81v, 96; Harriss, 'Financial Policy', 169.

[57] The articles declared, for example, that fees were not to be paid to Duchy officers unless

These measures, and the ethos which inspired them, had an immediate and dramatic effect. The clear annual value of the Lancastrian estates increased from an average of £11,000 under Henry IV to £13,000, and this jump in revenue was apparent from the first year of the reign.[58] The new emphasis on the financial worth of the Duchy was complemented by Henry's determination to make more systematic use of these improved revenues as a material resource in government. The annual sum paid into the royal chamber by the receiver-general of the Duchy—which had averaged £1,120 under Henry IV—leapt in the first year of the new reign to £4,500, a sum more than twice the size of the greatest direct contribution made by the Duchy to royal finances since 1399.[59] Between 1413 and 1422 the chamber received an average of £4,400 a year from Lancastrian revenues, and in 1420 the receiver-general paid out as much as £8,200.[60]

For the first time, therefore, the Lancastrian estates were making a substantial contribution to the funds available for the financing of royal policy. For the king in his capacity as lord of an affinity, however, the fact remained that financial stringency was incompatible with extracting the maximum political advantage from his estates; one or the other had to be chosen as the guiding administrative principle. Henry IV had seen the Duchy's value in terms other than the purely financial, giving priority to its role as a source of loyal service and political support. He had therefore been content to allow its administration to be largely self-regulating, and its revenues to be almost entirely absorbed by the huge cost of the annuities that maintained the affinity. Henry V's decision to maximize his income from the Lancastrian lands reversed the priorities which governed the management of the Duchy, its affinity, and its relationship with the king. His policies demonstrated that the Lancastrian retinue could no longer count on the level of material reward and special concessions that it had consistently enjoyed under Henry IV.

the latter ensured that their duties were adequately fulfilled, either by themselves or by a suitable deputy. Fixed procedures were established for the hearing of local accounts, so that a full and fair charge should be made and then recorded, together with the discharge, by a standard form of indenture. An attempt was made to ensure officers' accountability for the good management of the king's property, and to eliminate the possibility either of bribery or of ministers using their authority for their own financial benefit. There was to be no concentration of Duchy power at a local level in the hands of individuals: the authority of even the most influential local officers was to be checked by the supervision of others, or by a system of joint responsibility. Lastly, priority was to be given by local receivers to the payment of income due to the king; only after this were annuities to be issued, 'sique le Roy soit primerement paiez de ces que luy affiert': DL42/17 pt. 2 fos. 105v–106v; Harriss, 'Financial Policy', 169.

[58] Averages calculated from DL29/728/11987–92; DL29/729/11993–12005; DL29/730/12006–15; DL29/731/12016–26; DL29/732/12027–31. See also the figures quoted in Harriss, 'Financial Policy', 169–70.

[59] See above, Ch. 2.2; DL28/4/7–8.

[60] DL28/4/8–11.

The new king's concern for greater efficiency in terms of the carefully regulated collection of the maximum possible income itself ensured that the duties rather than the benefits of Duchy office-holding took precedence. The affinity also lost some of its cocoon of privilege in terms of the money assigned for the payment of annuities. Not only did Henry give royal income unquestioned priority over such payments, but increases in the Duchy revenues available to him were also achieved by decreasing the number of annuities assigned on Duchy lands. Whereas under Henry IV the trend underlying the yearly totals spent on the payment of annuities was consistently, if gradually, upward, under Henry V the same trend was just as consistently and more rapidly downward. The annual totals of annuity payments recorded under Henry IV average £8,000;[61] under his son the figure is £5,600.[62] In achieving this, however, Henry did not allow the structure of the retinue he inherited from his father to be undermined. Annuities were not summarily cancelled; the majority of Henry IV's grants were confirmed in 1413 by the new king.[63] Instead, reductions were achieved by a process of natural wastage, so that the place of a retainer who died was not automatically filled by the grant of a new annuity. A graphic demonstration of this process is provided by an account of annuities payable at certain Duchy lordships in the year 1421–2.[64] Out of a total of 66 annuitants, 3 had died during the accounting year; 33 were noted to be 'senex'; and of the remaining recipients of fees, 8 were women.[65] In other words, the 'active' core of the retinue supported by these lordships was now a group of 22 men; in 1400 the same lands had provided annuities for more than 130 'active' retainers.[66]

[61] DL29/728/11987–92; DL29/729/11993–12005; DL29/730/12006–15; DL29/731/12016–18.

[62] DL29/731/12019–26; DL29/732/12027–31; cf. Harriss's calculations in 'Financial Policy', 169. [63] See, for example, DL42/17 pt. 1 fos. 1v–6v, 9–26.

[64] DL29/738/12113. The account does not conform to the traditional division of the northern and southern circuits because it was made after substantial parts of the Duchy were enfeoffed by Henry V (for which, see below, Ch. 2.4). It covers the lordships of Higham Ferrers, Leicester, the collection of lands known as the 'south parts', and various individual manors. The account also records annuities paid by the receiver-general, which have not been included in the totals cited here in order to allow the figures to be compared directly with those gathered from the account for 1400 cited below, n. 66.

[65] Four of the 33 aged annuitants were also female. The women receiving annuities were, in general, either widows of former Duchy retainers or noblewomen (including the duchess of Clarence and Joan, Lady Bergavenny). Annuities paid by the receiver-general show exactly the same pattern, with 2 dead and 6 aged retainers, as well as 1 woman, among the 15 annuitants.

[66] DL29/738/12096. This figure does not include the 17 female annuitants in 1400. The account of 1400 gives no indication whether any of the retainers should be classed as 'senex', but, in view of the retaining policies of Henry IV and his father during the preceding few years, it is highly unlikely that such men would constitute more than a tiny fraction of the total. An earlier stage in the ageing process which overtook the affinity under Henry V is demonstrated in a Duchy annuity roll for 1415–16, when 6 of the 82 annuitants at the Lancaster receipt and 3 of the 17 at Halton were marked 'senex': DL28/27/6.

Moreover, the policy behind these figures appears to have been planned more carefully than a simple blanket reduction in expenditure. As Henry IV's Lancastrian affinity aged, Henry V took the opportunity not only to reduce but also to reshape it. Analysis of the accounts of individual honours reveals that the gradual reduction in spending on annuities did not follow a uniform pattern; some areas lost proportionately more than others. Some receipts, in fact—those of Sussex, Norfolk, Bolingbroke, and the collection of lands known as the 'south parts'—maintained a fairly consistent burden of annuities throughout the two reigns.[67] It is worth noting that these honours all fall within the southern circuit, away from the traditional Lancastrian heartland in the north, and where the scale of Lancastrian retaining had always been relatively circumspect. It was the northern areas of the Duchy, where annuity payments had consumed almost five-sixths of the available revenue under Henry IV, and which produced an overall deficit in all but one of the years from 1399 to 1407,[68] that sustained the bulk of the reduction in expenditure. There, each receipt's average annual spending on annuities fell by between 25 and 50 per cent during the reign.[69] It seems that, while Henry wished to preserve the affinity as 'a thin web of Lancastrian allegiance all over England',[70] he was not prepared to continue using almost all of the Duchy revenue in the north to sustain a retinue there on the vast scale of his father's affinity.

This unwillingness to maintain the affinity in the style to which it had become accustomed since 1399 reflects the revised role which the Lancastrian retinue was to play under the new regime. Lancastrian service retained its military significance, making an important contribution to Henry's French expeditions.[71] Nor was the general service of the retinue in peacetime rejected in favour of 'new men'; traditions of

[67] DL29/728/11991; DL29/729/11993–4, 11997, 11999, 12002, 12005; DL29/730/12007, 12009, 12013, 12015; DL29/731/12016, 12018–19, 12021, 12023, 12026; DL29/732/12031. The 'south parts' in this context were specific estates grouped together for accounting purposes, as opposed to the southern circuit of the Duchy as a whole, which included all Lancastrian lands south of the Trent.

[68] DL29/728/11987–8; DL29/729/11995–6, 12001, 12004, 12006.

[69] DL29/731/12017, 12019A, 12021A, 12022, 12024; DL29/732/12029.

[70] Walker, *The Lancastrian Affinity*, 37.

[71] See, for example, the number of Duchy retainers from Staffordshire and Derbyshire who served on Henry's campaigns: below, Ch. 7.1. The Duchy registers record a reminder in Oct. 1416 that all Duchy annuitants should have served on Henry's last campaign at Calais, and that payment should only be made to those who had performed this duty: DL42/17 pt. 2 fo. 51v; Harriss, 'Financial Policy', 169. For examples of annuities being stopped on the grounds of absence from the Calais expedition, see DL29/738/12108; see also DL28/27/6 for an annotated list of annuitants at the receipt of the county palatine, recording which were present at Harfleur. The principle that the payment of annuities depended on the performance of military service had been established under Henry IV (see above, Ch. 2.2), although it is probably fair to assume that, like other financial prescriptions, it was more effectively enforced under Henry V.

Lancastrian service continued to be accepted and valued by the new king. Nevertheless, the Duchy affinity had lost the exclusive hold on the king's confidence which it had enjoyed under Henry IV. The specifically 'Lancastrian' resources available to the crown, in terms of both revenue and service, were effectively exploited and duly rewarded, but now firmly within the context of the unification of the political nation under a more comprehensive and unambiguously royal allegiance. Henry's emphasis on his leadership of the community of the realm made necessary a process of distancing himself from his 'special relationship' with a specific retinue.

The fact that the Duchy was now only one of many resources at the king's disposal was reflected in changes to the Duchy personnel. There was, certainly, much continuity. Some men who had held high office under Henry IV did so again after 1413; Robert Waterton, for example, who had been chief steward in the north from 1407, became chamberlain of the Duchy in 1416.[72] Some men who had entered Henry's establishment as prince from a background of local Duchy office-holding were promoted to greater eminence after his accession; Roger Leche, who held the stewardship of Tutbury and the High Peak under Henry IV, became chief steward of the North Parts in 1413.[73] For the first time, however, men previously unconnected with the Duchy were appointed to Lancastrian office at a high level. Hugh Mortimer, for example, who had been chamberlain of Henry's household as prince of Wales, was appointed chamberlain of the Duchy on the new king's accession despite the fact that he had not previously been involved with the Duchy administration.[74] For the first time, the Duchy, though still an independent entity, was becoming fully integrated on equal terms with other aspects of the government and polity. Whereas previously the Duchy had constituted an exclusive pool of privileged servants of the king who were then deployed throughout the royal administration, the boundaries between 'Lancastrian' and 'royal' service were now permeable at all levels.

Yet the theoretical 'special relationship' between king and Duchy remained, and, just as Henry IV's attitude to his Lancastrian retainers had become a focus for criticism of his rule, so his son was able to demonstrate his commitment to his aims in national government through his treatment of his own men and estates. Henry IV had in 1399 optimistically promised that he would 'live of his own'. The fact that 'his own' constituted the crown lands together with his Lancastrian

[72] Somerville, *History of the Duchy*, 417.

[73] DL42/17 pt. 3 fo. 1; Somerville, *History of the Duchy*, 419.

[74] Somerville, *History of the Duchy*, 417; cf. J. Catto, 'The King's Servants', in Harriss (ed.), *Henry V*, 93.

possessions put the Duchy at the centre of debates about the financing of royal government.[75] The cost of rewarding the men who had secured him the throne meant that Henry could not fulfil his promise, since annuity payments consumed almost all the Duchy's disposable income; his failure to keep his word, compounded by financial mismanagement, contributed to the domestic crises of the reign, including growing parliamentary unwillingness to comply with requests for taxation.[76] Henry V's vindication of his claim to renewed financial assistance from his subjects was his restoration of the 'good governance' which his father had failed to provide.[77] In this sense, his overhaul of the finances and administration of the Duchy can be seen as a 'showpiece' example of his intention to restore the competence and efficiency of royal government, designed to reinforce the confidence of political society in the authority of his kingship.[78]

4. THE DUCHY OF LANCASTER UNDER HENRY VI

By 1422, Henry V had succeeded in integrating traditions of Lancastrian service into a united body politic, and in maximizing the potential of the Duchy as a financial resource in national government. His provisions for the management of the Lancastrian estates after his death initiated a policy towards the Duchy which was to be pursued throughout his son's reign—a policy which represented a significant blow to its role as a political resource under the personal control of the monarch.

Like many of those who followed him to France, Henry V made a settlement of his estates for the performance of his will before his departure on campaign in 1415.[79] On 22 July, Duchy lands worth a clear annual total of £6,000 were granted in trust to a group of sixteen feoffees.[80] With the exception of the lands from the Hereford heritage

[75] See above, Ch. 2.2; Wolffe, *The Royal Demesne*, 51, 73–7.

[76] McFarlane, *Lancastrian Kings and Lollard Knights*, 93–101; Harriss, 'Financial Policy', 160–2; Harriss, *Cardinal Beaufort*, 30–2.

[77] Harriss, 'Financial Policy', 160, 162–79.

[78] The same principle is evident in Henry's determination that royal justice should be seen to be a credible, impartial, and effective force in the shires. Whereas Henry IV had been prepared to use his control of judicial process in support of his Lancastrian retinue, and therefore to some degree to compromise his theoretically impartial authority as king, Henry V made a point of demonstrating during the judicial visitations he instituted in 1414 that Duchy retainers could expect no special treatment. See E. Powell, *Kingship, Law, and Society* (Oxford, 1989), 208–16, 224–8, and below, Ch. 6.2.

[79] See, for example, the feoffment made by Sir Ralph Shirley in June 1415 in case of his death abroad: LRO 26D53/2545.

[80] The feoffees were Henry Chichele, archbishop of Canterbury, Henry Beaufort, bishop of Winchester, Thomas Langley, bishop of Durham, Richard Courtenay, bishop of Norwich, Edward, duke of York, Thomas, earl of Arundel, Thomas, earl of Dorset, Ralph, earl of Westmorland, the knights Henry Fitzhugh, Henry Lescrope, Roger Leche, Walter

included in this settlement, these estates were then leased back to the king, so that the effect of the feoffment on the management of the Duchy during Henry's lifetime was limited.[81] On 31 August 1422, however, Henry died, and possession of the enfeoffed estates passed to the nine surviving feoffees for the performance of the will made by the king a year earlier.[82]

At the same time, therefore, as personal royal leadership was lost to the Duchy with the succession of a nine-month-old baby, the administrative unity of the Lancastrian estates was disrupted by Henry V's settlement. Nor were these estates the only ones to be lost to the central Duchy administration. The terms of Henry's marriage to Catherine de Valois in 1420 provided her with a dower settlement worth 10,000 marks, part of which was made up in 1422 by a grant of Duchy lands including the honours of Leicester and Hertford, the lordship of Knaresborough, and the castles of Melbourne and Pleshey.[83] Both the queen and the feoffees appointed their own officials to run the estates which they had been granted, although their establishments retained close associations, and sometimes shared personnel, with that of the Duchy.[84] The administrative procedures of the Duchy itself were altered to reflect its diminished responsibilities. So few lands were left in the crown's possession that the division into two circuits between north and south was abandoned, and a single auditor appointed.[85]

Investigation of the management of the Duchy estates in the reign of Henry VI is hampered by the fact that many fewer records survive than are extant for the reigns of his father and grandfather. Some auditor's and receiver-general's accounts survive for the lands in the hands of the king, as well as some auditor's accounts for the enfeoffed lands, but these cannot compare with the almost complete series of valors

Hungerford, and John Phelip, and Hugh Mortimer, John Wodehous, and John Leventhorp. The enfeoffed lands included the whole of the Hereford heritage as well as some Lancastrian estates (mostly those which had belonged to the families of Ferrers and Lacy); they included Halton in Cheshire, Clitheroe in Lancashire, Tickhill in Yorkshire, Bolingbroke in Lincolnshire, and Higham Ferrers in Northamptonshire: J. Nichols (ed.), *A Collection of all the Wills . . . of the Kings and Queens of England* (London, 1780), 236; *CPR 1413–16*, 356–7; Somerville, *History of the Duchy*, 199, 339; cf. DL29/732/12033.

[81] *CCR 1413–19*, 385–7; Somerville, *History of the Duchy*, 199–200.

[82] Those still alive were Chichele, Beaufort, Langley, Dorset (now duke of Exeter), Westmorland, Fitzhugh, Hungerford, Wodehous, and Leventhorp: Somerville, *History of the Duchy*, 200–1; Harriss, *Cardinal Beaufort*, 127.

[83] Catherine also received lands from the crown and the duchy of Cornwall. Henry IV had intended his widow, Joan, to receive a dower settlement from the Duchy, but his instructions were not carried out. DL29/132/12035; DL28/29/1; Nichols (ed.), *A Collection of all the Wills . . . of the Kings and Queens of England*, 204; Somerville, *History of the Duchy*, 199, 207, 339–40.

[84] Somerville, *History of the Duchy*, 202–3, 207–8; Harriss, *Cardinal Beaufort*, 323–4.

[85] Somerville, *History of the Duchy*, 201, 434; and see, for example, DL29/732/12036.

available for the period 1399 to 1422.[86] There is a good series of Duchy
registers and rolls for the reign, but these refer only to grants and
ordinances concerning the lands held by the king; nothing is known
about the activities of the feoffees except where the king subsequently
confirmed their actions.[87]

Despite these limitations, some general points can be made. Under
Henry IV the political value of the Lancastrian affinity had been made
the priority over the potential of the Duchy estates as a financial
resource. Henry V, while recognizing the political worth of the Lancastrian retinue, had begun to assimilate it into the polity as a whole under
unquestionably royal rather than private leadership, a process which
allowed him to exploit Duchy revenues with an efficiency which had not
been politically possible for his father. The fact that the terms of Henry
V's will dispersed the Lancastrian estates between his widow, his heir,
and his feoffees both demonstrated the king's willingness to use the
Duchy primarily as a financial resource, and ensured that the existence
of the Duchy affinity as a distinct entity in national politics would be
further compromised.[88] Even had Henry VI inherited the throne in
1422 as an assertive adult, his father's testamentary arrangements
meant that it would not necessarily have been easy to maintain the
coherence of the Duchy connection, since he had lost direct control of
a significant part of its territorial base.

As it was, during the fifteen years of Henry's minority, the authority
of the crown, though in theory residing in the person of the young king,
was represented and administered by a council composed of the greater
lords of the realm.[89] In the absence of personal royal leadership, it is
perhaps unsurprising that Duchy revenues, and not what remained of
the Duchy retinue in the shires, should during this period remain the
prime concern in its management. The success of this conciliar regime
was a considerable achievement, given how fundamental the role of an
active king was to the functioning of the polity, but by the mid-1430s
the strains were beginning to show.[90] In 1436, the powers of govern-

---

[86] Receiver-general's accounts: DL28/5/2; DL28/5/6–7. Auditor's accounts, king's lands:
DL29/732/12036; DL29/733/12038; DL43/15/13; DL28/29/1; DL29/733/12042. Auditor's
accounts, feoffees' lands: DL29/732/12033; DL43/16/2; DL29/732/12034; DL29/733/12037,
12039–41.   [87] DL42/18; DL37/8–29.

[88] His decision to use his private resources to provide for his wife and the fulfilment of his
last wishes also reflects his consistent determination to make full and proper use of 'his own'
before calling on the national resources of the crown: see above, Ch. 2.3.

[89] For the minority government, see R. A. Griffiths, *The Reign of King Henry VI* (London,
1981), pt. 1; B. P. Wolffe, *Henry VI* (London, 1981), pt. 2; Harriss, *Cardinal Beaufort*, chs. 6–
12; J. L. Watts, *Henry VI and the Politics of Kingship* (Cambridge, 1996), 111–35.

[90] This was especially the case once the death of the duke of Bedford in 1435 removed the
mediating authority which had previously contained the rivalry between the duke of
Gloucester and Cardinal Beaufort: Harriss, *Cardinal Beaufort*, 214–28, 236–7; Wolffe, *Henry
VI*, 67–8, 79; Griffiths, *Henry VI*, 39–46.

ment began to be transferred from the council to the independent person of the king.[91] It rapidly became apparent, however, that Henry's rule would not emulate the success of his illustrious father, and that the Duchy would receive little more active leadership from the king as an adult than it had during his minority. The fact that Henry made no attempt, at what was ostensibly the start of his majority, to reclaim his Lancastrian inheritance from his father's feoffees formed an early indication that the king was failing to take up the reins of power.[92] In fact, it seems that the reign as a whole was to be characterized by regimes controlled not by the king but by others on his behalf, successively the dukes of Suffolk, Somerset, and York and, in the later 1450s, Henry's queen. The nature of Henry's failings will be discussed in detail shortly,[93] but if it is accepted that his government continued to be managed for him after the end of the minority, rather than being controlled by his personal authority, it is evident that the political significance of the Duchy as the basis for an affinity subject to that personal authority could not effectively be revived. It is in any case clear that under the regimes of Henry's adult reign, as had been the case during his minority, the administration of the Duchy was largely predicated on its financial value.

As in 1413, it seems that those who already received a Duchy annuity had their fees confirmed at the beginning of the new reign, but Henry V's policy of instituting a virtual moratorium on new grants and allowing natural wastage to slim down the retinue seems to have been continued. Almost all the local receipts, within both the enfeoffed lands and those still in the possession of the crown, show a gradual decline in annuity payments: fees paid by the Norfolk receiver, for example, fell from £331 in 1428 to £153 in 1439; in the enfeoffed lands in Lancashire annuities fell from £386 to £198 in the same period; and at Tutbury annuities made up a total of £242 in 1433 and only £130 six years later.[94] At the same time, the practice of paying substantial sums from the Duchy into the royal household was maintained. Between 1437 and 1443 the receiver-general of the estates held by the king paid an

---

[91] Harriss, *Cardinal Beaufort*, 274–5; Wolffe, *Henry VI*, 80–1, 87–92; Griffiths, *Henry VI*, 231–6.

[92] By 1437 the feoffees had controlled the Duchy estates entrusted to them for fifteen years. When Henry V came to the throne, he had had no compunction about ignoring provisions made in his own father's will, including the instruction that the latter's widow should be endowed from the Duchy: McFarlane, *Lancastrian Kings and Lollard Knights*, 112–13; Somerville, *History of the Duchy*, 175.

[93] See below, pp. 45–9.

[94] For these specific figures, see DL29/732/12033, 12036; DL29/733/12041–2. For the other receipts, see references in n. 86 above. Grants of annuities were not completely stopped—see below, p. 96, for example, for a grant to Thomas Tuddenham of the reversion of a fee of 80 marks—but such cases appear to have been extremely rare.

annual average of £3,300 to the treasurer of the household.[95] Between 1437 and 1439 this consisted of a formalized annuity of 5,000 marks.[96] In January 1440 it was enacted in parliament that all surplus revenues of the unenfeoffed part of the Duchy should be appropriated to the household for a period of five years (subsequently extended for a further three), although in practice the amounts received remained largely the same.[97]

Nor did the enfeoffed estates escape the financial demands of the crown. From 1422, the feoffees made substantial loans to the government, which exceeded those received from any other source in the first ten years of the reign. This seems to have suited both the crown, which needed the revenue, and the feoffees themselves, represented principally by Cardinal Beaufort, whose estate in the lands was prolonged by the consequent delay in accumulating enough funds to fulfil Henry V's will.[98] In 1440 the feoffees, only three of whom were still alive, were also compelled to agree to cede the surplus revenue of the estates they held to the household.[99] This turned out to be the opening move in an ultimately successful attempt by Suffolk's regime to repossess the enfeoffed Duchy lands in the name of the now adult king. Despite Beaufort's resistance, the feoffment formally ended at the beginning of 1443.[100] Queen Catherine had died six years earlier, so that now for the first time since 1422 all the Duchy lands were reunited in the possession of the crown.[101]

Suffolk had won the support of the Commons in his manœuvres to regain the enfeoffed estates on the understanding that the finances of the household would benefit.[102] It rapidly became clear, however, that the Commons' expectations would not be fulfilled. Nor was a new

---

[95] DL28/5/2.

[96] G. L. Harriss, 'The Finance of the Royal Household, 1437–60', unpublished D.Phil. thesis (Oxford, 1953), 33–5.

[97] Harriss describes this as a change in form not substance: ibid. 35, 37–8; *Rot. Parl.*, v. 7; Hardy (trans. and ed.), *Charters of the Duchy*, 200–1.

[98] Somerville, *History of the Duchy*, 204; Harriss, 'Finance of the Royal Household', 38; Harriss, *Cardinal Beaufort*, 184, 194, 206, 223–4, 232, 234, 244, 246, 258, 278, 287, 307, 324.

[99] The three surviving feoffees were Cardinal Beaufort, Archbishop Chichele, and Lord Hungerford, all of them elderly: Hardy (trans. and ed.), *Charters of the Duchy*, 202–6. For the negotiations, see Harriss, 'Finance of the Royal Household', 38–40; Harriss, *Cardinal Beaufort*, 307–8; Somerville, *History of the Duchy*, 204–5.

[100] It was argued that all loans made by the feoffees had been repaid, and that they had over the years received more than enough funds to carry out Henry V's will. Moreover, they were reminded that 'the seid Feffees have no title ner interesse therynne, but only upon trust', the fear being that if two of the three elderly surviving feoffees should die, a fee simple would be created and the estates could be alienated from the crown. Beaufort already seems to have acquired some sort of personal interest in the enfeoffed lands in Norfolk. *Rot. Parl.*, v. 56–9; *CPR 1436–41*, 276–7; Harriss, 'Finance of the Royal Household', 40–53; Harriss, *Cardinal Beaufort*, 288, 308, 323; Somerville, *History of the Duchy*, 205–7.

[101] Somerville, *History of the Duchy*, 208.

[102] Harriss, *Cardinal Beaufort*, 308, 323.

Duchy affinity about to be created under the leadership of an adult and, in theory at least, active king. Instead, a substantial part of the Lancastrian estates was immediately enfeoffed to a new group of trustees, this time for the performance of Henry VI's wishes. By four charters dated between 1443 and 1445, Duchy lands worth nearly £4,000 a year were granted to a group of thirty-one feoffees.[103] These estates were subsequently demised back to the king, but their revenues were no longer paid into the wardrobe. Instead, they were used to support Henry's new foundations at Eton and Cambridge.[104]

More lands were lost to the central administration of the Duchy in 1446 in the wake of the king's marriage. As part of a dower settlement worth 10,000 marks, Margaret of Anjou was granted lands worth £2,000 a year from the Duchy, including Kenilworth Castle and the honours of Leicester, Tutbury, and the High Peak.[105] Between the queen's endowment and the foundations of the colleges, very little of the Duchy revenues remained in the possession of the crown.[106] This circumstance provoked significant tensions during the successive attempts to bring royal finances under control in the early 1450s. The resumption act of 1450 provided that the surplus revenues of the unenfeoffed Duchy lands should be put towards the expenses of the household, and such payments were made in 1450–1 and 1451–2. However, the feoffment was so extensive that these sums totalled little more than £300.[107] An attempt was made at the parliament following the first

[103] The lands included estates in Northamptonshire, Norfolk, Leicestershire, Yorkshire, South Wales, and Sussex. The feoffees were the archbishops of Canterbury and York, the bishops of London, Lincoln, Bath and Wells, Salisbury, and Worcester, the earls of Suffolk and Northumberland, Viscount Beaumont, the lords Hungerford, Cromwell, and Sudeley, Sir Edmund Hungerford, Sir John Beauchamp, the esquires James Fiennes, Edward Hull, John Hampton, John Noreys, John St Lo, William Tresham, John Vampage, and Richard Alred, and the clerks John Somerset, Henry Suer, John Langton, Richard Andrew, Adam Moleyns, Walter Lyhert, Walter Sherrington, and John de la Bere. Knaresborough and Pickering, and lands in Derbyshire and Staffordshire including Newcastle-under-Lyme were added to the new feoffments in 1449. Henry's 'will' ('voluntatem') in this context does not seem to be intended to mean his last will. Somerville, *History of the Duchy*, 210–11, 340; *Rot. Parl.*, v. 70–3; Hardy (trans. and ed.), *Charters of the Duchy*, 220–40; Harriss, 'Finance of the Royal Household', 67; J. L. Watts, 'Domestic Politics and the Constitution in the Reign of Henry VI, c.1435–61', unpublished Ph.D. thesis (Cambridge, 1990), 209 n.

[104] Each college was granted £1,000 a year in 1444, with an extra annual sum of £400 for King's and 400 marks for Eton added in 1446: Harriss, 'Finance of the Royal Household', 67–8; Somerville, *History of the Duchy*, 221; Watts, *Henry VI*, 167–71, 185–6.

[105] Margaret was also granted an annuity of £1,000 from Duchy revenues. She received a further annuity of 500 marks from the Duchy, which had previously been paid to the duke of Gloucester, in 1447. Somerville, *History of the Duchy*, 208–9, 340; *Rot. Parl.*, v. 118–20; Harriss, 'Finance of the Royal Household', 81, 237–9, 248–9.

[106] Cf., for example, Harriss's point that in 1446 the exchequer had to meet the entire burden of the expenditure of the wardrobe from its own resources, with no help from the Duchy, for the first time in nine years: 'Finance of the Royal Household', 83.

[107] Other payments may have been made from the same source in later years, although the accounts which would provide evidence of this have not survived; nevertheless, any sums

battle of St Albans in 1455 to resume the enfeoffed Duchy lands, and the Yorkists seem to have secured £1,000 from those estates in 1454–6.[108] When the act of resumption was eventually passed, however, both the queen's endowment and Henry VI's feoffments were safeguarded by exemption clauses, as they had previously been in 1450 and 1453.[109]

Under all the various regimes of Henry VI's reign, therefore, the management of the Duchy estates was predicated on their use as a financial resource. They were used to provide endowments for the queens Catherine and Margaret, and, initially at least, were used as some support for the expenditure of the royal household, a popular demonstration of the accepted principles of good financial governance in return for the financing of the war in France.[110] From the mid-1440s, however, the practice of using the king's private resources to meet some of his own costs was discontinued in favour of devoting almost all available Duchy revenues to an entirely private project.[111] Henry V's attempt to use the Duchy revenues as one source of support for an unquestionably public and national Lancastrian crown had effectively been abandoned.

The use of the Duchy estates to support an extensive regional affinity created around the king's lordship had also been abandoned, by taking Henry V's policy of letting the retinue age to its logical conclusion. Margaret of Anjou may have tried to create a new affinity around her midland estates of Tutbury, Leicester, and Kenilworth during the later 1450s, but, in the absence of virtually all the records of her administration, it is impossible to be sure. Certainly it seems that few of the region's gentry proved willing to fight on her behalf.[112] Nevertheless, there remained one overtly political element in the management of the Duchy, in that Duchy office conferred substantial authority on individuals in the localities. Under Henry IV and Henry V, Duchy stewardships had been filled by leading gentry members of the Lancastrian retinue in each region, their activities closely scrutinized by their royal lord.[113] Under Henry VI, these powerful local offices were filled

---

involved could only have been on the same negligible scale: DL28/5/6–7; Harriss, 'Finance of the Royal Household', 118–19, 157–9.

[108] Harriss, 'Finance of the Royal Household', 175–6.

[109] Somerville, *History of the Duchy*, 219–20; Harriss, 'Finance of the Royal Household', 176, 249, 251. [110] See above, pp. 37–8; Harriss, *Cardinal Beaufort*, 308.

[111] Harriss argues that 'at a time when increased charges on the revenue were threatened from both domestic and foreign commitments, the application of the majority of the Duchy of Lancaster revenues to the royal colleges [was] indefensible': 'Finance of the Royal Household', 112.

[112] Only one account drawn up by her receiver-general survives, for the year 1452–3: DL28/5/8. For detailed discussion of this issue, see below, pp. 300–1.

[113] See above, Chs. 2.2 and 2.3, and below, Chs. 3, 6, 7.1.

for the first time by members of the nobility. This was a significant change in the administrative structure of the Duchy, and one which has important implications for analyses of Henry's government as a whole.

Recent accounts of the reign have sought to illuminate the inadequacies of Henry's kingship by investigating the conundrum of his character. The picture of the king as a saintly and innocent recluse, familiar from hagiographic legend, has been challenged.[114] B. P. Wolffe argued that Henry was capable of intervening decisively in the affairs of the realm, but was inconsistent, vacillating, often irrational and suspicious, and lacking in judgement, a 'dangerous compound of force-fulness and weakness'.[115] Recent consensus, however, has sought a compromise between Henry the saint and Henry the autocrat, suggest-ing that, while the king's pacific and merciful nature dictated the course of English policy in France, he played little part in directing the exer-cise of royal authority in England.[116] The general conclusion has been, whatever view is taken of Henry's role in policy-making, that the king's imprudent generosity and vulnerability to pressure from those around him allowed members of his court to exercise undue influence on the direction of government, while enriching themselves with the spoils of royal patronage. The chief culprit during the 1440s has been identified as the earl of Suffolk, who, it is argued, emerged as the leader of a court faction based in the royal household, which included few of the ancient nobility and which dominated the authority and resources of the crown. It was by Suffolk and his servants that 'true power was exercised'.[117]

The evidence of Duchy office-holding, however, offers little support to this picture of the domination of the king and the exclusion from government of the nobility by a 'court clique' under Suffolk's leader-ship. In 1437, the year when the formal trappings of the minority were removed, and the point at which Suffolk's court party is supposed to have begun to establish its grip on government,[118] there was a concerted

---

[114] B. P. Wolffe, 'The Personal Rule of Henry VI', in Chrimes *et al.* (eds.), *Fifteenth-Century England*, 30–1, 44; Wolffe, *Henry VI*, 3–25; Griffiths, *Henry VI*, 2–6.

[115] Wolffe, *Henry VI*, 106–10, 125–6, 132–3 (quotation from 133).

[116] Griffiths, *Henry VI*, 248–54.

[117] Quotation from Griffiths, *Henry VI*, 304. For this interpretation of Suffolk's role in the polity, see ibid. 281–6, 301–4, 329–67. Wolffe, in his biography of the king, accords Henry a greater role in the direction of government (a view which he had stated forcibly in an earlier article: see 'The Personal Rule of Henry VI', 36–44, and above, n. 115); he describes Suffolk as the 'chief agent of Henry's policies', accusing him of 'sins of omission' in failing to advise the king wisely (*Henry VI*, 220, 223–4). However, he too emphasizes Suffolk's acquisitiveness and self-aggrandizement (ibid. 98–105, 109–13, 116, 220–9). C. L. Kingsford, writing in 1925, has been a lone voice in arguing that Suffolk was 'a man of lofty sentiment and principle . . . made the subject for the foulest and most persistent slander', who, 'had his genius been equal to his understanding, or his fortune to his merits', 'might have saved England from long years of disaster': *Prejudice and Promise in Fifteenth-Century England* (Oxford, 1925), 146, 176.

[118] Griffiths, *Henry VI*, 231–40, 275–82.

and far-reaching reorganization of the chief regional offices of the Duchy. This is usually taken to be one example of the appropriation of the crown's resources by Suffolk and the household,[119] but the most striking aspect of the reallocation of office is the fact that the major beneficiaries were members of the regional nobility. It is true that Suffolk himself secured the chief stewardship of the North Parts of the Duchy, and that relative newcomers to the peerage, such as Ralph, Lord Cromwell, and John, Lord Beaumont, were appointed to influential offices; also included, however, were members of the greater nobility such as the earls of Stafford and Salisbury. The overhaul of Duchy office-holding in 1437 seems in fact to represent not a partisan takeover by a court faction but a considered attempt to use Duchy resources to reinforce existing regional hierarchies.

The earl of Stafford, who controlled the most significant territorial stake in the north midlands apart from that of the king himself, had held the stewardship of Tutbury and the master forestership of Needwood during the king's pleasure since 1435, but in 1437 he received life appointments as steward of Tutbury, master forester of Needwood and of Duffield Frith, and steward of the Cheshire lordship of Halton.[120] The earl of Salisbury had been granted the Duchy stewardship of the honour of Pontefract in 1425 and that of the honour of Tickhill in 1432, but in 1437 his regional dominance was substantially reinforced by the conversion of his office at Pontefract to a life grant, and by his appointment, also for life, to the stewardship of Blackburn in Lancashire.[121] Cromwell, who had established himself during the previous decade as the leading figure in Nottinghamshire and the north-east midlands, was in 1437 appointed steward of the Duchy lordship of Pickering in east Yorkshire.[122] In the same year, Beaumont was appointed to the Duchy stewardships of the honour of Leicester and the lordship of Castle Donington, grants which made his dominance in the south-east midlands as unassailable as Cromwell's in the north-east of the region.[123] It was also in 1437 that the local interests and Duchy offices

---

[119] Griffiths, *Henry VI*, 233, 342–3.

[120] DL42/18 pt. 1 fos. 33v, 59–59v; Somerville, *History of the Duchy*, 510, 539, 542, 546, 556.

[121] These stewardships included the offices of constable and, where applicable, master forester. The Blackburn office was held jointly with Sir John Stanley: DL42/18 pt. 1 fos. 92, 93v–94; pt. 2 fo. 83v; Somerville, *History of the Duchy*, 501, 507, 513, 515, 518, 528–9. Griffiths acknowledges the fact of the appointments of Stafford and Salisbury, but does not see this as part of the same process as the grants to members of 'the court', arguing that 'the more outlandish (at least in the eyes of aspiring courtiers) of the duchy offices were not half so attractive, partly because they frequently lay in areas ruled by powerful magnates. Thus . . . Salisbury . . . became steward of the lordship of Tickhill' and 'the honour of Tutbury was under the control of the earl of Stafford': *Henry VI*, 343.

[122] Somerville, *History of the Duchy*, 533; DL42/18 pt. 1 fo. 48v. For Cromwell, see below, Ch. 7.2.

[123] The honour of Leicester included lands in both Leicestershire and Northamptonshire.

of Suffolk and William Phelip, later Lord Bardolf, were accommodated into a single hierarchy of authority in East Anglia.[124] In none of these cases did Duchy appointments allow interlopers to intrude into established structures of power; rather, they bestowed added authority on those who already played a legitimate role in regional rule.

The local power conferred by Duchy office was therefore divided up systematically between leading members of the regional nobility to create a series of territorial blocs under magnate control. Under normal circumstances, possession of the Lancastrian estates meant that the king had an important role to fulfil in the rule of the regions, but it was a role which Henry VI was showing no signs of tackling. In this context, the distribution of Duchy office in 1437 seems to have represented an attempt to 'manage' local power structures by annexing the private resources of the king in support of the local authority of private individuals—the nobility in their role as regional lords—in order to buttress the part they were having to play in national government, since the king was failing to relieve them of the public responsibilities which they had undertaken during his minority.[125] By 1437, therefore, profound abnormalities were already evident in Henry's rule, since, at the point when he should have begun to take over control of government from those who had managed it on his behalf during his childhood, the scope of their management was in fact being extended to include the king's private inheritance as well as his public authority.

The conclusion that this reorganization of the Duchy's local influence was a systematic policy of reinforcing regional hierarchies, involving leading members of the nobility, is not easy to reconcile with the argument that royal authority was usurped during this period by a self-serving and exclusive household clique. An alternative analysis of Henry's kingship has recently been proposed, however, which offers a political context into which the evidence of the management of the

Beaumont's power was further reinforced in 1440 when he secured the stewardship of the Duchy in Lincolnshire. DL42/18 pt. 1 fos. 48, 97–97v, 138; Somerville, *History of the Duchy*, 563, 572, 576, 586. Significantly, the 'new' nobles Beaumont and Cromwell were able to achieve this eminence not because they were usurping the regional influence of the 'traditional' nobility, but because their developing spheres of interest were located in areas of the midlands which had previously been dominated by the king through the Duchy, and where there was therefore a power vacuum under Henry VI: see below, Ch. 7.

[124] For the structure of power in East Anglia at this point, see below, Chs. 3 and 4; for details of the grants to Suffolk and Phelip in 1437, see below, pp. 88–92.

[125] This policy of using Duchy offices to reinforce and to manage local power structures continued throughout the reign. Significantly, when the Yorkist nobles secured control of government in 1460, the major Duchy stewardships were immediately redistributed among their number, Warwick being the chief beneficiary: Somerville, *History of the Duchy*, 421, 429, 493, 511, 514, 524, 540, 551, 564, 572, 576, 586, 594.

Duchy fits more readily.[126] It is difficult to demonstrate from surviving administrative evidence the extent of the king's active involvement in the making of policies carried out in his name, so that the attempts of Wolffe and Griffiths to attribute particular decisions to Henry's personal will, while simultaneously maintaining that he was almost indiscriminately susceptible to the influence of those around him, must remain speculative or, at best, provisional.[127] It has been suggested that the only coherent approach which can account for the nature of the successive regimes over which Henry presided and for the inconsistencies in previous accounts of the reign lies not in discussion of his ultimately unknowable character, but in investigation of his role within the polity; and, further, that in this context the most consistent feature of Henry's rule was his complete failure to exercise any independent royal authority.[128] The most fundamental aspect of the late medieval constitution was that the universal authority of the crown both guaranteed all other authority in the realm, and represented the interests of the realm as a whole.[129] For this universal royal authority to function, however, it had to be exercised, and exercised independently, for only through the independent power of the king could the diverse interests of his individual subjects be reconciled in the general good of the 'common weal'.[130] John Watts argues that, from the point in the later 1430s at which Henry is usually assumed to have taken up the reins of government, the king 'was not the initiator of his so-called "personal rule"', and that 'the impetus for royal activity came not from within, but from below'.[131] The survival of a formal council after 1437 therefore represents not the 're-establishment . . . of traditional royal rule',[132] but an attempt by the lords, in the absence of any self-assertion on Henry's part, 'to realize the pressing need for royal leadership by using the tools available to them'.[133]

[126] See Watts, *Henry VI*. What follows is, necessarily, a truncated summary of a complex argument.

[127] This argument seems in part to be a result of separating the issue of patronage from that of policy. Wolffe, for example, remarks that 'it is hard to believe that in the 1440s Henry weighed the consequences of granting any petition which reached him, or refused it'. Nevertheless, he argues that Henry's policy-making was conducted independently of such external influences, so that Suffolk in 1450 was merely the 'scapegoat' for the failure of the king's own French policy: Wolffe, *Henry VI*, 113, 223, 228.

[128] Watts, *Henry VI*, 9–11, 103–11, 363–6, and chs. 5–7, *passim*.

[129] E. H. Kantorowicz, *The King's Two Bodies* (Princeton, 1957), 363; G. L. Harriss, *King, Parliament, and Public Finance in Medieval England to 1369* (Oxford, 1975), 129–30, 510–11; Watts, *Henry VI*, 13–39; see above, Ch. 1.

[130] Watts, *Henry VI*, 74–80.

[131] Ibid. 132–3.

[132] Griffiths, *Henry VI*, 277.

[133] Watts, *Henry VI*, 135. Watts suggests that 'even when [the king] was involved directly in decision making, he seems merely to have supplied bland approbation. It may, indeed, seem strange that the councillors bothered to consult the king at all, but it should be remembered

This premiss prompts a radical reassessment of the nature of Suffolk's government during the 1440s. Watts suggests that, far from using his court position to monopolize access to the king for his own mercenary ends, Suffolk's leadership of the household represented an attempt to create an artificial active royal persona around the almost totally passive person of the king, and thus reconstitute the structures of 'normal' royal rule.[134] In this venture, it is argued, he secured the support of the territorial nobility, whose regional authority was essential to the maintenance of the effective power of the crown, and whose vested interests lay in the restoration of the royal lordship which underpinned the hierarchies of power within which they operated.[135] Consensus among the lords was essential if Suffolk's regime were to have any chance of exercising the judicial powers of the crown in the context of regional conflicts involving members of the nobility. Ultimately, the artificial royal lordship created by Suffolk through the household proved unable to impose lasting settlements on magnate rivalries; only the universal representation provided by the independent authority of an active king could provide adequate arbitration and enforce reconciliation between the disparate interests of his leading subjects.[136] Nevertheless, in the short term, Suffolk was able to combine his leadership of the royal household with the support he commanded among his fellow nobles to provide a semblance of active royal rule.

This reassessment of the regime of the 1440s provides a coherent context—as previous analyses of the reign do not—for the conclusion that the regional authority inherent in the major Duchy offices was in 1437 delegated to leading members of the territorial nobility. If that year marked the emergence of Suffolk as the leader of a broadly based attempt to create a workable regime around a king who was unwilling or unable to exercise his personal authority, then the harnessing of the regional power of the Duchy in support of magnate rule in the localities becomes comprehensible, as a necessary complement to the nobility's crucial role in constituting a semblance of royal authority at the centre. In the chapters that follow, further consideration will be given to the

---

that royal will, in which an apparently normal adult king would be expected to have the controlling share, remained the only legitimate basis for public action': ibid., 148.

[134] Ibid. 155, 162–71.
[135] Ibid. 172–80, 221–40; see also J. L. Watts, 'The Counsels of King Henry VI *c*.1435–1445', *EHR* 106 (1991), especially 189–90; and see above, Ch. 1. This interpretation finds considerable support in Harriss's account of events in the late 1430s and early 1440s: see Harriss, *Cardinal Beaufort*, 292–5, on the fact that 'there is no indication that [the king] initiated or directed policy or did more than give his official approval' during the late 1430s, and 306–9, 316–24, 344–52, for the establishment of Suffolk's regime with substantial noble support and without significant direction from Henry.
[136] Watts, *Henry VI*, 176–9, 195–9.

implications of the Duchy's role in local political structures for analyses of the nature of Henry's kingship.[137]

Under the first two Lancastrians, the financial and political aspects of the Duchy—the Duchy revenues and the affinity they supported—were largely interdependent. Henry IV relied heavily on his Lancastrian retinue in the acquisition and defence of his throne and in his government. The financial administration of the Duchy was therefore necessarily subjugated to the demands of the affinity, and he was unable to use his estates as a significant source of revenue. Henry V, unlike his father, was free from the particular insecurity of the usurper, and proved immensely able at uniting the polity around his leadership. In this context, the Lancastrian retinue could gradually be assimilated into broader structures of power, allowing the Duchy administration to focus instead on maximizing financial efficiency. After 1422, however, the effects of Henry V's will and the incapacity of his son meant that the Duchy ceased to function as a single entity, and, as the Lancastrian retinue dwindled, the interdependent relationship between the value of the estates in financial and in political terms broke down. By the end of Henry VI's reign, the revenues of the Duchy had been appropriated more explicitly to the private purposes of the king than at any point during the century. At the same time, the Duchy hierarchy of office, no longer connected to an extensive nationwide affinity but still extremely influential in regional power structures, had become an integral part of the system of national government. The appropriation of Lancastrian office by the nobility ensured that the territorial interests of the Duchy would be assimilated into the national body politic which, in the absence of a king who could exert his own authority either in central government or in the regions, was trying to find a workable means of preserving the illusion of normal political life.

[137] See below, Chs. 4, 5, 7.2, 8.

Part II

The Crown, the Duchy of Lancaster, and the Rule of the Localities
East Anglia, 1399–1461

3

1399–1430
The Lancastrian Crown in East Anglian Politics

I. PATTERNS OF LORDSHIP IN EAST ANGLIA TO 1399

From the moment of his usurpation, Henry IV faced the challenge of establishing confidence among his subjects in the public quality of Lancastrian rule, and thereby both demonstrating and reinforcing his claim to the universal authority of the crown. Success in the attempt would be vital to the survival of the regime; but it had to be combined with the management of his private local lordship in areas where the Duchy of Lancaster made him a substantial landowner.[1] The form which this problem took, and the complexity of the task of resolving it, varied considerably from region to region with differences in the patterns of landholding within which the Duchy estates were located, and differences in the degree of local influence which the Lancastrian connection had already developed by 1399.

In this context, the extensive and valuable Lancastrian estates in East Anglia presented an unusual set of circumstances. In other areas where the Duchy enjoyed a significant territorial stake, such as the north midlands,[2] the task which confronted Henry was that of accommodating his personal lordship over a powerful local affinity within his management of the wider regional and national powers of the crown. The Duchy lands in East Anglia, however, had not been used to develop any substantial political connection in the region before 1399. There was therefore no immediate local tension between the new public authority of the Lancastrian crown and a pre-existing pattern of private Lancastrian lordship. The opportunity was there for Henry to put the potential power which the Duchy estates represented to political use for the first time; to discover whether his possession of substantial estates in the region, with few political strings yet attached, could be used from his position as king to strengthen rather than compromise the crown's role in local affairs.[3]

[1] See above, Ch. 1.
[2] See below, Ch. 6.
[3] Parts of this section appeared in an earlier form as 'The Duchy of Lancaster and the Rule of East Anglia, 1399—1440: A Prologue to the Paston Letters', in R. E. Archer (ed.), *Crown, Government and People in the Fifteenth Century* (Stroud, 1995), 53–78.

Map 1. Duchy of Lancaster estates in East Anglia

The Duchy of Lancaster lands in East Anglia were concentrated in a compact group of estates in northern Norfolk.[4] This territorial stake was a particularly valuable one, in the context both of the Duchy as a whole, and of tenurial patterns within the shire. The average clear annual value of these lands during Henry IV's reign was £960, a figure exceeded only by receipts at the Lancastrian strongholds of Tutbury, Lancaster, and Bolingbroke, and the particularly rich conglomeration of manors known as the 'south parts'.[5] The Lancastrian lands divided, administratively and historically, into two groups. The manors of Gimingham, Thetford, Methwold, Beeston Regis, Tunstead, and Rodmere, and the hundreds of Gallow and Brothercross, known as the lands of the honour of Lancaster, had come to Gaunt as part of his wife's inheritance, having originally been acquired by Thomas of Lancaster from Earl Warenne in 1319.[6] The manors of Aylsham, Wighton, Fakenham, Snettisham, and the hundreds of Erpingham, North Greenhoe, and Smithdon were added in 1372 as part of the compensation which Gaunt received in exchange for his earldom of Richmond.[7] Although the Lancaster and 'Richmond' estates continued to be accounted separately, in practice the lands functioned as a unified 'Norfolk receipt'.[8] In territorial terms, they also formed a compact and unified sphere of interest.

Within the context of East Anglia as a whole, the Duchy lands potentially held great political significance. Though Norfolk and Suffolk formed a compact territorial bloc and were administered together under a joint shrievalty,[9] there were fundamental tenurial and political differences between the two. Norfolk was characterized by fragmented and diffuse tenurial patterns.[10] No magnate possessed sufficient estates to dominate the county, apart perhaps from the duke of Lancaster, and even then, because the Duchy lands were concentrated in the northern part of the shire, it would not necessarily be easy to extend

---

[4] See Map 1, p. 54.

[5] Valuations in Norfolk ranged between £847 (in 1411–12) and £1,035 (in 1402–3). The equivalent annual averages for these other receipts were, at Tutbury, £1,550; at Lancaster £1,480; at Bolingbroke £1,140; and in the South Parts, £1,020: DL29/728/11987–8, 11991, 729/11993–7, 11999, 12001–2, 12004–5, 730/12006–9, 12011–15, 731/12016–18.

[6] The Warenne family regained possession of the estates between Thomas's execution in 1322 and the death of the last Earl Warenne in 1347, when they reverted to Henry of Grosmont: R. Somerville, *History of the Duchy of Lancaster*, i (London, 1953), 26, 36; S. Walker, *The Lancastrian Affinity* (Oxford, 1990), 184–5.

[7] W. Hardy (trans. and ed.), *The Charters of the Duchy of Lancaster* (London, 1845), 26–31; Somerville, *History of the Duchy*, 52–3; Walker, *The Lancastrian Affinity*, 185.

[8] See references in n. 5 above.

[9] *List of Sheriffs for England and Wales*, PRO Lists and Indexes, 9 (1898), 87.

[10] B. M. S. Campbell, 'The Complexity of Manorial Structure in Medieval Norfolk: A Case Study', *Norfolk Archaeology*, 39 (1986), 225–61; A. H. Smith, *County and Court: Government and Politics in Norfolk, 1558–1603* (Oxford, 1974), 3.

Lancastrian lordship across the county as a whole.[11] In Norfolk, there-fore, the gentry had the opportunity for a wide range of independent action. Lordship was a desirable commodity, eagerly sought and fully exploited, but in the absence of a dominant territorial interest the balance of power essentially rested with the gentlemen of the shire. Lords might seek to extend the range of their authority by winning the service of these men, but the focus of political activity remained with the gentry themselves. This 'openness' in political society was reinforced by the county's significant mercantile presence at Norwich and the ports of Yarmouth and Lynn, by its commercial and agri-cultural wealth, by its relative proximity to London, and by the lawyers of the area.[12] These men formed a notoriously numerous element with-in the local population; they flourished on the litigation that was the inevitable result of fragmented tenurial patterns, and contributed to it themselves when they sought to convert their professional earnings into the status and power conferred by land ownership.[13] Thus, territorial interests were sufficiently fluid to offer the possibility that 'new men' would be able to establish themselves among the landowning classes, and the area did not lack candidates seeking to tread that path.

The geopolitics of Suffolk were very different from those of Norfolk. Whereas the estates of the Duchy dominated northern Norfolk, there was no significant Duchy presence in Suffolk; and whereas the duke of Lancaster had no rivals in terms of his territorial stake in Norfolk, Suffolk was composed of a complex of interlocking magnate estates. The lands of the Mowbrays and the de la Poles formed large territorial blocs;[14] the Mortimer honour of Clare gave the earls of March (and subsequently the duke of York) a substantial foothold in the county, and the sphere of influence in northern Essex of the de Vere earls of Oxford extended into southern Suffolk.[15] Political society in Suffolk,

---

[11] In this context, it is significant that the northern and western part of Norfolk, within which the Duchy lands lay, was economically and geographically distinct from the central and southern area of the shire. The light soils of the north and west supported an economy based largely on sheep and grain, whereas cattle farming and dairy production predominated on the heavy soils of central and southern Norfolk. As Hassell Smith comments, this tended to mean that 'in each region the inhabitants developed their own identity and community of interests'. Moreover, the fact that land ownership was more widely based in the latter area, together with the greater degree of economic diversification, meant that lordly control was likely to be more difficult to establish: Smith, *County and Court*, 3–8. [12] Ibid. 3–14.

[13] *Rot. Parl.*, v. 326–7; Smith, *County and Court*, 3; E. W. Ives, *The Common Lawyers of Pre-Reformation England* (Cambridge, 1983), 330–44; C. Carpenter, *Locality and Polity* (Cambridge, 1992), 97, 123–4. See below, Ch. 4.5, for discussion of the careers of William Paston, William Winter, and John Heydon, three such lawyers who established their families among the region's gentry.

[14] See Map 1, p. 54, and below, pp. 83 and 101.

[15] P. A. Johnson, *Duke Richard of York 1411–60* (Oxford, 1988), 14; D. MacCulloch, *Suffolk and the Tudors: Politics and Religion in an English County 1500–1600* (Oxford, 1986), 55; see Map 1, p. 54.

though lacking any significant Duchy influence, was thus much more clearly lord-centred than that of Norfolk.[16]

Geographically, then, East Anglia formed a compact bloc, but, in political terms, no magnate enjoyed the landed predominance which would straightforwardly allow the region to be governed as a single sphere of influence. The territorial balance of power suggested that under normal circumstances the rule of Suffolk would be competed for or divided up by whoever controlled the de la Pole and Mowbray estates, and that in Norfolk the Duchy lands provided the key to harnessing the support of the substantial local gentry. Anyone who aspired to the rule of the entire region would have to find some way of marrying the power of the Duchy in northern Norfolk with that of the noble estates in Suffolk.

This was a challenge for which Gaunt had shown no appetite. Despite the financial value of the East Anglian lands, their political significance in the years before 1399 had never rivalled that of Tutbury, Lancaster, Bolingbroke, or even less valuable areas. In a sense, Norfolk offered John of Gaunt no ready focus for such activity. Rich though they were, his East Anglian estates contained no *caput honoris* which could function as a political, as well as administrative and domestic, centre in the same way as the Lancastrian castles in the midlands and the north. The consolidation of his landed interest in the area through the Richmond exchange was also relatively recent, so that there were no deep-rooted traditions of Lancastrian allegiance to exploit in the establishment of a political connection. Further, the geographical balance of the Duchy as a whole placed Norfolk on the periphery, and certainly Gaunt himself rarely visited the county.[17] As has already been suggested, the shire was in any case not one which naturally lent itself to the establishment of one dominant lordship. The extent of Gaunt's estates made him the only plausible claimant to exercise authority over the whole county, but he does not seem to have attempted the difficult task of seeking to rule the numerous and wealthy gentry. Though more than willing to reap the benefits of 'good lordship' when and where it was available, the gentry of Norfolk were therefore left with the real possibility of maintaining their independence and with an unusual latitude for political manœuvre.[18]

Gaunt's retaining in the area fell into two broad categories. The associations he made among the more eminent members of local society during the 1370s and 1380s seem to have been inspired primarily by his

---

[16] Cf. MacCulloch, *Suffolk and the Tudors*, 53.

[17] Walker, *The Lancastrian Affinity*, 184.

[18] R. Virgoe, 'The Crown and Local Government: East Anglia under Richard II', in R. Virgoe, *East Anglian Society and the Political Community of Late Medieval England* (Norwich, 1997), 30–1.

need for military service. Knights such as John Plays, Thomas Morieux, and Thomas Erpingham served in Gaunt's company on campaign abroad, but at home they did not represent any coherent association of specifically Lancastrian interests.[19] Nor did they hold Duchy office; the lack of an honorial centre in the region also meant a dearth of the honorial appointments which were so important to the structure of the affinity in other areas.[20] The men who did hold posts within the Duchy constituted the second category of Gaunt's local retainers. The offices of steward, receiver, and feodary of the duke's Norfolk lands were essentially administrative and were filled by lesser gentlemen of the shire, many of them lawyers.[21] An association of activities and interests, enhanced by prolonged administrative and professional co-operation, is more readily identifiable among these men than among the more eminent Lancastrian retainers.[22] However, the fact that many of them were also involved in county administration, and many simultaneously served other employers in similar professional capacities, suggests that too much emphasis should not be placed on Gaunt's lordship as the focal point for this grouping within local society. Service to an absentee lord offered many advantages, but need not have represented either an exclusive association or even membership of a 'Lancastrian affinity' in the sense in which it existed elsewhere.[23]

The impression remains that Gaunt was less concerned with maximizing the political potential of his Norfolk estates than with exploiting their extensive revenues as a source of cash, albeit while maintaining a certain Lancastrian presence in the shire.[24] Even when the proportion of his East Anglian income assigned to the payment of annuities rose dramatically during the 1390s, this does not seem to have been the result of a newly ambitious retaining strategy in the area, but the consequence of a substantial grant to his son-in-law John Holand, combined with the recruitment of a few young esquires and the gift of fees to some members of his household.[25] Henry of Bolingbroke had

---

[19] Simon Walker has characterized these men as 'a miscellaneous collection of knightly retainers, scattered over East Anglia, who had little in common except a shared desire to profit from the duke's service': *The Lancastrian Affinity*, 186–7, and appendix I.

[20] Somerville, *History of the Duchy*, 97–8, 111–13; see below, Ch. 6.1, for the situation in the north midlands.

[21] Prominent among them, for example, were Edmund Gournay, Edmund Clippesby, John Winter, and John Methwold: Somerville, *History of the Duchy*, 377; Walker, *The Lancastrian Affinity*, 191.

[22] See below, pp. 62–4, for detailed discussion of this group.

[23] Walker, *The Lancastrian Affinity*, 191–4.

[24] Ibid. 187–8.

[25] Annuities accounted for just under a third of the clear value of the Norfolk receipt during the 1390s, which was double the proportion so used during the preceding decade. Holand was granted an annuity of 200 marks in Mar. 1391: DL29/310/4980; DL29/728/11985; Walker, *The Lancastrian Affinity*, 203–4, 307.

slightly stronger connections with the area. His principal residence at Peterborough lay nearby, and the region was represented in his retinue most prominently by his butler John Payn, and by Sir Thomas Erpingham, who had moved into Henry's service by 1390 and subsequently became one of his closest associates.[26] However, their regional origins remained largely incidental to their roles in the earl's service during the 1390s; indeed, they spent substantial parts of the decade with him on his expeditions overseas.[27] Any local links which Henry forged through his relationship with them can only have been relatively insubstantial. The conclusion remains that Gaunt showed no inclination to attempt the difficult task of establishing his dominance in East Anglia. The Lancastrian presence in the region, though by no means negligible, therefore took the form of a disparate collection of retainers whose allegiance was not—indeed, was not required to be— exclusive, and whose local influence as a coherent and identifiable group was, at most, occasional. The reaction of Norfolk landed society to the crisis of 1399 certainly testifies more to its independence than to any overriding political attachment. Apart from Henry's household men such as Erpingham and Payn, the Lancastrian army included only two of Gaunt's East Anglian retainers, the esquires John Reymes and Edmund Barry. On the other side, only one local knight—Sir William Elmham—joined the bishop of Norwich in support of the king.[28] 'The rest of the Norfolk gentry', Simon Walker concludes, 'maintained a characteristic neutrality and did nothing.'[29]

2. 1399–1430: THE ESTABLISHMENT OF A CROWN CONNECTION

In 1399, patterns of lordship in East Anglia presented Henry IV with a political *carte blanche*. His own Norfolk estates provided him with a territorial base which would potentially allow him greater direct

---

[26] Walker, *The Lancastrian Affinity*, 203–4; E. L. T. John, 'Sir Thomas Erpingham, East Anglian Society and the Dynastic Revolution of 1399', *Norfolk Archaeology*, 35 (1970), 96; L. T. Smith (ed.), *Expeditions to Prussia and the Holy Land made by Henry, Earl of Derby*, Camden Society, new series, 52 (London, 1894), p. xcii. For Erpingham, see below, pp. 64–5. Payn has been identified with the local esquire John Payn of Helhoughton, who received an annuity at the Duchy's Norfolk receipt from 1399. However, there seem to have been two John Payns, since Henry's butler died in 1402, while John Payn of Helhoughton was still receiving his annuity in 1425: Walker, *The Lancastrian Affinity*, 203; NRO NRS 3347 m. 3; NRS 3355 m. 3; see below, p. 63.

[27] Both Payn and Erpingham accompanied Henry to Prussia in 1390–1, and to Prussia and the Holy Land in 1392–3: Smith (ed.), *Expeditions to Prussia*, pp. xcii, 302.

[28] DL42/15 pt. 1 fo. 70; Walker, *The Lancastrian Affinity*, 206. For Reymes, see A. L. Raimes, 'Reymes of Overstrand', *Norfolk Archaeology*, 30 (1952), 29–31.

[29] Walker, *The Lancastrian Affinity*, 206.

involvement in local society than his predecessors as king, but the fact that his father's political interest in the region had been sporadic and superficial meant that his new public authority was not constrained by the Duchy's role in pre-established local hierarchies of private power. This fluidity in the power structures of Norfolk was matched by a similar situation in Suffolk. The combined effects of chance and political miscalculation meant that the various alternative candidates for regional lordship suggested by tenurial patterns in Suffolk were, temporarily at least, not in active contention. Indeed, if Gaunt had not established his supremacy in East Anglia by the end of the fourteenth century, it was not because he had faced consistent rivalry from these sources. William Ufford, earl of Suffolk, had been the major power in the region in the 1370s, adding to his own substantial estates the share of the Bigod lands which his wife inherited from her father Thomas of Brotherton. On Ufford's death without direct heirs in 1382, however, the Bigod inheritance was reunited in the hands of Thomas of Brotherton's other daughter, Margaret, who remained in possession until her death in 1399.[30] The Ufford earldom passed to the courtier Michael de la Pole, but his impeachment in 1386–7 left Suffolk leaderless, and Norfolk without serious contenders for control of the shire.[31]

During the early years of the next century, this situation was further accentuated, leaving a remarkable political vacuum in the region. Thomas Mowbray, duke of Norfolk, inherited the Bigod lands from his grandmother Margaret of Brotherton in March 1399 but, already in exile, he died six months later, leaving a 15-year-old heir. The latter's involvement in Archbishop Scrope's rebellion in 1405, before he had secured full livery of his estates, resulted in another minority which lasted until the end of the reign.[32] Michael, second de la Pole earl of Suffolk, was of age and in possession of his inheritance, having been restored to his father's title in 1398, but his political ambitions, and certainly his influence, seem to have been extremely limited.[33] Among the nobles with more peripheral interests in the region, the earl of March died in 1398, followed in 1400 by the earl of Oxford and in 1402 by Lord Scales, who held lands in Norfolk and Suffolk as well as Essex and Cambridgeshire: all three left minor heirs.[34] Thomas, Lord Bardolf, whose territorial interests centred on the honour of Wormegay in

[30] R. E. Archer, 'The Mowbrays', unpublished D.Phil. thesis (Oxford, 1984), 31; Virgoe, 'The Crown and Local Government', 29–30; *Complete Peerage*, vi. 40–1.

[31] *Complete Peerage*, xii. 438–40; Virgoe, 'The Crown and Local Government', 30.

[32] *Complete Peerage*, ix. 604–5; Archer, 'The Mowbrays', 104–5. See below, Ch. 4.3, for detailed discussion of the position of the Mowbrays in East Anglia.

[33] *Complete Peerage*, xii pt. 1, 441; Virgoe, 'The Crown and Local Government', 30; A. L. Brown, 'Reign of Henry IV', in S. B. Chrimes *et al.* (eds.), *Fifteenth-Century England* (Manchester, 1972), 7. See below, Ch. 4.1, for discussion of the de la Poles in East Anglia.

[34] *Complete Peerage*, viii. 450; x. 233–4; xi. 504.

western Norfolk, joined Mowbray in Scrope's rebellion and forfeited his estates to the crown.[35] Henry therefore had the chance to exploit his Lancastrian territorial interests from his new position as king without having to accommodate the authority of those with rival claims to local lordship, and with his own landed interest reinforced by control of a handful of forfeitures and wardships.

The circumstances in East Anglia within which Lancastrian interests were operating in 1399 were therefore somewhat anomalous. In some senses, however, this was also true of the king's relationship with those interests. As has already been suggested, the Lancastrian affinity in East Anglia, such as it was, differed significantly from its counterparts in other areas. Elsewhere, in the traditional centres of Duchy influence, coherent networks of Lancastrian gentry had developed under Gaunt's lordship, within which hierarchies of authority were created and reinforced by grants of office in the castles, honours, and forests belonging to the duke. In those areas, the Lancastrian affinity had played a significant part in local politics during the previous reign, and assumed a greater eminence after 1399 without a radical change in the nature of its role in regional patterns of authority (albeit with potentially profound implications for Henry's authority as king).[36] In Norfolk, where Gaunt's limited retaining had lacked consistent political focus, the Lancastrian connection was made up of a few members of the greater gentry and a number of lesser gentlemen with a tradition of administrative service to the Duchy. It is hard to discern in this disparate group any clear sense of a common political identity in the years before Henry's accession, especially in the context of a society where 'horizontal' links among the independent-minded gentry rivalled 'vertical' connections with the various noble sources of lordship in political importance.[37] In East Anglia, therefore, not only was Henry taking command of the resources of the Duchy for the first time; not only was he seeking to annex those resources to the crown for the first time; but he also faced the challenge of establishing Lancastrian authority for the first time as a coherent and significant regional presence. Though this was by no means a straightforward task, the temporary abeyance of magnate influence and the absence of clearly defined structures of Lancastrian lordship in its private sense gave Henry an unusual opportunity to develop a regional authority which, from its inception, could be unequivocally royal.

On his accession, Henry made no immediate changes to the Duchy establishment in East Anglia. Though annuity payments at the Norfolk

[35] Ibid. i. 420.
[36] See above, Chs. 2.1 and 2.2, and below, Ch. 6.
[37] Cf. Carpenter, *Locality and Polity*, 287–90.

receipt leapt in the first year of the reign from the £295 which they had averaged during the 1390s to more than £520,[38] there does not seem to have been any significant alteration in the structure or size of the retinue. Part of the increase in the cost of annuities was accounted for by the fact that, although John Holand's rebellion in 1400 removed his 200 marks from the total, Gaunt had granted his son Thomas Beaufort an annuity of 300 marks from the Norfolk revenues in January 1399.[39] The remainder was almost entirely the result of increasing the fees received by those already retained in the area, part of Henry's general distribution of largesse during the first years of his rule.[40] The composition of the relatively small group of lesser gentlemen who had been responsible for the administration of the Duchy estates under the previous regime continued largely unchanged, and there is no sign that Henry implemented any radically new policy in the management of his local resources. Rather, in the absence of any significant personal involvement in the area, he put his trust in existing traditions of Lancastrian service, such as they were.

However, even if the personnel of the Duchy administration remained static, the size of their rewards and the scale of their influence increased significantly, and this in itself had a profound impact on local society. During the 1390s men such as the lawyer John Winter of Town Barningham had combined professional service to the Duchy with office in local government.[41] His Duchy employment was by no means exclusive: he also acted for the Staffords in the area, as well as using his legal expertise in the service of the city of Norwich.[42] Nevertheless, his connections with other Lancastrian servants combined the professional, both within the Duchy and in other contexts, with the personal. His sister married the esquire John Reymes, who had been retained by Gaunt since 1392, and he himself married the sister-in-law of Bolingbroke's butler, John Payn.[43] For Winter, and for the other Duchy retainers in the region, 1399 brought greater responsibility and greater eminence, and therefore endowed the personal and professional network within which they operated with a correspondingly

---

[38] Both figures include grants of land: Walker, *The Lancastrian Affinity*, 307; DL29/738/12096.

[39] DL42/15 fo. 69, DL42/16 pt. 2 fo. 1v; cf. *CPR 1401–5*, 98.

[40] DL29/738/12096; Walker, *The Lancastrian Affinity*, appendix I; Brown, 'Reign of Henry IV', 19–20.

[41] He was receiver of the Lancastrian estates in Norfolk from 1396, and served as escheator in 1392 and 1397: Walker, *The Lancastrian Affinity*, 289; *List of Escheators for England and Wales*, PRO Lists and Indexes, 72 (1971), 86.

[42] Walker, *The Lancastrian Affinity*, 192; W. Hudson and J. C. Tingey (eds.), *The Records of the City of Norwich*, 2 vols. (Norwich, 1906–10), ii. 41, 53.

[43] Walker, *The Lancastrian Affinity*, 194, 279; John, 'Sir Thomas Erpingham', 103; C. Richmond, *The Paston Family in the Fifteenth Century: The First Phase* (Cambridge, 1990), 72.

greater significance. Winter was appointed to every commission of the peace in Norfolk for the first six years of the reign, for example, and represented the shire in parliament five times.[44] In 1408 he became steward of the Duchy in East Anglia, a position which he held until his death six years later.[45]

His career has many parallels among his local associates. John Payn, who had been appointed chief butler of England immediately on Henry's accession, served in parliament and as a JP in 1401. In September 1399 he was granted the constableship of Norwich castle, and on his death in 1402 he was succeeded in this office by John Reymes, who sat in the parliaments of 1404 and 1406.[46] John Gournay, son and heir of Gaunt's former local steward Edmund Gournay, served once as escheator, twice as sheriff, and twice as knight of the shire before his death in 1408.[47] Edmund Oldhall, receiver of the Duchy lands since 1398, joined Gournay in parliament in 1404, and was elected again with Winter in 1411. He sat on the Norfolk commission of the peace from 1406, and held office twice as escheator and twice as sheriff.[48] Sir Robert Berney had acquired the stewardship of the manor of Gimingham from Gaunt in 1398, and Henry granted him a Duchy annuity of £40. Berney was twice appointed sheriff, and served on three commissions of the peace and in two parliaments during the reign.[49]

The influence of these Lancastrian retainers and officials was overwhelmingly concentrated in Norfolk, where the Duchy interest they represented was based, and where such rapid advancement could be

[44] He was not appointed to the peace commissions of 1407–8, but served again from 1410 until his death in 1414. He served as MP in 1401, 1404, 1407, 1410, and 1411. *CPR 1399–1401*, 561; *1405–8*, 494; *1408–13*, 483; *Return of the Name*, 261, 265, 272, 274, 277.

[45] Somerville, *History of the Duchy*, 594. He received an annuity of 5 marks from the Duchy from 1399: DL29/738/12096.

[46] *Return of the Name*, 261, 265, 269; *CCR 1402–5*, 241–2; *CPR 1399–1401*, 561; John, 'Sir Thomas Erpingham', 103; J. L. Kirby (ed.), *Calendar of Signet Letters of Henry IV and Henry V (1399–1422)* (London, 1978), 55. John Payn received an annuity of 10 marks from the Duchy lands in Norfolk from 1399. John Reymes was granted £20 a year from the customs at Great Yarmouth in 1399; in July 1405 this, and the three pipes of wine he also received there, were replaced by a Duchy fee of £30, paid at the Norfolk receipt, on top of the £10 he already received from the Duchy: NRO NRS 11071 m. 3; NRS 3347 m. 4; DL42/16 pt. 2 fo. 9v; *CCR 1399–1402*, 12–13.

[47] Escheator in 1401; sheriff in 1399 and 1408; MP in 1399 and 1404. G. E. Morey, 'The Administration of the Counties of Norfolk and Suffolk in the Reign of Henry IV', unpublished MA thesis (London, 1941), 268; Somerville, *History of the Duchy*, 377; *List of Escheators*, 86; *List of Sheriffs*, 87; *Return of the Name*, 258, 267. Gournay died in office as sheriff in 1408; his replacement, at the king's suggestion, was Ralph Ramsey, for whom see below, at n. 50: Kirby (ed.), *Calendar of Signet Letters*, 150.

[48] Escheator in 1405 and 1411; sheriff in 1401 and 1413: Somerville, *History of the Duchy*, 596; *Return of the Name*, 267, 277; *CPR 1405–8*, 494; *1408–13*, 483; *List of Escheators*, 86; *List of Sheriffs*, 87.

[49] Sheriff in 1406 and 1410; JP in 1399 and twice in 1410; MP in 1399 and 1401: Walker, *The Lancastrian Affinity*, 289; DL42/15 pt. 2 fos. 56, 59v; DL29/738/12096; *List of Sheriffs*, 87; *CPR 1399–1401*, 561; *1408–13*, 483; *Return of the Name*, 258, 263.

accommodated fairly readily by an already relatively heterogeneous county society. Their activities did not, in general, extend into Suffolk. Nevertheless, even though the Duchy had no territorial stake in Suffolk, and though an adult earl of Suffolk, however uninfluential on the wider political stage, was resident and active there, Lancastrian interests were not completely absent from the rule of the shire. Suffolk was represented in parliament three times during the reign by Sir John Strange, a Lancastrian retainer since the 1370s who became controller of the royal household in 1406; twice by Sir Andrew Botiller, whose wife was Thomas Erpingham's niece; and once by Ralph Ramsey, a relation by marriage of Sir Robert Berney, who had been retained by Henry before his accession. Ramsey also served twice as sheriff, while Strange served twice as escheator and on Norfolk commissions of the peace in 1401 and 1406.[50]

Thus, if the Lancastrian presence in East Anglia in the years before 1399 had been 'ill-defined',[51] the establishment of the new regime threw it into sharp focus, as Henry placed increasing responsibilities in the hands of the men who had looked after his father's local interests. Crucially, these were men who had been retained for their personal and administrative competence, rather than for their place in local politics; this was a network formed through professional associations and ties of family and locality, in which Lancastrian service played one part among many, rather than a political connection bound together by loyalty to the Duchy. Their promotion after 1399 did not, therefore, represent the promotion of a partisan interest within the region, but the appointment to office of local men on whose competence the king could rely in the service of the Lancastrian crown. This process allowed Henry's private resources in the region to be assimilated into his public authority as king to create a connection broader than the Duchy interest, though incorporating and intrinsically linked to it, which was to dominate East Anglia during the following decades.

Fundamental to these developments was the political role played at a local and a national level by Sir Thomas Erpingham, unquestionably the most eminent Lancastrian retainer in the region. His home at Erpingham lay in the heart of Duchy territory in northern Norfolk, and his history of Lancastrian service was long and distinguished. He had been retained by Gaunt in 1380, before moving into his son's service by the beginning of the following decade, and in 1398 was one of the

---

[50] Strange: MP in 1404 (twice) and 1406; escheator in 1403 and 1407; Botiller: MP in 1404 and 1410; Ramsey: MP in 1402; sheriff in 1403 and 1408. *Return of the Name*, 264, 266–7, 270, 275; Walker, *The Lancastrian Affinity*, 282; A. Rogers, 'The Royal Household of Henry IV', unpublished Ph.D. thesis (Nottingham, 1966), 680; John, 'Sir Thomas Erpingham', 102, 104; *List of Sheriffs*, 87; *List of Escheators*, 86; *CPR 1399–1401*, 561; *1405–8*, 494.

[51] Walker, *The Lancastrian Affinity*, 206.

select group who followed Henry into exile. In October 1399 he was appointed chamberlain of the household by the new king, a post he exchanged in 1404 for a brief tenure of the stewardship of the household.[52] By 1399 Gaunt had already granted him fees of £20 and 40 marks in Norfolk, as well as the keeping of South Erpingham hundred; he also received an annuity of 100 marks from Henry, assigned at the Cambridgeshire manor of Soham.[53] Under the new regime, his resources and his authority in his native area increased substantially. From 1400 he received additional annual sums of £80 from the issues of Norfolk and Suffolk and £40 from the fee-farm of Norwich, and from 1402 a further 100 marks from the fee-farm of Cambridge; in 1405 he was also granted the alien priory estate of Tofts.[54] More significantly, he was a major beneficiary of the crop of noble minorities in the first year of the reign. The custody of the central Mowbray estate of Framlingham Castle was committed to Erpingham in November 1399.[55] Four years later, he was granted custody of the castle and honour of Clare and all other Mortimer lands in Norfolk, Suffolk, and Essex during the minority of the earl of March.[56] During the early years of the reign, therefore, Erpingham controlled the major part of the territorial interests of two of the greatest landowners in the region, vastly extending his sphere of influence from his hereditary power base in the Duchy heartlands of northern Norfolk across East Anglia into Suffolk.

Erpingham's influence on regional affairs is unmistakable from the earliest years of the reign. He was named to every commission of the peace in Norfolk, and figured prominently on a huge variety of other local commissions.[57] In 1403, to take one example, he was appointed with the earls of Northumberland and Worcester and the keeper of the privy seal to settle a longstanding dispute between the bishop of Norwich and the town of King's Lynn.[58] His appearance in such select company reflects his closeness to Henry and his consequent eminence at court, but the fact that he was the only local representative on the

---

[52] See above, pp. 58–9; *DNB*, suppl. II, 189–90; John, 'Sir Thomas Erpingham', 96; Rogers, 'Royal Household', 678, 687.   [53] DL42/15 fos. 22, 67v; *CPR 1401–5*, 47.

[54] *CPR 1399–1401*, 274; *1401–5*, 47; *1405–8*, 18; *CCR 1399–1402*, 460.

[55] The grant included the hundred of Loes and the manors of Kelsale and Soham in Suffolk, as well as Hanworth, Framingham, and Suffield in Norfolk. Erpingham was to be constable of Framlingham Castle, receiving an annual fee of £40: *CPR 1399–1401*, 93, 224; *1401–5*, 16; *CFR 1399–1405*, 31, 47, 62.

[56] In Nov. 1399 custody of the Mortimer lands had been granted to a group of trustees, including Erpingham, headed by the earl of Northumberland. Northumberland acquired sole control in 1401, but Erpingham was granted the keeping of the East Anglian lands in Nov. 1403: *CFR 1399–1405*, 22, 233–4; *CPR 1401–5*, 256, 326.

[57] For commissions of the peace, see *CPR 1399–1401*, 561; *1405–8*, 494; *1408–13*, 483. For other appointments, see *CPR 1399–1401*, 561; *1401–5*, 128, 274, 280, 503; *1405–8*, 152, 154, 200, 494; *1408–13*, 65, 181, 205, 222, 226, 483.

[58] *CPR 1401–5*, 274; Kirby (ed.), *Calendar of Signet Letters*, 189.

commission demonstrates the implications of that eminence for his regional influence. Also unmistakable in these years are Erpingham's associations with the local men whose service to the Duchy had recommended them for positions of greater responsibility under the new Lancastrian regime. Such links were in part the natural corollary of their shared role in local administration. In 1402, for example, Erpingham was appointed to a special commission in Norfolk with Sir John Strange, John Payn, John Gournay, and John Reymes,[59] and such joint appointments were frequent, as the presence of Duchy officials and retainers on both regular and special commissions remained high. However, Erpingham's involvement with these men was personal as well as official. He made consistent use of their service in his own transactions. Strange, Gournay, Robert Berney, John Winter, Edmund Oldhall, and Nicholas Wichingham, steward of the Duchy by 1401,[60] all acted as mainpernors or trustees for Sir Thomas, and Winter, Berney, and Andrew Botiller each held office as his deputy constable of Dover Castle.[61] Erpingham repaid this service in kind, acting as feoffee, for example, for Strange, Botiller, and Wichingham, as supervisor for the will of Winter's father, and as a witness for Winter himself.[62] Indeed, these names recur again and again, acting together in various combinations and various capacities in the legal transactions that were the stuff of local landed society. Entirely characteristic were a feoffment made by Andrew Botiller in 1401, to trustees who included Erpingham, Strange, Berney, and Winter, and another made by John Winter in 1409, when his quitclaim of Town Barningham to a group which included Berney and Oldhall was witnessed, among others, by Erpingham.[63]

It is clear that from 1399 onwards Duchy connections played a central role in shaping East Anglian affairs. However, in the context of a region where magnate lordship had not played a defining role in the development of social and political networks during the preceding decades, this did not represent the triumph of Lancastrian 'ins' over non-Lancastrian 'outs', but the forging of new links through key individuals between East Anglian political society and the Lancastrian crown. The sudden reordering of priorities after 1399 gave Duchy service prime significance, but the Lancastrian retainers who acquired

[59] *CPR 1401–5*, 128.

[60] Somerville, *History of the Duchy*, 594.

[61] *CFR 1399–1405*, 31, 233; *1413–22*, 12; *CCR 1399–1402*, 170; John, 'Sir Thomas Erpingham', 103–4; Morey, 'Administration of the Counties of Norfolk and Suffolk', 250, 302. Botiller was later to become one of the executors of Erpingham's will: E. F. Jacob (ed.), *The Register of Henry Chichele*, 4 vols. (Oxford, 1938–47), ii. 380.

[62] *CCR 1399–1402*, 332, 392; John, 'Sir Thomas Erpingham', 103–4; *CCR 1405–9*, 522, 524.

[63] *CCR 1399–1402*, 392; *1405–9*, 524. See also BL Add. Ch. 14128; *HMC Lothian*, 52–3; *CCR 1399–1402*, 305; *1405–9*, 279, 385, 462–3. For earlier associations between this group, see Magdalen College Guton deeds 23A and 1566; NRO Le Strange A16; NRO Phi/23.

a new eminence did not jettison old friends and associates. Crucially for its ability to represent the region, the 'Lancastrian' network which emerged therefore did not depend solely on previous connections with the new king, but was shaped also by the dynamics of the local society within which it operated. The case of Sir Simon Felbrigg perhaps represents the most obvious, and most extreme, example of this process. He had served abroad under Gaunt in the 1380s, but by the following decade had entered the service of Richard II, and became one of the East Anglian knights most closely associated with the king during the 1390s. In 1395 he became Richard's standard bearer and a knight of his chamber, and secured a collection of valuable grants in Norfolk.[64] The change of regime in 1399 stripped him of most of this acquired wealth and influence,[65] but seems to have left unaffected his association with Thomas Erpingham, whose home at Erpingham lay only a few miles from Felbrigg Hall in northern Norfolk. Despite the dramatic divergence of their political careers—while Erpingham joined Henry in exile, Felbrigg accompanied Richard to Ireland—the two men remained closely involved with each other in their local context both during and after the crisis. Indeed, Felbrigg was one of the feoffees to whom Erpingham entrusted his estates before his departure in 1398.[66] After 1399, this association naturally connected Felbrigg with the network which was developing around the Duchy and dominating the region's administration. He was a feoffee, for example, for both Botiller and Winter in the transactions cited above, and he was a regular member of the commission of the peace from 1407.[67] This Ricardian knight eventually became a direct beneficiary of Duchy patronage, when in 1410 he received a life grant of licence to hunt in all Duchy lands.[68]

As Felbrigg's career suggests, Thomas Erpingham remained a key figure within the development of the region's power structures as the

[64] The grants he received included the constableship of Framlingham Castle in 1399, which he was to lose to Thomas Erpingham only months later. C. Given-Wilson, *The Royal Household and the King's Affinity* (New Haven, 1986), 165, 201–2, 283; J. D. Milner, 'Sir Simon Felbrigg KG: The Lancastrian Revolution and Personal Fortune', *Norfolk Archaeology*, 37 (1978), 85–6.

[65] Henry confirmed Felbrigg's annuity in Nov. 1399, but he lost his offices: John, 'Sir Thomas Erpingham', 102.

[66] Ibid.; Milner, 'Sir Simon Felbrigg', 86.

[67] See above, n. 63; *CPR 1405–8*, 494; *1408–13*, 483.

[68] BL Add. Ch. 70687. J. D. Milner suggests that Felbrigg was never reconciled to the new Lancastrian regime which, Milner argues, rejected and ostracized him. In the light of Felbrigg's close and continuing involvement with the Lancastrians of East Anglia, as well as the fact that he received several substantial grants from the Lancastrian kings (although admittedly never rivalling the scale of his acquisitions under Richard II), this argument seems overstated. However, it is true that, very unusually, when Felbrigg made his will in 1440 he left masses to be said for Richard's soul, and made no mention of the dynasty he had served since 1399: Milner, 'Sir Simon Felbrigg', 86–7, 89–90; NRO WKC1/336/1a.

reign went on, a role underpinned by his status and connections within local political society, his eminence within the Duchy, and his influence in government at the centre.[69] However, though Erpingham's regional authority vastly increased in the years after 1399, and despite his control of the Mowbray and Mortimer interests, the ability of a knight to dominate such a large, prosperous, and disparate society would always remain to some extent limited. Despite his custody of the Mowbray lands in northern Suffolk and the Mortimer estates in south-western Suffolk, for example, Erpingham never sat on the commission of the peace in the county; his authority seems to have remained firmly concentrated in Norfolk. Instead, Erpingham's influence became part of a hierarchy of authority in the area which was created through, and remained fundamentally connected to, the powers of the crown.

In this process, the Duchy continued to play an integral role, though not an exclusive one. The arrival in the area of the king's half-brother Thomas Beaufort, for example, was the result not of involvement with the Duchy, but of his acquisition of forfeited noble estates. However, it was his association with the increasingly influential political connection focused around the Duchy and headed by Erpingham which made his regional lordship rapidly and powerfully effective. Beaufort had acquired some connections with East Anglia and with the Duchy in the area before Henry's accession. Gaunt had chosen to assign his annuity of 300 marks at the Norfolk receipt, and in 1398 Richard II had granted him the Fitzalan lordship of Castle Acre in Norfolk.[70] It was only from 1405, however, that he began to be actively involved in the region, when he was granted the lands in western Norfolk forfeited by the rebel Thomas, Lord Bardolf.[71] These estates, of which the most significant was the honour of Wormegay, were not outstandingly valuable or extensive, certainly in comparison to those of the duchies of Lancaster and Norfolk or the earldom of Suffolk.[72] Nevertheless, despite Beaufort's close relationship to the new king, as the youngest son of a recently legitimized family he had inherited a very limited landed estate.[73] For him, therefore, the Bardolf inheritance constituted a highly significant territorial interest, which, despite his later eminence

---

[69] John, 'Sir Thomas Erpingham', 104; Richmond, *The Paston Family*, 69 n.

[70] See above, p. 62; *CPR 1396–9*, 414.

[71] Custody of the lands was committed to him in August, and he obtained a life grant from the following October: *CFR 1399–1405*, 316; *CPR 1405–8*, 105.

[72] The estates were valued in the grant at 250 marks annually. For a later listing and valuation of the Bardolf estates, see NLW Peniarth MS 280, fos. 56–7.

[73] Gaunt had left Thomas 1,000 marks in cash, but lands worth only £17 per year in reversion. His wife's lands in Lincolnshire and Yorkshire were worth a further £40 p.a., although she did not come into possession of her inheritance until 1413. A. J. Elder, 'A Study of the Beauforts and their Estates, 1399–1450', unpublished Ph.D. thesis (Bryn Mawr, 1964), 69–71; G. L. Harriss, *Cardinal Beaufort* (Oxford, 1988), 6–7; *CFR 1413–22*, 22–3.

in government, was to remain his greatest stake in the localities.[74] Moreover, with many of the noble interests in the area in abeyance, and with Duchy influence effectively in the hands of men of substantially lesser status, Beaufort's presence at Wormegay, combined with his position at court, made his lordship a force to be reckoned with.

His new authority was most immediately felt in the area around the Bardolf lands. By February 1406 he was already heading a commission to investigate insurrection in the nearby town of King's Lynn, an appointment which he shared with Thomas Erpingham and with John Winter, John Gournay, and Edmund Oldhall, all prominent in local government through their connections with the Duchy.[75] However, the royal grants Beaufort acquired during these years suggest that the king intended his authority to be established more securely in East Anglia as a whole. From September 1406 until October of the following year, for example, during the vacancy of the see of Norwich, Beaufort had the keeping of the temporalities of the bishopric, and in April 1407 he secured the farm of the town of Dunwich in Suffolk.[76] Most significantly, in May 1408 his life grant of the Bardolf lands was converted into a hereditary estate.[77] Since Beaufort's death without issue in 1426 could not reasonably have been anticipated eighteen years earlier, it seems likely that Henry intended his half-brother's presence in East Anglia to be permanent. Certainly, his consistent appointment to the commission of the peace in Norfolk from October 1406, and in Suffolk from 1411, made him the highest-ranking JP in the region apart from the duke of York in Norfolk and the earl of Suffolk in both counties.[78] The fact that the authority of both these men was to some degree compromised—York's by the marginality of the region to his territorial interests and Suffolk's by his lack of influence at court—made Beaufort's presence all the more significant. By 1410, the only laymen appointed with the bishop of Norwich to borrow money for the king in East Anglia were Beaufort and Erpingham, a commission which reflects not only the influence of the two men, but also their developing personal association. Erpingham's nephew William Phelip, who was also to become his heir, entered Beaufort's service, and it was presumably through the latter's influence that Phelip married Joan, daughter and co-heir of Lord Bardolf, by 1408.[79] This alliance ensured

---

[74] Harriss, *Cardinal Beaufort*, 162–4, 353.

[75] The other commissioners were the lawyers John Cokayn and William Lodyngton, and the local knight John Inglesthorpe: *CPR 1405–8*, 152. For Winter, Gournay, and Oldhall, see above, pp. 62–3.

[76] *CFR 1405–13*, 45, 71–2; *CPR 1405–8*, 445.

[77] *CPR 1405–8*, 443.

[78] *CPR 1405–8*, 494, 497; *1408–13*, 483, 485.

[79] *CPR 1408–13*, 205; *1405–8*, 448. Phelip was the son of Erpingham's sister Juliana, who had married Sir William Phelip of Dennington, Suffolk. He had received an annuity of £20 from

that, even should the Wormegay estates revert from Beaufort control to their previous owners, the potential power they represented would still reinforce rather than challenge the structures of authority which had developed in the region since 1399.

These were structures to which the authority of the crown was fundamental. Because existing traditions of Duchy service in East Anglia had been non-partisan and in many senses non-political, Henry had been able to use them to tap into a broadly based local network which could provide the Lancastrian crown with effective service in the government of the region. That network had now acquired the lordship of Thomas Beaufort, significantly a 'royal' rather than a territorial magnate, in the sense that his power derived from his proximity to the king and from royal grants and appointments rather than from the personal inheritance of a landed stake in the region. Beaufort's role was not, however, the only royal element in local power structures; the prince of Wales had significant associations with the region which became closer and more influential as the reign progressed. Prince Henry's territorial interest in Norfolk was based on the duchy of Cornwall lordship of Castle Rising.[80] This estate, only a few miles from King's Lynn, lay close to the Bardolf lands held by Beaufort, his uncle, who had served under his command in Wales, and with whom his association in government became much closer in the latter half of the reign.[81] The prince's authority might therefore be expected to have buttressed Beaufort's attempts to establish himself in the region, and this undoubtedly proved to be the case. However, Prince Henry's own involvement in East Anglia—in terms of both his landed interest and his connections with the leading local gentry—also became much deeper during the following years.

Thomas Erpingham, whose prominence among the closest associates of the king had been marked in the early years of the reign, subsequently became increasingly associated with the prince of Wales, and it was to make way for the development of the prince's role in East Anglia that Erpingham gave up several key appointments in the region from 1405. After the rebellion of Thomas Mowbray in that year, Erpingham was not reappointed to the keeping of Framlingham Castle, and in 1409 he surrendered the custody of the Mortimer lands. The

the Duchy receipt in Norfolk since 1403: John, 'Sir Thomas Erpingham', 104; DL29/310/4981; DL42/16 fo. 43; NRO NRS 11061 m. 3. For Phelip in Beaufort's service, see below, p. 74. Phelip is also to be found in the king's service in 1406: POPC, i. 290 (calendared in Kirby (ed.), *Calendar of Signet Letters*, 125–6).

[80] Prince Henry retrieved the property by a judgment in chancery in 1403 from the duke of York, to whom his father had mistakenly granted the property in tail male: *CCR 1402–5*, 8, 30–1.

[81] Harriss, *Cardinal Beaufort*, 16, 43–67; P. McNiven, 'Prince Henry and the English Political Crisis of 1412', *History*, 65 (1980), 1.

new beneficiary in both cases was Prince Henry,[82] and it seems clear that the grants reflected and underpinned his growing links with the region, in which Erpingham's service played a key part, rather than any fall from grace of the latter. Erpingham retained possession of three Mowbray manors in Norfolk, and received an annuity of 100 marks from the prince at Framlingham.[83] His stewardship of the king's household had ceased in November 1404; from 1410, he was present in the prince's household, and on Henry's accession in 1413 was immediately appointed steward of the new royal establishment.[84]

Moreover, Erpingham was not the sole East Anglian presence in the prince's retinue. One of John Winter's professional interests was the stewardship of the duchy of Cornwall, an office he held until 1402, and this connection brought him into the service of Prince Henry.[85] In the early years of the reign he was controller of the prince's household, an office which he exchanged in 1403 for that of receiver-general.[86] The man with whom he exchanged office was John Spenser, a Norfolk esquire who had been attached to Henry's household since at least 1401.[87] The keeping of the prince's 'secret treasury' was entrusted to another Norfolk esquire, John Wodehous, whose service with the prince on campaign in Wales was rewarded in his native area with his appointment as steward of Castle Rising.[88] This East Anglian element in Henry's household was further reinforced by the presence of Erpingham's nephew John Phelip, the younger brother of Beaufort's retainer William.[89] Unsurprisingly, it is clear that at a local level Phelip, Spenser, and Wodehous fitted seamlessly into the network in which

---

[82] *CPR 1405–8*, 23; *CFR 1405–13*, 150–1.

[83] *CFR 1399–1405*, 315, 320–1; *CPR 1405–8*, 21; SC6/997/20. Similarly, in return for the offices of constable of Dover Castle and warden of the Cinque Ports which he also surrendered to Henry in 1409, Erpingham was granted a further £100 a year assigned on the prince's Lincolnshire estates: *CPR 1408–13*, 57; W. R. M. Griffiths, 'The Military Career and Affinity of Henry, Prince of Wales', unpublished M.Litt. thesis (Oxford, 1980), 208.

[84] Rogers, 'Royal Household', 721; *CPR 1413–16*, 120.

[85] For Winter's connections with the Duchy, see above, pp. 62–3.

[86] From 1403 Winter also received a fee of £20: Griffiths, 'Henry, Prince of Wales', 116–17, 217.

[87] In 1403, when Spenser took over from Winter as controller, the prince granted him £20 a year. On Henry's accession to the throne in 1413, Spenser became cofferer of the royal household and subsequently keeper of the great wardrobe. Griffiths, 'Henry, Prince of Wales', 116–17, 215; E. de L. Fagan, 'Some Aspects of the King's Household in the Reign of Henry V', unpublished MA thesis (London, 1935), 191, 246.

[88] Wodehous was acting as Henry's treasurer in 1401 and again in 1407–8; he received an annuity of £40 from the prince: Griffiths, 'Henry, Prince of Wales', 121–4, 174, 217. He may also have been related to Thomas Erpingham, though the exact relationship is not clear: F. Blomefield, *An Essay towards a Topographical History of the County of Norfolk*, 11 vols. (London, 1805–10), vi. 414.

[89] Phelip's association with the prince can also be dated to the early years of the reign, since his annuity was increased in 1406 from its previous level of £10 to 40 marks: Griffiths, 'Henry, Prince of Wales', 213; *CPR 1413–16*, 92.

Erpingham and Winter were so prominent. When John Phelip was granted the alien priory estate of Horstead in Norfolk in 1409, for example, his mainpernors were Sir John Strange and John Spenser.[90] Spenser had also acted as surety the year before for a group including Simon Felbrigg and Edmund Oldhall in a local transaction involving Erpingham, William Phelip, and John Gournay.[91] When, in 1413, the bishopric of Norwich fell vacant, the temporalities were committed to Erpingham, Winter, Wodehous, and Spenser, for whom Oldhall acted as mainpernor.[92]

When Prince Henry succeeded his father, therefore, his connections with East Anglia meant that his relationship with the local Duchy interest was significantly different from his relationship with the Duchy as a whole. The new king, unlike his father, had been brought up as heir to an inheritance broader than the specifically Lancastrian, and his retinue in the years before 1413 had been formed around his possession of royal rather than Lancastrian estates. In general, his accession marked a distancing of the personal ties between the king and his Duchy retainers, and a reappraisal of the uses to which the crown could put its Lancastrian resources, emphasizing financial concerns more than political.[93] Some of these general changes manifested themselves in East Anglia. Henry for the first time appointed to high Duchy office men who had no previous direct involvement with its administration, a notable example being the appointment in 1413 of John Wodehous as chancellor of the Duchy, an office to which he added the stewardship of the Lancastrian lands in East Anglia in 1415 after the death of John Winter.[94] In this particular case, however, Wodehous's lack of previous Duchy office seems far less striking than his involvement with a close-knit local group in which connections with Duchy service were strong and in which Henry himself in fact had a more significant interest than his father.

This exceptional relationship between the Duchy in East Anglia and the new king may also have had repercussions for the financial management of the Duchy in the region. The trend in the Duchy as a whole from 1413 was for revenues to increase and annuity payments to fall, reflecting Henry's determination to maximize his Duchy income as well as his lack of personal commitment to maintaining the Lancastrian affinity as it stood.[95] It may be no coincidence, though the figures are

---

[90] Phelip shortly afterwards surrendered Horstead in favour of his uncle Erpingham, while retaining the reversion: *CFR 1405–13*, 145; *CPR 1408–13*, 80–1.

[91] *CCR 1405–9*, 385. For Felbrigg, Oldhall, and Gournay, see above, pp. 63, 67.

[92] *CFR 1413–22*, 12.

[93] See above, Ch. 2.3.

[94] DL42/17 fo. 38; Somerville, *History of the Duchy*, 389, 594.

[95] See above, Ch. 2.3.

not dramatic enough to be conclusive, that Norfolk was the only one of the major receipts in which the reverse was the case: revenues fell slightly while the sum spent on annuities marginally increased.[96] It is possible that in East Anglia, very unusually, Henry was prepared to compromise the exploitation of his financial resources in the interests of investment in personnel, although much of the consistency in the level of annuity payments may, in fact, be attributable to the presence of Erpingham, who in 1415 added to his already substantial assignments at the Norfolk receipt a further £100 in exchange for an annuity which Henry had previously granted him in Lincolnshire.[97]

Whatever the significance of this financial evidence, it is clear both that Henry had developed a closer association with the Duchy in East Anglia than in many other areas, and, further, that this association was stronger than his father's links with the region. This circumstance is an important indication that the nature of the Duchy presence in East Anglia under Henry IV was qualitatively different from its role in many other areas. The network which developed in the region from 1399, though focused around Lancastrian retainers and Duchy officials, was not straightforwardly part of the 'Lancastrian affinity' in the sense in which the term is usually understood—that of a political connection formed and defined by traditions of service to private Lancastrian lordship—but a political connection which was broadly representative of the region as a whole and which had developed through service to the Lancastrian king rather than to the duke of Lancaster. The local influence of the prince of Wales, whose commitment to the maintenance of royal authority rather than to his private Lancastrian inheritance was evident throughout his political career, formed part of a hierarchy which connected the gentry of East Anglia, through various interests including that of the Duchy, to the power of the crown. Thus, the prince's own local following facilitated the assimilation of the Duchy in East Anglia into a new conception of Lancastrian lordship as an unmistakably national and royal authority. Henry's accession to the

---

[96] The annual clear value of the estates during the reign averaged £880 (compared to £960 under Henry IV); annuity payments (including fees assigned at Soham in Cambridgeshire) averaged £680 (compared to £670 under Henry IV). The other major receipts sampled were Tutbury, Lancaster, Bolingbroke, Pontefract, Leicester, Higham Ferrers, and the 'south parts': DL29/728/11987–8, 11991, 729/11993–7, 11999, 12001–2, 12004–5, 730/12006–9, 12011–15, 731/12016–19, 12019A, 12021, 12021A, 12022–5, 732/ 12027, 12029–31; DL43/15/12; Somerville, *History of the Duchy*, 339. When a new partition of the Bohun lands was made in 1421, Henry acquired the manors of Fulmerston in Norfolk and Elmsett, Somersham, and Offton in Suffolk, valued at a total of nearly £75. The lands of the Hereford heritage had been annexed to those of the Duchy in 1414, and this arrangement was continued after the new partition. Hardy (trans. and ed.), *Charters of the Duchy*, 151, 172–82.

[97] NRO NRS 3354 m. 2; DL28/27/8; *CPR 1413–16*, 404; see above, n. 83.

throne allowed the expanding 'crown–Duchy connection' to develop into a network of overwhelming regional dominance.

The blossoming of this network in East Anglia both during Henry V's reign and under the rule of the lords he appointed to govern after his death took place very clearly under the developing local lordship of Thomas Beaufort, who had been granted the earldom of Dorset in 1412 and whom Henry created duke of Exeter four years later.[98] Not only did the eminence of his new estate mean that he headed every commission of the peace appointed in Norfolk and Suffolk from his elevation to the dukedom in November 1416 until his death ten years later, but from 1418 until 1423 in Norfolk, and from 1417 until 1422 in Suffolk, he was the only nobleman named as a JP.[99] This isolation on the peace commission owed much to the fact that other potential noble JPs were fighting in France, but it is striking and significant that Beaufort continued to be appointed despite his own service abroad from 1418 to 1422.[100] In 1415 he became formally involved with the Duchy when he was named as one of the feoffees to whom Henry committed part of the Lancastrian estates, a settlement which included the East Anglian lands.[101] His local influence was further reinforced in 1417 when he was granted custody of the estates of the earl of Oxford during the minority of the latter's son and heir, who became a member of Beaufort's household.[102] In 1425, he added to this wardship the keeping of the Mortimer lands in East Anglia, which passed to the crown during the minority of Richard, duke of York.[103]

Notes made by William Worcestre of members of Beaufort's household testify to the influence of the latter's lordship in both Norfolk and Suffolk. Of the twenty-two names mentioned by Worcestre, the majority were those of knights and esquires from East Anglia, including both William Phelip and the earl of Oxford.[104] It is true that Beaufort's

---

[98] *Complete Peerage*, v. 201–2; *CPR 1416–22*, 53.

[99] *CPR 1416–22*, 456, 460; *1422–9*, 566.

[100] Harriss, *Cardinal Beaufort*, 101–4. Beaufort seems to have taken some pains to maintain contact with East Anglia. The accounts of the corporation of Norwich record payments made to messengers bringing letters and news to the city from Beaufort in France in 1416 (when he was serving as captain of Harfleur) and in 1420: Hudson and Tingey (eds.), *Records of the City of Norwich*, ii. 62–3; Harriss, *Cardinal Beaufort*, 81–3.

[101] Somerville, *History of the Duchy*, 199, 339. For the significance of the feoffment, see above, Ch. 2.4.

[102] *CPR 1416–22*, 110; *CCR 1413–19*, 395; J. H. Harvey (ed.), *William Worcestre: Itineraries* (Oxford, 1969), 355.

[103] In the same year Beaufort also reacquired the temporalities of the see of Norwich during another vacancy: *CFR 1422–30*, 85, 108.

[104] Sir William Oldhall, William Calthorp, Sir John Carbonell and his son Sir Richard, Sir William Wolf, Sir John Shardelowe, Sir William Drury, Sir Robert Clifton, Sir John Curson, Gilbert Debenham, and Thomas Boys: Harvey (ed.), *Worcestre: Itineraries*, 354–5, 358–9. See also the many bequests to members of his household in Beaufort's will: J. Nichols (ed.), *A Collection of all the wills . . .* (London, 1780), 250–63.

increased eminence in his nephew's government meant that he became a more remote figure in local politics after 1413; certainly his appearances on local commissions other than those of the peace dwindled as his responsibilities in government grew.[105] However, the extensive following which he commanded among the East Anglian gentry represented his authority effectively in the region, and, in turn, their local influence was reinforced by connections with his regional lordship and with Henry's royal overlordship.

At the head of this group, Thomas Erpingham and his family also reaped local benefits from the change of regime. In 1415, after the deaths of Michael, earl of Suffolk, and his eldest son at Harfleur and Agincourt, custody of the de la Pole estates was granted to Erpingham and William Phelip together with the dowager countess.[106] Erpingham continued his regular membership of the Norfolk commission of the peace, and from 1423, under the rule of the lords of the minority council among whom Beaufort was prominent, Phelip was regularly appointed to the Suffolk bench.[107] In 1426, a commission to treat for a loan in the two counties, equivalent to that issued to Beaufort, Erpingham, and the bishop of Norwich in 1410, was this time issued to the bishop, Beaufort, Erpingham, and Phelip,[108] an appointment which reflects Phelip's emergence as the natural heir of the authority of the leading members of the crown–Duchy connection. John Phelip, William's younger brother, benefited particularly from his personal association with the king,[109] although his political activity in East Anglia was more circumscribed than that of his brother. As a younger son who would inherit neither the Phelip lands at Dennington nor the Erpingham estates, John's territorial interests, greatly increased by several royal grants, were concentrated elsewhere.[110] Nevertheless, he remained closely associated with his older brother and with Beaufort. In 1415 John too became a feoffee in the Duchy, and in the same year he married the 11-year-old daughter and heir of Thomas Chaucer, the Beauforts' cousin and close ally. His career was cut short a few months later, however, by his death at Harfleur.[111] John Wodehous was another

---

[105] Harriss, *Cardinal Beaufort*, chs. 4 and 5; and see *CPR 1413–16* and *1416–22*.

[106] *CPR 1413–16*, 383–4.

[107] *CPR 1413–16*, 421; *1416–22*, 456; *1422–9*, 566, 570; *1429–36*, 625; *1436–41*, 590–1.

[108] *CPR 1422–9*, 355.

[109] See above, p. 71. Phelip remained a member of Henry's household after 1413: E101/407/10.

[110] For grants to Phelip of custody of lands see, for example, *CPR 1413–16*, 67, 131–2, 257, 328, 361 (properties in Berkshire, Bedfordshire, Dorset, Gloucestershire, Buckinghamshire, Sussex, Southampton, Kent, and Suffolk); see also J. L. Kirby (ed.), *Calendar of Inquisitions Post Mortem*, xx (London, 1995), 111–13.

[111] Somerville, *History of the Duchy*, 339; *CPR 1413–16*, 356; *Complete Peerage*, xi. 395; J. H. Wylie and W. T. Waugh, *The Reign of Henry the Fifth*, 3 vols. (Cambridge, 1914–29), ii. 47. M. M. Crow and C. C. Olson (in *Chaucer Life-Records* (Oxford, 1966), 69, 86–7, a reference for

of the East Anglian group whose service to Henry brought him advancement. As well as his appointment to Duchy office, he was named a feoffee and an executor in Henry's will; he was appointed chamberlain of the exchequer for life in 1415, and became chancellor to Queen Catherine.[112] This activity at court did not curtail his involvement in regional affairs. He represented Norfolk in parliament three times during the reign, and was appointed to the commission of the peace in the shire from 1415, while, again, royal grants helped to enhance his local territorial interests.[113]

The power of this extended network in regional affairs under Henry V and in the years immediately after his death was clearly profound, a conclusion reinforced by the legal records for the area from the early part of the century.[114] However, there is little to suggest that this dominance provoked instability or confrontation. It is not easy to interpret judicial records as quantitative evidence of conflict within political society during the first two decades of the century—even leaving aside the difficulties arising from the nature of the evidence—since the King's Bench records, the major source for disputes involving landowners, are

which I am indebted to Professor Christopher Brooke) argue that no contemporary proof has been found to support the identification of Chaucer's mother Philippa as Katherine Swynford's sister, although they agree that the two women were both members of the household of Gaunt's second wife. However, McFarlane's evidence for the family relationship between Chaucer and the Beauforts is convincing: 'Henry V, Bishop Beaufort and the Red Hat, 1417–1421', in K. B. McFarlane, *England in the Fifteenth Century* (London, 1981), 89–91, 97.

[112] See above, p. 71; *CPR 1413–16*, 336, 365; Somerville, *History of the Duchy*, 199, 389.

[113] In 1413, for example, Wodehous was granted the keeping of alien priory estates at Welles, Norfolk, and Paunfield, Essex: *CPR 1413–16*, 52, 421; *1416–22*, 456; *Return of the Name*, 284, 290, 297.

[114] In July 1422, for example, the Norfolk esquire Edmund Swathyng successfully brought a plea of novel disseisin against one John Vergeons over lands in Reymerston, despite the latter's claim that he held the property jointly with Erpingham, Felbrigg, Wodehous, Oliver Groos, and others (JUST1/1533 m. 1. Groos had been retained by Gaunt in the 1390s: Walker, *The Lancastrian Affinity*, 270.). In July 1424, however, he himself was in turn accused of novel disseisin, this time in Craneworth, by a group including the veteran Duchy servant Edmund Barry and the second-generation Lancastrian William Oldhall, who won their case with damages of £30. (For Barry's service to Henry IV during the invasion of 1399, see above, n. 28. Oldhall, son of Edmund Oldhall, the Duchy receiver in East Anglia, was a member of Beaufort's household: see above, n. 104, and C. E. Johnston, 'Sir William Oldhall', *EHR* 25 (1910), 715.) In February of the next year the Reymerston case again reared its head. Vergeons had by this time died, but Erpingham and the others he had named brought a retaliatory plea of novel disseisin against Swathyng over the same group of lands. Swathyng protested that he had already won a favourable judgment concerning the estates, and further argued that the jury had not been fairly selected since the sheriff who had impanelled them, Miles Stapleton, was married to the daughter of Simon Felbrigg and related to Oliver Groos. Despite the fact that the official inquiry to settle the matter confirmed the latter point, the court found against Swathyng, who was required to pay another £43 in damages (JUST1/1539 mm. 1, 2v–4). As he had obviously feared, the array of local authority and influence he faced proved overwhelming. See also JUST1/1541 m. 1v: in July 1429 a jury impanelled by the undersheriff William Dallyng was disbanded because of suspicions that it had been selected to favour John Wodehous, the plaintiff in the case.

sparse for these years and may not be complete.[115] Even so, while allowing for possible losses, the fact that both the surviving records of King's Bench and the relatively full series of assize rolls for the period contain almost no major cases from the region seems to support the suggestion that the early years of the century were a period of marked stability in East Anglia. Certainly, it seems that the crown–Duchy network in the region was sufficiently broad and authoritative to offer scope for the representation and reconciliation of a large part of the variety of interests within local political society. In 1425, for example, when Walter Aslak was in dispute with William Paston, the parties were brought to negotiation by Thomas Erpingham.[116] Paston's chosen arbitrators included William Phelip, Oliver Groos, and Thomas Derham, a lawyer retained by the Duchy who was Beaufort's steward at Wormegay; Aslak's nominees were headed by Simon Felbrigg and Robert Clifton, a member of Beaufort's household.[117] In fact, the settlement agreed by these negotiators broke down, and Paston claimed that Erpingham was 'a myghty and a gret supportour of the seyd Walter . . . ageyn the seyd William'.[118] However, the fact that Paston had been prepared to accept Erpingham's arbitration in the first place, and that he could clearly hope for support from sources very close to Sir Thomas, since the latter's nephew was his principal representative, suggests that Paston's version of events may be less than impartial.[119]

Another element in the failure of this arbitration may have been the death of Thomas Beaufort in 1426. His authority, which was closely associated with that of the crown and yet integrally connected with the dynamics of local politics, provided an effective means for the resolution of disputes in which both sides had access to support from within the crown–Duchy network. This was a necessary function if the connection were to command as broad a following as possible within the region. His intervention could involve direct arbitration; he adjudicated a dispute

---

[115] Carpenter, *Locality and Polity*, 364, 707.

[116] For an account of the dispute, see E. Powell, *Kingship, Law, and Society* (Oxford, 1989), 93–4.

[117] DL28/4/6; SC6/945/9. Phelip, Groos, and Derham were appointed with Sir Henry Inglose. For Felbrigg, Groos, and Clifton, see above, p. 67 and nn. 104, 114. The other men named by Aslak were Sir Brian Stapleton and John Berney of Reedham.

[118] *PL* Davis, i. 7–12 (Gairdner, ii. 12–18).

[119] Paston, who had been retained as legal counsel by the Duchy at least since 1420 (DL28/4/11), seems in fact to have enjoyed substantial connections with Erpingham and his associates: see, for example, JUST1/1533 m. 1; JUST1/1539 mm. 2v–4; JUST1/1543 m. 2; *CCR 1409–13*, 229; *1422–9*, 465. According to Aslak, it was Paston who had brought the case to Erpingham's attention. Aslak's account further suggests that if Sir Thomas did favour his own case, this was because Erpingham found Paston's demands excessive ('Sire Thomas thought that this was a merwelouse askyng and unskylfull'): *PL* Davis, ii. 505–6. For detailed discussion of William Paston's career and his family's place within the political society of northern Norfolk, see below, Ch. 4.5.

between Sir John Carbonell and John Ryplay in 1411, and in 1415 he and the bishop of Norwich were nominated to settle disagreements among the inhabitants of King's Lynn about the government and liberties of the town.[120] In other cases he assumed the role of umpire, to provide authoritative judgment in the last resort if the nominated arbitrators failed to reach a settlement: in 1426, for example, he was to make an award between Robert FitzRalph and Margaret Baroun if the negotiations of Sir John FitzRalph and Oliver Groos foundered.[121] It may be that this more remote involvement was characteristic of the later years of Beaufort's career, as his responsibilities in government became more pressing, and as the increasing eminence of men such as Erpingham and his nephews provided an extended hierarchy of local authority to which recourse was available.[122]

It has been argued that fifteenth-century lords 'achieved comprehensive control through comprehensive representation and vice versa. . . . The dream of every nobleman was surely the unchallenged rule of the locality, in which case everybody would be, in some sense, a part of his following, because everybody would look to him for justice . . . the distinction between the affinity and the local *communitas* would all but disappear'.[123] The crown–Duchy connection in East Anglia during the early years of the fifteenth century had never been a lordly affinity in the conventional sense, developing instead through a combination of pre-existing local associations (both 'horizontal' and 'vertical') and royal authority (manifested and delegated both directly and through the king's possession of the Duchy). It seems that this anomalous political structure came remarkably close to achieving 'comprehensive control through comprehensive representation'. The crown–Duchy network had multifarious connections throughout the disparate political society of East Anglia, combined with a hierarchy of authority which apparently offered sufficient scope for the settlement of conflict and the realization of interests within the region. This capacity to represent the region as a whole was made possible not only by the nature of the network itself, but also by the anomalous circumstances of local politics during these years. The absence of any alternative noble lordship in the area at the beginning of the period meant that no *exclusive* commitment was required by association with the Duchy interest, since it faced no competing source of lordship. This circumstance allowed its connections to permeate local political society. Service to other non-competitive political interests was completely compatible with ties to

---

[120] *CCR 1409–13*, 294; E210/4896.

[121] *CCR 1422–9*, 265.

[122] For examples of Erpingham acting as an intermediary between central government and East Anglian society under Henry V, see *POPC*, ii. 246–8, 272–4.

[123] J. L. Watts, *Henry VI and the Politics of Kingship* (Cambridge, 1996), 67.

the Lancastrian crown; Oliver Groos, for example, was retained by Michael, earl of Suffolk, during the reign of Henry IV,[124] while Edmund, the younger brother of John Winter, took a fee from John, duke of Norfolk, in 1429.[125] It was this combination—broad and wide-ranging political associations developing in the absence of competition for local influence between sources of private lordship—which allowed this network the 'unchallenged rule of the locality', and made it a proper vehicle for the universal and public authority of the crown. This was emphatically not a 'royal affinity' in the partisan and divisive mould of Richard II's Cheshire retinue.[126]

The anomalous local circumstances which had allowed the network to flourish would not last indefinitely, however. It had been the political vacuum in Suffolk caused by noble forfeitures and minorities which had allowed the crown–Duchy connection to broaden its scope from its Norfolk roots to embrace the wider society of the region as a whole. By the end of Henry V's reign, a new East Anglian nobility was emerging, represented principally by William de la Pole, earl of Suffolk, who came of age in 1417, and John Mowbray, heir to the dukedom of Norfolk, who succeeded to his estates in 1413 (although he was not to take possession of the bulk of his inheritance in East Anglia until his mother's death in 1425).[127] However, the potential repercussions of this development within local politics were temporarily contained by Henry's military campaigns, which both united his nobility in a common cause and removed them from the country for prolonged periods. East Anglia was particularly well represented in Henry's forces, and the fact that the young nobles of the region were campaigning in an army in which the experienced soldiers Beaufort and Erpingham played leading roles can only have reinforced perceptions of the domestic local hierarchy.[128]

There were, of course, changes within the crown–Duchy connection in East Anglia during these years. John Reymes, for example, died by 1411, followed by John Winter in 1414 and Edmund Oldhall in 1417.[129] It is clear, however, that the network was nevertheless expanding, and maintaining its coherence, as a younger generation emerged within

---

[124] SC6/996/20; E101/46/24; H. Nicolas, *History of the Battle of Agincourt* (London, 1833), 339; see above, n. 114.

[125] Archer, 'The Mowbrays', 345. See JUST1/1541 m. 22 for Winter acting with Norfolk in July of that year. [126] For which, see above, Ch. 1.

[127] *Complete Peerage*, xii pt. 1, 443; *CCR 1409–13*, 390–1; *CFR 1422–30*, 114–15.

[128] See E101/51/2, muster roll of the army at Southampton in 1417, for companies led by the Earl Marshal, the earls of Suffolk and March, William Phelip, and Brian Stapleton. For the military service of Beaufort and Erpingham, see *Complete Peerage*, v. 201–3; *DNB*, suppl. II, 190. In 1415 Beaufort and Erpingham, with Lord Fitzhugh, were empowered to receive the surrender of Harfleur: Harriss, *Cardinal Beaufort*, 81.

[129] Morey, 'Administration of the Counties of Norfolk and Suffolk', 289; Richmond, *The Paston Family*, 72; Somerville, *History of the Duchy*, 596.

the same political orbit. John Winter's brother and heir Edmund, for example, who held office as escheator, sheriff, JP, and MP,[130] shared his brother's local associations. In 1419 Edmund acted as a witness with Thomas Erpingham and the Duchy retainer Sir Edmund Barry when Simon Felbrigg made a grant of his estates to John Wodehous and other feoffees. When Wodehous died in 1431, Winter married his widow.[131] Edmund's son-in-law, the lawyer John Heydon, was to become one of the principal servants of William Phelip; initially retained as a Duchy apprentice-at-law, Heydon was later to hold high Duchy office.[132] Sir Thomas Tuddenham, later closely associated with Heydon, also developed connections with the crown–Duchy network at this time. Tuddenham inherited his estates at Eriswell, Suffolk, as a minor in 1415, and his wardship was granted to John Wodehous. Three years later, Tuddenham married Wodehous's daughter Alice.[133] In 1425 Tuddenham became Duchy steward in East Anglia when his father-in-law relinquished the office in his favour.[134] He also became a member of Beaufort's household, a position probably also secured through Wodehous's influence.[135] The later notoriety of Thomas Tuddenham and John Heydon, arising from their involvement in local affairs in the 1440s, will be discussed in detail below,[136] but it is important to note here that they each had an impeccable pedigree in the service of the Lancastrian crown and were among the heirs of a political connection which had dominated the region peacefully since the beginning of the century.

The greatest changes to overcome this evolving network were the deaths of Thomas Beaufort in 1426, and of Thomas Erpingham two years later.[137] In one sense, the existing local hierarchy was little disturbed by these losses, since William Phelip inherited the landed interest of both men. As his uncle's heir, Phelip acquired the Erpingham

[130] Escheator in 1410, 1417, and 1422; sheriff in 1418; JP in 1422; MP for Norfolk in 1420, 1421, 1422, 1427, 1429, and 1437: *List of Escheators*, 86–7; *List of Sheriffs*, 87; *CPR 1416–22*, 456; *Return of the Name*, 295, 300, 303, 313, 316, 330.

[131] *CCR 1419–22*, 41; Richmond, *The Paston Family*, 84.

[132] Richmond, *The Paston Family*, 90; W. J. Blake, 'Fuller's List of Norfolk Gentry', *Norfolk Archaeology*, 32 (1961), 272; Somerville, *History of the Duchy*, 425; see below, pp. 91, 95–6. Phelip and Heydon were associated certainly by 1431. Heydon later became one of Phelip's executors: *CFR 1430–7*, 59; Jacob (ed.), *Register of Henry Chichele*, ii. 598.

[133] *CFR 1413–22*, 205–6; Kirby (ed.), *Calendar of Inquisitions Post Mortem*, xx. 240–2; R. Virgoe, 'The Divorce of Sir Thomas Tuddenham', in R. Virgoe, *East Anglian Society* (Norwich, 1997), 117–18.

[134] Tuddenham, who had received livery of his estates in Mar. 1423, was to hold the stewardship for life, with reversion to Wodehous: DL42/18 pt. 2 fo. 61; *CCR 1422–9*, 27.

[135] Harvey (ed.), *Worcestre: Itineraries*, 355.

[136] See Chs. 4 and 5.

[137] *Complete Peerage*, v. 205; *DNB*, suppl. II, 190. Both men seem to have suffered periodic illness in the years before their deaths: J. Anstis, *The Register of the Most Noble Order of the Garter*, 2 vols. (London, 1724), ii. 88–9, 100, 102.

estates in north Norfolk, and took over the keeping of the Duchy hundred of Erpingham.[138] Beaufort died childless, and the Bardolf honour of Wormegay therefore reverted to the crown, but in 1437 it was restored to the Bardolf heiress and her husband Phelip, who was subsequently summoned to parliament as Lord Bardolf.[139] More importantly, however, Beaufort's death severed the link that had connected the local hierarchy directly to its royal overlord. Phelip, though promoted to the nobility, was no more than one among several nobles on the newly repopulated East Anglian stage. The fact that Phelip did not secure the Wormegay estates for a decade after Beaufort's death, and that they were farmed during these years by William, earl of Suffolk,[140] indicates the profound effect which the revival of local noble interests was to have on regional society. Moreover, these new magnates were attempting to secure their political inheritances not merely without the benefit of the key players who had previously connected local power structures directly to the crown, but without the benefit of any active kingship at all. The relationship between public and private interests in the region, which had been so successfully negotiated during the first three decades of the century, was again in flux. Once again, the powers of the crown were to play a vital role in the establishment of a new local order.

---

[138] Phelip was also granted the keeping of the London house and the alien priory lands which his uncle had held: *Cal. IPM*, iv. 203–4; *CFR 1422–30*, 247–8; DL43/16/2.

[139] Phelip was chief executor of Beaufort's will. *CCR 1435–41*, 374–5; *CPR 1436–41*, 117–18; *Complete Peerage*, i. 420.

[140] *CFR 1430–7*, 33, 60–1; see below, pp. 86, 89.

4

1430–1450

The Duke of Suffolk and the Rule of East Anglia

I. 1430–1437: THE RISE OF SUFFOLK'S LORDSHIP

As the heirs of the East Anglian nobility took possession of their inheritances, the political abnormalities of the early part of the century gradually disappeared, so that several lords again competed for influence in Norfolk, and the great territorial blocs of the de la Pole and Mowbray estates in Suffolk once more formed the basis for active political interests. However, this return to the ostensible status quo could no longer be a straightforward reassumption of inherited authority, since the rule of the two shires had in the meantime passed to a political network which was intrinsically connected both to the crown itself and to the crown in the particular guise of the Duchy. This new factor in local politics constituted little problem for those nobles whose territorial stakes in the region were peripheral to the bulk of their estates. The local lordship of the earl of Oxford and the duke of York, to whom the Mortimer estates passed on the death of the earl of March in 1425,[1] for example, would be limited in any circumstances, since their political activity was focused elsewhere. For the earl of Suffolk and the duke of Norfolk, on the other hand, East Anglia formed the heart-land of their 'country'. For them, the establishment of their authority in the region was a fundamental prerequisite of any wider political influence, and it was therefore for them that the power of the crown–Duchy network constituted a significant challenge.

With the deaths during the 1420s of Henry V, Thomas Beaufort, and Thomas Erpingham, the members of this network lost the hierarchy which had provided them with leadership, and had embodied their direct association with royal authority. Nevertheless, the cohesion of the connection was not immediately undermined, since it was so broadly based and deeply rooted in regional gentry society. The way was open for any contender for local rule to attempt to win the service of this powerful but now leaderless affinity; indeed, success in the attempt was essential if any nobleman were to impose his authority on the region as a whole. It was such success which laid the foundations

[1] *Complete Peerage*, viii. 453.

for the emergence of the lordship of William de la Pole, earl of Suffolk, as the controlling interest in local politics.

The first appearance of de la Pole interests in East Anglia had been marked by the marriage of the courtier Michael de la Pole to Katherine, daughter and heir of the Suffolk knight John Wingfield.[2] In 1385, three years after the death of William Ufford, earl of Suffolk, de la Pole was granted the vacant earldom, and was endowed with a substantial portion of the Ufford inheritance. His estates now formed a concentrated bloc in central and north-eastern Suffolk, together with several scattered but valuable manors in Norfolk.[3] Only a year after his creation as earl, however, de la Pole was impeached in parliament. Despite Richard II's efforts to save his favourite, de la Pole's escape into exile in 1387 was followed by the forfeiture of his estates; he died two years later. His son Michael recovered possession of his inheritance by 1392, and in 1398, when the acts of the Merciless Parliament were annulled, he was restored to the earldom of Suffolk.[4] On Henry IV's accession, the acts of 1398 were in turn revoked, so that the forfeiture of the first de la Pole earl was technically in force once more, but the second earl's career during the 1390s had been inconspicuous and uncontroversial, and within days the new king restored his title.[5]

Michael de la Pole's career followed much the same path under the new regime as it had under the old. He was active in his local area; he was appointed to every commission of the peace in Norfolk and consistently headed the list of JPs in Suffolk, as well as appearing on various special commissions in both counties.[6] Yet he was never an influential figure in national politics, and even in a local context it was clear both that greater authority was wielded by men closely connected with the king—the crown–Duchy connection under the emerging leadership of Beaufort—and that the earl of Suffolk presented no challenge to that dominance. He did command the service of local gentlemen; his retinue on campaign in France in 1415, for example, included Oliver Groos and

---

[2] On Wingfield's death in 1360, de la Pole acquired a group of estates in north-eastern Suffolk, including the manor of Wingfield, which was to become the family's principal residence in the area: *Complete Peerage*, xii pt. 1, 440; L. E. James, 'The Career and Political Influence of William de la Pole, First Duke of Suffolk, 1437–50', unpublished B.Litt. thesis (Oxford, 1979), 231, 239.

[3] *Complete Peerage*, xii pt. 1, 438; R. Virgoe, 'The Crown and Local Government', in R. Virgoe, *East Anglian Society* (Norwich, 1997), 30; James, 'Career and Political Influence', 231–2, 234.

[4] *Complete Peerage*, xii pt. 1, 439–41; M. McKisack, *The Fourteenth Century* (Oxford, 1959), 442–6, 451–2, 457, 467, 485.

[5] *Complete Peerage*, xii pt. 1, 441; Virgoe, 'The Crown and Local Government', 30; *CPR 1399–1401*, 160.

[6] *CPR 1399–1401*, 561, 564; *1401–5*, 519; *1405–8*, 494, 497; *1408–13*, 483, 485; *1413–16*, 421, 423; and see, for example, *CPR 1401–5*, 114, 128, 288, 291; *1405–8*, 154, 200, 231, for appointments to special commissions (frequently commissions of array).

John Clifton.[7] However, those of his followers who were also active in local government were the men who combined his service with connections associating them with the crown–Duchy group, Oliver Groos being a notable example.[8]

By 1415, therefore, a de la Pole earl of Suffolk had been resident and politically active (in however limited a sense) in East Anglia for nearly a quarter of a century. During that time, he had not sought to rival the regional influence of Beaufort, Erpingham, and the network they headed, but had accommodated himself to their growing dominance, and showed no resentment towards the regime which had promoted them. Indeed, the strength of de la Pole support for Henry V's military campaigns is striking. In 1415 both the earl and his eldest son Michael led substantial companies to France, which included among their number the latter's younger brother William.[9] This campaign initiated developments which would profoundly change the political significance of the de la Pole earldom. In September 1415 Suffolk died at Harfleur, and on 13 October his eldest son was granted immediate livery of his estates.[10] Twelve days later, the new earl was one of the few English casualties at Agincourt, and the title passed to his brother William who was, at 19, still a minor.[11] The latter's control of his inheritance was further curtailed by the fact that his father and brother had both left widows for whom provision would have to be made, and also by the claims of his brother's three daughters.[12] Despite these obstacles, the earl rapidly secured possession of the bulk of the de la Pole estates. In October 1416 he was granted control of the marriages of his nieces, but in the event this proved superfluous, since by 1422 two had died and the third had entered a convent, abandoning her right to her inheritance.[13] His mother died in 1419, less than a year after his own minority had formally ended.[14] By the early 1420s, the only part of the

[7] E101/46/24 m. 1; H. Nicolas, *History of the Battle of Agincourt* (London, 1833), 338–9; for Groos and Clifton, see above, pp. 76–7, and below, p. 99.

[8] Groos served as sheriff in 1409: *List of Sheriffs for England and Wales*, PRO Lists and Indexes, 9 (1898), 87.   [9] E101/46/24.

[10] *Complete Peerage*, xii pt. 1, 442; J. L. Kirby (ed.), *Calendar of Inquisitions Post Mortem*, xx (London, 1995), 134–6; *CPR 1413–16*, 364. The normal legal processes were to be circumvented because both the king and the new earl were on campaign abroad.

[11] *Complete Peerage*, xii pt. 1, 442–3; Kirby (ed.), *Calendar of Inquisitions Post Mortem*, xx. 138–40.

[12] Isabel, widow of William Ufford, earl of Suffolk, was also still alive and in possession of dower lands of which the de la Poles held the reversion; she died, however, in 1416: *CFR 1413–22*, 144; Kirby (ed.), *Calendar of Inquisitions Post Mortem*, xx. 184–5.

[13] *CPR 1416–22*, 48; *CCR 1419–22*, 247. By July 1422 Katherine de la Pole was already resident in Bruisyard nunnery, Suffolk, although the abbess was ordered not to allow her to make profession until she reached her majority, because of her potential inheritance. By August of the following year, however, she had become a nun, and her estates had formally passed to the earl: *CFR 1422–30*, 43–4.

[14] *CFR 1413–22*, 273; *CCR 1413–19*, 461.

de la Pole estates not in the earl's control was the dower of his sister-in-law, and, of the East Anglian lands, she held only two manors.[15] William de la Pole therefore held his father's territorial stake in the region almost in its entirety, and with it such traditions of de la Pole service as already existed, of limited political significance though they were.

During the following three decades, the earl developed a degree of influence in both local and national politics which his father had not begun to approach. His increasing importance in Henry VI's government owed much to his military career in France.[16] At a local level, though, the crucial distinction between the limited authority which his father had enjoyed and the ascendancy achieved by Suffolk was his association with, and eventual appropriation of, the crown–Duchy interest which had dominated the region in the early part of the century. Suffolk's connection with the leading members of this network began as soon as he inherited the earldom. In December 1415, custody of the de la Pole estates during the earl's two-year minority was committed to a group of trustees headed by Thomas Erpingham and William Phelip.[17] This appointment was probably a reflection of the local eminence of Erpingham and his nephew rather than the result of any particularly close connection between them and the previous earl; although Michael de la Pole had served on many commissions with members of the crown–Duchy connection, and although Erpingham acted as a feoffee for him in 1410, there is little evidence of any very close or consistent personal association.[18] However, there was no immediate opportunity for Suffolk to forge any more significant relationship with the leading figures in East Anglian politics in a domestic context, since he spent the greater part of the 1420s on campaign in France.[19] He returned to England in 1430, and in November of the following year was nominated to the minority council, an appointment which seems to have been the result of a nascent political association

[15] She also held the hundreds of Stow and Hartismere: *CCR 1413–19*, 263–5; *CPR 1413–16*, 402–3. For the very different effects of multiple dowers on the Mowbray inheritance, see below, Ch. 4.3.

[16] Suffolk achieved positions of considerable authority during his service in France, becoming admiral of Normandy in 1419, governor of Chartres in 1424, and lieutenant of Caen and Cotentin in 1430. His rewards included the title of count of Dreux, which he received in 1425: *Complete Peerage*, xii pt. 1, 444–5; *DNB*, xlvi. 50–1.

[17] The other trustees named were the dowager countess Katherine and the clerks Robert Bolton and Thomas Frampton: *CPR 1413–16*, 383–4; see above, p. 75. Both Bolton and Frampton were apparently in de la Pole service: see, for example, *CCR 1405–9*, 72; *1413–19*, 266–7.

[18] For such commissions, see, for example, *CPR 1401–5*, 128; *CPR 1405–8*, 231; *CPR 1413–16*, 409; for Erpingham as feoffee, see *CCR 1413–19*, 266–7.

[19] *Complete Peerage*, xii pt. 1, 444–5.

with the duke of Gloucester.[20] This connection should not, however, obscure the fact that Suffolk had already allied himself with Beaufort interests by his marriage, late in 1430, to Alice Chaucer.[21] The earl's new wife was the widow of Thomas Montague, earl of Salisbury, under whose leadership Suffolk had served in France.[22] More importantly in this context, however, Alice was the daughter and heir of Thomas Chaucer, whose substantial political influence from 1399 until his death in 1434 was closely linked to that of his cousins, the Beauforts.[23] Further, Alice's first husband had been Sir John Phelip, the younger of Thomas Erpingham's nephews. Although Phelip had died when she was only 11 years old, the connection had not been forgotten.[24]

Suffolk's marriage, which took place soon after his return to England, formed one of his first opportunities since taking possession of his inheritance to involve himself actively in domestic political life. By marrying Alice Chaucer, he allied himself in his local area with the powerful association of interests which had developed around Beaufort and Erpingham. However, the fact that the active involvement of the crown in regional affairs was limited by the king's minority, and that both Beaufort and Erpingham had recently died, meant that there was considerable room for manœuvre within local structures of lordship. In the years that followed, Suffolk reinforced and greatly extended his connections with the crown–Duchy network in East Anglia, and thereby established his own lordship as the authority which would succeed Beaufort and Erpingham in leadership of the network, and therefore of the region.

This process began as early as February 1431, when the Bardolf estates of the honour of Wormegay were granted at farm to Suffolk.[25] Through this grant, the earl secured control of the territorial stake which had underpinned Beaufort's local authority. Moreover, the estates greatly increased his own landed interest in the region, since the de la Pole properties in Norfolk consisted only of scattered individual manors. His mainpernors for the grant included the Suffolk knight

---

[20] R. A. Griffiths, *The Reign of Henry VI* (London, 1981), 40; J. L. Watts, *Henry VI and the Politics of Kingship* (Cambridge, 1996), 156–7.

[21] Licence to marry was granted on 11 Nov.; arrangements for the settlement of lands on the couple had been concluded a month earlier: *CPR 1429–36*, 86; BL Harl. Ch. 54.1.9.

[22] *Complete Peerage*, xii pt. 1, 444, 447.

[23] G. L. Harriss, *Cardinal Beaufort* (Oxford, 1988), 20, 39, 67, 120, 145, 271, 391–2. For details of Thomas Chaucer's career, see J. S. Roskell, *Parliament and Politics in Late Medieval England*, 3 vols. (London, 1981–3), iii. 151–91.

[24] An annuity of £100, for example, was paid at the exchequer to Suffolk and his wife specifically in her capacity as widow of John Phelip, and in 1440 the couple secured a grant in tail of the manors of Nedding and Kettlebaston in Suffolk which had previously been granted to Alice and Phelip shortly before the latter's death in 1415: E101/514/6 m. 1; *CPR 1436–41*, 400; Suff. RO T1/2/1/1; for Phelip's career, see above, pp. 71–2, 75.

[25] *CFR 1430–7*, 33, 60–1.

John Shardelowe and the Norfolk esquire Thomas Hoo, both of whom had been members of Beaufort's household.[26] In other words, Suffolk was immediately picking up the threads of the local Beaufort connection to which his marriage gave him access, in terms of both land and personnel. Suffolk's association with Thomas Tuddenham, for example, was already established by 1435, when the earl joined Thomas Hoo among Tuddenham's feoffees in his Norfolk manor of Oxburgh.[27] Tuddenham was to become one of Suffolk's most influential supporters during the following years.[28]

Nor did Suffolk extend his lordship only to those who had been members of Beaufort's household. He rapidly formed connections also among the wider crown–Duchy network with which Beaufort had been associated. In 1432, for example, he acted as feoffee for the widow of a Norfolk esquire with Simon Felbrigg, Oliver Groos, and Brian and Miles Stapleton.[29] Moreover, in the few years since the deaths of Beaufort and Erpingham, the crown–Duchy group in East Anglia had not lost its coherence, its dominant role in local government, or its capacity to represent a wide range of interests in the region.[30] Suffolk's rapid acquisition of the service of prominent individuals such as Tuddenham and Hoo therefore naturally brought him into contact with a broader local network, as well as giving members of that network access to his lordship. The earl's regular appointment to the commission of the peace in Suffolk from 1422 and in Norfolk from 1430, as well as his nomination to a variety of special commissions in the area from the latter year, reinforced this contact with the crown–Duchy connection, which continued to be strongly represented in local administration.[31]

---

[26] See n. 25 above; J. H. Harvey (ed.), *William Worcestre: Itineraries* (Oxford, 1969), 355, 359 (Shardelowe); J. Nichols (ed.), *Collection of all the wills . . .* (London, 1780), 262 (Hoo). Hoo was Suffolk's chief steward at Costessey in 1431–2, and was the only person outside the earl's family to whom the latter was paying an annuity in 1436. Shardelowe and Hoo were both in fact already associated with Suffolk by Oct. 1430, when they served as feoffees for the earl, and acted with him in land settlements made to provide a jointure for his new wife: C. Richmond, *The Paston Family* (Cambridge, 1990), 239 n.; E163/7/31 pt. 1; E210/5796; BL Harl. Ch. 54.1.9.

[27] *CCR 1429–35*, 361–2. For Tuddenham's service to Beaufort, see above, p. 80. Tuddenham acquired Oxburgh in 1434 on the death of Joan Streche, when the estates which she had inherited from her grandfather Sir John Weyland were divided between the co-heirs Tuddenham and Sir John Knyvet: F. Blomefield, *An Essay towards a Topographical History of the County of Norfolk*, 11 vols. (London, 1805–10), vi. 172–3.

[28] See below, Ch. 4.2. For further examples of Tuddenham's links with Suffolk during the 1430s, see *CCR 1435–41*, 62, 102.

[29] *CPR 1429–36*, 197.

[30] See, for examples of the continued operation of this network in private transactions and on public commissions: *CPR 1429–36*, 50, 126, 137, 351, 521; *CFR 1430–7*, 121.

[31] *CPR 1416–22*, 460; *1422–9*, 570; *1429–36*, 621, 625; *1436–41*, 586, 590–1; *1441–6*, 474, 478–9; *1446–52*, 592, 595.

Suffolk's increasing authority in East Anglia, intrinsically linked as it was to his burgeoning associations with the crown–Duchy network, brought him into rivalry with William Phelip, who had both a specific claim to the Wormegay estates in right of his wife Joan Bardolf, and a general one to leadership of the region as Erpingham's heir and as one of Beaufort's closest associates.[32] With Erpingham, Phelip had held the custody of Suffolk's lands during his short minority,[33] but there is little evidence of further direct association between the two in a local context in the years immediately after the earl's return to England—the time at which the latter was securing his stake in the political connection left by Beaufort, which Phelip might have hoped to inherit. Their relationship was by no means, or perhaps not at all, straightforwardly antagonistic. Together, for example, they dominated the king's household establishment from 1433, when Phelip, who had held office as chamberlain since the previous year, was joined by Suffolk as steward.[34] Nevertheless, at a local level the potential conflict between their respective lordships remained unresolved until 1437. In that year, a series of political manœuvres resulted in an accommodation which extended Phelip's territorial stake in the area, while establishing Suffolk's authority as the dominant regional lordship.

Their first direct confrontation was precipitated by a conflict of authority not in East Anglia but in the Thames Valley, where Suffolk held the Chaucer lands of his wife's inheritance.[35] Thomas Chaucer's territorial interest in the area had been reinforced by his office as steward and constable of the honour and castle of Wallingford, one of the duchy of Cornwall estates which had been assigned in dower to Queen Catherine. In June 1434 he surrendered the original grant so that he could be reappointed together with his son-in-law Suffolk, and after Chaucer's death in 1435 the earl held office alone.[36] However, the queen died on 3 January 1437, and the following day Phelip, making use of his position in the household and the access to the personal authority of the king which it allowed, secured a grant of the stewardship and constableship of Wallingford for himself.[37] Phelip was not able to maintain this encroachment on Suffolk's regional influence, but neither was the earl able to vindicate his sole right. On 22 February, 'by deliberation of the council', the Wallingford offices were granted to Suffolk and Phelip together in survivorship.[38] It has been suggested that

---

[32] See above, pp. 69–70, 74, 80–1.

[33] See above, n. 17.

[34] Griffiths, *Henry VI*, 41, 43.

[35] *CFR 1430–7*, 239–40.

[36] *CPR 1429–36*, 346–7; W. R. M. Griffiths, 'The Military Career and Affinity of Henry, Prince of Wales', unpublished M.Litt. thesis (Oxford, 1980), 60.   [37] *CPR 1436–41*, 32.

[38] *CPR 1436–41*, 44, 61.

Phelip challenged Suffolk over this issue in order to put pressure on the earl over his continued occupancy of the Bardolf inheritance;[39] certainly, it was only a few months after the Wallingford settlement that the possession of Wormegay apparently became a subject for negotiation. Suffolk's farm of the Bardolf lands, which he had held since 1431, was renewed for a further seven years on 15 July 1437.[40] Three days earlier, Phelip had secured the farm of the lordship of Swaffham, a manor adjoining the Bardolf estates in western Norfolk.[41] Four months later, on 11 November, Phelip and his wife finally received a hereditary grant of the Wormegay lands, which had been surrendered by Suffolk for the purpose;[42] two days after that, Phelip surrendered the custody of Swaffham so that it could be granted for life to Suffolk.[43] It is hard to avoid the conclusion that an exchange had been negotiated to allow Phelip to recover his wife's inheritance, while preserving the earl's recently enhanced authority in Norfolk.

This interpretation is supported by the evidence of the reorganization of the Duchy in the same year,[44] a process in which accommodation was again reached between the claims of Suffolk and Phelip. Phelip, because of his longstanding connection with the Duchy in the area, might have expected to dominate its administration. Equally, Suffolk's increasing authority in the region in general, and his connections with Duchy-based interests in particular, made him a rival whose claims could not be ignored. In the event, offices were again shared between the two men. The reorganization began with the Duchy's central administration. When Sir John Tyrell died in 1437, it was Suffolk who, on 23 April, succeeded him as chief steward of the North Parts of the Duchy during the king's pleasure.[45] On 11 May, this appointment was reinforced with a life grant of the chief stewardship of the lands held by the Duchy feoffees in the north.[46] On the same day, Phelip was appointed chief steward for the feoffees in the south and Wales, and on 12 May he received a grant of the parallel office in the lands still held by the king in the south.[47]

---

[39] Watts, *Henry VI*, 159 n. 139.

[40] *CFR 1430–7*, 345.

[41] Swaffham was part of the earldom of Richmond, which had been held by the duke of Bedford until his death in 1435: *CFR 1430–7*, 336.

[42] *CPR 1436–41*, 117–18. It seems to have been with these estates that Phelip acquired the title of Lord Bardolf: *Complete Peerage*, i. 420.

[43] *CPR 1436–41*, 133.

[44] For which, see above, pp. 45–7.

[45] DL42/18 fo. 47.

[46] His office in the lands held by the king was converted into a life grant on 17 May: DL42/18 fo. 47.

[47] DL42/18 fo. 47v. Though the feoffees in theory made their own appointments, the royal confirmations in the Duchy registers note that they acted 'ad instanciam et rogatum

With the principal Duchy stewardships divided evenly,[48] there remained the issue of the East Anglian offices. Although Thomas Tuddenham had succeeded his father-in-law John Wodehous as local Duchy steward in 1425, Phelip had subsequently been appointed to the same office by the feoffees, who held all the Duchy estates in the region apart from those of the Hereford heritage (which had been assigned as part of Queen Catherine's jointure and which continued to be administered separately after her death).[49] On 15 November 1437—two days after Phelip had surrendered Swaffham to Suffolk, and four after Suffolk had resigned his possession of Wormegay to Phelip—Phelip gave up his office as Duchy steward in East Anglia to make way for the reappointment of Tuddenham, who, though a member of Thomas Beaufort's household at the same time as Phelip, had rapidly developed associations with Suffolk during the 1430s rather than entering Phelip's service.[50] This exchange of office may well, therefore, have formed part of the compromise designed to protect the earl's interests in Norfolk after his surrender of Wormegay, and once again there was compensation for Phelip within the local Duchy administration. John Puttok, a Suffolk lawyer who had been prominent in Phelip's service since the later 1420s,[51] had been in office as Duchy feodary in East Anglia during pleasure since February, but on 13 November this was converted into a life appointment.[52] In May 1438, Reginald Rous—another lawyer, from Phelip's home manor of Dennington in Suffolk, whom the latter had employed certainly since

---

serenissimi domini Regis' (DL42/18 fo. 47v). Somerville concludes that 'the higher appointments at least were made by the feoffees upon request upon the king's behalf' (and thus were, of course, as susceptible as any other appointments to influence on the king from within his household); in fact, the two administrations were never fully separated, but remained interdependent: R. Somerville, *History of the Duchy of Lancaster*, i (London, 1953), 202–3; see above, p. 39.

[48] It was Phelip, rather than Suffolk, who secured the stewardship in the half of the Duchy where his own lands lay, and which would therefore reinforce his regional interests. It could be argued, however, that Suffolk's stewardship of the north gave him enough authority to extend his regional influence significantly. Suffolk and Phelip also shared the Duchy stewardship in the Thames Valley; on 25 Apr., they were appointed joint chief stewards of the Duchy estates in Oxfordshire, Berkshire, and Buckinghamshire for life, in survivorship. Significantly, the grant was backdated to 22 Feb., the day on which their joint office at Wallingford had been granted: DL42/18 fo. 47v.

[49] See above, p. 80; Somerville, *History of the Duchy*, 339–40, 594; DL29/732/12035. It is not clear when Phelip was appointed, but he was certainly in office by 1437.

[50] DL42/18 fo. 94; see above, pp. 80, 87.

[51] *CFR 1422–30*, 194, 208–9. Puttok was later to be an executor of Phelip's will. He is described during the 1420s and early 1430s as 'of Suffolk', but by 1437, when he and John Heydon stood as sureties for Phelip when he acquired the keeping of Swaffham, he is referred to as 'of Thweyt, Norfolk': E. F. Jacob (ed.), *Register of Henry Chichele* (Oxford, 1938–47), ii. 598; James, 'Career and Political Influence', 242; *CFR 1430–7*, 334, 336.

[52] Somerville, *History of the Duchy*, 598; DL42/18 fos. 51v, 94.

1431[53]—became receiver and steward of the lands of the Hereford heritage in East Anglia.[54]

Apart from the initial controversy over the Wallingford stewardship, this series of compromises had apparently been effected without direct confrontation between the two men. Indeed, they had too many associations in common, both as the leading representatives of the household on the council, and at a local level as associates of Thomas Beaufort, for their interests to diverge sufficiently for any rivalry to become overt opposition. Nevertheless, it seems clear that the settlements of 1437 represented a watershed in the development of their political relationship, and that it was only from that year onwards that their regional interests were fully assimilated into a single political connection. The personal links between the earl and Phelip became much closer; the latter, for example, became chief feoffee for Suffolk in his Thames Valley estates in February 1438.[55] A new degree of co-operation is evident also among their followers. Before 1437, those of Beaufort's former retainers who moved into Suffolk's service—men such as Hoo and Tuddenham—were those who had not apparently forged close personal associations with Phelip. From 1437 onwards, some of Phelip's most trusted servants began for the first time to act with and for the earl. By July 1438, the lawyer Rous was being employed by Suffolk as well as by Phelip;[56] by 1440, John Heydon, Phelip's deputy as chief steward of the South Parts of the Duchy, and later executor of his will, was also closely associated with the earl, who in that year supported Heydon unequivocally when he incurred the enmity of the duke of Norfolk.[57] Closer connections were also developing between individual members of the East Anglian network who had found themselves on opposite sides of the temporary divide between Suffolk and Phelip. When, in 1437, Thomas Tuddenham was granted the farm of an alien priory estate in Norfolk, Heydon and Rous acted as his sureties.[58] This was the beginning of an association between the

---

[53] *CFR 1430–7*, 59; James, 'Career and Political Influence', 242–4. Rous was also appointed an executor of Phelip's will: Jacob (ed.), *Register of Henry Chichele*, ii. 603.

[54] DL42/18 fo. 101v. Somerville lists Rous's office as the Duchy receivership at this point: Somerville, *History of the Duchy*, 594, 596.

[55] Among the other feoffees was Sir Thomas Tuddenham. Phelip had been among the feoffees named by Suffolk in 1424, but this appointment, in the company of Thomas Erpingham, probably reflects his interest as a former custodian of the de la Pole estates. Certainly, Phelip's prominence in the settlement of 1438 suggests that it was significant in the context of the manœuvres of the previous year. *CPR 1436–41*, 166; BL Harl. Ch. 54.1.8.

[56] E403/731 mm. 8, 10; James, 'Career and Political Influence', 243–4.

[57] Somerville, *History of the Duchy*, 430; James, 'Career and Political Influence', 244. Heydon had been in Phelip's service at least since 1431: *CFR 1430–7*, 59. For his associations with the crown–Duchy network in East Anglia, see above, p. 80. For the Lyston–Wingfield dispute in 1440, in which Heydon and Suffolk were involved, see below, pp. 108–10.

[58] *CFR 1430–7*, 337.

three which was to prove close, enduring, and, in the case of Tuddenham and Heydon, notoriously influential.[59]

A compromise had therefore apparently been reached in 1437 which
enabled Suffolk and Phelip to wield their respective authorities over the
crown–Duchy connection in East Anglia in co-operation rather than in
uneasy parallel. However, the very fact that co-operation had been
achieved left Suffolk with the upper hand. Grants of office and land
may have been divided equally, but in the region where the territorial
interests of the two men were concentrated the extent of the earl's lands
overshadowed Phelip's estates. In government, where they both had
access to the personal authority of the king through their positions in
the household, Suffolk was by 1437 clearly in the ascendant, enjoying
substantial support in the council and maintaining good relations with
both Gloucester and Cardinal Beaufort.[60] In the event, Phelip was to
die in 1441,[61] but it seems clear that the pre-eminence of Suffolk's lordship had in any case been firmly established during the previous four
years.[62]

This analysis reverses the traditional account of the basis of Suffolk's
power in East Anglia. His regional dominance during the 1440s is
usually attributed to the fact that his stranglehold on the royal
administration and his influence over the malleable king allowed him a
degree of local control unwarranted by his own territorial stake in the
area. This, it is argued, made it possible for him to usurp the rule of the
region from the Mowbray dukes of Norfolk, to whom local leadership
naturally and traditionally belonged.[63] However, Suffolk's regional
authority was not an artificial creation made possible by the earl's
influence in central government, but a development rooted in patterns
of power which had dominated the area since the beginning of the
century. Suffolk's control of East Anglia in fact pre-dated his control of
the king's government. Indeed, his regional power provided the secure

[59] See below, Chs. 4.3, 4.4, 4.5, 5, *passim*.

[60] Harriss, *Cardinal Beaufort*, 270–1, 293–4; Griffiths, *Henry VI*, 233–4; B. P. Wolffe, *Henry VI* (London, 1981), 104; Watts, *Henry VI*, 160, 162–3.

[61] *CFR 1437–45*, 165. Phelip held all his estates jointly with his wife Joan Bardolf, who therefore retained possession of them until her death in 1447. Phelip's only daughter, Elizabeth,
died very shortly after him in 1441. Control of the Bardolf lands during the minority of her
son Henry therefore passed to her husband, John, Viscount Beaumont (whose own territorial
interests were based in Lincolnshire and the east midlands). Henry died in 1451, but
Beaumont retained custody of the estates until his younger son, William, finally took posses-
sion of the inheritance as Lord Bardolf in 1460. *CCR 1441–7*, 18–22; *CFR 1445–52*, 45; *CPR 1436–41*, 558, 569; *1446–52*, 451; *CCR 1454–61*, 465; Watts, *Henry VI*, 173 n. 206. For a list of
the lands inherited by William Beaumont from Joan Bardolf, William Phelip, and Thomas
Erpingham, see NLW Peniarth MS 280, fos. 56–7.

[62] Harriss, *Cardinal Beaufort*, 323, 330–1; Griffiths, *Henry VI*, 280–2; Watts, *Henry VI*, 164–6.

[63] See, for example, Wolffe, *Henry VI*, 121–3; Griffiths, *Henry VI*, 585–6; R. L. Storey, *The End of the House of Lancaster* (London, 1966), 54–7.

basis from which he was able to extend his influence at a national level
from the later 1430s onwards. The implications of this reassessment of
Suffolk's local authority for analyses of his role in national politics and
of the nature of Henry's rule will be discussed in detail in the following
section, but it is immediately clear that the picture of a household
clique intruding into regional politics during the 1440s may have to
be redrawn.[64] Moreover, the fact that Suffolk was able to establish himself in East Anglia by achieving the leadership of a network which was
closely connected to the power of the crown and the private estates of
the king, and to retain its undisputed leadership even after the king had
reached his majority, forms an early indication of the abnormalities of
Henry's kingship which were to manifest themselves in the regimes of
the 1440s and 1450s.

2. 1437–1447: THE DE LA POLE AFFINITY

Suffolk had achieved the rule of East Anglia, not by usurping authority
which should have been another's, but by assuming the role that had
been Thomas Beaufort's at the head of the crown–Duchy connection in
the region. Moreover, the earl's own local status further reinforced
this dominance. Beaufort's influence over the region as a whole had
not depended fundamentally on a hereditary stake in the area, but had
been made possible by a temporary abeyance of the landed interests
which would, under normal circumstances, dominate the county of
Suffolk and participate in the rule of Norfolk.[65] By contrast, the political
ascendancy which Suffolk's connections with the crown–Duchy network gave him in Norfolk was complemented by the fact that he
held one of the two major territorial blocs in Suffolk in his own right.
His hereditary interest in one county therefore provided a solid foundation for his acquired interest in the other, and this twofold source of
authority allowed his influence to spread across the entire region.

However, the emergence of Suffolk's leadership did not mark the
straightforward transformation of the crown–Duchy connection in East
Anglia into a conventional magnate affinity. Close links with royal
authority had been an important element in the development of this
network since 1399, and Beaufort's local influence had been intrinsically associated with his proximity to the crown.[66] This fusion of public
and private power, and the direct involvement of the crown in the

[64] See above, pp. 47–9, for the suggestion that Suffolk's regime cannot adequately be
described as a 'court clique' at a national level either.

[65] See above, pp. 59–61, 68–70, 74–5, 77–8.

[66] See above, pp. 68–70.

region's political structures, did not disappear with the emergence of Suffolk's lordship. Indeed, they could not disappear, so long as control of the Duchy estates remained crucial to the rule of the county of Norfolk. Nevertheless, because of the peculiarities of Henry VI's kingship, the local role played by royal authority could not be reconstituted in the form in which it had existed earlier in the century. The relationship between public power and private influence was instead eventually to become a major source of political tension in the region.

Suffolk's 'management' of the king's authority from the late 1430s had considerable implications for the earl's regional influence, since he enjoyed a degree of access to the powers of the crown which made his local control almost unassailable.[67] However, the fact that his lordship was already established as a substantial force in the region, and was based on leadership of a connection that was genuinely representative of local society, means that this reinforcement of his authority should not be seen as an intrinsically sinister development. Rather, the consolidation of Suffolk's power in East Anglia in 1437 formed one part of the systematic delegation of regional rule to members of the territorial nobility in that year.[68] His role in central government did in a sense compromise his personal lordship in East Anglia, in that his business at court, together with the fact that his wife's lands in the Thames Valley offered convenient access to London, seems to have meant that he spent little time on his own estates.[69] Nevertheless, in another sense this served to recreate the situation, which had earlier proved so important to the developing regional dominance of the crown–Duchy network, in which the members of that network enjoyed close links with the authority of the crown through the lordship of a magnate closely involved in royal government. Indeed, these circumstances were reproduced in a more exaggerated form, since Suffolk was not only closely associated with the king, as Beaufort had been, but also, in the absence of a properly functioning monarch, effectively represented the authority of the crown.[70] His local servants therefore had vast resources at their disposal with which to bolster the earl's regional authority, as well as their own, despite the infrequency of their lord's personal appearances in the area.

The combination of Suffolk's role in national government and his local dominance produced a complex redoubling of the problems which

---

[67] Although see below, Ch. 4.4, for Thomas Daniel's use of his lesser but independent access to the king's authority to challenge Suffolk's regional hegemony during the 1440s.

[68] See above, pp. 45–7. For the monopolization of regional hierarchies in Staffordshire and western Derbyshire by the duke of Buckingham during the 1440s and 1450s, see below, Ch. 8.

[69] The Commons in 1450, for example, described Suffolk as 'of Ewelme in the Countee of Oxonford', one of the Chaucer properties: *Rot. Parl.*, v. 177.

[70] Watts, *Henry VI*, 158–80.

Henry IV had faced in attempting to reconcile his royal authority with his private regional lordship—problems which, ironically, he had negotiated successfully in East Anglia.[71] By the end of the 1430s, Suffolk had emerged as a threefold source of authority in the region. His control of government meant that he was responsible for the management of the public authority of the crown. Equally, it meant that he also represented the local interests of the king in his private capacity as duke of Lancaster. At the same time, his own private lordship in the region was of prime significance in local affairs. In other words, where Henry IV had encountered difficulties in combining management of his private resources with his public responsibilities as king, Suffolk was now faced with the task not only of supervising his own personal territorial interests, but also of attempting to represent the universal and public authority of the crown which under normal circumstances would guarantee his local power. Further, he also had to manage the private resources of the king without compromising that universal and public authority on which the stability of the realm depended. He was now in control of all the components involved in the make-up of local power structures, not because private interests were being allowed to run riot, but because the polity was forced to find alternative ways of managing itself when faced with a king who utterly failed to engage with his public responsibilities. Fundamental to Suffolk's chances of success in this complex role was his command of the crown–Duchy connection—now developing into what might more accurately be termed the de la Pole affinity—which had, after all, originally been formed out of an amalgam of public and private interests, and which remained a cohesive and broadly representative body.

As had been the case when this network emerged earlier in the century, the Duchy provided a structure of authority and a source of patronage for the advancement of Suffolk's evolving affinity. Of central importance were Thomas Tuddenham and John Heydon, who had been involved with the Duchy since the beginning of their careers, but who now acquired some of the most eminent offices within its administration.[72] Tuddenham was raised to the highest ranks of the Duchy hierarchy in 1443, when Suffolk surrendered his office as chief steward in the North Parts so that he could be reappointed for life jointly with Sir Thomas.[73] At around the same time, Heydon exchanged the office he already held in the South Parts for its equivalent in the north to become their deputy.[74] Their control of the Duchy interest was

---

[71] See above, Ch. 3.2.
[72] For the earlier careers of Tuddenham and Heydon, see above, p. 80.
[73] 29 Sept. 1443: DL37/11 nos. 31, 32.
[74] DL28/5/2 fo. 117v; Somerville, *History of the Duchy*, 425.

also greatly extended at a regional level. Tuddenham had been restored
to the local stewardship in East Anglia in 1437; in 1443 he exchanged
this grant for a joint appointment with Heydon, again for life.[75] On the
same day, Tuddenham was made 'chief steward' of the East Anglian
lands for life, with full powers 'as fully and wholly as any other chief
steward of our said Duchy'.[76] The creation of this new office is a
remarkable indication of the political significance which the Duchy had
acquired in East Anglia, from unpromising beginnings, since 1399. An
honorific hierarchy of Duchy office had finally been created in the
area, despite the physical lack of honorial centres and the absence of a
traditional *cursus honorum*, to reflect the vastly increased status of the
local Duchy-based connection.

Nor were grants of office the only advantages which these men
secured through their association with the Duchy. The granting of
annuities from Duchy revenues had long since ceased to be common
practice, and fees that were still being paid, therefore, were mostly those
which had been granted years before whose recipients had not yet died.
In 1446, however, Tuddenham was granted the unusual privilege of the
reversion of one such annuity, a sum of 80 marks.[77] John Heydon and
Reginald Rous, both lawyers, were also able to expand their landed
interests in the area by leasing Duchy properties. The manor of Beeston,
on the north Norfolk coast, had been farmed by Simon Felbrigg since
1437; when he died in 1442, the lease was acquired by Heydon, whose
home at Baconsthorpe lay close by.[78] In 1437 Reginald Rous secured the
farm of the manors of Offton, Elmsett, and Somersham, part of the
Hereford heritage, in his home county of Suffolk.[79]

This domination of the Duchy interest also gave these men substantial practical authority in the region. On three occasions in 1445–6,
Tuddenham and Heydon were appointed by the Duchy council to
arbitrate in local disputes involving Duchy tenants. In two of the cases,

---

[75] 24 Nov. 1443: DL37/11 no. 15.

[76] 'adeo plene et integre sicut aliquis alius capitalis senescallus eiusdem ducatus nostri':
DL37/11 no. 14. Somerville does not mention the creation of this new office for Tuddenham.
The latter also held the stewardship of the manor of Gimingham (in office Oct. 1443):
DL37/11 no. 79.

[77] The annuity was assigned on the account of the receiver-general: DL37/13 no. 18; and
see above, Ch. 2.4.

[78] DL42/18 fo. 74v; DL28/5/2. (For Felbrigg's longstanding association with the Duchy
connection in the area, see above, p. 67.)

[79] For the Duchy's acquisition of these manors, see above, Ch. 3.2 n. 96. The grant of the
lease was made at the request of William Phelip. Rous shared the farm with William Rous and
John Andrew, who were both to be active in Suffolk's service during the 1440s. Andrew, a
lawyer, had longstanding connections with the de la Poles, and was related to Thomas
Tuddenham. DL42/18 fo. 75; James, 'Career and Political Influence', 234, 244; R. Virgoe,
'The Murder of James Andrew: Suffolk Faction in the 1430s', in Virgoe, *East Anglian Society*,
110–11.

their responsibilities consisted of negotiating with the counsels of the duke of Gloucester[80] and the earl of Northumberland,[81] whose tenants were in conflict with those of the Duchy. The third case was a complex dispute in Norfolk over rights of common, in which the tenants' grievances were compounded by conflicting claims made to the properties by various parties, including Oliver Groos, Henry Inglose, Miles Stapleton, and the priors of Holy Trinity, Norwich, and of Bromholm.[82] The disputants eventually submitted to the arbitration of the Duchy council, which appointed a commission to act on its behalf, headed by Tuddenham and Heydon.[83] The settlement which they awarded in 1446 included the ratification of some of the property rights claimed and the dismissal of others—an indication of the extensive authority over their fellow Norfolk gentry which Tuddenham and Heydon enjoyed as the local representatives of the Duchy.

This authority was reinforced by their connections with Suffolk and the royal household. Tuddenham's prominence in Suffolk's service[84] brought him grants which further increased his local resources. He profited from his access to the crown's resources: when Simon Felbrigg died, for example, Tuddenham acquired his share of an annuity of 100 marks from the fee-farm of Norwich.[85] He also enjoyed the benefits of Suffolk's private lordship. The earl granted the farm of Swaffham, which he had acquired in 1437, to Sir Thomas, whose manor of Oxburgh lay nearby.[86] Tuddenham also acquired office at court, becoming keeper of the great wardrobe in 1446, and in local government; he had been sheriff in 1432, and thereafter played a variety of roles, serving three times as MP for Norfolk, being appointed to every commission of the peace in the county between 1434 and 1450, and appearing on a remarkable proportion of the special commissions in the area during that period.[87] Heydon, too, became a prominent figure in

---

[80] DL37/13 no. 106. Thomas Shuldham, Duchy receiver in the area from 1443 (see below, at n. 91), was the third commissioner appointed.

[81] DL37/13 no. 134. In this instance, they were appointed with William Cotton, receiver-general of the Duchy from 1445 (DL37/2 nos. 45–6).

[82] DL37/2 no. 100; DL37/13 nos. 55, 76, 83.

[83] The other commissioners were Shuldham, Cotton, and John Prisot, a lawyer retained by the Duchy (for whom, see Somerville, *History of the Duchy*, 451).

[84] For evidence of this very close association during the 1440s see, for example, *CPR 1436–41*, 433; *1441–6*, 427; *CCR 1435–41*, 374–5; *1441–7*, 443; *1447–51*, 38–9, 136–7.

[85] The annuity was shared with Sir John Clifton, who had received the original grant with Felbrigg: *CPR 1441–6*, 403.

[86] James, 'Career and Political Influence', 243. It is possible that Suffolk in fact allowed Tuddenham to retain a position he already held at Swaffham, since the petition against him by the town's inhabitants in 1451 asserted that he had been steward there for sixteen years, in other words since 1435: *PL* Davis, ii. 528 (Gairdner, ii. 231).

[87] *CPR 1446–52*, 4; *List of Sheriffs*, 87; *Return of the Name*, 321, 327, 333 (MP in 1432, 1435, and 1442); *CPR 1429–36*, 621; *1436–41*, 146, 149, 198, 266, 504, 535, 574, 576, 586; *1441–6*, 61, 77, 92, 431, 474; *1446–52*, 139, 299, 592. Tuddenham had represented the county of Suffolk,

local administration; he represented Norfolk in the parliament of 1445, served consistently as a JP from 1441, and appeared as a special commissioner almost as frequently as Tuddenham.[88] Reginald Rous was appointed to the commission of the peace in Suffolk in 1439 and served regularly throughout the 1440s.[89]

These three were the most prominent of a larger group of men associated with Suffolk who were active in the administration of East Anglia. The earl's steward John Ulveston held office as escheator in 1442, and was consistently appointed as a JP in Suffolk from the following year.[90] The esquire Thomas Shuldham became receiver of the Duchy in East Anglia in 1443; his association with Tuddenham was already close by 1435, when he became one of the latter's feoffees at Oxburgh.[91] Prominence in official structures of power also, of course, conferred authority in informal hierarchies. When (probably during the 1430s or early 1440s) John Bekyswell and Thomas Derham quarrelled over a disputed rent, the award of their arbitrators, one of whom was Thomas Shuldham, was to be guaranteed by Thomas Tuddenham as umpire.[92]

It is this group of men most intimately associated with the earl who have usually been identified as members of a court clique trading on Suffolk's influence in government to intrude into the region's power structures.[93] However, it is clear both that these men were not intruders within East Anglian political society, and that Suffolk's affinity was made up of a network of associations which spread throughout the region. The crown–Duchy connection of which he had inherited the leadership had itself been extraordinarily broad, and Suffolk's local dominance ensured that new generations and new families were also drawn into his political orbit. Among the greater East Anglian landowners associated with Suffolk, for example, was Thomas, Lord Scales. Scales's opportunities to build up a personal following in the area during the previous two decades had been limited by regular absences

where the family seat at Eriswell lay, in the parliament of 1431. His subsequent elections in Norfolk reflect the decisive shift in his political interests to that county, where his Duchy office gave him substantial powers and where he acquired the manor of Oxburgh, which was to become his principal residence. *Return of the Name*, 319; Blomefield, *History of the County of Norfolk*, vi. 172, 175.

[88] *Return of the Name*, 334; CPR *1436–41*, 146, 149, 199, 586; *1441–6*, 77, 474; *1446–52*, 138, 139, 299, 592. By 1447 Heydon was also acting as steward of the duke of Buckingham's lands in Norfolk: C. Rawcliffe, *The Staffords* (Cambridge, 1978), 204.

[89] CPR *1436–41*, 590–1; *1441–6*, 478–9; *1446–52*, 595.

[90] James, 'Career and Political Influence', 233; *List of Escheators for England and Wales*, PRO Lists and Indexes, 72 (1971), 87; CPR *1441–6*, 478–9; *1446–52*, 595.

[91] DL37/10 no. 25; CCR *1429–35*, 361–2.

[92] C1/10/324. The petition is dated to the chancellorship of John Stafford as bishop of Bath and Wells (1424–43).

[93] See, for example, Griffiths, *Henry VI*, 584–6.

on campaign in France. By the later 1440s, however, he had clearly become involved at a local level with the de la Pole interest, and was acting as a feoffee for the earl.[94] Suffolk was also associated in a variety of local transactions during the 1430s and 1440s with members of the region's gentry such as Sir John Clifton, Sir Miles Stapleton, Sir John Heveningham, Sir Andrew Ogard, John FitzRalph, Thomas Brewes, William and John Harleston, William Calthorp, and Edmund Wichingham,[95] many of whom were also active in local office.[96] Clifton was retained by Suffolk, who acted as his chief feoffee and later overseer of his will;[97] Stapleton was married to the earl's niece, and Suffolk was godfather to FitzRalph's son.[98]

Although it was no longer the case, as it had been earlier in the century, that the various other noble interests in the area were in abeyance, Suffolk's local and national dominance was such that the political effect was in fact very similar. Leaving aside for a moment the significant exception of the duke of Norfolk, which will be considered in detail shortly,[99] the other lords with a territorial stake in East Anglia stood no chance of challenging Suffolk's regional rule. For the lesser landowners, as had been the case within the earlier crown–Duchy network, their association with the earl therefore remained compatible with service to other, non-competitive, sources of lordship. John Harleston and Edmund Wichingham, for example, were both connected during the 1440s with the duke of York, in whose service Andrew Ogard was highly influential and from whom Lord Scales and John Clifton also received fees.[100] Nevertheless, their local ties with

---

[94] *Complete Peerage*, xi. 505–6; *CPR 1446–52*, 111; *CCR 1447–54*, 38–9, 212–14. See, for example, KB27/722 Coram Rege rot. 79v, for Scales acting with Tuddenham, Heydon, and Brian Stapleton in 1441. See also NRO MS 15677 (Scales, Tuddenham, and Heydon acting as co-feoffees in 1445).

[95] See, for example, *CPR 1441–6*, 427; *1446–52*, 111; *CCR 1429–35*, 361–2; *1435–41*, 62, 102; *1441–7*, 443; *1447–54*, 38–9, 120–1; *CFR 1445–52*, 27–8; E210/7164; DRO D231M/T425; W. Rye (ed.), *A Calendar of the Feet of Fines for Suffolk* (Ipswich, 1900), 303.

[96] During the 1430s and 1440s, FitzRalph, Heveningham, Brewes, Stapleton, and Calthorp all served as sheriff, and Brewes, Stapleton, and William Harleston as escheator. Clifton and Wichingham were appointed to the commission of the peace in Norfolk, and Heveningham, Brewes, and John Harleston in Suffolk, while Stapleton acted as JP in both counties. *List of Sheriffs*, 87; *List of Escheators*, 87; *CPR 1429–36*, 621, 625; *1436–41*, 586, 590–1; *1441–6*, 474, 478–9; *1446–52*, 592, 595.

[97] Clifton also named Thomas Tuddenham among the overseers of his will, made just before his death in 1447, while John Heydon, who had been chief steward of Clifton's estates since 1434, was appointed an executor: Richmond, *The Paston Family*, 239 n.; R. Virgoe, 'Inheritance and Litigation in the Fifteenth Century: The Buckenham Disputes', in Virgoe, *East Anglian Society*, 136–8; R. Virgoe, 'The Earlier Knyvetts: The Rise of a Norfolk Gentry Family', in Virgoe, *East Anglian Society*, 166, 174 n.

[98] James, 'Career and Political Influence', 248; *CFR 1437–45*, 313.

[99] See below, Ch. 4.3.

[100] Harleston was receiver of York's East Anglian lands at some time during the 1440s. James, 'Career and Political Influence', 238–9, 253 n.; A. R. Smith, 'Aspects of the Career of

Suffolk should not be obscured by the range of other associations they enjoyed.

Like the crown–Duchy connection out of which it had developed, therefore, the de la Pole affinity combined public and private interests within a broadly representative local network. Inherent in this amalgam of various sources of authority were significant tensions between the different aspects of Suffolk's local rule, but the compound authority which resulted seems initially to have been powerful and representative enough to contain them. Unlike the crown–Duchy connection, however, Suffolk's dominance did not remain uncontroversial. As the 1440s went on, local disputes increasingly began to disrupt East Anglian political society. This development has usually been attributed to the supposed intrusion of household men into local power structures, but it has become clear that the de la Pole affinity did not in fact derive their regional power primarily from their influence at court. Rather, from about 1440 the whole edifice of Suffolk's local control was subjected to external challenge—a development which was to expose and intensify the tensions within Suffolk's position in regional society.

3. 1437–1447: THE CHALLENGE TO SUFFOLK'S LORDSHIP

The establishment of a power base in the region was as vital for the Mowbray duke of Norfolk—whose main estates, like William de la Pole's, lay in Suffolk—as it had been for Suffolk himself. Norfolk's challenge for a share in local rule, which began around 1440, exposed the contradictions inherent in Suffolk's position. The aim of every local magnate—a role which formed one aspect of Suffolk's multifaceted authority—was to defeat or neutralize by accommodation the regional pretensions of his rivals in order to achieve and maintain control of his 'country'. Such an accommodation might in normal circumstances be negotiated under the aegis of the universal and public authority of the crown; in East Anglia the king's private responsibilities as duke of Lancaster would also play a crucial role in determining the balance of power between rival interests in the region. However, because of the abnormalities of Henry VI's kingship, both the public power of the crown and the private authority of the king as duke were represented by Suffolk himself. In his personal capacity, Suffolk had every incentive to oppose and if possible to overcome Norfolk's attempts at self-assertion, particularly because his comprehensive local control had hitherto been maintained from some distance. His responsibilities in national govern-

Sir John Fastolf (1380–1459)', unpublished D.Phil. thesis (Oxford, 1982), 3, 103; P. A. Johnson, *Duke Richard of York* (Oxford, 1988), 17; Griffiths, *Henry VI*, 670–1.

ment left him little time for the personal supervision of local affairs which would be necessary either for the development of a political accommodation with his rival, or for the defence of his interests against sustained challenge. In his public capacity, however, with his responsibility for the management of royal authority, it was necessary for Suffolk to acknowledge Norfolk's claim to an interest in local rule, which was, after all, based on a significant territorial stake in the region. If he did not, the tenurial and political complexion of the region would no longer be adequately represented, and royal government depended for its efficacy, and its ability to secure regional stability, on its reflection and exploitation of the realities of local power structures. It is to this quandary, caused by the confusion of public and private authority in the hands of a private person, that the increasing strains in East Anglian society evident during the first half of the 1440s can largely be attributed.

The Mowbray estates in East Anglia were concentrated around Framlingham Castle in eastern Suffolk, in a rich and compact bloc which spilled over the border into south-eastern Norfolk. These lands had belonged during the thirteenth century to the Bigod earls of Norfolk, and had subsequently been granted by Edward II to his brother Thomas of Brotherton.[101] On the latter's death, the inheritance passed to his two daughters. The elder, Margaret, had married John, Lord Segrave; the pourparty of the younger passed to her daughter Joan, the wife of William Ufford, earl of Suffolk. When Joan died in 1375, Margaret of Brotherton became sole heir to the entire Bigod inheritance, including the earldom of Norfolk.[102] Margaret's daughter had married the Lincolnshire baron John, Lord Mowbray, and their son Thomas therefore stood to inherit not only his father's estates, but also the Segrave and Brotherton lands to which his mother was heir. It was in recognition of these prospects that, when the earldom of Norfolk was elevated to a dukedom in 1397, Thomas Mowbray was created duke on the same day as his grandmother Margaret was promoted to the rank of duchess.[103]

However, the new duke was never to take possession of his East Anglian estates. When Margaret died in March 1399, Thomas Mowbray had already been in exile for five months, and he died in Italy in September of the same year.[104] His son and heir, Thomas, was 15 when his father died. He was granted livery of his estates early, in 1403, but two years later he was executed for his involvement in the Scrope

---

[101] Archer, 'The Mowbrays', 28–9; *Complete Peerage*, ix. 596–7.

[102] *Complete Peerage*, ix. 599–600; Archer, 'The Mowbrays', 31.

[103] *Complete Peerage*, ix. 601. The Mowbrays had already in 1377 acquired the earldom of Nottingham: Archer, 'The Mowbrays', 58.

[104] *Complete Peerage*, ix. 603–4. For his IPM, see J. L. Kirby (ed.), *Calendar of Inquisitions Post Mortem*, xix (London, 1992), 100–1.

rebellion, and his lands were forfeited to the crown.[105] His 13-year-old brother and heir, John, was taken into the royal household in 1410, and then in 1411 entrusted to the guardianship of Ralph Neville, earl of Westmorland.[106] John Mowbray was finally allowed to take possession of his estates in March 1413.[107]

During almost the whole of Henry IV's reign, therefore, no adult Mowbray heir secured full possession of the range of estates which the family had inherited. In East Anglia, the Brotherton lands instead played a significant role in extending the territorial influence of the leaders of the crown–Duchy connection. Thomas Erpingham held Framlingham Castle from 1399 until 1403. After Thomas Mowbray's forfeiture in 1405, Erpingham continued to hold three Mowbray manors in Norfolk, while the lordship of Framlingham was granted to the prince of Wales.[108] Moreover, the minorities did not constitute merely a temporary interruption to the local power of the Mowbrays, since their interest in East Anglia was recently acquired, and its undoubted political potential had yet to be realized. The estates of the Lords Mowbray themselves lay not in East Anglia, but primarily in Lincolnshire, around the chief family residence at Epworth in the Isle of Axholme.[109] The inheritance of the Brotherton lands represented a chance to extend Mowbray power substantially, through the acquisition of large and extremely valuable estates in a new area.[110] Valuable though the lands were, however, they supported no established local following, and therefore offered the Mowbrays no ready-made political role. Between 1338 and 1382 the inheritance had been divided, and for the rest of the fourteenth century it was controlled by Countess Margaret, the scope of whose lordship, despite her remarkable dynamism, was inevitably limited by the fact that she was elderly and female.[111] The Mowbrays therefore faced the task of building virtually from scratch a political interest in the area which would adequately reflect the status and potential power inherent in their newly acquired territorial stake. The longevity of Margaret of Brotherton meant that the start of this process had to be deferred. Though there is some

---

[105] *CPR 1401–5*, 322, 328; *CFR 1399–1405*, 320; *Complete Peerage*, ix. 603–5; Kirby (ed.), *Calendar of Inquisitions Post Mortem*, xix. 101–10.

[106] Before 1410 Mowbray's wardship was in the hands of the king's mother-in-law, the countess of Hereford: *Complete Peerage*, ix. 604–5; *CPR 1408–13*, 167–8, 220, 307.

[107] *CCR 1409–13*, 390–1. He inherited as Earl Marshal, earl of Norfolk and of Nottingham, Lord Mowbray and Segrave, since the dukedom of Norfolk had not been restored to the family after Thomas Mowbray's forfeiture in 1399: *Complete Peerage*, ix. 605.

[108] See above, pp. 65, 70–1; cf. Kirby (ed.), *Calendar of Inquisitions Post Mortem*, xix. 103–4.

[109] Archer, 'The Mowbrays', 152, 333.

[110] In 1395, the Brotherton lands in Norfolk and Suffolk were worth over £1,400: ibid. 54.

[111] Ibid. 31, 34. Margaret was over 60 when the Brotherton lands were reunited in her hands: *Complete Peerage*, ix. 599–600.

evidence that Thomas Mowbray began to forge associations among the East Anglian gentry during the 1390s in anticipation of his future role in the region,[112] the fact remained that when he became duke of Norfolk in 1397 he held virtually no property in East Anglia. When his grandmother eventually died at the age of nearly 80, Mowbray was no longer in a position to take advantage of his inheritance.[113]

When John Mowbray took possession of his estates in 1413, therefore, he became the first Mowbray earl of Norfolk to have the opportunity to capitalize on the political potential of the Brotherton lands in East Anglia. In the event, this opportunity was curtailed by the effects of providing dowers for two young and well-connected Mowbray widows, which severely depleted his East Anglian inheritance for a prolonged period.[114] The estates assigned in 1400 to Elizabeth Fitzalan, widow of Thomas, duke of Norfolk, originally included Framlingham Castle itself. Although she was subsequently forced to exchange the latter, because of its strategic importance, for properties in the midlands, she retained a valuable group of East Anglian lands, including Bungay Castle.[115] For Constance Holand, widow of Thomas, Earl Marshal, the disgrace of her husband's treason was considerably mitigated by the fact that Henry IV was her uncle.[116] On her marriage she had been granted a group of manors in Norfolk and Suffolk from her husband's inheritance (which was at that point in the possession of the crown) valued at an annual sum of £200, and when she was widowed in 1405 her possession of these properties for life was immediately confirmed.[117] Rowena Archer's study of the estate accounts extant for the life of John Mowbray led her to conclude that 'the most striking feature . . . is the proportion of manors in the hands of the two dowagers'.[118] Of the seventy-seven properties listed in the accounts, only slightly more than half were in Mowbray's control, and in East Anglia this depletion was particularly severe: between them, Elizabeth and Constance held eighteen manors in Norfolk and Suffolk, leaving the earl in possession of only seven.[119]

---

[112] See below, at n. 129.

[113] See above, at n. 104.

[114] Fortune had, in a similar situation, favoured William de la Pole, who was able rapidly to consolidate his possession of his estates despite the claims of two dowagers and his three nieces: see above, pp. 84–5.

[115] Elizabeth was the sister and co-heir of Thomas, earl of Arundel. According to the valuations in the original grant of July 1400, the Suffolk properties she retained were worth £430 annually. *Complete Peerage*, ix. 604; *CPR 1399–1401*, 399; *CCR 1399–1402*, 165–6; Archer, 'The Mowbrays', 92 and table VI.

[116] Constance was the daughter of Henry's sister Elizabeth by her first husband John Holand, duke of Exeter: *Complete Peerage*, ix. 605.

[117] *CPR 1399–1401*, 402; *CPR 1405–8*, 38.

[118] Archer, 'The Mowbrays', 148.

[119] Ibid. 148–9; cf. Kirby (ed.), *Calendar of Inquisitions Post Mortem*, xix. 103–4.

It is perhaps unsurprising, therefore, that John Mowbray made little political impact in East Anglia, since, holding so few of the family's local estates, he was in no position to impose his lordship—a circumstance which he seems to have recognized. The Earl Marshal in fact spent a considerable proportion of the years between 1415 and 1425 serving in France,[120] but on his periodic returns to England he seems to have visited East Anglia relatively rarely, dividing his time instead between London and the Mowbray residence at Epworth in Lincolnshire, where his wife kept her household during his absences.[121] Mowbray had been named to the commissions of the peace in Norfolk and Suffolk from 1414, in recognition of his family's territorial stake in the area, but received no other local appointments.[122] His mother Elizabeth died in 1425; the reversion of her dower lands gave Mowbray control of a substantial stake in East Anglia for the first time, and, in the same year, he was restored to the dukedom of Norfolk.[123] However, these developments do not seem to have prompted him to any greater political activity in the area. It was entirely characteristic of his regional interests that, when he died in 1432 at Epworth, he asked to be buried there, on the Isle of Axholme.[124]

By 1432, the Mowbray dukes of Norfolk had therefore had little chance to stake their claim to the rule of East Anglia. Their immediate local prospects seemed little better. The duke's son and heir was, at 17, still a minor;[125] Constance Holand still held a significant proportion of the family's East Anglian estates; and the jointure settlement of John Mowbray's widow, Katherine Neville, gave her the greater part of her husband's lands including Axholme itself and the bulk of the Mowbray manors in Norfolk.[126] Constance died only a year after the new duke

---

[120] *DNB*, xxxix. 221.

[121] The relative political unimportance of East Anglia for Mowbray is also indicated by the fact that, while he used his estates in the region extensively as a source of cash and supplies for his military expeditions, comparatively few of his retinue were drawn from the area: Archer, 'The Mowbrays', 177, 190, 235, 237, 343–5.

[122] *CPR 1413–16*, 421, 423; *1416–22*, 456, 460; *1422–9*, 566, 570; *1429–36*, 621, 625.

[123] *CFR 1422–30*, 84, 114–15; R. E. Archer, 'Parliamentary Restoration: John Mowbray and the Dukedom of Norfolk in 1425', in R. E. Archer and S. Walker (eds.), *Rulers and Ruled in Late Medieval England* (London, 1995), 99–116.

[124] N. H. Nicolas (ed.), *Testamenta Vetusta*, 2 vols. (London, 1826), i. 223. Christine Carpenter has suggested that during the later 1420s, the only period of his political life when he remained in England for a protracted period and when he was therefore in a position to pursue his local interests, Mowbray attempted to extend his regional influence from his power base in Leicestershire across into eastern Warwickshire. This confirms the impression that the duke's domestic political concerns focused on the east midlands rather than on his estates in East Anglia: C. Carpenter, *Locality and Polity* (Cambridge, 1992), 380–8.

[125] Custody of the Mowbray estates was granted to the duke of Gloucester, and the marriage of the minor heir to Anne, countess of Stafford: *CFR 1430–7*, 117, 143, 230–1.

[126] Katherine was the daughter of Mowbray's former guardian the earl of Westmorland. In Norfolk, she held the manors of Forncett, Lopham, Suffield, Earsham, Hanworth, and Little Framingham. *Complete Peerage*, ix. 607; *DNB*, xxxix. 221–2; R. E. Archer, 'Rich Old Ladies:

secured livery of his estates, but the extensive lands held by Katherine Neville were lost to the Mowbrays; she died in 1483, having outlived all her Mowbray descendants.[127] With Axholme in the hands of the dowager duchess, Framlingham became for the first time the chief residence of a Mowbray duke of Norfolk. The extent of his mother's dower, particularly in traditional areas of Mowbray influence, meant that it was more vital than ever for the duke finally to realize the political potential of his rich East Anglian inheritance. By 1436, however, when he came of age,[128] the local dominance of the crown–Duchy connection was already being reinforced by the leadership of the earl of Suffolk, a process which left little room for the claims of a lord who was still, in effect, a newcomer to the region. The turbulence of the area during the 1440s and 1450s—usually interpreted as the result of John Mowbray's attempts to maintain his family's natural regional dominance against the artificial influence of Suffolk's household men—instead owed much to Mowbray's attempts to establish his lordship as a new regional authority in the face of a deeply rooted and broadly based structure of power of which Suffolk had inherited the leadership.

The Mowbrays had not been entirely without a following in East Anglia in the years before 1436. The first duke had begun to establish some connections among the knights of the region in the last years of his life. Thomas, Lord Morley, Sir George Felbrigg, and Sir John Inglesthorpe, for example, were all granted fees by Thomas Mowbray in the late 1390s, and Felbrigg and Sir William Elmham were among those nominated by the duke to administer his estates during his exile.[129] However, the minorities in the family during Henry IV's reign meant that these nascent connections were all but lost,[130] and the local Mowbray interest was effectively represented only by the professionals involved in the administration of the family's estates. Of these men, some were natives of the area. John Lancaster of Bressingham in Norfolk, for example, had been in Mowbray service since 1389, and became receiver of the duke's estates in Norfolk and Suffolk.[131] Others prominent among the family's retainers in the region, however, had not been drawn into Mowbray service by local associations, but had been

The Problem of Late Medieval Dowagers', in A. J. Pollard (ed.), *Property and Politics: Essays in Later Medieval History* (Gloucester, 1984), 29; *CCR 1429–35*, 204–5, 208–14.

[127] *CFR 1437–45*, 24; Archer, 'Rich Old Ladies', 24–5.

[128] *CPR 1429–36*, 603; *CCR 1435–41*, 29–30.

[129] Archer, 'The Mowbrays', 75, 284, 339–40; S. Walker, *The Lancastrian Affinity 1361–99* (Oxford, 1990), 205–6.

[130] A certain continuity is perhaps suggested by the fact that in 1415 Simon Felbrigg became one of John Mowbray's feoffees. He was not, however, retained by Mowbray. Rowena Archer notes that most of the force raised by the Earl Marshal to join the rebellion of 1405 seems to have been drawn from the north. *CPR 1413–16*, 319–20, 333; Archer, 'The Mowbrays', 130 n.   [131] Archer, 'The Mowbrays', 339, 350.

'transplanted' into the area as a result of their employment. Richard Steresacre, who was retained in 1390 and became closely associated in Mowbray service with John Lancaster, acquired his lands in Suffolk only in the early years of the new century, and Robert Southwell, the Earl Marshal's receiver-general from 1413 and treasurer at Framlingham from the following year, came originally from Southwell in Nottinghamshire.[132] From the beginning of the reign of Henry V, there was again some tentative expansion in the Mowbray following in East Anglia, as John Mowbray began to recruit the service of some local landowners. Sir Simon Felbrigg acted as his feoffee, while Sir John Jermy and Sir John Heveningham served in his retinue in France.[133] However, these men by no means formed a coherent group, nor did their Mowbray associations play a pre-eminent part among the wealth of their local connections. Service to the largely absentee Mowbrays, like employment by John of Gaunt for the East Anglians of the 1380s and 1390s,[134] seems to have been a local option offering some potential benefits, while remaining compatible with a variety of other regional associations. Both Felbrigg and Edmund Winter, who was associated with John Mowbray from the late 1420s, for example, were prominent members of the crown–Duchy connection in the area.[135]

Among the few men who became more closely involved with Mowbray lordship, some were those whose own lands lay close to Framlingham. Living in the shadow of Framlingham Castle made the potential power of the Mowbrays hard to ignore, but these men also had the greatest chance of consistent local contact with the family, and may therefore have recognized that they were well placed to gain maximum advantage from the service of even a frequently absent lord. Sir Robert Wingfield, whose home at Letheringham lay three miles from Framlingham, is perhaps the most obvious example. John Mowbray had been his guardian during his minority; Wingfield served with Mowbray in France during the 1420s, and married Elizabeth, the daughter of Thomas Mowbray's widow Elizabeth Fitzalan by her second husband Robert Goushill.[136] Wingfield later became Mowbray's

---

[132] Archer, 'The Mowbrays', 354; R. Hawes and R. Loder, *The History of Framlingham* (Woodbridge, 1798), 397. Robert Southwell's son Richard followed his father into Mowbray service and consolidated the family's position among the East Anglian gentry: G. E. Morey, 'East Anglian Society in the Fifteenth Century: An Historico-Regional Survey', unpublished Ph.D. thesis (London, 1951), appendix, 93; *PL* Davis, ii. 76–7 (Gairdner, ii. 254–5).

[133] See above, n. 130; E101/51/2 m. 21; Archer, 'The Mowbrays', 285.

[134] Walker, *The Lancastrian Affinity*, 206; see above, Ch. 3.1.

[135] Winter received a fee from Mowbray from 1429, and was one of his attorneys in England when the duke led Henry VI's coronation expedition to France the following year: Archer, 'The Mowbrays', 209, 345; see above, p. 79.

[136] Archer, 'The Mowbrays', 279; BL Add. Ch. 17209; *DKR*, 48, 'Calendar of French Rolls, Henry VI' (London, 1887), 276.

steward, and received from him a life grant of the manor of Hoo, which adjoined Letheringham.[137] A marriage alliance also served to bind the Howard family closely to the Mowbrays, despite the fact that their lands around Stoke-by-Nayland lay further south, near the Essex border. Sir Robert Howard, probably a member of John Mowbray's household, married Mowbray's sister Margaret between 1415 and 1420. Their son Sir John was to be prominent in the service of the third Mowbray duke.[138]

During the 1420s, therefore, John Mowbray formed a variety of associations within East Anglian society, but he could claim to be the sole, or even the principal, lord of few local gentlemen. His status in the region does seem to have benefited to some degree from his acquisition in 1425 of his mother's dower lands and of the dukedom of Norfolk. In 1428, for example, when the negotiations arranged by Thomas Erpingham between William Paston and Walter Aslak had broken down, the dispute was finally settled by the award of 'the right high and myghty prynce the Duc of Norffolk'.[139] However, though it has been argued that 'the restoration to the dukedom naturally made him a leader in his shire',[140] the extent of this leadership should not be over-estimated. In this particular case, Mowbray's intervention may have owed much to the fact that he had personal connections with both parties, rather than to any universal recognition accorded to his regional lordship.[141] Moreover, the upper ranks of the region's power structure were temporarily in a state of flux, since Beaufort and Erpingham had recently died and the earl of Suffolk had not yet returned to England. Indeed, before Norfolk's award, appeals had also been made in the course of the Paston–Aslak dispute to the dukes of Gloucester and Bedford—an apparently unequivocal demonstration that Norfolk was not the 'natural leader' to whom appeal would immediately and auto-matically be made in local matters.[142]

It seems clear that by the time of his death in 1432 John Mowbray's

---

[137] Hawes and Loder, *History of Framlingham*, 49; Storey, *End of the House of Lancaster*, 226.

[138] The marriage was eventually to bring the Howards the dukedom of Norfolk: A. Crawford, 'The Career of John Howard, Duke of Norfolk, *c.*1420–85', unpublished M.Phil. thesis (London, 1975), 9, 12–13; see below, pp. 178, 180.

[139] The quotation is from Paston's earlier memorandum: *PL* Davis, i. 10 (Gairdner, ii. 15); for the dispute, see above, p. 77, and for the settlement, see *CCR 1422–9*, 393–4.

[140] Archer, 'The Mowbrays', 286.

[141] Aslak had fought in France in Mowbray's retinue in 1417. The lawyer Paston had been retained as legal counsel by the duke, had been steward of his properties in East Anglia before 1425, and in that year was 'wyth Ser John Jermy, knyght, and othre of the counseill of the seyd Duk of Norffolk in hys lordshipes in Norffolk and Suffolk thanne to hym falle by the deth of the right worthy and noble lady hys modyr': E101/51/2 m. 21; *PL* Davis, i. 10 (Gairdner, ii. 15).

[142] *PL* Davis, i. 10 (Gairdner, ii. 14); Davis, ii. 505–7.

following in East Anglia was neither large nor a particularly coherent regional presence. His son's minority, relatively brief though it was, can only have exaggerated this situation at a time when Suffolk's appropriation of the crown–Duchy connection was gathering momentum. The third duke, however, unlike his predecessors, was forced to concentrate his involvement in regional politics in East Anglia, and therefore compete with the rival authority of the de la Pole interest. The result of this confrontation was a clear indication that Mowbray lordship, newly aggressive though it might be, could not match the traditional authority, closely connected to the regional power of the crown, of the affinity which Suffolk commanded.

Hostility between the two nobles grew rapidly during the 1430s, when a longstanding dispute between Norfolk's servant Richard Steresacre and Suffolk's retainer James Andrew resulted in the murder of the latter, apparently at the instigation of Robert Wingfield and Gilbert Debenham, both associates of Mowbray.[143] Wingfield and Debenham were pardoned, at Norfolk's request, in 1439. However, it seems clear that, at least by 1441, the duke could not reliably secure the same kind of protection for his lesser followers.[144] Another local dispute around this time, also involving Robert Wingfield, provided more dramatic evidence of the limitations of Norfolk's lordship when confronted with the pervasive influence of the de la Pole affinity. Wingfield became involved during the late 1430s in a dispute with the Suffolk esquire Robert Lyston over possession of the manors of Badingham, Dallinghoo, and Creting St Peter, which lay near both Letheringham and Framlingham itself.[145] The estates had belonged to Sir Richard Carbonell, whose death in 1430 was followed shortly afterwards by that of his baby son. An inquisition *post mortem* held in the autumn of 1432 named Robert Wingfield as the heir, though without explaining the nature of his title; Robert Lyston seems to have claimed the manors as the heir of an earlier Sir William Carbonell.[146] Lyston claimed in 1438 that Wingfield had expelled him from the properties six years earlier— a move with which the uninformative IPM of 1432 was presumably connected—and that, after he had won his case for their recovery at a special assize, Wingfield seized the manors again.[147] Again Lyston took

[143] Virgoe, 'The Murder of James Andrew', 109–11. Andrew, a lawyer of some prominence in Suffolk politics, was killed in July 1434. His quarrel with Steresacre, over land in Baylham, had remained unsettled for twenty years. Suffolk and Norfolk were both summoned before the council in Feb. 1435 as a result of the incident: *POPC*, iv. 300–1.

[144] Virgoe, 'The Murder of James Andrew', 112–13.

[145] For Lyston's account of the dispute, see E28/65 m. 1 and *CPR 1436–41*, 475–6.

[146] C139/53/11; *Calendar of Inquisitions Post Mortem in the Reign of Henry VII*, i (London, 1898), 295.

[147] Unless otherwise specified, all details are taken from KB27/714 Coram Rege roti. 123v, 124; E28/65 m. 26.

the issue to court, and again he won; Wingfield then 'procured and excitid the wurthi prince the Duke of Norffolk to putte oute ageyn the seid Robert Lyston', claiming that Norfolk was his feoffee in the estates. In this attack, Lyston alleged, his evidences of title were stolen. Again Lyston won his case in court, bringing the damages he had been awarded to a total of over 700 marks.[148] Wingfield's response was to bring a charge of assault against him in Nottinghamshire, as a result of which Lyston was outlawed in July 1440 for non-appearance in court.[149] Norfolk's lordship did prove useful to Wingfield in these manœuvres: when Lyston's property became forfeit to the crown for outlawry, Norfolk persuaded the Treasurer, Cromwell, to grant him the 700 marks for which Wingfield was liable, as part payment of the wages which the duke was owed for his military service on the Scottish border; Norfolk then released Wingfield from his obligation to pay the debt.[150]

However, Lyston had support from within the de la Pole affinity, notably from Reginald Rous, who was acting as his attorney, and John Heydon, who seems to have been among the feoffees at Badingham from whom Lyston acquired the property as the heir of Sir William Carbonell.[151] Confronted with opposition from Suffolk's men, Norfolk's influence proved woefully inadequate. The duke's success in rescuing Wingfield from the necessity of paying the damages awarded by the courts was short-lived. His scheme resulted in 'greet hevyng an shovyng be my lord of Suffolk and all his counsell for to aspye hough this mater kam aboute'.[152] Lyston appealed to the council, and in November 1440 was granted a pardon of outlawry and restitution of his goods.[153] This success with the council formed part of a much wider victory. Not only had Lyston consistently won favourable verdicts in the courts, but in June 1440 a commission for Wingfield's arrest was issued, and in the following September he was committed to the Tower, where he spent

---

[148] The figure of 700 marks is quoted in the letter to John Paston referring to the case; the sums detailed in Lyston's petition add up to 920 marks. The exchequer accounts record the sum as £493 (about 740 marks). *PL* Davis, ii. 22 (Gairdner, ii. 47); E28/65 m. 1; E403/751 mm. 4–5.

[149] Lyston had been accused in the Michaelmas term of 1439 of assaulting one of Wingfield's servants. KB27/714 Coram Rege rot. 90; KB27/718 Coram Rege rot. 69.

[150] Norfolk's action is reported on 1 Nov. 1440 (when Wingfield's opponent is referred to as 'John Lyston'). *PL* Davis, ii. 22 (Gairdner, ii. 47); cf. E403/751 m. 5. The duke had been warden of the east march and captain of Berwick in 1437–8: *DNB*, xxxix. 223.

[151] James, 'Career and Political Influence', 262; *Cal. IPM Henry VII*, i. 295. Lyston's mainpernors when the assault case brought by Wingfield reached court in Nov. 1440 included Heydon, Rous, and John Andrew. (Wingfield failed to pursue the case, and Lyston was allowed to go *sine die*.) William Phelip and Thomas Tuddenham also seem to have been involved in supporting Lyston against Wingfield, probably as Lyston's feoffees: C81/1369/4 (a reference for which I am indebted to John Watts).

[152] *PL* Davis, ii. 22 (Gairdner, ii. 47).

[153] E28/65 m. 1; *CPR 1436–41*, 458; E403/751 mm. 4–5.

the next nine months.[154] More remarkably, Norfolk himself seems to have spent some time in the Tower.[155] Certainly, in July 1440 he was required to bind himself in the massive sum of 10,000 marks to remain in the king's household until he found security of the peace not to harm John Heydon.[156] This humiliating penalty, imposed at the suit of a mere lawyer (and one, moreover, from his own 'country'), together with the duke's inability to protect the interests of his retainer, testifies to the fact that Norfolk could not hope to match the power wielded, at a local and a national level, by the East Anglian connection under the lordship of the earl of Suffolk.

Other disputes in which Norfolk was involved during the 1440s confirm this impression. The manors of Stockton and Geldeston, which lay a few miles from the Mowbray castle at Bungay, were held by the esquire Ralph Garneys. His title was challenged by the duke,[157] who seized the properties in March 1438 and retained possession of them for the next three years.[158] At the end of 1443 Norfolk returned to the offensive: in December, his men felled trees and hunted in Garneys's park, and in the spring of 1444 the duke turned his attentions to the issue of water rights. In March, Norfolk's men were said to have stopped water flowing through Garneys's fulling mill; in May, they allegedly damaged, and diverted the river away from, two of his water mills.[159] However, the Garneys family was not without powerful connections. Ralph's father William, who had served Michael de la Pole in the early years of the century, had by the end of his life secured the services of William Phelip as his chief feoffee, and Ralph himself seems to have revitalized these associations, notably with John Heydon, who

---

[154] The commission was issued to the JPs and sheriff of Norfolk and Suffolk, together with Lord Scales: *CPR 1436–41*, 451–2; *CCR 1435–41*, 395, 420. In Nov. 1440 Wingfield failed to appear in King's Bench to satisfy Lyston of his damages because he was in the Tower. He finally answered the summons in the Michaelmas term of 1441, after his release, and was promptly committed to the Marshalsea: KB27/718 Rex rot. 34.

[155] Storey, *End of the House of Lancaster*, 226.

[156] *CCR 1435–41*, 381.

[157] Colin Richmond suggests that the tension between Norfolk and Garneys could have developed because Garneys's mother was Elizabeth Bigot, a descendant of the Bigod earls of Norfolk, and Stockton and Geldeston were among the Bigot properties she inherited. Norfolk did complain later in the dispute that he was being 'gretely hyndred and hurt of his enheritaunce'; in 1455, when the case came to court (see below, Ch. 5 n. 111), he argued that his great-grandmother Margaret of Brotherton had been in possession of them until unjustly disseised by Elizabeth Bigot's grandfather John. Richmond, *The Paston Family*, 138, 147–8; C81/1484/58; KB27/778 Coram Rege rot. 51.

[158] KB9/249 m. 108; KB27/734 Rex rot. 3v; KB27/738 Rex rot. 4. The allegation was made in 1444, and the disseisin attributed to a group of Norfolk's men including Gilbert Debenham, William Brandon, Edmund Fitzwilliam, and John Tymperley. It was later asserted that in Nov. 1441—in other words when Garneys regained the properties—Norfolk accepted his homage for the manors as held of the Mowbray manor of Forncett: KB27/778 Coram Rege rot. 51; see below, Ch. 5 n. 111.

[159] KB9/249 mm. 108, 112; KB27/738 Rex roti. 4–5.

was among his feoffees at Stockton and Geldeston.[160] Certainly his access to the powers of the crown outstripped Norfolk's. On 2 June 1444 Garneys secured a commission of *oyer* and *terminer* to investigate his complaints against the duke, and another on 10 September.[161] On 29 September, at Norfolk's request, the commission was ordered also to consider the duke's complaints against Garneys, but four days later this instruction was halted by signet letter.[162] On 24 December, after a petition from Norfolk, the order was given for the investigation of his grievances to proceed, but the composition of the commission, which was headed by Sir John Clifton and Garneys's feoffee Sir John Heveningham, remained weighted against the duke.[163] Indeed, in the autumn of 1445 Norfolk's men were indicted in King's Bench both for the disseisin of 1438 and for the attacks on Garneys's property in 1444; they submitted no defence, and were therefore convicted.[164] Garneys was charged with attacking Norfolk's property at Mettingham, but was acquitted; the local jury explicitly endorsed his claim that his actions had been a legitimate reassertion of his rights in the face of infringements by Norfolk's men.[165] The implication that Garneys had won the support of the de la Pole interest is compounded by the fact that, when he died childless in 1446, the disputed manors were acquired by Suffolk himself.[166]

Norfolk's inability to turn the appointment of special commissions to his advantage was merely one facet of his lack of influence within regional administration during the 1440s. While offices and commis-

---

[160] Richmond, *The Paston Family*, 143, 145–6; KB27/778 Coram Rege rot. 51. When Ralph had earlier quarrelled over the inheritance with his uncle Peter, the arbitrators who settled the dispute included Reginald Rous and John Puttok. In 1435, Garneys and Heydon were together named as feoffees of the manor of Bradeston in Norfolk by John Berney of Reedham in a settlement in which the de la Pole connection was also represented by John Heveningham, Miles Stapleton, and Thomas Brewes. *CCR 1435–41*, 109; NRO NCC Reg. Doke fos. 157–8; for Heveningham, Stapleton, and Brewes, see above, at n. 95; for Bradeston, see below, Ch. 5 at n. 49.   [161] *CPR 1441–6*, 290, 337.

[162] *CPR 1441–6*, 338; C81/1373/20.

[163] C81/1484/58; C81/1374/5; *CPR 1441–6*, 338; *CCR 1435–41*, 109; Richmond, *The Paston Family*, 144. (I am very grateful to Dr Simon Walker and Dr John Watts for the signet letter references.) The composition of the four commissions varied slightly, but all included Clifton and Heveningham, as well as the lawyers John Markham and William Yelverton, and the esquire Robert Clere. The elder Sir John Heveningham in fact died during the summer of 1444 (C. Richmond, *John Hopton: A Fifteenth-Century Suffolk Gentleman* (Cambridge, 1981), 235 n.) but, on this evidence, his son seems to have assumed his father's active role in local society virtually immediately. For Clifton and Heveningham's connections with Suffolk, see above, at nn. 95, 97. Heveningham senior was also the brother-in-law of James Andrew, who had been killed by Norfolk's men in 1434: Virgoe, 'The Murder of James Andrew', 111; *POPC*, iv. 300–1.

[164] KB9/249 mm. 108, 112; KB27/738 Rex. roti. 4–5.

[165] KB27/738 Rex rot. 40; KB9/248 m. 63.

[166] Norfolk made no further attempt on them until 1453. Richmond, *The Paston Family*, 147–8; C1/25/77; C1/26/164; and see below, Ch. 5 n. 111.

sions in East Anglia were consistently held by men connected with Suffolk,[167] the representation of Norfolk's affinity in equivalent positions was almost negligible. Of the local gentry most closely associated with the duke, only Gilbert Debenham sat on the commission of the peace in either county during the 1440s;[168] moreover, Debenham had previously been associated with Thomas Beaufort, and as late as 1438 had apparently been in conflict with Norfolk over a matter which was settled through the intervention of the earl of Suffolk.[169] None of the sheriffs appointed during the decade were closely connected with the duke. Of the escheators, only John Tymperley (who served in 1439–40) was a prominent Mowbray servant,[170] and even his affiliation is questionable given that, certainly by the later 1440s, he was also establishing associations with Suffolk and his affinity.[171] Suffolk's influence permeated landed society in the region; his control of local administration through his position in government was therefore reinforced by his network of connections in the locality. This meant that, despite his ducal status and his extensive lands, Mowbray could find no adequate niche for his lordship.[172] It is perhaps no surprise, therefore, that when William Burgeys asked for William Paston's advice about a rent he was disputing with Reginald Rous, the judge told him under no circumstances to take legal action, ' "for zyf thu do," he seyd, "thu xalte hafe the werse, be thi cawse never so trewe, for he is feid wyth myn lord of Sowthfolke and mech he is of hese consel, and also thu canste no man of lawe in Northfolke ne in Sowthfolke to be wyth the a-zens hym" '.[173]

The effects of Suffolk's hegemony were compounded by the fact that Norfolk's management of the already limited political resources he had in the region proved singularly inept. The Wingfields, for example,

---

[167] See above, Ch. 4.2.

[168] Debenham was a JP for Suffolk in 1440, 1442–5, and 1448–9. *CPR 1436–41*, 590–1; *1441–6*, 478–9; *1446–52*, 595.

[169] *CCR 1435–41*, 232. When Debenham appeared in court on a murder charge in the autumn of 1438, his pledges were John Tymperley and John Wyndham, both at that stage associated with John Mowbray; the following Easter, his mainpernor (for the same indictment) was Thomas Tuddenham: KB27/710 Coram Rege rot. 71v.

[170] See, for example, KB9/1050 mm. 97–8. Tymperley held free warren at Eyke for life by grant of the duke: KB9/252/2 m. 16.

[171] In Nov. 1447, for example, Tymperley was one of a group of feoffees which included Scales, Tuddenham, and Rous to whom the manor of Babingley, Norfolk, was granted by another group including Suffolk, Heydon, and Heveningham. By the 1450s, however, Tymperley was taking part in Norfolk's attempts to seize Stockton from the duchess of Suffolk: *CPR 1446–52*, 111; C1/26/164.

[172] This analysis of the situation was apparently common currency by the end of the 1440s. A contemporary poem, using the heraldic devices of Norfolk and Suffolk respectively, declared that 'The white Lioun is leyde to slepe | Thorough the envy of the Ape Clogge': T. Wright (ed.), *Political Poems and Songs*, 2 vols. (London, 1859–61), ii. 222.

[173] The report must have been made in 1444 or earlier: *PL* Davis, ii. 518. (*PL* Gairdner, ii. 48, misreads 'myn lord of Sowthfolke' as 'Northfolke'.)

were one of the few local families for whom the duke's lordship was of paramount importance, and whose connections with the Mowbrays were both close and longstanding. In 1440–1, Robert Wingfield had been working closely with Norfolk in the effort to overcome the de la Pole connections of Robert Lyston.[174] Only three years later, however, the duke and Wingfield were completely estranged, and they continued at loggerheads throughout much of the rest of the decade. After his defeat by Lyston, it seems likely that Wingfield began to turn away from Norfolk's ineffective lordship towards that of Suffolk, whose support lay behind Lyston's success.[175] This at least seems to be the most likely explanation of the fact that in August 1443 Norfolk decided to reclaim the manor of Hoo, which his father had granted for life to Wingfield, by seizing the property.[176] The duke also mounted an assault on Wingfield's home at Letheringham during which, Wingfield claimed, evidences belonging to him were stolen, together with other property which he valued at nearly £5,000.[177] On 26 November 1443, Norfolk was forced to bind himself in the sum of £2,000 to keep the peace towards Wingfield, and to appear before the council in the following April.[178] The matter was then submitted to the arbitration of the bishop of Norwich, the earl of Suffolk, and Chief Justice Fortescue.[179] The settlement which they imposed in May 1444 allowed Norfolk to retain possession of Hoo, but in return the duke was forced to grant Wingfield the manor of Weston by Baldock in Hertfordshire, and to confirm his position as chief steward of the

[174] See above, pp. 108–10.

[175] Watts, *Henry VI*, 202.

[176] The disseisin was alleged to have been carried out on 21 Aug. 1443 by a group of men described as 'of Framlingham', led by Sir Robert Conyers: KB9/1050, m. 97; KB27/734 Rex rot. 3; KB27/735 Rex rot. 37.

[177] E28/82. According to Wingfield, Norfolk's men were armed with 'gonnes and other engynes and instrumentes'. The petition in which the attack is reported was submitted in July 1452. However, the reference to the arbitrators in the case, who included William de la Pole as earl of Suffolk and Sir John Fortescue as chief justice, makes it clear that the incident took place between early 1442, when Fortescue took office, and late 1444, when Suffolk was elevated to the rank of marquis. There is another report of Norfolk's attack on Letheringham in 1448, when a commission of *oyer* and *terminer* was appointed to investigate the matter. The details of the incident given here include the allegation that property was stolen by Norfolk's men both from Wingfield and from William Brandon. Brandon was in 1443 indicted by Wingfield for assaulting his family in the course of the dispute over Hoo; it seems highly unlikely that, around the same time, he was sufficiently closely associated with Wingfield to share his fate at the hands of the duke's forces. By 1448, however, Brandon had changed sides, and had become Wingfield's chief supporter in his confrontations with Norfolk. Brandon later married Wingfield's daughter Elizabeth. Wingfield and Brandon may well, therefore, have been attempting in 1448 to 'backdate' their association. Storey, *End of the House of Lancaster*, 260; *CPR 1446–52*, 236; KB9/1050 m. 97; KB27/735 Rex rot. 37; KB9/257 mm. 41–4, 53, 58; S. J. Gunn, *Charles Brandon, Duke of Suffolk c.1484–1545* (Oxford, 1988), 2, 46, 48; and see below, pp. 114–15.

[178] *CCR 1441–7*, 196.

[179] E28/82.

Mowbray lands in Suffolk for life. Wingfield was also awarded 3,500 marks in damages.[180]

Only three years, therefore, after the limitations of his lordship had been publicly demonstrated in the course of Wingfield's dispute with Lyston, Norfolk attempted to assert his authority over his own retainer with a startling show of force, which proved not only an inadequate means of achieving his aims but also actively damaging in political terms. Though the duke did retrieve the disputed manor, he paid a high price: he was forced to make significant concessions to Wingfield, imposed by the authority of arbitrators who included his local rival Suffolk. His actions also made certain the loss of Wingfield's service, a defection he could ill afford given the limited range of his following in East Anglia. In November 1444 Sir Robert joined Suffolk's expedition to escort Margaret of Anjou back to England, and subsequently entered the service of the new queen.[181] Though Margaret attempted to negotiate a reconciliation between Wingfield and Norfolk,[182] relations between the two remained uneasy.

A second crisis developed in their relationship in 1447–8, and in this instance too the duke's authority was severely compromised. In December 1447 and January 1448, Wingfield and his son Robert, with their associate William Brandon who had also been prominent in Norfolk's service earlier in the decade, were indicted in King's Bench for a series of offences including assault, theft, and threatening behaviour.[183] The central charges against them, however, which seem to have precipitated this judicial campaign, constituted a series of challenges to Norfolk's authority which the duke had apparently been unable to control. It was alleged that on 6 December Richard Hadilsay,

[180] The confirmation in office was made on 1 May, and the grant of Weston three days later. In 1452, however, Wingfield claimed not yet to have received 'any peny' of the 3,500 marks. Presumably as a result of the arbitration, Norfolk's men were acquitted on charges of expelling Wingfield from Hoo in July 1444. E28/82; *CCR 1441–7*, 213, 215; KB27/735 Rex rot. 37v.

[181] James, 'Career and Political Influence', 263; C. Monro (ed.), *The Letters of Queen Margaret of Anjou . . .*, Camden Society, old series, 86 (London, 1863), 155–6. Wingfield was named in a Commons petition to the parliament of 1450, together with others including the duchess of Suffolk, as one of those who 'hath been of mysbehavyng aboute youre Roiall persone'. The fact that Thomas Daniel (for whom, see below, pp. 120–3) was one of the others named indicates that this was not a specifically de la Pole group, but Wingfield's inclusion nevertheless demonstrates his new connections with the court. By May 1450, for example, Wingfield seems to have been a member of Somerset's retinue. (The evidence for this in the calendar of the French Rolls refers to 'Robert Wingfield of Sussex'; it seems probable that this is a misreading for 'Suff'.) *Rot. Parl.*, v. 216; *DKR*, 48, 'Calendar of French Rolls, Henry VI', 383.

[182] Monro (ed.), *Letters of Queen Margaret*, 155–6 (a letter from the queen to Norfolk, written at the request of Wingfield and his sons. In it, she asks the duke to 'have theym towards yor good lordship', and to show them 'tenderness and faver', despite the fact that there are 'certein matiers that ye fynde yow agreved and displeased in as yet').

[183] KB9/257 mm. 41–4, 53–6, 58–62.

Norfolk's chaplain at Framlingham, complained to the duke of threats made against him by Wingfield's son Robert, who was also at that point staying at the castle.[184] Norfolk, in his capacity as JP for Suffolk, ordered Robert to bind himself to keep the peace towards Hadilsay; the esquire refused, and was sent to Melton gaol on the duke's orders. Three hours later, on Wingfield's instructions, William Brandon rescued Robert from prison.[185] Norfolk subsequently secured letters patent from the king ordering Brandon and the younger Wingfield not to come within seven miles of his person. Both nevertheless spent Christmas at Letheringham, well within the forbidden radius from the duke's household at Framlingham.[186] On 10 January, according to the indictments, Wingfield broke into the close of the duke's retainer Edmund Fitzwilliam; the following day he hunted without permission in Norfolk's park at Soham.[187] Also on 11 January, he entered Hadilsay's room at Framlingham to steal a royal pardon which the chaplain had obtained when outlawed on a charge brought by Wingfield.[188]

Norfolk's recourse to judicial action in response to this apparently concerted insubordination again emphasized the inadequacy of his own authority. The special commission of *oyer* and *terminer* to investigate Wingfield's actions issued on 18 December, presumably at Norfolk's request, included Suffolk's men John Heydon and Reginald Rous, as well as Sir John Heveningham and the Duchy lawyer John Prisot.[189] On 23 January, Wingfield was summoned into King's Bench to show why, in the light of the charges against him, he should not forfeit a bond he had made in 1447 to keep the peace; he pleaded not guilty, but on the day appointed for the hearing produced a royal pardon.[190] Six months later, the efficacy of Wingfield's de la Pole connections was even more apparent. Sir Robert made a formal complaint about Norfolk's earlier attack on Letheringham, and it was presumably as a result of this that

---

[184] KB9/257 m. 41.

[185] This episode was allegedly repeated—unless these are confused accounts of a single incident—on 8 Jan., when Robert Wingfield jr. was again reported to be in Melton gaol on Norfolk's orders, this time for refusing to bind himself to keep the peace towards William Thetford, who had made the original complaint of threatening behaviour in December with Hadilsay. He was rescued, on his father's orders, by Brandon and three other gentlemen: KB9/257 m. 44.

[186] KB9/257 m. 53.

[187] Ibid. Fitzwilliam had been in Mowbray service since 1428: Archer, 'The Mowbrays', 345.

[188] KB9/257 m. 44. Sir Robert was also alleged to have entered a house at Wickham Market in armed pursuit of Norfolk's treasurer John Leventhorp, declaring that he would give 500 marks to have his head: KB9/257 m. 44 (and for Leventhorp as treasurer, Suff. RO V5/18/2/1).

[189] *CPR 1446–52*, 137.

[190] The pardon, which was granted on 14 Feb., specifically included all sureties of the peace forfeited by Wingfield and his mainpernors. The latter group included two gentlemen of the king's household, John Trevilian and Henry Langton—a significant indication of the change in Wingfield's political affiliations during the 1440s. KB27/747 Rex rot. 7; *CPR 1446–52*, 130.

the duke was committed to the Tower on 28 August. During the six days of his imprisonment, a special commission, including both Suffolk and Scales, was appointed to investigate the incident.[191] The dispute was still continuing in 1452, when Wingfield complained to the council that Norfolk had forcibly retaken the manor of Weston by Baldock which he had been granted in exchange for Hoo,[192] and seems to have ended only with Wingfield's death.[193]

Nor was Wingfield the only member of the Mowbray affinity to become alienated from the duke. It has already been noted that the duke also lost the loyalty of the Suffolk esquire William Brandon,[194] and a similar pattern is apparent in the case of John Wyndham, who was an esquire in Norfolk's service at least by 1439, and who was among the Mowbray servants who were alleged to have carried out the assault on Hoo in August 1443.[195] Shortly after this, however, Wyndham began to develop associations with Suffolk and his local followers,[196] and by 1450 he was named with Tuddenham and Heydon among the principal de la Pole servants against whom a campaign of local complaint was being orchestrated.[197] He later married the dowager Lady Heveningham, a remarkably advantageous match which Wyndham seems to have

[191] The commission was issued on 1 Sept.: *CPR 1446–52*, 236; Storey, *End of the House of Lancaster*, 227; R. Flenley (ed.), *Six Town Chronicles of England* (Oxford, 1911), 123.

[192] The attack was alleged to have taken place on 5 June 1452; Wingfield's petition was considered on 20 July: E28/82.

[193] There is some difficulty over the date of Wingfield's death. The Calendar of Fine Rolls records the issue of a writ of *diem clausit extremum* in July 1452, but his will, printed in *Testamenta Vetusta*, is dated Oct. 1452 and probate recorded in Nov. 1454. Moreover, in the Michaelmas term of 1452, Wingfield was summoned into King's Bench over a debt of 800 marks claimed by Norfolk: *CFR 1452–61*, 3; Nicolas (ed.), *Testamenta Vetusta*, 275; KB27/766 Rex rot. 39v. Wingfield's sons seem to have re-established good relations with Norfolk. The eldest, John, became steward to the duke on his father's death (a transfer of office which Hawes and Loder record as having taken place in 1454: *History of Framlingham*, 394); Robert and Thomas Wingfield were among the duke's men holding Stockton against the duchess of Suffolk in the later 1450s: C1/26/164.

[194] See above, pp. 114–15; though for Brandon's later relations with the duke, see below, Ch. 5 at n. 116.

[195] NRO WKC1/348; KB9/1050 mm. 97–8. Wyndham had also joined Norfolk as a mainpernor for Wingfield in his dispute with Lyston in 1439: KB27/714 Coram Rege rot. 124v.

[196] In fact, Wyndham was already closely associated with John Heydon as early as Oct. 1443, when the latter was entrusted with the legal arrangements for Wyndham's purchase of the Norfolk manor of Wicklewood. In June of the following year, Wyndham's feoffees in the manor included not only the Mowbray servant John Tymperley, but also Thomas Tuddenham, John Heydon, and Thomas Shuldham. Wyndham joined Tymperley in the Babingley feoffment of Nov. 1447 (see above, n. 171). His purchase of the reversion of Simon Felbrigg's lands from the latter's widow, a transaction which had been completed by the end of 1451, was to make Wyndham a near neighbour of John Heydon in the heart of the Duchy territory of northern Norfolk: NRO WKC1/304/1, 4; WKC1/336/6–7; WKC1/337–9.

[197] William Wayte wrote to John Paston on 6 Oct. 1450 that the commons of Norwich should 'crye vp-on my Lord for justice of these men that arne indyted, and telle here names, in speciall Todenham, Heydon, Wyndam, Prentys': *PL* Davis, ii. 49 (Gairdner, ii. 177).

secured through the good offices of the duchess of Suffolk.[198] While it is true that the superior attractions of de la Pole lordship might well have been enough to undermine the Mowbray affinity even without mismanagement on Norfolk's part, what evidence there is of the duke's actions (most dramatically in the case of Wingfield) suggests that his political maladroitness may have played a significant role in the defection of some of his closest associates among the East Anglian gentry.

Indeed, it is revealing of Norfolk's lack of discernment that in the late 1430s he acquired the service of the local esquire John Belsham, a murderer whom not a single other landowner in the region, gentle or noble, was prepared to support. During the 1420s and 1430s, Belsham was indicted for an extended series of crimes including three murders, as well as assaults and counterfeiting.[199] These charges do not seem to fit the general pattern of fifteenth-century gentry crime, in which both the alleged incident and the ensuing judicial process typically formed elements of wider disputes within local society. Philippa Maddern points out that, very unusually, no associates were indicted with Belsham on any of these many charges, and that no mainpernors ever stood surety for him. She concludes that Belsham had an individual tendency towards violence, which his local society neither accepted nor supported.[200] The exception in that society, however, seems to have been the duke of Norfolk. In July 1438, Belsham appeared in court accused of murdering one Alice Lowell, and was committed to Bury St Edmunds gaol. On 8 September, Norfolk himself appeared at the gaol and forcibly removed Belsham from custody, despite the protests of the gaoler, who was subsequently fined for his prisoner's 'escape'.[201] In 1443, Belsham was named as another of the duke's gentlemen who took part in the assault to recover Hoo. In contrast to the earlier indictments, where he is named as an esquire of Hadleigh, Belsham is here described as 'late of Framlingham'.[202] It seems that Norfolk was prepared to acquire the service of a man whose criminal career had made him a virtual outcast from local political society—and, indeed, then to employ him in an action which alienated one of the duke's principal retainers and achieved very little else. The implication is that, although Suffolk's dominance made it extremely difficult for Norfolk to make any significant impression on the rule of the region during the 1440s, this situation was compounded by the duke's own misjudgements.

Whatever the limitations of Norfolk's attempts to establish his own

---

[198] *PL* Davis, i. 255–7 (Gairdner, ii. 288–9); Richmond, *John Hopton*, 237.

[199] For detailed discussion of his career, see P. C. Maddern, *Violence and Social Order: East Anglia 1422–1442* (Oxford, 1992), 154–66.

[200] Ibid. 162–3.

[201] KB9/232/1 m. 97.

[202] KB9/1050 mm. 97–8.

lordship in the region, Suffolk's response to this challenge to his local authority was uncompromising. Under normal circumstances, any lord would use all the means at his disposal to defend his local rule against incursions by a rival, and this consideration seems to have been the decisive factor in Suffolk's strategy, despite the fact that he was operating in circumstances which were far from normal and that the means at his disposal included all the resources of the crown. It is more than possible that the complex nature of Henry's failings as king concealed the dangers of this approach,[203] since Suffolk may not have appreciated fully the confusion of public and private authority inherent in his position, and so may not have been explicitly aware of the extent of the responsibility for maintaining royal authority which had devolved on to his shoulders. He may therefore have considered East Anglia straightforwardly as an arena for his private lordship. It is also possible that the divergence between the efficacy of Suffolk's and Norfolk's respective lordships disguised the significance of the problem. It could well have seemed to Suffolk, from his position in command of a long-standing, broad, and cohesive local following, that the claims of Norfolk—whose fledgling political connection was managed with an incompetence which alienated support as fast as it won it—to be represented in regional rule were of negligible validity.

Nevertheless, mismanaged and unsuccessful though they were, Norfolk's assaults on power structures in East Anglia did expose the strains under which Suffolk's rule operated. While the claims of the latter's local following to represent their 'country' went unchallenged, it was possible for the crown, whose authority underwrote their rule, to be seen to be fulfilling its duty of universal representation. Once the challenge had been made, and especially once it had been slapped down, the mirage of universal representation was destroyed. When it became clear that the crown offered no prospect of recourse independent of Suffolk's lordship, then the duke of Norfolk, however unsuccessful and ill judged his attempts to assert himself, inevitably provided focus and leadership for those in the region whose interests had not been satisfied by Suffolk's rule. Moreover, because the authority of the king—which, in representing the common interest of the entire realm, was able to contain the methods by which individual interests were pursued—had been to some degree compromised, the shared confidence in the workings of the system, which restrained the tendency towards conflict and violence inherent in a competitive political society, was similarly eroded.

Henry IV had faced similar problems in Staffordshire in the second half of his reign, when the dominance in local administration of his

---

[203] Watts, *Henry VI*, 364–5.

private Duchy affinity, which was not broad enough to represent the shire as a whole, provoked a violent response from those excluded from regional government.[204] In East Anglia, the development of an extensive, wide-ranging, and unquestionably royal affinity had meant that it had previously been possible to contain the potential tensions between the public and private elements of the king's regional power. During the later 1440s, once Norfolk's challenge had exposed the fact that the de la Pole affinity could not claim to embody the united interests of the area as a whole, this containment was no longer possible. Moreover, the problem was compounded by the anomalous nature of Suffolk's authority. Henry IV's problems in Staffordshire may have stemmed from his failure to accommodate his private lordship within his public authority, but at least he was the rightful possessor of both. Suffolk—as a nobleman attempting to impersonate the public power of the crown at the same time as managing the king's private interests as duke of Lancaster, and maintaining his own private regional influence—faced a daunting political task from what was now being revealed as a position of extreme vulnerability. These circumstances help to explain the increasing division in local society apparent in East Anglia during the last years of Suffolk's rule.

4. 1447–1450: THE POLITICS OF CONFRONTATION

Suffolk's lordship in East Anglia came under increasing pressure during the 1440s because of Norfolk's local rivalry. From about 1447, however, these strains apparently became more profound, and as a result Suffolk's authority seems, almost for the first time, to have become a force in local society which was more divisive than cohesive. A significant element in the increasingly confrontational politics of the region during the late 1440s was the fact that Suffolk faced a challenge to his local authority from inside, as well as outside, the system of government he had created. Suffolk had succeeded in developing and maintaining a workable regime by establishing his own lordship over the royal household. This control over the king and his immediate environment seems to have allowed the earl to contain the potentially disastrous effects of Henry VI's passivity, which meant that the powers of the crown were undiscriminatingly responsive to the demands of all who could reach him.[205] Impressive though Suffolk's control was, however, it was not a monopoly. Others could, and did, secure access to the

---

[204] See below, Ch. 6.2.
[205] See discussion above, pp. 47–9; Watts, *Henry VI*, 158–80.

authority and the bounty of the crown,[206] and this had implications within local, as well as national, politics. The deficiencies of Henry VI's kingship had allowed Suffolk to develop the influence which his affinity already enjoyed at a local level into a virtual hegemony. Nevertheless, because the power wielded directly by the crown in Norfolk was unusually great, those deficiencies also provided a means by which de la Pole rule in the county could be challenged.

The household esquire Thomas Daniel, for example, has often been identified as a member of Suffolk's 'court clique'.[207] It has been assumed that any prominent member of the household in the 1440s, and especially one who secured royal office in East Anglia, must have been closely associated with the apparently all-powerful duke.[208] However, the element most consistently evident in Daniel's involvement in the region is in fact his opposition to the de la Pole affinity.[209] Norfolk, who had failed to secure independent access to the powers constituted by the royal household, seems to have identified this political rarity, a household man who owed nothing to Suffolk, as a potentially valuable ally.

Daniel first intruded into the affairs of East Anglia in November 1446 when he secured his appointment to the shrievalty; in the following two years he also appeared on the commission of the peace in Norfolk.[210] By 1447 his first appearances in the Paston letters demonstrate both his growing importance in the area, and the fact that he was already challenging, rather than reinforcing, Suffolk's regional influence. In a letter probably written in the summer of 1447, Edmund Paston described how 'Steward, the chiffe constable' had 'enqueryd me of the rewle of myn master Danyell and myn lord of Suffulke, and askyd wheche I thowte schuld rewle in this schere, and I seyd bothe, as I trowh, and he that suruyuyth to hold be the uertue of the suruyuyr'.[211] The fact that Daniel's appearance in the region involved the acquisition, in dubious circumstances, of estates whose rightful owners were closely involved with the de la Pole affinity ensured that his relations with Suffolk's men would be hostile and confrontational.

The manors of Rydon, Grimston, Congham, and Gayton in western

[206] Watts, *Henry VI*, 216–21.

[207] Daniel entered the royal household in 1441–2, and within five years had become an esquire of the body: James, 'Career and Political Influence', 122.

[208] See, for example, *PL* Gairdner, i. 94; Wolffe, *Henry VI*, 122; Morey, 'East Anglian Society', 420–1, 440; Crawford, 'Career of John Howard', 13, 16; R. L. Friedrichs, 'Ralph, Lord Cromwell and the Politics of Fifteenth-Century England', *Nottingham Medieval Studies*, 32 (1988), 220.

[209] This was certainly the case until the mid-1450s. For the latter years of the reign, see below, pp. 183–4.

[210] *List of Sheriffs*, 87; *CPR 1446–52*, 592. Daniel was originally from Cheshire: Griffiths, *Henry VI*, 369.   [211] *PL* Davis, i. 147–8 (Gairdner, ii. 79–80).

Norfolk had been the central estates of the Wodehous family in the early years of the century, and John Wodehous's stewardship of the nearby duchy of Cornwall lordship of Castle Rising reinforced this territorial interest.[212] It was at Rydon that Alice Wodehous married Thomas Tuddenham in 1418, and that John Wodehous died in 1431.[213] The latter's heir, Henry, intended to use these manors to provide a jointure for his prospective bride, Elizabeth Daniel, and so required his feoffees to grant them in trust to Elizabeth's brother Thomas. Once title to the estates had been legally transferred to Daniel, however, Henry Wodehous discovered that Elizabeth had already married.[214] Daniel then refused to restore the manors to Wodehous, and was clearly exploiting his access to the king to reinforce his position. In April 1447 the king's esquire Thomas Daniel was, for his good service, granted leave to fortify his manor of Rydon, together with the hereditary right of free warren in all his estates at Rydon, Grimston, Congham, and Well Hall in Gayton.[215] A year later it was reported in Norfolk that he was out of favour at court and that, whether as cause or consequence, Suffolk's ascendancy was unchallenged.[216] By September 1448, however, Daniel's political fortunes had clearly recovered, since he was able to secure a grant of the reversion of the stewardship of Castle Rising; unusually, he seems to have acquired control of the lordship immediately.[217]

This usurpation of the traditional area of Wodehous interest immediately brought him into conflict with members of the de la Pole

---

[212] Blomefield, *History of the County of Norfolk*, ii. 543–4. Griffiths, 'Henry, Prince of Wales', 65–6, 174, 217. The Wodehous manor house at Rydon lay only a mile from Castle Rising: Harvey (ed.), *Worcestre: Itineraries*, 253.

[213] Virgoe, 'The Divorce of Sir Thomas Tuddenham', 118; Somerville, *History of the Duchy*, 389. Wodehous's father had married the heiress of Sir Thomas Fastolf, prompting a move of the family's principal residence to her manor of Kimberley in central Norfolk (Blomefield, *History of the County of Norfolk*, ii. 544), but Rydon seems to have retained its importance to the family.

[214] Wodehous's feoffees included Sir Thomas Tuddenham, Sir John Clifton, and Oliver Groos: *Rot. Parl.*, v. 340–1; see also *CCR 1447–54*, 354–5. It is not clear when the negotiations for Wodehous's marriage to Elizabeth Daniel took place. Blomefield reports that Henry conveyed the manors to Daniel during 1449–50, but Daniel was apparently in possession much earlier (see below, at n. 215). As Blomefield also notes, John Paston had released his rights in the estates to Daniel in Nov. 1446. If Paston was one of Wodehous's feoffees, this may have formed part of the settlement for the proposed marriage. The date seems plausible, since it was in 1446 that Daniel held office (as sheriff) in the area for the first time. Blomefield, *History of the County of Norfolk*, viii. 383, 428, 443; *CCR 1441–7*, 443. For Daniel and the Pastons, see below, pp. 140–1.

[215] *CChR 1427–1516*, 80.

[216] Margaret to John Paston, Apr. 1448: *PL* Davis, i. 222 (Gairdner, ii. 86).

[217] Presumably with the co-operation of Ralph, Lord Cromwell, who had a life grant of the office. The grant to Daniel, which again was hereditary, included the offices of constable of the castle and warden of the chase within the lordship: *CPR 1446–52*, 203; *PL* Davis, ii. 34 (Gairdner, ii. 137).

affinity, notably Thomas Tuddenham, whose own estate at Oxburgh lay nearby, and whose early career owed much to his guardian and father-in-law John Wodehous.[218] By October 1450, when Thomas Denys was charged with holding Rydon 'for Danyels sake' against a group of gentlemen who included Henry Tuddenham and Henry and John Wodehous, he alleged 'that this was the first porpose of Tudenham and Heydon whils thei regned, to gete this place'.[219] Daniel's aggressive hostility to the de la Pole affinity was further demonstrated by another long-running territorial dispute—his attempt to seize the Norfolk manor of Bradeston from the custody of Osbert Mundford and associates including Thomas Tuddenham—in which he became involved shortly after Suffolk's fall.[220]

Daniel, who has aptly been described as politically the 'most supple' of the household esquires,[221] was clearly prepared to exploit a variety of associations, but in the context of East Anglian politics his first affiliation was with the duke of Norfolk. Norfolk does not seem to have played any part in Daniel's initial appearance in the region, but by 1448 their association was sufficiently close for Daniel to become a feoffee in the duke's East Anglian lands.[222] The combined opposition of these two men—one excluded from the structures of power through which Suffolk's control was maintained, the other a member of the very establishment through which Suffolk's power was constituted—was clearly

---

[218] For the importance to Tuddenham of his association with Wodehous, see above, Ch. 3.2 at nn. 133–5. Tuddenham divorced Alice Wodehous in 1436, but the circumstances of the annulment—Alice had admitted that her baby was the result of a liaison with her father's chamberlain—seem to have meant that Tuddenham's relations with her family were not adversely affected. He was still acting as chief feoffee, for example, for Henry Wodehous in 1440, and as witness for Jerome Wodehous in 1442. Virgoe, 'The Divorce of Sir Thomas Tuddenham', 117–18; *CPR 1436–41*, 385; *CCR 1441–7*, 302–3.

[219] Denys warned that 'if ye help not now Tudenham and Heydon shal achieve in their desese the conquest that thei coude neuer achieve in their prosperite': *PL* Davis, ii. 46 (Gairdner, ii. 173–4). Tuddenham is also reported to have protected a Gayton man who killed one of Daniel's tenants there in 1446–7. Also in the autumn of 1450, Daniel was summoned to find security of the peace for his conduct towards Henry Wodehous, but claimed he dared not appear 'owing to the indisposition of divers lieges of the king'. Henry Wodehous's petition in the second parliament of 1455, asking the king to annul the feoffment made to Daniel and to restore his estates, was granted. A proviso was added, however, that Daniel was not to be answerable for any revenues from the lands for the period in which they had been in his possession: *PL* Davis, ii. 526–7 (Gairdner, ii. 214); *CPR 1446–52*, 413; *Rot. Parl.*, v. 341.

[220] For detailed discussion of this dispute, see below, pp. 165–8.

[221] James, 'Career and Political Influence', 123. E. F. Jacob describes him as 'politically ambidexterous': *The Fifteenth Century* (Oxford, 1961), 497.

[222] *CPR 1446–52*, 145. The feoffment included some properties in Surrey, Sussex, Huntingdonshire, and London. Since this settlement coincides with the report of Daniel's temporary fall from favour (see above, n. 216), it is possible that his links with Norfolk for him represented an attempt to secure some sort of insurance for his local interests. However, he may already have been associated with the duke by the previous summer, since in Aug. 1447 one Henry Parker of Ipswich was alleged to have sought maintenance for his claim to a manor at Hintlesham by enfeoffing Norfolk, Oxford, and Daniel in the property: KB9/256 mm. 20–1.

not enough to undermine the rule of the de la Pole affinity in East Anglia. Nevertheless, it was enough to demonstrate that the affinity could not claim to be universally representative of the region, and in the absence of any possibility of intervention by impartial royal authority, the opposition of those excluded from Suffolk's lordship posed a serious threat to local stability.[223] Indeed, Daniel's involvement in the region demonstrated both the extent of that threat, and the difficulty Suffolk faced in attempting to maintain control of local government on behalf of a king whose power was apparently at the disposal of anyone who could secure access to him. After a decade of Suffolk's rule at the head of a connection which had dominated the region since the beginning of the century, Daniel, a mere esquire with no hereditary stake in the area, had been able to defy the de la Pole affinity to acquire and retain substantial local estates by fraud. In 1447 he was even being discussed as a serious rival to Suffolk's local power.[224] The only basis for Daniel's intrusion into the region was his access to royal authority through his position in the king's household, and his success was an extraordinary demonstration of how vulnerable even the most solidly established political structures could be when they were not underpinned by the independent power of the crown. This vulnerability struck at the heart of the entire edifice of government Suffolk had created. His control of Henry's environment could never be complete, and therefore his rule could always be challenged by anyone who could secure access to the supreme authority of the infinitely malleable king.[225]

The significance of Daniel's challenge to Suffolk's local rule was compounded by the problems in central government which developed during the last years of the decade. The deepening crisis in national affairs, and particularly the surrender of Maine in 1448, seems to have lost Suffolk much of the noble support which had been vital to such legitimacy as his rule could claim in the absence of an active king. This loss of consensus meant that Suffolk's position at the head of government became increasingly embattled.[226] In this context, the exposure of the structural flaws in his authority which Daniel's intrusion into East Anglian affairs represented became even more threatening. At the same time, the breadth of Suffolk's responsibilities meant that he was unable

[223] It is perhaps indicative of increasing local tension that, though Suffolk nominated Norfolk as a prospective knight of the garter in 1445 and 1446, he was no longer prepared to do so in 1447. (Norfolk was finally elected after Suffolk's death in 1450.) J. Anstis, *The Register of the Most Noble Order of the Garter* (London, 1724), ii. 127, 129–30, 132–3, 142–3.

[224] See above, at n. 211. By 1448 Margaret Paston was referring to him as 'my lord Danyel': *PL* Davis, i. 223 (Gairdner, ii. 87).

[225] See Watts, *Henry VI*, 216–21, for the rise in the later 1440s of a 'series of *parvenus*', of whom Daniel was one, who 'used their access to the king and their leverage over Suffolk to obtain prominence at the centre or opportunities in the localities'.

[226] Ibid. 240–51.

to seek to control this division within his own 'country' through careful personal supervision. Instead, he seems to have attempted to tighten his grip on the region by increasing the powers of his local affinity and bringing in reinforcements from the wider resources at his disposal.

During the last two years of the decade, the regional authority of Thomas Tuddenham, for example, was significantly extended. In May 1449, he was appointed for the first (and, as events turned out, the only) time to the commission of the peace in Suffolk.[227] That this represented a serious attempt to increase Tuddenham's sphere of influence from Norfolk across the entire region is apparently confirmed by the fact that four months later he was also named to a commission appointed to borrow money for the king in Suffolk.[228] It was the first time that Tuddenham had been a member of such a commission in the county, despite the fact that they had been appointed regularly throughout the 1440s.[229] Indeed, virtually none of the various special commissions to which he had been named in the area had had any jurisdiction in Suffolk. Moreover, the enhanced authority which Tuddenham enjoyed in Suffolk as a result of his appointment as a JP was explicitly associated with his representation of the local interests of the crown, since he appeared on the commission in his capacity as the local steward of the Duchy.[230]

Other appointments made during these years also indicate that the newly elevated duke of Suffolk was attempting to use his control of crown resources and his lordship over the royal household to defend his local authority. Tuddenham was joined on the 1449 commission of the peace by another newcomer to the bench, Philip Wentworth, a household esquire who had abandoned his Yorkshire roots during the 1440s to settle in East Anglia, and who had served as sheriff for Norfolk and Suffolk in 1447–8.[231] Perhaps most tellingly, the sheriff appointed to succeed Wentworth in 1448 was Giles St Lo, a household esquire originally from the south-west; his successor in 1449 was John Say, an esquire of the body who had recently been granted the reversion of the Duchy chancellorship, but whose local interests were concentrated in Cambridgeshire and his native Hertfordshire. Neither—these appointments apart—had any connection with East Anglian affairs.[232]

---

[227] *CPR 1446–52*, 595.
[228] *CPR 1446–52*, 299.
[229] *CPR 1436–41*, 504; *1441–6*, 61–2, 68, 92, 431.
[230] *CPR 1446–52*, 595.
[231] James, 'Career and Political Influence', 121; *List of Sheriffs*, 87.
[232] In the absence of other evidence, I am assuming that Giles St Lo was a member of the same family as his contemporary John St Lo, an esquire of the body from Somerset. *List of Sheriffs*, 87; Griffiths, *Henry VI*, 332, 480; J. C. Wedgwood, *History of Parliament: Biographies of the Members of the Commons House 1439–1509* (London, 1936), 737; Somerville, *History of the Duchy*, 390.

The suggestion that this attempt to reinforce Suffolk's regional control was an expression of authority in crisis is supported by the fact that it seems to have been accompanied by the involvement of at least some of his servants in a serious outbreak of disorder in Norfolk. As Suffolk's support among the greater nobility faltered, and his political dependence on the household establishment therefore grew, it may be that he was increasingly left with little choice but to acquiesce in attempts by members of that establishment to further their own regional interests, in however unruly or disruptive a fashion.[233] Early in 1448, for example, the courtier Robert Hungerford, Lord Moleyns, seized John Paston's manor of Gresham in Norfolk.[234] Eight months later, when Paston's initial attempts to recover the property through negotiation and legal action had proved fruitless, he sent his wife to occupy a 'mansion' in the town.[235] In January 1449 Moleyns's men (said by the Pastons to be a heavily armed force numbering a thousand) mounted an assault on the house, which was badly damaged in the attack, and expelled Margaret Paston. In all, Moleyns was able to retain possession of the estate for three years, despite the fact that his claim seems to have had little substance in terms of the letter of the law, and that he had had no previous involvement in the affairs of East Anglia, which was, after all, considerably removed from his own power base in Wiltshire and Somerset.[236] Significantly, an important element in

---

[233] Cf. Watts, *Henry VI*, 219–20.

[234] For all details given below, see *PL* Gairdner, i. 42–4; *PL* Davis, i. 51–3, 233–4; ii. 29–30 (Gairdner, ii. 99–100, 111–12, 127–30); Richmond, *The Paston Family*, 47–59; KB9/262 mm. 45–6 (the earl of Oxford's report on the events of Jan. 1449); for further discussion of the Gresham affair and the Paston evidence, see below, Ch. 4.5.

[235] There is some confusion about the identity of the house in which Margaret Paston took up residence. Paston's later petition to parliament (*PL* Davis, i. 52 (Gairdner, ii. 127)) claimed merely that he had decided to 'inhabite hym in a mansion with-in the seid town'. M. A. Rowling has argued, citing Oxford's report on the matter in King's Bench in the autumn of 1449, that Paston had in fact taken his own manor back from Moleyns, and was being deliberately ambiguous in order to conceal his own use of force (M. A. Rowling, 'New Evidence on the Disseisin of the Pastons from their Norfolk Manor of Gresham, 1448–1451', *Norfolk Archaeology*, 40 (1989), 302–8; KB9/262 mm. 45–6). While this is one (though not the only) possible interpretation of Oxford's submission, a letter from Margaret to John Paston (*PL* Davis, i. 226 (Gairdner, ii. 101)) casts some doubt on Rowling's conclusion. Though the letter is undated, it was clearly written during the course of the Gresham dispute, and seems to belong to the period when Margaret was in residence there, since she asks her husband 'to gete som crosse bowis, and wyndacis to bynd them wyth, and quarell, for zwr hwsis here ben so low that there may non man schete owt wyth no long bowe thow we hadde neuer so moche nede'. However, the same letter makes clear that Moleyns's men were still in possession of the Pastons' property: 'Partryche and his felaschep arn sore aferyd that ze wold entren azen up-on hem, and they haue made grete ordynawnce wyth-jnne the hwse, as it is told me'. (Rowling argues, not entirely convincingly, that this letter in fact dates from much later in 1449, during the period when Margaret was at the nearby manor of Sustead: 'New Evidence', 305.)

[236] Gresham had belonged to Moleyns's wife's family before it was bought by William Paston. For a detailed discussion, see below, Ch. 4.5; for the Hungerford estates, see *Complete Peerage*, vi. 613.

Moleyns's intervention in the region was the fact that John Heydon was 'of my lordes councell'.[237] The dispute led Margaret Paston to conclude by May 1449 that 'but if ze have my lord of Suffolkys godelorchyp qhyll the werd is as itt is ye kan never leven jn pese wyth-owth ye have his godelordschep'.[238] Her interpretation—and the suggestion that Suffolk may have had to condone disruptively self-interested behaviour in the localities on the part of his supporters at court to shore up his threatened authority in national government—are lent further force by the fact that the household men Philip Wentworth and Edward Hull (the former a member of Suffolk's local affinity, the latter intervening in the region for the first time) pursued property disputes against the Pastons' ally Sir John Fastolf with particular aggression during the last years of the decade.[239]

Suffolk had attempted, in response to Daniel's challenge to his regional authority, to reinforce his own local power by extending the influence of the household in East Anglia. This, and the involvement of one of his leading retainers in a violent dispute in support of a complete outsider to the region, can only have reinforced the impression (first created by Norfolk's unsuccessful attempt to establish his own lord-ship) that the virtual stranglehold on local administration enjoyed by Suffolk's affinity did not adequately reflect the full range of regional interests. This was particularly significant in the context of the with-drawal of the lords from participation in government during much of 1448 and 1449, which meant that it was during this period that Suffolk's regime most resembled the popular image of a court clique.[240] The failure of the duke's rule in a national context could do nothing but underline the fact that his local lordship could no longer represent regional society as a whole, and, almost for the first time, was becom-ing implicated in serious local disorder.

The events of 1447 to 1450 demonstrated, for the first time in East Anglia under the Lancastrian dynasty, and in an extreme form, the difficulties faced by local political society when the public authority of the crown was compromised by too close an association with private interests. In one sense, Suffolk enjoyed every possible advantage in the

---

[237] *PL* Davis, ii. 30 (Gairdner, ii. 112).

[238] Margaret was reporting to her husband what 'sondery folkys have seyd to me', but it was clearly a judgement with which she concurred. The year is not entirely certain, but Davis's suggestion of 1449 is far more convincing than Gairdner's of 1463, and the sentiments expressed are certainly appropriate to the former year. Paston re-entered Gresham in Oct. 1449, but was again expelled by Moleyns's men during the chaotic beginning of 1450. *PL* Davis, i. 235–6; *PL* Gairdner, i. 42–4; ii. 127–30; iv. 75; Richmond, *The Paston Family*, 59–63.

[239] A. R. Smith, 'Litigation and Politics: Sir John Fastolf's Defence of his English Property', in A. J. Pollard (ed.), *Property and Politics* (Gloucester, 1984), 63–7; Smith, 'Aspects of the Career of Sir John Fastolf', 126–8, 142, 204–6. For Fastolf and the Pastons in relation to Suffolk's local rule, see below, Ch. 4.5.   [240] Watts, *Henry VI*, 240–6.

rule of his 'country'. His estates in Suffolk gave him a power base from which to dominate that county; his administration of the Duchy gave him control of the pre-eminent territorial stake in Norfolk; his appropriation of the crown–Duchy connection gave him an extraordinarily broad local following; and his leadership of the government which he had constituted around the passive figure of Henry VI gave him the resources of the royal administration with which he could turn his local rule into virtual regional hegemony. Every possible advantage, that is, except the one without which local stability could not be guaranteed: the independent and universal authority of an active monarch. Indeed, Suffolk's 'advantages' constituted a particularly acute form of the problems inherent in the management of regional royal authority, which Henry IV had been able to avoid in East Anglia because of the development of a Duchy-based political connection under the aegis of the crown, but which had troubled his kingship in areas such as the north midlands. If the concept of the king directly controlling substantial territorial interests in the localities held the potential for constitutional disruption, the risks were vastly increased when a nobleman, however able, wielded such power on the king's behalf.

Under these circumstances, Suffolk's achievement was considerable. For a decade, he had managed the government of the realm for an incapable king, and at the same time, and from a distance, maintained his lordship as the dominant force in East Anglia. The evidence of the region's politics supports the suggestion that the conventional analysis of Suffolk's rule during the 1440s must be significantly revised. In East Anglia, at least until 1447, his overwhelming local dominance was based on his legitimate inheritance of a connection which was intrinsically linked to the power of the crown in Norfolk as embodied in the Duchy of Lancaster; this, combined with his own territorial influence in Suffolk, formed the basis of an affinity which was remarkably cohesive and broadly representative of regional society. After 1447, it was not so much Suffolk's own actions which tainted the legitimacy of his power in East Anglia, but the circumstances in which he was forced to operate.[241] Magnate rule of the localities depended fundamentally on the underlying universal authority of the king. To Suffolk fell the unhappy task of acting simultaneously in both capacities, of embodying both noble and royal authority. The increasing conflict in Norfolk and Suffolk in the later 1440s reflects his attempts to shore up his regional power base as the tensions inherent in his anomalous position began to emerge under the continuing strain of Henry's vacuity.

---

[241] See, in a national context, Watts, *Henry VI*, 198: 'Suffolk had, in a sense, accroached the royal power, though it is difficult to see what royal power there could have been without his efforts or those of someone like him; as it was, there was precious little even for him to use.'

5. EAST ANGLIA IN THE 1440S: THE PASTON EVIDENCE

This account of East Anglian politics in the 1440s has emerged from an examination of Suffolk's rule in the context of pre-existing patterns of regional authority, undertaken largely through analysis of the formal records of local political society, both private—notably the surviving evidence of property transactions—and public, especially the records of the judicial system. It therefore differs from previous accounts of the region's politics during this period not only in many of its conclusions but also in the nature of its principal sources, since little reference has so far been made to the evidence provided by the correspondence of the Paston family. The letters offer a unique insight into the realities of local politics—the manœuvres which lay behind the formal records— and it is therefore hardly surprising that they have been seen as the key to an understanding of East Anglian political society during the majority of Henry VI. 'What makes our view of East Anglia in the mid-fifteenth century so exceptionally translucent,' Ralph Griffiths has suggested, 'is, in three words, the Paston Letters.'[242]

Exceptional though they undoubtedly are, however, the translucence of the evidence which the letters provide is open to question. Their very uniqueness means that the task of establishing a proper understanding of the context in which they were written is at the same time crucially important and particularly problematic. The letters offer us extraordinary access to the Pastons' world; but they also make us the Pastons' friends in any attempt to investigate the society in which the family lived and the politics in which they participated. These are not, of course, new observations: Bertram Wolffe, for example, takes care to point out that 'assertions made in . . . the Paston Letters cannot always be taken at their face value'.[243] However, the extent to which the Paston evidence has determined both the nature and the conclusions of previous accounts of the region's politics is striking. A great deal of attention has been paid, for example, to East Anglian affairs from 1440, when the evidence of the letters begins, but relatively little to the preceding decades when the Pastons are not available as guides—an imbalance which has allowed the misidentification of Suffolk's affinity as an intruding household clique to dominate discussions of the area in the 1440s and 1450s.[244] In fact, the letters only begin to provide sub-

---

[242] Griffiths, *Henry VI*, 584.

[243] Wolffe, *Henry VI*, 121–4 (quotation from 124).

[244] See, for example, Wolffe, *Henry VI*, 121–4; Griffiths, *Henry VI*, 584–8; R. Virgoe, 'The Crown, Magnates and Local Government in Fifteenth-Century East Anglia', in Virgoe, *East Anglian Society*; Smith, 'Aspects of the Career of Sir John Fastolf'; Smith, 'Litigation and Politics'; Storey, *End of the House of Lancaster*, 54–7; and Richmond, *The Paston*

stantial evidence of local politics from 1448 onwards. It has already been suggested that by this point the region was becoming seriously disturbed because of the increasing insecurity of Suffolk's regime at both a local and a national level, but, despite this, the Paston evidence from the late 1440s and early 1450s has been used retrospectively to establish the nature of East Anglian politics during the 1440s as a whole. The Pastons' principal opponents in the region at the end of the decade, Sir Thomas Tuddenham and John Heydon, have been identified as the chief local representatives of what has been described as Suffolk's 'systematic and illegal exploitation of his position'[245] throughout the period of his supremacy in government; and the indictments which the Pastons were instrumental in initiating against Tuddenham and Heydon in 1450–1 have been used as the basis for describing the pair's misdeeds in the preceding decade.[246] The charges laid against Tuddenham and Heydon in the wake of Suffolk's fall will be discussed in detail later,[247] but a re-examination of the Pastons' experiences and of the letters themselves up to 1450 may help to establish whether they do in fact provide incontrovertible evidence of the 'abuse and prostitution of royal power' in East Anglia during the 1440s by Suffolk and his affinity,[248] and therefore whether the analysis of Suffolk's rule offered in the preceding chapters can be sustained in the face of the Pastons' testimony.

The family's origins lay at Paston in north-east Norfolk. Clement Paston, who died in 1419, was a 'good pleyn husbond'—possibly even a bondman—but he was able to provide his son with an education, and William Paston embarked on a distinguished legal career which culminated in his appointment as Justice of Common Pleas in 1429.[249] From the 1410s onwards, William began to use the money and influence which his profession brought him to establish himself and his family within local landed society, buying property and acquiring more through his marriage in 1420 to Agnes, daughter and heir of the local knight and Lancastrian retainer Edmund Barry.[250] Indeed, given the importance of the Duchy of Lancaster within local political networks in the early years of the century, it is unsurprising to find that his marriage was not the only connection which William Paston developed with

Family. Richmond does discuss the decades before 1440, but his focus is, self-evidently, the Pastons; and he accepts the fact of Suffolk's 'tyranny' in the region in the 1440s: *The Paston Family*, 227, 233–5.

[245] Richmond, *The Paston Family*, 235; see also 46.
[246] See, for example, Griffiths, *Henry VI*, 584–92.
[247] See below, pp. 156–60, 164–5.
[248] The phrase is Wolffe's: *Henry VI*, 227.
[249] *PL* Davis, i, pp. xl–xliii, lii–liii; Richmond, *The Paston Family*, pp. xvi–xvii, 13–14.
[250] Richmond, *The Paston Family*, pp. xvi–xvii, 31–4, 117–19; for Barry, see above, Ch. 3.1 at n. 28.

Duchy interests. He had been retained as legal counsel to the Duchy by 1420, and was closely associated with leading members of the crown–Duchy network which dominated the region.[251] Paston itself was held of the Duchy manor of Gimingham—something which was to complicate William's attempt to create a manorial lordship there, given that royal interests were involved—and the area into which he was extending his territorial interests was the hundred of North Erpingham, also part of the Duchy, which lay in the Lancastrian heartlands of northern Norfolk.[252]

In many ways, this must have seemed an opportune place and time for an ambitious lawyer to be seeking to acquire the stake in local political society which could be secured only through land ownership and the lordship associated with it.[253] The opportunities for land acquisition offered by the relatively fluid tenurial make-up of Norfolk, combined with the wealth which could be accumulated in the area through commerce and the law, meant that, in contrast with some other parts of England, social mobility was a characteristic feature of this local society.[254] Indeed, several of the leading members of the crown–Duchy network in the first two decades of the century had risen from humble backgrounds through their professional service to the Lancastrian dynasty.[255] In the following two decades, changes within this network offered the next wave of 'new men' substantial opportunities. It has already been suggested that the deaths of Thomas Beaufort in 1426 and Thomas Erpingham in 1428, and those of John Winter in 1414 and John Wodehous in 1431, removed key players from various levels in the region's power structures—losses which were made all the more significant, given the crown's role in the region, by the absence of active royal leadership after the death of Henry V in 1422.[256] The fact that Beaufort, Erpingham, and Winter all died without direct heirs meant that patterns of landholding, as well as patterns of lordship, seemed likely to change significantly.[257]

However, the rapid creation of a substantial estate through purchase was always likely to lead to complications. First, in a society where land

---

[251] DL28/4/11; see above, Ch. 3.2 n. 119.

[252] The process of establishing a manor at Paston was not completed until the mid-1460s: Richmond, *The Paston Family*, 1–12. For North Erpingham hundred, see above, Map 1, p. 54.

[253] Carpenter, *Locality and Polity*, 244, and *passim*; Richmond, *The Paston Family*, ch. 1.

[254] See above, pp. 55–6; see also comments on regional variation in the land market in Carpenter, *Locality and Polity*, 147.

[255] See above, pp. 62–3.

[256] See above, pp. 79–81.

[257] Famously, a remarkable number of the region's leading landowners died without male heirs in the late 14th and early 15th cents. Simon Felbrigg was to be another, in 1442; William Phelip left a daughter, who died very shortly after him in 1441. See above, Ch. 4.1 n. 61, and Ch. 4.2, at n. 78; Blomefield, *History of the County of Norfolk*, iv. 86–8.

was the basis of political power and social status and its possession therefore the subject of intense competition, the purchaser would have to face the possibility that his title, however sound in terms of law, might be challenged by the residual claims of the heirs of former owners.[258] If, as Colin Richmond has commented, 'land was so much more than economics',[259] it could also be said that the unchallenged ownership of land was a matter of so much more than legal technicality, particularly where rights acquired by purchase rather than inheritance were concerned.[260] Secondly, an ambitious newcomer seeking to create an estate for himself would almost inevitably end up trampling on the toes of other landowners in the region, and would therefore have to establish himself in the face of at least some local opposition.[261] William Paston was to encounter difficulties on both of these fronts as a result of his attempt to acquire the manor of East Beckham in northern Norfolk.

East Beckham had been bought in 1379 by William Winter. Like William Paston several decades later, Winter was the son of a husbandman, who had established his family among the region's gentry by investing the profits of his professional service in land. Also like William Paston, Winter's territorial interests were concentrated in North Erpingham hundred, around his chief estate of Town Barningham.[262] Winter died in 1397, but his eldest son, John, became a highly influential figure in Norfolk as one of the leading members of the crown–Duchy network in the early years of the fifteenth century. When he died in 1414, his brother Edmund inherited his estates. Though not a prominent royal and Duchy servant as his brother had been, Edmund held several important local offices in the 1410s and 1420s. By the 1430s, however, his career in local government was apparently on the wane, and with it his family's influence in the region.[263]

The story of East Beckham is a complex one, which Colin Richmond has patiently unravelled. The manor had been lost to the Winters in 1415 when it was sold, in order, it seems, to pay for the performance of unfulfilled provisions in William Winter's will.[264] This was exactly the kind of disposition of an estate for religious purposes which appealed to landowners on their deathbeds and to their heirs not at all; it must have rankled all the more with Edmund Winter by the 1430s, when his own fortunes were on the slide and when William Paston's campaign to turn

---

[258] Carpenter, *Locality and Polity*, 119–20, 127–8, 283–5.

[259] Richmond, *The Paston Family*, 42.

[260] See Colin Richmond's comments on the claims of the Winters and the Moleyns to East Beckham and Gresham (*The Paston Family*, 52–3, 91), which are discussed below, pp. 133, 138.   [261] Carpenter, *Locality and Polity*, 147.

[262] Richmond, *The Paston Family*, 64–72.

[263] See above, pp. 62–3, 80; Richmond, *The Paston Family*, 72–3, 83–5.

[264] Richmond, *The Paston Family*, 74–82.

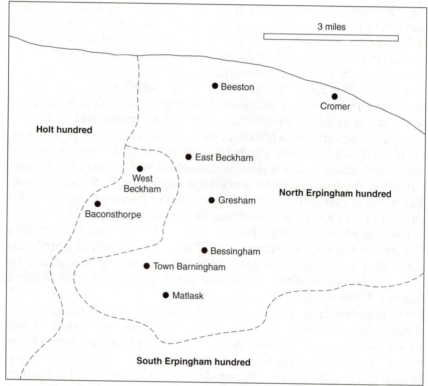

Map 2. The Pastons and their neighbours in northern Norfolk

his professional influence and earnings into landed power was gathering momentum virtually on Winter's doorstep.[265] The purchaser of East Beckham in 1415, using money he made in the fishing industry, had been William Mariot of Cromer, but in 1434 he drowned at sea, and his widow was forced to offer East Beckham for sale in the attempt to pay off his debts. According to Joan Mariot's later account, Edmund Winter expressed his interest but could not compete with William Paston, who rapidly entered into an agreement to buy the manor. As Richmond has suggested, 'in 1434 the Pastons must have appeared to Edmund as the usurpers of the Winters in North Erpingham Hundred. Irked, beyond endurance, he may have seen, as we are perhaps entitled to see, the contest for East Beckham as the family's last stand.'[266]

Edmund Winter entered East Beckham in December 1434, before

[265] Edmund was forced to sell the manor of Egmere near Walsingham, where his father had lived, in 1425; among Paston's acquisitions in the area in the 1420s were Cromer and Gresham in North Erpingham hundred, and Oxnead in the neighbouring hundred of South Erpingham, which he bought in 1419: Richmond, *The Paston Family*, pp. xvi–xvii, 70, 84.
[266] Ibid. 82, 87–8; quotation from 85.

Joan Mariot's sale to William Paston had been completed. The fact that atavistic claims such as Winter's to East Beckham were not rendered harmless by legal purchase is demonstrated by the verdict in Edmund's favour delivered by a jury of influential local men in 1436. However, although Paston had lost the first round, and although he could not stop the dispute dragging on for the next decade, his star was rising while Winter's was falling, and he found an answer to all of Winter's manœuvres. In 1438–9 Judge William appealed to the arbitration of the earl of Suffolk; the earl's decision that the law should take its course in an action of novel disseisin brought against Winter, despite the obstacles the latter had put in its way, seems in practice to have been favourable to the Paston side, since the resulting verdict went their way in 1441. However, Paston's chances of taking immediate advantage of this victory were scuppered by the death of Joan Mariot in 1440, and her son John's subsequent defection to the opposing camp (for understandable reasons given that the legal battle to retain East Beckham was using up all the profits he might hope to make by completing its sale to William Paston).[267] Winter's first priority seems to have been to prevent Paston acquiring the manor; although John Mariot's decision to turn his back on the uncompleted sale compromised Winter's chances of retaining the manor for himself, it greatly strengthened the case against Paston, and Winter therefore seems to have been happy to accept Mariot as his 'front-man'.[268]

However, the political cards remained stacked in Paston's favour. Suffolk was again called in to arbitrate at the end of 1443, but the chances of a settlement seem to have foundered on Judge William's unwillingness to abandon proceedings in the courts. His confidence appears to have been justified, since a verdict was returned in his favour in 1444. However, this success was followed almost immediately by William Paston's death. In the following year, through a collusive action with Simon Gunnor, Paston's lessee at East Beckham who had clearly also now changed sides in the dispute, Mariot recovered the manor. The Pastons were not to secure the profits of the property until 1503.[269] This sudden reverse in the Pastons' fortunes raises important questions. First, why was Judge William's death such a crucial turning-point in the course of this dispute? And, second, what light can the intricacies of the dispute shed on the Pastons' situation in the later 1440s, and by extension on the evidence of the state of local politics which their letters provide?

[267] Ibid. 88, 90–6.

[268] Winter had not, for example, challenged the Mariots' possession of the manor between 1415 and 1434; only when Paston—who represented a threat to the Winters' local position in a way the Mariots did not—appeared as a purchaser did he launch his challenge.

[269] Richmond, *The Paston Family*, 101–4.

William Paston's death had a profound effect on his family's immediate situation within local political society. Judge William's career had brought him wealth and a network of important political associations; he was attempting the complex task of building his family a landed estate in the region, but he had the legal expertise and the connections necessary to pursue his ambitions successfully. His son and heir John, in his early twenties when William died, could not hope to match his father's influence, in the short term at least.[270] In other words, when the letters begin in earnest in the later 1440s, the family were struggling with a situation in which they had been rendered suddenly exposed and vulnerable.[271] Up to 1444, by contrast, William Paston had been able to acquire a substantial amount of property, by various means including sharp practice where necessary, and to defend it against his rivals.[272] In this respect at least, it is clearly important not to overgeneralize about the negative aspects of the Pastons' experience within local political society during the period of Suffolk's dominance.

The second question which suggests itself, in the attempt to place the East Beckham dispute within the wider context of East Anglian politics, is to ask who was in a position to take advantage of the Pastons' sudden vulnerability in 1444. The loss of Judge William was clearly a severe blow to the Pastons' immediate prospects, but neither Edmund Winter nor John Mariot was in a particularly strong position, in terms of their local influence, to reassert their claims. In fact, the key figure in the Pastons' difficulties at East Beckham in 1444–5, and the further problems they encountered in the later part of the decade, may well have been John Heydon. The enmity between Heydon and the Pastons has usually been explained in terms of the supposed intrusion of Suffolk's household clique into East Anglian affairs. Suffolk's servants, it is argued, were unscrupulous thugs who pursued their own and their lord's ambitions by terrorizing the region's gentry—a typical (if untypically well-documented) example being the misfortunes of the Paston family.[273] The possibility that the Pastons might have been a *particular* target of Heydon's hostility, rather than unfortunate victims of a generalized reign of terror, has barely been considered. It has already been demonstrated that the identification of Suffolk's affinity as an intruding court clique cannot be sustained; the history of the East

---

[270] *PL* Davis, i, pp. liii–liv; Richmond, *The Paston Family*, pp. xvi–xvii, 12, 103–4.

[271] It was after William's death, for example, that the friar John Hauteyn was able to trouble the family over his claim to Oxnead: *PL* Davis, i. 233–4; ii. 520–2 (Gairdner, ii. 60–1, 74, 100); Richmond, *The Paston Family*, 42–6.

[272] For discussion of Judge William's manœuvres see, Richmond, *The Paston Family*, 34–42.

[273] Ralph Griffiths, for example, calls Tuddenham and Heydon 'Norfolk bullies'; R. L. Storey talks of the 'exploits of the Tuddenham gang'; E. F. Jacob describes Heydon as a 'professional desperado': Griffiths, *Henry VI*, 305; Storey, *End of the House of Lancaster*, 57; Jacob, *The Fifteenth Century*, 503.

Beckham dispute provides a context in which the conflict between Heydon and the Pastons in the later 1440s is both more explicable, and more complex in terms of distinguishing 'right' from 'wrong', than has usually been assumed.

John Heydon was married to the daughter of Edmund Winter. In 1436 he had acted as mainpernor for his father-in-law in the course of legal proceedings relating to East Beckham.[274] Ties of kin would therefore have encouraged him to view William Paston and his ambitions for his family with some hostility; and this sentiment must undoubtedly have been reinforced by consideration of his own position within local landed society. Heydon's home lay at Baconsthorpe, only a couple of miles from his father-in-law's estate at Town Barningham in one direction and from the Winters' former property at East Beckham in another. Heydon too was a lawyer seeking to establish himself and his family among the region's leading gentry, and was also therefore attempting to expand his landed stake in the area. It is not easy to reconstruct the chronology or the details of Heydon's acquisitions, but from the list of properties he held at his death in 1479 it is clear that his territorial ambitions were focused in Duchy of Lancaster territory in the north of the shire, in the hundreds of North and South Erpingham and in Holt, Greenhoe, and Gallow which adjoined them to the west. It seems likely that several at least of these properties were acquired in the 1440s and 1450s when his career was at its height.[275]

The rapid expansion of the Pastons' landed power in the area therefore threatened Heydon's growing influence just as much as it did the waning interests of his father-in-law Winter. The distribution of Heydon's estates in fact suggests that the small area in which Baconsthorp and East Beckham lay constituted the 'front line' where the growing power of the Pastons further east met the developing landed interests of Heydon to the west. Moreover, the challenge to Heydon–Winter interests which William Paston's attempt to acquire East Beckham represented was substantially reinforced in 1440 by the marriage of Paston's eldest son John to the heiress Margaret Mautby, an alliance which brought into the family the manors of West Beckham,

---

[274] See above, p. 80; *CCR 1435–41*, 64; Richmond, *The Paston Family*, 90 n. 99.

[275] See Map 2, p. 132. Heydon seems to have inherited the manors of Woodhall in Baconsthorp and Loverds in Heydon, both in South Erpingham hundred. By the time of his death he also held the manors of Saxlingham in Oulton and Oulton Hall and Leches in Oulton, in South Erpingham hundred; Northrepps in North Erpingham hundred; Losehall in Hempstead, Bodham Hall, and Braunches in Salthouse, all in Holt hundred; Pensthorp in Gallow hundred; Thursford in Greenhoe hundred, and lands in Great Walsingham, also in Greenhoe. He also held five manors in the south of the shire (Bokenhams in Carleton Rode, Boseviles in Bunwell, Launds in Tibenham, Hockham, and Hackford). C140/72/72; see also Blomefield, *History of the County of Norfolk*, v. 130, 140, 284; vi. 244, 260, 373, 504–5; vii. 120; viii. 151; ix. 367–8 (although note that information given here is not always reliable).

Matlask, and Bessingham. These estates, together with William Paston's manor of Gresham, purchased in 1427, surrounded Baconsthorpe on three sides.[276] Colin Richmond comments that the Mautby estates 'were so placed that Edmund Winter must have felt thoroughly beleaguered',[277] but the same is equally true of Heydon, even if Heydon's rapidly developing career offered him more reassurance than his father-in-law's failing one.

Heydon's professional success, in particular his service to the Duchy of Lancaster and his connections first with William Phelip and later with the earl of Suffolk,[278] gave him increasing influence in the region in the late 1430s and early 1440s, and it is not unreasonable to suppose that he had a hand in what successes Edmund Winter and subsequently John Mariot were able to achieve in their attempt to frustrate William Paston's acquisition of East Beckham. However, it is clear both that Judge William retained the upper hand, and that Suffolk's weight was not being thrown behind Paston's opponents. If Heydon did continue to support Winter's challenge after 1436—and it is clear that it would have been in his interests to do so—he could not, it seems, in the end compete with Judge William's influence and connections. However, William Paston's death coincided with a crucial point in the development of Heydon's career. In 1441 he had been appointed to the commission of the peace in Norfolk, and served consistently thereafter; in 1442 he acquired the lease of the Duchy manor of Beeston, which lay close to East Beckham and Cromer in North Erpingham hundred; most importantly, in November 1443 he was appointed, with Thomas Tuddenham, to the stewardship of the Duchy in East Anglia.[279] Whatever the vulnerability of William Paston's young heir in 1444, it might seem surprising that either Edmund Winter—who had not played a substantial part in the rule of the region since the 1420s—or John Mariot—the son of an indebted Cromer fisherman—should be in a position to deprive his family of East Beckham so convincingly by the end of the following year. The one person who *did* have the influence to secure the manor for John Mariot, and who was both a close associate of the Winters and the possessor of landed interests which

---

[276] John and Margaret Paston did not secure possession of Bessingham and Matlask until 1446, after the death of Margaret's grandmother; West Beckham did not come to the Pastons until 1479 when Margaret's uncle Edward Mautby died. Nevertheless, the threat to the interests of John Heydon and Edmund Winter represented by the Pastons' acquisition of even the reversion of these manors would have been immediately apparent. *PL* Gairdner, ii. 51; Richmond, *The Paston Family*, 102–3, 127–34.

[277] Richmond, *The Paston Family*, 134; see also 121: 'It is evident that the Mautby marriage was a vital aspect of William Paston's campaign to make North Erpingham Hundred Paston territory'.

[278] For which, see above, pp. 80, 91–2.

[279] See above, pp. 95–8.

were also at risk from the expansion of the Paston estate within this small corner of Erpingham hundred, was John Heydon.[280]

This conclusion must remain speculative in the absence of direct evidence linking Heydon with Mariot's case in 1444–5.[281] However, what is not in question is the next phase of conflict which engulfed John Paston and his family. In February 1448 Robert Hungerford, Lord Moleyns, seized the Pastons' manor of Gresham, an action in which he clearly had the support of John Heydon.[282] On the face of it, this was a surprising and extraordinarily aggressive incursion into the region by a courtier whose estates lay in Wiltshire and who had had no previous involvement in the affairs of East Anglia. Seen in these terms, Moleyns's sudden interest in Gresham has proved hard to explain; it has usually been depicted as a particularly extreme manifestation of the almost random acquisitiveness of members of the court regime in the 1440s, and of the propensity of Suffolk's leading associates in East Anglia to support illegal seizures of property.[283] However, the Pastons were later to allege that the initiative behind the attack came not from Moleyns but from Heydon[284]—a claim which makes a great deal of sense in the context of more than a decade of conflict precipitated by the Pastons' territorial expansion in northern Norfolk.

Gresham lay at the heart of the same small area where Heydon's

---

[280] Heydon's marriage to Eleanor Winter was in crisis in 1444, according to Margaret Paston's report to her husband in July of that year, but the cause of the estrangement— Eleanor seems to have borne a child by someone else—appears to have meant that it did not cause a rupture between Heydon and his wife's family. Certainly, when Edmund Winter wrote his will in 1448 he appointed Heydon as his supervisor and left him a bequest, but made no mention of Eleanor. Ralph Griffiths cites Margaret's letter as evidence that Heydon's 'harsh treatment of his first wife and their young child seemed to confirm to members of the Paston family that here was a particularly unmannered and vicious gentleman who represented Suffolk's regional dominance', but it is striking that Margaret in fact offers no comment, hostile or otherwise, on what she has 'herde seyne' of Heydon's conduct. The paragraph is perhaps worth repeating in full: Margaret writes that 'Heydonnis wyffe had chyld on Sent Petyr Day. I herde seyne that herre husbond wille nowt of here, nerre of here chyld that sche had last nowdyre. I herd seyn that he seyd zyf sche come in hesse precence to make here exkewce that he xuld kyt of here nose to makyn here to be know wat she is, and yf here chyld come in hesse presence he seyd he wyld kyllyn. He wolle nowt be intretit to haue here ayen in no wysse, os I herde seyn.' (Heydon's marriage has many parallels with that of Thomas Tuddenham, who also separated from his wife because she had given birth to a child as a result of an adulterous affair. She subsequently entered a convent, while Tuddenham remained on good terms with her family.) *PL* Davis, i. 220 (Gairdner, iii. 255–6); NRO NCC Reg. Wilbey, fo. 147; Richmond, *The Paston Family*, 171 n. 16; Griffiths, *Henry VI*, 585–6; for Tuddenham, see above, Ch. 4.4 n. 218.

[281] It should, however, be noted that the letters are in several instances not the comprehensive sources we might expect; see, for example, the case of Thomas Daniel: below, p. 140.

[282] *PL* Davis, ii. 29–30 (Gairdner, ii. 112); Richmond, *The Paston Family*, 53.

[283] See above, pp. 125–6; Richmond, *The Paston Family*, 147–8; and, for example, Griffiths, *Henry VI*, 587–8.

[284] See the petition to the chancellor printed in *PL* Davis, i. 55–6, and the indictment brought against Moleyns and Heydon in 1450: KB9/265 mm. 44–5.

father-in-law Edmund Winter had jostled for position with William Paston, only a couple of miles from Heydon's home at Baconsthorp, from the Mautby manors of Bessingham and Matlask of which John and Margaret Paston had secured possession in 1446, and from the disputed estate at East Beckham, now back in the hands of John Mariot.[285] It had belonged at the end of the fourteenth century to Margery Bacon, wife of William Moleyns. Its history had parallels with that of East Beckham, in that Margery had given instructions for her executors to sell the manor, giving her grandson and heir first refusal; he ultimately defaulted on the complex arrangements made to pay for the estate, and the feoffees arranged for its sale to another purchaser—William Paston—in 1427.[286]

Where the case of Gresham differed from that of East Beckham was that the purchase was completed; in strict legal terms, Paston's title seems to have been good. However, as Colin Richmond remarks, the Moleyns family were left with 'an attachment, of no ultimate legal use, but a spur to action if time and occasion were propitious . . . We are face to face, I think, with this family's reluctance to give up what once it had held, in this case recently and in this case too with not even the intention of letting go what it held. If possession is nine parts of the law, atavistic commitment has to be the tenth.'[287] By 1448, this attachment belonged to Robert Hungerford, in right of his wife Eleanor Moleyns. However, the person for whom time and occasion seem to have been particularly propitious was John Heydon. The expansion of the Paston family's estates in North Erpingham hundred, and the threat to Heydon's landed interests which it represented, had been checked by the death of Judge William in 1444 and John Mariot's subsequent recovery of East Beckham in 1445.[288] It seems entirely likely that Heydon would have wished to press home his advantage now that John Paston had been forced on to the back foot, and Gresham offered the perfect opportunity. Heydon's connections at court gave him access to Moleyns; his legal expertise gave him the means to make the most of Moleyns's claim. Though Moleyns himself was undoubtedly a sudden intruder into the region, his assault on Gresham forms part of a long-term battle for local supremacy between neighbours and rivals in this part of northern Norfolk, in which Heydon was now the key player. The suggestion that the Gresham affair can only be properly understood in the context of the earlier conflict at East Beckham is further reinforced by the fact that Edmund Winter's son John, John Mariot, and Simon Gunnor (William Paston's turncoat lessee at East Beckham) were all involved with Heydon in supporting

[285] See Map 2; and above, n. 276.   [286] Richmond, *The Paston Family*, 47–53.
[287] Ibid. 52–3.   [288] See above, at n. 269.

Moleyns and the men who were occupying Gresham in his name during 1448 and 1449.[289]

John Heydon therefore had his own pressing reasons—interrelated concerns for his own landed interests and those of his relatives—for his hostility to the Pastons and their territorial expansion in his corner of northern Norfolk. To characterize him as a representative of the court regime exploiting his access to Suffolk to victimize defenceless members of the local gentry is to ignore the fact that he was himself a prominent member of the local gentry, well connected in the region, who found after 1444 that he had the opportunity and the influence to gain the upper hand over a weaker opponent in a long-running dispute, just as William Paston had been able to do until his death in that year. If Heydon was indeed instrumental in John Mariot's victory at East Beckham, he was after all supporting Mariot's right to retain his own manor against the challenge of a would-be buyer whose purchase had never been completed.[290] Moleyns's claim to Gresham was clearly substantially weaker than Mariot's to East Beckham, and the methods he employed were both more extreme and more violent.[291] As has already been suggested, his occupation of the manor provides a major example of the increasingly pronounced disorder which developed in the region as Suffolk's control faltered at the end of the decade.[292] Nevertheless, it was also the assertion through direct action—albeit of an unusually violent and disruptive kind—of a claim which would at least have been comprehensible to contemporaries, even if not strictly arguable by the letter of the law, and which had important implications in the context of a continuing struggle for local influence in which Heydon's interests were closely involved. In this sense, Heydon's support for Moleyns does not fall so far outside the parameters of the normal functioning of gentry society in the period as previous assessments of his 'criminal activities' have concluded.

It also has to be said that John Paston's search for support in the

---

[289] Edmund Winter had died in Feb. 1448, nine days after Moleyns's seizure of Gresham. *PL* Davis, ii. 30 (Gairdner, ii. 112); Richmond, *The Paston Family*, 107. Moleyns was said to be spending Shrovetide in 1449 at 'Jon Wynterys plase': *PL* Davis, i. 228 (Gairdner, ii. 131), and see also i. 237 (omitted in Gairdner).

[290] For the status of Paston's purchase, see Richmond, *The Paston Family*, 115. It is evidence of William Paston's perhaps unscrupulous and certainly overbearing methods that he had persuaded Joan Mariot to hand over all evidences relating to the manor in 1435, despite the fact that he did not yet have any legal title to them: Richmond, *The Paston Family*, 35–6, 88–9; see also *PL* Davis, ii. 11 (Gairdner, ii. 64).

[291] In this context, it is significant that, unlike Mariot, Moleyns was not able to retain possession of the manor after 1451, although it must also be noted that his ability to pursue the dispute was curtailed thereafter because of the fact that he was captured while serving in France in 1452 or 1453; he did not return to England until 1459: Richmond, *The Paston Family*, 60–1.

[292] See above, Ch. 4.4.

wake of the reverses he suffered after his father's death added to the complexity of his family's situation in the late 1440s. Heydon's close association with Suffolk clearly precluded any realistic hope that help might be forthcoming from that quarter, and John Paston's response seems to have been to attach himself to the rival lordship of Thomas Daniel. By 2 April 1448, Margaret Paston was asking her husband 'to send me wurd hw ze spede in zwr mater twchyng Gressam, and hw Danyel js jn grace', and added the request 'that I may ben recommawndyd to my lord Danyel'.[293] The connection was still in place two years later; in May 1450, when a parliament was being held at Leicester, Thomas Denys informed John Paston that 'My Maister Danyell desireth yow thedir'.[294]

This relationship raises two important points in relation to the wider analysis of the Pastons' situation in the late 1440s and the status of the evidence provided by the letters. First, though Moleyns's behaviour at Gresham seems to have been both aggressive and unscrupulous, it was equalled if not exceeded in these respects by that of Daniel at Rydon.[295] Therefore, though the Pastons were victims of one courtier intruding into the region in the increasingly disordered circumstances of the late 1440s, they were prepared to offer their support to another who was inflicting the same kind of treatment on another prominent Norfolk family. This is not a conclusion which it would be easy to draw from the letters; perhaps unsurprisingly, the Pastons themselves give little sense of the activities of their 'lord Danyel', which can only be pieced together from other evidence. Secondly, their association with Daniel involved the Pastons in a broader pattern of conflict within the region. Daniel's duplicity over the Rydon estates, in which John Paston was prepared to offer him support,[296] earned him the enmity not only of Henry Wodehous but also of Wodehous's brother-in-law Thomas Tuddenham. Paston's support for Daniel, and Tuddenham's association with John Heydon, meant that the conflict caused by Daniel's incursion into western Norfolk and that precipitated by Paston expansion in the north of the shire would necessarily become intertwined, a

[293] *PL* Davis, i. 223 (Gairdner, ii. 87).

[294] *PL* Davis, ii. 38 (Gairdner, ii. 150).

[295] For which, see above, pp. 120–1. Daniel's claim to Rydon seems to have been wholly fraudulent; William Worcestre reports that in 1454 Henry Wodehous decided to demolish the manor house rather than risk it falling into Daniel's hands again: Harvey (ed.) *Worcestre: Itineraries*, 253.

[296] In Nov. 1446 Paston released to Daniel his right in the manors of Rydon, Grimston, Well Hall, and Congham, which suggests that he may have been a feoffee for Wodehous. This quitclaim may simply have formed part of the settlement for the proposed marriage between Elizabeth Daniel and Henry Wodehous or, given that it is not a general quitclaim on behalf of a group of feoffees, it may represent evidence of Paston's willingness to collude with Daniel's fraud. Whatever the significance of this particular deed, it is clear that Paston was supporting Daniel in his possession of the properties in the late 1440s. *CCR 1441–7*, 443.

connection reinforced by the fact that Heydon's father-in-law Edmund Winter had married Tuddenham's mother-in-law Alice Wodehous after she was widowed in 1431.[297] In other words, by the time the Paston letters begin to survive in significant numbers, what had been a dispute over the competing local interests of the Pastons and the Winters in northern Norfolk had become a broader conflict in which Thomas Daniel and the Pastons were pitted against Thomas Tuddenham and John Heydon.

Read in this context, the letters describe not the hijacking of local power structures by an exploitative court clique, but a comprehensible local dispute rendered unusual in its scope and implications by the wider political context of the years 1447–50 and by the involvement of the 'intruders' Daniel and Moleyns. Nor does this evidence support the charge that the duke of Suffolk was systematically abusing his power in the region. Suffolk's interventions in the East Beckham dispute in 1438 and 1443 seem, so far as it is possible to tell, to have been studiedly impartial. Further, it is striking that he was apparently unable or unwilling to force a settlement. This—unlike the conflict resulting from the duke of Norfolk's attempts to establish himself in the area—was a dispute *within* the political network of which Suffolk had inherited the leadership. Though this should in theory have put him in a position to arbitrate effectively, it is important to note that this was a network which had been established through close associations with the public authority of the crown and with the king's private local interests in his capacity as duke of Lancaster. Suffolk was, of course, having to manage both of these manifestations of royal authority in the region on behalf of the king, and his success in establishing himself at the head of the crown–Duchy network played a crucial part in allowing him to fulfil this complex role. However, the peculiarities of this situation may, even before the crisis years of 1447–50, have meant that Suffolk was not able to be as authoritative as might be expected under normal circumstances in the exercise of his lordship over his own servants and associates, who played such a crucial part in sustaining his hybrid power in the region in the absence of an active king. The dispute between William Paston and Edmund Winter was therefore essentially left to take its course. Until 1444, that meant success for the greater political and professional resources of Judge William; after his death, it meant that his son could find little answer to the increasing local influence of John Heydon.

Certainly, it is Heydon, not Suffolk, who appears to be the villain of

---

[297] Alice's first husband, John Wodehous, had died in 1431. Edmund and Alice both died in 1448; their wills are NRO NCC Reg. Wilbey, fos. 147, 150. See above, Ch. 4.4 at n. 213; Richmond, *The Paston Family*, 83 n., 107.

the piece from the Pastons' point of view. Heydon and Tuddenham are together the targets of the Pastons' hostility between 1448 and 1451— significantly the point at which the Heydon–Paston and Tuddenham– Daniel disputes had become intertwined—but by 1455, when the Pastons were no longer unequivocal supporters of Daniel, John Paston was still struggling against 'Heydon and his dyscyplis' but was prepared to remark of Tuddenham that 'he gaff me no cawse of late tyme to labor ageyns him'.[298] Though Suffolk's power is reported to be over-whelming—as in Margaret Paston's famous remark that 'sondery folkys haue seyd to me that they thynk veryly but if ze haue my lord of Suffolkys godelorchyp qhyll the werd is as itt is ye kan neuer leven jn pese wyth-owth ye haue his godelordschep'[299]—he is not explicitly the target of the Pastons' complaints. It is possible that it would not have been easy to criticize members of the nobility directly even in private correspondence;[300] even so, it is perhaps worth quoting in full the passage from which Margaret's remark is taken. In a letter to her husband in May probably of 1449, she writes:

And I haue spokyn wyth the sexteyn and seyd to hym as ye bad me that I xuld don, and he axid me ryt feythfully hw ye sped jn zowr materys. I told him that ze haddyn fayre be-hestys, and I seyd I hopyd that ze xuld don rytz well ther-jn; and he seyd he supposyd that D. wold don for zou, but he seyd he was no hasty laborere jn non mater. He seyd be hys feyth he wost qhere a man was that laboryd to hym for a mater ryth a long tym, and alwey he be-hestyd that he wold labore itt effectualy, but qhyll he sewyd to hym he kowd never haue remedy of his mater; and than, qhan he thowth that he xuld no remedy haue

---

[298] James Gloys had reported to Paston that 'It is seyde be Heydon and his disciples that my Mayster Yeluerton and ye and my Mayster Alyngton shuld haue do oon Ser John Tartyssale, parson of the Estchirche of Warham and chapeleyn to the Priour of Walsyngham, to put in to the parlement a bille of diuers tresons don be my lord of Norwich, Ser Thomas Tudenham, and John Heydon, and ye shuld haue set to your seales; and if that Heydon had be vj howres fro the parlement lengere than he was there had be graunted an oyere determynere to haue enquere of hem, &c.' Gloys comments that this is 'a slandrows noyse', 'which I suppose is do to bryng you ought of the conceyte of the pepyll, for at this day ye stand gretly in the countreys conceyte'. Paston replied that 'this is the furst day that I herd of any seche, but I wold wete the namys of hem that vttere this langage and the mater of the bill. As for my lord of Norwych, I suppose ye know I haue not vsid to meddel wyth lordis materis meche forther than me nedith. And as for Ser Thomas Todynham, he gaff me no cawse of late tyme to labour ageyns hym, and also of seche mater I know non deffaut in hym.' *PL* Davis, i. 84–5, and ii. 124 (Gairdner, iii. 45–7). For Daniel and the Pastons in the 1450s, see below, pp. 172–6, 183–4.

[299] *PL* Davis, i. 236 (Gairdner, iv. 75, where the letter is misdated to 1463). It could be argued that, if Margaret felt the need to articulate this point explicitly in a letter to her husband as late as 1449, Suffolk's power could not have been as all-consuming as has some-times been supposed; Paston must have felt he had a realistic hope of effective help from other quarters—presumably, and, by this evidence, misguidedly, from Daniel—if he needed to be told the advice of 'sondery folkys' that they 'thynk veryly' that Suffolk's was the only lordship worth having.

[300] See below, pp. 175–6, for a case involving the duke of Norfolk.

to sew to hym, he spak wyth Fynys that is now Speker of the Parlment, and prayid hym that he wold don for hym jn his mater, and zaf hym a reward, and wyth-jnne ryth schort tym after his mater was sped. And the sayd sexteyn and other folkys that ben yowre ryth wele willerys haue kownselyd me that I xuld kownsell zou to maken other menys than ye haue made to other folkys that wold spede yowr materys better than they haue don thatt ye haue spoken to ther-of be-for this tym. Sondery folkys haue seyd to me that they thynk veryly but if ze haue my lord of Suffolkys godelorchyp qhyll the werd is as itt is ye kan neuer leven jn pese wyth-owth ye haue his godelordschep. Therfor I pray you wyth all myn herth that ye wyll don yowre part to haue hys godelordschep and his love jn ese of all the materis that ye haue to don, and jn esyng of myn hert also. For be my trowth I am afferd ellys bothen of these materys the qhyche ye haue jn hand now, and of othere that ben not don to yett but if he wyl don for zou and be yowr godelord.

Several points emerge from this passage taken as a whole. First, Thomas Daniel—'D.'—is clearly not providing the help for which the Pastons must have hoped in their attempt to counter the influence of Heydon and reclaim Gresham from Moleyns. Second, the duke of Norfolk is not even mentioned in the context of the Pastons' need for effective lordship—something which reinforces the suggestion that he remained a fairly marginal figure in the politics at least of Norfolk, if not of the region as a whole, in the late 1440s. But, third, it is also clear that Margaret at least does not see Suffolk as the malign force behind the manœuvres against her family. Though she may believe that 'qhyll the werd is as itt is ye kan neuer leven jn pese wyth-owth ye haue his godelordschep', she counsels not despair but an attempt to win 'hys godelordschep and his love jn ese of all the materis that ye haue to don'. This may well have seemed something of a forlorn hope in view of the close association between the duke and their enemy Heydon, but it was clearly not beyond the bounds of possibility in the way that it surely would have been had the Pastons seen Suffolk either as the cause of their misfortunes, or as a figure so compromised by his leadership of a corrupt clique as to render Heydon's activities indistinguishable from the effects of the duke's lordship.[301]

---

[301] Margaret's report of a conversation she had with Barow, one of Moleyns's men at Gresham, three months earlier reinforces this point. Barow told her that 'he had lever than xl s. and xl that his lord had not commawndyd hym to com to Gressam, and he seyd he was rytz sory hidderward in as meche as he had knowleche of zw be-fore; he was rytz sory of that that was don'. 'I seyd to hym,' Margaret wrote, 'that he xuld haue compascion on zou and other that were dissesyd of her lyvelode, in as meche as he had ben dissesyd hym-self; and he seyd he was so, and told me that he had sewyd to my lord of Suffolk dyuers tymys, and wold don tyl he may gete his gode azen. I seyd to hym that ze had sewyd to my Lord Moleynys dyuers tymys for the maner of Gressam syth ze wer dissesyd, and ze cowd neuer gete no resonabyl answere of hym, and ther-fore ze entred azen as ze hopid that was for the best. And he seyd he xuld neuer blame my lord of Suffolk for the entre in his lyvelode, for he seyd my seyd lord was sett ther-up-on be the informacion of a fals schrew. And I seyd to hym in lyke wyse is the

The causes and context of the reverses which the Pastons suffered in the later 1440s therefore seem to have been far more specific than has hitherto been suggested. In the light of this conclusion, the assumption that the Pastons' situation was representative of the general experience of the East Anglian gentry and that it can be used to demonstrate wholesale abuses on the part of Suffolk's regime appears to be highly problematic. Ralph Griffiths, in attempting to use the letters in this way, argues that 'their laments are substantially confirmed by other evidence',[302] but it is striking that in most accounts of East Anglian landed society in the 1440s the only other evidence cited is that relating to the Norfolk knight Sir John Fastolf.[303] The consensus has been that Fastolf was the victim of what Colin Richmond has termed a 'vendetta' on the part of the duke of Suffolk. Suffolk and his servants, it is alleged, used their position to harass Fastolf and to cause him substantial losses in their attempt to enrich themselves through the illegal acquisition of property which was rightfully his.[304] As in the case of the Pastons—with whom Fastolf developed increasingly close connections as the decade went on[305]—the assumption has been that his experience was typical of the oppressions of Suffolk's regime. Anthony Smith, for example, in his detailed study of Fastolf's career, argues that 'Fastolf's relations with Suffolk illuminate English political history by illustrating the domestic misgovernment that the Duke encouraged'; indeed, Sir John 'was only one of many men in East Anglia who had suffered injustice during Suffolk's supremacy, even if he was one of the most important'.[306]

However, once again, the conclusions to be drawn from Fastolf's experiences may not be as straightforward as they at first appear. Fastolf did suffer losses at the hands of the duke himself and of members

mater be-twyx the Lord Moleynys and zou: I told hym I wost wele he sett neuer ther-vp-on be no tytyl of rytz that he hadde to the maner of Gressam, but only be the informacion of a fals schrew. I rehersyd no name, but me thowt be hem that thei wost ho I ment': *PL* Davis, i. 229 (Gairdner, ii. 132–3). Though this was clearly a tense conversation—Margaret made it clear in a later letter that she did not trust Moleyns's men (*PL* Davis, i. 232 (Gairdner, ii. 96))—the sense remains that it was the 'fals schrew' Heydon who was behind Moleyns's involvement in a dispute in relation to which Suffolk had not yet taken any action. By Oct. 1450, William Wayte was warning John Paston bluntly to 'be ware of Heydon, for he wold destroyed yow, be my feyth': *PL* Davis, ii. 48 (Gairdner, ii. 176).

[302] Griffiths, *Henry VI*, 584.

[303] See, for example, ibid. 584–9; Wolffe, *Henry VI*, 122–3; Storey, *End of the House of Lancaster*, 54–6; Richmond, *The Paston Family*, 147.

[304] Smith, 'Litigation and Politics', 63–8; 'Aspects of the Career of Sir John Fastolf', chs. 4 and 5; Richmond, *The Paston Family*, 233–40, and quotation from 227.

[305] William Paston had been associated with Fastolf, to whom Margaret Paston was related, since at least 1436. During the 1440s John Paston became one of his principal local servants: see Richmond, *The Paston Family*, 122–3, and ch. 7.

[306] Smith, 'Aspects of the Career of Sir John Fastolf', 167, 144; see also references above at n. 303.

of his affinity, and he undoubtedly felt himself to have been greatly wronged; but examination of the disputes in which he was involved, in the context both of the relationship between the law and landowning politics and of the particular circumstances of Henry VI's government in the 1440s, suggests that Fastolf's troubles—like those of the Pastons—cannot necessarily be taken as a paradigmatic example of the effects of a systematically corrupt regime. It is clear, for example, that the position of Fastolf himself within East Anglian political society was far from typical, and that the peculiarities of his situation played a significant part in the difficulties he faced.

Fastolf was a career soldier who made a substantial fortune through his service in France and who sought from 1415 onwards to acquire a major territorial stake in his native East Anglia, in particular in eastern Norfolk and Suffolk around his manor of Caister.[307] Like William Paston, therefore, Fastolf was trying to convert new wealth into landed power, in Fastolf's case with an extraordinarily ambitious programme of purchase.[308] And like William Paston, therefore, Fastolf was always likely to run into trouble from rival claimants to his estates and from those whose interests he threatened. His closest East Anglian associates in the 1430s and 1440s were men with whom he had served in France, including Sir Henry Inglose, Sir John Clifton, Sir Andrew Ogard, and Sir William Oldhall.[309] This was a group which enjoyed strong connections within the crown–Duchy network in the region, of which Suffolk was now acquiring the leadership, and with Suffolk himself.[310] Fastolf had served with the earl in France; he joined Suffolk on the commission of the peace in Norfolk from 1437, and indeed bought the manor of Cotton in Suffolk from him in 1434.[311] There was therefore no enmity inherent in the relationship between the two men from the outset, nor any a priori incompatibility between their interests. Indeed, a notable feature of Fastolf's career in East Anglia is that he ran into so little difficulty over his purchases in the three decades during which he was building up his estate. Between 1415 and 1445 he spent more than £12,500 on properties in Norfolk, Suffolk, and Essex, with what Smith has described as 'the most startling period of investment in land'

---

[307] A. R. Smith, ' "The Greatest Man of That Age": The Acquisition of Sir John Fastolf's East Anglian Estates', in R. E. Archer and S. Walker (eds.), *Rulers and Ruled* (London, 1985), 137–8; 'Aspects of the Career of Sir John Fastolf', pp. vii, 1–23.

[308] See Smith, 'Aspects of the Career of Sir John Fastolf', 12–13: 'That a period [1439–45] in which around £1500 was spent on new property can be described as one in which investment slowed down (in comparison with the heady days of the early 1430s) emphasizes the immense scale of the investment in land which Fastolf undertook.'

[309] Ibid. 3, 103, 107–8; Richmond, *The Paston Family*, 207.

[310] See above, Ch. 3.2 nn. 104, 114, and p. 99.

[311] Smith, 'Acquisition of Sir John Fastolf's East Anglian Estates', 146; 'Aspects of the Career of Sir John Fastolf', 29, 138; *CPR 1436–41*, 586; *1441–6*, 474; *1446–52*, 592.

occurring in the first half of the 1430s.[312] Yet during this time he was not seriously troubled in his possession of any of his estates, despite the fact that there were flaws in his title to more than one of the properties.[313]

Given the difficulties which attended any attempt to establish a major landed estate by purchase, this territorial expansion unhampered by conflict or serious challenge was remarkable. It has already been suggested that the social and political structures of East Anglia were unusually fluid. Though this could in some circumstances result in unusual volatility within local society, changes at various levels within power structures in the region meant that there was particular room for manœuvre within local political society in the 1420s and 1430s, from which Fastolf may have benefited.[314] It must also be said that Fastolf's purchases represented a significant accumulation of *potential* local power, but were not accompanied by any immediate attempt to translate that potential into active local lordship, since Fastolf was in France for much of the time.[315] The immediate political impact of his programme of acquisition on local hierarchies and networks was therefore limited. It is perhaps significant, therefore, that Fastolf first began to experience minor setbacks from the late 1430s onwards—the point at which the earl of Suffolk was establishing himself at the head of local networks and of government at the centre, and also the point at which Fastolf finally retired from service in France.[316] It was not until this point, in other words, that the question of whether Fastolf's stake in East Anglia could be accommodated within a political structure dominated by the earl of Suffolk became a pressing one.

The answer to this question, at least in the later 1430s and earlier 1440s, seems to have been that it could. The issues which caused problems between Fastolf and Suffolk in these years arose in areas which were potentially of particular sensitivity, and yet the conflict remained relatively limited. Tensions first seem to have emerged not in fact over Fastolf's land acquisitions, but over the wardship of the daughter and heir of Fastolf's nephew Sir Robert Harling.[317] The

[312] Smith, 'Acquisition of Sir John Fastolf's East Anglian Estates', 137; 'Aspects of the Career of Sir John Fastolf', 7–8. Fastolf inherited lands worth £46 per year from his father; by 1445 the clear annual value of his estates in England exceeded £1,000: K. B. McFarlane, 'The Investment of Sir John Fastolf's Profits of War', in his *England in the Fifteenth Century* (London, 1981), 185.

[313] For the defects in Fastolf's title to Fritton and to Titchwell, see below, pp. 148, 150.

[314] See above, pp. 79–81.

[315] Smith, 'Aspects of the Career of Sir John Fastolf', pp. vii, 2–9; McFarlane, 'Investment of Sir John Fastolf's Profits of War', 187.

[316] See above, Ch. 4.2; McFarlane, 'Investment of Sir John Fastolf's Profits of War', 178.

[317] Smith, 'Aspects of the Career of Sir John Fastolf', 135–6. Thomas Tuddenham was the son of Robert Harling's sister Margaret, and was therefore first cousin to the heiress Anne Harling; however, there is no evidence that he became involved in the dispute which

Harling estates included four manors in the hundred of Lothingland in eastern Suffolk, a region in which both Fastolf and the earl had a substantial territorial stake.[318] Lothingland hundred itself, and properties at Lowestoft and Gorleston within it, formed part of the de la Pole estates.[319] Fastolf's purchases in the area included estates in Lowestoft and Gorleston as well as Bradwell, Fritton, and Hobland, all in Lothingland, and several properties in the adjoining hundred of Flegg to the north, where he was building a new home for himself at Caister; together, they formed a concentrated and valuable estate in an area of substantial importance to Suffolk's local lordship.[320] It might therefore have been expected that the two men would be in competition for a wardship such as that of Anne Harling, whose estates lay in an area of interest to both of them. Instead, though Suffolk acquired the wardship by grant of the king in 1437, he sold the rights to Sir John Clifton, who sold them on to Fastolf.[321] The dispute which then developed in the early 1440s concerned not the wardship itself but the payments to be made between the three men.[322]

The Harling dispute has parallels with the disagreement which arose in the 1440s as a result of Fastolf's purchase of the manor of Cotton from Suffolk. The sale took place in 1434, when Suffolk needed to raise a substantial sum of money to pay off his ransom. The earl had been born and baptized at Cotton, and sold it only because he was forced to do so by financial difficulties.[323] It seems unlikely that he was happy to accept Fastolf's purchase as a permanent interruption to his family's possession of the manor, and Suffolk's widow did finally reclaim the estate from Fastolf's executors in 1469.[324] However, during the 1440s the earl made no direct attempt to repossess Cotton. The dispute which arose—like that over the Harling wardship—concerned the payment for the property, which had been made by instalments in the later 1430s.[325]

developed between his lord Suffolk and his great-uncle Fastolf: Blomefield, *History of the County of Norfolk*, i. 319; xi. 207.

[318] Smith, 'Aspects of the Career of Sir John Fastolf', 19, 136.

[319] James, 'Career and Political Influence', 232 and fig. 1.

[320] Smith, 'Acquisition of Sir John Fastolf's East Anglian Estates', 138; 'Aspects of the Career of Sir John Fastolf', 10–11, 15–23.

[321] Fastolf later claimed that the wardship should never have been the king's to grant, since the lands were in the hands of feoffees and Robert Harling had therefore held no lands of the king: *PL* Davis, ii. 152 (Gairdner, iii. 94); Smith, 'Litigation and Politics', 65; 'Aspects of the Career of Sir John Fastolf', 136–7; for Clifton's close connections with both Suffolk and Fastolf, see above, pp. 99, 145.

[322] The arguments were still continuing in the mid-1450s: Smith, 'Litigation and Politics', 64–5; 'Aspects of the Career of Sir John Fastolf', 137–8.

[323] Smith, 'Acquisition of Sir John Fastolf's East Anglian Estates', 146, 150; Richmond, *The Paston Family*, 235–6; Kirby (ed.), *Calendar of Inquisitions Post Mortem*, xx. 268.

[324] C. Richmond, *The Paston Family in the Fifteenth Century: Fastolf's Will* (Cambridge, 1996), 119–20.

[325] Anthony Smith comments that 'there was room for confusion about this transaction',

It seems likely that Suffolk's financial problems in the later 1430s and early 1440s played a significant role in the disputes over both Cotton and the Harling wardship; a complicating factor in clarifying the details of the payments made by Fastolf in the latter case, for example, was the fact that Suffolk himself owed Fastolf 250 marks.[326] Certainly, in both cases conflict remained limited to disagreement about the money that had changed hands; Suffolk did not seek to regain control of the estates themselves.

Tensions undoubtedly rose between Suffolk and Fastolf as the 1440s went on. The earl challenged Fastolf's possession of the manors of Hellesdon and Drayton in Norfolk, and seems to have caused him financial losses there. Fastolf's title seems to have been good; Suffolk's challenge may have had less to do with his apparently spurious claim to the properties than with the fact that they lay only a couple of miles from his manor of Costessey, a property which was valuable but isolated in terms of the distribution of the other de la Pole estates. Indeed, Fastolf's purchases in East Anglia during the 1430s had been concentrated in this area near Norwich; as well as Hellesdon and Drayton, he owned manors at Saxthorpe, Guton, Felthorpe, and Hainford and property in Norwich itself.[327] In this context, it seems possible that in this case at least Suffolk's aggression may have been defensive in intent.[328] It was not only with Suffolk, however, that Fastolf came into conflict during these years. He was involved in litigation with Suffolk's sister Isabella, Lady Morley, during the early 1440s, as well as a dispute with Gilbert Debenham over possession of the manor of Fritton in Lothingland, which Fastolf, knowing that its title was defective, had bought cheaply.[329] In 1444 the Priory of Hickling in Norfolk contested Fastolf's right to an annual rent of 25 marks which he had bought in 1428 and which had previously been paid regularly and without demur; this was the start of a dispute which remained unresolved at Fastolf's death.[330]

but concludes that the dispute 'was encouraged by Suffolk's servants' as part of what he sees as their campaign of harassment against Fastolf: Smith, 'Aspects of the Career of Sir John Fastolf', 138–9; see also 'Litigation and Politics', 66.

[326] Smith, 'Aspects of the Career of Sir John Fastolf', 137.

[327] Smith, 'Acquisition of Sir John Fastolf's East Anglian Estates', 138–9, 141; 'Litigation and Politics', 67; 'Aspects of the Career of Sir John Fastolf', 131–5; Richmond, *The Paston Family*, 239.

[328] Suffolk's wife and son did succeed in securing possession of the estates in the 1460s: Richmond, *The Paston Family*, 240; *Fastolf's Will*, 140–50.

[329] Smith concludes that Fastolf's dispute with Lady Morley related to the goods of Robert Sargeaunt, a wool chapman, who owed them both money: Smith, 'Aspects of the Career of Sir John Fastolf', 139–40, 181–4; 'Litigation and Politics', 61–2.

[330] It is not clear why the Priory suddenly contested Fastolf's right to the rent, though it seems likely that the conflict owed something to Fastolf's souring relations with Thomas, Lord Scales, who was lord of the manor of Hickling and patron of the Priory. Smith, 'Litigation and Politics', 60–1, 65; 'Aspects of the Career of Sir John Fastolf', 192–202. See

However, it is clear, first, that it is perhaps the lack of conflict in which Fastolf was involved before the later 1430s that is surprising, given the scale of his attempt to break into structures of landed power in the region, rather than the fact that he encountered difficulties from that point onwards; and, second, that he was not unsuccessful in his own defence during these years. Though the dispute about payment for the Harling wardship was still rumbling on in the mid-1450s, as was the Hickling Priory case, the disagreement over the payment for Cotton was resolved in Fastolf's favour in 1443, and he was able to defeat Debenham over Fritton in 1441.[331] It was not until 1447 that Fastolf began to experience serious reverses including the temporary loss of some of his properties. It has already been suggested that it was from this point onwards that political structures became more unstable both at the centre and in East Anglia as Suffolk's position at the head of government became more exposed and his power correspondingly more brittle,[332] and these circumstances may help to shed some light on the difficulties which Fastolf experienced.

Significantly, in two of the major disputes which erupted from 1447 Fastolf faced challenges from members of the royal household who were newcomers to the region and who were able to use their access to the king to pursue their interests. As has already been demonstrated, the years from 1447 to 1450 were marked by household intervention in the region of a kind which had not occurred earlier in the decade, and which seems to have been both a symptom of Suffolk's growing difficulties in maintaining control of the household-based regime which he had created at the centre, and a result of his attempts to use the resources of the household to shore up his power in the face of these difficulties.[333] During these years, therefore, a previously stable system of rule was beginning to break down both at the centre and in East Anglia, circumstances which created conditions of particular volatility in a region already characterized by social mobility and tenurial fluidity. These conditions were also likely to leave the recently acquired estates of the ageing and childless Sir John Fastolf particularly vulnerable.[334]

---

the handwritten postscript of Scales's letter to Fastolf, written in January possibly of 1452, saying that, if Fastolf had been as faithful and kind to him since he returned to England as he had been in France, there was no one of his estate for whom Scales would do so much. The clear implication is that this has not been the case: Magdalen College Hickling MS 104. (Gairdner's abstract completely reverses the sense of this: *PL* Gairdner, ii. 82.)

[331] Debenham was to cause Fastolf trouble again in 1455–7. Smith, 'Aspects of the Career of Sir John Fastolf', 138, 181–4, 188.   [332] See above, Ch. 4.4.

[333] See above, pp. 122–6.

[334] Fastolf was now nearly 70. P. S. Lewis remarks that for Sir Edward Hull, who challenged him over Titchwell, and for a number of other people, Fastolf's 'lands seemed easy prey and his ability to protect them diminishing': P. S. Lewis, 'Sir John Fastolf's Lawsuit over Titchwell 1448–55', *Historical Journal*, 1 (1958), 3.

In the case of the Norfolk manor of Titchwell, the courtier Sir
Edward Hull was exploiting the fact that Fastolf's title to the property
was less than watertight. Hull was the son of a west country esquire who
rose to become an esquire of the body by 1438, a feoffee of the Duchy
of Lancaster in 1443, a knight of the body by 1445, and one of the
queen's carvers by 1448.[335] It was in the autumn of 1448 that an
inquisition held in Norfolk alleged that Hull's wife Margery and her
sister were the heirs to Titchwell. Though Fastolf immediately
traversed the inquest, forcing a review of its findings, the manor had
already been taken into the king's hands, and in December Hull was
granted its farm.[336] Fastolf's other antagonist from within the household was Philip Wentworth, an esquire originally from Yorkshire who
settled in East Anglia during the 1440s. Their dispute over possession
of the manors of Beighton in Norfolk and Bradwell in Suffolk began in
November 1447, significantly the point at which Wentworth secured his
appointment as sheriff of Norfolk and Suffolk.[337] In this case, unlike
that of Titchwell, Fastolf's title seems to have been sound; however, as
we have already seen, legal title acquired by purchase was not necessarily proof against the challenge of 'atavistic' hereditary claims, and it
was a claim of this kind—that of Thomas Fastolf, heir of Sir Hugh
Fastolf from whom Sir John had bought the two manors—on which
Wentworth's challenge was based.[338] Wentworth secured a grant for his
brother-in-law Robert Constable of the wardship of Thomas Fastolf,
despite Sir John's complaint that he should have had the wardship as
the boy's guardian, and inquisitions held in 1449 then declared that
Beighton and Bradwell were rightfully part of Thomas's inheritance. As
in the case of Titchwell, Fastolf immediately traversed the inquests, and
this time managed to secure the farm of the manors himself.[339]

Fastolf therefore became a target for household men who saw opportunities for themselves in East Anglia in the volatile circumstances of
the late 1440s. A further problem facing him was that—as the Pastons
discovered when they looked to Daniel for lordship—the search for
allies by either side in a conflict might lead to disputes becoming inter-
connected. For example, Fastolf had during the 1440s rented the
manor of Caister Bardolf from the Bardolf heiresses Anne and Joan, the
latter the widow of William Phelip. When Joan Bardolf died in 1447,

[335] He held several appointments in France in the 1440s, but Lewis comments that he
seems to have been in England 'rather more than usual in the period 1447–50': 'Sir John
Fastolf's Lawsuit', 3–4.

[336] Ibid. 3; Smith, 'Litigation and Politics', 63.

[337] Smith, 'Aspects of the Career of Sir John Fastolf', 204; see above, Ch. 4.4 at n. 231.

[338] Note Anthony Smith's suggestion that Fastolf's opponents in this case 'may also have
had sympathy, and possibly information, from some branches of the Fastolf family': 'Aspects
of the Career of Sir John Fastolf', 205–7.

[339] Smith, 'Litigation and Politics', 64; 'Aspects of the Career of Sir John Fastolf', 204–5.

Fastolf became embroiled in a dispute with her executors, prominent amongst whom was John Heydon. Though the details of the conflict remain obscure, Smith comments that Fastolf regarded it as the most important of the disputes to be brought before the judicial hearings of 1450.[340] It may be no coincidence that it was in 1447 that Heydon spoke in defence of Hickling Priory in the course of its litigation with Fastolf, even though he was not acting as the Priory's attorney, and that he also seems to have helped Edward Hull and Philip Wentworth in their challenges to Fastolf from this point onwards.[341] The association between Fastolf and the Pastons is also likely, of course, to have encouraged Heydon to view Fastolf with hostility.[342]

The interaction between these various disputes has been seen as the result of the operation behind the scenes of the co-ordinating hand of Suffolk.[343] Given that there is no direct evidence to show that this was a concerted campaign of harassment initiated by the duke, this proposition requires careful scrutiny. It is important to remember that Heydon, and Fastolf's other opponents, were independent protagonists within local and national politics as well as servants and associates of Suffolk. Suffolk's will did not dictate their every action—perhaps particularly during the increasingly troubled years at the end of the decade—just as his fall in 1450 did not remove their influence at a stroke. Fastolf did not recover Titchwell, for example, until after Edward Hull's death in France in 1453; he lost Bradwell to Wentworth in the same year, and his dispute with Hickling Priory remained unresolved throughout the 1450s.[344]

Nevertheless, it is clear that Fastolf's relationship with Suffolk did deteriorate in the later 1440s. In 1447 Suffolk occupied Fastolf's manors at Dedham in northern Essex, and retained possession of the properties until his fall from power three years later.[345] Fastolf's acquisition of the estates in 1428 had been technically sound, but yet again this is a case where the claims of hereditary attachment caused

---

[340] Heydon had been associated with William Phelip at least since the early 1430s. Smith, 'Aspects of the Career of Sir John Fastolf', 156–7; see above, Ch. 4.1 at n. 57.

[341] Smith, 'Litigation and Politics', 63–5; 'Aspects of the Career of Sir John Fastolf', 195, 198, 206; Lewis, 'Sir John Fastolf's Lawsuit', 7–8.

[342] Fastolf seems to have provided the Pastons with practical assistance in their attempt to defend their property at Gresham; when Margaret Paston wrote to her husband of the need to acquire some crossbows for this purpose, probably in 1448 or 1449, she added that she supposed 'ze xuld have seche thyngis of Sere Jon Fastolf, if ze wold send to hym': *PL* Davis, i. 226 (Gairdner, ii. 101); see also her letter of 28 Feb. 1449, asking John to 'speke to Sere Jon Fastolf for the harneys that ze hadden of hym': *PL* Davis, i. 232 (Gairdner, ii. 96).

[343] Smith, 'Litigation and Politics', 63–7; 'Aspects of the Career of Sir John Fastolf', 140, 143, 195; Richmond, *The Paston Family*, 227, 234–5.

[344] Lewis, 'Sir John Fastolf's Lawsuit', 18–19; Smith, 'Litigation and Politics', 68–70; 'Aspects of the Career of Sir John Fastolf', 192, 209.

[345] Smith, 'Litigation and Politics', 66–7; 'Aspects of the Career of Sir John Fastolf', 126.

difficulties for an owner whose title was based on purchase. Suffolk's grandfather Michael de la Pole had acquired the properties, which had formerly belonged to the Ufford earls of Suffolk, by grant of Richard II, but lost them again when he was impeached in 1388.[346] As Colin Richmond has suggested, it seems that Suffolk regarded Dedham as 'going with' his earldom, much as the duke of Norfolk seems to have viewed the manors of Stockton and Geldeston when he seized them from Ralph Garneys.[347] However, the timing of Suffolk's assertion of his claim requires explanation, given that he had not troubled Fastolf's possession during the preceding two decades. It is possible that the initiative operated from the bottom up, rather than from the top down as has usually been assumed—in other words, rather than Suffolk masterminding a campaign against Fastolf, it is possible that increasing hostility between the latter and Suffolk's local associates drew the duke into more overt conflict with Fastolf than had characterized their relationship in the later 1430s and early 1440s.[348] John Heydon would be a prime suspect for this co-ordinating role; it was in 1447 that he became personally involved, as Joan Bardolf's executor, in conflict with Fastolf,[349] and encouraging Suffolk to take action at Dedham might have offered Heydon an effective way to bring pressure to bear on Fastolf in relation to other issues.

Alternatively—or perhaps simultaneously—Suffolk himself may have had his own reasons for wanting to put pressure on Fastolf. It has already been suggested that the significance of the challenge to Suffolk's rule at a local level represented by the duke of Norfolk and in particular by the household esquire Thomas Daniel in the later 1440s was compounded by the fact that Suffolk's position in central government was at the same time becoming increasingly embattled because of growing divisions over foreign policy. It may be that Suffolk's difficulties at both of these levels seemed to coincide in the person of Fastolf. As has already been demonstrated, Fastolf's acquisition of his East Anglian estate had not been intrinsically incompatible with Suffolk's lordship and the crown–Duchy network over which he established his authority, but by the later 1440s local and financial tensions between Suffolk and Fastolf had grown.[350] At the same time, Fastolf was prominent among a group of old soldiers who were increasingly disaffected with the military policies of Suffolk's government and who stood to lose heavily in

---

[346] James, 'Career and Political Influence', 231; Smith, 'Aspects of the Career of Sir John Fastolf', 128; Richmond, *The Paston Family*, 237–8.

[347] Richmond, *The Paston Family*, 238; for Norfolk, see above, pp. 110–11.

[348] Cf. Watts, *Henry VI*, 219: 'Far from being the co-ordinator of an empire of crime, Suffolk may have been the unwilling front-man for ungovernable underlings.'

[349] See above, at n. 340.

[350] See above, pp. 146–8.

terms of land and money as a result of the surrender of Maine, which was finally effected in 1448 after three years of negotiations.[351] Significantly, it was in the early part of 1447 that the previously secret plan to cede Maine was becoming more widely known, and therefore that the possibility of public opposition from men such as Fastolf began to pose a serious threat to Suffolk's position.[352] It is possible either that these circumstances prompted Suffolk to act against Fastolf in East Anglia, or that they encouraged him to respond to pressure from his servants in the region to do so.

Whether the initiative behind the difficulties in which Fastolf found himself from 1447 onwards came from above or below, or a combination of the two, it is certainly clear that his position in regional society was not one which gave him a realistic chance of defending his interests successfully against such well-connected opponents. The very reason that we know so much about Fastolf's problems in the late 1440s is that he was living in London, at his home in Southwark, as he did for most of the time between his retirement from France in 1439 and his move to his house at Caister by the summer of 1454, and he therefore had to deal with his interests in East Anglia by exchanging letters with his servants and representatives there.[353] If, as Anthony Smith has commented, 'throughout the 1440s Fastolf's influence in East Anglia was not as great as one would expect it to have been' in the light of his territorial eminence in the region,[354] this state of affairs cannot straightforwardly be attributed to hostility between Suffolk and Fastolf without also taking into account the fact that the latter was in no position to develop such influence while his personal involvement in the society and politics of the region remained so limited.[355] Suffolk had built up his lordship in the 1430s by establishing himself at the head of a broad and broadly representative regional network; his regional authority could therefore be sustained despite his prolonged, perhaps almost continual, absences in London and the Thames Valley, because it was represented and embodied by his local servants and associates.[356] Fastolf's chief East Anglian associates, on the other hand, were prin-

---

[351] Watts, *Henry VI*, 223–33; McFarlane, 'Investment of Sir John Fastolf's Profits of War', 188–9; Smith, 'Aspects of the Career of Sir John Fastolf', 122–3; Lewis, 'Sir John Fastolf's Lawsuit', 20.

[352] Watts, *Henry VI*, 227–32; C. Holmes, 'East Anglia and the Royal Court, 1440–1450', unpublished BA dissertation (Cambridge, 1993).

[353] McFarlane, 'Investment of Sir John Fastolf's Profits of War', 178; Richmond, *The Paston Family*, 243; and see *CCR 1447–54*, 398, for Fastolf described in 1452 as 'of Suthwerk, Surrey'.

[354] Smith, 'Aspects of the Career of Sir John Fastolf', 140.

[355] Though land conferred potential power, the active development and exercise of lordship was necessary to make that power a reality: see Carpenter, *Locality and Polity*, 287–9, 312–14, 358–9, and *passim*.

[356] See above, Chs. 4.1 and 4.2.

cipally a group of men with whom he had fought in France. In so far as they were part of a network during the 1440s, it was Suffolk's network; and, by the increasingly turbulent last years of the decade, whatever political coherence they might once have had as a group was all but lost.[357] Fastolf was therefore represented in the region by the lesser men who served him—men such as Thomas Howes, John Berney, William Jenney, and John Paston (although Paston too spent most of the late 1440s and early 1450s in London).[358] Though effective in terms of looking after Fastolf's business, at least in an administrative sense, this small group was in no sense an affinity with political muscle within the region. Fastolf himself was appointed to very few local commissions during the 1440s, and acted as feoffee or executor for very few members of the local gentry.[359] It is noticeable, in the context of his problems in East Anglia, that when Fastolf's title to properties he had bought in London was challenged he had no difficulty defeating his opponents, even though the property market in the capital was complex and intensely competitive, and even though his legal position in those cases was less than sound.[360] In London, where he lived and where he was politically active, he was able to defend his purchases successfully; in East Anglia, where he was not resident and where his political activity was limited, his influence was far less secure.

This last point is an important reminder that the experiences of Sir John Fastolf and of the Paston family can reveal a great deal about political society in East Anglia in the 1440s, and by extension about the governing regime as a whole, so long as we remember that they were specific experiences informed by specific circumstances. The unique evidence of the letters has encouraged both an assumption that the Pastons and their patron Fastolf were representative of the generalized experience of their class and their region, and a tendency to accept their account of the world in which they lived without determining what was distinctive about their perspective. However, it is only through an exploration of what was particular about their experience, through all the different kinds of evidence at our disposal, that the relationship between that experience and its wider context becomes clear. The com-

---

[357] See above, Ch. 4.2 at nn. 95, 97, 100, and below, Ch. 5 at nn. 9, 22, for the political affiliations of Clifton, Ogard, and Oldhall, for example.

[358] Richmond, *The Paston Family*, 227–8, 231–8.

[359] Fastolf was appointed to the Norfolk commission of the peace from 1437, but his only appointments to special commissions in the region were to inquire into uncustomed boats and merchandise in 1440 and 1442. (Fastolf owned a fleet of ships and had substantial commercial interests, particularly at Yarmouth: McFarlane, 'Investment of Sir John Fastolf's Profits of War', 195–6.) *CPR 1436–41*, 413, 586; *1441–6*, 108, 474; *1446–52*, 592. See also Smith, 'Aspects of the Career of Sir John Fastolf', 102, 105, 120–1, 140 (though note that Smith attributes Fastolf's lack of official appointments to Suffolk's hostility).

[360] Smith, 'Aspects of the Career of Sir John Fastolf', 169–80.

plexity of the Paston correspondents' character and circumstance and of their social and political relationships, something which is apparent throughout the correspondence, should raise questions about the one-dimensional villainy which is often ascribed to their opponents. Indeed, the events of 1450–1 were to demonstrate not the representative nature of the experiences of John Paston and John Fastolf, but their political isolation.

5

1450–1461
The Struggle for Control

Margaret Paston's analysis in May 1449 of the irresistible power of 'my lord of Suffolkys godelorchyp'[1] seemed to be based on sound advice. Less than a year later, however, the unthinkable had happened: Suffolk had lost his position at the head of government, leaving his affinity, whose dominance in local politics during the previous decade had been overwhelming, for the first time vulnerable and exposed. The hybrid authority which had controlled the region since 1437 was once again divided, as control of the de la Pole estates fell to the dowager duchess and her young son, and the duke of Somerset took over the guidance of Henry's government. Those who had opposed the de la Pole affinity, represented principally by Norfolk and Fastolf, lost no time in seeking to capitalize on the situation to obtain redress for their grievances and the removal of their opponents from positions of power, and, in so doing, to establish their own authority in East Anglia in place of Suffolk's.

The early months of 1450 were chaotic and confused. Suffolk was impeached on 7 February,[2] and his opponents in Norfolk saw the opportunity for which they had been waiting. On 16 April Fastolf instructed his servants to collate information concerning all the injuries done him by John Heydon over the last thirteen years, explaining that he had not taken legal action before because 'the world was alway set after his rule'.[3] Clearly, the world now seemed to be changing. By the end of the first week in May Suffolk was dead, and John Paston, prominent among those with grievances against Tuddenham and Heydon, was being advised that 'yef ye purpose to come hydre [to parliament] to put vp youre bylles, ye may come now in a good tyme; for now euery man that hath any, they put theyme now jnne'.[4] On 1 August, a general commission of *oyer* and *terminer* was appointed for

---

[1] See above, Ch. 4.5 at n. 299.

[2] *PL* Gairdner, ii. 120–7. A month later, however, it was being reported in Norfolk that 'the Duke of Suffolk is pardonyd and hath his men azen waytyng up-on hym, and is rytz wel at ese and mery, and is in the Kyngys godegrase and in the gode conseyt of all the lordys as well as ever he was': *PL* Davis, i. 237 (Gairdner, ii. 136).

[3] *PL* Gairdner, ii. 137.

[4] *PL* Davis, ii. 37 (Gairdner, ii. 148).

Norfolk and Suffolk, headed by the duke of Norfolk and John de Vere, earl of Oxford.[5] For the first time in sixteen years, the commission of the peace appointed in Norfolk in October included neither Tuddenham nor Heydon,[6] and Tuddenham also lost his place on the bench in Suffolk, as did the de la Pole steward John Ulveston.[7]

Nevertheless, by the beginning of 1451 it was clear that, despite these setbacks, Suffolk's affinity was surviving the loss of its lord, and that, though his East Anglian servants had lost much of their influence in government, their local authority remained substantial. In September 1450, for example, John Heydon was in a position to help Osbert Mundford recover the manor of Bradeston from Thomas Daniel, who still enjoyed Norfolk's support.[8] In the following month, rumours abounded of the efforts of Tuddenham and Heydon to secure themselves the favour of those who had replaced Suffolk about the king, notably the duke of York, about whom Judge Yelverton sent word to John Paston that 'ze shuld not spare but gete yow hese goodlordshep'. It was said that Tuddenham and Heydon were offering more than £2,000 for Sir William Oldhall's good lordship, and that Heydon would spend another £1,000 'rather thanne he shuld fayle of a shiref this yeer comyng for his entent'.[9] Legal manœuvres continued throughout the winter,[10] but by March Suffolk's men had seized the initiative. At the beginning of that month it was reported that the earl of Oxford, William Yelverton, and John Paston had been indicted in Kent for maintenance of the commission of *oyer* and *terminer* in Norfolk, news which served to encourage local rumours that Tuddenham and Heydon 'shuld haue a-geyn the rewle in this contre assmych as euer thei had, or more'. They were said to be 'well cheryshid' with the king, and rumour had it that Heydon was to be knighted.[11] In April Fastolf was instructing his chaplain Thomas Howes to keep his allies in Norfolk steadfast in the face of the support Tuddenham and Heydon would muster at the

---

[5] *CPR 1446–52*, 388.

[6] *CPR 1446–52*, 592.

[7] *CPR 1446–52*, 595. Tuddenham had been a JP in Suffolk only since 1449; Ulveston had served consistently since 1443.

[8] *PL* Gairdner, ii. 145. In the indictments brought against him in Norwich that autumn, Heydon was accused of leading an insurrection; he claimed that the charge was a malicious misrepresentation of his assistance of Mundford: KB27/758 Rex rot. 9. For Daniel and Norfolk, and the Bradeston dispute, see below, pp. 165–8, 172.

[9] *PL* Davis, ii. 47–51 (Gairdner, ii. 174–6, 181). Oldhall's political origins lay with the East Anglian Duchy-based connection, for which, see above, Ch. 3.2 n. 104, but he was by this time closely associated with York.

[10] See *PL* Gairdner, ii. 145, for Worcestre's notes of sessions held during this period at Swaffham, Norwich, and Lynn.

[11] *PL* Davis, i. 239–41; ii. 67–8 (Gairdner, ii. 223–5, 227–8, 230). In January Oxford had written to the sheriff expressing his displeasure at reports 'that trow favour in your office to the pople that hath compleyned by many and grete horible billes agayn certeyn persones shuld not be shewid at this next Sessions at Lenn': *PL* Gairdner, ii. 203–4.

sessions,[12] but all such encouragement proved inadequate. The success of Suffolk's men at the final sessions at Walsingham on 3 May 1451 was overwhelming.[13] By February 1452 Tuddenham and Heydon were again being appointed to special commissions in the region, and three years later both men were reinstated as JPs in Norfolk.[14]

This survival of the de la Pole affinity seems remarkable in the context of analyses of Suffolk's power which argue that his government was based on control of a court clique, and that this corrupt regime allowed his followers in East Anglia briefly to usurp the natural sphere of influence of the Mowbray dukes of Norfolk. However, if Suffolk's affinity is seen instead as a broadly based connection which owed as much to his association with, and inheritance of, a traditional pattern of authority that had developed during the first two reigns of the century as it did to his power in central government, its survival is more readily comprehensible. Suffolk's lordship had undoubtedly bestowed unprecedented eminence on his closest East Anglian associates, but it had not *created* their local influence. Thomas Tuddenham's political pedigree, as we have seen, reached back to these earlier roots; thanks to his connections with John Wodehous and Thomas Beaufort, he had been an effective presence in the region before Suffolk had even begun to make his mark as a local lord.[15] Correspondingly, Suffolk's fall did not remove the entire source of his servants' authority. Though Tuddenham was forced to surrender his position in the central administration of the Duchy,[16] neither he nor John Heydon lost their offices in East Anglia, and they therefore retained control of the substantial influence which the Duchy conferred in Norfolk.[17]

The importance of this Duchy connection was demonstrated at the sessions of May 1451. First, Justice Prisot, who had been retained by the Duchy as legal counsel at least since 1445, moved the location of the hearings. Thomas Howes attributed this decision to the fact that if they 'had be holden at Norwich as they bygonne, he supposed it shuld

---

[12] *PL* Gairdner, ii. 233.

[13] Ibid., ii. 145, 239.

[14] *CPR 1446–52*, 537; *1452–61*, 671–2. By Sept. 1452, when another *oyer* and *terminer* commission was appointed in Norfolk headed by the duke of Norfolk and the earl of Oxford, the other commissioners included both Tuddenham and Heydon: *CPR 1452–61*, 55. For their return to the peace commission, see below, at n. 124.   [15] See above, p. 80.

[16] Tuddenham was replaced as chief steward of the North Parts, an office which he had held jointly with Suffolk, by Lord Cromwell. This transfer of office did not, however, take place until 1451. Heydon had been deputy chief steward in the north, but had surrendered the appointment in 1446. DL37/19 no. 41; R. Somerville, *History of the Duchy of Lancaster*, i (London, 1953), 425.

[17] Anthony Smith, for example, attributes Heydon's readiness to ignore a writ *certiorari* obtained by Fastolf in May 1450 to 'the confidence Heydon placed in the power and authority he derived from [Duchy] office' (in the hundred of South Erpingham): 'Aspects of the Career of Sir John Fastolf', unpublished D.Phil. thesis (Oxford, 1986), 164.

nat so fast passe to th'entent of Tudenham and Heydon and ther felawes . . . but enjorned to Walsingham, wher they have grettist rule'.[18] Walsingham, in northern Norfolk, lay in the heart of Duchy territory, and according to Howes was 'the most parcial place of alle the shire'. There Tuddenham and Heydon had gathered a reported 400 horsemen, as well as all their 'frendez, knyghteys, and esquiers, and gentilmen that wolde in nowise do other wise than they wolde'. To oppose this impressive array, 'ther was nat one of the pleyntyfs ner compleynuantez ther', apart from the persistent John Paston.[19] Unsurprisingly, their grievances did not find a sympathetic hearing. Howes reported that 'Prisot wolde suffre no man that was lerned to speke for the pleyntyfs, but took it as a venom, and took them by the nose at every thred woord whiche myght weel by knowe for open parcialte'.[20]

Moreover, though Tuddenham and Heydon were the most prominent of Suffolk's local servants, in terms both of the authority they enjoyed during the 1440s and therefore of the hostility they provoked in 1450, the deep roots of the de la Pole affinity spread widely throughout East Anglian society, and this broader network suffered little in practical terms from the events of 1449–50. Indeed, it was these men who made up the fabric of local government, and the duke of Norfolk's following was not extensive or authoritative enough to offer an alternative hierarchy. For example, though Tuddenham, Heydon, and Ulveston lost their positions on the commission of the peace, Lord Scales, Miles Stapleton, John Heveningham, Thomas Brewes, John

---

[18] Somerville, *History of the Duchy*, 451; *PL* Gairdner, ii. 238. Norwich was a focus of particular hostility to Tuddenham and Heydon and their closest associates, largely, apparently, because Heydon, as recorder of the city in 1437, had become involved in two long-standing disputes, one between rival factions within the city government, and the other between the city corporation and the cathedral priory over their competing jurisdictions. The latter dispute (which had been in progress at least since 1417 and was not settled until 1524) resulted in the liberties of the city being taken into the king's hands between 1443 and 1447. Heydon's involvement with one of the Norwich factions and his close association with the prior, John Heverlond, inspired a series of indictments presented in 1450 by the opposing faction in the city, alleging that Heydon, with Tuddenham, Ulveston, and others, had conspired to maintain the prior's case, to subvert justice in the city, and to extort money from the citizens: KB9/267 mm. 23–5; for the Norwich disputes, see P. C. Maddern, *Violence and Social Order* (Oxford, 1992), 175–205, and R. L. Storey, *End of the House of Lancaster* (London, 1966), appendix III.

[19] *PL* Gairdner, ii. 239.

[20] Ibid. Tuddenham, Heydon, and John Andrew had, for example, been indicted at Norwich before Norfolk, Oxford, and Yelverton on 2 Mar. 1451 for having in Sept. 1438 extorted £105 from John Fastolf by threatening and assaulting three of his servants; on 3 May, before Scales and Prisot at Walsingham, they were acquitted. Similarly, Heydon, Andrew, and John Ulveston were indicted on the same day at Norwich before Norfolk and his associates for having in Apr. 1449 broken Fastolf's close at Beighton; and were then acquitted at the Walsingham hearing before Scales and Prisot: KB27/766 Coram Rege roti. 90–90v; KB27/790 Coram Rege rot. 58.

Harleston, Philip Wentworth, and even Reginald Rous did not.[21] The *oyer* and *terminer* commission of August 1450 itself included Scales, Heveningham, and Andrew Ogard as well as Norfolk, Oxford, and Fastolf; though Ogard was connected with both Fastolf and the duke of York, he had also been associated in a local context with Suffolk.[22] Such apparent ambiguity was common, and Norfolk was therefore forced to seek the support of many gentlemen whose connections with Suffolk, though very real, had not been too unequivocally intimate. In August 1450, for example, Miles Stapleton and Thomas Brewes were apparently co-operating closely with Norfolk and Oxford.[23]

Though such men were probably more than willing to distance themselves from Suffolk, Tuddenham, and Heydon during the uncertain months of 1450, their support subsequently ebbed away from Norfolk and his followers, reverting instead to previous affiliations as the political tide turned in the spring of the following year. 'To knowe some of your feynt frendes', Howes wrote to Fastolf in May 1451 in a letter describing the Walsingham sessions that acquitted Tuddenham and Heydon, 'at that tyme that my Lord Norffolk sat at Norwich up on the oyer determyner, Sir John Hevyngham myht nat fynde it in his hert to go iiij. furlong from his duellyng to the shirehouse, but now he cowd ryde from Norwich to Walsyngham to syt as one of the Commyssioners.' Heveningham was apparently not alone in this defection. Howes continued: 'As to the rule of other, that ye wolde have supposed your wellewillers, how they have byhavyd them at Walsyngham, I shall sende yow woord . . . But this I knowe well, that they founde none obstacle ner impedyment in ther consciens in all your matter.'[24] By June, Stapleton too had clearly demonstrated his allegiance to the de la Pole interest, becoming joint custodian of Suffolk's lands.[25]

This continuing support among the gentry was paralleled at a higher level. Suffolk's regime had relied fundamentally on the support of the nobility, but that support had been compromised by the deteriorating situation in France in 1448–9, and by the following year noble consensus could no longer sustain the position in government of Suffolk himself. John Watts has suggested that the events of 1450 were the result of a

[21] *CPR 1446–52*, 592, 595. For Suffolk's associations with this group, see above, Ch. 4.2. For Wentworth, see above, Ch. 4.4 at n. 231.

[22] See above, n. 5; Smith, 'Aspects of the Career of Sir John Fastolf', 103.

[23] *PL* Davis, ii. 42–4 (Gairdner, ii. 163–5).

[24] *PL* Gairdner, ii. 239.

[25] *CFR 1445–52*, 220; see below, at n. 32. Andrew Ogard, too, seems to have abandoned his associations with York in favour of his connections at court by the beginning of 1452. P. A. Johnson comments that during the later 1440s Ogard had 'drifted away from York towards the royal household': P. A. Johnson, *Duke Richard of York* (Oxford, 1988), 90; J. L. Watts, *Henry VI and the Politics of Kingship* (Cambridge, 1996), 289 n. 123.

dramatic divergence between popular conceptions of the governing regime, shared and articulated by some of the Commons in parliament, and the principal concerns of the lords. He argues that by early 1450 the preservation of order was the consideration uppermost in the minds of the nobility, as well as the masking of their own role in making the policies which had provoked such widespread discontent.[26] In the spring of 1450, in the face of an explosion of popular anger, these concerns dictated the sacrifice of Suffolk, but they did not dictate the abandonment of the underlying political structures which had made government possible during the previous decade—in fact, quite the reverse, given that the fundamental problem of the king's inadequacy remained, in a more acute form than ever now that it had been exposed by Suffolk's fall. Despite the traumatic events of 1450, therefore, the attempt to constitute royal authority on the king's behalf through the co-operation in government of the greater nobility and of the royal household continued, and action against Suffolk's adherents was severely limited.[27]

The survival at a local level of the de la Pole affinity as a coherent group and its acquisition of new noble leadership is entirely consistent with this analysis. In the summer of 1450, the duke of Somerset assumed the leadership of the king's government by securing the confidence and participation both of the nobility and of the household establishment.[28] The duke seems to have reconstituted the basis of power which had sustained Suffolk's rule as best he could, while accommodating the exigencies of a political context rendered increasingly complex by the crisis of 1450.[29] If Somerset had essentially inherited Suffolk's role in government, albeit a role significantly altered by the effects of the recent crisis, there was every reason why the de la Pole affinity, with its substantial links through the Duchy to the authority of the crown, should look to the duke for support.

There was certainly no 'hostile' attempt to appropriate or manipulate Suffolk's territorial interests. Custody of the de la Pole estates during the minority of his son was committed in May 1450 to the dowager duchess, who seems to have played a key role in maintaining the affinity both in the immediate aftermath of her husband's fall and during the following years.[30] By the end of the year, moreover, Lord Scales was prepared to extend his lordship openly to Tuddenham and Heydon,[31]

[26] Watts, *Henry VI*, 233–4, 240–8.

[27] Ibid. 260–6, 282–3.

[28] Johnson, *Duke Richard of York*, 83, 89; Watts, *Henry VI*, 282–90.

[29] Watts, *Henry VI*, 284–94.

[30] *CFR 1445–52*, 154; C. Richmond, *The Paston Family in the Fifteenth Century: The First Phase* (Cambridge, 1990), 240–1.

[31] *PL* Gairdner, ii. 189–90. Their opponents seem not to have been entirely certain about the strength of this association, while apparently fearing the worst, since Fastolf reports that 'it ys lyke that grete labour and speciall pursute shall be made to the Lord Scalys that he wolle

with whom he had, of course, been frequently associated during the previous decade. On 1 June 1451, custody of the de la Pole lands which had not been assigned in dower to the duchess was transferred to Scales and Miles Stapleton, whose mainpernors for the grant were Suffolk's former servants John Ulveston and Humphrey Forster of Ewelme.[32] This grant effectively marked the re-emergence of the de la Pole affinity, remarkably unscathed at a local level, if somewhat bruised in a national context,[33] under the new leadership of Scales and the duchess. By 1453–4, the duchess's accounts included payments for the service of a familiar roll-call of old associates: Tuddenham, Heydon, Rous, Ulveston, Andrew, William Harleston, Miles Stapleton, John Hevening-ham, Thomas Brewes, and Philip Wentworth.[34] The local political connection which these men embodied long pre-dated the regime of the 1440s. Although those amongst them whose links with Suffolk himself had not been so close as to be incontrovertible might have prevaricated during the dangerous months of 1450, longstanding associations were rapidly reassembled.

The breadth of the East Anglian gentry network on which the de la Pole interest continued to draw and the noble support it was able to attract after 1450 suggest that it may be necessary to re-examine the local campaign against Suffolk's men in 1450–1, which has been characterized as an 'East Anglian movement . . . of general complaint', in which Sir John Fastolf 'encouraged and helped the common people to seek redress along with him' for 'the way Suffolk's associates had oppressed the ordinary people'.[35] Popular hostility to Suffolk and his local representatives does seem to have existed in the region; Yelverton told Fastolf in November 1450, for example, that 'here ys a

meynteyn the seid Tuddenham and Heydon in all he can or may' at the Lynn sessions in Jan. 1451, and John Bocking writes 'God graunte . . . that an outas and clamour be made upon the Lord Scalez, preying hym for well of the cuntre, neyther susteyn ner help hym ner Heydon in no wyse': *PL* Gairdner, ii. 196, 206.

[32] *CFR 1445–52*, 220. Duchess Alice had been assigned dower on 24 Dec. 1450. In November she had also been granted the keeping of the disputed manor of Stockton (for which, see above, pp. 110–11). In the spring of 1453, custody of the de la Pole estates was restored to the duchess, who had successfully petitioned for the implementation of letters patent granted in 1444 which declared that, if the duke died, his wife should have custody of the heir and his inheritance: *CCR 1447–54*, 209–15, 217; *CFR 1445–52*, 181; *Rot. Parl.*, v. 394.

[33] John Watts mentions the duchess of Suffolk as one of those who 'were not restored to obvious favour for some time' by Somerset's regime after 1450, for example. Thomas Tuddenham lost his office as keeper of the great wardrobe at the end of 1450. However, his successor was William Cotton, with whom he had been associated in the administration of the Duchy for some years, and by July 1451 Tuddenham was able to secure a pardon for all but £200 of the £1,400 fine which had been awarded against him in Norfolk: Watts, *Henry VI*, 289; *CPR 1446–52*, 408, 455; G. E. Morey, 'East Anglian Society in the Fifteenth Century', unpublished Ph.D. thesis (London, 1951), 444.

[34] BL Eg. Roll 8779 mm. 8–9.

[35] Smith, 'Aspects of the Career of Sir John Fastolf', 147–8.

marveyllous disposed contree, and manye evylle wylled peple to Sir Thomas Tuddenham and Heydon'.[36] However, the detailed reports in the Paston letters of the machinations of Suffolk's servants should not obscure the fact that their opponents were undertaking parallel operations to orchestrate proceedings against them. Whatever judgement we make about the objectivity of the Paston correspondents' analysis of the mood of the commons, for example, it is clear that wherever popular hostility did exist, it was being harnessed and orchestrated in the interests of their campaign.[37]

William Wayte, for example, writing to John Paston in October 1450, recommended that 'Swhafham men be warned to mete with my seyd lord [of York] . . . and putte sum bylle vn-to my lord of Syr Thomas Tudenham, Heydon, and Prentys, and crye owte on hem . . . and calle hem extorcionners, and pray my lord that he wyll do sharp execucyon vp-on hem'. William Yelverton's advice, reported in the same letter, was that the mayor, aldermen, and commons of Norwich should lobby York in like manner, 'and late yt be don in the most lamentabyl wyse; for, syr, but yf my lord here sum fowle tales of hem and sum hyddows noys and crye, by my feyth thei arne ellys lyke to come to grace'.[38] This appeal to concepts of the common weal was reinforced by emphasis on the threat of public disorder. Fastolf was trying to arrange that the duke of Norfolk and 'alle knyghtes and escuyers of the same cuntre' should inform the council 'how the cuntre of Norffolk and Suffolk stonde right wildely withowt a mene may be that iustice be hadde', in order to achieve the specific objectives that Stapleton should be appointed as sheriff and that the sessions of *oyer* and *terminer* should be held as planned.[39]

[36] *PL* Gairdner, ii. 189 (although it is also clear that this is exactly what Fastolf would have wanted to hear).

[37] See above, Ch. 4.5, for discussion of the reliability of the evidence of the Paston letters. In this case, however, it seems more than possible, in view of the popular uprisings which swept the south of England in 1450, that the correspondence does accurately reflect the tenor of public opinion. Nevertheless, this conclusion should not obscure the manipulation of popular feeling by Fastolf and his associates detailed below.

[38] *PL* Davis, ii. 47–8 (Gairdner, ii. 175).

[39] *PL* Davis, ii. 51 (Gairdner, ii. 182). (For Stapleton's brief association with Norfolk, Fastolf, and their supporters, see above, at n. 23.) The risk was, of course, that if the specific objectives were not achieved and the dire predictions of disorder then failed to materialize, the credibility of those who had made them would be seriously undermined, a risk articulated in a memorandum of Paston's from this time: 'For as meche as the oyer and termyner is thus restreynyd, not wythstandyng the wrytyngys and all the materis vtterid be my lord of Oxenford, but if ther folow sumwhat lyke to the perell lyke to be conceyved be maters that so worn vtterid and be the seyd wrytyngys ellis shal it gretly sowndyn ageyns the worchep and the weel of all the personys, lordis and other, that eyther have wreten or vtterid owght, and lyke wyse of hem in whos name seche materis hath ben vtterid soo that hereaftyre whan they have ryght gret nede to be herd and to be wel spedde they shul the rather fayle thereof bothen, and here enemyes the heyer vp and the more bold, &c.' *PL* Davis, ii. 525–6 (Gairdner, ii. 213).

By the end of the year, Scales was attempting to undermine this political campaign by calming public criticism of Suffolk's men: '. . . the Lord Scales meyntenyth Syr Thomas Tudenham in all that he may goodly, but he wyll not awowyt', Wayte reported on 3 January, 'but he shall come don to the oyre determinere sekerly, and for to make an ende atwex Syr T. Tudenham and Swafham . . . And so my mayster [Yelverton] vnderstandeth that yf Swafham and he werne accorded that thei shuld sette lytyll be Norwych.'[40] This letter makes explicitly clear the vital role in the plans of Fastolf and his allies played by a credible claim to represent the common weal, both to convince the government that action, in the form of redress of grievance, was necessary to pre-serve order, and also to rebut charges that their campaign was partisan contrivance. Yelverton's response to the possible pacification of Swaffham was that the supposedly spontaneous 'public outcry' should be further reinforced. He instructed Paston to ensure 'that ther be atte Lenn a sufficiaunt fellawshep to-gedyr and that ther be madde a grette noyse vp-on the Lord Scales bothe of Tudenham and Heydon and for all thoo that arne of that sekte'. Wayte reported that, if the bailiff of Swaffham had not told the council that unless judicial action proceeded 5,000 Norfolk men were ready to rebel, Tuddenham and the others would have been pardoned, 'for ther was made a gret suggestion that it hadde be don of grette malyce'.[41]

This carefully orchestrated campaign allowed Fastolf, under the aegis of Norfolk, and his allies—those who had failed to establish them-selves within the de la Pole affinity, or who had come into conflict with the local interests of Suffolk and his men—to exploit popular hostility to Suffolk's leading supporters in order to reinforce a campaign prompted by their personal grievances. Suffolk's place at the head of government undoubtedly allowed his affinity to wield immense power in local politics, power which his followers could and did exploit to promote and enrich themselves, but, as has already been suggested, the Paston-derived picture of the universal oppression of regional society may be misleading. In this context, a document printed by Gairdner which bears the heading 'These be names of men that arne myschevesly oppressed and wronged by Sir T. Tudenham and Heydon and here adherentes' is particularly telling.[42] It forms part of the evidence gathered by the Pastons and their associates during 1450 and 1451 as they sought to demonstrate the wrongs done by Suffolk's men during the preceding decade and to secure the punishment of those responsible, a campaign in which no stone was apparently left

---

[40] *PL* Davis, ii. 60–1 (Gairdner, ii. 207–8). By 9 Jan. Scales's mediation appeared to have failed: *PL* Davis, ii. 63 (Gairdner, ii. 211).
[41] *PL* Davis, ii. 60–1 (Gairdner, ii. 207–8).
[42] *PL* Gairdner, ii. 216–7.

unturned, as accusations were brought forward of crimes dating back as far as the late 1430s.[43] The list begins promisingly enough with the names of Fastolf and Justice Yelverton, and rapidly moves through familiar gentry names such as Paston, Berney, and Jenney. However, it is not long before the catalogue loses much of its impetus; names which could have carried only very little weight appear beside the generalized 'Homines de Swafham', and the list concludes with the far from triumphant 'Item, many men indyted in Norffolk and Suffolk be Tudenham and Heydon, &c.'. It is striking that the names cited form a compact group of associates all intimately connected with the Pastons at this point, and who therefore feature prominently in the correspondence. The document seems therefore to support the contention that the grievances which this small group took such pains to present as general and concerned with universal justice were in fact much more specific and personal. In the case of the Norfolk manor of Rydon, for example—the 'conquest' that was 'the first purpose of Tudenham and Heydon whils thei regned'—all the surviving evidence indicates that it was Thomas Daniel's occupation (enforced at least in October 1450 by a 'garyson') which was the usurpation, and that if Tuddenham and Heydon were helping their friend Henry Wodehous to recover the manor, they were not without justice on their side.[44]

Indeed, overt demonstration of the fact that political manipulation and opportunism were not the sole preserve of the de la Pole affinity is provided by Thomas Daniel's response to Suffolk's fall. Daniel, characteristically, played no part in the lengthy attempts to bring Tuddenham and Heydon to justice for their alleged crimes. Instead, he pursued his policy of self-aggrandizement in opposition to Suffolk's affinity in East Anglia, which had first surfaced in his appropriation of the Wodehous lands,[45] in a policy of direct action. He embarked on a second territorial dispute in which he was again the aggressor and Suffolk's men again defenders of the wronged party. The manor of Bradeston in eastern Norfolk had long been associated with Duchy and de la Pole interests. By the beginning of the century the manor, which had originally belonged to the Caston family, had descended to the Carbonells of Badingham in Suffolk, who were associated with the local crown–Duchy connection through their service to Thomas Beaufort.[46] When Sir John Carbonell made his will in 1423 he left a bequest to his

---

[43] These included charges that Tuddenham and Heydon were 'conspiring' together as early as 1434–5, which seems implausible given the relatively uneasy relationship between Suffolk and Phelip, their respective lords, until 1437: *PL* Davis, ii. 526–7 (Gairdner, ii. 214–15); KB9/267 mm. 25, 61; KB9/272 mm. 3–4; see above, pp. 88–92.

[44] See above, pp. 120–2; *PL* Davis, ii. 45–6, 48 (Gairdner, ii. 173–4, 176).

[45] See above, pp. 120–2.

[46] Both Sir John Carbonell and his son Richard were members of Beaufort's household: J. H. Harvey (ed.), *William Worcestre: Itineraries* (Oxford, 1969), 355.

fellow Beaufort retainer William Phelip;[47] four years later Sir John's heir Richard granted Bradeston to Thomas Tuddenham, with whom he too had shared membership of Beaufort's household.[48] Tuddenham's tenure at this point was brief, since Sir Richard's death in 1430 was followed swiftly by that of his son, and the estate passed to John Berney of Reedham, the right heir of the Castons, who settled the manor in 1435 on his eldest son Thomas by a feoffment to trustees who included John Heydon, John Heveningham, Miles Stapleton, and Thomas Brewes.[49] When Thomas died in 1441, only a year after his father, his son was still a minor. Custody of Bradeston first passed to the bishop of Norwich, under whose authority Heydon was acting as steward of the manor in the early 1440s.[50] When the bishop died in 1445 the keeping of the manor was acquired by Suffolk,[51] but by 1447 Bradeston had been granted to a group of trustees including Thomas Tuddenham and Osbert Mundford, the stepfather of the heir John Berney.[52] Daniel's decision to seize this manor,[53] with its immediate importance to key members of the de la Pole connection and its longer association with members of the crown–Duchy network, represented not merely

[47] Phelip's manor of Dennington lay only a couple of miles away from Badingham: Richmond, *The Paston Family*, 151, 151 n.; see above, Ch. 3.2 n. 104.

[48] Richmond, *The Paston Family*, 151, 152 n.; BL Add. Roll 26849 mm. 6, 8. Tuddenham and Richard Carbonell were related by marriage. There is some uncertainty about the exact identity of Carbonell's wife, but Colin Richmond convincingly suggests that she was the sister of Tuddenham's wife Alice Wodehous. Tuddenham was supervisor of Sir Richard's will: Richmond, *The Paston Family*, 152–3 n.

[49] NRO NCC Reg. Doke, fos. 157–8; BL Add. Roll 26849 m. 18v; Richmond, *The Paston Family*, 152–4. For the de la Pole associations of Heveningham, Stapleton, and Brewes, see above, Ch. 4.2 at nn. 95, 98.

[50] The bishop is recorded as holding his first court in the manor because of the minority of the heir less than a fortnight after Thomas Berney's death. John Heydon's stewardship is noted on the court rolls of 1442 and 1444: BL Add. Roll 26849 mm. 25–7.

[51] E. B. Fryde, D. E. Greenway, S. Porter, and I. Roy (eds.), *Handbook of British Chronology*, 3rd edn. (London, 1986), 262; BL Add. Roll 26849 m. 31 (first court held by Suffolk, Jan. 1446).

[52] Mundford held one third of the manor as part of the dower of his wife, Thomas Berney's widow Elizabeth, and the remaining two-thirds jointly with the other trustees, during the minority of Elizabeth's son John. Suits were therefore brought against Daniel in King's Bench in the names of both Mundford and John Berney. BL Add. Roll 26849 mm. 32, 37; NRO NCC Reg. Doke, fos. 157–8; F. Blomefield, *An Essay towards a Topographical History of the County of Norfolk* (London, 1805–10), vii. 217–18, and xi. 125; KB27/766 Coram Rege roti. 46v, 55v; KB27/770 Coram Rege rot. 59v; KB27/790 Coram Rege rot. 102v; *PL* Davis, ii. 78–9 (Gairdner, ii. 256–7).

[53] The basis of Daniel's claim to Bradeston has proved difficult to recover, but on the evidence of his behaviour over the Wodehous lands, it need not have been substantial. His interest in Bradeston may have been prompted by the fact that Robert Lethum, one of his closest local supporters (for whom, see below, pp. 173–4), held lands as of the manor of Bradeston at Wilton-by-Blofield which lay close by. Lethum was consistently in trouble at Bradeston's manorial court from at least 1447 for offences such as encroachment and enclosure, and consistently failed to appear to answer the charges, both of which circumstances indicate that he was challenging the authority of the lords of the manor: BL Add. Roll 26849 mm. 24, 32, 34, 36, 37v, 39, 39v, 40.

opportunistic acquisitiveness but a profound challenge to the authority of Suffolk's men at a time when they found themselves suddenly vulnerable.[54]

By April 1450 word had reached Mundford that Daniel intended to claim the property by a forcible entry. Scales, who was shortly to emerge as the new lord of Suffolk's affinity, and whose tenant Mundford was, professed to believe that Daniel was 'come in-to this cuntre for non other cause but for to haue such as the Kyng hath gifen hym in Rysyng', but made it clear that he would act against him if it proved otherwise.[55] Despite Daniel's assurances to Scales that he would 'be wel gouerned in tyme commyng', he entered Bradeston shortly afterwards.[56] On 7 September, Mundford reclaimed the manor with the help of John Heydon, and by 6 October William Wayte considered that 'there is non other remedy but deth for Danyell'.[57] However, around this time Daniel was able to secure the support of the earl of Oxford as his pledge for a court summons.[58] Only slightly more than a year later he had recovered his position to such an extent that he was reported to have secured the good lordship not only of the duke of Somerset but also of Lord Scales himself, a development which was rumoured to offer the prospect of an accommodation with Tuddenham and Heydon and even the possibility that 'he shall be suffred to entre in-to Brayston and kepe it'.[59] The agreement, perhaps unsurprisingly, failed to materialize, and in February 1452 Daniel again took the manor by force, this time claiming the support of the duke of York. The latter, however, refused to be implicated in Daniel's ambitions and

[54] John Paston's association with Mundford via his relationship with the Berneys meant that, in this dispute, he and the much reviled Tuddenham and Heydon were unlikely allies: *PL* Davis, ii. 78–9 (Gairdner, ii. 256–7); Richmond, *The Paston Family*, 137, 155.

[55] *PL* Davis, ii. 34–5 (Gairdner, ii. 137–8). For Daniel's office at Castle Rising, see above, Ch. 4.4 at n. 217.

[56] The entry was made during the Leicester parliament, which was held in May and June 1450: *PL* Davis, ii. 35 (Gairdner, ii. 138); *PL* Gairdner, ii. 145, 256 n.

[57] *PL* Gairdner ii. 145; *PL* Davis, ii. 48 (Gairdner, ii. 176).

[58] Oxford bound himself in 100 marks to produce Daniel in the Wodehous case cited above, Ch. 4.4 n. 219. The earl was pardoned payment for Daniel's non-appearance: *CPR 1446–52*, 413.

[59] Richard Southwell, writing on 18 Dec., remarked further that 'whethir it be thus or non I can not say. Neuerthelesse me thinketh ye shall sone knowe if Mounford will agree that he shall entre in-to Brayston, and if that be trewe all the remenaunt shall seme the more likly': *PL* Davis, ii. 76–7 (Gairdner, ii. 254–5). It is presumably to this brief period that a letter among the Magdalen College MSS should be assigned, in which Scales asks Sir John Fastolf to show his 'goode maistershippe' to John Dowebyggyng (whom Scales describes as 'my servaunt' but who is consistently encountered elsewhere in Daniel's service; see below, n. 85), who had been outlawed for debt because he was bound to Fastolf on Daniel's behalf in the sum of £100. There is no indication in the letter of the year in which it was written, but the date of 8 Jan. means that 1452 is plausible, since it falls between Daniel's reported association with Scales in Dec. 1451 and his re-entry into Bradeston in Feb. 1452, which marked the re-opening of hostilities with the de la Pole connection: Magdalen College Hickling MS 104; *PL* Gairdner, ii. 82.

immediately disavowed any interest in the manor.[60] By the following May all suggestion of a *rapprochement* with Scales had disappeared.[61] In November 1453 Mundford was back in possession; by 1459 Daniel had apparently been convicted of trespass against Mundford and fined almost £70.[62] The next mention of the matter in the surviving correspondence dates from November 1460, five months after Mundford's execution at Calais, when his family learned 'that Danyell is comen to Rysyng Castell and hes men make her bost that her mastre shal be a-yene at Brayston wythinne shorte tyme'.[63]

In this case, as in the dispute over the Wodehous lands, the de la Pole affinity responded to, rather than represented, a policy of aggressive self-aggrandizement. Moreover, this situation seems to be broadly representative of the pattern throughout the 1440s, when—with the notable exception of the assault on Gresham—the worst excesses of disorder were provoked by Daniel's ambition and Norfolk's misjudgements.[64] It would appear, therefore, that the proceedings against Suffolk's servants in 1450–1 represented the efforts of a small group of landowners to obtain redress not for universal wrongs, but for their specific grievances against members of a broad grouping whose longstanding local dominance had been further reinforced by Suffolk's eminence in national government during the 1440s. In the prosecution of these efforts, they looked to the lordship of the duke of Norfolk, for whom the fall of Suffolk represented the opportunity finally to make his claim to regional rule effective. However, just as Fastolf, Yelverton, and their allies were defeated by the resources and resilience of the de la Pole affinity, so Norfolk's success proved to be extremely limited.

In this context, it is worth re-examining in some detail a proclamation made by the duke during this period.[65] Norfolk declares that he has

---

[60] *PL* Davis, ii. 77–8. Indictments were brought against Daniel by Mundford and John Berney in King's Bench in the Michaelmas term of 1452: see above, n. 52.

[61] The bishop of Norwich reported that Scales was well disposed towards John Paston, 'and wol do [for] yow that he can, so that ye wold for-sake Danyell': *PL* Davis, ii. 81 (Gairdner, ii. 265).

[62] *PL* Davis, i. 79 (Gairdner, ii. 312–13); KB29/88 m. 33.

[63] *PL* Gairdner, i. 185; *PL* Davis, i. 262 (Gairdner, iii. 53, where the letter is misdated to 1455); Richmond, *The Paston Family*, 155. Daniel's continued tenure of Castle Rising is as obscure as the original grant. On 4 Mar. 1456, after Cromwell's death (the point at which Daniel was to have first taken office there according to the terms of his grant, which he had clearly pre-empted), custody of the lands of the lordship of Rising was granted for 20 years to Henry Bourchier and Thomas Sharnburne, by mainprise of Henry Tuddenham of Oxburgh; in June of the same year, Scales was appointed to the keeping of the castle, with an instruction that he should live there for its safe-keeping. Nevertheless, in 1457 and 1458 Daniel was still being referred to as 'of Rysyng Castle'. However, note that Daniel apparently abandoned his hostility to Scales and the former Suffolk affinity in the later 1450s. *CFR 1452–61*, 152; *CPR 1452–61*, 287, 396–7; *PL* Gairdner, iii. 133; see below, pp. 183–4.

[64] See above, Chs. 4.3 and 4.4.

[65] *PL* Gairdner, ii. 258–9. Gairdner suggests that 'the intended royal visit to Norfolk mentioned in the end of this proclamation appears to tally best with the date of April

been sent by the King to investigate the 'oryble wrongis' that have been reported in 'this contre', and that those responsible will be duly punished. He continues:

Also hit ys opunly puplysschid that serteyne servaunts of the Lord Scales schulde in his name manasse and put men in feer and drede to compleyne to us at this tyme of the seide hurts and greves, seynge that we wolde abyde but a schort tyme her, and aftir our departynge he wolde have the rewle and governaunce as he hath had affore tyme. We lete yow wete that nexst the Kynge our soverayn Lord, be his good grace and lycence, we woll have the princypall rewle and governance throwh all this schir, of whishe we ber our name whyls that we be lyvynge, as ferre as reson and lawe requyrith, hoso ever will grutche or sey the [contrary]; for we woll that the Lord Scales, Sir Thomas Tudenham, Sir Mylis Stapylton, and John Heydon have in knowleche, thowh our persone be not dayly her, they schal fynde our power her at all tymes to do the Kynge our soverayn Lord servyse, and to support and mayntene yow alle in your right that ben the Kyngs trewe lige men. For hit may non ben seyde nay, but that her hath ben the grettest riotts, orryble wrongs and offences done in thise partyes by the seide Lord Scales, Thomas Tudenham, Mylis Stapilton, John Heydon, and suche as ben confedred on to theym that evir was seen in our dayes . . .

The conventional analysis of Mowbray power in the period—that 'the inherent landed strength and traditional authority of the dukes of Norfolk' were merely 'temporarily eclipsed' by Suffolk's rule during the 1430s and 1440s[66]—suggests that this declaration marks a stage in the natural re-emergence of Norfolk's lordship in the years after 1450, and, incidentally, forms a rare and useful exposition of the realities of noble power in the localities.[67] However, this rarity may have significant implications for analysis of the particular reality to which the proclamation refers.

Norfolk's explicit self-assertion is unique among the Paston letters. Lords may be *reported* to be more or less powerful in straightforward terms,[68] but in their own dealings with the men of their 'country', noblemen convey their authority obliquely through the tone of their

---

1452'. Both Storey and Griffiths, however, argue that it should be dated to Feb. 1451 and related to Norfolk's appointment as a commissioner of *oyer* and *terminer*. Storey, *End of the House of Lancaster*, 248; R. A. Griffiths, *The Reign of Henry VI* (London, 1981), 591 n.

[66] R. Virgoe, 'The Crown, Magnates, and Local Government in Fifteenth-Century East Anglia', in R. Virgoe, *East Anglian Society* (Norwich, 1997), 90.

[67] For discussion of this proclamation in the context of an analysis of local lordship, see Watts, *Henry VI*, 64–6.

[68] See, for example, *PL* Davis, i. 147 (Gairdner, ii. 80): 'He enqueryd me of the rewle of myn master Danyell and myn lord of Suffulke, and askyd wheche I thowte schuld rewle in this schere'; and *PL* Davis, i. 236 (Gairdner, iv. 75): 'sondery folkys have seyd to me that they thynk veryly but if ze have my lord of Suffolkys godelorchyp qhyll the werd is as itt is ye kan never leven jn pese'.

communications, rather than by articulating it directly.[69] It is true that the duke's proclamation is also unusual in that it is a general and public statement at a time of local and national upheaval, which may help to explain his untypically overt approach.[70] Nevertheless, even if his tone is purely a function of the critical nature of the moment, the conclusion must remain that it is the expression of lordship in crisis. Under normal circumstances a lord's authority remained largely unarticulated and undefined, yet implicit in his every word. Here there may be an analogy with the military power of the nobility. The creation and maintenance of lordship depended fundamentally on the ability to raise military support that was inherent in the possession of land. By the late medieval period, however, the maintenance of 'worshipful' lordship depended largely on the manipulation of this power as an implicit force, rather than on its practical implementation. The appearance of a lord at the head of an armed following, as opposed to the worshipful attendance of his retinue, in fact regularly signalled instability within political society, whether it was an attempt to create and enforce especially rapidly a lordship which had not previously existed in a particular area, or a response by a lord who felt his authority to be threatened or challenged in his 'country'.[71] It may be that explicit articulation of authority was as much a sign of lordship under pressure as was overt military display.

Certainly, the circumstances in which Norfolk found himself in 1451–2 correspond more closely with the pattern outlined above than has usually been argued, since the duke, faced with the task of establishing a new lordship in the area, had failed during the preceding decade to create any significant sphere of authority independent of Suffolk's virtual hegemony in the 'schir of whishe we ber our name' or its twin, in which the bulk of the Mowbray lands actually lay. It may not be stretching interpretation too far to see a reflection of these circumstances in the language of this proclamation. Norfolk accuses Scales's men of claiming

[69] For example, Lord Scales in *PL* Davis, ii. 34–5 (Gairdner, ii. 137–8): 'seyng the said Osberd is my tenaunt and homager it is my part to holde with hym rather than with Danyell in hise right, which I wylle do to my pouer . . . And in cas that he wold do wrong to the lesse gentilman in the chirre, it shal not lye in hise pouer, be the grace of God.'

[70] However, comparison with Lord Moleyns's letter to the tenants of Gresham in 1449 suggests that even in such circumstances Norfolk's approach was unusual. Moleyns chooses to assert his lordship (which was far from securely established in the specific context of the disputed possession of Gresham) not through confrontational language, but through the expansive tone of inherent authority: 'Trusty and welbeloued frendys, I grete yowe well, and putte yowe all oute of doute all that ye haue doon for me . . . I will . . . saue yowe harmeles ayenst all thoo that wold greue yowe, to my power. And as hertly as I can I thanke yow of the gud wyl ye haue had and haue toward me; and as to the tytyll of rigth that I haue to the lordship of Gressam schal with-in short tyme be knoweyn, and be the lawe so determynyd that ye schal all be glad that hath ought me youre gud wyll ther-in.' *PL* Davis, ii. 521 (Gairdner, ii. 99).   [71] C. Carpenter, *Locality and Polity* (Cambridge, 1992), 625.

that their lord will continue to enjoy the 'rewle and governaunce *as he hath had affore tyme*', and asserts that instead 'we *woll have* the princypall rewle'.[72] This might have been a tenable position for Norfolk in the immediate wake of Suffolk's fall in 1450—to expect that he would finally be able to claim his rightful position now that the 'undue' influence of Suffolk had been removed from both the national and the local political stage—but, coming as it does at least a year later, his assertions seem to be a clear indication that he had failed to establish his authority any more successfully in the absence of the supposedly crucial figure of Suffolk. Instead, it is only too clear that the de la Pole affinity has survived under Scales's leadership, and that this proclamation in fact forms a partisan declaration of intent on Norfolk's part. What begins as a call for 'the trowthe' about crimes committed by 'any persone of what estat, degre, or condicion he be' has by the end of the document become an assertion that 'hit may non ben seyde nay' that in fact Scales, Tuddenham, Stapleton, and Heydon are the guilty parties, and an instruction to make 'billiz of your grevance' on that basis.[73]

A lord who had secured the undisputed rule of his 'country' could perhaps legitimately assume that his own interests coincided with those of the regional 'common weal', since comprehensive authority could only be maintained by a credible claim to represent the collective interests of all those who were subject to that authority.[74] However, every indication suggests that this was not the position from which Norfolk was operating. The duke had had the opportunity to establish his control over East Anglian society and had manifestly failed, since his chief opponents were still, by his own admission, able to inspire 'feer and drede' in his 'country'. His theoretical status as the leading noble of the region was, after Suffolk's death, unquestionable, and, now that the king's government was no longer being directed by his local rival, there was no reason why he should not have been able to gain access to the powers of the crown in support of his regional authority. Nevertheless, he was apparently unable to translate this opportunity into effective political dominance. During the crisis of 1450–1, for example, when the de la Pole affinity was temporarily in disarray, many of its members were apparently willing to co-operate with Norfolk, but the duke seems to have failed completely to take advantage of this co-operation to forge more broadly based and substantial connections among the leading gentry. By 1453, when Norfolk headed a commission to treat for a loan in East Anglia, not one of the other men appointed

---

[72] My italics. In the first quotation, Norfolk is reporting the words of Scales's men, but makes no attempt to refute this part of their claims, an impression reinforced by the future tense of the second sentence.   [73] *PL* Gairdner, ii. 259.

[74] See above, p. 6; Watts, *Henry VI*, 67.

was a political ally of his.[75] Instead, his fellow commissioners were the bishop of Norwich, who had been closely associated with Suffolk,[76] and Scales, Tuddenham, and Stapleton, men who embodied the continuing influence of the de la Pole connection.

This failure seems to have been the result not only of the inadequacy of Norfolk's local following, but also, once again, of the duke's mismanagement of what resources he did command. By the beginning of 1453, the depredations of men closely linked to Norfolk himself inspired the region's gentry to unite in a chorus of complaint more general than any provoked by the alleged oppressions of Tuddenham and Heydon. Ironically, this crisis seems to have been largely the result of Norfolk's alliance with the disruptive figure of Thomas Daniel, made in the late 1440s in an effort to circumvent the local effects of Suffolk's political dominance at the centre.[77] In December 1451 a rift between Norfolk and Daniel was reported, coinciding with the latter's association with Somerset and his negotiations with Scales. Various lords, as well as Norfolk's mother, were said to have written to the duke 'for to have Danyell in his favour a geyne', a development ascribed to Somerset's influence. These interventions were apparently successful, since it seems to have been shortly afterwards that Daniel married Norfolk's niece Margaret Howard at Framlingham Castle.[78] The duke lent active support to Daniel's territorial ambitions; according to William Worcestre, his claims to Rydon were made 'with the help and power of John Duke of Norfolk', which included the assistance of 'a large armed force of the duke's'.[79] However, the most dramatic implications of their alliance seem to have related to the political dealings of the duke himself. By 1452, not only had Suffolk's men succeeded in retaining their position, but Norfolk had lost the support of those gentlemen who, having found no place in the de la Pole affinity, had in 1450 formed his natural constituency. In this process, a crucial part seems to have been played by his association with Daniel.

A memorandum drafted by John Paston in 1452 is explicit on the subjects of both the change in the duke's intimate circle, and the reasons that lay behind it:

Itt is to remembre vndere hos rule that the gode lord is at this day, and whiche be of his new cownseyll. Item, that . . . his old cownseyl and attendans . . . be

---

[75] *CPR 1452–61*, 52.

[76] Griffiths, *Henry VI*, 285, 348, 486, 645; Watts, *Henry VI*, 210–11, 225 n., 227 n., 232 n., 241 n., 247 n., 248 n.   [77] See above, Ch. 4.4.

[78] The marriage is dated to the thirtieth year of the reign (Sept. 1451–Aug. 1452); it is therefore possible that it took place before the estrangement reported in December, although a later dating seems more likely given the evident strength of their association from 1452 onwards. *PL* Gairdner, ii. 145; *PL* Davis, ii. 76–7 (Gairdner, ii. 254–5); Blomefield, *History of the County of Norfolk*, ix. 54.   [79] Harvey (ed.), *Worcestre: Itineraries*, 253.

avoydyd . . . Item, be the demenyng of the . . . sescionys [of the peace] was verily conseyvid be the jantylmen of the shyere that it was set of purpose to have be indytementys defowlyd seche personys as were of the old cownseyl wyth the seid lord, and seche as kepe Wodhows lond, or seche as help or confort Osbern Munford . . . in his rygth of the manere of Brayston, of whiche he is now late wrongfully dyssesyd; and generally to have hurt all othere that wold not folwe the oppynyons of the seyd new cownseyll . . .[80]

The common element linking the disputes in which Wodehous and Mundford were involved was the fact that in each case Daniel was their opponent. The identification of their interests with those of Norfolk's ousted 'old cownseyl', as a generalized group that 'wold not folwe the oppynyons' of the duke's new advisers, demonstrates that it was Daniel 'vndere hos rule' Norfolk was now operating, and who had alienated the latter's traditional supporters.[81]

The immediate focus of Paston's concern, and the principal subject of the memorandum quoted above, was the activities of a group of gentlemen led by Charles Nowell and Robert Lethum. This 'gret multitude of mysrewled people', according to the complaints to be found among the Paston letters and the returns of judicial hearings in February 1453,[82] had been responsible for a series of assaults, robberies, and forced entries in 1452, including an attack on Paston himself, as well as a conspiracy to have many 'men of gode name and fame' indicted for riot and rebellion.[83] Paston's direct involvement may mean that the impression the correspondence gives of universal outrage at the activities of this 'criminal gang' may be somewhat exaggerated. It is clear, however, both from the letters and from the records of King's Bench, that a broad range of local landed interests were prepared, at least temporarily, to abandon otherwise deep-seated differences to form an unlikely alliance against Nowell and his associates. Gilbert Debenham, Richard Southwell, and John Paston himself had figured prominently in opposition to Suffolk's men during the 1440s and in the immediate aftermath of the duke's fall, but by 1452 their names appear on the lists of gentlemen who informed against Nowell and Lethum in the company of those of Scales, Tuddenham, Stapleton, Rous, and Wyndham, the leading lights of the de la Pole connection.[84]

What is also clear is that the 'riottys felowshipp' which had provoked

[80] *PL* Davis, i. 72–4 (Gairdner, ii. 273–5).

[81] For Daniel's disputes with Wodehous and Mundford, see above, pp. 120–2 and 165–8.

[82] *PL* Davis, i. 59 (Gairdner, ii. 267); KB9/85/2 (Norfolk), and KB9/118/1–2 (Suffolk). An *oyer* and *terminer* commission had been appointed on 8 Jan.: *CPR 1452–61*, 60. See also KB9/271 mm. 43–4.

[83] Nowell and his associates were alleged to have arranged for Roger Chirche, one of their own number, to be arrested so that he could then name their opponents as his supposed co-conspirators: *PL* Davis, i. 58–63 (Gairdner, ii. 267–72).

[84] *PL* Davis, i. 75 (Gairdner, ii. 307–8); KB9/85/2 m. 17v; KB9/118/1 m. 36v.

this remarkable alliance were servants of Thomas Daniel. Nowell had been appointed bailiff of Bradeston by Daniel after the expulsion of Mundford,[85] and those who were accused of riot at his instigation were said specifically to be 'notable and thryfty men that were well willid to the seyd Munford for the seid maner of Brayston'.[86] What is not clear from the Paston evidence, but emerges from the judicial records of the *oyer* and *terminer* commission of 1453, is that Nowell and Lethum were as closely involved with the duke of Norfolk as they were with his ally Daniel. The records of the hearings in Norfolk offer only oblique references to this relationship; Nowell and his accomplice John Radcliff are described in some of the indictments as esquires 'late of Framlingham'.[87] The records of the Suffolk commission offer more explicit evidence.[88] According to these indictments, Daniel's men had joined forces with some of Norfolk's retainers to carry out repeated attacks on de la Pole property.[89] Their incursions into Suffolk's parks and attacks on his servants were alleged to have begun in February 1450 and to have been renewed during the summer and autumn of that year.[90]

In other words, Norfolk seems to have attempted, from early 1450, to assert his authority over the de la Pole interest in Suffolk by using aggressive tactics in which Daniel and his men played a vital role. By 1452, Daniel was pursuing his own concerns in Norfolk by directing the same degree of aggression against men who were the duke's 'natural' supporters.[91] In this context, the willingness of men such as John

---

[85] *PL* Davis, i. 73 (Gairdner, ii. 274). In one of the indictments heard before the commission of 1452, Nowell is described as an esquire 'late of Bradeston'; indicted with him was John Dowebyggyng, 'late of Rydon', who had been in Daniel's service at least since his fraudulent dealings with Henry Wodehous. In 1453 Daniel and Nowell were indicted at the manorial court of Bradeston for breaking the close there and stealing horses, cattle, and sheep: KB9/85/2 m. 17; *Rot. Parl.*, v. 340–1; BL Add. Roll 26849 m. 39.

[86] Roger Chirche, who had been persuaded to make a confession in order to implicate these men, was also to be secured a pardon 'be the mene of Danyell': *PL* Davis, i. 73, 79 (Gairdner ii. 274, 312).   [87] KB9/85/2 m. 37.

[88] This difference between the judicial records of Norfolk and Suffolk—that members of the gentry appear as protagonists in their own right in accounts of incidents in Norfolk, and as servants of noblemen in the context of disputes in Suffolk—is a specific demonstration of the general contrast between the geopolitical characteristics of the two shires, for which see above, pp. 55–7.

[89] The men indicted included Mowbray retainers such as John Howard, Edmund Fitzwilliam, John Framlyngham, and Thomas Chambre, as well as Charles, Otwell, and Arthur Nowell. All the above were described as 'late of Framlingham Castle': KB9/118/1 m. 22; KB9/118/2 m. 165.

[90] KB9/118/1 mm. 8, 22, 28–9; KB9/118/2 mm. 16–17. The duchess of Suffolk had accused John Howard, the Nowells, and others of trespasses (presumably connected with their incursions into her properties) in the Michaelmas term of 1452: KB27/766 Coram Rege roti. 71v, 76.

[91] At some point between Jan. 1450 and Mar. 1454 Daniel was also claiming to have been named Fastolf's heir, a 'sclaundre' which was 'noyous grete vexacion' to Fastolf and his feoffees: C1/19/115.

Paston to co-operate with longstanding opponents becomes explicable, and the scale of Norfolk's political mismanagement apparent. Paston's letter of April 1452 to the sheriff, John Clopton, demonstrates his bafflement at his lord's abrupt abandonment of the men who had served him during the previous decade, as well as Norfolk's failure to provide the access for communication of grievance that was essential to the operation of responsive, and therefore successful, lordship.[92] Having reported Nowell's attack on him, Paston writes that this

was to me strawnge cas, thinking in my conseyth that I was my lordis man and his homagere or Charlis knew hys lordschipe and that my lord was my god lord . . . I thowt also that I had neuer geff cawse to non of my lordis hous to ow me evill will, ne that ther was non of the hows but I wold haue do fore as I cowd desire animan to do for me, and yet will, except my aduersare. And thus I and my frendis haff mwsid of this, and thowt he was hired to do thus, and this notwithstanding, assone as knolech was had of my lordis coming to Framingham, neuer attemptid to procede ageyns him as justis and law wuld, but to trust to my seyd lord that his Hyghnes wold se this punischid . . . and dayly hath be redy with such jentilmen as dwelle here-a-bought that can record the trought to haue come compleyn to my lord, but we haue had contynually tydyngis of my lordis comyng heder that causid vs for to a-bide there-vp-vn, besechyng your gode maystershep that ye wull lete my lord haue knowlech of my compleynt . . .[93]

The overwhelming impression of the duke which emerges from these documents is of a lord whose grasp of the political realities of his 'country' was far from firm. His absence and his failure to communicate with the gentlemen of the area when they were waiting to convey urgent complaints and to petition for redress in effect constituted an abdication of his responsibilities. Because of the reciprocal nature of lordship and service, this also represented a lost opportunity to assert, demonstrate, and reinforce his authority. Local lordship having failed them, the gentlemen of Norfolk and Suffolk took their complaints instead to the king.[94] This mismanagement reinforces suggestions in the Paston evidence that Norfolk had been manipulated by his 'new cownseyll': 'Item, to remembre,' the memorandum of 1452 continues, 'how suttely the seyd Chirche was be his owyn assent led to my lord of Norffolk be his owyn felashep, to the entent to accuse and defame seche as they lovyd nott.'[95] The implication that the duke was ignorant of

---

[92] *PL* Davis, i. 66–7 (Gairdner, ii. 261–2). See also John Osbern's report to the bishop of Norwich that he 'trostid to my lord of Norffolkes lordchep and ritewesnesse that he wold see that Charles shuld be scharply correctyd for hese trespasse and mysrewle, or ellis the jentelmen of the shire must to-giddyre purvey a-nodyre meane': *PL* Davis, ii. 80–1 (Gairdner, ii. 265).

[93] *PL* Davis, i. 67 (Gairdner, ii. 261–2).

[94] *PL* Davis, i. 58–63; ii. 530–1 (Gairdner, ii. 263–4, 267–72).

[95] *PL* Davis, i. 73 (Gairdner, ii. 274).

the activities of Nowell and his followers may owe much to dutiful adherence to the topos of noble 'ritewesnesse', since any good lord would immediately act to correct any wrongs of which he was appraised. But whether Norfolk had been unwittingly manœuvred into furthering Nowell's plans, or whether he was an informed participant, the conclusion remains the same: his management of the matter had been inadequately informed or inadequately considered, and either way had succeeded in alienating some of his closest gentry supporters and in demonstrating the deficiencies of his lordship.[96] Indeed, the fact that his leadership had proved a particularly disruptive element in local politics was implicitly acknowledged during the hearings of 1453, when all the main protagonists requested securities of the peace from their opponents. The sums demanded ranged from 100 marks to £2,000; the sole exception was the case of Norfolk himself, who was required to bind himself to keep the peace towards the duchess of Suffolk in the vast sum of £10,000.[97]

Although in this local context Norfolk had alienated his natural constituency among the gentry, at a national level he was able to secure some concessions from the regime headed by the duke of Somerset. Somerset's establishment of an authoritative government in the wake of Suffolk's fall depended fundamentally—as had Suffolk's regime before it—on the widespread support it was able to command among the lords. The failure of Suffolk's rule, however, meant that it was necessary for Somerset to try to distinguish the regime which he headed from its predecessor in the light of the criticisms which had erupted in 1450, despite the underlying continuity in political structures. Somerset's appeal to noble consensus therefore necessitated the conciliation of those few magnates who had been in some sense excluded from the regime of the 1440s, a prime example being Norfolk himself, whose

---

[96] It is worth noting that, even by 1455, Norfolk was making the elementary mistake of attempting to force a non-local parliamentary representative (the Suffolk esquire John Howard) on the fiercely independent-minded political society of Norfolk: see below, n. 115.

[97] Daniel was among the duke's mainpernors: KB9/118/2 mm. 24, 167. In Dec. 1453, Norfolk was bound in a recognizance to the king in the even greater sum of £12,000 to appear in chancery the following March, and in the meantime to keep the peace towards the duchess of Suffolk: *CCR 1447–54*, 476. It is tempting to see this combination of disruptiveness and mismanagement as characteristic not only of Norfolk himself, but also of his followers. In Aug. 1452, for example, John Dowebyggyng, a servant of Daniel's and therefore at this point also of the duke himself, led a raid on the home of the de la Pole steward John Ulveston, allegedly intending to murder him. Having laid an ambush, the party were said to have sent one of their number into the house to ask for Ulveston, only to learn from his wife and son that he was not there. 'It is a shrewed turne that he is not at home,' the would-be assassins are reported to have said on hearing the news, 'our iourney is evyll lost. But as for him we shull have our purpose an other tyme well inowe and as for his sone late us smyte of his right arme and than shalle he never do so moche harme as his fader hath do.' This revised plan, too, was thwarted: Ulveston's wife, who had clearly smelt a rat, had already made her escape, taking her son with her. KB9/118/1 m. 36.

opposition, such as it was, to Suffolk's government, as well as his temporary association with York during the crisis of 1450–1, had been prompted by his inability to obtain a stake in the rule of East Anglia in the face of Suffolk's local hegemony.[98] Somerset's response to the crisis of order in Norfolk and Suffolk therefore seems to have been to back 'all the competing factions at once'.[99] Both Norfolk and Scales, for example, among many other lords including Somerset himself, were appointed to the commission of *oyer* and *terminer* which sat in February 1453.[100] Despite Norfolk's presence on the commission, the hearings unleashed a flood of indictments relating to the activities of Nowell, Lethum, and their associates, as well as an attempt to implicate some of the duke's most prominent followers, including the Nowells, in the organization of Cade's rebellion.[101] However, Norfolk was able to prevent process of exigent being awarded against them in February and again in April,[102] and to secure pardons even for men such as John Framlyngham and William and Hugh Ashton who had been among those accused of treason.[103]

Nevertheless, this evenhandedness was not enough to satisfy Norfolk's expectations that he would assume the rule of the region once Suffolk was removed. Though Norfolk did enjoy a new degree of access to the powers of the crown, his failure to establish his authority over the de la Pole affinity and its survival as a powerful local rival meant that this access could not be exclusive, given that Somerset's government could only attempt to accommodate, rather than discriminate between, the demands of competing local factions. Moreover, without substantially privileged access to royal authority, Norfolk stood little chance of achieving local dominance, since his small and partisan following could not match the broad network of longstanding connections which constituted the de la Pole interest, and which was now reinforced by those gentlemen who had been alienated from Mowbray lordship by Norfolk's alliance with Daniel. Under these circumstances, it was always likely that York, who had since 1450 consistently aligned

---

[98] Watts, *Henry VI*, 236–40, 275–6, 291–2; see above, Ch. 4.3.

[99] Watts, *Henry VI*, 298–9. In Mar. 1452, Norfolk was granted a pardon for all offences he had committed and fines he had occurred: *CPR 1446–52*, 530.

[100] *CPR 1452–61*, 60. John Watts argues that large-scale judicial commissions such as this one, in which sixteen lords were appointed to hear indictments in thirteen counties, played a vital part in Somerset's attempt to reassert the king's legitimate authority at the head of his united nobility: *Henry VI*, 290–1.

[101] Sir William Ashton, Edmund Fitzwilliam, Charles and Otwell Nowell, Hugh Ashton, John Radcliff, Thomas Chambre, and John Framlyngham were indicted, among others, with Sir William Oldhall at the Suffolk hearings for treasonably conspiring to make York 'king and governor' of the realm: KB9/118/1 m. 30; see also KB9/271 m. 117; KB27/770 Rex rot. 3.

[102] KB9/118/2 mm. 163–4.

[103] KB9/118/2 m. 241; KB27/770 Rex rot. 3; *CPR 1452–61*, 70, 75.

himself with popular criticism of Suffolk and his adherents,[104] would attract Norfolk's support when he renewed his challenge to Somerset at the end of 1453.[105]

Norfolk certainly seems to have supposed that York's protectorate offered a renewed opportunity to gain the upper hand against the de la Pole affinity, and to recoup some of the ground he had lost during 1452–3. The hearings of February 1453, for example, had coincided with a failed attempt on Norfolk's part to control the shire election in Suffolk. On 12 February, a group of Mowbray retainers led by Thomas Daniel, John Howard, and William Ashton, alleged to have numbered 600 men, went to the county court at Ipswich to participate in the election. When the officials of the pro-de la Pole sheriff, Thomas Sharnburne, refused to co-operate with their wishes, Norfolk's men took matters into their own hands and nominated John Wingfield and Daniel himself as the county's representatives.[106] This drastic intervention achieved little. The election was declared invalid, and at the shire court a month later the names of Philip Wentworth and Gilbert Debenham were returned instead.[107] Moreover, the sheriff's return of the writ for the original election, declaring that he had been prevented from holding the shire court 'be cause of manas and thretes', initiated proceedings against Daniel and his companions in the court of Common Pleas.[108]

This setback provoked no immediate response from Norfolk. By April 1454, however, York had established his supremacy in government in place of Somerset, and Norfolk rapidly took the opportunity to reopen the matter. On 27 May, he submitted a petition to York and the other lords of the council, recounting how, fifteen months earlier, his

[104] Griffiths, *Henry VI*, 685–6, 688–94; B. P. Wolffe, *Henry VI* (London, 1981), 240–8, 252–4; Johnson, *Duke Richard of York*, 85–92; Watts, *Henry VI*, 261, 266–74.

[105] Norfolk at this point submitted a petition charging Somerset with treason: *PL* Gairdner, ii. 290–2.

[106] These details are taken from Sharnburne's account of the incident: KB27/775 Coram Rege rot. 20v.

[107] Wentworth was closely associated with the de la Pole interest, and although Debenham had been a Mowbray servant, he was one of the gentlemen alienated from the duke during this period (see above, at n. 84). As Roger Virgoe notes, few, if any, Mowbray supporters were present at this second election. R. Virgoe, 'Three Suffolk Parliamentary Elections of the Mid-Fifteenth Century', in Virgoe, *East Anglian Society*, 55–6; C219/16/2 m. 55.

[108] E28/84. Despite Sharnburne's protestations, it seems more than likely—as Virgoe points out—that, however Norfolk's men comported themselves, the sheriff would have sought to delay the election to avoid the influence of such a substantial Mowbray contingent. Nevertheless, the other activities of Daniel and his men at around the same time suggest, first, that Sharnburne's admittedly partial account of their aggression is not inherently improbable, and secondly that Norfolk's men could by no means claim to represent the voice of the shire, since they had alienated such a broad section of local political society (see above, pp. 172–6). Indeed, their 'election' was blatantly partisan and hamfistedly imposed, since, as Sharnburne was able to point out, Daniel held no lands in Suffolk and was therefore unqualified to represent the county: KB27/775 Coram Rege rot. 20v.

servants had legitimately and peacefully attended the Suffolk election, only to be victimized by Sharnburne who was 'ymagynyng and purposyng to make knyghtes of the shire aftyre hys owne intent and for hys syngler covytyse'.[109] His request that his men should be allowed to appear in court by attorney was granted, and when the case finally appeared in King's Bench in February 1455, during the very last days of the first protectorate, William Ashton and sixteen of the others were allowed to go *sine die* on a legal technicality.[110] Norfolk also chose the period of York's government to present his claim to the manors of Stockton and Geldeston, which he had signally failed to make good during the 1440s, to the courts.[111]

York's ascendancy during 1454 and the latter part of 1455 after the first battle of St Albans[112] also gave Norfolk a substantially enhanced

[109] E28/84. This petition gives the date of the disputed election as 19 Feb. (the Monday after St Valentine). However, as Roger Virgoe demonstrates, the date given in KB27/775 Coram Rege rot. 20v (the Monday *before* St Valentine) seems to be the correct one: Virgoe, 'Three Suffolk Parliamentary Elections', 63 n. 18. The petition (but not the attached list of Norfolk's men) is printed in *POPC*, vi. 183–4.

[110] Ashton and the others (who included Edmund Fitzwilliam) claimed there was no case to answer because only the tenor of Sharnburne's return, and not the return itself, had been submitted to the court: KB27/775 Coram Rege rot. 20v. In the autumn of the same year, the duke's esquire John Radcliff received a general pardon, which allowed him to escape charges which had been brought for his part in the Mowbray attacks on de la Pole property in 1450: KB27/778 Rex roti. 25, 28; for the attacks, see above, at n. 90. For the end of the protectorate, see Griffiths, *Henry VI*, 739.

[111] Norfolk seems to have taken the properties briefly during 1453, when the duchess's accounts record both his intrusion and a payment to Philip Wentworth for re-establishing her possession (BL Eg. Roll 8779 mm. 4, 9). The duke's supposed feoffees in the manor (Thomas Bourchier, archbishop of Canterbury, Henry, Viscount Bourchier, and John Southwell) then presented their petition in the summer of 1455. Norfolk's decision to take his case to law at this point in the long-running dispute indicates that he expected a favourable hearing from the courts under York's regime, a not unreasonable assumption, given that his chief representative, the archbishop, had recently taken office as chancellor and therefore presided over the court of chancery where the plea was initially heard. However, York's unwillingness to maintain overtly partisan causes is evident from the fact that Norfolk faced opposition not only from the attorneys of the duchess of Suffolk, who had held the manors since 1450, but also from lawyers representing the king, who supported the duchess's account of the descent of the properties but argued that they should have been taken into the king's hand after Suffolk's death. Norfolk's claim does seem to have been weak. He argued that the Mowbrays had possessed the manors until unjustly disseised first by the Bigots and then by their descendants the Garneys. However, the king's attorney was able to demonstrate that both Norfolk's father and the duke himself had accepted the Garneys' homage for the manors (as held of Norfolk's manor of Forncett). Perhaps frustrated by his lack of legal success, Norfolk resorted to more direct methods, in which he was again assisted by his enhanced influence under York. In 1456 the duke's servant Richard Southwell, who had been appointed to the escheatorship, seized the manors from the duchess. She petitioned the chancellor in August of that year, and seems to have won her case (presumably after Bourchier's departure from office two months later) and been restored to possession of the properties. Norfolk later seized the estates once again, although the precise date of this attack is not clear. KB27/778 Coram Rege rot. 51; C1/25/77; C1/26/164; see above, pp. 110–11.

[112] Norfolk and Oxford did not take part in the battle because they arrived a day too late: *PL* Gairdner, iii. 30.

stake in the administration of the East Anglian shires. Appointments to local office during these years show a consistent degree of Mowbray influence which was unprecedented during the 1440s and highly unusual during the 1450s. The sheriff appointed in November 1454 was Robert Wingfield's son John, who had returned to Norfolk's service after his father's death.[113] John Wingfield's brother Robert represented Suffolk in the parliament of July 1455 together with William Jenney, who had been associated with the campaign against the de la Pole affinity in 1450–1;[114] the MPs for Norfolk were the Mowbray retainers Roger Chamberleyn and John Howard.[115] The escheator in 1454 was William Brandon, who had also apparently been reconciled with the duke,[116] and in the following year Brandon was succeeded by Norfolk's servant Richard Southwell.[117]

Norfolk was therefore able to profit from his association with York to pursue longstanding grievances and to reinforce his own local authority. He seems to have acted in the expectation that York would offer him partisan support in his struggle to assert the local rule which he appears to have assumed was his by right. However, York's ability to fulfil Norfolk's hopes was limited by the fact that his regime, as had Somerset's, depended fundamentally on commanding broad support among the lords.[118] Partisan intervention in regional affairs would have jeopardized the survival of this consensus. Though Norfolk was a prominent member of the Yorkist council in 1454, therefore, so was his local rival Scales,[119] and, at a local level, though Mowbray servants

[113] *List of Sheriffs for England and Wales*, PRO Lists and Indexes, 9 (1898), 87; and see above, Ch. 4.3 n. 193.

[114] *PL* Davis, ii. 48 (Gairdner, ii. 176); *PL* Gairdner, ii. 190–3, 252.

[115] In June the duchess of Norfolk had written to ask John Paston to support their nomination, explaining that 'it is thought right necessarie for diuers causes that my lord haue at this tyme in the parlement suche persones as longe vnto him and be of his menyall seruauntz'. The election indenture confirms that the process was dominated by Mowbray servants. Norfolk's influence prevailed despite the fact that Howard's election was far from uncontroversial. It was reported that Howard was not acceptable 'in asmeche as he hadde no lyvelode in the shire, nor couersaunt', and that 'it is an evill precedent for the shire that a straunge man shulde be chosyn, and no wurshipp to . . . my lord of Norffolk to write for hym; for yf the jentilmen of the shire will suffre sech inconvenyens . . . the shire shall noght be called of seche wurshipp as it hathe be'. The extent to which the duke was still struggling to assert his authority against that of his dead rival is demonstrated by the fact that he responded to complaints about Howard's nomination by declaring that 'the shire shulde have fre eleccion, soo that Ser Thomas Todenham were noght nor none that was toward the Duc of Suffolk': *PL* Davis, ii. 117, 119–21 (Gairdner, iii. 34, 38–9); C219/16/3 m. 36.

[116] Brandon was certainly back in favour with Norfolk by July 1455, when the duke granted him, for his good service, the custody and marriage of the heir of John Clippesby. It seems plausible that his reconciliation with the duke took place at the same time as that of the sons of Brandon's close associate Robert Wingfield. BL Add. Ch. 14974; see above, Ch. 4.3 n. 193.

[117] *List of Escheators for England and Wales*, PRO Lists and Indexes, 72 (1971), 88; *PL* Davis, ii. 76–7 (Gairdner, ii. 254–5); *PL* Gairdner, iii. 21.

[118] Griffiths, *Henry VI*, 725–8; Watts, *Henry VI*, 307–8, 317–21.

[119] Watts, *Henry VI*, 309 n. 212.

dominated the offices of the royal administration, Tuddenham and Heydon were still able to secure places on special commissions in the area.[120]

Moreover, Norfolk's position during these years seems to have been based on a profound misreading of the political complexion of the 'country' he aspired to rule. His estates in Suffolk were at least as substantial as those which maintained the de la Pole affinity there, but his avowed intention to secure for himself 'the princypall rewle and governance throwh all this schir, of whishe we ber our name'[121] took no account of the fact that his own territorial stake in Norfolk was not significant enough to support that degree of authority.[122] The key to the rule of the shire was control of the Duchy of Lancaster estates, which remained firmly in the hands of the longstanding representatives of Duchy interests in the area, Thomas Tuddenham and John Heydon.[123] Norfolk undoubtedly gained the upper hand in local affairs under York's protectorate, but this did not represent the restoration of the traditional power of a territorial magnate previously excluded from government. Rather, the duke had tried and failed during the previous fifteen years to establish an effective local lordship in the face of a well-established regional interest reinforced by both royal and noble power; York's regime offered him an opportunity finally to make some headway.

Unsurprisingly, given the territorial balance of power in the two shires, Norfolk's ascendancy was limited. It was also short-lived. Tuddenham and Heydon had been reappointed to the commission of the peace in March 1455, after the collapse of York's first protectorate; they kept their places on the bench in the commissions issued after the end of the second protectorate in 1456.[124] Indeed, from this point on, it ceased to be possible for any of the interests competing for dominance in East Anglia to secure local control by winning privileged access to the central powers of the crown. It seems that the collapse of even the illusion of a workable national authority constituted in the person of the king meant that, between 1456 and the beginning of 1459, whether the political initiative rested with the queen or with York, such legitimacy as the regime could claim for itself and such power as it could wield lay in the public authority of the crown as constituted and represented by the unified body of the lords.[125] Though it was such noble

---

[120] *CPR 1452–61*, 148, 257.

[121] See above, p. 169.

[122] This was particularly the case given that his mother held in dower most of what Mowbray manors there were in Norfolk: see above, Ch. 4.3 at n. 126.

[123] Tuddenham's association with the local Duchy stewardship now dated back 30 years: see above, p. 80. [124] *CPR 1452–61*, 671–2.

[125] For discussion of the constitutional issues on which this suggestion is based, see Watts, *Henry VI*, 335–41.

support that had previously allowed Suffolk, Somerset, and York at various times to direct the king's government, the dislocation of the polity was now so severe and so explicit that consensus was the only basis for any effective rule, and no single interest could easily exclude its rivals without forfeiting its claim to exercise legitimate authority.[126] Therefore, though Norfolk's interests had 'naturally' rested with York and the principle of the rule of the lords (because his local influence was restricted by men whose power had originally derived from their access to the personal authority of the king), and though Scales's connections with the household drew him into association with the queen and her attempts to reassert the personal authority of the crown, both were included in government during this period.[127] This analysis of national power structures is supported by the evidence of East Anglian local government. The commission of array issued in Norfolk in September 1457, for example, was comprehensively representative, including Norfolk himself, Oxford and Fastolf, their longstanding opponents Scales, Tuddenham, and Stapleton, and the maverick figure of Thomas Daniel.[128]

Despite both sides' need to maintain a broader consensus during these years, the convoluted course of high politics seems to have facilitated the gradual restoration of traditional divisions and alliances among the East Anglian gentry after the trauma caused by Daniel and his followers in 1452–3. Proceedings against Lethum and Nowell continued in 1454,[129] but by the summer of 1455 Gilbert Debenham, who had been alienated from Norfolk because of the influence of the duke's 'new cownseyll', was back in the Mowbray household, and John Paston had also clearly returned to the duke's political orbit.[130] Moreover, the

[126] See Watts's argument that 'if Margaret wanted the recognition of the wider political community, then she had to invite broadly based counsel. In doing so, however, her independent power was to a large extent dissolved in the overwhelming authority attached to the *persona publica* of her husband: an authority whose execution belonged to the lords. This meant that, in practice, she was forced to defer to assemblies founded on a principle of noble unity, which—on past form—were likely to favour compromise. The position of those who had been working all along for noble unity, on the other hand, was the very obverse of that of the queen. To acquire an effective practical authority, they had to take account of Margaret and her growing party; especially when the king, symbol of their own unity, was with her': *Henry VI*, 340–1.

[127] Both Norfolk and Scales were, for example, summoned to attend the council in the autumn of 1458: J. L. Watts, 'Domestic Politics and the Constitution in the Reign of Henry VI', unpublished Ph.D. thesis (Cambridge, 1990), 347 n. 363.

[128] The commission issued in Suffolk included York, Norfolk, John Wingfield, and Gilbert Debenham (for whose return to Mowbray service, see below, n. 130), as well as Philip Wentworth, Thomas Brewes, and John Hopton, all associated with the de la Pole affinity: *CPR 1452–61*, 402. For other broadly based commissions, see ibid. 407, 409, 490–1.

[129] *PL* Davis, i. 75–80 (Gairdner, ii. 307–14); KB9/272 m. 52; KB27/774 Rex rot. 30v (where Lethum was allowed to go *sine die*, on a legal technicality, on a charge of procuring the insurrection which Roger Chirche had attempted to stir up, for which see above, n. 83).

[130] *PL* Davis, i. 72; ii. 118, 120 (Gairdner, ii. 273; iii. 35, 39).

alliance between the de la Pole affinity and erstwhile Mowbray servants provoked by the activities of Lethum *et al.* seems to have disintegrated. York's ascendancy, and the consequently artificially enhanced influence of Mowbray interests at a local level in 1454, seem to have left Tuddenham and Heydon, the most prominent of Suffolk's former servants in the region, temporarily more vulnerable than at any point since 1450–1. Early in 1454 some of the charges which had been brought against them in 1450 were revived in King's Bench;[131] in November a burgess of Lynn cited a legal technicality to secure the reversal of an outlawry which Tuddenham had secured against him seven years before;[132] in the same month a case in which judgment had been given for Scales and Tuddenham against inhabitants of Swaffham in 1452 was reopened, again on a plea that the decision was invalid because of legal inaccuracies;[133] and several local men took the opportunity to attack Tuddenham's estates.[134] This renewed vulnerability encouraged longstanding enmities to resurface. By July 1455 Heydon and John Paston, for example, were again at loggerheads. Even so, the effect of the events of 1452–3 was perhaps evident in the fact that Paston was moved to remark of Tuddenham that 'he gaff me no cawse of late tyme to labour ageyns him'.[135]

This reversion to traditional alliances may well have been facilitated by the fact that developments in national politics seem to have provoked a change in Thomas Daniel's role in the region. Daniel's local opposition to the de la Pole affinity had been made possible by his independent access to the same authority from which they derived much of their influence—the powers of the crown as made available

---

[131] These included the allegations of maintenance and extortion made by Fastolf, and the charges arising from Heydon's involvement with the faction-ridden corporation of Norwich (for which, see above, n. 18), as well as accusations that Heydon, with Suffolk, had been conspiring in the interests of France in 1440, and that Tuddenham and Heydon had helped Suffolk to plan the death of the duke of Gloucester in 1447. Tuddenham had in fact been acquitted on one such charge by a Norwich jury in Feb. 1453: KB9/272 mm. 2–5; KB27/762 Rex rot. iv.

[132] The outlawry, secured for non-payment of a debt of £20, was revoked on the grounds that the original writ had not mentioned the town from which the defendant came, information which was required by the Statute of Additions: KB27/774 Coram Rege rot. 84v.

[133] In the spring of 1451 Scales had charged the men with stealing 600 of his sheep from Swaffham, and had eventually been awarded £97 damages; the accused unsuccessfully argued that the sheep were only temporarily in Scales's custody and in fact belonged to Tuddenham, from whom they were confiscated as the penalty for failing to appear to answer charges which the accused had brought against him at the Swaffham court in Oct. 1450. The appeal against the decision was not settled in 1454–5, but continued in the courts until Jan. 1457 when Scales released his claim to the damages, a settlement which seems to support the argument that the regime the queen was constructing at this point could not afford—at least in East Anglia—to offer universal protection to the partisan interests of those associated with the court: KB27/774 Coram Rege rot. 120.

[134] KB27/782 Coram Rege roti. 6–7, 67, 88–88v, 107.

[135] *PL* Davis, i. 85 (Gairdner, iii. 46–7).

through the royal household.[136] In the later 1450s, however, the very principle of rule by the personal authority of the king was in dispute, a situation which left no room for competition between rival suitors to that authority. The interests both of Daniel and of the de la Pole affinity lay in the restoration of a more personal royal authority, just as the interests of Norfolk's traditional supporters, who had suffered as a result of their exclusion from access to the person of the king, lay with any alternative to that personal royal authority, and therefore with attempts to represent the political community by other means.[137] During these years, therefore, Daniel's association with the political circle around the queen, which included men such as Scales, Tuddenham, and Heydon, seems to have led to a loosening of his ties with Norfolk and a reorientation of his local interests.[138] By August 1456 he was in a position to ask Scales to write on his behalf to John Paston,[139] and when, at the end of that year, Daniel became involved in a local property dispute, his opponent indicted Scales, Tuddenham, and Heydon as his accessories.[140] In October 1457 Daniel was included with Scales, Tuddenham, and Wentworth on a local commission to investigate a report of slanderous utterances about the king, queen, and prince, to which Norfolk was not named.[141] Thereafter, where Daniel's name is mentioned by the Paston correspondents, it is unequivocally linked with those of Tuddenham, Heydon, and their allies.[142]

[136] See above, Ch. 4.4.

[137] Daniel had already in 1452 learnt that, despite his alliance with Norfolk, he could hope for little from York, since the very basis on which York claimed power meant that the duke could not allow himself to be seen to be overtly partial. (See above, at n. 60, for Daniel's attempt to claim York's support for his seizure of the manor of Bradeston, and York's immediate disavowal of the matter.) This conclusion must have been reinforced in the summer of 1455, when Henry Wodehous's account of Daniel's fraudulent dealings over Rydon finally received a favourable hearing at the Yorkist parliament (his complaint having first been presented to parliament in 1450): see above, Ch. 4.4 n. 219; *CCR 1447–54*, 354–5.

[138] The epithet 'late of Framlingham' was still among the aliases used to describe Daniel in Nov. 1457, but it seems clear that his Mowbray links had already been significantly eroded at this point: *CPR 1452–61*, 396–7. For the de la Pole affinity in the queen's party, see below, pp. 185–6.

[139] *PL* Davis, ii. 158 (Gairdner, iii. 100). Daniel had been associated with Scales briefly at the end of 1451: *PL* Davis, ii. 77 (Gairdner ii. 255), and see above, at n. 59.

[140] In the spring of 1457 Daniel was indicted in King's Bench for seizing the manor of Stanhoe in north-west Norfolk from his namesake Thomas Daniel of Walsoken on 23 Dec. 1456. Daniel of Walsoken brought charges against Daniel, Scales, Tuddenham, and Heydon in the Michaelmas term of 1457: KB9/285 m. 65; KB27/786 Coram Rege roti. 40–40v, 53, 70.

[141] *CPR 1452–61*, 404. In Sept. 1458, Daniel and his associate Robert Lethum were also accused, with John Wyndham, Thomas Shuldham, and Thomas Sharnburne, of maintaining a false indictment brought by John Andrew against Fastolf's servant Thomas Howes, an offence which had allegedly taken place during the summer of 1457. Howes and Andrew had been in dispute for several years; an arbitration between them was in progress in Mar. 1454. BL Add. MS 27444 fo. 57 (and see the abstract—which does not list all the accused—printed in *PL* Gairdner, iii. 133); Magdalen College Fastolf MS 52(1). For the affiliations of Andrew, Wyndham, Shuldham, and Sharnburne, see above, pp. 98, 109 n., 116–17, 178–9.

[142] In Oct. 1460, for example, Friar Brackley suggested to John Paston that he should try

The return to the longstanding division in East Anglian society between the de la Pole affinity, newly reinforced by the support of Daniel, and those who looked to Norfolk for lordship was further clarified by the increasingly confrontational politics of the last two years of the reign, as division in government solidified into outright opposition. The withdrawal of York and the Nevilles from the regime in the face of the queen's self-assertion in 1459 did not win the support of Norfolk who, though sympathetic to the Yorkist manifesto, was not sufficiently embroiled in the Yorkist cause to be prepared to commit himself to open rebellion.[143] Nevertheless, although Margaret ensured that Norfolk was actively involved in the government and defence of his 'country',[144] it is clear that her regime restored the upper hand locally to the men most closely associated with her, the de la Pole connection.[145] During 1458–9, both their influence at a national level and their local power were substantially reinforced. Under the financial resettlement initiated by the queen at the end of 1458, Tuddenham became the treasurer of the royal household. Scales, who in 1459 was reported to be attending on the prince of Wales, was in 1460 placed in charge of the

to secure a commission for the arrest of Tuddenham, Heydon, Wentworth, Andrew, Daniel, and Wyndham. Perhaps indicative of this reconciliation is the fact that in May 1458 Daniel's servant Charles Nowell was able to secure a general pardon which allowed him to escape further legal process against him for his violent activities of 1452–3 (for which, see above, pp. 173–5), including the murder of Philip Berney: *PL* Davis, ii. 212–13 (Gairdner, iii. 227–8); KB27/790 Rex rot. 43v.

[143] Norfolk was present at the parliament of Nov. 1459 which attainted York, Rutland, March, Salisbury, and Warwick: *Rot. Parl.*, v. 351; Griffiths, *Henry VI*, 823–5. John Watts comments that almost no lords were at this stage prepared to join York in opposition to the queen 'who, for the first time, seemed to offer all the major ingredients of public authority', and argues that 'it is fairly clear that [Margaret's government] exercised a genuine public authority' and 'seems . . . to have aimed at a broad base of support': *Henry VI*, 349–55.

[144] For commissions to Norfolk during 1459 and the first half of 1460, see *CPR 1452–61*, 494–5, 558, 560–1, 566, 603, 606. The duke reportedly spent Easter 1460 at Caister for the safekeeping of the coast against a possible landing by Warwick. In Dec. 1459 Norfolk was also granted an annual sum of £50 owed by Ramsey Abbey to the earl of Salisbury and forfeited on his attainder: *PL* Davis, ii. 334 (Gairdner, iii. 212); *CCR 1454–61*, 418.

[145] See *CPR* references above, n. 144, for the strong representation of this connection on commissions of the period. Though the duchess of Suffolk had had the forethought to marry her son, the de la Pole heir, to York's daughter, she too was reported to be a supporter of the queen. Friar Brackley wrote in Oct. 1460 that the duchess, as well as Tuddenham, Heydon, and their allies, were 'Regine et Principi maxime fauorabiles'. This analysis of the duchess's allegiance seems entirely plausible, although it must be remembered that Brackley had an interest in promoting his conclusion that 'maxime expediens est parti Regis et Comitis Warwicie subtrahere, diminuere, et pocius opprimere vires omnium illorum predictorum'. Moreover, her son's marriage demonstrates that the duchess was keeping her options open; in Oct. 1460, for example, the young duke and his wife were petitioning York, on Duchess Alice's instructions, to secure particular nominations for the shrievalty. *Complete Peerage*, xii pt. i, 448; *CAD*, iv. 26–7 [A6337–A6343] (these deeds suggest that the marriage took place early in 1458); J. A. F. Thomson, 'John de la Pole, Duke of Suffolk', *Speculum*, 54 (1979), 528–9; *PL* Davis, ii. 210, 213 (Gairdner, iii. 226, 228).

defence of the city of London.[146] Heydon was a member of the committee which drafted the act of attainder against the Yorkists.[147] At the regional level, local offices were dominated by men associated with the de la Pole/court nexus. William Calthorp, the sheriff appointed for Norfolk and Suffolk in November 1458, was succeeded the following year by Philip Wentworth.[148] Wentworth also represented Suffolk in the parliament of 1459 with William Tyrell, the Duchy steward in Essex who was retained in de la Pole service, while John Wyndham sat for Norfolk with the local esquire Edmund Blake, an usher of the king's chamber.[149]

The evidence of the commissions of the peace is harder to evaluate, not least because no commissions survive for Norfolk between March 1458 and March 1460, while the existence of five separate commissions for Suffolk in the same period reveals some odd inconsistencies. Reginald Rous, for example, who had appeared on every commission of the peace in Suffolk since 1439, was named to only two of the commissions appointed during this period.[150] Similarly, the name of John Andrew, who had been a JP since 1445 with the single exception of the commission of October 1450, disappeared from the commission in January 1459. He was restored to the list of JPs appointed on 18 June and 8 August, only to be omitted once more fourteen days later, before reappearing in March and May 1460.[151] Nevertheless, it is clear that neither man was consistently losing his place in local government—both were, for example, appointed to the anti-Yorkist commission of array in December 1459[152]—and the interruption to their service on the local bench may simply have reflected the fact that the old guard of the de la Pole connection was surrendering the local limelight to younger men such as Philip Wentworth, who enjoyed both de la Pole associations and close links with the queen.[153] Moreover, the nomination to

---

[146] Griffiths, *Henry VI*, 858; Watts, 'Domestic Politics and the Constitution', 370 n.; Watts, *Henry VI*, 356 n.; *PL* Davis, ii. 185 (Gairdner, iii. 196). Scales had been associated with the queen since the early 1450s: Johnson, *Duke Richard of York*, 238.

[147] Storey, *End of the House of Lancaster*, 187; Griffiths, *Henry VI*, 824.

[148] *List of Sheriffs*, 87.

[149] *Return of the Name*, 353. William Tyrell was the son of John Tyrell, who had been chief steward of the north parts of the Duchy under the minority government. William held office as Duchy steward in Essex, Hertfordshire, Middlesex, Surrey, and London from 1437 (and jointly with his elder brother Thomas from 1440). He was receiving a £10 annuity from the de la Pole estates in 1454: Somerville, *History of the Duchy*, 605; BL Eg. Roll 8779 m. 6. For Blake, see Griffiths, *Henry VI*, 329, and *CPR 1452–61*, 536.

[150] He was appointed in Jan. 1459, omitted on 18 June and 8 Aug. 1459, restored to the commission of 20 Aug., and then dropped again in 1460. *CPR 1436–41*, 590–1; *CPR 1441–6*, 478–9; *CPR 1446–52*, 595; *CPR 1452–61*, 677–8.

[151] See all references in n. 150.

[152] *CPR 1452–61*, 560–1.

[153] Wentworth was named to every commission of the peace during this period apart from that of Jan. 1459: *CPR 1452–61*, 677–8.

the commission of the peace in both counties in March 1460 for the first time of the young duke of Suffolk and of the courtier Viscount Beaumont, who had controlled the Bardolf inheritance since 1447 but had previously held virtually no local appointments, provides a clear demonstration that the fortunes of the de la Pole affinity and of the court were closely linked, and that the queen's ascendancy enhanced the local influence of both.[154]

Members of the same group also became the beneficiaries of the Yorkist forfeitures. In December 1459 Wentworth was granted the offices of chief steward and constable at York's honour of Clare in Suffolk, while Edmund Blake became receiver and porter of the castle there, and steward of the remaining possessions of York and Salisbury in Suffolk and Essex.[155] Meanwhile, although Norfolk was co-operating with Margaret's government, some at least of his followers in East Anglia were not entirely trusted by the regime. John Paston was told that, while 'Wyndham, Heydon, Todynham, Blake, W. Chambirleyn, Wentworth, han late commyssyonys to take for tretowrys and send to the next gayl alle personys, fawtourys, and weelwyllerys to the seyd [Yorkist] lordys', 'ze haf none of commyssyonys directid to zow . . . for ze bene holdyn fauowrabil'.[156]

The change of government precipitated by the Yorkist invasion and the battle of Northampton in July 1460 reversed the local, as well as the national, balance of power. Scales was killed in London on 25 July.[157] Two days earlier, March, Warwick, and Salisbury had written to all officials in Norfolk to explain that they had issued letters instructing that no one should 'robbe or dispoile' Tuddenham, Heydon, Wyndham, and Andrew, but wanted the people to be informed that 'we, ne noon of us, intende not to favour or tendre hem, or any other of suspecte fame, but rather to corecte suche be the lawe, for we made our seid letters soly for kepyng of the pease and justice, and not for favour of suspecte condicione'.[158] By October Margaret Paston was reporting that 'the pepyll reporte full worchepfully of my lord of Warwyk', and that 'they haue no fer her but that he and othyr scholde schewe to gret favor to hem that haue be rewyllerys of thys contre be-for tyme'.[159] Despite these apprehensions, none of the de la Pole connection appeared on the commission of the peace appointed for

---

[154] *CPR 1452–61*, 677–8. For Beaumont and the Phelip–Bardolf inheritance, see above, Ch. 4.1 n. 61. His only local appointment before 1460 was as a commissioner *de walliis et fossatis* in Norfolk in 1452: *CPR 1446–52*, 582.

[155] *CPR 1452–61*, 536.

[156] *PL* Davis, ii. 185 (Gairdner, iii. 196).

[157] *Complete Peerage*, xi. 507; J. Gairdner (ed.), *Three Fifteenth-Century Chronicles*, Camden Society, new series, 28 (1880), 75 (where the date is given as 20 July).

[158] *PL* Gairdner, iii. 221–2.

[159] *PL* Davis, i. 259 (Gairdner, iii. 239).

Norfolk in November, which was headed by York, Norfolk, Warwick, and Salisbury and included Mowbray men such as Roger Chamberleyn and John Paston.[160]

The Yorkist settlement agreed at the parliament of 1460 won the support of the duke of Norfolk, and the young duke of Suffolk also threw in his lot with his father-in-law.[161] The Yorkist victory in 1461 sealed the fate of the East Anglian connection which had developed its local influence through close personal association with the Duchy of Lancaster and the Lancastrian dynasty. Although it seemed briefly that the duchess of Suffolk's successful negotiation of the political upheavals might secure the fortunes of her servants,[162] by December the new king had sent specific instructions that indictments of Tuddenham and Heydon should be encouraged in Norfolk.[163] Tuddenham was executed in February 1462; Thomas Daniel and Philip Wentworth had been attainted in parliament three months earlier.[164] John Heydon— perhaps unsurprisingly for this adroit political trimmer—survived, but his power in the region was severely curtailed by his removal, after almost two decades in office, from the local stewardship of the Duchy. After twenty years during which he had consistently filled a variety of offices in local government, he is glaringly conspicuous by his absence from the appointments of 1461 onwards.[165] Other members of the de la Pole affinity weathered the change of dynasty with less disruption to their careers: Miles Stapleton, William Calthorp, and Edmund Wichingham retained their places on the commission of the peace in Norfolk, for example, as did Reginald Rous and Thomas Brewes in

[160] *CPR 1452–61*, 671–2.

[161] *Complete Peerage*, xii pt. i, 448; Gairdner (ed.), *Three Fifteenth-Century Chronicles*, 76–7; Griffiths, *Henry VI*, 872; Watts, 'Domestic Politics and the Constitution', 385, 387 n. Suffolk's allegiance was presumably decided by the marriage alliance he had made; it is also worth noting John Watts's point that by 1461 'the sense of ideological conflict or dynastic rivalry had more or less given way to the perception of a war between North and South', and that the queen had become 'indelibly associated with an interest which was patently more regional than national': *Henry VI*, 360–2.

[162] In June 1461 John Paston received a report from Norwich that 'it is toolde here that Tudenham and Heydon haue a pardon of the Kyng and that they schal come vp to London with the Lady of Suffolk to the coronacion'. The duchess's interests were safeguarded by a provision made in the first parliament of the new reign. *PL* Davis, ii. 237 (Gairdner, iii. 278); *Rot. Parl.*, v. 470.

[163] *PL* Davis, i. 277; ii. 262–3 (Gairdner, iv. 15, 20).

[164] Gairdner (ed.), *Three Fifteenth-Century Chronicles*, 78; *Rot. Parl.*, v. 480. For Tuddenham's will, see N. H. Nicolas (ed.), *Testamenta Vetusta* (London, 1826), i. 297–8. Wentworth was executed in May 1463: Gairdner (ed.), *Three Fifteenth-Century Chronicles*, 79.

[165] John Neville, Lord Montague, was appointed steward of the Duchy lands in Norfolk, Suffolk, and Cambridgeshire on 21 July 1461; he was immediately appointed to the commission of the peace in Norfolk, and to that in Suffolk from 1464: Somerville, *History of the Duchy*, 594; *CPR 1461–7*, 568, 572–3; *List of Sheriffs*, 87; *List of Escheators*, 88; *Return of the Name*, 358.

Suffolk.[166] Though the fortunes of the leaders of the de la Pole affinity were irretrievably associated with those of the court, these latter men, members of the extraordinarily broad local connection, had been able to avoid committing themselves too unequivocally, just as they had in 1450.[167]

Indeed, as had also been the case in 1450, de la Pole associations permeated local society to such an extent that it was impracticable to exclude from regional administration everyone thus 'tainted'. However, whereas in 1450 local structures of power had survived the loss of the duke of Suffolk remarkably intact, and the dominance of the de la Pole affinity had continued, the events of 1461 had a much more profound effect on the political life of the region. The leaders of that affinity were removed, and the Duchy lands, from which they had derived much of their local power, were—though still a private estate distinct from the crown lands—no longer the personal inheritance of the king. The advent of a new, active, Yorkist monarch, and simultaneously of a new generation among the local nobility as the duke of Suffolk emerged from the shadow of his mother and as the 17-year-old Mowbray heir succeeded his father,[168] marked the end of sixty years during which the region had been dominated by a recognizably Lancastrian connection which had evolved since 1399. It was the beginning of a period of change in the political complexion of the region which was to culminate in the extinction of the Mowbrays and the emergence of the Howards as the controlling interest in East Anglia.[169]

---

[166] *CPR 1461–7*, 568, 572–3. For the connections of these men with de la Pole interests, see above, pp. 91, 99.

[167] See above, pp. 159–62.

[168] *PL* Davis, i. 279 (Gairdner, iv. 25); *DNB*, xxxix. 224–5.

[169] *Complete Peerage*, ix. 608–15; D. MacCulloch, *Suffolk and the Tudors* (Oxford, 1986), 53–73.

Part III

The Crown, the Duchy of Lancaster, and the Rule of the Localities
Derbyshire and Staffordshire, 1399–1461

6

1399–1414
King and Duchy

1. THE LANCASTRIAN AFFINITY IN THE NORTH MIDLANDS TO 1399

The Duchy of Lancaster estates in Derbyshire and Staffordshire, and the problems of political management with which they confronted Henry IV in 1399, present a marked contrast to the situation in East Anglia. The Norfolk lands, which had been acquired relatively late in the Duchy's history, were peripheral to the main focus of Lancastrian regional interests and were used mainly as a financial rather than a political resource.[1] Because the potential local influence inherent in the possession of the Duchy estates had not previously been exploited there, Henry was able to start from scratch in developing an unequivocally royal lordship in the region which fully incorporated his private territorial interests without compromising the universal authority of the crown. The north midlands, on the other hand, formed part of the Duchy heartlands in terms of both geography and politics. There, Henry inherited from his father an extensive and powerful affinity which played a leading role in local politics, and which offered the new king substantial military support both in 1399 and in the crises of the early years of the reign. In Derbyshire and Staffordshire, therefore, the tension between Henry's private authority and his new public responsibilities was at its most intense and most explicit. The task of establishing the Lancastrian monarchy while preserving regional power structures in which private Lancastrian lordship played such a key role was a complex and delicate one.

The honours of Tutbury and Duffield, which dominated south-western Derbyshire and eastern Staffordshire,[2] had been among the first properties annexed to what was eventually to become the Duchy.

---

[1] See above, Ch. 3.1.

[2] The honours included, in Staffordshire, the castle of Tutbury, the forest of Needwood, and the manors of Rolleston, Marchington, Barton, Agardsley, and Uttoxeter; and in Derbyshire, the forest of Duffield, the hundreds of Appletree, Wirksworth, and Repton, and a collection of manors stretching from Scropton in the south up to Hartington and Matlock on the edges of the Peak: R. Somerville, *History of the Duchy of Lancaster*, i (London, 1953), 7; DL29/728/11987; see Map 3, p. 194.

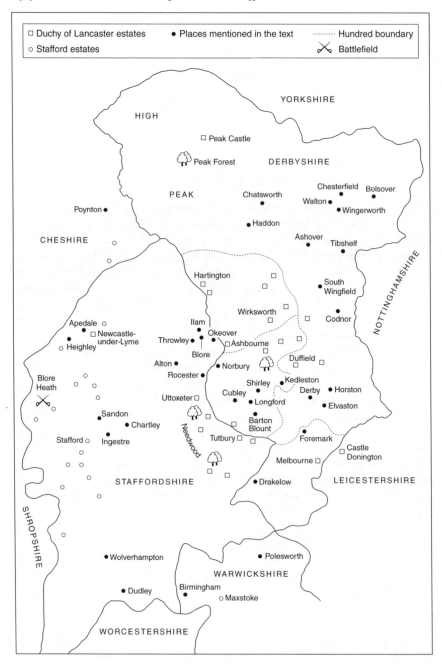

Map 3. Duchy of Lancaster estates in Derbyshire and Staffordshire

They were forfeited by Robert Ferrers, earl of Derby, after his rebellion in 1266, and granted to Henry III's son Edmund, first earl of Lancaster.[3] In 1372 Duchy interests in the area were further consolidated by the addition of the lands received by John of Gaunt in exchange for the earldom of Richmond; these included the castle and honour of the High Peak which dominated north-west Derbyshire.[4] These estates represented one of the greatest concentrations of Lancastrian territorial interests outside the palatinate itself.[5] Tutbury was the largest single receipt in the Duchy, worth on average £1,760 a year during the 1390s.[6] However, Gaunt had chosen not to exploit the area as a source of cash, the strategy he adopted for his rich but peripheral lands in Norfolk,[7] but instead used this revenue to create and sustain an affinity which made the north midlands a focal point of Lancastrian political activity. By the 1390s, the Tutbury receiver was paying an average of just over £600 each year in annuities,[8] and these financial rewards were supplemented by the plethora of prestigious offices at Gaunt's disposal in his three castles and two forests in the region. While, as elsewhere in the Duchy, the receivers' duties fell to professional administrators, the offices of steward and constable of the castles at Tutbury, Melbourne, and the High Peak and the master forestships of Needwood and Duffield Frith were filled by members

---

[3] Somerville, *History of the Duchy*, 3–7. Edmund had already in 1265 acquired Melbourne Castle, which lay just beyond the southern edge of the Ferrers lands in Derbyshire, from Simon de Montfort. In 1267 the manor of Newcastle-under-Lyme in north-west Staffordshire, which had previously belonged to the crown, was added to his endowment, and in 1279 he surrendered two Welsh lordships in return for a further grant of Ferrers lands, consisting of the manor of Ashbourne and the wapentake and manor of Wirksworth in Derbyshire. The midlands estates acquired by the marriage in 1294 of Edmund's son Thomas to Alice Lacy, heiress of the earl of Lincoln, lay mainly further east, in Nottinghamshire and Leicestershire; however, they included Castle Donington just inside the Leicestershire border, only a few miles from Melbourne and not far from Tutbury itself. *CPR 1258–66*, 424; Somerville, *History of the Duchy*, 8, 14, 18–19, 22; J. R. Birrell, 'The Honour of Tutbury in the Fourteenth and Fifteenth Centuries', unpublished MA thesis (Birmingham, 1962), 17; T. F. Tout, 'The Earldoms under Edward I', *TRHS*, new series, 8 (1894), 147.   [4] Somerville, *History of the Duchy*, 52–3.

[5] The north midland estates were rivalled in this respect only by Duchy holdings in Yorkshire: DL29/728/11987.

[6] This average represents the clear value of the estates. The equivalent figure for Henry IV's reign is £1,550: figures calculated from S. Walker, *The Lancastrian Affinity* (Oxford, 1990), appendix IV; DL29/728/11987–8; DL29/729/11995–6, 12001, 12004; DL29/730/12006, 12008, 12011–12, 12015. The Tutbury receipt accounted for the revenues from all the lands mentioned above, including the High Peak and Melbourne Castle, although both retained an administrative identity independent of the Ferrers estates. (This practice of preserving an administrative distinction between lands of different provenance seems to have been universal within the Duchy; see above, Ch. 3.1 at n. 8, for the separate accounts of the 'Lancaster' and 'Richmond exchange' lands within the Norfolk receipt.)

[7] See above, Ch. 3.1. It seems that Gaunt's predecessor Henry of Grosmont may have treated the north midlands estates primarily as a financial resource, since the annuities he is known to have granted in the area (a total of £82) constituted only a small fraction of the receipt's income: Walker, *The Lancastrian Affinity*, 215.

[8] Walker, *The Lancastrian Affinity*, appendix IV.

of the local gentry.[9] This hierarchy of office gave the affinity in the region a coherent structure entirely lacking in this period amongst the Lancastrians of East Anglia, where there was no *caput honoris*, and therefore no significant official presence above the administrative level.[10] Further, this structured affinity was given focus by the frequent presence of Gaunt himself and of members of his family at the various Lancastrian residences in the area. The duke was a regular visitor to the region; his second wife Constance of Castile spent long periods at Tutbury until her death in 1394, and Bolingbroke and his children used the castle periodically thereafter.[11] The region was also well represented in the duke's household. Sir Walter Blount, a knight of Gaunt's chamber in the 1380s and his chamberlain during the 1390s, had been constable of Tutbury castle since 1373 and master forester of Needwood at least since 1380. The Derbyshire knight Hugh Shirley joined the household during the 1390s, as did Sir John Dabridgecourt, master forester of Duffield Frith; the esquire Peter Melbourne, constable of Melbourne Castle, had been a member since the previous decade.[12] Nor was the duke's household the only Lancastrian establishment in which there was a midlands presence; Shirley's wife was among Constance of Castile's principal attendants, and Blount married one of the noblewomen who had accompanied the duchess from Spain.[13]

This diversity of roles within Lancastrian service was, by the 1390s, paralleled by the range of connections linking the men who made up the core of the Duchy affinity. Prominent among this group were a number of gentry families whose manorial seats lay in south-west Derbyshire, close both to each other and to Tutbury—among them the Blounts of Barton Blount and the Shirleys of Shirley, together with the Cokayns of Ashbourne, the Montgomeries of Cubley, the Cursons of Kedleston, the Longfords of Longford, and the Poles of Hartington, as well as the Okeovers of Okeover, just over the Staffordshire border.[14]

---

[9] Somerville, *History of the Duchy*, 98–100, 377, 381–3.

[10] See above, Ch. 3.1, and Ch. 4.2 at n. 76, for the subsequent recognition of the newly enhanced political importance of the Duchy affinity in East Anglia by the creation in 1443 of the position of 'chief steward' in the region—an office of equivalent status to those which had always existed within the Lancastrian honours in the midlands.

[11] Walker, *The Lancastrian Affinity*, 216–17; Somerville, *History of the Duchy*, 65.

[12] Blount and Shirley were each left 100 marks in Gaunt's will, of which Blount, Dabridgecourt and Melbourne were among the executors. Walker, *The Lancastrian Affinity*, 217; Somerville, *History of the Duchy*, 364, 377, 381–2; J. Nichols (ed.), *Collection of all the Wills* . . . (London, 1780), 159, 163.

[13] Walker, *The Lancastrian Affinity*, 217; E. A. Ayres, 'Parliamentary Representation in Derbyshire and Nottinghamshire in the Fifteenth Century', unpublished MA thesis (Nottingham, 1956), 2–3; *DNB*, v. 257.

[14] All these manors lay within the hundred of Appletree or the neighbouring soke of Wirksworth, both of which belonged to the Duchy, apart from Okeover which lay only a couple of miles from Ashbourne but on the opposite bank of the river Dove (see Map 3, p. 194).

Also included were some with further-flung estates, such as the Foljambes and the Wendesleys, whose homes at Walton and Wingerworth lay a couple of miles from Chesterfield in north-east Derbyshire, as well as Dabridgecourt, a naturalized Hainaulter who became involved with the region from the early 1380s through his office at Duffield.[15]

Members of this group are consistently to be found acting with and for each other in legal transactions during the 1380s and 1390s;[16] unsurprisingly, some were also related by marriage. John Curson of Kedleston, the steward of Tutbury during the later 1390s, married Sir Nicholas Montgomery's daughter Margaret. Their daughter, another Margaret, became the wife of Thomas Okeover, while Montgomery's son and heir, also Nicholas, was married to the daughter of Sir Nicholas Longford.[17] Sir John Cokayn, nephew of the lawyer John Cokayn whom Gaunt appointed chief steward of the North Parts of the Duchy, married Hugh Shirley's daughter Isabel, and their son, another John, married Joan, daughter of John Dabridgecourt.[18]

It is a striking feature of this group that their territorial interests were concentrated in Derbyshire, and—despite the fact that John Curson's son and heir was later to marry a daughter of the Staffordshire knight and Lancastrian retainer John Bagot[19]—that their links with those of Gaunt's retainers whose estates lay primarily to the west of Tutbury were less numerous and less intimate. Indeed, the Staffordshire com-

---

[15] For all these families in Lancastrian service, see Somerville, *History of the Duchy*, 364, 366–7, 377, 381–2; Walker, *The Lancastrian Affinity*, 216, 264, 267, 269, 273, 275–6, 278, 281, 284. Dabridgecourt, whose grandfather had come to England in the service of Edward III's queen Philippa of Hainault, held the manor of Elvaston in Derbyshire, which he seems to have acquired from the Willoughbys of Wollaton through his marriage to Maud, widow of Sir Richard Willoughby. After Dabridgecourt's death the manor was acquired by the Blounts. E. F. Jacob (ed.), *The Register of Henry Chichele* (Oxford, 1938–47), ii. 650; S. J. Payling, *Political Society in Lancastrian England* (Oxford, 1991), 34, 242; DRO D518M/E4, E6. For the Blounts and Elvaston later in the century, see below, Ch. 8 at n. 209.

[16] See, for example, DRO D158M/T16; DRO D231M/T161, T306; DRO D258 Box 54/1 hb; DRO D518M/T57; DCL I. H. Jeayes (ed.), 'Descriptive Catalogue of the Charters and Muniments in the Possession of R. W. Chandos-Pole esq. at Radbourne Hall', 175 [425], 177 [431], 179 [435–6, 438–9], 185 [457]; I. H. Jeayes (ed.), *Descriptive Catalogue of Derbyshire Charters* (London, 1906), 10 [76], 44 [344], 86 [677], 210–11 [1692–3], 240–1 [1921, 1924, 1926–8], 270 [2130], 306 [2415–16]; *CPR 1391–6*, 98; *CCR 1392–6*, 367; J. G. Bellamy, 'The Parliamentary Representation of Nottinghamshire, Derbyshire and Staffordshire in the Reign of Richard II', unpublished MA thesis (Nottingham, 1961), 374.

[17] I. Rowney, 'The Cursons of Fifteenth-Century Derbyshire', *Derbyshire Archaeological Journal*, 103 (1983), 108; Huntington Library HAP box 2, folder 1.

[18] There has been some confusion over the identities of the various John Cokayns; for clarification, see C. Carpenter, *Locality and Polity* (Cambridge, 1991), 111 n. To add to the confusion, John Dabridgecourt had two daughters named Joan; the other married Hugh Willoughby (see below, Ch. 8 n. 209, and Jacob (ed.), *Register of Henry Chichele*, ii. 53). For the John Cokayn who was Gaunt's steward, see Somerville, *History of the Duchy*, 367–8.

[19] The marriage took place in 1410: Bellamy, 'Parliamentary Representation', 16; G. Wrottesley, 'A History of the Bagot Family', *Collections for a History of Staffordshire*, new series, 11 (1908), 55, 117.

ponent of the Duchy retinue formed less of an identifiable and close-knit group than its more extensive counterpart in Derbyshire and the Tutbury borderlands. The duke's principal retainers in Staffordshire were men who had fought for him on his campaigns in Spain during the 1380s, including John Bagot himself as well as the knights Thomas Beek, William Newport, John Ipstones, and Thomas Aston.[20] Only Beek held Duchy office in the region,[21] however, and, though these men maintained significant connections with fellow Lancastrians across the region, their domestic careers remained comparatively independent of the Duchy circles which dominated Derbyshire and the eastern border of Staffordshire.[22]

This imbalance between the two parts of the Duchy affinity in the region was mirrored in the political complexion of the two counties. Christine Carpenter has argued in her study of fifteenth-century Warwickshire that 'regionalism was a key factor' in the history of the latter shire, which 'was in fact a wholly artificial creation, consisting of a number of areas, each of them facing outwards to the neighbouring county'. She points out that, 'although one would not expect a county to constitute a geographical and economic unit, Warwickshire is more fragmented than most', and goes on to suggest that 'in some sense this applies to all the midland counties and is due to the artificiality of their original shiring'.[23] Derbyshire and Staffordshire are certainly among the counties to which this analysis applies. The politics of the region were profoundly influenced by the fact that the shire boundaries did not delineate discrete geo-political units, but were merely one element in broader territorial and political structures across the region. In this, the north midland counties differed significantly from East Anglia, an area which formed a coherent political entity within which the two shires of Norfolk and Suffolk were characterized by clearly distinguishable political and tenurial traits.[24] In the north midlands, regional power structures had no 'natural' shape. Instead, they had to be given shape through the interaction of the various territorial interests in the region, expressed through the formation of private networks and hierarchies, with the public framework of local government.[25] This meant that changing political circumstances could affect not only the make-up of local power structures, but the structures themselves across the entire region.

---

[20] Walker, *The Lancastrian Affinity*, 225, 263. Aston's annuity was paid at the Cheshire receipt of Halton: DL29/738/12096.

[21] As steward of Newcastle-under-Lyme: Somerville, *History of the Duchy*, 377.

[22] Their appearances in the corpus of deed evidence quoted above, n. 16, for example, are extremely limited.   [23] Carpenter, *Locality and Polity*, 25–6.

[24] See above, Ch. 3.1.

[25] C. Carpenter, 'The Duke of Clarence and the Midlands: A Study in the Interplay of Local and National Politics', *Midland History*, 11 (1986), 25–6.

In administrative terms, Derbyshire and Staffordshire were two completely independent entities—indeed, their official structures of power faced in opposite directions, since Derbyshire's shrievalty was shared with its eastern neighbour Nottinghamshire, and Staffordshire's was periodically combined with Shropshire to the west.[26] In tenurial terms, however, this situation was almost exactly reversed. The extensive and valuable estates of the honour of Tutbury, the dominant territorial interest in the region, straddled the Derbyshire–Staffordshire border, so that eastern Staffordshire and western Derbyshire together naturally tended to form a political unit. This lack of correspondence between the administrative and tenurial structures of the region meant that a consistent degree of Lancastrian influence in the official hierarchies of local government in both shires was by no means inevitable, but would depend on the relationship of political interests and networks in the Tutbury region with those of western Staffordshire and eastern Derbyshire.

In Derbyshire, the pattern of landholding facilitated the growth of Lancastrian influence and the affinity through which it was embodied. While the Duchy's territorial dominance was unchallengeable in the west of the shire, which was therefore firmly linked to Staffordshire through the Tutbury lands, the east would always be susceptible to influence from Nottinghamshire. Indeed, the only other magnate family resident in the county were the Greys of Codnor, the bulk of whose midlands estates lay further east in Nottinghamshire rather than in Derbyshire itself.[27] Nevertheless, the Greys were closely associated with Gaunt, who himself held estates and retained several important local figures in Nottinghamshire.[28] Eastern Derbyshire was therefore incorporated into a Lancastrian sphere of influence stretching from Tutbury across into Nottinghamshire, and Lancastrian interests were able to dominate the official representation of the shire, including the dual shrievalty.[29]

[26] Staffordshire was, however, a single shrievalty throughout the Lancastrian period: *List of Sheriffs for England and Wales*, PRO Lists and Indexes, 9 (1898), 103, 127.

[27] S. M. Wright, *The Derbyshire Gentry in the Fifteenth Century* (Chesterfield, 1983), 4.

[28] John, Lord Grey, and one of his sons served abroad under Gaunt's command. The Duchy held several manors in Nottinghamshire, and the overlordship of the Yorkshire honour of Tickhill also dominated the north of the county. Walker, *The Lancastrian Affinity*, 211; Payling, *Political Society*, 120.

[29] *List of Sheriffs*, 103; *Return of the Name*, 240–1, 244, 247, 249, 252, 255; *CPR 1391–6*, 436; *1396–9*, 96, 233, 435; *List of Escheators for England and Wales*, PRO Lists and Indexes, 72 (1971), 110; Walker, *The Lancastrian Affinity*, 210–11; Payling, *Political Society*, 119. Cf. the situation in Warwickshire under the first two Lancastrian kings, when Duchy interests in Staffordshire and Leicestershire meant that the king was able to extend his regional control across the shire borders into north and east Warwickshire, and men from the 'Duchy' shire of Leicestershire dominated the dual shrievalty of Warwickshire and Leicestershire: Carpenter, *Locality and Polity*, 361–2, 366–7, 371–2.

In Staffordshire, the political complexion was very different. The Lancastrian estates were clustered in the east of the county, with Newcastle-under-Lyme a lone outpost in the north-west, and Gaunt held no lands across the border in Shropshire which could help to incorporate western Staffordshire into a broader sphere of Duchy influence. Moreover, Staffordshire—unlike Derbyshire—offered a range of alternative sources of magnate lordship. The shire boasted a number of baronial seats—those of the lords Audley at Heighley, the lords Furnival at Alton, the lords Ferrers at Chartley, the lords Basset at Drayton Basset, and the Suttons at Dudley.[30] Most significant was the presence of Hugh Stafford, earl of Stafford, whose extensive estates in western Staffordshire and in Shropshire allowed him to dominate the part of the county where Gaunt had no territorial stake.[31] During the 1380s the substantial Stafford affinity had a controlling interest in the administration of the shire virtually as overwhelming as that of the Lancastrians in Derbyshire,[32] and Gaunt seems to have been happy to acquiesce in this partition of the region. His relations with the Staffords were generally warm—Earl Hugh had fought under Gaunt's command—and there seem to have been some links between their retinues: both Sir John Ipstones and Sir Thomas Aston, for example, had been retained by Stafford before moving into Gaunt's service.[33]

This political accommodation was disrupted by Stafford's death in 1386. His son and heir Thomas was granted livery of his estates in 1389, but died childless three years later, to be succeeded by his brother William, who died in 1395 before reaching his majority. The earldom passed to a third brother, Edmund, then aged 17.[34] The effects of this succession of Stafford minorities were compounded by the deaths in 1390 and 1391 of Ralph, Lord Basset, and Nicholas, Lord Audley, both without direct heirs.[35] Gaunt was the obvious candidate to fill this

[30] The Suttons of Dudley were not strictly of baronial status at this point; John Sutton was created Lord Dudley in 1440. *Complete Peerage*, i. 339–40; v. 587–91, 315–17; ii. 3; iv. 479–80.

[31] C. Rawcliffe, *The Staffords* (Cambridge, 1978), 11, 191–2.

[32] *List of Sheriffs*, 127; *Return of the Name*, 205–6, 209, 211, 213, 215, 218, 221, 224, 226, 229, 232, 235, 238, 240; *CPR 1381–5*, 139, 245, 251; *1385–9*, 82, 254; *1388–92*, 135, 138, 342, 344, 525, 527; Walker, *The Lancastrian Affinity*, 212–13. Bellamy notes that not only was Lancastrian representation in the county administration in Staffordshire a fraction of what it was in Derbyshire, it was also more limited than in Nottinghamshire. Of the 31 Duchy men who became MPs in the three counties during Richard II's reign, for example, 16 sat in Derbyshire, 9 in Nottinghamshire, and only 6 in Staffordshire: 'Parliamentary Representation', p. xvii.

[33] Walker, *The Lancastrian Affinity*, 214, 225; Bellamy, 'Parliamentary Representation', pp. xxix, 3.

[34] Rawcliffe, *The Staffords*, 9, 11–12; *Complete Peerage*, xii pt. 1, 180.

[35] Ralph Basset left his properties in the region to his nephew Sir Hugh Shirley, but the bequest was of dubious legitimacy, and many of the estates were subsequently secured by the Staffords, who were descended from a sister of Basset's grandfather. The Audley barony was revived in 1405 for Nicholas's great-nephew and co-heir John Tochet. Walker, *The Lancastrian*

political vacuum, and indeed the decade was marked both by an increased proportion of Lancastrian office-holders in Staffordshire and by rising expenditure on annuities at the Tutbury receipt.[36] These years did not, however, mark a straightforward extension of the duke's dominance from Derbyshire into Staffordshire. Simon Walker has argued persuasively that, at the same time as Richard II was establishing a power base in his new principality of Chester,[37] he was also seeking to create some sort of a personal following for himself across the Cheshire border in Staffordshire. Richard retained Thomas, the young earl of Stafford, in 1389 and, during the following years, some leading members of the Stafford affinity including the esquire William Walsall, a prominent figure in local administration, to whom the king subsequently granted the constableship of Stafford Castle and custody of the Audley estates.[38] In the months after Gaunt's death Richard turned his attention to the Duchy affinity itself, retaining John Dabridgecourt and Thomas Wendesley in April 1399.[39] During the later 1390s the king also seems to have been grooming his nephew Thomas Holand for a leading role in the midlands. Holand was granted most of the Beauchamp estates in 1397, and it was to him that the honour of Tutbury itself was apportioned on Gaunt's death in 1399.[40] It was undoubtedly in Staffordshire that Lancastrian interests were most vulnerable but, significantly, even in Derbyshire they were coming under attack during the later 1390s. Sir Nicholas Clifton, Holand's steward in Derbyshire and from 1396 constable of the royal castle at Bolsover, was able consistently to outmanœuvre Gaunt's retainer Thomas Foljambe in a local property dispute, despite Foljambe's attempts to secure redress, which were pursued throughout the 1390s with the duke's support.[41]

However, the events of 1399 demonstrated that Richard's attempts to establish his own lordship in the region had enjoyed only limited success—both Dabridgecourt and Wendesley, for example, joined the invading Lancastrian army[42]—and vindicated Gaunt's management of his north midlands following. As Simon Walker points out, support for Bolingbroke in Staffordshire may in fact have been reinforced by

---

Affinity, 222; *Complete Peerage*, i. 340; ii. 3–4; E. P. Shirley (ed.), *Stemmata Shirleiana* (London, 1873), 1, 33–4; Rawcliffe, *The Staffords*, 192.

[36] *Return of the Name*, 240, 242, 245, 248, 250, 253, 256; *CPR 1391–6*, 437; *1396–9*, 235; Walker, *The Lancastrian Affinity*, 224–6, 308–9; Rawcliffe, *The Staffords*, 201.

[37] For Richard II and Cheshire, see above, Ch. 1.

[38] Walsall held the Audley wardship jointly with John Delves, a fellow Stafford retainer: Walker, *The Lancastrian Affinity*, 216, 228; J. C. Wedgwood, *Staffordshire Parliamentary History*, William Salt Archaeological Society (London, 1917–18), 107; *CFR 1391–9*, 11.

[39] *CPR 1396–9*, 534, 558.

[40] Walker, *The Lancastrian Affinity*, 231; *CPR 1396–9*, 200; Somerville, *History of the Duchy*, 135. [41] Walker, *The Lancastrian Affinity*, 229–31.

[42] See below, n. 44.

Richard's decision to grant Tutbury to Holand, since the local reputation of the latter's family had been tarnished by his uncle's murder of the Stafford heir fourteen years earlier.[43] Nevertheless, the scale of the region's representation in Henry's forces in 1399 seems to indicate clearly that any hostility to the Holands merely supplemented the positive force of Lancastrian allegiance in the area. Wages were paid from the central revenues of the Duchy for the military service during the crisis of forty knights, esquires, and gentlemen. Of these forty, sixteen were from Derbyshire and Staffordshire, a figure more than twice the number from any other single region.[44] The status of the north midlands as one of the pre-eminent areas of Duchy influence had been re-emphasized, and the Lancastrians of the area reaped the benefits of their loyalty in the years after 1399.

2. 1399–1414: THE LANCASTRIAN AFFINITY AND THE LANCASTRIAN CROWN

Henry's lordship over the Duchy retinue in Derbyshire and Staffordshire played a significant part in securing his military success in 1399, but in the following years it became clear that it would not necessarily be a straightforward task to accommodate this private lordship within his public authority as king. Henry was confronted with the problem of combining his need to exploit the confirmed loyalty of his retainers in the face of repeated rebellion (as well as his responsibility to reward them for their service) with his need to avoid alienating any of his other subjects or destabilizing established local power structures. The fact that he was facing military challenges to his rule also meant that he had little opportunity to give close attention to the maintenance of this delicate equilibrium. His immediate response in the north midlands in the first troubled years of the reign was simply to reward the continuing loyal service of his Lancastrian following.

Annuity payments at Tutbury, which had averaged around £600 a year during the early 1390s, reached £830 by September 1400 and only

[43] John Holand killed Ralph, eldest son of Hugh, earl of Stafford, in a brawl during the Scottish campaign of 1385. Thomas Holand, now duke of Surrey, was granted custody of Tutbury Castle and honour, Lancaster Castle and honour, and other northern lands including the castles of Liverpool, Halton, and Kenilworth, in Mar. 1399: Walker, *The Lancastrian Affinity*, 231; Rawcliffe, *The Staffords*, 11; Somerville, *History of the Duchy*, 135.

[44] The men recorded were the knights Thomas Beek, John Cokayn, Walter Blount, Thomas Aston, Thomas Wendesley, John Dabridgecourt, and Nicholas Montgomery, the esquires Simon Fraunceys, Roger Bradbourne, Thomas Foljambe, Thomas Gresley, Henry Bothe, John Curson, Thurstan del Boure, and Thomas Cokefield, and the gentleman John Normanton: DL42/15 fo. 70; DL28/4/1–2; DL29/728/11987–8. The overwhelming importance of the north midlands to the military resources at Henry's disposal was further emphasized during the rebellion of 1403: Payling, *Political Society*, 136.

a year later came to a total of more than £1,000—a figure which, when added to the 500 marks assigned at Tutbury to Gaunt's widow, accounted for virtually the entire revenue of what was the Duchy's richest receipt.[45] The initial increase can be attributed partly, perhaps mostly, to Gaunt's concern to reinforce his affinity in the region in the last years of his life.[46] However, the dramatic inflation in the cost of the Tutbury retinue after 1399 was the direct result of Henry's distribution of generous rewards to the men who had formed the backbone of his invading army.

Some money was expended on the payment of new annuities to men who had not previously been formally retained by the Duchy. The Frounceys of Foremark and the Gresleys of Drakelow, for example, lived in the Lancastrian heartlands of south-west Derbyshire and both families actively supported Henry in 1399.[47] Both were to be financially rewarded: the esquire Simon Frounceys was granted £12 a year in 1401, and Sir Robert Frounceys and Sir Thomas Gresley £40 and £26 respectively in 1406, all at the Tutbury receipt.[48] These substantial grants to knightly families which had not previously had any formal connection with the Duchy were the exception rather than the rule, however. Most of the new Lancastrian retainers were relatively uninfluential local gentlemen who were paid only small sums.[49]

This recognition of the broader base of the Lancastrian connection in the region was not accompanied by any serious attempt to expand the Duchy's constituency among the local élite. Even the grants to Gresley and the Frounceys reinforced rather than challenged the status quo, since they represented exactly the same geographical interests as the established core of the local affinity. Instead, additional sums were distributed to the existing group of leading Lancastrians. Gaunt had

---

[45] During Henry IV's reign, annuity payments, including the assignment to Duchess Katherine, averaged £1,380 a year; the average annual clear value of the receipt was £1,550. When other 'foreign' payments, including those to the Duchy's receiver-general, were deducted, the receipt in fact showed a deficit (ranging from £6 to £220) in six of the ten years for which accounts survive: Walker, *The Lancastrian Affinity*, appendix IV; DL29/728/11987–8; DL29/729/11995–6, 12001, 12004; DL29/729/730/12006, 12008, 12011–12, 12015; for the over-extension of the Tutbury revenues, see above, pp. 28–9.

[46] See above, Ch. 2.1.

[47] Thomas Gresley and Simon Frounceys (a Derbyshire esquire for whom no other reference has so far been found, but who was almost certainly a member of the same family) were both paid for their service during Henry's return to England: see above, n. 44. Thomas Gresley had also fought with Gaunt in Gascony: DL29/728/11985.

[48] Simon Frounceys was also granted in 1401 the wardship of the hundred of Gresley in Derbyshire, which he later exchanged for an annuity of 17 marks. Robert Frounceys had been retained in Nov. 1399 as a king's knight with an annuity of £62 from the fee-farm of Nottingham, a sum which the Duchy annuity replaced when Nottingham was granted to the new queen in dower: DL42/15 pt. 1 fo. 91v, pt. 2 fo. 1; DL42/16 pt. 3 fos. 17, 71; DL29/738/12096; DL28/27/9; *CPR 1399–1401*, 64.

[49] See DL29/738/12096.

paid Sir Hugh Shirley two annuities of 100 marks and £20; in 1400 Shirley acquired the constableship of Castle Donington with an additional annuity there of 40 marks, and in 1402 the master forestership of Duffield Frith.[50] Sir William Newport and Sir John Cokayn had each received 20 marks annually from Gaunt; Newport was granted an annuity of £40, and Cokayn the town of Ashbourne, worth £60, by the new king.[51] The annuity paid to Peter Melbourne, the constable of Melbourne Castle, was increased dramatically from £10 to 100 marks in November 1399, and the Derbyshire esquire John Curson of Kedleston received an annuity of £20 in addition to his fee as steward of Tutbury.[52] Roger Leche of Chatsworth in Derbyshire, who had been a member of Henry's household at least since 1398, was granted an annuity of 100 marks from the High Peak in September 1399.[53]

The policy of rewarding those who had already proved their worth in Lancastrian service dictated not only the distribution of financial grants from the Duchy, but also appointments to local office. The direct association between the leading gentry families of the region and the Lancastrian crown seems to lie behind the fact that office-holding in the two shires was characterized during the first half of the fifteenth century by the consistent reappointment of a relatively small number of gentry families.[54] In counties where various noble interests were competing for local rule, the need to secure the representation of those interests in shire administration could result in a comparatively high turnover of office among a broad section of the gentry, as lords sought to place their men in positions of influence.[55] In counties where the

[50] The Donington annuity was later changed to a grant of a dovecot at the castle and 25 marks a year: Walker, *The Lancastrian Affinity*, 281; DL29/738/12096 m. 5; DL29/212/3248; DL42/15 fos. 8v, 10v, 23, 96, 98.

[51] Newport received his grant in Nov. 1399, Cokayn in Oct. 1400: Walker, *The Lancastrian Affinity*, 267, 276; DL29/738/12096 m. 6; DL42/15 fo. 87.

[52] Somerville, *History of the Duchy*, 377, 381; Walker, *The Lancastrian Affinity*, 275; DL42/15 fos. 6v, 8v.

[53] In 1399 Leche was also granted the reversion of lands in the Peak worth £24 a year which were currently held by Sir Thomas Wendesley: DL28/1/10 m. 30v; DL 29/738/12096; DL42/15 pt. 2 fos. 63v–64.

[54] In Derbyshire, for example, 19 gentry families provided JPs between 1399 and 1422, and 13 between 1423 and 1461; 7 families provided sheriffs in the first period and 8 in the second (although these latter figures are distorted by the fact that the shrievalty was shared with Nottinghamshire). In Staffordshire, where the Duchy was one of the two major powers, 18 families provided JPs between 1399 and 1422, and 16 from 1423 to 1461; 17 families provided sheriffs in the first period and 24 in the second: *List of Sheriffs*, 103, 127; CPR *1399–1401*, 557–8, 564; *1401–5*, 516; *1405–8*, 490, 497; *1408–13*, 480, 485; *1413–16*, 418, 423; *1416–22*, 451, 459; *1422–9*, 561, 569; *1429–36*, 615, 624; *1436–41*, 581, 590; *1441–6*, 469, 478; *1446–52*, 588, 595; *1452–61*, 663–4, 677. Cf. Wright's comments on Derbyshire: *The Derbyshire Gentry*, 95–8, 110–12; Payling's conclusions for Nottinghamshire: *Political Society*, ch. 5; and Carpenter, *Locality and Polity*, 274–5.

[55] For example, Warwickshire, where 36 families provided JPs between 1429 and 1460, and 31 provided sheriffs between 1430 and 1509. Although the periods covered do not match

Duchy was the leading landed interest, however, the fact that the king's territorial dominance was matched by his complete control of royal appointments meant that men connected with the Duchy were the obvious candidates for local office. It also meant that the concentration of regional power in the hands of an élite group of Lancastrian retainers was an obvious means of delegating the king's personal authority in the locality. The appearance of such an élite within a Duchy-dominated shire such as Nottinghamshire should not, therefore, be taken to indicate that it was the norm for local rule to be dominated by a small group of greater gentry.[56]

This is not to say that office-holding was necessarily unduly restricted in 'Duchy' shires, since if the Lancastrian connection were a broad and representative network within gentry society, as it was in Derbyshire and eastern Staffordshire, the consistent appointment of leading Lancastrians in local administration would be a legitimate reflection of the structure of that society.[57] Nevertheless, the task of managing the king's regional resources in the context of local government was by no means straightforward. Though the extent of the Lancastrian lands gave Henry potentially far more direct power in the region than any of his royal predecessors, his new responsibilities as king meant that he would not—indeed, could not, given his exalted position in the judicial hierarchy—be as closely involved in the minutiae of local politics as previous Lancastrian lords.

Henry responded to this complex situation by the simple expedient of effectively handing over the government of the region to the extensive and powerful group of Lancastrians whose support had been so crucial to his success in 1399. Initially at least, this policy resulted in only a slight intensification of the situation which had existed for most of the previous reign, before the upheavals of the later 1390s. In Derbyshire, where the Lancastrians had already held the controlling interest in the government of the shire, their dominance was now overwhelming. While the status of Richard, Lord Grey of Codnor was recognized by his appointment to head the commission of the peace, on which room was also made for John Tochet, heir to the Audley barony, and Thomas Neville, younger brother of the earl of Westmorland, who had married the Furnival heiress,[58] the main body of the commission

exactly, it is clear that the number of families involved is significantly greater: Carpenter, *Locality and Polity*, 275 n., and discussion, 272–7.

[56] Cf. Payling, *Political Society*, 216–20.

[57] Cf. ibid. 119–20.

[58] Tochet was appointed to the commission of the peace from 1401 until his death in 1408, and Neville from Jan. 1406 until his death in Mar. 1407; he was then replaced on the commission by John Talbot, who had married Neville's daughter and heir: *Complete Peerage*, i. 340–1; v. 589–90; *CPR 1399–1401*, 557–8; *1401–5*, 516; *1405–8*, 490; *1408–13*, 480.

was made up of leading members of the Lancastrian affinity. Those who had previously served as JPs—men such as Nicholas Montgomery, Thomas Wendesley, John Curson, Thomas Foljambe, and Peter de la Pole—still formed the backbone of the commission but were joined, in various combinations, by others who had not served during the 1390s: Roger Leche, Hugh Shirley, Nicholas Longford, John Cokayn, John Dabridgecourt, Robert Fraunceys, Peter Melbourne, and John Blount. Sir Thomas Rempston, the leading Lancastrian in Nottinghamshire and Leicestershire, whose authority was spreading across the midlands, also became a regular member of the commission.[59] Leche, Fraunceys, and Montgomery also served as sheriff during the reign, Montgomery on three occasions, and most of the remaining appointees were Lancastrians from Nottinghamshire.[60] The joint escheatorship followed the same pattern, with Cokayn, de la Pole, and the lawyer Henry Bothe, who was to become the Duchy's local attorney, among the Derbyshire appointments.[61] Remarkably, all but one of the thirteen men who represented the shire in the parliaments of the reign were directly connected with the Duchy.[62]

This almost total domination of local office was mirrored in the composition of special commissions appointed in the county. When, for example, a commission was issued in 1402 to reassure the shire about Henry's intentions to uphold the law, Grey and Tochet headed the list of commissioners, but the remaining places were filled by Wendesley, Shirley, Montgomery, Leche, and Rempston.[63] The personal authority

[59] *CPR 1391–6*, 436; *1396–9*, 96, 233, 435; *1399–1401*, 557–8; *1401–5*, 516; *1405–8*, 490; *1408–13*, 480. Rempston had been in Henry's service since at least 1389, and followed him into exile in 1398. His local influence was substantially increased by his appointment in 1400 as keeper of Nottingham Castle and Sherwood Forest, and his Duchy offices as steward of the honour of Leicester and, from 1401, of Castle Donington on the Leicestershire–Derbyshire border. He was married to the widow of Sir Godfrey Foljambe, the grandson of Gaunt's steward of Tutbury. *CPR 1399–1401*, 353; Somerville, *History of the Duchy*, 366, 381, 563, 572; Payling, *Political Society*, 59, 121–4, 239. See also Carpenter, *Locality and Polity*, 366, for Rempston's membership of the peace commission in Warwickshire, apparently as an extension of his influence in Leicestershire. For Duchy territorial interests in Leicestershire, see E. Acheson, *A Gentry Community* (Cambridge, 1992), 16–17.

[60] Leche was appointed in 1400, Fraunceys in 1406, and Montgomery in 1405, 1409, and 1413. *List of Sheriffs*, 103; Payling, *Political Society*, 119–34, 244–5.

[61] Cokayn was appointed in 1405, de la Pole in 1412, and Bothe in 1403 and 1409. Bothe was appointed Duchy attorney in Derbyshire in 1411. *List of Escheators*, 110; DL42/16 pt. 3 fo. 65.

[62] The men elected were Walter Blount, John Curson (twice), Thomas Gresley, Peter de la Pole, John Cokayn (twice), Roger Leche (twice), Nicholas Longford, Roger Bradbourne, Roger Bradshawe, John Strelley, Thomas Okeover, Nicholas Montgomery, and Robert Fraunceys. Only Strelley had no formal connections with the Duchy, and he was associated with the prince of Wales: W. R. M. Griffiths, 'The Military Career and Affinity of Henry, Prince of Wales', unpublished M.Litt. thesis (Oxford, 1980), 173. Bradbourne and Bradshawe both received an annuity from the Duchy; for the others, see above, pp. 196–7, 203–4. DL29/738/12096; DL29/738/12099; *Return of the Name*, 258, 260, 262, 265–6, 268, 271, 276.

[63] *CPR 1401–5*, 129. For other Lancastrian-dominated special commissions in Derbyshire,

of these Lancastrians in the region was clearly substantial. In May 1402, when a dispute between the burgesses of Leicester, Derby, and Nottingham was put to arbitration, it was Thomas Rempston and John Curson who were appointed to negotiate a settlement.[64] Their influence was also growing, as royal grants further increased the resources at their disposal. The keeping of Horston Castle in south-east Derbyshire, for example, was granted to John Curson in 1400; John Dabridgecourt was among those to whom the alien priory of Tutbury was granted in 1403; and Roger Leche, John Dabridgecourt, John Blount, and John Foljambe all received wardships of escheated lands.[65]

In Staffordshire, as in Derbyshire, Henry's consolidation of the existing Duchy retinue resulted, initially at least, in a re-creation of the political balance that had characterized much of the previous reign, which in this case meant that the Lancastrians took a share in local rule. The strength of Lancastrian representation in the county had been reduced by the death in 1394 of Sir John Ipstones,[66] and although Sir Robert Fraunceys emerged to replace him as a leading Duchy retainer active in shire administration, the Lancastrian presence was, after the upheavals of the 1390s, once more rivalled by that of the Stafford affinity under the developing leadership of Edmund Stafford, who received livery of his estates in 1399.[67] Like his father, the new king seems to have been happy not to overstretch his resources by attempting to dominate Staffordshire, but instead to accommodate the local power of the Stafford earldom. Lancastrian interests were represented by Thomas Aston and Robert Fraunceys on the commission of the peace, by Fraunceys and William Newport in the shrievalty, and by Fraunceys, Aston, and John Bagot in parliament.[68] Nevertheless, their

see *CPR 1399–1401*, 83, 213, 463, 521; *1401–5*, 130, 137–8, 286–7; *1405–8*, 66, 150, 154, 229; *1408–13*, 63, 182.

[64] *CPR 1401–5*, 89.

[65] Blount was granted custody of the lands of William Ipstones during the minority of his heir in Nov. 1399; Foljambe was granted wardships in 1402 and 1403, and Dabridgecourt in 1401. Leche secured the keeping of the lands of his neighbour Richard Vernon of Haddon certainly before 1405. Thomas Rempston's appearance among the office-holders of the shire (for which, see above, at n. 59) can also be traced largely to his acquisition of lands in wardship, since in Nov. 1399 he was granted custody of the midland estates of the young Thomas Mowbray, which included properties in Derbyshire as well as Leicestershire and Warwickshire. *CPR 1399–1401*, 179; *CFR 1399–1405*, 24, 28, 161, 214, 235; DL42/15 pt. 2 fo. 73v; DL42/15 pt. 1 fos. 85–85v.

[66] Ipstones was murdered in the course of a long-running dispute with the Peshales and the Swynnertons of Staffordshire: Walker, *The Lancastrian Affinity*, 226–7.

[67] *CPR 1396–9*, 500; *CCR 1399–1402*, 229–30. Stafford had already been appointed to the commission of the peace in 1397: *CPR 1396–9*, 235. For the Stafford affinity as an active and cohesive group during these years, see for example SRO D1721/1/1 fos. 25, 25v, 272.

[68] Fraunceys and Aston were both named as JPs in 1399 and 1401; Newport was appointed sheriff in 1401 and Fraunceys in 1402; Fraunceys sat in the parliaments of 1399 and 1400, on the first occasion with Aston and on the second with Bagot: *CPR 1399–1401*, 564; *List of Sheriffs*, 127; *Return of the Name*, 259, 261.

influence was wielded in tandem with Stafford himself, who headed the list of JPs, and his leading retainers. The Staffords' steward John Knightley and their former receiver-general Nicholas Bradshawe were regular members of the commission of the peace, while Robert Mauveisin, one of the earl's annuitants, also found a place on the bench, despite his long-running feud with the Lancastrian John Bagot.[69] Mauveisin secured the shrievalty in 1400, and William Walsall served as both escheator and knight of the shire in 1402.[70] A similar balance between adherents of Lancaster and Stafford was maintained on special commissions appointed during the opening years of the reign.[71] It seems clear that this co-operation extended to informal, as well as formal partnerships; in 1401, for example, when Fraunceys and Newport acted as mainpernors for John Bagot, they were joined by Walsall and the Stafford retainer John Delves.[72] Indeed, the degree of co-operation evident was such that it would perhaps be artificial to draw too distinct a line between the two groups. Sir Thomas Aston, for example, seems to have maintained close links in the early years of the reign with the Staffords, by whom he had previously been retained.[73]

Henry had placed his trust in the existing Duchy affinity, and in co-operation with the earl of Stafford had re-established the political balance achieved in the region during the 1380s. It remained the case that, while the Tutbury retinue was created around estates which straddled the border between Staffordshire and Derbyshire, the groups of Lancastrians active in the government of each of the two counties did not, with the sole exception of Robert Fraunceys, overlap; and further, that this reflected the fact that the Lancastrians of Derbyshire maintained a dominant role in the affairs of their shire which was reinforced by their association with the powerful Duchy interests in Nottinghamshire and Leicestershire, while the less numerous Lancastrians of Staffordshire participated in the rule of their county by its earl.

However, this reconstructed political balance in the north midlands was not to last. In July 1403 the earl of Stafford was killed fighting for Henry at the battle of Shrewsbury, leaving a baby son as his heir.[74] The

[69] Bradshawe had been the Staffords' receiver-general during the 1390s, and had also been retained by Henry by 1398. For commissions of the peace, see n. 59 above; SRO D641/1/2/40a; Rawcliffe, *The Staffords*, 201, 216; Walker, *The Lancastrian Affinity*, 225–6.

[70] For Walsall in Stafford service, see above, at n. 38. *List of Sheriffs*, 127; *Return of the Name*, 263; *List of Escheators*, 152.

[71] *CPR 1399–1401*, 44, 210; *1401–5*, 127, 130, 138, 297.

[72] *CCR 1399–1402*, 319, 324. Delves, as the earl's esquire, received an annuity of 20 marks from Edmund Stafford: SRO D641/1/2/48; *CPR 1401–5*, 347, 385. Fraunceys, with Robert Mauveisin, also witnessed the confirmation of Nicholas Bradshawe's grants from the earl after the latter's death: *CPR 1401–5*, 270.

[73] See above, at n. 33; SRO D260/M/T/7 bundle 2 unnumbered deed (9 Henry IV); SRO D1721/1/1 fos. 25v, 272–272v; Rawcliffe, *The Staffords*, 196.

[74] *Complete Peerage*, xii pt. 1, 181; ii. 388.

powerful Stafford affinity, which dominated the western half of Staffordshire, was left leaderless, and the political vacuum thus created was further intensified by the death of John Tochet, Lord Audley, in 1408, leaving his 10-year-old son to succeed him.[75] Henry's best chance of restoring the political equilibrium of the region would perhaps have been to grant custody of the Stafford lands for the duration of the heir's long minority to a candidate who represented a potential source of local lordship. Instead, he gave the keeping of the estates to his new queen as part of her dower settlement.[76] With the vast resources of the Stafford earldom effectively in abeyance, Henry seems to have assumed that this political gap in the rule of Staffordshire could be bridged by allowing his own retainers, while maintaining their co-operation with the Stafford affinity, to take over the leadership of the shire as their counterparts in Derbyshire had done. Indeed, in the troubled years after 1403 when Henry can have had little opportunity to give detailed consideration to such localized difficulties, the transfer of power in Staffordshire wholly to his trusted Duchy affinity may have seemed the ideal solution to the problem of the Stafford minority. However, his willingness to allow his men to dominate official appointments in the years after 1403 in fact served to demonstrate that Duchy resources in Staffordshire were too limited, in terms of both territory and personnel, adequately to represent the shire as a whole.

Between Sir Humphrey Stafford's tenure of the shrievalty in 1403–4 and the appointment of John Delves in 1410, all but one of the county's sheriffs were Duchy retainers.[77] What is more striking is that, during the five years when Lancastrians were nominated, both Robert Fraunceys and William Newport served twice; both, moreover, had also held the shrievalty earlier in the decade.[78] Such monopolization of the most important local office in the royal administration, not only by representatives of one political interest but by so few individuals, indicates that the Duchy's stake in the shire was dangerously narrow, especially when the local influence of the individuals themselves was far from

[75] Wardship of the Audley estates was granted to William Roos of Hamelak, whose sphere of influence primarily lay further east and north, in Nottinghamshire, Lincolnshire, and eastern Yorkshire. Thomas Neville, Lord Furnival, had died a year earlier, but was immediately succeeded by John Talbot, the husband of his daughter and heir: *Complete Peerage*, i. 340–1; v. 590–1; *CPR 1408–13*, 76.

[76] Queen Joan was also granted the marriage of the earl's son Humphrey. She seems to have left the Stafford administration largely intact. In 1412 she leased the Staffordshire lands to Ralph Neville, earl of Westmorland, whose daughter was to marry the young Earl Humphrey. *CPR 1401–5*, 328, 347–9, 369, 378, 476; SRO D641/1/2/48; SRO D1721/1/1 fo. 297; *Complete Peerage*, ii. 389.

[77] The exception was the experienced administrator William Walsall in 1406: *List of Sheriffs*, 127.

[78] Fraunceys was appointed in 1402, 1404, and 1408, and Newport in 1401, 1405, and 1407. The other Lancastrian to serve was Thomas Aston in 1409–10: *List of Sheriffs*, 127.

unassailable. Fraunceys's main territorial interest in Staffordshire was property which his wife held for life in dower, while Newport was the first member of his family to achieve local eminence of any kind.[79] This concentration of office in the hands of the small Duchy circle is equally evident in the shire's representation in parliament. Two Stafford men sat in the parliament of 1403–4, but Humphrey Stafford is the only non-Lancastrian to appear in the surviving returns after that year, as Fraunceys, Bagot, Aston, and Newport divided the places between them.[80]

It was becoming increasingly apparent that Henry had handed over control of Staffordshire to his relatively narrow group of retainers who were based almost exclusively in the east of the county. Henry does seem to have made some concession to the fact that the personnel of the Duchy in Staffordshire was so limited, in that some new faces were introduced into the administration of the shire during this period. However, the new appointees were chosen not from among the non-Lancastrian gentry of the county, but instead from the Duchy affinity in Derbyshire. The Lancastrian connection in the latter shire had undergone some changes in the years since Henry's accession. The casualties at the battle of Shrewsbury in 1403 included not only the earl of Stafford but also two of the leading Derbyshire Lancastrians, Walter Blount and Hugh Shirley.[81] Other leading retainers of the Duchy also died during this period, and Henry redistributed the offices left vacant among other members of the affinity. After Shirley's death, his office of constable at Castle Donington was granted to Robert Fraunceys, who

[79] Ayres, 'Parliamentary Representation', 101; Wedgwood, *Staffordshire Parliamentary History*, 170.

[80] Walsall and Ralph Stafford were the shire's MPs in 1403; Fraunceys and Bagot served in the parliament of 1404; Aston sat with Stafford in 1406, and Bagot returned, this time with Newport, in 1407. No returns survive for Staffordshire for the remaining years of the reign: *Return of the Name*, 265–77. Unusually for a man of knightly status, Bagot also served twice as escheator, in 1406–7 and 1408: *List of Escheators*, 152–3.

[81] The Duchy retainer Nicholas Longford was another of those killed: Somerville, *History of the Duchy*, 364; Shirley (ed.), *Stemmata Shirleiana*, 34; W. W. Longford, 'Some Notes on the Family History of Nicholas Longford, Sheriff of Lancashire in 1413', *Transactions of the Historic Society of Lancashire and Cheshire*, 86 (1934), 61. Henry's response to their loss demonstrates his unwillingness to compromise the independence and influence of the most prominent Lancastrian families. Blount was succeeded by his adult son John, but Hugh Shirley's heir Ralph was only 13, and his wardship was granted to Shirley's widow Beatrice (despite the fact that all wardships falling to the crown had been assigned to the payment of the expenses of the royal household). Beatrice also continued to receive the annuity of 100 marks which she and her husband had jointly been granted from the Tutbury estates. Sanchia Blount, Sir Walter's widow, retained possession of the Duchy manor of Hartington in the Peak district, worth more than £100, which Henry had granted to her and her husband in 1399. In 1409 she was also granted pasture rights in various Duchy parks in Derbyshire. DL42/15 pt. 2 fo. 11v; Shirley (ed.), *Stemmata Shirleiana*, 37, 40; DL29/738/12096; DL29/738/12100; DL42/16 pt. 2 fo. 37; pt. 3 fo. 137.

was becoming a near-ubiquitous figure in local administration.[82] Walter Blount's offices, the constableship of Tutbury and the master forestership of Needwood, passed in 1403 to Nicholas Montgomery, but five years later he was replaced by Sir Walter's son John.[83] In 1405 the chief stewardship of the Peak was granted for life to Roger Leche, and in the same year, on the death of John Curson, Leche also became steward of Tutbury.[84] Through these grants, John Blount, Leche, and Fraunceys emerged as the new leading members of the Duchy connection in the region.

In this context, it is striking that, of the Derbyshire men, it was Blount and Leche who followed Fraunceys into participation in the administration of Staffordshire. This development was first manifested in changes to the commission of the peace in the latter shire. The commission continued to be headed by Lord Furnival until his death in 1407, together with the Lords Burnell and Audley, and the earl of Stafford's men—Bradshawe and Knightley—retained their places. The representation of the Staffordshire Lancastrians on the bench was reinforced in 1406 by the appointment of the Duchy retainer John Bagot, but in the same year Roger Leche was also nominated for the first time, to be joined four years later by John Blount.[85] Neither Leche nor Blount had ever held royal office in Staffordshire before. In 1407 Blount also acquired the stewardship of the Duchy manor of Newcastle-under-Lyme in north-west Staffordshire from Thomas Beek, who had held the office since the 1380s.[86] Blount's incursion into the shire may also have been related to his family's acquisition of a territorial stake in the region in 1406, when John Sutton of Dudley died. Dudley had been married to Blount's sister Constance, and custody of their 6-year-old son and his valuable estates was granted to his maternal grandmother, Blount's mother Sanchia.[87]

[82] Shirley had also taken over the master forestership of Duffield from John Dabridgecourt in 1402; after Shrewsbury, the office reverted to its former incumbent: Somerville, *History of the Duchy*, 556, 573; DL42/15 pt. 2 fos. 7v, 14v.

[83] John Blount was also paid an annuity of £60 at the Tutbury receipt from 1403. Somerville, *History of the Duchy*, 541, 546; DL42/15 pt. 2 fos. 6–7; DL42/16 pt. 3 fo. 148v.

[84] The office of chief steward of the Peak seems to have been hived off from that of chief steward of the North Parts of the Duchy, since Leche's predecessor in office was said to be Richard Gascoigne in his capacity as chief steward in the north. Thomas Wendesley, the steward of the Peak, had also been killed at Shrewsbury, and his office was granted to Ralph Staveley, a member of Henry's retinue since the 1390s. The keeping of Horston Castle, which John Curson had also held, was granted to Richard, Lord Grey, whose own castle at Codnor lay only a few miles away. Somerville, *History of the Duchy*, 539, 550–1; DL42/16 pt. 3 fos. 14, 21–21v; Payling, *Political Society*, 136 n.; DL42/15 pt. 2 fo. 8v; DL28/1/10 m. 30v; Walker, *The Lancastrian Affinity*, 225; DL29/738/12096; *CPR 1405–8*, 20.

[85] *CPR 1405–8*, 497; *1408–13*, 485.

[86] Beek was said to be 'en volente de lesser lestat qil ad el dit office'; he died at the beginning of the following year: DL42/16 pt. 3 fo. 116; Somerville, *History of the Duchy*, 377, 550.

[87] *Complete Peerage*, iv. 479; *CPR 1405–8*, 273; *CFR 1405–13*, 48.

The Lancastrian retinue had never been a universally representative force in Staffordshire but, despite this, it was now being given a near-monopoly of royal office in the county.[88] For the gentry from western Staffordshire, who were largely unrepresented in local government, the incursion into the shire of the Derbyshire Lancastrians—and especially Blount, with his office at Newcastle-under-Lyme and his family's control of the Sutton of Dudley lands—was an overt demonstration that their claim to a stake in regional rule had not merely been ignored by the royal administration, but actively passed over. For some, it seems to have been the last straw.

The dominance of the Duchy had been as evident in judicial process as it was in the royal administration,[89] and among the families to have suffered in the courts under the local Lancastrian regime were the Erdeswicks of Sandon in Staffordshire. Thomas Erdeswick had inherited the manor of Bramshall near Uttoxeter from his mother Margaret, the daughter and heir of James Stafford, and had successfully defended his title against a counter-claim by Sir Humphrey Stafford of

[88] This appropriation of local government by a few individuals connected with the Duchy when Lancastrian interests formed only one part of the shire's political make-up was very different from the concentration of office in the hands of the leading Lancastrians of Derbyshire and Nottinghamshire, where the fact that the Duchy affinity was a broadly representative local network made them legitimate recipients of delegated royal authority: see above, pp. 204–5.

[89] See, for example, cases won by Lancastrians in JUST1/1514 mm. 65v, 66, 70; JUST1/814 m. 8. In the autumn of 1406, the abbot of Burton on Trent complained in King's Bench of attacks on his property involving among others William Shirley, the Duchy parker of Rolleston, and allegedly instigated by Sir Thomas Gresley. It was alleged that the men had repeatedly broken into the abbey's close, claiming that the land was common pasture, and assaulted the monks and their servants. They had also refused an offer of arbitration and threatened to kill the abbot if he took the case to law. Despite this, the abbot requested the appointment of a commission of *oyer* and *terminer*, and three of the accused were arrested; however, they were immediately rescued. Sir Nicholas Montgomery intervened, and persuaded Shirley and the others to accept the arbitration of legal counsel representing the abbey, the Duchy, and Montgomery himself, but they insisted that before this could happen, the abbot should stop the hearing by the commission and pay all expenses incurred. The abbot, according to his later complaint, was so afraid that, 'cordo doloroso et flendo', he agreed and asked the justices to supersede the sessions. They complied—not, according to the abbot, so much because of his request but because they too were 'perturbati et compulsi' by the threats of the accused. Shirley and his companions were therefore released *sine die*. Unfortunately for the abbot, when this complaint reached King's Bench, it was respited with a writ of *nisi prius*; when the case was heard at Stafford in March 1407, the jury acquitted all the defendants. Gresley is not named in the King's Bench indictment, but is specifically mentioned in the commissions of *oyer* and *terminer*. He also exchanged recognizances in the sum of 1,000 marks with the abbot at the time when the commissions were due to sit. His dispute with the abbey, which lay only a couple of miles from his manor of Drakelow, was of long standing; a document among the Gresley charters (wrongly headed as charges made against the abbey by Gresley) details enclosures carried out by Thomas to the detriment of the abbey during the late 1390s: KB27/582 Rex rot. 9; *CPR 1405–8*, 150, 156; I. H. Jeayes (ed.), *Descriptive Catalogue of the Charters and Muniments of the Gresley Family* (London, 1895), 80–2 [363], 85 [377–8].

Southwick in 1377.[90] Stafford's son, another Sir Humphrey, was not himself a Duchy retainer but was one of the representatives of the Stafford interest active with the Lancastrians in the rule of the shire,[91] and was quick to take advantage of the opportunities offered him by the new regime. Stafford brought a case of novel disseisin against Erdeswick and his son Hugh, and in July 1401 Erdeswick complained that he was being so threatened and harassed by Stafford that he could not secure a fair hearing. Both men were summoned to appear before the king and council, bringing with them all the evidence relating to the ownership of Bramshall.[92] However, this intervention clearly failed to settle the dispute, and in 1404 the case came to judgment. This time, despite Erdeswick's plea that he had already won his case almost thirty years before, the Staffordshire jury found for Sir Humphrey. Erdeswick was fined and ordered to relinquish the manor.[93]

Thomas Erdeswick lived on until 1410,[94] but in the last few years of his life his son Hugh emerged as the leader of a group of gentlemen from the disenfranchised west of Staffordshire, whose hostility to the power and privileges of the Lancastrian retinue was overt and explicit.[95] Erdeswick began his challenge to the authority of the Duchy affinity in 1408, supported principally by Thomas Swynnerton, whose family's feud with the Lancastrian John Ipstones had led to the latter's murder during the previous reign, and by the brothers John, Thomas, and William Mynors, members of a Uttoxeter family who had served Thomas of Lancaster in the early fourteenth century but who had since failed to prosper and had lost all connection with the Duchy.[96] Their campaign began in February 1408 with attacks on Duchy tenants at Newcastle-under-Lyme, the lone Lancastrian manor in north-west Staffordshire, where John Blount had been in office as steward for just

[90] JUST1/814 m. 3 (printed in G. Wrottesley (ed.), 'Extracts from the Plea Rolls of the Reigns of Richard II and Henry IV', *Collections for a History of Staffordshire*, 15 (1894), 117–18). I am indebted to Fran Bumpus for her help in distinguishing the Staffords of Southwick and Hook from their various namesakes.

[91] See above, pp. 209–10; Wedgwood, *Staffordshire Parliamentary History*, 165–6.

[92] *CCR 1399–1402*, 350, 365–6. Erdeswick also accused Stafford in 1402 of withholding written evidence from him: Wrottesley (ed.), 'Extracts from the Plea Rolls of the Reigns of Richard II and Henry IV', 106.

[93] JUST1/814 m. 3v; Wrottesley (ed.), 'Extracts from the Plea Rolls of the Reigns of Richard II and Henry IV', 117–18.

[94] E. Powell, *Kingship, Law, and Society* (Oxford, 1989), 209; CHES3/26/4 (IPM).

[95] For a discussion of Erdeswick's challenge to the Lancastrians in the context of the judicial policies of Henry IV and Henry V, see Powell, *Kingship, Law, and Society*, 208–11.

[96] Erdeswick's brothers Robert and Sampson were also active in his support: *Rot. Parl.*, iii. 630; Walker, *The Lancastrian Affinity*, 227; Canon Bridgeman, 'A History of the Family of Swynnerton of Swynnerton', *Collections for a History of Staffordshire*, 7 pt. II (1886), 44–51; Powell, *Kingship, Law, and Society*, 209–10; J. R. Maddicott, *Thomas of Lancaster* (Oxford, 1970), 42, 46, 339; KB9/113 m. 45.

three months.[97] Blount arrived in the town to hold a court session in May, and, on hearing the complaints against Erdeswick and Swynnerton, he ordered an inquiry. This never took place, according to the mayor because the town's officers had been threatened 'de lour vies'. Blount's intervention provoked further attacks on those who had brought the indictments at Newcastle, and an attempted assault at Lichfield on Blount himself.[98] His response was to call in the Duchy chief steward in the north, Robert Waterton, who arrived in Newcastle-under-Lyme to hear the charges against Erdeswick in the following October. Waterton authorized Blount to arrest Erdeswick and his followers, who found sureties that they would appear before the king and council.[99] The next day, however, the attacks on Duchy tenants began again.

During the first months of 1409, Erdeswick and the Mynors brothers moved their campaign into Lancastrian territory in the eastern half of the shire, with assaults not only on tenants but also on minor officials of the Duchy, attacks on the Duchy mills at Uttoxeter, and a blockade of the fields around the town, William Mynors allegedly threatening that no one should dare pass them on pain 'de perdre son teste, les jaumbes de son fitz, ses servantz et ses biens'. On 25 February, they attacked Nicholas Montgomery's manor at Cubley, across the border in Derbyshire.[100] The following day, in response to this concerted attack on Duchy servants and property, Henry issued a commission to Montgomery himself, Robert Fr8ceys, William Newport, and Thomas Gresley to arrest Erdeswick and the three Mynors.[101]

Erdeswick's assaults on the Lancastrian regional establishment in 1408–9 coincided with one of the bouts of severe illness which had afflicted the king periodically since 1405.[102] Just as the pressure of the rebellions in the earlier years of the reign may have prevented Henry from formulating a more sophisticated response to the loss of Edmund

[97] Blount was appointed on 28 Oct. 1407; the first attack led by Erdeswick was alleged to have taken place on 10 Feb. 1408. Somerville, *History of the Duchy*, 550; *Rot. Parl.*, iii. 630.

[98] Blount escaped, thanks to a warning from a 'gentillhomme de honour'. This account of the allegations, unless otherwise noted, is taken from the Lancastrians' petition to parliament, which also appears as an indictment among the records of King's Bench: *Rot. Parl.*, iii. 630–2; KB9/197 m. 7. See also KB9/113 mm. 2, 27, 45.

[99] See *CCR 1405–9*, 417 for the issue of writs to Blount, Erdeswick, and John and William Mynors on 21 Nov. 1408.

[100] Before setting out from Uttoxeter on this raid, they were said to have broken into the house of John Pasmere, a Duchy forester who, according to the Lancastrians' petition, had been in Lancastrian service for forty-six years. The unfortunate Pasmere was also alleged to have been assaulted six weeks later.

[101] *CPR 1408–13*, 64.

[102] Henry was seriously ill in June 1408 (after which 'he was never the same man again', according to McFarlane) and during the winter of 1408–9: P. McNiven, 'The Problem of Henry IV's Health 1405–13', *EHR* 100 (1985), 747; K. B. McFarlane, *Lancastrian Kings and Lollard Knights* (Oxford, 1972), 103.

Stafford as a partner in local government, now, when the dominance of the Duchy affinity was clearly causing conflict in regional society, the king was again prevented from focusing his complete attention on the complexities of local politics. It is impossible to know whether Henry's reaction would have been less simplistic had he not been to some degree incapacitated but, whether it was the product of conviction or of desperation, his first intervention in response to the disorder in Staffordshire was unequivocally partisan. His order that Erdeswick should be arrested by a commission composed of four of the leading local Lancastrians demonstrated the king's complete support for his Duchy retainers, his willingness to reinforce their local hegemony by entrusting to them the management of the crisis, and his unwillingness to reconsider the balance of power in the shire despite the fact that Duchy domination was clearly causing profound instability.

The king's action apparently succeeded in antagonizing a much broader section of local society than had yet supported Erdeswick, who a month after the appointment of the commission was able to launch his most serious attack so far on the Lancastrians. Erdeswick, Swynnerton, and the Mynors brothers were joined by Erdeswick's uncle, William Venables of Kinderton in Cheshire. Despite the fact that Venables himself received an annuity from the Duchy honour of Halton, it seems likely that his Cheshire origins were significant, since the county had never been a traditional focus of Lancastrian interests and had recently been used by Richard II to challenge Lancastrian domination in the north-west and by Henry Percy as a recruiting ground for his assault on the regime.[103] Indeed, Venables's elder brother had been killed fighting for Percy in 1403, although Henry seems to have regarded William as trustworthy since he was immediately allowed to inherit his brother's forfeited estates.[104] Also in Erdeswick's company was John Delves, who had been active in the administration of the shire with the Lancastrians, but whose manor of Apedale lay near the isolated Duchy manor of Newcastle-under-Lyme, firmly in the 'non-Lancastrian' part of the shire, and who also had substantial links with Cheshire.[105] On 27 March

---

[103] Venables had been granted £20 a year by Henry in 1399: DL29/738/12096. For Cheshire during the previous reign, see above, Ch. 1. Hotspur had been justiciar of Chester: Griffiths, 'Henry, Prince of Wales', 6, 62.

[104] The king granted an annuity of £40 to the widow of Sir Richard Venables on 8 Sept. 1403, and two days later William received a grant of his estates: *CPR 1401–5*, 256, 259.

[105] See above, at n. 72; *List of Escheators*, 152; Wedgwood, *Staffordshire Parliamentary History*, 207. It may be no coincidence that, though Delves was nominated as sheriff in Nov. 1409, he was immediately replaced by the Lancastrian Thomas Aston. The Cheshire connection may also account for the participation of Thomas Stanley, the son of Sir John Stanley of Knowsley, who had acquired an interest in Staffordshire through his marriage to the heiress of Sir John Ardern of Elford: *List of Sheriffs*, 127; Wedgwood, *Staffordshire Parliamentary History*, 203.

this group gathered their supporters at Rocester, across the river from the Lancastrian strongholds of south-west Derbyshire, and declared their intention to destroy Sanchia Blount's house at Barton Blount. Erdeswick challenged John Blount to meet him in single combat or, if he preferred, to fight six against six, twelve against twelve, or twenty against twenty. The Lancastrian petition recounts these allegations with a tone of outraged innocence; it is clear, however, that Blount met Erdeswick's challenge with a similar display of force.[106]

It seems that no serious violence resulted from this show of strength, but during further skirmishes in the following months two men died.[107] It was apparent that decisive action was needed, and Henry's response was uncompromising. In January 1410, a lengthy petition was presented to parliament detailing the Lancastrians' version of events since 1408. The king immediately ordered that the petition should be converted into an indictment in King's Bench and that Erdeswick, Venables, and the others should be arrested. The extraordinary proviso was added that, if the accused failed to appear immediately to answer the charges, they should be summarily convicted.[108] In the face of this ultimatum, most of those charged surrendered.[109]

Henry's support of his retinue had therefore been absolute. In the following years, however, it does seem finally to have been recognized that it was too risky and too provocative to allow his policy of letting the Duchy dominate Staffordshire to continue unchecked. Hugh Erdeswick received a pardon in February 1411,[110] and, though Henry was apparently not prepared to allow Erdeswick himself to hold local office, the royal appointments made in Staffordshire in the years after the crisis of 1409–10 were less uncompromisingly Lancastrian. The shrievalty was not held by a Duchy retainer for the rest of the reign, and John Delves was appointed sheriff in November 1410, despite his indictment with Erdeswick only ten months earlier.[111] This may have

[106] This emerged during the judicial inquiries at the beginning of Henry V's reign: KB9/204/2 m. 41.

[107] *Rot. Parl.*, iii. 631–2; KB9/113 m. 27. Indictments brought at the beginning of the next reign suggest that Erdeswick took another large force from Newcastle-under-Lyme into Derbyshire to challenge Blount in May 1409, and was again met with forceful resistance: KB9/113 m. 45.

[108] *Rot. Parl.*, iii. 632.

[109] Pardons were issued to Venables in Dec. 1410 and to Delves, Swynnerton, and Stanley (with Erdeswick) in Feb. 1411: *CPR 1408–13*, 269, 275–7; KB27/597 Rex rot. 11; G. Wrottesley (ed.), 'Extracts from the Cheshire Plea Rolls of the Reigns of Edward III, Richard II and Henry IV, and from the De Banco and Coram Rege Rolls of Richard II and Henry IV', *Collections for a History of Staffordshire*, William Salt Archaeological Society, 16 (1895), 86–7; Powell, *Kingship, Law, and Society*, 210–11.

[110] *CPR 1408–13*, 276.

[111] The other sheriffs appointed after 1409 were Thomas Giffard and Thomas Dethick: *List of Sheriffs*, 127. There are no surviving Staffordshire returns for the parliaments of 1410, 1411, or 1413. The only commission of the peace appointed during this period was in the

been the result of a change of policy on the part of the king himself, but it seems likely that the strategy was influenced by the fact that between January 1410 and November 1411 government was largely in the hands of the prince of Wales,[112] whose relationship with the region differed significantly from that of his father.

After Henry IV's accession to the throne in 1399, his son's endowment as prince of Wales, duke of Cornwall, and earl of Chester gave the latter markedly different territorial interests from those represented by the Lancastrian retinue. Prince Henry spent much of the early part of the reign in his own county palatine of Chester and campaigning in the counties of the Welsh marches, including Shropshire, and his affinity reflected this sphere of influence.[113] There was, of course, a substantial degree of continuity between the prince's retinue and his father's. The Staffordshire Lancastrian knight William Newport served under the prince (from whom he received a substantial annuity) in his Welsh campaigns, for example, and Prince Henry confirmed the fee that Richard II had granted at Chester to the Duchy retainer Thomas Wendesley as steward of Macclesfield.[114] Nevertheless, inasmuch as Prince Henry had any connection with Staffordshire, it was as an extension of his interests in the counties of Shropshire and Cheshire, a geographical balance which corresponded closely with the interests of Erdeswick and his supporters and not at all with those of the leading local Lancastrians. Indeed, Erdeswick's uncle William Venables had been retained at the prince's Chester receipt since 1401.[115] The prince had no reason to be hostile to the Duchy retinue, but, as the legitimate heir of the reigning king rather than a usurper dependent for his success on his private following, he did not share his father's overriding concern to exploit and to reward Lancastrian service in its partisan sense. He had no incentive to place the interests of the Duchy affinity above any of the

immediate aftermath of the indictments, in June 1410, and is less conciliatory than the nominations to the shrievalty, since the controversial figure of John Blount was appointed for the first time. The Stafford stalwart William Walsall was also a novice JP. *Return of the Name*, 275, 277; *CPR 1408–13*, 485.

[112] McFarlane, *Lancastrian Kings and Lollard Knights*, 107–8; G. L. Harriss, *Cardinal Beaufort* (Oxford, 1988), 50–7.

[113] Griffiths, 'Henry, Prince of Wales', 6, 19, 133–5, 205–17.

[114] Newport received 40 marks a year and Wendesley 100 marks. The prince also retained the Erdeswicks' opponent Sir Humphrey Stafford: Griffiths, 'Henry, Prince of Wales', 134–5, 197, 212, 215, 217; see above, at nn. 92–3.

[115] Prince Henry also retained Hugh Venables in 1412. John Kingsley esquire had also been retained by the prince at Chester in 1401, and a John Kingsley joined Erdeswick and Venables in their assault on Blount. Positive identification is difficult, especially as there was also a John Kingsley among Percy's rebel forces in 1403; but if there were some connection between these three Kingsleys it would reinforce the idea, suggested by Venables's career, that some members of the prince's Cheshire retinue supported Erdeswick's opposition to the overwhelming power of the Lancastrians in Staffordshire. Griffiths, 'Henry, Prince of Wales', 210, 216; *CPR 1401–5*, 257.

other resources at his disposal, and a positive inducement not to do so if such a policy had provoked serious disorder by excluding a substantial section of local society from regional government.[116]

It may therefore be significant that in 1411, under the administration of the prince and his supporters in the council, the bailiff of the Duchy liberty in Staffordshire was indicted for obstructing royal officers in the execution of their duties, a suit which clearly indicated that the local priorities of the crown were (or, at least, could publicly be seen to be) rather different from those evident earlier in the reign.[117] Prince Henry lost control of government at the end of 1411, but his father's ill health became more severe in the autumn of the following year,[118] and there was no reversal of the newly conciliatory policy in the rule of Staffordshire. It seems that during the last years of the reign a somewhat uneasy truce was maintained. The king had leapt to the defence of his retinue but, despite this uncompromising stance, his policy of allowing the Lancastrians complete control of the shire had subsequently been modified. Erdeswick had made his point, and, although he had won no direct share in local rule for himself, he was prepared for the moment to eschew further aggression.

Nevertheless, the shire was far from quiet. The Mynors, for example, refused to make their peace with the crown and continued their campaign of violence. Thomas and Robert Mynors were killed in 1411 when they were disturbed by the local posse in an attack on Wolverhampton church,[119] and their brothers, John and William, embarked on a series of revenge attacks on the town.[120] It is clear, however, that the Mynors were now operating alone,[121] and that the Duchy affinity was no longer their target. Erdeswick seems to have been content to bide his time and to concentrate on consolidating his local following.[122] He may have been encouraged to play this waiting game by the prospect of the accession in the not too distant future of the prince of Wales, who could plausibly be expected to introduce a more

---

[116] Cf. Carpenter, *Locality and Polity*, 367–8.

[117] KB27/602 Rex rot. 22v.

[118] McNiven, 'The Problem of Henry IV's Health', 747; McFarlane, *Lancastrian Kings and Lollard Knights*, 103.

[119] Powell, *Kingship, Law, and Society*, 211; KB9/113 m. 11.

[120] The Mynors, who were described in the indictment as 'notorii latrones et depredatores insidiatores viarum et depopulatores agrorum', were said to have damaged local mills and threatened the inhabitants of surrounding villages in an attempt to cut off Wolverhampton's food supplies: B. H. Putnam (ed.), *Proceedings Before the Justices of the Peace in the Fourteenth and Fifteenth Centuries* (London, 1938), 311–17.

[121] The commission issued for their arrest in Dec. 1411 included not only the Lancastrians Roger Leche and William Newport but also the Mynors' former allies John Delves and Thomas Swynnerton: *CPR 1408–13*, 376.

[122] Erdeswick and his brothers Robert and Sampson were retaining substantial numbers of local yeomen during these years: KB9/113 mm. 2, 40.

universally representative regional administration than that established by his father.[123]

Erdeswick's hopes were vindicated when he represented Staffordshire in the parliament held two months after the new king's accession; two years later he was appointed to the commission of the peace.[124] Meanwhile, Henry V had emphasized his commitment to creating a universal, rather than a specific and partisan, concept of Lancastrian service by an appointment which would have been unthinkable only a few years before: in July 1413 John Mynors became bailiff of the Duchy liberty in Staffordshire.[125] However, the transition to the new regime was not as smooth as this assimilation of formerly disruptive elements into the Duchy and the royal administration would suggest. Indeed, the conflict which developed in Staffordshire during 1413–14 emphasizes the extent to which the clear-cut division between Lancastrians and non-Lancastrians in the shire had already broken down during the period of truce in the last years of the reign of Henry IV.

Erdeswick's recruiting drive during the final years of the reign suggests that he was preparing to assume the leadership of western Staffordshire, an area in which few potential sources of lordship had been available since the death of the earl of Stafford in 1403 and the subsequent domination of the county hierarchy by the Duchy retinue from the east of the shire.[126] Erdeswick must have supposed that his campaign against the Lancastrians had established him as the leading contender to represent the west of the county once Henry V's new regime was in place, but in 1413 a rival emerged, in the shape of Edmund Ferrers of Chartley. Ferrers's father Robert had been in possession of Chartley Castle in central Staffordshire since 1381, but seems to have been almost completely politically inactive, receiving no

---

[123] The prince's accession could reasonably have been expected in the near future because of Henry IV's poor health: see above, n. 102.

[124] *Return of the Name*, 279; *CPR 1413–16*, 423. Erdeswick eventually became sheriff in 1423: *List of Sheriffs*, 127.

[125] He also received a grant of an £8 annuity at the Tutbury receipt. William Mynors became a yeoman of the new king's household. Both brothers were finally pardoned, as 'dilecti servientes nostri', for the events of 1408–10, as well as for the indictments brought by the inhabitants of Wolverhampton. Somerville, *History of the Duchy*, 548; DL28/27/6; *CPR 1413–16*, 172; KB27/597 Rex rot. 11; Powell, *Kingship, Law, and Society*, 213–14; Wrottesley (ed.), 'Extracts from the Cheshire Plea Rolls', 87. See J. L. Kirby (ed.), *Calendar of Signet Letters of Henry IV and Henry V* (London, 1978), 181, for evidence of Henry's willingness to support the interests of the Mynors.

[126] See Carpenter, *Locality and Polity*, 288, for the possibility of a gentry family assuming the leadership of a region 'in exceptional circumstances, where there were no resident nobility, or a vacuum caused by, for example, confiscation or minority', and Wright, *The Derbyshire Gentry*, 66–8 (also below, p. 257), for Sir Richard Vernon achieving such authority in the Peak district of Derbyshire later in the century.

royal appointments from Henry IV.[127] His death a few days before that of the king allowed his son Edmund to inherit the Ferrers lands and the potential power in the region which they embodied.[128] Edmund had made his first appearance in local administration when he was named to a commission appointed to arrest the Mynors brothers in 1411.[129] His ambition to achieve greater regional authority was unmistakable. As soon as he received livery of his estates he began to retain supporters from among the esquires and yeomen of the region, among them John Meverell of Throwley, Edmund Basset of Blore, and Ralph Basset of Cheadle.[130] Moreover, Ferrers had the considerable advantage of long-standing associations with the new king.[131]

Erdeswick was clearly aware of the threat which Ferrers represented to his own nascent sphere of influence. It seems that there had been some tension even before Robert Ferrers's death, since one of Robert Erdeswick's men was later indicted for the assault of a Ferrers servant in 1412.[132] When Edmund Ferrers took possession of his inheritance, serious conflict between the two broke out almost immediately.[133] In September 1413 Erdeswick mustered his men and rode to Chartley, only a few miles from his own home at Sandon, where he held the fields outside the manor for two days.[134] On that occasion one of Ferrers's tenants was assaulted and imprisoned until a ransom was paid, and other attacks on Ferrers's men followed.[135] According to Erdeswick, Ferrers was also parading his military resources in the fields between Sandon and Chartley, and similarly harassing Erdeswick's servants. It was also alleged that Ferrers's brothers planned an ambush for Erdeswick himself on his journey to attend Joan Mauveisin at a loveday concerning her dispute with John Bagot. The plot was foiled when Erdeswick was warned, but the messenger he sent in his place was abducted, assaulted, and robbed.[136]

---

[127] The Ferrers lands were concentrated in south Staffordshire and north Warwickshire: Carpenter, *Locality and Polity*, 32.

[128] *Complete Peerage*, v. 316–17.

[129] *CPR 1408–13*, 376.

[130] KB9/113 mm. 11, 28, 41.

[131] Ferrers is described as Prince Henry's butler in 1405, and his chief butler in 1408: *CCR 1402–5*, 456; *1405–9*, 422; Powell, *Kingship, Law, and Society*, 212.

[132] KB9/113 m. 6.

[133] An early source of tension may have been the appointment in July 1413 of Erdeswick and his ally Thomas Giffard to investigate complaints about intimidation by Ferrers's associates Richard and Nicholas Peshale of Newport, Shropshire. When Giffard tried to make the arrest in Jan. 1414, the Peshales resisted; Nicholas escaped, and Richard was only taken with the assistance of Robert Erdeswick: *CPR 1413–16*, 112; KB9/113 mm. 3–4. For Ferrers's association with the Peshales, see *Rot. Parl.*, iv. 32, and Powell, *Kingship, Law, and Society*, 241.

[134] KB9/113 m. 14.

[135] KB9/113 mm. 1, 26, 45.

[136] *Rot. Parl.*, iv. 32. For the feud between the Mauveisins and the Bagots, see above, at

Attempts were made to bring this growing conflict to arbitration, and it is in this context that the newly developed divisions within the Duchy affinity are visible for the first time. The emergence of a new power in western Staffordshire was now clearly inevitable. The Lancastrian affinity played an important role in attempting to keep its emergence peaceful, but, within that process, the sympathies of individual Duchy retainers were not uniformly distributed. Indeed, the efficacy of the 'cooling-off' period at the end of the previous reign is demonstrated by the fact that several Lancastrians were prepared to act for Erdeswick, despite the scale of previous hostilities. Initial overtures were made on Erdeswick's behalf by mediators who included the Duchy knight William Newport.[137] Bonds were exchanged, and arbitrators chosen. Ferrers was to be represented by the Erdeswicks' longstanding opponent Sir Humphrey Stafford, the Lancastrian John Bagot, whose lands had been raided by Erdeswick (perhaps spurred on by his connection with the Mauveisins), and the lawyer John Savage. Erdeswick's nominees were his uncle William Venables, the Lancastrian John Cokayn and, perhaps most surprisingly, the Duchy retainer Thomas Gresley, despite the fact that his daughter was married to the brother of Erdeswick's erstwhile enemy John Blount.[138]

Despite these efforts, the loveday thus arranged failed—according to Erdeswick, because Ferrers mounted an attack on his opponent's home. Erdeswick alleged that he escaped their murderous intent only because the situation was calmed by the intervention of Thomas Gresley.[139] The violence not only continued but intensified: Sampson Erdeswick, a lawyer, was pursuing his brother's business in the courts when he was assaulted by Ferrers's servants and horribly mutilated.[140]

n. 69. Erdeswick's assistance to Joan Mauveisin may have been motivated not only by his recent opposition to the local Lancastrians, of whom John Bagot was a leading representative, but also by his current rivalry with Edmund Ferrers. In 1410, Joan Mauveisin had leased her manor of Mauveisin Ridware for eight years to Ferrers, possibly in an attempt to secure his support for her cause; Erdeswick may therefore have seen the ongoing dispute as an opportunity to demonstrate that his authority carried more weight than that of his rival: BL Add. Ch. 58192.

[137] *Rot. Parl.*, iv. 32. Perhaps significantly, Newport had been one of the local Lancastrians most closely associated with the prince of Wales during the previous reign: see above, at n. 114.

[138] Powell, *Kingship, Law, and Society*, 241–2; G. Wrottesley (ed.), 'Extracts from the Plea Rolls of the Reigns of Henry V and Henry VI', *Collections for a History of Staffordshire*, William Salt Archaeological Society, 17 (1896), 51; KB9/113 m. 47v; F. Madan, 'The Gresleys of Drakelow', *Collections for a History of Staffordshire*, William Salt Archaeological Society, new series, 1 (London, 1898), 52, 240.

[139] *Rot. Parl.*, iv. 32.

[140] 'c'est assavoir articles de ses pees trencheront & ses jambes, brais, & mains par diverses horribles plaies couperont & debrusseront, par ount sez nerves sount devenuz secchez, & il claudant & mahemez a toutz jours, & ses articles issint coupes misteront en le bouche de dit Sampson, & apres ovesq; eux asporteront, & luy pur mort lesseront': *Rot. Parl.*, iv. 33.

Erdeswick's response was swift. On 1 April 1414, with his brothers, his uncle, and supporters from Staffordshire and Cheshire, he raided Chartley and assaulted Ferrers's servants, one of whom died.[141]

This attack on Chartley marked the climax of the conflict. It coincided with the culmination of the new king's judicial initiatives to restore public order and re-emphasize the efficacy of royal authority. The opening of parliament at Leicester at the end of April was accompanied by the arrival there of the court of King's Bench on what was to become a 'full-scale judicial visitation of the midlands'.[142] The presence of this physical manifestation of authoritative royal justice almost immediately began the process of resolving the dispute between Ferrers and Erdeswick. When the Leicester parliament opened, both sides presented petitions, and when King's Bench arrived at Lichfield in May indictments relating to the dispute were submitted; both parties were charged with the illegal granting of liveries as well as the violence of the preceding months.[143] The resulting legal process continued in the courts until the following year, but the royal intervention in the area ended the violence between Erdeswick and Ferrers. The main protagonists secured pardons, and many of those involved in the conflict were removed from the region when they joined the Agincourt campaign.[144]

In Staffordshire, therefore, the overwhelming authority of the limited Duchy retinue had been attacked, and subsequently compromised, under Henry IV, and the resulting political vacuum provoked a brief explosion of violence between rival contenders for local power at the beginning of the next reign. In Derbyshire, where the Lancastrian hegemony was more longstanding and far more representative of the composition of the shire, the change of regime was marked by much less controversy. The dominance of the Duchy in the county had been so complete, and the threat to its authority from potential rivals—and correspondingly the need to maintain a united Lancastrian front—so insubstantial, that the only local conflict of any note under Henry IV (apart from Thomas Gresley's longstanding dispute on the Staffordshire border with the abbey of Burton on Trent)[145] had flared up within the Lancastrian affinity itself, although its causes remain somewhat obscure. In 1405–6 trouble seems to have developed between Roger

---

[141] Hugh, Robert, and Roger Erdeswick were accompanied by, among others, William, Hugh, and Ralph Venables, Thomas Giffard, and John Kingsley: *Rot. Parl.*, iv. 32; KB9/113 mm. 1, 39, 46.

[142] Powell, *Kingship, Law, and Society*, 168–70, 173–7.

[143] *Return of the Name*, 281; *Rot. Parl.*, iv. 32–3; Powell, *Kingship, Law, and Society*, 175–6; KB9/113 (see membrane references above).

[144] Powell, *Kingship, Law, and Society*, 214–16; KB27/614 Rex roti. 4v, 30v; *Complete Peerage*, v. 317–18.

[145] For which, see above, n. 89.

Leche and several of his neighbours. It was alleged that armed confrontations took place between Leche and his fellow Lancastrian Ralph Staveley in the autumn of 1405, and between Leche and the young esquire Richard Vernon of Haddon at the beginning of the following year.[146] The conflict with Staveley may be explained by the fact that around this time Leche was extending his influence further into north-west Derbyshire, where Staveley's interests were concentrated. A few weeks after the alleged incident, for example, Leche acquired the newly created office of chief steward of the High Peak, where Staveley had been local steward since 1403.[147] Vernon, only 16 at the time of the reported conflict, was the son of one of Richard II's knights. Leche had been granted custody of Vernon and his lands when his father died, a circumstance which again might suggest a plausible background to dispute.[148] There was also trouble between Leche and John Cokayn at Ashbourne, the latter's power base on the southern edge of the Peak, in 1410.[149]

The ambivalent position of the Duchy affinity in relation to this conflict is perhaps suggested by the fact that the strongly Lancastrian jury which presented these indictments in 1414 identified Leche as the aggressor in two of the cases, but as the victim in the third.[150] It is possible that Leche had provoked some resentment among the established Lancastrian families of the region because of the speed with which he had risen from relatively obscure origins to a position of eminence at not only local but also national level. Having joined Henry's establishment as an esquire during the 1390s, he rose to become controller of the royal household by 1404, and in 1407 steward of the household of the prince of Wales—a career at court matched by few of the Duchy affinity in the north midlands after the deaths of

---

[146] KB9/204/2 m. 41.

[147] Leche had also been granted some Duchy lands in the area previously held by the former steward of the Peak Thomas Wendesley, who died in 1403: see above, at n. 84.

[148] Leche also brought a suit against Vernon's brother William for alleged offences against the statute of liveries in 1410: J. S. Roskell, 'Sir Richard Vernon of Haddon, Speaker in the Parliament of Leicester, 1426', *Derbyshire Archaeological Journal*, 82 (1962), 44; *CPR 1396–9*, 524; see above, n. 65; KB27/598 Coram Rege rot. 94.

[149] KB9/204/2 m. 41. Cokayn and Leche were both imprisoned in the Tower in Oct. 1411 (*CCR 1408–13*, 243–4), and it has been suggested (Payling, *Political Society*, 131, 191 n.) that they were arrested because of their confrontation in Aug. 1410. However, the elapse of more than 12 months between incident and arrest and the lack of any other evidence of the original dispute means that the two events may be unrelated. Nevertheless, there is no other ready explanation for the imprisonment. Other commentators (see, for example, McFarlane, *Lancastrian Kings and Lollard Knights*, 108; Griffiths, 'Henry, Prince of Wales', 171) have assumed, perhaps more convincingly, that, because of Leche's connection with Prince Henry, the arrests were related to the latter's impending fall from power and his rivalry with his younger brother Thomas.

[150] It was alleged that Staveley attacked Leche, but that the latter was responsible for threatening Vernon and Cokayn.

Walter Blount and Hugh Shirley.[151] His affiliation with Prince Henry during the second half of the reign may also have distanced him somewhat from the majority of the Derbyshire Lancastrians, who were more closely associated with the king. Nevertheless, it is clear that, for the most part, the Duchy connection in Derbyshire during Henry IV's reign co-operated closely with each other both in the administration of the shire and in private transactions.[152]

In Derbyshire, therefore, the new king inherited a broad connection which had dominated the shire during the previous reign as one part of a Duchy sphere of influence which extended south and eastwards into Leicestershire and Nottinghamshire.[153] Its counterpart in Staffordshire was more limited, and Henry had already demonstrated that he was not prepared to allow its power in local government to be artificially enhanced by privileged access to royal authority, as his father had done with disruptive results. The challenge he faced was that of preserving the stability of power structures across the region, in which the Duchy retinue under the personal lordship of the king played such a significant part, while simultaneously seeking to establish the Lancastrian crown as an incontrovertibly public and universally representative authority.

[151] A. Rogers, 'The Royal Household of Henry IV', unpublished Ph.D. thesis (Nottingham, 1966), 680; Griffiths, 'Henry, Prince of Wales', 170–1.

[152] See, for example, DRO D37M/RL1; DRO D77M/374, 388; DRO D258 Box 7/8 t; DRO D779B/T80–6; NA DDFJ 1/64/133, 1/77/1; DCL Jeayes (ed.), 'Descriptive Catalogue of the Charters . . . at Radbourne Hall', 193 [486–7], 197 [495–6]; DCL Every 3340, 3388; BL Stowe ch. 64; Jeayes (ed.), *Derbyshire Charters*, 26 [201], 99 [803], 151 [1231], 186–7 [1505], 197 [1585], 241 [1931], 242 [1980], 250–1 [1983], 262 [2081], 270 [2131], 342 [2714]; *CCR 1405–9*, 275.

[153] Cf. Payling, *Political Society*, 119–37.

7

1414–1440
Crown and Nobility

1. 1414–1422: POLITICAL ASSIMILATION AND ROYAL RULE

At the beginning of Henry V's reign, the Duchy remained the dominant interest across Derbyshire and eastern Staffordshire. The new king immediately demonstrated that he was not about to compromise or undermine traditions of Lancastrian service in the region: in the north midlands, as elsewhere in the Duchy, Henry confirmed the vast majority of his father's grants of fees and office.[1] It was clear that he intended to maintain direct control of those regions where the Duchy was legitimately the dominant territorial power and fully represented the area's political make-up. Nevertheless, the events of the last years of his father's reign and of 1413–14 indicated that he was not prepared to condone the monopolization of power by the Lancastrian retinue in areas where that was not the case. Moreover, his lack of a longstanding association with many of the Duchy retainers in the area, and the effect of his protracted campaigns in France, meant that his regional lordship was more distant and less personal than that of his father. This provided the context for the unification of the region under an authority that was unambiguously royal and public rather than private and partisan.

There were few immediate changes in the overall structure of the Duchy connection around the honour of Tutbury after Henry's accession, although there was a significant adjustment in the balance of power between individuals, as the upper hand among the Lancastrians in the region shifted from the personal following of the old king to that of his son. The previously ubiquitous Robert Fraunceys, for example, played relatively little part in local government under the new regime.[2] The most striking feature of the first years of the reign was the continuing rise of Roger Leche, who had been closely associated with the prince of Wales in the second half of the previous reign.[3] He had been an integral part of the Lancastrian network which had dominated the area in the years before 1413, but after Henry's accession he enjoyed a

[1] See above, Ch. 2.3 at n. 63.
[2] Fraunceys was appointed to commissions of array in Derbyshire and Staffordshire, and to the Staffordshire commission of the peace once, in 1417: *CPR 1413–16*, 408; *1416–22*, 198, 212, 459. [3] For Leche's earlier career, see above, pp. 32, 204, 211.

new degree of personal authority which made him unquestionably the leading non-noble figure in the region.

In April 1413 Leche's offices as steward of Tutbury and the High Peak were confirmed, and at the same time he was granted the chief stewardship of the North Parts of the Duchy, an appointment which reinforced and extended the influence he already derived from his local Lancastrian office.[4] Two months later his son Philip became master forester of Duffield Frith.[5] During the next two years Leche received several valuable grants in the region, including the keeping of Lancastrian lands in the High Peak and custody of the royal manor of Bolsover in north-east Derbyshire.[6] This increasing territorial influence was reinforced by his role in local government. Leche was consistently appointed as a JP and to a variety of special commissions in both Staffordshire and Derbyshire, and represented the latter shire in two of the first three parliaments of the reign; in the third, his place was taken by his son.[7] In April and May 1416 this remarkable career culminated in his appointment as treasurer of England and chamberlain of the Duchy of Lancaster.[8]

It is tempting to view Leche's rapid promotion as an attempt to establish a regional hierarchy linking the Duchy affinity to the crown, as had proved possible in East Anglia. There, a broad and influential political connection had been created on the basis of the Duchy estates without compromising the universal and public nature of royal authority, through the development of a hierarchy which offered the regional lordships of Thomas Erpingham and Thomas Beaufort as mediators of royal power.[9] In the north midlands, on the other hand, the Duchy retinue had been established under private Lancastrian lordship and changed relatively little after 1399, so that it was subject much more directly to the personal lordship of the king. There is no evidence that Walter Blount, Hugh Shirley, or John Curson in the early years of Henry IV's reign, or latterly Robert Fraunceys, John Blount, or Leche himself, could exercise the degree of regional authority over their peers enjoyed by Erpingham in East Anglia.

[4] DL42/17 pt. 3 fo. 1; R. Somerville, *History of the Duchy of Lancaster*, i (London, 1953), 418, 539, 551. Leche was also one of the Duchy feoffees named in the settlement made by the king in July 1415: Somerville, *History of the Duchy*, 199, 417; see above, Ch. 2.4 n. 80.

[5] DL42/17 pt. 3 fo. 4; Somerville, *History of the Duchy*, 556.

[6] The Bolsover grant was made to Leche jointly with his son Philip. Leche also received the keeping of the alien priory of Hinckley, Leicestershire, and of the lands of Nicholas Longford during his heir's minority, as well as custody of the manor of Daventry in Northamptonshire for ten years. He was also granted an annuity of £30 to add to the 100 marks he already received from the Duchy: *CFR 1413–22*, 43, 107, 137; DL28/27/6; DL42/17 pt. 1 fo. 53; DL29/731/12017.

[7] *CPR 1413–16*, 113, 178, 408, 418, 423; *Return of the Name*, 278, 281, 283.

[8] *CPR 1416–22*, 9; Somerville, *History of the Duchy*, 417; DL42/17 pt. 3 fo. 22.

[9] See above, Ch. 3.2.

The rapid enhancement of Leche's personal influence in the region after 1413, combined with his increasing influence in national government, was therefore a significant departure from previous patterns of local authority. However, if Henry did intend to establish him as an intermediary between the crown and the region to facilitate the absorption of Henry's private Lancastrian lordship into his public authority as king, it was an attempt which was destined to fail. Leche died in November 1416, and his son Philip—who in any case had by no means inherited all his father's office and influence—was killed in France four years later, leaving his three sisters as his heirs.[10] Even had Leche survived, it is questionable how long the balance of power thus created could have been sustained, or, indeed, whether the king would have persisted with a policy similar to the one he was pursuing in East Anglia.

Henry's conciliatory treatment of Hugh Erdeswick in Staffordshire had demonstrated that he was fully aware of the problems his father had created by making no attempt to alter the nature or scope of the Duchy affinity and its place in local society in response to changing circumstances.[11] Even in Derbyshire and eastern Staffordshire, where the Duchy affinity continued to operate as a broad and cohesive network,[12] there is some evidence that the new king was taking care that the regime should be inclusive rather than unnecessarily limited. In a region where the Duchy retinue was wide-ranging and genuinely representative, there were no obvious 'outsiders', but there were some individuals among the gentry who had previously played little part in local rule. Sir Thomas Gresley, for example, was associated with many of the Lancastrian families of Derbyshire, most notably the Blounts, and had himself been retained by the Duchy in 1406.[13] Despite these Lancastrian connections, it is striking that Gresley played almost no role in regional government under Henry IV.[14] After 1413, however, he was immediately included in the administrative hierarchy, and was appointed to all three major local offices during the course of the

[10] E. A. Ayres, 'Parliamentary Representation in Derbyshire and Nottinghamshire in the Fifteenth Century', unpublished MA thesis (Nottingham, 1956), 65, 110, 112.

[11] See above, pp. 208–16.

[12] See, for example, continuing associations between Lancastrian families during Henry V's reign in *CCR 1413–19*, 270–1; *HMC Rutland*, 52; S. M. Wright, *The Derbyshire Gentry in the Fifteenth Century*, Derbyshire Record Society, 8 (Chesterfield, 1983), 212 (deeds 1419–20); I. H. Jeayes (ed.), *Descriptive Catalogue of Derbyshire Charters* (London, 1906), 10 [80], 101 [823], 157 [1280], 222 [1769], 251 [1984], 319 [2539]; DRO D231M/T22, T169, T308, E451, E5120; NA DDFJ 1/64/156, 8/5/3–4; DCL I. H. Jeayes (ed.), 'Descriptive Catalogue of the Charters . . . at Radbourne Hall', 199 [507]; LRO 26D53/343.

[13] Gresley's daughter Margaret was married to Sir Thomas Blount. Ayres, 'Parliamentary Representation', 23; see above, Ch. 6.2 at n. 138.

[14] Gresley represented Derbyshire in parliament in 1400, but held no other major office in Derbyshire or Staffordshire during the reign: *Return of the Name*, 260.

reign.[15] In 1421 his enhanced status was confirmed by his appointment to Duchy office as steward, constable, and master forester of the High Peak; his son John became master forester of Duffield Frith.[16]

There was, however, one important development in the balance of local power which Henry was apparently unwilling or unable to recognize while promoting Leche to a position of regional leadership. Richard Vernon held extensive estates stretching from Haddon on the southern edge of the Peak in Derbyshire across to Harlaston in Staffordshire and on into Cheshire and Shropshire.[17] This territorial configuration was markedly different from the traditional heartlands of Duchy power around Tutbury on the south Derbyshire–Staffordshire border, but overlapped significantly with the landed interests in northern Derbyshire of Roger Leche, whose manor of Chatsworth lay only a few miles from Haddon. As has already been discussed, Leche had been granted Vernon's wardship during his minority, and relations between the two apparently became less than cordial even before Vernon came of age in 1411.[18]

Between 1413 and 1416, when it seemed that Leche might become the crucial element in a new regional hierarchy which would help to reconcile the king's private lordship with his public responsibilities, Vernon was accorded no place in local administrative structures. It is inconceivable, given the extent of his estates, that he could have been ignored indefinitely, and striking that his public career began immediately after Leche's death. It seems likely, given the earlier tension between the two men and the overlap of their territorial interests, that it was hostility on Leche's part which barred Vernon from local office. Only weeks after Leche's death in November 1416, Vernon was appointed to the shrievalty in Staffordshire, and he was named to the commission of the peace in the shire from the following year.[19] Even this accommodation of Vernon's interests was only partial, however.

---

[15] He was elected MP for Staffordshire in the first parliament of the reign, and for Derbyshire in 1414, 1417, and 1421; he served as sheriff in Derbyshire in 1418 and in Staffordshire in 1422; he joined the peace commission for the first time in Derbyshire in 1420, and in Staffordshire in February 1422: *Return of the Name*, 279, 283, 289, 292, 296; *List of Sheriffs for England and Wales*, PRO Lists and Indexes, 9 (1898), 103, 127; *CPR 1416–22*, 451, 459. See also his appointments to special commissions in both counties: *CPR 1413–16*, 178; *1416–22*, 72–3, 198.

[16] DL42/17 pt. 1 fos. 74–74v; pt. 3 fos. 56v–57; Somerville, *History of the Duchy*, 551, 556 (where John Gresley's appointment as master forester of Duffield and Thomas Gresley's master forestership of the Peak are confused). Thomas Gresley was also granted the farm of the herbage of lands in the Peak which had previously been held by Roger Leche: DL42/17 pt. 3 fo. 48.

[17] J. S. Roskell, 'Sir Richard Vernon of Haddon', *Derbyshire Archaeological Journal*, 82 (1962), 43–4.

[18] Ibid. p. 44; see above, p. 223.

[19] *List of Sheriffs*, 127; *CPR 1416–22*, 459. In 1419 he also represented Staffordshire in parliament: *Return of the Name*, 292.

The offices he acquired were confined to Staffordshire, rather than extending into Derbyshire where his authority would have challenged the sphere of influence of Leche's heir. It was not until after Henry V's death that Vernon was able to extend his official influence into the latter shire. Once Leche had gone, there is no readily apparent explanation of the exclusion of Vernon from the rule of a county in which he held substantial estates, unless Leche's presumed personal antipathy to him was shared by the king, who might therefore have chosen to limit his influence within the Derbyshire hierarchy.

The failure to accommodate Vernon in local power structures during the first three years of Henry's reign suggests that Leche's authority in the region might not have been tenable indefinitely, at least in the form in which it seems to have been conceived. It is hard to imagine that Vernon, like Erdeswick before him, would not eventually have protested forcefully about his exclusion from local office.[20] It is arguable that Leche's position would have required modification in any case, since even his meteoric career had not provided him with the status and range of resources which Thomas Beaufort and Thomas Erpingham together could muster in support of their leadership of the crown–Duchy connection in East Anglia. Moreover, their authority had not had to contend with the claims of potential rivals to a stake in regional rule, since fate and the absence of a pre-existing Duchy affinity had made East Anglia something of a *tabula rasa* for the Lancastrian monarchy.[21]

In the event, after 1416 Henry made no attempt to advance a single individual in Leche's place, although the Montgomery family did benefit substantially from the reallocation of his offices. Like Leche, the Montgomeries had been stalwart Lancastrians under both Gaunt and Henry IV, and were prominent members of the close-knit Duchy connection in south-west Derbyshire, but after 1416 they achieved a new eminence among the Lancastrians of the region. On Leche's death, Sir Nicholas Montgomery became steward of Tutbury, and his son, another Nicholas, succeeded John Blount as constable of Tutbury and master forester of Needwood in 1418.[22] Both men were already active in local administration; Sir Nicholas had been appointed sheriff of Derbyshire and Nottinghamshire in the first year of the reign, and his

---

[20] However, since Vernon's exclusion seems to have been personal, he would not necessarily have found a natural constituency among the local gentry to support his protest, as Erdeswick did in championing the cause of an unrepresented region.

[21] See above, Ch. 3.

[22] See above, pp. 196–7, 206; DL42/17 pt. 3 fos. 23–23v, 27v; Somerville, *History of the Duchy*, 539, 542, 546. The younger Nicholas had joined his father as a Duchy annuitant in 1414, when he was granted a fee of £20; in addition he was granted the 40 marks payable to the Duchy each year by Hugh Shirley's widow Beatrice for the wardship of her son Ralph: DL28/27/6; DL42/17 pt. 1 fo. 32v.

son represented Derbyshire in parliament in 1414 and 1416.[23] However, after 1416 their enhanced authority was clearly apparent. Both Montgomeries were regularly appointed to the commission of the peace in Derbyshire from 1418, and in 1420 the younger Nicholas joined the bench in Staffordshire—the first time a member of the family had been appointed to office in the shire, reflecting the extension of their interests into the county through their recent appointments to Duchy offices at Tutbury.[24] Substantial though this promotion was, however, the Montgomeries could not rival the concentration of authority, or the degree of influence in central government, which Leche had enjoyed earlier in the reign.

In Derbyshire, therefore, Henry's attempt to promote Roger Leche to a position of regional leadership potentially comparable to that of Beaufort and Erpingham in East Anglia was undermined by Leche's death, even before possible flaws in the policy had a chance to show themselves unequivocally. After 1416, Henry made no further attempt to create a hierarchy of authority linking the crown to the Duchy affinity in the region through a few key individuals. In a sense, preoccupied as he was with war in France, it was probably easier not to do so, since the Lancastrian affinity in Derbyshire and eastern Staffordshire was still operating as a cohesive group even without such individual leadership, and apart from Leche there were few local men with whom Henry had longstanding personal associations, and who would therefore present themselves as obvious candidates for enhanced local authority.

In Staffordshire, as in the years before 1413, the relationship between the Duchy and local power structures was rather different from the situation in Derbyshire. The Lancastrians of the Tutbury area were not excluded from the rule of the shire,[25] but Henry was clearly concerned that they should not be allowed to dominate the west of the county, which had gone unrepresented for much of the previous reign. The assimilation of Hugh Erdeswick into local government was the most overt demonstration of this concern, signalling that the division provoked under Henry IV by the blanket imposition of Duchy authority across the whole shire would not be allowed to recur.[26] Moreover, the accommodation of Erdeswick was not the token acceptance of one

---

[23] *List of Sheriffs*, 103; *Return of the Name*, 281, 287.

[24] *CPR 1416–22*, 451, 459. I am assuming that the 'Sir Thomas Montgomery jr' who appears in the printed listing of the commission of the peace for July 1420 is a mistake for Sir Nicholas, who appears thereafter. Both Montgomeries also appeared on a variety of special commissions in Derbyshire: see *CPR 1413–16*, 178, 408; *1416–22*, 72–3, 143, 197, 211, 252.

[25] The Tutbury officials (Leche, and subsequently the Montgomeries) continued to hold office in the county, as did Sir John Bagot. For Leche and the Montgomeries, see references given above, nn. 4, 22; for Bagot, see *List of Sheriffs*, 127; *CPR 1416–22*, 212, 251, 270, 459.

[26] See above, Ch. 6.2 at n. 124, for Erdeswick's appointments to local office; he also appeared on special commissions in the shire: *CPR 1416–22*, 198, 251, 459.

previously troublesome individual. Others associated with him were also appointed to local office. John Delves, for example, who had been active in Erdeswick's support during the confrontations of 1409, rose to a new prominence, serving twice as sheriff and three times on the commission of the peace.[27] Nor were other interests in the shire ignored. It was in Staffordshire that the growing regional influence of Richard Vernon was eventually recognized in the second half of the reign, while John Meverell, who had been among the first local retainers of Edmund Ferrers of Chartley and who had never before held local office, represented the shire in parliament in 1414 and served as sheriff in 1417.[28]

Despite the promotion of men such as Meverell, the personal authority of Edmund Ferrers remained limited in the wake of his confrontation with Erdeswick in 1413–14.[29] The combined effect of Erdeswick's confrontation with the Duchy affinity, his campaign of recruitment during the last years of Henry IV's reign, and his decision to attack Ferrers as soon as the latter inherited his lands, before he had had a chance to establish a coherent following, seems to have meant that Erdeswick was able to undermine Ferrers's position and secure his own as a leading figure in regional affairs. While Erdeswick consolidated his influence in Staffordshire, Ferrers served in France until 1422.[30] Indeed, the role of Henry's French campaigns in calming the tensions which had emerged in the region during the previous reign must not be overlooked. The leading figures from both Staffordshire and Derbyshire who served in France included not only Ferrers, but also Richard, Lord Grey of Codnor, and his son John, Roger and Philip Leche, John Blount, John Bagot, John Dabridgecourt, Thomas and John Gresley, the elder and the younger Nicholas Montgomery, Richard Vernon, Nicholas Longford, Ralph Shirley, and members of the Cokayn, Foljambe, and Staveley families.[31] The fact that these influential men were periodically, and in some cases almost con-

---

[27] Delves served as sheriff in 1415 and 1420, and as JP in 1413, 1415, and 1420. He was also appointed escheator in the first year of the reign: *List of Sheriffs*, 127; *CPR 1413–16*, 423; *1416–22*, 459; *List of Escheators for England and Wales*, PRO Lists and Indexes, 72 (1971), 152. See also Delves's appointment to commissions of array in the shire: *CPR 1416–22*, 198, 212. For his involvement in the conflict of 1409, see above, Ch. 6.2 at n. 105.

[28] See above, at n. 19; *Return of the Name*, 282, 284; *List of Sheriffs*, 127.

[29] For which, see above, pp. 219–22.

[30] *Complete Peerage*, v. 318. Even when Ferrers returned, he made little immediate attempt to resume the task of establishing himself as a major independent power in Staffordshire, preferring instead to concentrate his energies on his Warwickshire estates and his association with the earl of Warwick: C. Carpenter, *Locality and Polity* (Cambridge, 1992), 314–17, 377–8; see below, pp. 237–8.

[31] E101/47/39; E101/51/2; *DKR* 44, 'Calendar of French Rolls, 1–10 Henry V' (London, 1883), 546, 555, 564, 568, 570–1, 581, 624; *DKR* 41, 'Calendar of Norman Rolls, Henry V' (London, 1880), 693, 730, 745; H. Nicolas, *History of the Battle of Agincourt* (London, 1833), 357, 375–6, 380–4; PRO Lists and Indexes, Suppl. Series, ix pt. 2, 'Warrants for Issues, 1399–1485' (New York, 1964), 383–94; cf. Wright, *The Derbyshire Gentry*, 8.

tinuously, out of the country, engaged together in the national enterprise of foreign conquest, meant that the animosities of the previous
reign could more easily be forgotten, and that Erdeswick, for example,
was able to establish his stake in regional rule gradually and peacefully
while his former opponents were occupied abroad.[32]

Indeed, the experience of Lancastrians and non-Lancastrians
fighting together on a national campaign, away from the particular
context of regional politics, facilitated the more general assimilation of
the Duchy affinity into local political society under a Lancastrian lordship that was now more comprehensive and unambiguously royal. As
Lancastrian allegiance in its specific, private sense gradually became
less relevant in the context of the new regime, so Henry's general
policy of letting the retinue itself slim down through a process of
natural wastage could be pursued without controversy, even in an area
like the north midlands, where his father had devoted almost all of the
Duchy's regional income to the payment of fees.[33] Between 1400 and
1413, annuity payments at Tutbury and the High Peak had averaged
more than £1,110 a year, but under Henry V the equivalent figure was
£730. This average figure was the result of a gradual decrease as the
retinue aged, so that by 1420 the Duchy was paying out only £480.[34]
The decline in the number of Lancastrian annuitants in the region did
not, however, mean that the Duchy network which dominated
Derbyshire and eastern Staffordshire was breaking up. Rather, it was
being assimilated into a united Lancastrian body politic, within which
the operation of Lancastrian lordship in its private capacity was increasingly redundant.

Whereas the reign of Henry V was marked in East Anglia by the consolidation of the broadly representative crown–Duchy connection
which had developed since 1399,[35] in the north midlands the Lancastrian affinity had already existed as a coherent and influential force in
1399, and reached the height of its powers under Henry IV, whose
association with many leading local figures was close and longstanding.
Under his successor, and especially after the death of Roger Leche,
this personal connection with the king was to a large extent lost, and
correspondingly it became clear that in areas where the Duchy affinity
could not claim to be territorially dominant or universally representative, it would have to accommodate other interests. Whereas in Norfolk

---

[32] For the beneficial effects for domestic order of the departure of former disputants and
troublemakers on campaign, see E. Powell, *Kingship, Law, and Society* (Oxford, 1989),
229–40; Carpenter, *Locality and Polity*, 369–71.

[33] See above, Ch. 2.3.

[34] DL29/728/11988; DL29/729/11995–6, 12001, 12004; DL29/730/12006, 12008, 12011–12,
12015; DL29/731/12019A, 12021A, 12022; DL43/15/11; DL29/732/12027, 12029.

[35] See above, Ch. 3.2.

and Suffolk the crown–Duchy connection came to embody the fabric of power in the region, Henry V's success in Derbyshire and Staffordshire was to manage his Duchy affinity so that it became merely one part (albeit a vitally important one) of the fabric of power. These contrasting situations in East Anglia and the north midlands seem, however, to have produced similar effects within local society. In both regions, Henry V's reign was a period of considerable stability. The initial confrontation in Staffordshire between Erdeswick and Ferrers was rapidly resolved and an enduring settlement reached under the watchful eyes both of the king himself and of the earl of Warwick, now the major power immediately to the south of the county, who had been appointed umpire in the attempted arbitration between the two rivals.[36] Thereafter, there is no evidence of significant conflict within landed society.

In other words, while the personal connection between the king and the local Lancastrians diminished with the accession of Henry V, this allowed the Duchy affinity to be assimilated peacefully into a re-configured structure of regional power which took account of the differing situations in Derbyshire on the one hand, where Duchy men were still the dominant local grouping, and Staffordshire on the other, where a variety of interests could now claim a stake in the rule of the shire. This analysis of Henry's success should perhaps include the qualification that it is impossible to know how he would have dealt with the re-emergence of an adult Stafford earl to claim a share in the rule of Staffordshire, although, in the light of his general willingness to work closely with the nobility, and to exploit rather than override existing territorial interests in regional rule, there is nothing to suggest that he would have resisted the resumption of the west of the shire into a reconstituted Stafford sphere of interest.[37] As it was, Henry died before

[36] Warwick was also temporarily appointed to the commission of the peace in the shire in 1413 and 1415: G. Wrottesley (ed.), 'Extracts from the Plea Rolls of the Reigns of Henry V and Henry VI', *Collections for a History of Staffordshire*, 17 (1896), 51; *CPR 1413–16*, 423. Warwick's participation in the settlement of the Ferrers–Erdeswick dispute seems to have been one aspect of a more general move northwards on his part. During the previous reign the earl had had little involvement in north Warwickshire, but under Henry V (who, as his treatment of Erdeswick demonstrated, was much more prepared than his father had been to countenance the idea of partnership with other interests in the rule of the midlands) Warwick began to develop his authority in the north of the county. Despite the Ferrers–Erdeswick case, however, Warwick's active participation in Staffordshire affairs remained limited during Henry V's lifetime because, as Christine Carpenter suggests, 'the two major powers in the west and north midlands, which, in the absence of an adult earl of Stafford, were respectively Warwick himself and the king as duke of Lancaster, had achieved such full control of their own spheres that each was able to seal his area of authority off from the other': *Locality and Polity*, 315, 367–9.

[37] For Henry's relations with the magnates in general, see G. L. Harriss, 'The King and his Magnates', in G. L. Harriss (ed.), *Henry V* (Oxford, 1985); for his partnership with Warwick in the rule of the midlands, see above, n. 36; for his concern that the Staffordshire administration should reflect the composition of local political society, see above, pp. 230–1.

the end of Stafford's minority, and the loss of his personal leadership initiated a further phase in the evolution of the regional balance of power.

2. 1422–1440: THE GROWTH OF NOBLE LORDSHIP

The immediate impact of Henry V's death on local power structures was limited but, in conjunction with other developments, it created a situation in which there was substantial potential for significant change. With the accession of the infant Henry VI, the authoritative leadership which had underpinned the rule of the Duchy connection in Derbyshire and enforced a sustainable distribution of power among the various gentry interests in Staffordshire was lost. This coincided with the re-emergence of several potential sources of noble lordship which had been in abeyance during most of the two previous reigns, with the return of Edmund Ferrers of Chartley from France and the end of lengthy minorities in the families of Stafford and Sutton of Dudley.[38] The abeyance of these interests in southern Staffordshire had been a major factor in allowing the county to be drawn into a broadly co-ordinated pattern of interests which linked Staffordshire with its eastern neighbour Derbyshire through the Tutbury borderlands. The fact that those nobles whose estates straddled south Staffordshire and north Warwickshire had been temporarily out of active contention in local politics meant that this area could be neutralized as a dividing line between the unchallenged control of the earl of Warwick in Warwick-shire and that of the king, wielding a combination of royal and Duchy power, in Staffordshire.[39] Now, however, the balance of power in Staffordshire was again in flux.

Ostensibly, one of the most significant developments was the coming of age of Humphrey, earl of Stafford, who received livery of his estates in 1423.[40] The disturbances in Staffordshire in the first decade of the century had been closely related to Henry IV's failure to respond adequately to the loss of Edmund Stafford and the consequent unbalancing of the regional distribution of power during his son's lengthy minority. Under Henry V, a balance had been found between the Duchy and the rest of the shire so that the leading gentry of western Staffordshire shared regional rule with the Lancastrians from

---

[38] See above, p. 231; *Complete Peerage*, ii. 388; iv. 479.

[39] The close association between Henry V and Warwick meant that this division of power worked extremely smoothly. Henry used Warwick to keep a local eye on the settlement of the troubles in Staffordshire in 1413–14: see above, at n. 36, and Carpenter, *Locality and Polity*, 315–16, 366–70.

[40] *CPR 1422–9*, 75; *CCR 1422–9*, 89.

the east of the county under royal overlordship.[41] The re-emergence of an adult Stafford earl might therefore have been expected to precipitate profound change in local politics. In fact, the immediate impact made by Earl Humphrey was limited, largely because his mother held in dower and in her own right the bulk of the estates to which he was heir.[42] The earl's coming of age was not marked, for example, by his appointment to the Staffordshire commission of the peace.[43] Rather than emerging immediately as an independent source of local authority, he seems to have been accommodated within a developing hierarchy which profoundly changed the political shape of the region. Under Henry V, Staffordshire had been incorporated into a broad sphere of influence under royal direction stretching eastwards across the midlands, which was based on the king's possession of the Duchy estates.[44] Though the connections between eastern Staffordshire and western Derbyshire remained, the loss of the personal leadership of an adult king in 1422 and the re-emergence of noble interests in the west and south of Staffordshire meant that the shire's politics were gradually reoriented southwards to Beauchamp-controlled Warwickshire.

At the lowest level of this developing hierarchy, there emerged in Staffordshire during the 1420s and early 1430s a small group of esquires and gentlemen—notably the lawyer Robert Whitgreve, John Harper, Thomas Arblaster, and Humphrey Cotes—who became mainstays of the county's administration at its lower levels. None of these men ever held the shrievalty, but between them they filled a significant proportion of the remaining local offices. Whitgreve, for example, served as escheator in 1427, 1431, and 1434, and was appointed to commissions to negotiate loans in the shire in 1430 and 1431.[45] A king's serjeant since 1423, he was also appointed receiver at Tutbury in 1432.[46] Harper held the escheatorship in 1428 and 1432, represented the county in parliament in 1431, and was appointed to the commission of the peace from

---

[41] See above, pp. 230–1.

[42] Anne, countess of Stafford, had first been married to Thomas, the third earl, who died young (his death swiftly followed by that of his brother William, the fourth earl). Anne subsequently married their next brother, Edmund, fifth earl of Stafford. Having been widowed twice, she had therefore received two separate thirds of the Stafford estates in dower. In her own right she was heir to half the Bohun inheritance. In fact the countess held only a comparatively small proportion of the Stafford lands in Staffordshire, but she held most of the Warwickshire estates, and it is clear that her son's overall position considerably affected his ability to consolidate his authority in the region. *CCR 1392–6*, 38–40, 47–8; *1402–5*, 212–15; 226–36; C. Rawcliffe, *The Staffords* (Cambridge, 1978), 12–18; Carpenter, *Locality and Polity*, 321.   [43] *CPR 1422–9*, 569.

[44] See above, Ch. 7.1.

[45] He went on to serve as escheator twice more, in 1438 and 1441: *List of Escheators*, 152–3; *CPR 1429–36*, 51, 127.

[46] DL42/18 pt. 1 fo. 13; Somerville, *History of the Duchy*, 543.

1430.[47] Arblaster was elected knight of the shire four times;[48] Cotes was appointed to the escheatorship in the first year of the reign.[49]

It is clear that, as these men became increasingly active in local administration, they did so as associates in the service of the young earl of Stafford. By December 1426, when Stafford made a settlement of his lands, Whitgreve and Harper were among his feoffees.[50] Arblaster, whose father had been retained by Earl Edmund, also acted with Harper as a feoffee for the earl in 1430 and 1435, and had been appointed steward of the Stafford lordship of Newport in Wales by 1434.[51] The earl's mother appointed Harper to the stewardship of her lands in 1428, and by the early 1430s Cotes was serving as one of the Stafford bailiffs in Staffordshire.[52] These men are consistently to be found acting together on business connected with the earl and his estates.[53] In this association with the newly revitalized Stafford interest they were joined by the two men who had emerged as the leading non-Duchy figures in the shire—Hugh Erdeswick, whose home at Sandon lay only a few miles from Stafford Castle, and Richard Vernon. Erdeswick was named as a feoffee by the earl in the settlement of 1426, and Vernon was acting for him in that capacity by 1430.[54]

Nevertheless, because of the earl's relative lack of resources during these years, few men were formally retained by him.[55] One exception was the esquire Philip Chetwynd of Ingestre, whose family had been connected with the Staffords since the previous century, and to whom the earl granted an annuity of 10 marks in 1431.[56] Chetwynd, too,

---

[47] Harper served as escheator again in 1439. He also joined Whitgreve on the loan commission of 1431. *List of Escheators*, 152–3; *Return of the Name*, 319; *CPR 1429–36*, 127, 624.

[48] In 1426, 1432, 1433, and 1435: *Return of the Name*, 311, 322, 325, 327.

[49] Cotes served as escheator again in 1440: *List of Escheators*, 152–3.

[50] SRO D1721/1/1 fos. 50v–51; *CCR 1422–9*, 318–19, 321–2.

[51] *CPR 1401–5*, 347; *1429–36*, 466; *CCR 1429–35*, 357–8; J. C. Wedgwood, *Staffordshire Parliamentary History*, William Salt Archaeological Society (London, 1917–18), 209–10; T. B. Pugh, *The Marcher Lordships of South Wales 1415–1536* (Cardiff, 1963), 287. In 1406–7 Thomas Arblaster senior was acting as constable of the dowager countess Anne's castle at Caldicot, and he later fought at Agincourt in the retinue of the countess's third husband William Bourchier: SRO D641/1/2/7; Nicolas, *History of the Battle of Agincourt*, 360; Rawcliffe, *The Staffords*, 14, 18.

[52] Pugh, *The Marcher Lordships of South Wales*, 291; SRO D641/1/2/53.

[53] Wm Salt Lib. HM Chetwynd bundle 7 unnumbered deeds (1427, 1435); *CCR 1422–9*, 326, 328; *1429–35*, 234, 357–8; *CPR 1429–36*, 284, 286.

[54] See references above, n. 50; *CCR 1429–35*, 357–8. For other examples of Erdeswick and Vernon acting in association with Stafford and his associates, see Wm Salt Lib. HM Chetwynd bundle 7 unnumbered deed (1435); SRO D1721/1/1 fo. 38; *CCR 1422–9*, 328.

[55] Robert Whitgreve was one of the few, receiving an annuity of 10 marks from May 1430, a fee which was assigned not on the earl's estates in Staffordshire but on the Welsh lordship of Newport: Pugh, *The Marcher Lordships of South Wales*, 156.

[56] The local influence of the Chetwynds had been limited earlier in the century because of the fact that by 1418 a succession of heirs had died young, leaving four widows simultaneously dowered from the family estates. G. Wrottesley (ed.), 'The Chetwynd Cartulary', *Collections*

acted in close co-operation with Whitgreve, Harper, Arblaster, and Cotes, and maintained links with Erdeswick and Vernon.[57] However, it is difficult to discern in this limited grouping, of which the core remained the four prominent local administrators, the development of a genuinely coherent affinity owing its primary allegiance to the earl of Stafford. It seems clear that this nascent Stafford connection was subsumed within a broader regional structure of power, which linked the affairs of Staffordshire closely to those of Warwickshire through Edmund Ferrers of Chartley and Richard Beauchamp, earl of Warwick.

Ferrers's local role had been limited after his abortive bid to assert his authority in 1413–14 and his subsequent departure on campaign in France. During this period abroad he served under Warwick, and on his return home in 1422 it became clear that this connection would prove highly significant for the affairs of the north midlands.[58] During the 1420s Ferrers began to assert his authority in north Warwickshire, one of his most notable achievements being the successful prosecution of his wife's claim to half of the valuable manor of Birmingham.[59] Both the identity of his new Warwickshire associates and the process by which the Birmingham dispute was resolved in his favour indicate that Ferrers was pursuing these ambitions under the aegis of the earl of Warwick.[60]

Indeed, Warwick had pressing reasons for wishing to extend his influence northwards, a strategy which a close alliance with Ferrers provided an ideal opportunity to pursue. Under the first two Lancastrians, the region had been effectively divided into two blocs—the north midlands controlled by the king through a combination of royal and Duchy power, and the west midlands under Beauchamp authority—and this 'mutual exclusion' meant that Warwick had had little need to concern himself with the northern borders of his 'country'.[61] However, the loss of the guiding hand of Henry V had coincided with the return of Ferrers and the majorities of the Stafford and Dudley heirs, as well as the arrival in the region of Joan Beauchamp of Bergavenny through her purchase

---

for a History of Staffordshire, William Salt Archaeological Society, 12 (1891), 256–60, 312–13 [77].

[57] Wm Salt Lib. HM Chetwynd bundle 7 unnumbered deed (1435); SRO D1721/1/1 fo. 38; *CCR 1422–9*, 326, 328; see below, p. 238.

[58] Carpenter, *Locality and Polity*, 314–15; J. H. Wylie and W. T. Waugh, *The Reign of Henry the Fifth* (Cambridge, 1914–29), iii. 131.

[59] Carpenter, *Locality and Polity*, 314–15, 377–8; *Complete Peerage*, v. 318.

[60] In 1431, for example, Ferrers married his daughter to the son and heir of Lord Clinton, a north Warwickshire nobleman who had been associated with the Beauchamps since the beginning of the century, and for whom Ferrers and Warwick together had acted as feoffees in 1420–1: see references in n. 59 above, and LRO DE2242/3 unnumbered indenture (10 Henry VI).

[61] Though note that the earl's close partnership with Henry in local rule did mean that he had begun to develop some involvement with Staffordshire political society: see above, at n. 36; Carpenter, *Locality and Polity*, 315–16, 366–72 (quoted phrase from 315).

of the Botetourt inheritance on the Warwickshire–Staffordshire border, all of which meant that this previously stable region now suddenly appeared extremely volatile, at least in prospect.[62] In order to protect his interests in Warwickshire, Beauchamp was forced to turn his attention northwards, and in the years after 1422 the combined authority of Warwick and Ferrers was to prove a highly effective link with Staffordshire political society.

The reappearance of Ferrers in regional affairs might have seemed likely to presage a renewal of hostilities with his old rival Hugh Erdeswick. In the event, no such problems surfaced, and a significant part in promoting this co-operation may have been played by the supra-regional authority of Richard Beauchamp. Warwick had been appointed to oversee the initial arbitration between the two, and although he subsequently developed close links with Ferrers there is also evidence that Erdeswick may have been serving the earl in some capacity as early as 1417.[63] Certainly, Ferrers and Erdeswick were operating in the same circles by the late 1420s, and by the middle of the following decade Ferrers had retained both Erdeswick and the latter's former ally John Mynors.[64]

Ferrers—and, through him, Warwick—forged such connections not only with Erdeswick but also with the other leading members of the Staffordshire grouping associated with the young earl of Stafford. By the mid-1430s, for example, Ferrers was retaining not only Erdeswick, but also Richard Vernon and Robert Whitgreve, the latter the most prominent of the group of men who were coming to dominate the shire administration.[65] The close co-operation within this extended regional hierarchy is clearly demonstrated by a settlement of various of his estates by Philip Chetwynd, himself a landowner with interests in both Warwickshire and Staffordshire. In February 1427, Chetwynd granted his Warwickshire manor of Grendon to a group of feoffees who included the earl of Stafford, Robert Whitgreve, and John Harper; the chief witness to the transaction was Edmund Ferrers of Chartley.[66] Two days earlier, Chetwynd had settled his manor of Ingestre in Staffordshire on feoffees who again included Whitgreve and Harper; among the witnesses this time were Hugh Erdeswick and Thomas Arblaster.[67]

[62] See above, p. 234; Carpenter, *Locality and Polity*, 316–17, 373.

[63] See above, n. 36; Carpenter, *Locality and Polity*, 316; BL Eg. Roll 8773 (under 'expenses of council').

[64] *CCR 1422–9*, 326, 328; E163/7/31 pt. 1. The latter reference is to the tax return made in 1436 by Edmund Ferrers's son and heir William. However, since he had only acquired the Ferrers estates in Feb. 1436, following his father's death in Dec. 1435 (*CFR 1430–7*, 244, 272; *Complete Peerage*, v. 318–19), it seems fair to assume that the document reflects primarily his father's retaining policy.   [65] E163/7/31 pt. 1; see above, pp. 235–6.

[66] Wm Salt Lib. HM Chetwynd bundle 7 unnumbered deed (1427) (cf. *CCR 1422–9*, 326).

[67] *CCR 1422–9*, 328.

It is therefore clear that the impact made in Staffordshire by the earl of Stafford in the 1420s and early 1430s was entirely within the orbit of a much wider regional hierarchy, in which Stafford and Edmund Ferrers played a supporting role to the authority of the earl of Warwick.[68] The interlocking of these three interests was evident after Ferrers's death in 1435, when his widow married Stafford's retainer Philip Chetwynd, whose uncle, John, was a Beauchamp annuitant.[69] Further, the focus of this hierarchy reflected the dominant interests of Warwick, the senior partner, in concentrating on Warwickshire. The extension of this broad sphere of influence into Staffordshire seems to have been achieved through an alliance with the gentry figures who had led the county before 1422, under the relatively loose overlordship of Ferrers and Stafford. It is striking that, in the Chetwynd feoffments cited above, it was in the settlement of the Warwickshire property that the two noblemen were involved; in the corresponding Staffordshire deed, their roles were filled by Erdeswick and, as fellow witnesses, two eminent local knights with longstanding Duchy connections, Roger Aston and John Bagot.[70] Nevertheless, the increasing influence of Warwick, Ferrers, and Stafford in the shire was recognized in 1430 by their appointment, in Ferrers's and Stafford's case for the first time, to the commission of the peace.[71]

It was also in 1430 that Richard Vernon was reappointed to the Staffordshire bench for the first time in ten years.[72] During the 1420s, Vernon had fitted easily into the emerging hierarchy associated with Stafford, Ferrers, and Warwick in Staffordshire,[73] but his attention was principally focused elsewhere, in Derbyshire, where structures of power were also changing. Just as Staffordshire politics were reoriented in

---

[68] Joan Beauchamp was also eventually more or less assimilated into this network, although her attempts to extend her personal authority caused considerable disruption in east Warwickshire in the later 1420s and in the north-west of the county in 1431–2. John Talbot, later earl of Shrewsbury, held the Furnival seat at Alton in north Staffordshire, as well as several manors in Derbyshire. In the few periods when he was not on campaign in France during the 1420s and 1430s, he showed little interest in the region, preferring to concentrate on his estates in Shropshire. Inasmuch as he did have any involvement in the area, it was as part of the Beauchamp–Ferrers–Stafford hierarchy, since he was married to Warwick's daughter. The lords Audley (whose estates were also based in Shropshire) and Dudley made little impression in the region, focusing their activities on service to the crown in France, Ireland, and Wales and at court. Carpenter, *Locality and Polity*, 320, 380–90; A. J. Pollard, 'The Family of Talbot, Lords Talbot and Earls of Shrewsbury in the Fifteenth Century', unpublished Ph.D. thesis (Bristol, 1968), 30, 240, 412; *Complete Peerage*, i. 337, 341; iv. 479; xi. 698–703.

[69] Wrottesley (ed.), 'The Chetwynd Cartulary', 261; Carpenter, *Locality and Polity*, 685; see above, at n. 56.

[70] See references above, nn. 66–7; for the Aston and Bagot families, see above, p. 198.

[71] *CPR 1429–36*, 624. See also Ferrers's and Stafford's appointments to special commissions in the county: *CPR 1422–9*, 355, 481; *1429–36*, 51, 127.

[72] *CPR 1429–36*, 624.

[73] See above, pp. 236, 238.

response to the pull of Beauchamp authority from the south after the loss of Henry V's personal leadership, so the balance of power in Derbyshire too began to alter, as the role of Tutbury as a focal point for the region as a whole began to wane. Vernon, for example, who had been forced before 1422 to concentrate on building up his authority in Staffordshire because of his exclusion from local government in Derbyshire,[74] began to assert himself as a major power in the latter shire from the beginning of Henry VI's minority.

In 1423, Vernon was appointed as a JP in Derbyshire for the first time; he was named to every subsequent commission of the peace in the shire until his death almost thirty years later.[75] He secured the Derbyshire shrievalty in 1424, and represented the county in the parliaments of 1422, 1426, and 1433, while his sons Richard and Fulk were elected knights of the shire in 1432 and 1437 respectively.[76] Vernon also appeared on a variety of special commissions appointed in Derbyshire.[77] This explosion of influence was reinforced in 1424 by his appointment as Duchy steward and master forester of the High Peak.[78] It may be that his sudden inclusion in royal and Duchy hierarchies in the region under the minority government owed something to his family links with the Beauforts,[79] although such recognition of his regional status was also undoubtedly long overdue; it is harder to explain his exclusion from local office under Henry V than his inclusion after 1422. The stewardship of the Peak corresponded closely with Vernon's territorial interests in Derbyshire, which centred on Haddon, on the southern edge of the Peak. This had, of course, also been true of Roger Leche of Chatsworth, who held the office earlier in the century, but Leche simultaneously held the stewardship of Tutbury, and his tenure of office therefore had the effect of drawing the Peak region even more closely into the established Lancastrian balance of power focused on the south-west of the county.[80] For Vernon, on the other hand, the stewardship of the Peak reinforced territorial interests ranging across Derbyshire and Staffordshire into Shropshire and Cheshire, which gave him little direct connection with the Duchy heartlands around Tutbury.[81] Vernon's acquisition of Duchy office thus both confirmed

---

[74] See above, pp. 228–9.

[75] *CPR 1422–9*, 561; *1429–36*, 615; *1436–41*, 581; *1441–6*, 469; *1446–52*, 588; Roskell, 'Sir Richard Vernon', 52.

[76] *List of Sheriffs*, 103; *Return of the Name*, 302, 310, 321, 324, 329.

[77] *CPR 1422–9*, 405; *1429–36*, 50, 126, 136.

[78] DL42/18 pt. 2 fo. 60; Somerville, *History of the Duchy*, 551–2.

[79] Vernon was the great-nephew and heir of Sir Fulk Pembrigge, who was closely connected with both Henry and Thomas Beaufort: J. S. Roskell, *Parliament and Politics in Late Medieval England* (London, 1981–3), iii. 179, 267.

[80] See above, pp. 211, 226.

[81] See Map 3, p. 194, and Roskell, 'Sir Richard Vernon', 43–5.

his status as a major player in the politics of the entire region, and marked the emergence of the Peak district of northern Derbyshire as an independent political centre of gravity which was no longer merely an adjunct to the focus of power at Tutbury.

Vernon's annexation of the Peak in support of his growing personal authority in the north of the county formed one of the first signs that the political coherence and geographical focus of the Duchy-dominated structure of power in Derbyshire were beginning to be disturbed. The powerful and close-knit gentry network based around the Lancastrian estates in the south-west of the shire was maintaining its cohesion both in private transactions and in local administration,[82] but the loss of Henry V meant that direct royal control of the north midlands, through a combination of the authority of the crown and the territorial dominance of the Duchy, could no longer be maintained. The opportunity for the development of significant noble lordship evident in Staffordshire during these years has already been discussed,[83] and this was mirrored further east in Nottinghamshire. It seems that the pressure of political developments in the latter shire began to have a substantial effect on the balance of power across the border in Derbyshire.

Eastern Derbyshire held the seat of the lords Grey of Codnor, who had been easily incorporated into the Duchy domination of the county under the first two Lancastrian kings. Their extensive involvement in royal service made them natural allies of the king in his role as duke of Lancaster, especially because the bulk of their midlands estates, further east in Nottinghamshire and Leicestershire, lay in counties where the Duchy also played a substantial local role.[84] Moreover, their service to the king frequently kept them away from the midlands, so that their opportunities to develop an independent sphere of influence in Derbyshire, even had they so wished, were limited.[85] In 1430, however,

---

[82] For the associations and activities of the Montgomeries, Blounts, Gresleys, Shirleys, Cokayns, Okeovers, Poles, Foljambes, Longfords, and Cursons, see DRO D231M/T379; D410M Box 15/654; DCL Jeayes (ed.), 'Descriptive Catalogue of the Charters . . . at Radbourne Hall', 207 [542]; DCL Every 3227, 3235, 3242–3, 3307, 3339, 3519; BL Add. Ch. 53621; Jeayes (ed.), *Derbyshire Charters*, 20 [156–7, 159], 171 [1393–4], 197–8 [1588, 1591–2]; Wright, *The Derbyshire Gentry*, 212 (deed 1430); *Return of the Name*, 302, 305, 310, 313, 315, 318, 321, 324, 326; *List of Sheriffs*, 103; *CPR 1422–9*, 561; *1429–36*, 615. However, note that conflict developed between the Longfords and Foljambes in the 1430s, a dispute which produced indications that the Duchy network as a whole was beginning to show signs of strain: see below, pp. 242–9. [83] See above, pp. 234–9.

[84] Wright, *The Derbyshire Gentry*, 4; Carpenter, *Locality and Polity*, 366; see above, Ch. 6.1 at n. 27.

[85] Richard Grey of Codnor held many offices, including those of chamberlain of England and admiral of the Fleet, and had an active diplomatic career. He served in Wales under Henry IV and in France under Henry V until his death in 1418. His son and heir John also served in France, and in 1427 was appointed Lieutenant of Ireland: *CPR 1399–1401*, 465; *1401–5*, 122–3, 285, 317, 483; *1405–8*, 84; *1416–22*, 384; *1422–9*, 397–8; *Complete Peerage*, vi. 127–9; cf. S. J. Payling, *Political Society in Lancastrian England* (Oxford, 1991), 90–1.

John, Lord Grey died, and was succeeded by his brother Henry,[86] who rapidly demonstrated that he had more extensive local ambitions than either of his predecessors, ambitions which were also potentially more viable now that the politics of the entire region were becoming increasingly fluid. Certainly, Henry Grey's ambitions in Derbyshire were immediately apparent. He was appointed to the commission of the peace in 1431, and by 1436 was retaining John Curson and Ralph de la Pole, both from families with longstanding Lancastrian connections and prominent roles in local administration.[87] In 1434 it was also alleged that during the preceding year Grey had distributed his livery to other Derbyshire gentlemen.[88]

It is clear, however, that Grey was not the only Nottinghamshire figure seeking to make an impact in eastern Derbyshire. Ralph, Lord Cromwell, had been a member of the commission of the peace in the shire since 1424, and in 1434 it was alleged that he too had been distributing his livery to members of the Derbyshire gentry.[89] In 1429 Cromwell also acquired the keeping of the royal manor of Bolsover, which lies just east of Chesterfield, a couple of miles from the Nottinghamshire border.[90] Nor was interest in the area confined to the nobility. Sir Henry Pierpoint, a leading member of the Nottinghamshire gentry, had held office as master forester of Duffield Frith from 1424 until 1428.[91] In this context it is striking that the only serious conflict to arise in the north midlands between 1422 and the mid-1430s developed in this part of the region. Whereas in Staffordshire and western Derbyshire the division of power between the Beauchamp–Ferrers–Stafford alliance and the Duchy connection around Tutbury apparently proved extremely successful, while Richard Vernon's control of the Peak gave him enough influence to straddle the two groups, and indeed the two counties, as a semi-independent figure, trouble broke out in eastern Derbyshire in the early 1430s as a result of incursions into the area by competing interests from Nottinghamshire.

The Foljambe family had, since the early years of the century, been one of the few members of the Duchy affinity in Derbyshire with territorial interests in the north-east of the county around Chesterfield.[92]

[86] *CFR 1430–7*, I, 18; *Complete Peerage*, vi. 130.
[87] *CPR 1429–36*, 615; E163/7/31 pt. I. John Curson was acting as chief steward of the lands of Grey's mother Elizabeth by 1432: NUL MiM 137/6; *Complete Peerage*, vi. 128–9.
[88] KB9/11 m. 15v; see below, at nn. 112, 114.
[89] *CPR 1422–9*, 561; KB9/11 m. 15v. For Cromwell, see Payling, *Political Society*, 95–8.
[90] *CFR 1422–30*, 272.
[91] Sir John Cokayn was appointed in the latter year: see below, n. 94. For the Pierpoint family, see Payling, *Political Society*, 21–2.
[92] Their home manor of Walton lay very close to the town: see above, Ch. 6.1 at n. 15, and Map 3, p. 194. The Foljambes had acquired Walton through Thomas Foljambe's marriage to Margaret, one of the two daughters and heirs of Sir John Loudham, at the end of the 14th cent.: cf. NA DDFJ 4/2/1–2.

During the 1420s, however, their local authority was challenged by the Nottinghamshire knight Henry Pierpoint.[93] Pierpoint had temporarily succeeded in intruding into Derbyshire power structures through his four-year tenure of Duchy office at Duffield Frith,[94] but his local ambitions were apparently focused on Chesterfield, which lay near his own Derbyshire property at Ashover, and where he seems to have been active as early as 1423.[95] Chesterfield was held by Joan Holand, countess of Kent, and in the early years of the century she had appointed John Foljambe her steward there.[96] In 1429, however, she farmed the property for a term of twenty years to Pierpoint, who three years later also leased the right to hold an annual fair in the town from the countess.[97] Thomas Foljambe seems to have resorted to direct action almost immediately after this second grant, attempting to prevent the collection of the profits of the fair held by Pierpoint in September 1432.[98] Later indictments relating to the incident alleged both that Foljambe assaulted Pierpoint, and that the latter responded in kind with an attack on Foljambe's son.[99]

Overt hostilities seem to have subsided during the following year, but at the beginning of 1434 the dispute again flared into violence. On 1 January, Henry Pierpoint was attending Chesterfield church with members of his family, including his son Henry and his brother-in-law Henry Longford, when Thomas Foljambe, jun. arrived, also accompanied by members of his family as well as by a large number of armed supporters.[100] Foljambe and his men attacked Pierpoint and his associates, and in the ensuing violence Henry Longford was killed, while Pierpoint was maimed and his son injured.[101] The incident—

[93] For previous discussion of the Pierpoint–Foljambe dispute, see Wright, *The Derbyshire Gentry*, 128–33, and Payling, *Political Society*, 199–200.

[94] Pierpoint's appointment at Duffield seems to have been controversial. The previous incumbent, Sir John Gresley, later claimed that his own appointment had been unlawfully superseded: Somerville, *History of the Duchy*, 556; DL42/18 pt. 2 fos. 60, 87; SC8/114/5698. Pierpoint had also been appointed to the Derbyshire bench in July 1418: *CPR 1416–22*, 451.

[95] Pierpoint may have secured possession of Ashover before his father's death in 1425; the manor was probably settled on him when he married Nicholas Longford's daughter Ellen: S. J. Payling, 'Inheritance and Local Politics in the Later Middle Ages: The Case of Ralph, Lord Cromwell, and the Heriz Inheritance', *Nottingham Medieval Studies*, 30 (1986), 78; NA DDFJ 1/64/153 (printed in Jeayes (ed.), *Derbyshire Charters*, 102 [827]).

[96] NA DDFJ 8/2/3 (John Foljambe in office as steward, 1407).

[97] KB9/11 mm. 18v–19.

[98] KB9/11 mm. 18v–19; C1/9/332.

[99] KB9/11 mm. 16v–17, 18–18v. Susan Wright dates Pierpoint's lease of the fair to 1433 (*The Derbyshire Gentry*, 130), and therefore does not connect the two allegations of assault. However, the indictments are all dated to the feast of the Exaltation of the Cross in 1432, the day on which the Chesterfield fair was traditionally held.

[100] Details of the incident are taken from KB9/11 mm. 14–15, 17 (cf. KB27/694 Rex rot. 2; KB27/698 Rex rot. 2). For Pierpoint and Longford, see Wright, *The Derbyshire Gentry*, 128; Payling, *Political Society*, 238. Thomas Foljambe, sen. had died in 1433: *CFR 1430–7*, 103, 150–1.   [101] William Bradshaw, another associate of Pierpoint, was also killed.

which is recounted in later indictments in a tone which suggests shock at the ferocity as well as at the location of the assault[102]—provoked the issue of a general commission of *oyer* and *terminer* headed by the duke of Bedford and the earls of Stafford and Suffolk.[103] The range of indictments received when the commission sat at Derby in the following April clearly indicates the profusion of interests jockeying for influence in the eastern part of the shire, and the resulting confusion in regional politics.

Two separate grand juries presented indictments before the commission. Pierpoint himself sat on one, with three other Nottinghamshire knights; the rest of the jury was composed of members of the Derbyshire gentry, including John Curson and John de la Pole, who were in 1433–4 acting with Pierpoint as feoffees for Nicholas Montgomery.[104] Pole and other jurors, including Ralph Shirley and Thomas Okeover, were also connected with the family of the murdered Henry Longford.[105] The presence of Pierpoint and his associates and the substantial representation of Nottinghamshire interests on the panel seem to indicate that it is possible to characterize the jury as a whole as pro-Pierpoint. The second jury included Sir William Plumpton, a relative of the Foljambes, as well as Derbyshire men including Richard Vernon and John Cokayn.[106] Vernon was closely associated with Foljambe at this point, and Cokayn, one of Vernon's closest allies, had been the beneficiary when Pierpoint was superseded in office at Duffield Frith. It therefore seems possible to view this panel as pro-Foljambe.[107] Though both panels agreed on the basic facts of the case, their sympathies

---

[102] Susan Wright makes the point that violence was an accepted element in medieval life and that 'the parish church was frequently the scene of open conflict in the fifteenth century' (*The Derbyshire Gentry*, 127–8). Nevertheless, neither the killing of men of gentle status nor acts of murder actually inside a church were common, and the detailed and largely non-formulaic account of the incident in the subsequent indictments suggests its unusual and shocking nature. (Cf. the murder of a London citizen in a church in the course of a violent dispute between Lord Strange and Sir John Trussell in 1417 which, K. B. McFarlane notes, 'caused a great stir'; those responsible were excommunicated and required to do 'elaborate penance': *Lancastrian Kings and Lollard Knights* (Oxford, 1973), 157–8.)

[103] *CPR 1429–36*, 353, 355. The records of the hearings indicate that, of the three, only Bedford and Stafford attended.

[104] KB9/11 m. 14; H. J. H. Garratt (ed.), *Derbyshire Feet of Fines 1323–1546*, Derbyshire Record Society, 11 (1985), 86 [1086]. The three Nottinghamshire knights were John Zouche, Hugh Willoughby, and Robert Strelley, for whom see Payling, *Political Society*, 20, 34–5, 46–7, 83.

[105] Jeayes (ed.), *Derbyshire Charters*, 197–8 [1588, 1591–2]; Wright, *The Derbyshire Gentry*, 242.

[106] KB9/11 m. 16v. Plumpton's mother Alice was the heiress of the Foljambes of Hassop, the main Foljambe line. Alice's father was the grandson of Sir Godfrey Foljambe, chief steward of John of Gaunt's lands in the 1360s; the Foljambes of Walton were a cadet branch of the same family. Somerville, *History of the Duchy*, 366; T. Stapleton (ed.), *The Plumpton Correspondence* (Gloucester, 1990), pp. xxvi–xxviii.

[107] Vernon paid an annuity of £1 to Foljambe, sen. from 1429 to 1432. Foljambe, jun. granted Vernon a lease certainly by 1436, and possibly as early as 1433, it being unclear whether NA DDFJ 1/81/6 is dated 19 (xix) or 11 (xi) Henry VI. The latter is possibly more

were reflected in their indictments. The 'Pierpoint' jury, for example, indicted Foljambe's lawyer for attempting to secure his acquittal from the murder charge, allegedly by improper means, at the Derby sessions of the peace in January 1434. The 'Foljambe' jury accompanied their account of the murder with an indictment relating to a retaliatory attack carried out the following day by Pierpoint's son on one of Foljambe's men, as well as charges against Pierpoint himself for his assault on Foljambe in 1432.[108]

It also seems possible to link Henry Grey of Codnor with the 'Pierpoint' jury. The panel included his retainer John Curson as well as others, including Henry Bradbourne, Henry Kniveton, and Ralph Shirley, with whom Grey seems to have been associated.[109] It is tempting, therefore, to view the 1434 proceedings in terms of rivalry for the rule of north-east Derbyshire between, on the one hand, interests based in eastern Derbyshire and Nottinghamshire led by Henry Grey and including Henry Pierpoint, and, on the other, the group which dominated western Derbyshire, led by Richard Vernon, in support of the Foljambes.[110] However, though this proposition has some relevance to the issues at stake, it is clear that it does not do justice to the full complexity of the situation.[111] The 'Vernon–Foljambe' jury, for example, sitting without Vernon and Cokayn, indicted its own missing colleagues for seeking to influence the election of knights of the shire by intimidation, while the 'Grey–Pierpoint' jury, in a reduced version omitting Pierpoint, indicted Henry Grey for the illegal distribution of liveries.[112] Indeed, the indictments for the granting of liveries made by both juries were so extensive that, as Susan Wright has commented, they 'comprehended most of the then politically active elements in the county'.[113]

likely, since a corresponding grant definitely dated to 1436 is for a term of three years, which would establish a consistent pattern if the lease had originally been granted in 1433; however, even if the lease was first granted in 1436, this would suggest that Vernon had at least not antagonized Foljambe in the 1434 dispute. Wright, *The Derbyshire Gentry*, 129, 249; NA DDFJ 1/81/4, 1/81/6 (printed in Jeayes (ed.), *Derbyshire Charters*, 184–5 [1494, 1496], with the latter grant dated to 19 Henry VI); see above, nn. 91, 94; KB9/11 m. 16v. For connections between Vernon and Cokayn, see Wright, *The Derbyshire Gentry*, 67.

[108] KB9/11 mm. 14–15, 16v–17; see above, at n. 99.

[109] KB9/11 mm. 14, 15v (panel, and Bradbourne associated with Grey); E163/7/31 pt. 1 (Curson); Wright, *The Derbyshire Gentry*, 169 n. 51 (Bradbourne, Kniveton, Shirley—although note Dr Wright's point that in the latter two cases an association with the Longfords might have had more immediate significance: ibid. 190 n. 63).

[110] Cf. Wright, *The Derbyshire Gentry*, 66–7, 130–1.

[111] Cf. ibid. 131–2.

[112] KB9/11 mm. 15v, 17v. The 'Foljambe' jury alleged that Vernon's appearance at the shire election in June 1433 with a group of armed men occurred the day after Grey had tried the same tactics, a sequence of events which would seem to corroborate the suggestion of competition between the two men for influence in the shire.

[113] Wright, *The Derbyshire Gentry*, 131. The accused included not only Grey, Vernon, and Foljambe, but also Ralph, Lord Cromwell, Joan Beauchamp, Lady Bergavenny, John Curson, Ralph Shirley, John de la Pole, and John Cokayn: KB9/11 mm. 15–15v, 17v.

The substance of these charges adds further confusion to any attempted division of local politics into two opposing factions, since among those alleged to have received liveries from Henry Grey in 1433, for example, were Richard Vernon and John Cokayn.[114] This may represent no more than overtures made by Grey to leading members of the west Derbyshire gentry, but it demonstrates that there was considerable fluidity in regional politics in the early 1430s.

There are further complications inherent in any attempt to characterize the conflict as competition between, on Foljambe's side, interests based in western Derbyshire and, on Pierpoint's, those of eastern Derbyshire and Nottinghamshire. Associated with Pierpoint in the dispute were gentry families from western Derbyshire, including not only the Longfords but also the Cursons and the Poles, all of whom had long been associated in Duchy circles with the Foljambes, the Cokayns, and the Vernons.[115] At the same time, Foljambe had apparently won the support of the Nottinghamshire knight Thomas Chaworth, who headed the 'Foljambe' grand jury, and who later stood bail with Vernon for Foljambe's lawyer.[116] Both of these circumstances suggest that the events of 1434 do not reflect a simple division between the east and west of the shire, but rather the attempts of various local interests to secure or enhance their own authority in the wake of the loss of royal leadership in the region since the death of Henry V. It is noticeable that, among the Duchy connection based around Tutbury, those families who developed associations with Pierpoint, such as the Longfords, the Cursons, and the Poles, had territorial interests firmly based in the south and west of the county. The incursions of Pierpoint and Grey in north-eastern Derbyshire therefore presented no direct challenge to their local sphere of influence, perhaps appearing to represent simply the possibility of new and potentially profitable alliances. Foljambe and Vernon, on the other hand, did have territorial interests in the east of the shire, Foljambe around Chesterfield and Vernon across the whole of the Peak district. For them, therefore, Pierpoint and Grey represented a substantial threat to their regional authority.

The wider political context, however, seems to indicate that this was not a case of blanket hostility on the part of Vernon and Foljambe to any incursion by Nottinghamshire interests, a conclusion which helps to explain the apparent contradiction of the presence of the

---

[114] KB9/11 m. 15v; among the other men named as having received liveries were Richard Shirley, esquire, and Robert Fraunceys, son of the Duchy retainer prominent in local politics earlier in the century. Further confusion is evident in the fact that when the murder charges came to court, Grey's retainer John Curson stood bail for some of those accused, in the company of William Vernon and Foljambe's attorney Richard Brown: KB27/698 Rex roti. 6, 28. For Brown, see Wright, *The Derbyshire Gentry*, 129.

[115] For references, see Ch. 6.2 n. 152, Ch. 7.1 n. 12, and above, n. 82.

[116] KB9/11 m. 16v; Wright, *The Derbyshire Gentry*, 129.

Nottinghamshire knight Thomas Chaworth on the 'Foljambe' jury. Chaworth's career was closely linked with that of Ralph, Lord Cromwell, who was during the 1430s establishing himself as a major power in Nottinghamshire.[117] From 1429, one of Cromwell's principal concerns in the region was to make good his claim to the Heriz inheritance, which included the manors of Tibshelf and South Wingfield, just south of Chesterfield in eastern Derbyshire. The rival claimant was Henry Pierpoint. Cromwell was immediately successful in establishing his possession of the estates, and in 1431 appointed feoffees in the disputed manors, who included Thomas Chaworth, Richard Vernon, and John Cokayn.[118] In this context, the appearance of these three men in 1434 as co-jurors on a panel sympathetic to an enemy of Pierpoint seems altogether less surprising.[119] Vernon's association with Cromwell must therefore have been a further element in his decision to support Foljambe against Pierpoint. The threat posed to Vernon by Pierpoint's attempt to establish himself around Chesterfield was substantially enhanced by Vernon's participation in the Cromwell–Pierpoint feud. It seems that Vernon had no objection to the participation of Nottinghamshire interests in the rule of eastern Derbyshire, as long as the interests concerned were those of his ally Cromwell. Cromwell's regional ambitions may also help to explain the fact that Henry Grey of Codnor can plausibly be associated with the 'Pierpoint' jury in 1434. Although conflict did not finally erupt between Grey and Cromwell until 1439,[120] it is not unreasonable to suppose that political tensions were building up earlier in the decade.

The conflict of 1434, therefore, cannot adequately be characterized either as simply a personal dispute between Foljambe and Pierpoint, or as the reaction of interests based in western Derbyshire to incursions into the east of the county from Nottinghamshire. Rather, it resulted from the complex interaction of specific grievances with broader developments in the political complexion of the region; different elements in Derbyshire society were forming associations with various interests in Nottinghamshire which were now, in the absence of a king able to use Duchy resources to control the region, beginning to compete for local influence. Indeed, the loss of royal leadership meant that the coherence of the Duchy connection itself was beginning to

---

[117] Cromwell had acted as a feoffee for Chaworth as early as 1423. Payling, *Political Society*, 96–7, 102–3; Payling, 'Inheritance and Local Politics', 75, 79.

[118] Payling, 'Inheritance and Local Politics', 67–73, 75–6; Payling, *Political Society*, 102–3; C. Richmond, *John Hopton* (Cambridge, 1981), 16–17.

[119] It is worth noting that when the 'Pierpoint' jury indicted Cromwell for the granting of liveries, Vernon and Cokayn were among the alleged recipients, although it is difficult to make any generalizations about the implications of the livery charges. KB9/11 m. 15v; see above, at n. 114.

[120] See below, pp. 250–1.

break down, as diverging regional interests and noble associations began to separate members of the 'Lancastrian' gentry.[121]

The difficulty in 1434 was that, caught between the territorial power of Vernon and the remains of the Duchy connection in the west of the shire, and the ambitions of Nottinghamshire figures such as Cromwell, Pierpoint, and Grey, eastern Derbyshire represented something of a political vacuum. The very fact that the Foljambes had resorted to violence so swiftly in their dispute with the Pierpoints, and had allowed it to go so far, suggests that eastern Derbyshire offered no recognizable hierarchy to which they could appeal or whose intervention to restore order they might expect. This interpretation seems to be borne out by the judicial proceedings of April 1434. None of the peers who headed the commission, Bedford, Suffolk, and Stafford, had any substantial territorial interests in the county, so that the hearings essentially represented the intervention of central government authority. The participation in the legal process of both Pierpoint and Foljambe, as well as of many other influential members of local society, demonstrates the effectiveness of that central authority;[122] but the fact that their participation was expressed in the formation of two rival and partisan juries indicates the scale of the confrontation and the lack of local resources to deal with it. Since there were apparently no informal means of conciliation available to the disputants, the conflict was taken directly into the court in a largely undiluted form.

The fact that the commission embodied 'external' national authority may also help to explain the apparent inconsistencies in the indictments presented by the two juries. All the charges which seem at odds with the general sympathies of the 'Foljambe' and 'Pierpoint' panels relate to the granting of liveries and the conduct of shire elections, issues which had little to do with the feud itself, but were of particular concern to central government.[123] These indictments may therefore have had more to do with the presence of the commission than with the violence of 1434. What the composition of the commission does not explain, however, is the fact that this intervention was successful, since, without the active participation of local interests in the attempt to enforce a compromise, the temporary imposition of an antagonistic legal process could expect to achieve little.[124] Nevertheless, the violence in the shire was effectively

---

[121] The division between Longford, supported by Curson and Pole, and Foljambe, supported by Cokayn and Vernon, cut right across traditional Duchy associations. It could perhaps be argued that Vernon's connection with the Duchy itself demonstrated signs of dislocation in traditional networks, since Vernon had only secured his office at the Peak after royal leadership had been lost in 1422, and since his stewardship there substantially altered the focus of political and territorial interests across the Tutbury region: see above, p. 241.

[122] Cf. the very much less effective intervention of York's regime in Derbyshire affairs in 1454: below, pp. 289–97; Wright, *The Derbyshire Gentry*, 136.

[123] See above, at nn. 112–14.

ended by the hearings before Bedford and Stafford,[125] despite their lack of a significant personal stake in the shire, and the arbitration begun in 1435 was achieved under initially the supervision, and subsequently the personal adjudication, not of a local figure but of the archbishop of York.[126]

This restoration of order becomes more comprehensible if the Pierpoint–Foljambe dispute is seen as one aspect of a wider conflict which was approaching resolution in 1434. The involvement of Vernon and the Foljambe group with Cromwell, and of Longford, Curson, and Pole with Pierpoint, demonstrates that the gentry of the Duchy network in western Derbyshire had already effectively conceded that they could not retain control over the east of the county, where their interests had always been relatively insubstantial, in the face of determined incursions from Nottinghamshire. The west of the shire had always been drawn through the honour of Tutbury into spheres of influence further west in Staffordshire, while the joint shrievalty meant that the east was pulled towards a political centre of gravity further eastwards in Nottinghamshire. Under Henry IV and Henry V, this potential division in Derbyshire society had been contained by the fact that the entire region, from eastern Staffordshire across Derbyshire and into Nottinghamshire and Leicestershire, had formed part of a power bloc under the control of the king through the Duchy lands and the affinity they supported. What the events of the early 1430s highlighted was that, as the influence of the Duchy as a unifying force across the region receded during the minority of Henry VI, eastern Derbyshire was emerging as an area increasingly separate from the west of the shire. Foljambe's actions in 1434 may have represented a last attempt to insulate his family's power base at Chesterfield from changes in the region's political make-up, but the battle was already lost.[127]

The issue that remained was the question of which Nottinghamshire figure would prevail. In 1429, Henry Pierpoint must have hoped to make the Chesterfield area his base in the shire, but it was also in that year that Cromwell made his move on the Heriz manors and secured the keeping of the royal manor of Bolsover.[128] By 1434 it was clear that Pierpoint would be no more successful in preserving his independent authority in the area than Foljambe. Cromwell had consolidated his

---

[124] Powell, *Kingship, Law, and Society*, 87–9, 97–9; E. Powell, 'The Restoration of Law and Order', in Harriss (ed.), *Henry V*, 58–60; cf. Wright, *The Derbyshire Gentry*, 136.

[125] Thomas Foljambe was eventually acquitted: KB27/694 Rex rot. 2v.

[126] *CCR 1429–35*, 365; *1435–41*, 32–4, 53.

[127] It is not clear how soon Foljambe was fully reconciled with the family of the murdered Henry Longford, but all trace of hostility had been dropped by the early 1450s, when Foljambe's son married Nicholas Longford's daughter: see below, Ch. 8 n. 211.

[128] See above, at nn. 90, 118.

ossession of the Heriz properties, while Pierpoint had not only lost his
chance to secure the estates but was also in increasing financial
difficulties.[129] However, though Pierpoint had been overwhelmed,
Henry Grey of Codnor still remained as a potential rival to Cromwell's
authority. Cromwell made no move against Grey until the end of the
decade. When he did, in 1439–40, a key role was taken by the Derbyshire esquire John Stathum, who had been one of the arbiters chosen by
Foljambe in his dispute with Pierpoint four years earlier.[130] In July
1440, a general commission of *oyer* and *terminer* was issued in response
to a complaint by John Stathum about attacks on himself and others by
Henry Grey.[131] Stathum, whose home at Morley lay only a few miles
from the Nottinghamshire border, was closely associated with Cromwell, and it was probably thanks to this connection that Stathum was in
1439 granted custody of the royal castle at Horston, which lay close to
Codnor and had been held by Grey's father earlier in the century.[132]
The implication that Cromwell was developing his regional interests at
Grey's expense is reinforced by the fact that, while Cromwell continued
his regular membership of the Derbyshire and Nottinghamshire commissions of the peace throughout the 1430s and 1440s, Grey lost his
place on the bench in both counties in 1439.[133]

This confrontation in eastern Derbyshire demonstrates the degree to
which the area had been drawn into the purview of competing noble
interests based in Nottinghamshire. The response to Stathum's petition
in 1440 also illustrates the regional implications of the young king's
failure to take up the reins of government, and of the consequent necessity for royal authority to continue to be constituted through the co-
operation of the nobility in conciliar government. While the regime as
a whole seems to have been based on a relatively broad noble consensus, it was becoming clear that regional power was unsustainable
without the political backing available only to those with representation
at court.[134] Grey's misfortune lay in trying to create a power base for
himself within the sphere of influence of Cromwell, who had been
among the leading members of the minority council as a close associate
of Cardinal Beaufort, and who from 1433 held the treasurership.[135]

---

[129] Payling, 'Inheritance and Local Politics', 75–9.

[130] *CCR 1429–35*, 365.

[131] *CPR 1436–41*, 450; Payling, *Political Society*, 195. For detailed discussion of this case, see
Payling, *Political Society*, 195–9, and S. J. Payling, 'Law and Arbitration in Nottinghamshire
1399–1461', in J. Rosenthal and C. Richmond (eds.), *People, Politics and Community in the
Later Middle Ages* (Gloucester, 1987), 143–6.

[132] Payling, *Political Society*, 195; *HMC De L'Isle and Dudley*, i. 216, 230; *CFR 1437–45*, 115;
see above, Ch. 6.2 n. 84.

[133] *CPR 1436–41*, 581, 588; *1441–6*, 469, 476.

[134] The duke of Norfolk was discovering the same thing in East Anglia: see above, Ch. 4.3.

[135] R. L. Friedrichs, 'Ralph, Lord Cromwell and the Politics of Fifteenth-Century

Cromwell's power at court, and Grey's lack of representation there, ensured that the latter suffered a humiliating defeat. Less than a week after the issue of the commission, Grey was ordered on pain of £1,000 to surrender to the Tower; a month later he bound himself in the same sum to keep the peace and to stay within three miles of London.[136] These penalties ensured that he was unable to be present in Derbyshire when the commission, which included Cromwell himself as well as his local associate Richard Vernon, held hearings there in September and October.[137] Grey and his men were indicted for a series of offences, including attacks on several of Cromwell's leading followers and on a park belonging to Cromwell himself.[138] In the following year Grey successfully petitioned for a general pardon, and also secured the removal of Cromwell from further hearings, arguing that he was 'mortal enemye to the said lord Grey and noon egal Juge'.[139] However, he was again required to find security of the peace in the sum of 1,000 marks, and these continuing financial penalties severely compromised his position in the arbitration which followed. Grey was forced to grant three manors to a group of Cromwell's nominees as a pledge that he would abide by the arbiters' award. The latter then stipulated that he should find a further £800 security, a sum which by this stage he was unable to raise. As a result, the manors were not restored to the Grey family until 1455.[140] Grey had suffered an overwhelming defeat at Cromwell's hands.[141] His complete exclusion from regional power structures does not, however, seem to have led to further disruption, since this devastation of his local resources was followed by his death in 1444, leaving a 9-year-old heir.[142]

Cromwell's ascendancy demonstrates not only the assimilation of eastern Derbyshire into the political orbit of the east midlands, but also, much more obviously than was the case in East Anglia, the policy adopted by the regime of the late 1430s of attempting to 'manage' the

England', *Nottingham Medieval Studies*, 32 (1988), 208–12; G. L. Harriss, *Cardinal Beaufort* (Oxford, 1988), 119–20, 139, 144–6, 182–4, 207, 219–20, 222, 230, 232–5, 246–7, 252–5.

[136] *CCR 1435–41*, 384, 388.
[137] *CPR 1436–41*, 450; Payling, *Political Society*, 195, 197.
[138] Payling, *Political Society*, 196, and see, for example, KB27/726 Rex roti. 3, 6v, 17v, 33v; KB27/730 Rex rot. 42v; KB27/742 Rex roti. 37–37v, 40–1.
[139] E28/67 mm. 7–8; Payling, *Political Society*, 197; *CPR 1436–41*, 507; *CCR 1435–41*, 471.
[140] Payling, *Political Society*, 198; C139/116 mm. 14, 15, 17.
[141] Significantly, Cromwell marked his victory over Grey in eastern Derbyshire (and over Henry Pierpoint, who finally capitulated over his claim to the Heriz estates in 1441) by establishing his lordship as a physical presence in the area through the construction of a house, begun in 1442–3, at the Heriz manor of South Wingfield, a few miles south of Chesterfield. The estate was to become one of his principal homes: R. L. Friedrichs, 'The Career and Influence of Ralph, Lord Cromwell, 1393–1456', unpublished Ph.D. thesis (Columbia, 1974), 205–6; Payling, 'Inheritance and Local Politics', 80–4.
[142] *Complete Peerage*, vi. 130.

rule of the regions by creating a series of territorial blocs under noble control.[143] This development embodied a significant change in the political complexion both of the country as a whole, and of the midlands in particular. Under the first two Lancastrian kings the direct connection between local society and the crown through the Duchy had been the major conditioning factor in the political structures of the north midlands. The nobility of the region had had little opportunity to exert consistent influence over local affairs, partly because of the fact that, by chance, several of the families which would normally have been contenders for local rule were affected by lengthy minorities, and partly because the Duchy affinity in the hands of the king was such a powerful presence that there was little scope for the development of independent noble interests.[144] By the late 1430s, however, the coherence of this balance of power was breaking down under the effects of a decade and a half without active royal direction. As the young king gave no indication that he was about to piece together again political structures which had depended so fundamentally on personal royal leadership, the territorial influence of the Duchy was in 1437 instead harnessed in support of regional power blocs under the control of magnates who were now having to embody the public authority of the crown in the localities, as well as managing their own private lordships. In eastern Derbyshire, Nottinghamshire, and Leicestershire, this meant turning to Cromwell and Beaumont, members of the minor nobility who were promoted to a local eminence unprecedented in their families' history. In Staffordshire and western Derbyshire, the obvious candidate for greater authority was the earl of Stafford, whose lordship was to prove a major element in regional politics from the later 1430s.

[143] See above, Ch. 2.4.   [144] See above, Chs. 6.2, 7.1.

8

1437–1461

The Duke of Buckingham and the Rule of the North Midlands

By 1440, eastern Derbyshire had been assimilated into structures of authority based in Nottinghamshire, while Staffordshire had been drawn during the 1420s and 1430s into a broad sphere of influence focused on Warwickshire, through a regional hierarchy formed by the connected lordships of Warwick, Ferrers, and Stafford. Western and central Derbyshire, though not directly subject to the influence of this noble coalition,[1] had been accommodated into the same pattern of local authority through the associations of this Staffordshire connection with the substantial remains of the Duchy affinity in both counties. During the later 1430s, however, this balance of power underwent several significant changes.

First, the earl of Stafford began to emerge from Warwick's shadow in the north midlands as an increasingly influential force in his own right. In 1435 the steward of Tutbury and master forester of Needwood, Nicholas Montgomery, died.[2] His offices were granted during pleasure to the earl, creating for the first time a direct link between the power of the Staffords in western Staffordshire and the territorial interests of the Duchy in the east, which extended across the border into Derbyshire.[3] These associations with the Duchy were reinforced in 1437, when Stafford was included in the sweeping reorganization of Duchy office-holding which established a series of magnate lordships across the midlands.[4] His stewardship at Tutbury was converted into a life grant, as was his office at Needwood, and in addition he was appointed for life to the master forestership of Duffield Frith.[5] His enhanced authority in Staffordshire and Derbyshire was further buttressed by a significant

---

[1] Neither Warwick nor Ferrers nor Stafford had significant lands in Derbyshire: C. Carpenter, *Locality and Polity* (Cambridge, 1992), 449; *Complete Peerage*, v. 320 n.; C. Rawcliffe, *The Staffords* (Cambridge, 1978), appendix A.

[2] This was the younger Nicholas Montgomery, who had succeeded his father as Tutbury steward in 1422: see above, Ch. 7.1 at n. 22; R. Somerville, *History of the Duchy of Lancaster*, i (London, 1953), 539, 546; DL42/18 pt. 2 fo. 57.

[3] DL42/18 pt. 1 fo. 33v; Somerville, *History of the Duchy*, 539, 542, 546.

[4] See above, pp. 45–7.

[5] The office at Duffield Frith was to be held jointly with the previous incumbent Sir John Cokayn: DL42/18 pt. 1 fos. 59–59v; Somerville, *History of the Duchy*, 539, 556.

stake in Cheshire, where he was granted the Duchy stewardship of Halton, also for life.[6]

For the first time since 1399, the extensive Lancastrian estates in Staffordshire and Derbyshire had been placed under noble control. The fact that the magnate to whom they were granted was the earl of Stafford meant that there was a real possibility that the two counties (eastern Derbyshire apart) could be united under a single noble lordship. This enhancement of Stafford's regional authority inevitably altered in his favour the balance of his coalition with Warwick and Ferrers. Where Stafford and Ferrers had previously enjoyed similar local status as junior partners under Warwick's overlordship, Stafford was now establishing a new degree of personal influence. His permanent acquisition of the Tutbury offices reinforced a trend which had begun with the death of Edmund Ferrers in 1435, when Stafford's seniority over the heir, William Ferrers, was underlined by the marriage of Ferrers's widow to Stafford's retainer Philip Chetwynd, which brought control of her share of the Ferrers estates more closely into Stafford's political orbit.[7]

Moreover, Duchy office was not the only addition to Stafford's regional influence. In 1438 the death of his mother allowed him for the first time to take control of the Stafford inheritance in its entirety.[8] In the same year, he consolidated his interests in north Warwickshire with the purchase of most of the estates of Lord Clinton, including Maxstoke Castle.[9] This dramatic increase in his territorial power was all the more significant in view of the loss of the earl of Warwick's personal involvement in the region from 1437, when he left England to take up his appointment as lieutenant-general and governor of Normandy.[10] Between 1435 and 1439, therefore, the earl of Stafford's regional authority was utterly transformed. Before these years, he had played only a supporting role in a local hierarchy created under the overlordship of Richard Beauchamp. During the later 1430s, Stafford acquired the means to become in his own right the leading force in a reconfigured north midlands, controlling a territorial bloc based in Staffordshire and stretching eastwards into Derbyshire and south into northern Warwickshire.[11]

[6] Somerville, *History of the Duchy*, 510.

[7] See above, Ch. 7.2 at n. 69.

[8] *CFR 1437–45*, 51; *CPR 1436–41*, 169, 233; Rawcliffe, *The Staffords*, 18.

[9] Carpenter, *Locality and Polity*, 321, 392–3. Stafford also received several royal grants of local land and revenue during this period. In May 1438 he received a life grant of the fee-farm of the town of Stafford, and of the keeping of Atherstone, a royal manor in north-east Warwickshire. In Dec. 1439 he was granted custody of estates belonging to the abbey of Vale Royal, which included lands in Derbyshire and Cheshire: *CPR 1436–41*, 161, 389; *CCR 1435–41*, 156; Carpenter, *Locality and Polity*, 393.

[10] Carpenter, *Locality and Polity*, 392; *Complete Peerage*, xii pt. 2, 381.

[11] This sphere of influence was further reinforced by Stafford interests to the north and west, in Cheshire and Shropshire: see Ch. 6.1 at n. 31, and above, at n. 6.

It is not at all clear whether Beauchamp could, in the long term, have accepted this transformation of the north midlands into an independent sphere of influence for his former protégé. In the event, Stafford's new authority was never tested by Warwick's return, since Beauchamp died in France in 1439. The loss of the man who had dominated midlands politics for much of the century, and the succession of a 14-year-old heir,[12] meant that the way was now clear for Stafford to turn the potential power of his estates and offices into political reality—to reassemble the Tutbury affinity and marry it with the connection which he had previously shared with Warwick and Ferrers, and which was now regrouping around his own lordship.[13] Earlier in the century Henry IV and, more successfully, Henry V had tried to fill the political vacuum left by the loss of Stafford lordship in western Staffordshire by extending their own regional control eastwards from the Duchy lands around Tutbury;[14] Stafford was now attempting the same process in reverse in order to fill the vacuum left in eastern Staffordshire and western Derbyshire by the loss of royal lordship over the Duchy. It was clear that this complex task would require skilled handling and sustained attention if it were to be an even temporarily viable form of regional rule. Henry IV, despite the range of resources available to him, had, after all, provoked significant regional disruption through an over-simplistic approach.[15] However, it was vital that Stafford should succeed in the attempt, since the kingship of Henry VI offered no prospect of effective recourse if the earl's control of the combined influence of his own and the Duchy estates should falter.

The enhanced authority of Stafford and his following was certainly apparent in the later 1430s. The earl's associate John Harper had been a member of the Staffordshire commission of the peace since the beginning of the decade, but in 1439 he was joined on the bench for the first time by his colleagues in Stafford's service, Robert Whitgreve and Thomas Arblaster.[16] In Derbyshire, the earl's hereditary stake had previously qualified him for little active involvement in local government,[17] but his office at Tutbury afforded him a new status in the shire. That this status did not automatically provide him with direct power, but would have to be developed into real authority in the county, is demonstrated by the fact that all the sheriffs between 1437 and 1441 were Nottinghamshire men, which suggests that Cromwell's domi-

---

[12] *Complete Peerage*, xii pt. 2, 382–3.
[13] Cf. Carpenter, *Locality and Polity*, 400, 405.
[14] See above, Chs. 6.2, 7.1.
[15] See above, Ch. 6.2.
[16] *CPR 1436–41*, 590; see above, pp. 235–6.
[17] I. D. Rowney, 'The Staffordshire Political Community, 1440–1500', unpublished Ph.D. thesis (Keele, 1981), 23–4.

nance in Nottinghamshire and eastern Derbyshire was during these years more than a match for Stafford's newly acquired influence in the latter shire.[18] Nevertheless, the earl was appointed to the Derbyshire commission of the peace for the first time in 1437,[19] a clear indication that the Tutbury stewardship had given him the means through which his authority could be extended into the county.

The personal influence of the men most closely associated with Stafford during the previous decade also increased. Robert Whitgreve, who had been receiver at Tutbury since 1432, was appointed to the stewardship of the Duchy manor of Newcastle-under-Lyme for life in 1437.[20] In May 1438 he was formally retained by Philip Chetwynd, whose personal influence had been increased by his marriage to Ellen, Lady Ferrers, and in 1442 Stafford granted Whitgreve the right to bear arms 'en signe de noblesse'.[21] Thomas Arblaster was granted the pannage of several royal chases in Staffordshire in 1439, while John Harper secured additional fees for his 'good counsel', including 10 marks granted by Stafford himself in 1441.[22] It also seemed that for the first time a coherent Stafford affinity might begin to emerge around these few trusted associates, as the earl began to make more substantial and extensive connections among the region's gentry. Richard Vernon and Hugh Erdeswick, prominent among the Staffordshire gentry who had collaborated with the authority of the Beauchamp-led coalition earlier in the decade, now formalized their associations with the earl: Erdeswick was acting as his chief steward in Staffordshire by 1438, while Vernon was granted an annuity in 1440.[23] The fact that they (and, indeed, Robert Whitgreve) had also been associated with Edmund Ferrers during the previous decade, but were now moving closer to Stafford, emphasizes the fact that the earl was in the ascendant over what had earlier been largely a common connection.[24]

[18] *List of Sheriffs for England and Wales*, PRO Lists and Indexes, 9 (1898), 103; S. J. Payling, *Political Society in Lancastrian England* (Oxford, 1991), 244–5; see above, pp. 247, 249–52.

[19] *CPR 1436–41*, 581.

[20] The grant was made to Whitgreve jointly with John Kingsley, who had held the office since 1420: DL 42/18 pt. 1 fos. 59v, 106v; Somerville, *History of the Duchy*, 550.

[21] Wm Salt Lib. HM Chetwynd bundle 7 unnumbered deed (1438); G. Wrottesley (ed.), 'The Chetwynd Cartulary', *Collections for a History of Staffordshire*, 12 (1891), 313; SRO D1721/1/11 fo. 123. For Chetwynd's marriage, see above, Ch. 7.2 at n. 69.

[22] *CFR 1437–45*, 95; *CCR 1435–41*, 130; Rowney, 'Staffordshire Political Community', 62. By the mid-1440s Harper was also being employed as auditor of the south Yorkshire estates of John Talbot, earl of Shrewsbury: A. J. Pollard, 'The Family of Talbot, Lords Talbot and Earls of Shrewsbury in the Fifteenth Century', unpublished Ph.D. thesis (Bristol, 1968), 309. See also the employment of Whitgreve, Harper, and Arblaster on special commissions in Staffordshire: *CPR 1429–36*, 523, 529; *1436–41*, 370, 505, 537; *1441–6*, 92; *CFR 1437–45*, 324; DL37/8 no. 76; DL37/10 no. 44; DL37/12 no. 60.

[23] SC6/988/12 m. 10v (cf. SRO D641/1/2/54); SRO D641/1/2/272 (cf. NLW Peniarth MS 280, fos. 11–12).

[24] See above, pp. 238–9.

Vernon's personal authority had by this point become so significant that he had in effect created his own regional lordship. His dominance in northern Derbyshire, founded on the potent combination of his own extensive territorial interests and his Duchy stewardship of the High Peak, was further reinforced in 1439 by his appointment as steward of the Derbyshire lands of John, duke of Norfolk.[25] His ascendancy among his fellow gentry is evident from the fact that by 1437 he himself was paying a fee to Hugh Erdeswick.[26] By 1440 his authority in the Peak was so overwhelming that seven landowners, including the controller of the king's household Sir Thomas Stanley, complained to the Duchy council that they had been unable to maintain their rights in the region in the face of opposition from Vernon.[27] This independent personal authority, of which his Duchy office formed a key element, meant that Vernon would play a crucial role in any attempt Stafford might make to establish himself at the head of a revitalized Duchy connection in the area.[28] The very fact that this powerful figure with his own 'country' in north Derbyshire chose this moment to formalize his association with the earl demonstrates the increasing status of the latter as a potential claimant to the rule of the entire region.[29]

Vernon and Erdeswick were joined by increasing numbers of other local gentlemen in forging formal connections with Stafford. John Hampton of Stourton, an esquire of the king's body whose father had been granted an annuity from the Stafford lands in 1406, was given a fee of 10 marks by the earl in 1442.[30] The esquires Ralph Egerton, Nicholas Longford, John Curson, and Henry Bradbourne were all granted annuities between 1440 and 1445, and John Cokayn was active

[25] See above, pp. 240–1; *HMC Rutland*, iv. 29. In 1443 his son Fulk was also appointed steward of the Duchy lands in Staffordshire and Derbyshire which had previously been under the control of Henry V's feoffees. Fulk had been granted the keeping of Shothill park in 1437, and in the following year was made constable of the Peak jointly with his father. In 1439 he was appointed bailiff of two Derbyshire wapentakes. DL37/10 no. 21; DL42/18 pt. 1 fos. 93v, 100v; *CPR 1436–41*, 366.

[26] Erdeswick's brother Sampson was also receiving a fee from Vernon: S. M. Wright, *The Derbyshire Gentry in the Fifteenth Century*, Derbyshire Record Society, 8 (Chesterfield, 1983), 249.

[27] *HMC Rutland*, i. 1–2. Vernon was summoned before the Duchy council, presumably as a result of this complaint, on 20 Feb. 1440: DL42/18 pt. 1 fo. 149.

[28] Vernon's status was reflected in the annuity he was granted by the earl, the large sum of £20: SRO D641/1/2/272.

[29] Vernon may also have felt his authority to be under pressure at this point as a result of Stanley's complaint against him earlier in the year. However, even if Vernon's decision to associate himself formally with Stafford was precipitated by his own temporary vulnerability, the implication remains that recourse to the earl's developing lordship might offer him effective support.

[30] Hampton's annuity was increased to £10 in 1444. An annuity of £50 which he had been granted from the fee-farm of Coventry in 1437 was in 1445 transferred to the revenues of Tutbury. SRO D641/1/2/48; D641/1/2/54–5; NLW Peniarth MS 280, fos. 20, 34; DL37/12 no. 42.

in the earl's service by 1439.[31] Of these men, Hampton in particular became increasingly eminent in local affairs, joining Whitgreve, Harper, and Arblaster at the administrative heart of Staffordshire politics. He represented the shire in parliament for the first time in 1437, and was to be elected twice more during the 1440s; in 1439 he joined the Stafford-shire commission of the peace.[32] Egerton and Curson also played some role in local government. Egerton had held the Staffordshire shrievalty during the 1430s, and subsequently received occasional appointments as a special commissioner in the county; he was also elected knight of the shire in 1442.[33] Curson had been sheriff of Derbyshire in 1436, and served several times as escheator and in parliament; from 1437 he was a regular member of the peace commission in the county.[34] The evidence of private transactions mirrors that of these public appoint-ments, in that the continuing association of the core of Stafford's connection—Vernon, Erdeswick, Whitgreve, Harper, and Arblaster—was accompanied by some degree of involvement on the part of the newcomers, most extensively in the case of John Hampton.[35] During this period Stafford also retained two lawyers, William Comberford (like Vernon, Erdeswick, and Whitgreve, another former Ferrers associate) and Ralph de la Pole.[36] Both combined their service to the earl with employment by the Duchy—interests which, at a local level, were now effectively one and the same—and the significance of these affiliations was reflected by their regular appointment to the commis-sion of the peace, Pole in Derbyshire and Comberford in Stafford-shire.[37]

This burst of retaining in the late 1430s and early 1440s indicates the significance of the earl's new regional resources and his consequent

---

[31] SRO D641/1/2/56; D641/1/2/15; NLW Peniarth MS 280, fos. 11, 18, 31, 35; A. Compton Reeves, 'Some of Humphrey Stafford's Military Indentures', *Nottingham Medieval Studies*, 16 (1972), 89; Rawcliffe, *The Staffords*, 233. Cokayn was the son of the John Cokayn who, until his death in 1438, had shared the master forestership of Duffield Frith with Stafford: see above, n. 5.

[32] Hampton sat in the parliaments of 1442 and 1449: *Return of the Name*, 330, 333, 339; *CPR 1436–41*, 590. See also his appointment to special commissions: *CPR 1436–41*, 505; *CFR 1437–45*, 214, 324; DL37/10 no. 46.

[33] Egerton was appointed sheriff in 1432, and had also represented Staffordshire in the parliament of 1429: *List of Sheriffs*, 127; *CFR 1437–45*, 214; *Return of the Name*, 317, 333.

[34] *List of Sheriffs*, 103; *List of Escheators for England and Wales*, PRO Lists and Indexes, 72 (1971), 111; *Return of the Name*, 305, 315, 321, 326, 332; *CPR 1436–41*, 581; *1441–6*, 469; *1446–52*, 588; *1452–61*, 663–4.

[35] See, for example, SRO D1721/1/1 fos. 38, 269v, 270; Wm Salt Lib. HM Chetwynd bundle 7 unnumbered deed (1442); *CCR 1435–41*, 185–6, 266–7, 268.

[36] Both were retained for 40s. in 1443: SRO D641/1/2/57; NLW Peniarth MS 280, fos. 25, 30; Rowney, 'Staffordshire Political Community', 41, 67; see above, pp. 245, 256.

[37] Somerville, *History of the Duchy*, 451, 453, 457; *CPR 1436–41*, 581; *1441–6*, 469, 478. Later in the decade, Buckingham appointed Pole his lieutenant in the lands of the honour of Tutbury in Derbyshire, and Comberford to the equivalent position in Staffordshire: NLW Peniarth MS 280, fo. 45.

intention to extend his local lordship. The fact that he was for the first time making connections among Derbyshire gentry families with traditions of service to the Duchy, such as the Longfords, Cursons, Poles, and Cokayns,[38] reflects the new foothold which the stewardship of Tutbury gave him across the Staffordshire–Derbyshire border. John Curson and Ralph de la Pole had also been associated during the previous decade with Henry, Lord Grey. Their move into Stafford's following in the years between Grey's political eclipse in 1440 and his death in 1444 seems to indicate that the earl now represented the obvious focus of noble authority in Derbyshire for those who were unwilling or unable to look east to the lordship of Cromwell.[39]

The earl's acquisition of an increasing stake in the rule of the north midlands was reflected in his enhanced status among the nobility. In 1441 he began to use the title of earl of Buckingham, which had originally been conferred on his maternal grandfather Thomas of Woodstock, the youngest son of Edward III.[40] The adoption of this style therefore implicitly emphasized his descent from royal stock, and it is inconceivable that he could have enhanced his standing among his peers in this way without the approval of Henry VI's government, represented primarily by the lords who dominated the household.[41] The new earl of Buckingham therefore seemed to have secured every possible advantage in support of his developing power in the north midlands. To his own estates he added the regional authority that was the legacy of his participation in the Beauchamp-led coalition which had dominated the area during the previous two decades; both these elements were further reinforced by support from central government, manifested most significantly in the grant of office at Tutbury, and reflected also in the earl's new title.

This wealth of resources at Buckingham's disposal in the attempt to unite Staffordshire and western Derbyshire under his rule was paralleled by the magnitude of the task facing him. In a similar situation, Henry IV and Henry V had been able to draw on the authority of the crown in seeking to bridge the gap left by the loss of

---

[38] For the Lancastrian associations of these families, see above, Ch. 6.1 at n. 14, and Ch. 7.2 n. 82.

[39] Henry Bradbourne was a third local gentleman to move from Grey's service to that of Stafford. The correlation between Grey's defeat and Stafford's acquisition of these retainers seems fairly explicit; John Curson, the first of the three to take a fee from the earl, was retained three months after the issue in 1440 of the special commission to investigate complaints against Grey: see above, Ch. 7.2 at n. 131; Wright, *The Derbyshire Gentry*, 68.

[40] *Complete Peerage*, ii. 388; vi. 474–5.

[41] A similar process is perhaps apparent in the case of John, Lord Beaumont, whose regional authority was vastly increased between 1437 and 1440 by a series of grants in Leicestershire and Lincolnshire, and whose new status was recognized in Feb. 1440 by his elevation to a viscountcy: *Complete Peerage*, ii. 62; *CPR 1436–41*, 380; see above, Ch. 2.4 at n. 123.

Stafford lordship in western Staffordshire. Buckingham, on the other hand, had to extend his private lordship into eastern Staffordshire and western Derbyshire by taking on the quasi-public responsibility of managing the Duchy estates on the king's behalf.[42] Despite the advantages he enjoyed, and despite the absence of significant rivals in the region, his efforts to enlarge his affinity and establish his rule in the years after 1437 were not an unqualified success.

While Buckingham's retaining policy suggested that he was concerned to gather around himself a more coherent local following, in practice it is hard to demonstrate that his lordship was percolating more broadly through regional society, or that it was successfully tapping into established structures of power. In Derbyshire in particular, which would have to be grafted on to the earl's inherited power base in Staffordshire if he were to establish himself as an adequate regional replacement for the king's lordship over the Duchy, his office at Tutbury should have given him an immediate entrée into the gentry network which dominated the western half of the county and was traditionally closely associated with the Duchy.[43] Despite this, and despite the fact that Buckingham did retain members of this Derbyshire network, such as Longford, Curson, and Pole, his authority seems to have remained a peripheral force in the shire. The related families of Blount and Gresley, for example, were key members of the Tutbury connection in Derbyshire and influential participants in local government.[44] This regional standing was recognized in the appointment of Sir Thomas Blount as Buckingham's deputy steward at Tutbury, but there is little evidence of any attempt by the earl to use this official connection to cultivate a personal relationship with the two families—an omission which seems particularly remarkable given that both the Gresleys and the Blounts also held properties in Staffordshire.[45] Nor

[42] The earl of Suffolk had faced the same challenge in East Anglia—that of securing the rule of the entire region by combining his private lordship in Suffolk with control of the Duchy in Norfolk: see above, Chs. 4.1 and 4.2.

[43] For this network, see above, Ch. 6.1 at nn. 14–15, and references in Ch. 6.2 n. 152 and Ch. 7.2 n. 82.

[44] See, for example, *CPR 1436–41*, 581; *1441–6*, 469; *List of Sheriffs*, 103, 127; *Return of the Name*, 314, 335, 338, 344–5; above, Ch. 7.1 n 13.

[45] For Blount holding office at Tutbury at least by 1439, see *Rot. Parl.*, v. 16; DL42/18 pt. I fos. 84v–85, 142–142v; DL37/10 no. 44. He was also appointed steward by Queen Catherine in the Duchy lordships, including Leicester, which formed part of her dower: LRO DE40/22/55; cf. E163/7/31 pt. I. Susan Wright states that Blount was retained by Buckingham during the 1440s, citing information from T. B. Pugh, but Carole Rawcliffe makes no mention of Blount in any connection with the Stafford retinue. The only evidence I have been able to find of any possible association between them during these years is a charter of 1443 involving Buckingham, to which Blount's brother-in-law Sir John Gresley was a witness. It is not clear whether Buckingham or the crown would have been responsible for the appointment of Blount as deputy steward of Tutbury, but in the absence of any other traceable connection between Blount and the earl, the crown would perhaps seem more likely. Buckingham's

was this an isolated example. Buckingham developed no association, for instance, with the Montgomeries of Cubley, the earl's predecessors in office at Tutbury.[46] It is hard to avoid the conclusion that Buckingham was failing to exploit the opportunity provided by his Duchy stewardship to reassemble Lancastrian networks in the region. His increased retaining seems to have brought him the service of a few individuals, rather than the core of a connection spreading through local society.[47]

Nor had the earl enjoyed resounding success in Staffordshire, ostensibly the centre of his regional interests. While Buckingham had assumed the leadership of the connection which he had previously shared with Edmund Ferrers under the overlordship of Richard Beauchamp, it rapidly became apparent, for example, that he had not won the support or even the acquiescence of Ferrers's heir William. The marriage of the dowager Lady Ferrers to Buckingham's retainer Philip Chetwynd had brought a considerable share of the Ferrers lands into Chetwynd's control and helped to consolidate Buckingham's authority over the Ferrers connection. For both these reasons, however, it probably found little favour with William Ferrers. This impression is reinforced by developments concerning the north Warwickshire manor of Birmingham. Edmund Ferrers's successful prosecution of his claim to the manor during the 1420s had been a clear indication of his importance in the regional hierarchy developing around the earl of Warwick.[48] After Ferrers's death, however, the rival claimant William Bermingham successfully brought an assize of novel disseisin against the widowed Lady Ferrers and her new husband, who subsequently made no attempt to reassert the Ferrers claim.[49] In effect, this represented an abandonment of Ferrers's interests in north Warwickshire by the Beauchamp–Stafford nexus. The commission for the assize which found in favour of Bermingham had substantial connections with Warwick, and, despite the enhancement of Buckingham's power by the end of the decade, the latter showed no inclination to revive Chetwynd's interests in the

failure to cultivate any connection with Blount, who was a crucial figure in Derbyshire–Staffordshire power structures, is paralleled by the earl's failure to develop an association during the 1440s with William Mountford, the key gentry figure in north Warwickshire. Wright, *The Derbyshire Gentry*, 71, 100 n.; SRO D1721/1/1 fos. 148v–149; Rowney, 'Staffordshire Political Community', 452; F. Madan, 'The Gresleys of Drakelow', *Collections for a History of Staffordshire*, new series, 1 (London, 1898), 49; A. Croke, *The Genealogical History of the Croke Family*, 2 vols. (Oxford, 1823), ii. 185–6; Carpenter, *Locality and Polity*, 409, 434.

[46] See Ch. 7.1 at n. 22, and above, at nn. 2–3; Wright, *The Derbyshire Gentry*, 71.

[47] Cf. Susan Wright's comments on the limitations of Buckingham's affinity in Derbyshire during the 1440s: *The Derbyshire Gentry*, 70–2. She is, however, prepared to accept that the earl's lordship was an effective force in some areas of the shire; see discussion below, pp. 272–5.

[48] See above, p. 237.

[49] Carpenter, *Locality and Polity*, 391, 406.

manor. The implication is that, because of the overlap between the
Ferrers connection and that of Buckingham, which had been consolidated by the Chetwynd marriage, William Ferrers himself may have
been considered to be largely redundant first to Warwick's and then to
Buckingham's management of the north midlands.[50] Certainly, Ferrers
seems to have become somewhat distanced from his father's former
ally. By 1445, when making a feoffment of property in Derbyshire, he
turned not to Buckingham, who would have been the obvious choice as
a trustee for someone with Ferrers's territorial interests, but to the
further-flung authority of John Sutton of Dudley and John, Viscount
Beaumont.[51]

Moreover, it became clear that Buckingham's dismissal of Ferrers's
interests had not left the latter without the means to exert any influence
on local affairs. In 1440 the dowager Lady Ferrers died,[52] and her son,
now restored to full possession of his estates, seems to have been able
to mount a challenge to Buckingham's regional control. In November
1441 Ferrers was for the first time appointed to the commission of the
peace in Staffordshire, and in the same month his associate Richard
Archer, a Warwickshire gentleman who had no connection with
Buckingham, secured the Staffordshire shrievalty.[53] This somewhat
belated recognition of Ferrers's claim to a stake in the government of
the shire may well have been a response to a show of strength on his
part, since earlier in the year he had been ordered to stop making
unlawful assemblies in the region.[54] The demonstration that Buckingham could not exclude from local rule a former ally whose concerns he
had decided to ignore was the first indication that a Stafford hegemony
was failing to materialize. Indeed, in view of the rift between Ferrers
and Buckingham, the deficiencies in the earl's affinity were indicated by
the fact that, when Ferrers chose Dudley and Beaumont as his feoffees
in 1445, among the witnesses were Stafford associates, including Henry
Bradbourne, Ralph de la Pole, and John Cokayn.[55]

In the context of Buckingham's problems with Ferrers, and of his
apparent failure to reconstitute the Duchy affinity under his own
leadership, it may be significant that, when further flaws in local
political structures were exposed by a dispute which began in the early

[50] Carpenter, *Locality and Polity*, 391.
[51] *CCR 1441–7*, 288–9. See below, at n. 89, for Ferrers's alliance with Henry Beauchamp
when the latter challenged Buckingham's interests in Warwickshire between 1444 and 1446.
[52] Wrottesley (ed.), 'The Chetwynd Cartulary', 261–2.
[53] *CPR 1441–6*, 478; *List of Sheriffs*, 127; Carpenter, *Locality and Polity*, 323, 408.
[54] *CCR 1435–41*, 422–3. The same process is evident in Warwickshire, where he was also
added to the commission of the peace in 1441: Carpenter, *Locality and Polity*, 406, 408.
[55] See reference above, n. 51. The Gresleys, who had not developed any association with
Buckingham in Derbyshire, were also connected with Ferrers in Staffordshire: reference
above, n. 51; *CCR 1441–7*, 188.

1440s, the protagonists included members both of traditionally Lancastrian families and of the former Ferrers retinue. Conflict developed in 1442 in the Peak district on the Staffordshire–Derbyshire border, the heartlands of Buckingham's newly formed power bloc. John Meverell of Throwley and Edmund Basset of Blore had been among the first local gentlemen retained by Edmund Ferrers in 1413.[56] Both families were also members of the gentry network which had evolved in the region under Henry V and during his son's minority, as the already broad Duchy connection was assimilated more fully into local society.[57] Within this network, both the Meverells and the Bassets were closely associated with their neighbours the Okeovers of Okeover, a connection which was still in evidence by 1439, when John Meverell's son Sampson acted as a witness for Thomas Okeover.[58] Meverell died in 1442, and within months his heir Sampson had quarrelled with both Okeover and Ralph Basset, the current owner of Blore.[59] The conflict seems to have begun with a dispute over tithes owed by Meverell to the church at Ilam, where the priest John Southworth was the nominee of Okeover, whose grandson and heir had just married Basset's daughter.[60] Southworth granted these tithes to Basset, a move to which Meverell furiously objected, responding in September 1442 with a raid on crops at Throwley belonging to Basset.[61] During the following two years the conflict intensified. In April 1444 Southworth, according to Meverell, 'without any atorite' ordered 'al the prestus in the contre that they schold do no scerves wen I or my wyeff were in any of tho kercus'.[62] Meverell appealed to the chancellor John Stafford, archbishop of

[56] See above, Ch. 6.2 at n. 130. In July 1415 John Meverell acted as a feoffee for Ferrers: LRO DE170/45/2.

[57] Associates of the Meverells and Bassets during the previous three decades included the Okeovers, the Fitzherberts, the Poles of Hartington, the Longfords, the Cursons of Kedleston, the Cokayns, the Montgomeries, and the Bradbournes: DCL Every 3242–3, 3307, 3519; DRO D231M/E451, T22–3, T169, T308, T379; LRO 26D53/190; BL Harl. MS 4028 fo. 93; BL Add. Ch. 53621; Wright, *The Derbyshire Gentry*, 212 (deeds of 1420 and 1430), 242 (deed of 1429).

[58] DRO D231M/T23 (printed in I. H. Jeayes (ed.), *Descriptive Catalogue of Derbyshire Charters* (London, 1906), 270 [2133]); and see, for example, DRO D231M/T379 (Jeayes (ed.), *Derbyshire Charters*, 20 [157]). For the Okeovers in the Duchy retinue earlier in the century, see above, Ch. 6.1 at n. 14, and Ch. 7.2 n. 82.

[59] J. C. Wedgwood, *Staffordshire Parliamentary History*, William Salt Archaeological Society (London, 1917–18), 181.

[60] Rowney, 'Staffordshire Political Community', 309; DRO D231M/F15 (Jeayes (ed.), *Derbyshire Charters*, 270 [2135]); cf. DRO D231M/E697, T380.

[61] CP40/731 rot. 559v; G. Wrottesley (ed.), 'Extracts from the Plea Rolls of the Reign of Henry VI', *Collections for a History of Staffordshire*, William Salt Archaeological Society, new series, 3 (1900), 167.

[62] BL Add. Ch. 27343 (dorse). Meverell's wife was Isabella, daughter of Sir Roger Leche, who, with her two sisters, inherited most of the Leche estates after the death of their brother Philip: see NA DDP 45/3; E. A. Ayres, 'Parliamentary Representation in Derbyshire and Nottinghamshire in the Fifteenth Century', unpublished MA thesis (Nottingham, 1956), 110.

Canterbury, whose service he had entered on his return from a military career in France, and in July the archbishop's commissioners duly excommunicated Southworth.[63]

Nor was this the only dispute to develop at this point within the same group of associates. Thomas Okeover had been among the feoffees who administered the estates of Nicholas Fitzherbert of Norbury during his lengthy minority.[64] During the early 1440s the now adult Fitzherbert quarrelled with Okeover and Ralph Basset over lands at Snelston in which Okeover had been enfeoffed and over rights of common at Norbury.[65] Fitzherbert submitted a petition to the chancellor complaining that Okeover and Basset had destroyed his close at Norbury in May 1443, and in June the accused were summoned before the council.[66] On that occasion judgment was reserved, and in July and November Basset and Okeover bound themselves to appear again to answer the complaints.[67] Basset responded in September with an indictment alleging that, five months earlier, Fitzherbert had broken into his property and stolen trees and underwood, while in the same term Fitzherbert brought a charge against Basset and Okeover for breaking his close at Norbury.[68] No progress in resolving these hostilities had been made by February 1444, when Fitzherbert secured the appointment of a commission of inquiry into his opponents' activities.[69]

Between 1442 and 1444, therefore, both of these disputes had caused significant local disruption and, in the course of both, appeals had been made to national authority in the person of the chancellor and through the courts. Despite all this, and despite the fact that the conflicts were taking place in the heart of his recently enlarged 'country', where he now represented not only his own private lordship but also the king in the guise of the Duchy, Buckingham made no attempt to restore peace, nor indeed to intervene at all. Significantly, when Meverell and Basset

[63] BL Add. Ch. 27343. For Meverell in Archbishop Stafford's service, see J. M. J. Fletcher, 'Sir Sampson Meverill of Tideswell, 1388–1462', *Journal of the Derbyshire Archaeological and Natural History Society*, 30 (1908), 2, quoting the inscription on Meverell's tomb. (The chancellor of England mentioned as Meverell's feoffee in C1/72/112 is presumably also Stafford.)

[64] DRO D231M/E451. Nicholas Fitzherbert, like the Meverells and Bassets, had connections with the Ferrers of Chartley, although Fitzherbert's were more recent. In Sept. 1440 William Ferrers leased his manor of Breadsall in Derbyshire to Fitzherbert and Henry Bothe: DCL I. H. Jeayes (ed.), 'Descriptive Catalogue of the Charters . . . at Radbourne Hall', 209 [558].

[65] C1/16/158; Rowney, 'Staffordshire Political Community', 311–12. Fitzherbert and Basset were apparently still on reasonably good terms in 1441, when they were co-witnesses to a feoffment by Ralph Shirley: BL Harl. MS 4028 fo. 93.

[66] C1/16/158; *POPC*, v. 290–1, 294–5.

[67] *POPC*, v. 295; *CCR 1441–7*, 153, 200.

[68] CP40/731 rot. 624v; Wrottesley (ed.), 'Extracts from the Plea Rolls of the Reign of Henry VI', 167; KB27/730 Coram Rege rot. 124v.

[69] *CPR 1441–6*, 246.

were brought to arbitration in 1444, the judge appointed was not Buckingham but John Sutton, Lord Dudley, who had made little effort to establish himself as a local magnate, preferring to concentrate his activities at court.[70] Unsurprisingly, this attempt to settle a two-year-old dispute by a nobleman who could exercise only limited regional authority was unsuccessful.[71]

Buckingham failed to take any action until the summer of 1445 when, rather than attempting to demonstrate his lordship by enforcing a settlement, his chosen response was blatantly partisan. Before this point, he had had no formal connection with Meverell or Fitzherbert, or with their common enemies Basset and Okeover. This lack of direct association with any of the competing families might have given Buckingham an ideal opportunity to exercise his lordship as a cohesive force in the region by attempting an arbitration. Indeed, given that his responsibilities included the management of the king's local interests on behalf of the crown, it was vital that, wherever possible, he should play a conciliatory rather than a divisive role, if the credibility of Henry's kingship as a universally representative public authority were to be preserved. Instead, in June 1445 the earl granted Ralph Basset an annuity of 10 marks.[72] Had the region been at peace, the range of Basset's local connections and the situation of his estates would have made him a welcome addition to Buckingham's following. As it was, with the grant of a single annuity the earl had taken sides in both disputes. If Buckingham's authority were now to be demonstrated in this context, it would have to be through confrontation rather than conciliation.

[70] H. S. Grazebrook, 'The Barons of Dudley', *Collections for a History of Staffordshire*, William Salt Archaeological Society, 9 (1888), 70 (quoting a deed of 1444 whereby 'Johannes Dns Dudley constuitur arbiter inter Sampsonum Meverell, Mil', et Radul' Basset, Mil''). For Dudley's career, see *Complete Peerage*, iv. 479; R. A. Griffiths, *The Reign of Henry VI* (London, 1981), 165–6, 281–2; Rowney, 'Staffordshire Political Community', 40.

[71] Rowney, 'Staffordshire Political Community', 15; see below, at n. 95.

[72] SRO D641/1/2/56. Carole Rawcliffe (*The Staffords*, 233) dates this grant to Oct. 1444, quoting NLW Peniarth MS 280, fo. 35 (which is printed in Compton Reeves, 'Humphrey Stafford's Military Indentures, 90). However, the Peniarth MS gives no specific date, unlike the SRO MS. Some indication of the approximate timing is given in the Peniarth MS by the fact that the grants seem to be listed in chronological order, but this too supports the SRO MS, since Basset's annuity appears among others dated to 1445. Ian Rowney follows Rawcliffe's dating of the grant to Basset, and therefore attributes the lifting of the excommunication of the latter's ally John Southworth in Oct. 1444 to Buckingham's intervention. This conclusion is harder to support if Buckingham's grant to Basset is redated to the following year, since there is no other evidence that the earl became involved in the dispute in 1444. Basset does seem to have had some association with Buckingham and his inner circle during the late 1430s (see SRO D1721/1/1 fos. 38, 269v), but this had apparently not been enough for him to be able to call upon the earl's intervention when the conflict began. Indeed, if the lifting of Southworth's excommunication is not attributable to Buckingham's influence, his gesture of support seems to have afforded Basset no practical help at all in his dispute with Meverell: Rowney, 'Staffordshire Political Community', 313; see below, pp. 270–2.

In the event, the earl's support provided little immediate benefit to Basset's cause, except perhaps for facilitating a temporary lull in hostilities.[73] No progress was made on resolving the vexed issue of the tithes or on bringing the disputants' legal and extra-legal manœuvrings to a halt.[74] The fact that Buckingham's intervention was late and largely ineffective minimized the tension between his responsibility for the Duchy and his apparent willingness to allow his authority to become a partisan force in the region, but it can have done little to substantiate his claim to undisputed local rule, a claim which had already been shaken by William Ferrers's self-assertion in 1441. By 1445 it was clear, therefore, that, despite all the advantages Buckingham enjoyed in the exercise of his local authority, his efforts to establish a coherent affinity and to extend his rule across Staffordshire and into Derbyshire were significantly flawed.[75] In part, this may be a reflection of the fact that in 1441 he was appointed captain of Calais, an office which necessitated his periodic absence abroad from 1442 onwards.[76] However, these absences were not frequent, and by 1442 the earl had already had the benefit of several years in which to establish his local rule, so that the limitations of his regional policies cannot be wholly, or even largely, ascribed to this appointment.[77] Rather, it seems that he was failing to establish his lordship as an authority which could adequately claim to represent or to control the north midlands.

Despite the signs of strain evident in Buckingham's 'country', the repercussions of these disputes were limited by the fact that the earl faced little challenge from potential rivals in Staffordshire and western Derbyshire. In 1444 that situation seemed to be changing, with the approaching majority and growing influence of the Beauchamp heir Henry, earl of Warwick. Beauchamp had been brought up in the royal household, where he was becoming a significant presence by the early 1440s.[78] The re-emergence of an adult earl of Warwick, and especially one with substantial influence at court, promised to be the most potent challenge Buckingham had yet faced to his regional authority, since Warwick and Stafford interests overlapped significantly in north

---

[73] Direct confrontation between the two sides seems to have stopped until Jan. 1448, possibly because of the fact that Basset seems to have spent a brief period at Calais in Buckingham's retinue: *DKR*, 48, 'Calendar of French Rolls, Henry VI', 370.

[74] According to Meverell, for example, Basset set dogs on his sheep at Throwley on 10 Oct. 1444. However, neither side in either dispute could secure their opponents' attendance in court to face charges. KB27/754 Coram Rege rot. 44v, and, for example, KB27/738 Coram Rege rot. 73v; KB27/742 Coram Rege roti. 102–102v.

[75] See below, pp. 273–4, for a discussion of local office-holding during these years.

[76] Rawcliffe, *The Staffords*, 20–1 (and for the dating of the appointment to 1441, see J. L. Watts, *Henry VI and the Politics of Kingship* (Cambridge, 1996), 201).

[77] Carole Rawcliffe comments that Buckingham, 'absorbed in political affairs at home, rarely visited Calais': *The Staffords*, 21.

[78] Griffiths, *Henry VI*, 298, 315; Watts, *Henry VI*, 196–7.

Warwickshire and south Staffordshire, and had within recent memory formed a single connection under Beauchamp overlordship.

The threat to Buckingham posed by Henry Beauchamp has been seen as more significant even than this, however. According to Somerville's *History of the Duchy*, on 23 October 1444 Beauchamp was granted in tail male the offices of steward and constable of the honour of Tutbury, master forester of Needwood and Duffield Frith, and steward, constable, and master forester of the High Peak.[79] Such a step—the hereditary grant of major Duchy office—was absolutely unprecedented. Since 1399, the management of the Duchy had required the negotiation of a complex relationship between the public authority of the crown and the king's personal lordship over his private resources. Now, when the king was manifestly unable to take personal control of either his national or his regional responsibilities, the latter had been dealt with on his behalf by using grants of Duchy office to reinforce noble rule in the regions. This process retained an element of public responsibility in that it was the participation of the nobility that made Henry VI's government viable, a role which a share of the king's private resources helped them fulfil. In other words, the systematic redistribution of Duchy office to members of the nobility in 1437 embodied an attempt to create a workable system for the rule of the regions.[80]

The grant to Beauchamp in 1444, however, has seemed to be exactly what the distribution of office in 1437 is usually taken to represent: the acquisition of overweening authority by court insiders.[81] During the preceding four decades the crown had had to tread very carefully in Staffordshire and Derbyshire in the management of the immense territorial power of the honours of Tutbury and the High Peak. Now their stewardships were apparently to be given in perpetuity to one noble family, creating a new and vastly extended Beauchamp power bloc in the midlands. This represented a permanent abdication on the part of the crown of any future control over some of the most influential offices within the king's personal patrimony. The implications of this extraordinary step have been seen as more profound still, because the young courtier Warwick was being promoted largely at the expense of Buckingham, who seven years earlier had received a life grant of the Tutbury offices. The Duchy lands in Staffordshire and Derbyshire were far more crucial to Buckingham's territorial interests than to Warwick's, and it is inconceivable that Buckingham could have been expected lightly to accept the alienation of their stewardship to a 19-year-old rival.[82]

[79] Somerville, *History of the Duchy*, 540.
[80] See above, Ch. 2.4; Watts, *Henry VI*, 172–4.
[81] For this interpretation of the appointments of 1437, see Griffiths, *Henry VI*, 342–3.
[82] Carpenter, *Locality and Polity*, 412–13.

The inevitability of Buckingham's opposition to such a grant, and the consequent disruption of existing political structures in the north midlands, has made it difficult to distinguish any coherent policy behind the promotion of Beauchamp. The most likely explanation has seemed to be, as Christine Carpenter suggests, that 'there was no policy at all behind the grant', and that it was the result simply of the 'indiscriminate generosity' available to all those around the king.[83] While this remains the most plausible analysis, recourse to the Duchy chancery rolls, Somerville's original source, sheds new light on the problem. What Somerville failed to record was that the grant to Warwick contained a qualifying clause. Beauchamp was to take possession of the offices in tail male 'immediately after the death of such person or persons who hold those offices or any one of them at present by our grant or that of any of our ancestors'.[84] Confirmation of the fact that Buckingham was not ousted from office can be found in the same roll: Thomas Blount is described in December 1444, two months after the grant to Beauchamp, as the deputy of Buckingham as steward of Tutbury.[85] In other words, while the proposed alienation in perpetuity of some of the Duchy's most powerful regional offices was an unprecedented step, demonstrating the extraordinary degree of self-aggrandizement available to those who could gain access to the king, the grant can no longer be seen as an example of the willingness of the court to ride roughshod over existing regional power structures and the claims of established territorial magnates.

All the same, even the acquisition of the reversion of his Duchy stewardships can hardly have endeared Warwick to Buckingham,[86] and there is evidence of hostility between the two. In April 1444, for example, Beauchamp secured the title of premier earl; five months later Buckingham, presumably unwilling to see his status superseded by a teenage rival, was elevated to a dukedom. In April 1445 Beauchamp too secured a dukedom, initiating a precedence dispute which could only be settled by the somewhat undignified arrangement that precedence should alternate annually between the two.[87] Nevertheless, the limited

[83] Carpenter, *Locality and Polity*, 412.

[84] 'immediate post decessum talis persone seu talium personarum que illa officia seu eorum aliquod occupant vel occupat in presenti ex concessione nostra seu aliquorum progenitorum nostrorum': DL37/12 nos. 23–4; for the documents in full, see H. R. Castor, 'New Evidence on the Grant of Duchy of Lancaster Office to Henry Beauchamp, Earl of Warwick, in 1444', *Historical Research*, 68 (1995), 225–8.

[85] DL37/12 no. 65.

[86] John Rous records in his celebration of the earls of Warwick, written in the 1480s, that Henry Beauchamp was made 'hygz stward of the duchre of Lanchastre', which suggests that the grant did make some impression on the consciousness of regional political society: J. Rous, *The Rous Roll* (reprint, Gloucester, 1980), paragraph 54. I am indebted to Dr John Watts for this point and reference.

[87] *Complete Peerage*, ii. 388; xii pt. 2, 383.

nature of the grant of Duchy office to Warwick helps to explain why this antipathy was not expressed in regional politics in Staffordshire or Derbyshire, where the years between 1444 and 1446 seem to have been a period of relative stability.[88] Such tranquillity would have been immensely difficult to reconcile with Beauchamp's supposed intrusion into the Tutbury stewardship; instead, it now appears that Buckingham's authority suffered no direct challenge during these years.

In Warwickshire, on the other hand, where Beauchamp was developing a power base with the support of the courtier lords Sudeley, Beauchamp of Powick, and the earl of Wiltshire, as well as of William Ferrers,[89] he undoubtedly represented a threat to Buckingham's stake in the balance of power. The nature and extent of Buckingham's interests in Warwickshire will be considered in detail later, but it is clear that he was far from reconciled to the development of the Beauchamp-led coalition.[90] Nevertheless, he seems to have made little attempt to respond to this direct pressure. Rather, members of his affinity in Warwickshire began to take matters into their own hands, a development which mirrors the duke's almost complete passivity in the face of the growing conflict on the Staffordshire–Derbyshire border between 1442 and 1444.[91] Buckingham had therefore failed either to demonstrate his authority by maintaining order within his own 'country', or to defend his lordship against the challenge of a rival. That challenge ended when Warwick died in June 1446, leaving a baby daughter to succeed him.[92] Since the reversion of the Tutbury offices had been bestowed on Beauchamp and the male heirs of his body, the entail was already broken, and the threat to Buckingham's future security removed.[93] Despite the fact that he once again enjoyed a free hand in the exercise of his influence throughout the region, Buckingham failed

---

[88] Cf. Rowney, 'Staffordshire Political Community', 314.

[89] Carpenter, *Locality and Polity*, 413–14.

[90] See below, pp. 275–6; Carpenter, *Locality and Polity*, 414–16. Warwickshire society suffered considerable disruption from the effects of this challenge to the status quo, and indeed of Beauchamp's inadequate control of the resources suddenly at his disposal. Carpenter demonstrates that all the Warwickshire affinities began to malfunction during the mid-1440s, and argues that 'the root of the whole problem was that Henry Beauchamp had been given responsibilities he was too young and too inexperienced to handle. These brought him into confrontation with the spheres of interest that had been established by others while he was still a minor, required him to ignore new gentry loyalties that had developed in the same period, and were backed up by a royal court that was now beginning to attract considerable resentment. Since Henry had the formidable weight of the court and at least part of his father's old following behind him, it was very difficult for anyone else to acquire the authority to ensure the stability that Henry himself was unable to provide': *Locality and Polity*, 416–20 (quotation from 420).

[91] Ibid. 415; see above, pp. 262–6.

[92] *Complete Peerage*, xii pt. 2, 384.

[93] For the implications of Beauchamp's death in the context of Warwickshire politics, see Carpenter, *Locality and Polity*, 420–3.

to impose his authority on local affairs any more effectively after Beauchamp's death than he had done in the years before 1444. He seems to have made almost no attempt either to expand or to consolidate his affinity; indeed, his somewhat piecemeal retaining of the earlier 1440s stopped altogether towards the end of the decade.[94] He also made no further move to intervene in the disputes in which his new retainer Ralph Basset was engaged, despite the fact that during these years they resulted in worsening disorder involving increasing numbers of local gentlemen on both sides.

Hostilities were resumed in January 1448, when Sampson Meverell ambushed the priest John Southworth and, allegedly threatening to kill him, forced him to release the disputed tithes to Meverell himself.[95] Meverell was immediately indicted for the attack, but the total absence of support available to his opponent Basset, who had been Buckingham's retainer for two and a half years, was demonstrated by the fact that the legal deadlock between the two sides, which had persisted since the first allegations were made in 1442, was now swiftly broken in Meverell's favour. The sheriff of Derbyshire in 1447–8 was Basset's other opponent Nicholas Fitzherbert—an appointment which itself was an indication either of the confusion in Buckingham's policy or of his lack of control in the shire—and the jury empanelled by Fitzherbert to hear the case against Meverell acquitted him.[96] Moreover, this apparent alliance between Meverell and Fitzherbert,[97] and the consequent conflation of the two disputes, seems to have been one manifestation of a more general widening of the conflict to involve other leading gentry figures.

It is difficult to ascertain where the sympathies of the gentry of western Derbyshire and eastern Staffordshire lay in relation to the continuing hostilities during the earlier 1440s. This is perhaps not surprising given that Basset and Okeover had previously been associated with Meverell and Fitzherbert within the same local network, which had developed from the Duchy connection during the previous three decades. Other members of this network therefore had close links with both sides.[98] Had effective leadership been available to

---

[94] Rawcliffe, *The Staffords*, 232–40.

[95] KB9/257 m. 10.

[96] *List of Sheriffs*, 103; Wrottesley (ed.), 'Extracts from the Plea Rolls of the Reign of Henry VI', 182; KB27/747 Rex rot. 23v; see above, p. 264.

[97] Fitzherbert was acting as a feoffee for Meverell by 1450: BL Add. Ch. 27510–11.

[98] Thomas Okeover's widowed daughter-in-law, for example, the mother of his grandson and heir Philip, was the sister of John Curson, who had joined Meverell as a witness for Okeover in 1439: Rowney, 'Staffordshire Political Community', 469; I. Rowney, 'The Cursons of Fifteenth-Century Derbyshire', *Derbyshire Archaeological Journal*, 103 (1983), 109; DRO D231M/T23. Sir John Cokayn, father of the Cokayn active in the 1440s, had with his neighbour and close associate Thomas Okeover been among the feoffees of Nicholas Fitzherbert's estates during his minority: DRO D231M/E451; cf. D231M/T308. A yet closer

negotiate and enforce a settlement earlier in the dispute—leadership which Buckingham's Duchy office should have enabled him to provide—such common interests surrounding the combatants should have helped to restore order and uphold any agreement.

In the absence of such leadership, however, it was becoming clear by 1448 that Meverell was winning substantial support from members of this network, including men who, like his enemy Basset, were retained by Buckingham. In July 1446, the witnesses of a transaction involving Henry Bradbourne's heir included not only Fulk Vernon and his brother-in-law John Cokayn, but also Sampson Meverell and Nicholas Fitzherbert.[99] In 1447, Meverell also acted as a witness for Richard Vernon, in the company of Cokayn, Bradbourne, Thomas Blount, and Nicholas Montgomery.[100] In the same year Montgomery expressed his confidence in the Meverells more emphatically still by marrying his daughter Elizabeth to Meverell's son and heir Thomas.[101] In 1448 this growing support was for the first time manifested in forceful intervention. Two weeks before Meverell's attack on Southworth, John Cokayn broke into the park at Okeover;[102] five months later, Nicholas Montgomery joined Meverell in a raid on Basset's property at Blore.[103] The association of Richard Vernon with Meverell's supporters was particularly significant because of the authority his Duchy stewardship gave him in the Peak, the region where the conflict was focused.

Indeed, the fact that Vernon was Buckingham's most eminent local retainer, and that Basset suffered significant reverses during this period, might seem to suggest that Buckingham had abandoned the latter's cause and thrown the weight of his affinity behind Meverell. However,

---

association between Cokayn and Okeover is suggested by Cokayn's description of the latter as his 'nepos' in 1414: DRO D231M/T22.

[99] Jeayes (ed.), *Derbyshire Charters*, 337 [2678]. Thomas Blount was also among the witnesses. For John Cokayn's marriage to Agnes Vernon, see A. E. Cokayne, *Cokayne Memoranda* (Congleton, 1873), 198.

[100] Jeayes (ed.), *Derbyshire Charters*, 304 [2394].

[101] L. Morsbach (ed.), *Mittelenglische Originalurkunden von der Chaucer-zeit bis zur Mitte des XV Jahrhunderts* (Heidelberg, 1923), 40–4; cf. BL Add. Ch. 27512.

[102] KB27/750 Coram Rege rot. 61v. Cokayn may have had his own quarrel with Okeover (R. L. Storey, *The End of the House of Lancaster* (London, 1966), 157; G. Wrottesley, 'An Account of the Family of Okeover of Okeover', *Collections for a History of Staffordshire*, William Salt Archaeological Society, new series, 7 (1904), 54), but in view of the timing of the attack and the evidence of association between Cokayn, Vernon, and Meverell, it seems fair to describe the events as part of the same conflict.

[103] CP40/751 rot. 61v; CP40/754 rot. 321; Wrottesley (ed.), 'Extracts from the Plea Rolls of the Reign of Henry VI', 182, 185. It also seems that the favours were being repaid; Meverell was one of a group of jurors accused of accepting bribes from Vernon in an assize of novel disseisin he was contesting in June 1448: Wrottesley (ed.), 'Extracts from the Plea Rolls of the Reign of Henry VI', 191–2. For details of this dispute between Vernon and Sir William Trussell over the Pembrigge inheritance, see Rowney, 'Staffordshire Political Community', 354–8. The jury of which Meverell was a member reversed an earlier decision in favour of Trussell, and awarded Vernon the huge sum of £2,080 in damages: ibid. 356.

there are several difficulties with such an analysis. First, Buckingham's history of inactivity in relation to the dispute, which persisted even after the apparently positive and partisan step of retaining Basset, makes such an enthusiastic espousal of Meverell's cause in 1448 hard to explain, particularly in the absence of any readily understandable motive for such a policy. Secondly, it is far from clear that Buckingham had the degree of influence over men such as Vernon and Cokayn necessary to direct events in the region. When a resolution was sought in 1447, for example, to a dispute over rights of pasture which had developed between John Gresley and Vernon's son William, the matter was 'sette in peese' not by Buckingham but by William Ferrers.[104] The fact that Vernon, the steward of the Peak, should turn for judgment not to Buckingham, who as steward of Tutbury was Vernon's immediate superior in the Duchy hierarchy, but to the duke's Staffordshire rival, is a clear demonstration of Buckingham's failure to exploit his Duchy office in support of his authority in eastern Staffordshire and western Derbyshire. Not only is it apparent that his lordship was not the first recourse of local gentlemen who found themselves in dispute, but, as it became increasingly clear that the causes of conflicts were being ignored or addressed only inadequately, the impression of growing confusion in regional politics is hard to escape. Ferrers's arbitration of 1447 between Gresley and Vernon produced only a temporary settlement, and by 1449 Ferrers himself was at odds with Richard Vernon and was forced to seek an arbitration with his erstwhile retainer.[105]

The extent of this political confusion has proved hard to explain in terms of previous analyses of Buckingham's regional influence. The territorial pre-eminence which the duke enjoyed through the combination of his Staffordshire estates and his office at Tutbury, coupled with the lack of serious rivals for local control once the threat posed by Beauchamp had been removed, has led historians to conclude that Buckingham's authority was the dominant force in the north midlands during this period.[106] When examining the details of Buckingham's rule, however, it proves difficult either to find examples of the duke's lordship successfully influencing local affairs, or to explain the increasing confusion in regional politics during the later 1440s. Buckingham's failure

[104] *HMC Rutland*, iv. 29.

[105] See above, Ch. 7.2 at n. 65; Carpenter, *Locality and Polity*, 426 n.

[106] Ian Rowney suggests, for example, that during the 1440s and 1450s, 'Staffordshire really was Stafford's shire', while Susan Wright argues that during that time the duke 'steadily moved into a pre-eminent position in the midlands'. Both they and Carole Rawcliffe discuss Buckingham's affinity in terms which suggest that it functioned as a coherent and powerful force in the region: I. Rowney, 'Government and Patronage in the Fifteenth Century: Staffordshire 1439–59', *Midland History*, 8 (1983), 66; 'Staffordshire Political Community', 49–50, 58–71; Wright, *The Derbyshire Gentry*, 68–72 (quotation from 69); Rawcliffe, *The Staffords*, 72–85.

to offer his retainer Ralph Basset any support in the face of renewed attack in 1448 has therefore been attributed to the duke's insecurity about his own influence over Richard Vernon and a consequent unwillingness to oppose him; the worsening violence during these years has been explained largely in terms of the increasing involvement of 'angry young men' such as the 'major thug' John Cokayn.[107]

However, to describe the events of the later 1440s in terms of the internal dynamics of Buckingham's affinity and the criminal tendencies of individuals does not explain or even acknowledge the scale of the problem. While it is true, for example, that Cokayn's prolonged exclusion from his inheritance eventually led him into a sustained career of violence, at this point he could still plausibly be seen simply as a young man with as yet unrealized prospects, who was acting in concert with several influential local landowners.[108] The tendency to minimize the wider political significance of the increasing disorder during the last years of the decade has largely been the result of a consistent overestimation of the degree of regional influence wielded by Buckingham. In Derbyshire, he had failed to take advantage of his Duchy office to draw the gentry networks in the west of the shire into his service.[109] In Staffordshire, although the close-knit group of lesser gentlemen who formed the core of his affinity dominated local government, he had made surprisingly little headway in extending his following. The increasing conflict seems to have developed because existing gentry networks proved unable to contain disagreements among their number, and were given no direction by Buckingham's nominal leadership. In other words, the delegation of Duchy authority to the duke, as a means by which his territorial dominance in western Staffordshire could be extended to control the east of the shire and western Derbyshire, seems to have created a power vacuum in the region because of the deficiencies of Buckingham's lordship.

This conclusion is supported by the evidence of local office-holding. The joint shrievalty of Derbyshire and Nottinghamshire had during the early years of the century been shared between Duchy men from both counties. During the 1440s, it was dominated by gentry from Nottinghamshire and eastern Derbyshire, a reflection of Cromwell's increasing influence in the east midlands. On the three occasions when

---

[107] Rowney, 'Staffordshire Political Community', 307, 316–18.

[108] For Cokayn's dispute with his mother and stepfather over the Cokayn estates, see below, at nn. 122–3, and for his later career, Carpenter, *Locality and Polity*, 115–16. Cokayn can only have been in his mid-twenties during the later 1440s, and there would have been no reason necessarily to assume that, as in fact happened, he would not come into his lands for another decade: *Locality and Polity*, 110, 111 n.

[109] Cf. Suffolk's success in a similar situation in establishing his authority over the powerful Duchy affinity in East Anglia: see above, Ch. 4.1.

the office did go to men from western Derbyshire, none were retainers of Buckingham, and in 1447 the nominee was the controversial figure of Nicholas Fitzherbert.[110] On the Derbyshire bench, the duke's influence seemed impressive at the beginning of the decade, since his retainers Vernon, Curson, and Pole were all regular appointees. While Buckingham's representation remained static, however, the most striking development during the later 1440s was the increasing influence both of Cromwell, who was joined on the commission by the Nottinghamshire knight Thomas Chaworth, and of the families of Blount and Gresley, neither of whom had developed close links with Buckingham.[111] In Staffordshire, remarkably, not one of the sheriffs during the 1440s was retained by the duke.[112] Though the Staffordshire commission of the peace was more impressively Stafford dominated, the duke's longstanding servants Arblaster, Harper, Whitgreve, Hampton, and Comberford all being regular members, the only representative of the leading gentry families of the shire on the bench was Sir Roger Aston.[113] The Astons had long been associated with both the Duchy and the Stafford earls, but, when Sir Roger died, his place was taken in 1449 by Sampson Meverell, whose appointment could well be taken as an indication of the influence of his ally Richard Vernon, but can only more problematically be associated with Buckingham.[114]

In other words, explanation of 'what appear at first sight to be contradictions' within political networks during these years need not depend only on 'the rather obvious point that the gentry were individuals'.[115] While this is undoubtedly true, it is also clear that gentry as individually resourceful and independent minded as those of Norfolk were eager to take advantage of the benefits of effective lordship where and when it was available to them.[116] The confused evidence of local associations in the north midlands during the later 1440s is a reflection not simply of a general unwillingness on the part of the gentry to commit themselves too firmly to any one network, but rather of the fact that reliable lordship was not available in the region. Such apparent political 'contradictions' in fact indicate growing incoherence within

[110] *List of Sheriffs*, 103; Payling, *Political Society*, 244–5; see above, pp. 264, 270. The other Derbyshire sheriffs were John de la Pole of Hartington in 1442 and Thomas Blount in 1446.

[111] Chaworth was first appointed in 1444; Thomas Blount, who had been a member of the commission since 1439, was joined by his son Walter and John Gresley in 1449: *CPR 1441–6*, 469; *1446–52*, 588; for Chaworth's connections with Cromwell, see above, Ch. 7.2 at n. 117; for the Blounts and Gresleys, see above, at n. 45.

[112] *List of Sheriffs*, 127; Rawcliffe, *The Staffords*, 232–40.

[113] *CPR 1441–6*, 478; *1446–52*, 595; see above, pp. 235–6, 257–8. The rest of the commission was made up of the lords Audley, Dudley, and Ferrers, with the addition of Suffolk and the bishop of Coventry and Lichfield in 1449, and lawyers including William Yelverton and Richard Bingham.   [114] *CPR 1446–52*, 595; see above, pp. 271–2.

[115] Wright, *The Derbyshire Gentry*, 71.

[116] See above, Part II, *passim*.

local power structures. By the later 1440s, the political confusion within formerly close-knit gentry networks and within the duke's retinue itself, exacerbated by Buckingham's failure to act in response to the increasing conflict within his 'country', means that his authority cannot be assumed to have been the dominant factor governing regional affairs, nor can men such as Vernon be taken to have acted within the context of a functioning 'Stafford affinity'. While the developing 'horizontal' affiliations of Vernon, Cokayn, Basset, and others can be traced throughout the period, it is far from clear where Buckingham stood in relation to any of them.[117]

The degree of confusion in local politics by the end of the decade is such that it is not even readily apparent what the duke was trying to achieve in the region. His failure to secure the rule of Staffordshire and western Derbyshire, despite all the resources at his disposal, suggests that it was perhaps the result not only of political mismanagement, but also of lack of interest. While this would represent an abandonment of the responsibilities inherent in his stewardship of the Tutbury lands—a serious dereliction of duty in the context of Henry VI's inadequacies— and while Staffordshire was the traditional heart of his patrimony, Buckingham did have a vast range of other estates. In Warwickshire, the duke had at the beginning of the 1440s been the obvious contender to succeed Richard Beauchamp, certainly in the north of the shire, where his substantial properties formed a natural link to his Staffordshire interests, but potentially also across the county as a whole.[118] If, for example, Buckingham saw Warwickshire as the focus of his midland concerns, and Staffordshire and Derbyshire as areas of secondary, peripheral interest, this would help to explain his failure to make his authority effective in the latter shires.

There are some indications that the duke was more interested, or at least more active, in Warwickshire affairs at the beginning of the decade than he was in those of the north midlands. While his son often visited Stafford Castle during the 1440s, Buckingham himself more frequently used his residence at Maxstoke in north Warwickshire.[119] Certainly, the duke was participating in land disputes in Warwickshire in the early 1440s, even initiating an arbitration in 1442–3, in sharp contrast to his inactivity in relation to the Basset–Meverell and Okeover–Fitzherbert

---

[117] Carole Rawcliffe revealingly suggests, in explaining that the number of fees paid from Buckingham's Staffordshire estates fell during the 1450s, that 'perhaps experience had by then taught Duke Humphrey that the indiscriminate granting out of annuities was simply not worthwhile' (*The Staffords*, 77). This had been precisely Buckingham's problem: indiscriminate retaining had failed to create a coherent and effective political connection, where a considered and discriminating policy might have succeeded.

[118] Carpenter, *Locality and Polity*, 393, 400–1.

[119] Rawcliffe, *The Staffords*, 66–7.

conflicts.[120] However, this activity in the end achieved little. Despite the progress which Buckingham made in developing a coherent connection in Warwickshire during the late 1430s and early 1440s, signs of strain were becoming apparent, as in Staffordshire and Derbyshire, from about 1443.

Tension developed in north Warwickshire between John Cokayn, who had been in the earl's service since the late 1430s, and Thomas Bate, a Warwickshire lawyer also associated with Buckingham.[121] Cokayn, whose father had died in 1438, had been deprived of most of the family estates by the combination of the large jointure settled on his mother and her remarriage to Bate—a greatly advantageous match for the latter and one possibly secured through Buckingham's good lordship.[122] In 1443 the dispute erupted into violence when Cokayn attacked Bate's home at Polesworth in north Warwickshire.[123] There seems to have been some attempt to establish a settlement between Cokayn and Bate in 1446, but, as Christine Carpenter comments, it was a conflict which 'should never have occurred at all, seeing that they had a common lord'.[124] When Henry Beauchamp began to assert himself in the shire from 1444, Buckingham's ability to control his own retainers seems to have been less than reliable.[125] By the end of the 1440s it was clear that, far from rebuilding Richard Beauchamp's hegemony in Warwickshire, Buckingham had 'failed to make the best of what he had, failed even to build an effective power base in the areas of the county that should have been his', through lack of effort in the south of the shire, and through a combination of misjudgement and mismanagement in the north and east.[126]

Christine Carpenter explains this failure in Warwickshire by suggesting that the duke's primary concerns lay in maintaining his authority in Staffordshire and Derbyshire,[127] but it has become clear that Buckingham was if anything more active as a regional lord in Warwickshire than he was further north. The overriding characteristic of his involvement in all three midland shires was a blend of deficient political skills and apparent uninterest. Indeed, it is far from clear to what extent

---

[120] Carpenter, *Locality and Polity*, 404–5, 429.

[121] See above, at n. 31; Carpenter, *Locality and Polity*, 405, 699.

[122] Carpenter, *Locality and Polity*, 102–3, 110; Rowney, 'Staffordshire Political Community', 316.

[123] KB9/250 m. 45; KB9/258 m. 4; Carpenter, *Locality and Polity*, 411, 431; Rowney, 'Staffordshire Political Community', 316.

[124] Carpenter, *Locality and Polity*, 431; Jeayes (ed.), *Derbyshire Charters*, 28 [218].

[125] Carpenter, *Locality and Polity*, 414–19; see above, at n. 91.

[126] Carpenter, *Locality and Polity*, 434. Buckingham's failure to secure any substantial representation of his own interests among office-holders in Warwickshire during the 1440s mirrors the situation in Staffordshire and Derbyshire (for which, see above, pp. 273–4): ibid. 410.

[127] Ibid. 401, 406, 422.

Buckingham was trying to participate in local rule at all by the mid-1440s. Much of the duke's time seems to have been spent not in the midlands but in the south-east, at his Essex manor of Writtle and at Tonbridge Castle in Kent.[128] Both allowed easy access to London and the court, where Buckingham seems to have been very active, witnessing over 75 per cent of royal charters issued in the years 1446 to 1449, for example.[129] The duke's frequent presence at court provides a compelling reason why Henry Beauchamp had not been able to supersede Buckingham's tenure of the Duchy stewardships at Tutbury, despite the unprecedented generosity of the reversionary grant he did secure.[130] Buckingham's connections with the royal household can only have been further increased by the fact that Tutbury and the High Peak were among the lands granted in 1446 to the queen as part of her dower.[131] However, prolonged attendance at court necessarily precluded detailed attention to the affairs of a region as far from the capital as the north midlands, and without detailed attention even the most powerful local lord might find it difficult to regulate regional government.[132] Buckingham's decision to concentrate his activity at court during the latter half of the decade, without having first consolidated his following in a region which by contemporary standards was relatively remote, meant that he effectively abandoned any chance he still had of establishing his rule

[128] Rawcliffe, *The Staffords*, 66–7. J. M. Thurgood concludes from the evidence of Buckingham's household accounts for the year 1452–3 that his two main residences at that point were Maxstoke and Writtle. The duke showed so little interest in the Stafford castles on the Welsh border, for example, that they were 'allowed to collapse into "colde, ruynous and decaid" heaps of rubble'. Some evidence of the duke's whereabouts is provided by NLW Peniarth MS 280, since some of the grants listed are recorded with a note of the place at which they were given. Though the sample cannot be said to be reliably representative, it is noticeable that three of the four grants dated at Maxstoke were given in 1442–3, when the duke seems to have been making some attempt to establish himself in north Warwickshire politics. All but two of the dated grants made between 1445 and 1450, on the other hand, were given at London or Writtle. J. M. Thurgood, introduction to M. Harris (ed.), 'The Account of the Great Household of Humphrey, First Duke of Buckingham, for the year 1452–3', Camden Miscellany, 28, 4th series, 29 (London, 1984), 5; Rawcliffe, *The Staffords*, 67; NLW Peniarth MS 280, fos. 21, 24, 30, 37, 39–43, 45.

[129] Watts, *Henry VI*, 257.

[130] The suggestion that Buckingham was closely involved in Suffolk's regime also supports Watts's argument that Henry Beauchamp's rapid rise to prominence was potentially as disruptive at court as it was in the midlands; he argues that the young earl 'became the focus for a developing network of court figures, headed by Lords Sudeley and Beauchamp of Powick', who 'threatened to create an alternative source of lordship in the household' and 'to disrupt the Beaufort-focused equilibrium among the nobility': *Henry VI*, 196–7.

[131] Somerville, *History of the Duchy*, 208, 340; *Rot. Parl.*, v. 118–20.

[132] The national and international concerns of John of Gaunt, for example, together with the sheer scale of his estates, seem to have meant that his ability to exercise consistent influence on local affairs was limited. Even the formidable regional control of Richard Beauchamp seems to have wavered during the mid-1420s, when he was away in France for lengthy periods: Carpenter, *Locality and Polity*, 378–88, 619–20; S. Walker, *The Lancastrian Affinity* (Oxford, 1990), chs. 4 and 5.

in the north midlands.[133] Indeed, it may be that the devolution of regional rule to members of the nobility as a strategy to deal with the effects of the king's incapacity was not in fact viable in the long term. The abnormalities of Henry's kingship meant that local power could only be secured if the magnate in question was active and influential at court.[134] The catch-22 was that, except in regions close to the capital, consistent attendance at court meant that local authority could not adequately be sustained.[135] Even had Buckingham shown more aptitude for the task of regional rule, it is possible that he would have encountered many of the same problems because of these conflicting demands on his attention.

It seems therefore that, although Buckingham made some attempt in the late 1430s and early 1440s to establish his authority throughout a power bloc extending from western Derbyshire through Staffordshire into north and east Warwickshire, the deficiencies of his political management, both within his own retinue and across the region as a whole, and his preoccupation with affairs at court meant that he comprehensively failed to achieve the rule of this 'country'. The conclusion must be that his lordship did not act as a political focus or agent of control in Staffordshire and western Derbyshire, while at the same time he dominated the political resources of the area through his own estates and his Duchy office to such an extent that no one else was able to offer effective leadership in his stead. Given that the Meverell–Basset dispute took place in the region where Richard Vernon held the local Duchy stewardship, and within the network of former Ferrers and Duchy connections of which he was a part, Vernon could perhaps have

---

[133] In 1449, for example, when county commissions composed of one lord and the two knights of the shire were appointed to distribute money respited from the last subsidy, Buckingham was not appointed in either Staffordshire or Derbyshire; the nomination instead went in Staffordshire to Dudley and in Derbyshire to Cromwell. It may also be a reflection of Buckingham's lack of interest in maintaining an active stake in local government that in 1448 John Hampton, the only one of the duke's retainers even to be nominated to the Staffordshire shrievalty during the decade, secured an exemption from taking office, forcing the incumbent, Thomas Ferrers of Tamworth, who was no friend of Buckingham's, to stay on for a second year. In this context, it may be significant that the duke was apparently quite happy to allow a prime role in the rule of north Warwickshire—ostensibly part of his 'country'—to be taken during the later 1440s by William Mountford, with backing from the court. *CFR 1445–52*, 121; Rowney, 'Staffordshire Political Community', 47; Carpenter, *Locality and Polity*, 422, 426–7; see above, n. 45.

[134] See above, pp. 250–1, for the destruction of Henry Grey's regional lordship by Cromwell, whose influence at court was a significant factor in the creation of his local sphere of influence.

[135] The duke of Suffolk, for example, managed to maintain control of East Anglian affairs for most of the 1440s, despite his inevitable preoccupation with national government, through his extensive and powerful affinity, but his task was made very much easier by the fact that his 'country' lay within relatively easy reach of London and the royal palaces in the Thames Valley, an area which was itself Suffolk's other main territorial base apart from East Anglia: see above, Chs. 4.2 and 4.3.

chosen to play a role as peacemaker despite Buckingham's unwillingness to act. However, his maverick political instincts led him instead to
join the fray, leaving local landowners with no effective recourse for the
representation of their interests and the resolution of disputes. Though
appeals were made to Dudley and to Ferrers as arbiters during the
1440s, both, with limited local resources, failed to achieve workable
settlements. Only Buckingham, representing his own private lordship
and the regional authority of the king, had the potential power to
enforce peace, and he was apparently unable or unwilling—perhaps
both—to do so. This situation provides an interesting contrast with that
in East Anglia, where the crown's resources had been vested in the duke
of Suffolk. Suffolk's control of the region proved to be highly effective
for much of the 1440s—indeed, it was so overwhelming that problems
eventually developed because those who could not be accommodated
within the de la Pole-dominated hierarchy were effectively excluded
from local political society.[136] In Staffordshire and western Derbyshire,
Buckingham's control of the region *should* have been overwhelming;
problems developed because his authority was ineffective, and there
was no one else to turn to. In this context, the failure of Buckingham's
lordship was the failure of all lordship.

From the autumn of 1448 onwards the increasing crisis of noble and
popular confidence in Suffolk's regime precipitated by the surrender of
Maine placed local hierarchies everywhere under increasing strain. In
East Anglia, Suffolk's attempt to tighten his grip on the region as his
government came under increasing pressure resulted in the first
significant signs of strain appearing in his local rule.[137] In the north
midlands, the failure of existing power structures to contain the
tensions in regional society had already become apparent earlier in the
decade, but, with the added insecurity of national crisis, the Meverell–
Basset dispute entered a yet more violent and more widely disruptive
phase. On 30 October 1449 John Cokayn, accompanied by his brother
William, Sampson Meverell's son Thomas, Richard Vernon's son
Thurstan, and a group of armed men, besieged Basset's home at Blore
and burned his crops. Cokayn and his supporters allegedly would have
burned the house as well, had not John Curson, Henry Bradbourne,
and Richard Bagot, 'heryng of his grete riot and route come thider to
thentent for to se pees kept' and persuaded them to leave.[138] The next
day, however, they returned and assaulted Basset and his servants. The
fact that Curson and Bradbourne were retainers of Buckingham might

---

[136] See above, Ch. 4.

[137] See above, Ch. 4.4.

[138] All details, unless otherwise noted, are taken from KB27/758 Coram Rege rot. 22
(calendared in Wrottesley (ed.), 'Extracts from the Plea Rolls of the Reign of Henry VI',
192–4); cf. SC8/96/4795–6.

suggest that the duke had at last decided to intervene in support of Basset, were it not for the fact that seven months later, having made no headway in obtaining redress, Basset took his complaint to parliament and, despite persistent efforts, was subsequently unable to secure his attackers' presence in court.[139] On 5 November William Cokayn led another assault, this time on the manor and park at Okeover. The attackers broke doors and windows 'with fourmes trestill and tabull dormant and brende them there' and, to add insult to injury, 'by the seid fyre rostyd parcell of the seid dere takyn in the seid park'. Cokayn returned a month later to hunt there again with Thurstan Vernon, and allegedly 'lafte in the seid park but v dere alyve'.[140] Again, it is difficult to accord Buckingham's lordship any active role in these developments.[141] Philip Okeover, too, chose not to appeal to the duke but to petition parliament in the following year.[142]

The degree to which Buckingham chose to focus his attention on developments at court rather than on the increasingly turbulent politics of the north midlands during the critical years at the end of the 1440s is striking, and confirms the impression that court affairs were his chief concern for much of the decade. John Watts has argued that the territorial nobility withdrew from participation in government during 1448 and much of 1449, as Suffolk's beleaguered regime faced worsening military and financial crises.[143] Only three members of the higher nobility are recorded as attending council meetings in the autumn of 1448 and the spring of 1449; unsurprisingly, Suffolk was a constant presence with, in 1448, York and, in 1449, Salisbury. Perhaps more surprising is the fact that, in both periods, it was Buckingham who made up the trio.[144] Even after two gentlemen from his midlands

[139] See above, at n. 31; KB27/758 Coram Rege rot. 22. Curson and Bradbourne were both married to sisters of Bagot, who was retained by Buckingham in 1455: SRO D641/1/2/60; Rowney, 'Staffordshire Political Community', 320, 450.

[140] All details, unless otherwise noted, are taken from KB27/758 Coram Rege roti. 79–79v (calendared in Wrottesley (ed.), 'Extracts from the Plea Rolls of the Reign of Henry VI', 196–7); cf. SC8/132/6597.

[141] At the time of the first attack Philip Okeover was away from home attending parliament in the service of Edward Grey of Groby, who had been associated with Buckingham in Warwickshire in the early years of the decade, although this association seems to have waned in the later 1440s. Thomas Okeover had by this stage gone to live on his second wife's estates in Nottinghamshire, leaving his Staffordshire properties in the hands of Philip, his grandson and heir: Carpenter, *Locality and Polity*, 401–5, 412, 422–3; Rowney, 'Staffordshire Political Community', 319; Wrottesley, 'Account of the Family of Okeover', 49–51.

[142] KB27/758 Coram Rege roti. 79–79v.

[143] Watts, *Henry VI*, 240–5.

[144] J. L. Watts, 'Domestic Politics and the Constitution in the Reign of Henry VI, c.1435–61', unpublished Ph.D. thesis (Cambridge, 1990), 266 n. 9; cf. his *Henry VI*, 243 n. 168. The fact that by 1447 Buckingham had appointed John Heydon as his steward in Norfolk (NLW Peniarth MS 280, fo. 42; Rawcliffe, *The Staffords*, 204) may also suggest a closer relationship with Suffolk than has previously been accepted. In 1450 Buckingham was clearly not widely perceived to be closely associated with Suffolk (J. Gairdner (ed.), *Three Fifteenth-Century*

'country', one of them his own retainer, had in the tense months after Suffolk's fall in 1450 presented petitions to parliament complaining of violent attacks perpetrated upon them by neighbours, the duke showed no more inclination to address himself to the problems of the region.[145] Instead, he presided over sessions held in Kent in August 1450 in the aftermath of Cade's rebellion.[146]

In this context, it is no surprise that Basset and Okeover should have joined the chorus of complaint in parliament after Suffolk's fall,[147] since it was clear that there was no local authority to which they could appeal for redress of their grievances. However, the sacrifice of Suffolk to popular anger over the failings of the regime of the 1440s did nothing to alter political structures in the north midlands. Buckingham had been a prominent member of the noble consensus which sustained Suffolk's government; he was a prominent member of the noble consensus which allowed the duke of Somerset to take up the reins of power in 1450.[148] He still controlled the Duchy offices at Tutbury, and one of the few remaining challenges to his territorial dominance in Staffordshire and western Derbyshire was removed by the death of William Ferrers in June 1450, leaving a young daughter as his heir.[149] With Buckingham's nominal authority acting as a dead weight at the top of regional hierarchies, no progress could be made in resolving disputes which had been allowed to fester for the best part of a decade, and which were becoming increasingly disruptive.[150]

Chronicles, Camden Society, new series, 28 (1880), 97), but this may have been part of a broader misconception of the nature of Suffolk's government; John Watts has pointed out that the participation of the nobility in Suffolk's household-based regime was not apparent to the Commons: *Henry VI*, 248–51.

[145] See above, nn. 139, 142, for the petitions of Basset and Okeover.

[146] Buckingham sat at the Kent sessions in the company of Chancellor Kemp and the archbishop of Canterbury: Storey, *End of the House of Lancaster*, 66–7; R. Virgoe (ed.), 'Some Ancient Indictments in the King's Bench referring to Kent 1450–2', in F. R. H. Du Boulay (ed.), *Documents Illustrative of Medieval Kentish Society*, Kent Archaeological Society, 18 (1964), 215, 221–2, 226; *PL* Davis, ii. 41 (Gairdner, ii. 161–2). Buckingham's political involvement in the south-east was increased in 1450 by his appointment as constable of Dover and warden of the Cinque Ports: *CPR 1446–52*, 336.

[147] John Paston was being advised at this point that it was a 'good tyme' to 'put up your bylles' to parliament, 'for now every man that hath any, they put theme now inne, and so may ye': *PL* Davis, ii. 37 (Gairdner, ii. 148).

[148] Watts, *Henry VI*, 172–80, 221–40, 282–90; above, pp. 160–1.

[149] *Complete Peerage*, v. 320. Custody of the Ferrers estates went to Lord Sudeley for the three years before the heiress Anne Ferrers was granted livery, although the Warwickshire lands were in fact in the hands of Ferrers's widow. Anne Ferrers was married to Sir Walter Devereux, but his territorial interests were focused in Herefordshire, and he showed little inclination to make political capital out of his wife's estates in Staffordshire. *CFR 1445–52*, 159; *CCR 1447–54*, 384–6; Carpenter, *Locality and Polity*, 451; Rowney, 'Staffordshire Political Community', 19–20.

[150] Buckingham's failure to concern himself actively with the affairs of the region during these years is epitomized by the fact that he seems not to have appointed a successor to Hugh

The deadlock is apparent in the judicial records of Michaelmas 1450. The petitions of Basset and Okeover were presented to King's Bench as indictments,[151] but in neither case could the accused be produced in court, and Meverell responded by accusing Basset of falsely conspiring to secure his indictment on the charges brought by John Southworth in January 1448.[152] The court also heard the backlog of indictments which had gone unanswered since 1442.[153] During the following months the failure of Basset's and Okeover's appeals to parliament became apparent as the superior local resources of Meverell and his supporters reasserted themselves.[154] Fines were imposed on John and William Cokayn for their trespass against Basset, for example, which came to the less than princely sum of 140 shillings.[155]

By September 1451, however, the regional balance of power had once again been altered, this time by the death of Richard Vernon. He was succeeded by his eldest surviving son William,[156] but it was clear that the latter could not hope immediately to inherit the huge degree of personal influence that his father had built up in the area during the previous three decades. He was not immediately appointed to the commission of the peace in his father's place, for example, nor did he inherit the stewardship of the High Peak, which had been so important in consolidating Vernon's power in northern Derbyshire.[157] The loss of one of Buckingham's most eminent local retainers (albeit one with whom the nature of his relationship is often hard to fathom) seems to have prompted the duke to focus some degree of renewed attention on the region.[158] During the latter half of the 1440s he had virtually

---

Erdeswick as steward of his lands in Staffordshire after the latter's death in 1451: Rawcliffe, *The Staffords*, 216; *CFR 1445–52*, 231.

[151] Local juries assessed their damages at 390 and 395 marks respectively: KB27/758 Coram Rege roti. 22, 79–80.

[152] KB27/758 Coram Rege rot. 40. Meverell carefully did not disclaim responsibility for any assault on Southworth, merely disputing the allegation that he had stolen 8 marks from him (and claiming £400 in damages).

[153] KB27/758 Coram Rege roti. 25, 46.

[154] When commissions were issued in Aug. 1450, for example, to make new tax assessments, the Staffordshire commissioners included both Richard Vernon and Sampson Meverell, as well as less controversial nominees such as Buckingham, Harper, and Comberford. Vernon was also appointed in Derbyshire, where Talbot and Cromwell headed the commission rather than Buckingham: *CFR 1445–52*, 171.

[155] Wrottesley (ed.), 'Extracts from the Plea Rolls of the Reign of Henry VI', 202.

[156] Vernon's sons Richard and Fulk had already died: *CFR 1445–52*, 231; J. S. Roskell, 'Sir Richard Vernon of Haddon', *Derbyshire Archaeological Journal*, 82 (1962), 52; Wedgwood, *Staffordshire Parliamentary History*, 192.

[157] *CPR 1452–61*, 663–4; DL37/21 nos. 30–1 (grant of office at the High Peak to Walter Blount. For discussion of Blount's role in local affairs during these years, see below, pp. 284–5).

[158] Apparently not enough, however, to appoint a steward of his estates there: see above, n. 150.

stopped retaining in Staffordshire and Derbyshire, but in the years after Vernon's death he began once again to grant new fees. There is little sign, however, that the duke was adopting a more coherent retaining policy than he had pursued during the 1440s. His first, and at this point the only, new recruit was John Gresley, in 1451.[159] This would have represented a useful broadening of his following, were it not for the fact that the Gresleys were still involved in a long-running dispute with the Vernons, whose power might have been diminished by the loss of Sir Richard, but who were still among the region's leading gentry and had been connected with the duke for the previous two decades.[160] As had been the case when Ralph Basset became a member of Buckingham's retinue, the duke made no attempt to intervene in the dispute in which his new retainer Gresley was engaged.[161]

Indeed, the Meverell–Basset feud itself showed no sign of abating. Basset had been among a group of Buckingham's retainers to whom the duke sent letters in May 1451, perhaps to summon them to attend on him when he was with the king at Kenilworth and Coventry with a 'greet felesship' in the following September.[162] This demonstration that Buckingham, in some contexts at least, still regarded himself as Basset's lord heralded no improvement in the latter's fortunes. In October 1452 Sampson and Thomas Meverell finally surrendered themselves to answer the charges laid against them, only to produce royal pardons.[163] A year later, the Meverells again broke into the park at Blore; by this

---

[159] By the following year Gresley's son Thomas was a page in the duke's household. Rawcliffe, *The Staffords*, 239; SRO D641/1/2/58. This John Gresley was the son of the Sir John Gresley who died in 1449: Madan, 'The Gresleys', 54, 57, 60.

[160] For the Gresley–Vernon dispute, see above, at n. 104. The attempted arbitration by William Ferrers in 1447 had failed to stop the conflict. In 1450, for example, the widow of one of Gresley's servants appealed William Vernon and his brother-in-law Hugh Davenport of the murder of her husband. Rowney, 'Staffordshire Political Community', 318; KB27/754 Coram Rege rot. 34v.

[161] Significantly, Gresley seems to have turned to Buckingham's lordship in the course of continuing hostilities between 1449 and 1451 with the abbey of Burton on Trent, which had a history of conflict with the Gresleys dating back to the beginning of the century (see above, Ch. 6.2 n. 89). The dispute prompted the issue of three commissions for the arrest of Gresley and his brothers between Mar. 1449 and May 1450. Gresley's appeal may have been a factor in prompting Buckingham to retain him, although the abbey also claimed the duke's protection. It is striking and entirely characteristic that, as Susan Wright remarks, 'Buckingham's "protection" and "good lordship" were apparently of small benefit to Gresley or to the abbey. Buckingham's warnings to the abbot . . . were ineffective . . . Neither apparently was Buckingham able to impose a settlement or to suggest any kind of compromise'. The dispute was still continuing in 1467. (For an attempted arbitration in 1455 by the prior of Holy Trinity, Repingdon, and others, see NUL MiDc 5 fo. 15v.) *CPR 1446–52*, 285–6, 385; Wright, *The Derbyshire Gentry*, 125; I. H. Jeayes (ed.), *Descriptive Catalogue of the Charters and Muniments of the Gresley Family* (London, 1895), 98.

[162] Letters were also sent to John Curson and Nicholas Longford, among others, but not, however, to Vernon: SRO D641/1/2/57; E404/68/97; M. D. Harris (ed.), *The Coventry Leet Book* (London, 1907–13), 263–6; Rowney, 'Staffordshire Political Community', 71.

[163] KB27/766 Rex rot. 8v.

stage Basset was also facing renewed hostility from Thomas Meverell's father-in-law Nicholas Montgomery.[164]

From 1453, however, this longstanding dispute took second place to a new conflict among the local gentry, which had its roots in the region's changing political hierarchies and which was decisively influenced by the increasingly dramatic developments within national government.[165] A marked feature of local politics in the few years since 1450 had been the increasing authority of Sir Thomas Blount's son Walter. Thomas Blount himself had been one of the most influential gentry figures in the region throughout the 1440s, holding office as deputy steward of Tutbury, as sheriff in both Staffordshire and Derbyshire, and as a regular member of the commission of the peace in the latter shire,[166] but during the early 1450s Walter became a significant local power in his own right. He joined his father on the bench in 1449, and represented Derbyshire in four out of the five parliaments between 1447 and 1453.[167] In 1449 he was also appointed bailiff of two Derbyshire wapentakes in succession to Richard Vernon's son Fulk, who had recently died.[168] In a society where land conferred power, such independent authority was rarely achieved by a gentry heir who had not yet come into his inheritance. Moreover, Blount's promotion was not derived from Buckingham's patronage, since Walter had no greater personal associations with the duke than his father Thomas.[169]

It is clear that Walter Blount's success was the result not only of his family's traditional regional influence but also of his own connections with the court, where he had been a household esquire since 1441.[170] In March 1453, for example, when John, Lord Dudley, was granted the farm of a wardship, Walter Blount was among his mainpernors.[171] More significantly, after Richard Vernon's death Queen Margaret appointed Blount to succeed him as steward, constable, and master forester of the High Peak, an office which had helped to sustain Vernon's pre-eminent position in northern Derbyshire, and which provided Blount with substantial personal authority.[172] It is possible that during this period he

---

[164] KB27/778 Coram Rege rot. 61; KB27/770 Coram Rege rot. 19v; see above, at n. 101.

[165] The course of this dispute is complex and many of its causes and implications are obscure. Much of the following must therefore remain provisional. For a detailed version of this argument, see H. R. Castor, ' "Walter Blount is gone to serve Traytours": The Sack of Elvaston and the Politics of the North Midlands in 1454', *Midland History*, 19 (1994), 21–39.

[166] See above, at n. 45; *List of Sheriffs*, 103, 127; *CPR 1436–41*, 581; *1441–6*, 469; *1446–52*, 588.

[167] *CPR 1446–52*, 588; *Return of the Name*, 335, 338, 344, 347.

[168] *CPR 1446–52*, 221.

[169] See above, at n. 45.

[170] D. A. L. Morgan, 'The House of Policy: The Political Role of the Late Plantagenet Household, 1422–1485', in D. Starkey (ed.), *The English Court: From the Wars of the Roses to the Civil War* (London, 1987), 50 n.   [171] *CFR 1452–61*, 29.

[172] The date of the queen's grant is not known, but it was confirmed by the king on 4 July 1453: DL37/21 nos. 30–1.

may also have come into contact with Richard Neville, who had secured the earldom of Warwick in 1449 in right of his wife, Henry Beauchamp's sister Anne, and who was until the middle of 1453 still closely connected with the court.[173] Certainly, in February 1451 Walter Blount stood bail for Robert Harecourt, who was at this point supported by Warwick as well as by other members of the court, when he appeared to face charges relating to the murder of Richard Stafford in Coventry in 1448.[174]

Blount had therefore succeeded in interpolating himself into regional political structures independently of his family's territorial interests, which he had not yet inherited, and independently of Buckingham who, nominally at least, dominated local society. The fact that a significant element in Blount's regional influence was provided by his acquisition of Duchy office demonstrates the extent of the duke's failure to exploit his own Tutbury stewardship as the focal point for a coherent affinity in eastern Staffordshire and western Derbyshire. Nor, as the king's representative in the region, was he ensuring that local society was adequately represented in the distribution of office, since Blount, who did not even yet control his own patrimony,[175] was hardly a sufficient substitute as steward of the Peak for the territorial eminence and political experience of Richard Vernon. The Peak stewardship conferred enormous influence in a part of Derbyshire where there were very few magnate interests, and it had allowed Vernon to develop his own independent regional lordship to become the single most powerful member of the gentry in the shire for much of the three decades before his death. Blount's appointment represented an extraordinarily rapid promotion, and dealt a severe blow to the regional aspirations of Vernon's heir William. The origins of the conflict which developed in Derbyshire in the early 1450s are obscure, but the degree of hostility directed specifically at Walter Blount seems to indicate that his meteoric rise was, or at least became, a particular cause of resentment.

The earliest indications of trouble suggest that the conflict originally focused not in fact on Blount and his family but on their relatives the

[173] Wright, *The Derbyshire Gentry*, 73; Carpenter, *Locality and Polity*, 439, 459, 466. For the complex and protracted division of the Beauchamp estates between Richard Neville, the earl of Shrewsbury, the duke of Somerset, and George Neville, Lord Latimer, the husbands of Anne Beauchamp and her three half-sisters, see Carpenter, *Locality and Polity*, 439–46.

[174] Blount's description in the record of the mainprise as 'of London' supports the suggestion that he was active at court at this point. His connection with Harecourt cannot have improved Blount's relationship with Buckingham, who was associated with the group supporting the Staffords. Wrottesley (ed.), 'Extracts from the Plea Rolls in the Reign of Henry VI', 198; for the Stafford–Harecourt feud, see Carpenter, *Locality and Polity*, 427–8, 454–6.

[175] This had significant implications in local politics. Unlike his father, for example, and although he had held office as MP and JP, Walter had not yet been appointed to the shrievalty, the most prestigious and powerful of the shire offices: *List of Sheriffs*, 103; Carpenter, *Locality and Polity*, 263–9.

Shirleys.[176] Ralph Shirley's grandfather, Sir Hugh, had been among the leading Duchy retainers in Derbyshire at the beginning of the century, but Ralph's father had spent most of his time in Nottinghamshire, and Ralph himself established the family seat at his wife's Leicestershire estate of Staunton Harold.[177] From the early 1450s Shirley properties in Derbyshire came under attack from a group of local gentry led by Sir Nicholas Longford. No evidence survives of the origin of the dispute, but in August 1450 the Shirley manor of Brailsford was raided by a group of yeomen from Longford.[178] There is no extant record of any further trouble until December 1452, when Nicholas Longford himself broke into the park at Shirley in the company of John Cokayn and Nicholas Montgomery.[179] The Shirleys had earlier in the century been engaged in a protracted dispute with Buckingham over the Basset of Drayton inheritance,[180] but it seems unlikely that the attacks by Longford were prompted by the duke. Even if Buckingham had the degree of control over his retainers necessary to initiate such a campaign—which is certainly not a straightforward assumption to make—it is hard to see why he would choose to reopen hostilities years after the matter seems to have been settled substantially in his favour. The fact that both of the Shirley properties attacked, Brailsford and Shirley, lay only a few miles from the manor of Longford in south-west Derbyshire suggests that Nicholas Longford's own local interests may have been the principal spur to his actions.

Certainly, the context of the Shirley–Buckingham dispute offers no clue as to why hostilities subsequently focused on the Blounts, and specifically on the person of Walter Blount. In July 1453, seven months after the attack on the park at Shirley, Ralph Twyford, a local gentleman closely associated with Longford, assaulted Walter Blount's brother Thomas at Derby.[181] There is no indication of the cause of the incident, although it may be significant that Walter Blount's prestigious Duchy office at the Peak, for which he may have been felt to be insufficiently qualified, had been confirmed less than a month earlier.[182] Indeed, these incidents provide unequivocal evidence of the dislocation

---

[176] Ralph Shirley's stepmother may have been a Blount; his second wife was Walter Blount's sister Elizabeth: LRO 72'30 vol. I, unnumbered deed (Dec. 36 Henry VI); E. P. Shirley (ed.), *Stemmata Shirleiana* (London, 1873), 1, 45, 397–8, 399–402.

[177] See above, Ch. 6.1 at n. 12, and Ch. 6.2 at n. 50; Shirley (ed.), *Stemmata Shirleiana*, 44, 46–7.

[178] KB9/12/1 m. 12.

[179] KB9/12/1 m. 10.

[180] Wright, *The Derbyshire Gentry*, 70–1; Rawcliffe, *The Staffords*, 12, 192.

[181] KB9/12/1 m. 15. The indictment describing the attack originally alleged that it had been carried out on the instructions of Nicholas Longford and John Curson, but the phrase was later crossed out.

[182] See above, n. 172.

which had occurred within the former Duchy network during Buckingham's tenure of the Tutbury stewardship, since the Shirleys and the
Blounts, leading members of the Lancastrian affinity in the first decades
of the century, were now being attacked by their erstwhile associates in
Duchy service, the Longfords, Cokayns, and Montgomeries.

Whatever its origins, the temper of the feud between Blount and
Longford was decisively exacerbated in the spring of 1454, a development which seems to have been closely related to the dramatic course
of events in national politics. At the end of 1453, a year in which the
government had come under increasing pressure, not least because of
the king's mental collapse, the duke of York challenged Somerset's
authority, and by April 1454 had secured the removal of his rival and
his own appointment as protector. During these months York won the
support of the Nevilles, including Richard, earl of Warwick, while
Buckingham, although included in the broadly based protectorate
administration established at the end of March 1454, had originally
been among the nobles who opposed York's manœuvres.[183]

It has been suggested that the establishment of York's protectorate
was a decisive moment in Derbyshire politics because Walter Blount
had by 1454 attached himself unequivocally to York's cause through the
service of Richard Neville, whose lordship was certainly to be the
decisive factor in Blount's career in the later 1450s.[184] R. L. Storey
argues, for example, that Blount 'apparently became a member of
[York's] household no later than 1454', citing as evidence a letter
written to Warwick by York, who notes that 'for the good lordship . . .
that for my sake ye owe and bere unto my servaunt Walter Blount
squier, ye desire me to geve him leve to be witholden with you as your
Marchall' at Calais.[185] Warwick was appointed captain of Calais in the
summer of 1455, so that York's letter, which is dated 15 October,
cannot have been written before October 1455, and probably dates from
later still, since Warwick was unable to take possession of Calais until
July 1456.[186] It is difficult, therefore, to see this as proof of Blount's
political affiliations more than a year before the letter can at the earliest

---

[183] Griffiths, *Henry VI*, 715, 719–28; Watts, *Henry VI*, 305–9; *PL* Gairdner, ii. 295–8.
Warwick had lost custody of the Despenser lands of the Beauchamp inheritance to Somerset
in June 1453: Carpenter, *Locality and Polity*, 466.

[184] See Storey, *End of the House of Lancaster*, 152; Wright, *The Derbyshire Gentry*, 73.

[185] Storey, *End of the House of Lancaster*, 152, 254; BL Cotton MS Vespasian F XIII no. 89
(printed in H. Ellis (ed.), *Original Letters Illustrative of English History*, 2nd series, i (London,
1969), 124–6).

[186] G. L. Harriss, 'The Struggle for Calais: An Aspect of the Rivalry between Lancaster and
York', *EHR* 75 (1960), 40–1, 46. David Morgan points out that another of York's retainers,
Sir Edmund Mulso, was also seconded from the duke's service to serve under Warwick at
Calais. Mulso's will was made at Calais in May 1458, and he was dead by Jan. 1459. Morgan
suggests that it may have been to replace Mulso that Warwick requested Blount's presence,
which would date the letter to Oct. 1458: 'The House of Policy', 53 n.

have been written.[187] In fact, there is no evidence that Blount was any more closely connected with Warwick than with other members of the court before the beginning of the protectorate. Nor does Blount seem to have become noticeably estranged from the bulk of his family's local gentry associates before the end of 1453.[188] It appears that, until this point, the sporadic demonstrations of hostility between Nicholas Longford and the families of Blount and Shirley caused relatively little regional disruption. That was to change in the spring of 1454.

In the north midlands, as elsewhere in the country, the 'Yorkist' regime immediately sought to restore the credibility and efficacy of the crown's authority. The first step was the reinforcement of the commission of the peace, with the appointment of Warwick to the bench in Staffordshire in April 1454 and of Warwick, York, and Shrewsbury to the Derbyshire commission in May.[189] These appointments constituted a significant change in regional power structures. The sources of authority previously available, in theory at least, to the gentry of the area—effectively Buckingham (whatever the deficiencies of his lordship) through his territorial power in Staffordshire and his stewardship of Tutbury, and indeed the crown itself in the guise of the Duchy—were inseparable from the authority of the court and the person of the king. Blount's court career had given him independent access to royal authority, which allowed him to carve out a substantial niche for himself in Buckingham's 'country', despite his lack of any close association with the duke.[190] Nicholas Longford had been retained by Buckingham for the past decade,[191] and before 1454 Blount had shown little appetite

---

[187] Susan Wright suggests that Blount entered Warwick's retinue, arguing that the earl 'finally joined York at the end of 1453, and Blount subsequently followed Warwick into York's service'. She too refers to York's letter, despite both the discrepancy in the dates, and the fact that the duke's comments are if anything more suggestive of Blount moving from York's service to Warwick's than vice versa: *The Derbyshire Gentry*, 73, 100, 180.

[188] See NA DDFJ 1/84/4 (printed in Jeayes (ed.), *Derbyshire Charters*, 200 [1616]) for Blount as a witness with William Vernon, John Cokayn, and John de la Pole in June 1453; DCL Every 3523 for Blount and co-feoffees including Ralph de la Pole and Nicholas Fitzherbert in Sept. 1453.

[189] York and Shrewsbury were also added to the Staffordshire commission in July 1454. Shrewsbury had come into his inheritance in 1453 on the death of his father, who had shown little interest in his Staffordshire and Derbyshire estates. The new earl's appointment to the peace commission was an early indication of his intention to develop Talbot influence in the region. Shrewsbury does not seem to have been closely involved with York, but was hostile to Somerset, whose sister-in-law Margaret was Shrewsbury's stepmother and had, with her husband, sought to disinherit him in favour of her own children. *CPR 1452–61*, 663–4, 677; Pollard, 'The Family of Talbot', 52–60, 65, 69–70; *Complete Peerage*, xi. 703.

[190] Blount's success in using the access to the king's authority offered by his position at court to establish his personal influence in the north midlands, despite the fact that he owed nothing to, and therefore represented a challenge to, the ostensible structures of power in the region, parallels Thomas Daniel's maverick career in East Anglia, for which, see above, Chs. 4.4, 5.

[191] See above, at n. 31.

for risking the possibility of a trial of strength with the duke—however remote, given Buckingham's erratic and often ineffectual role in local affairs—by responding to Longford's challenges. However, though Buckingham was not excluded from the Yorkist regime,[192] he was far from being in the ascendant, and the appointment of Warwick and York to the commissions of the peace signalled their determination to make royal authority, newly reconstituted independently of the person of the now totally incapable king, directly effective in the localities.

Blount, perhaps encouraged by contact with Warwick at court during the early 1450s,[193] seems to have decided that the new regime offered him a favourable political climate in which to pursue his local grievances. On 30 April 1454 he led a raid on the manor of Longford, accompanied by his brother Thomas and his cousin Nicholas Gresley.[194] If he had hoped to secure the protector's backing for his efforts, he was to be disappointed. York, like his predecessors Suffolk and Somerset, had been able to establish himself at the head of a viable government only by winning a broad basis of noble support.[195] In order to demonstrate the legitimacy of the authority he wielded as protector, and thus to reinforce the fragile consensus among the lords on which his power rested, the duke's primary concern in the localities was not to support partisan interests, but to display the impartiality of royal justice.[196] On 10 May, therefore, royal letters were issued summoning both Blount and Longford to appear before the council 'in all hast'.[197] Despite this even-handed response, Blount's decision to seize the initiative against his local rival under the auspices of the new regime seems to have been immensely provocative, inspiring Longford to a dramatic assault both on Blount himself and on the legitimacy of York's government. Longford's response to the summons clearly demonstrated that, at least in Derbyshire, the protectorate was neither immediately nor universally accepted as a legitimate and non-partisan delegation of royal authority.

York's attempt to present his government as an impartial and representative regime was somewhat compromised by the fact that the sheriff charged with delivering the summonses was John Gresley.[198] Gresley was the first Derbyshire gentleman to hold the joint shrievalty since

---

[192] Griffiths, *Henry VI*, 726–8.

[193] See above, at nn. 173–4.

[194] KB9/12/1/ m. 9 (misdated to 30 May in Storey, *End of the House of Lancaster*, 154). The indictment is printed in A. Carrington and E. M. Poynton, 'A Lancastrian Raid in the Wars of the Roses', *Journal of the Derbyshire Archaeological and Natural History Society*, 35 (1913), 244.

[195] Watts, *Henry VI*, 307–8, 319–21; Griffiths, *Henry VI*, 726–8.

[196] Cf. Carpenter, *Locality and Polity*, 467–75; Watts, *Henry VI*, 309–12.

[197] *POPC*, vi. 180.

[198] *List of Sheriffs*, 103.

Nicholas Fitzherbert in 1447–8, and had recently joined Longford as a member of Buckingham's retinue, both of which circumstances might in theory have reinforced the credibility of his authority in Longford's eyes. Nevertheless, he was Walter Blount's cousin, and his brother Nicholas had participated in Blount's recent attack on Longford's estates.[199] If the latter had any doubts about the justice he could expect from York's government, they would therefore have been compounded by the identity of the government's principal officer in the region. Gresley dispatched his servant Christopher Langton to deliver the royal letter to Longford at his manor of Hough in Lancashire.[200] Longford refused to receive the summons, and Langton left after being threatened by servants. The next day, however, he returned. Determined to deliver the letter, even if Longford refused to accept it, Langton placed it on a bench by the door, instructing the servants to tell their master what he had done, and rode away. This time, the Longfords' refusal to accept the authority of the sheriff and the government he represented was demonstrated more dramatically. Before Langton had reached the park gate, John Longford and a group of men overtook him. They had brought the royal letter, and tried to force the unfortunate Langton to eat it. When he said he would rather die, his attackers spat on the letter and made him tear it up—an explicit rejection of royal authority as represented by York's regime. Langton was put in the stocks at Hough, and then taken as a prisoner to Poynton in Cheshire, before eventually being moved to Longford on 27 May.

Derbyshire had by this point already experienced some reaction to the arrival of the summons; on 17 May the Blounts' tenants at Sutton were attacked by Richard and Edward Longford.[201] This raid offers an early indication of the breadth of regional support the Longfords could muster in their rejection of the government's intervention, since they were said to have been aided by William Vernon and John Cokayn.[202] The latter were both at Longford on 27 May when Langton arrived as a prisoner, as were Edmund and Roger Vernon, Edward Cokayn, and Ralph Fitzherbert.[203] On the following day, it became clear why

[199] The sheriffs between 1448 and 1453 were members of the Nottinghamshire families of Staunton, Willoughby, Clifton, Strelley, and Plumpton: *List of Sheriffs*, 103; Payling, *Political Society*, 244–5; see Ch. 7.1 n. 13, and above, at nn. 159, 194.

[200] All details, unless otherwise noted, are taken from KB9/12/1 m. 24 (printed in Carrington and Poynton, 'A Lancastrian Raid', 228–32). See also R. L. Storey's account of the episode, in *End of the House of Lancaster*, 152–5.

[201] KB9/12/1/ m. 23 (printed in Carrington and Poynton, 'A Lancastrian Raid', 232–6). Servants of Longford also raided Ralph Shirley's park at Shirley on 26 May: KB9/12/1 m. 8.

[202] John Curson, Nicholas Montgomery jr., and Nicholas Fitzherbert were also originally included in the indictment for the offence, but their names were later crossed out.

[203] Nicholas Montgomery jr. and Nicholas Fitzherbert were also originally included in the charge against this group: KB9/12/1 m. 24. Longford's force also included several knights and esquires from Cheshire and Lancashire, some of whom—such as Sir John Mainwaring and

Longford had assembled such substantial support. He mustered a force alleged by the Blounts to have numbered about a thousand, which included the Vernons and the Cokayns as well as Hugh Egerton and the younger Nicholas Montgomery, and rode to Derby, where they attacked Walter Blount's lodgings and the home of one of his servants.[204] The sheriff John Gresley met them in the market-place and sought to restrain them by reading the commission of the peace and a letter from York ordering that the peace should be kept. Longford and his associates treated Gresley with contempt, telling him that they would be restrained by no lord, sheriff, or royal minister; significantly, the indictment detailing their actions originally alleged that they added 'persone regie excepta', although the phrase was later crossed out.[205] Even if the emphasis on this distinction between the authority of the king himself and of York's officials acting in the king's name was a ruse on Blount's part to secure the duke's support, the willingness of Longford and his allies to challenge the authority of York's regime seems clear from their treatment of the sheriff, his servant, and the royal letters.[206]

That Longford's hostility was directed primarily at Walter Blount rather than at his family as a whole was already evident from the attack on his Derby lodgings. Confirmation of Blount's personal unpopularity was provided by the next target of Longford and his supporters, who left Derby and rode to the nearby manor of Elvaston.[207] The Blounts' family seat lay at Barton Blount, and it was this manor which had been attacked by Hugh Erdeswick when the Blounts became a focus of anti-Lancastrian feeling in the first decade of the century.[208] Elvaston had been acquired relatively recently by the family and, significantly, had been settled on Walter by his father by 1447.[209] Blount himself was

John Davenport, both of Cheshire—were also retained by Buckingham. As Susan Wright implies, however, it is difficult to regard this as substantive evidence that the duke instigated the attack. Longford himself, after all, owned estates in Cheshire and Lancashire, and it was at his manors in these counties that his supporters originally gathered. *The Derbyshire Gentry*, 137; KB9/12/1 m. 13.

[204] All details of the events of 28 May, unless otherwise noted, are taken from KB9/12/1 m. 13. The indictment is printed in A. Carrington and W. J. Andrew, 'A Lancastrian Raid in the Wars of the Roses', *Journal of the Derbyshire Archaeological and Natural History Society*, 34 (1912), 39–49. See also Storey, *End of the House of Lancaster*, 152–5.

[205] 'quod nullus dominus persone regie excepta nec aliquis vicecomes aut minister domini Regis esse eorum gubernator nec illos impediret': KB9/12/1 m. 13.

[206] For Longford's more wary attitude to divisions in central authority in the wake of the protracted upheavals of the following years, see below, at n. 273.

[207] All details of this attack are also taken from KB9/12/1 m. 13.

[208] See above, Ch. 6.2 at n. 106.

[209] It is not entirely clear how Elvaston came into the possession of the Blounts. At the beginning of the 15th cent. it was part of the estates of the Willoughbies of Wollaton which, because of the death of the childless Sir Richard Willoughby in 1369, had descended to his younger brother Hugh, a cleric. Hugh sought to disinherit the heirs of his younger half-

away, but the raiding party inflicted substantial damage on the house and its contents. Doors, windows, tables, bedhangings, and household utensils were broken or cut into pieces; accounts, deeds, and court-rolls were destroyed. More importantly, care was taken to emphasize that this violence was far from random or mindless: tapestries decorated with Blount's arms were cut into four, the attackers allegedly declaring that 'that seyd Walter Blount was gone to serve Traytours therefore his armus shall thus be quarterd'.[210] The identification of the protector and his government as 'Traytours' was a dramatic demonstration that, in some minds at least, York had not succeeded in establishing that his regime was a legitimate attempt to take on the public responsibilities of an incapable king, rather than the illegitimate accroachment of royal power by a partisan faction. Whether Blount had indeed 'gone to serve Traytours', or whether his final decision to commit himself to York had not yet been made when the raid on his home took place, his position by the time the indictments were presented in July was unequivocal. His rapid rise to personal power in the region, and the perception among his peers that he had associated himself with York by May 1454 (whether or not that was true), had left him virtually isolated in Derbyshire and Staffordshire. Members of the Longford, Vernon, Cokayn, Montgomery, Egerton, and Fitzherbert families had taken part in the attacks on his property; John Curson was accused of aiding and

brother Edmund in favour of his own children, who had, necessarily, been born out of wedlock. In this scheme he was assisted by Sir John Dabridgecourt, who had married Richard Willoughby's widow; their daughter Joan Dabridgecourt married Hugh Willoughby's eldest son. Hugh granted the manor of Elvaston to Dabridgecourt, and, shortly before the former's death in 1406, Edmund Willoughby's heir (confusingly, another Hugh) agreed not to challenge Dabridgecourt's possession in return for an annual rent of 10 marks. Elvaston seems to have been among the estates which Dabridgecourt's will ordered his executors to sell for the good of his soul, and was presumably bought by Sir John Blount, one of the supervisors of the will, since by 1417 it was Blount who was paying the rent for the manor to Hugh Willoughby. In 1442 the rent was paid by a group of feoffees, presumably to the use of Thomas Blount, headed by Sir Thomas Gresley; by 1447 it was Walter Blount who was responsible for the payment. When Walter came into the Blount inheritance on his father's death in 1456, he too seems to have settled the manor on his eldest son, for in 1472–3 Sir Hugh Willoughby's heir Robert was sueing the widow of William Blount (who had predeceased his father) for the return of Elvaston. In Sept. 1473 Walter Blount, now Lord Mountjoy, agreed to pay Robert Willoughby £80 in return for a quitclaim of Elvaston. (The Lathbury family also seems to have had some estate at Elvaston; this interest, too, passed to John Dabridgecourt and subsequently to the Blounts.) DRO D518M/T57; D518M/E4, E6, E7B, E8; NUL Mi 5/168/45; MiD 1770/3; Payling, *Political Society*, 34, 72, 242; E. F. Jacob (ed.), *The Register of Henry Chichele* (Oxford, 1938–47), ii. 53–4, 108–9; Croke, *History of the Croke Family*, 196, 202. I am indebted to Susan Wilkinson, of Nottingham University Library MS department, for allowing me to see the results of her research into the Willoughbies' transactions.

[210] Susan Wright rightly points out that this supposedly verbatim quotation 'may simply be the Blounts ensuring York's protection' (*The Derbyshire Gentry*, 136), but, as suggested above (at n. 206), unless the entire account in all its detail is wildly exaggerated, this speech is not inconsistent with other actions of Longford and his supporters.

abetting the raid on Elvaston, as was Longford's son-in-law Thomas Foljambe (although his name was later deleted from the indictment).[211] In such circumstances, when a significant proportion of the society within which Blount operated had perceived a connection between him and York and rejected both, Blount was left with no option but to throw in his lot with the protector. It is no coincidence that he was the only local gentleman to commit himself so early and so completely to York's cause.

The Longford–Blount dispute has been the subject of a variety of characterizations, and there has been little consensus about its nature and significance. Ralph Griffiths concluded that 'it is difficult to view these disturbances as anything but the product of local enmities',[212] while others have argued that the violence was a regional manifestation of the national division between York and Lancaster.[213] R. L. Storey, who devoted a whole chapter of *The End of the House of Lancaster* to the affair, suggested both possibilities, though he inclined towards the former as the more probable.[214] Recent analyses have suggested a version lying somewhere between explanations based on national 'party' politics and those which look solely to personal feuds. It is noticeable that many of the families ranged against Blount in 1454 were associated with Buckingham. Longford and Curson were his retainers, as was Hugh Egerton, while the Vernons and the Cokayns had been associated with the duke, albeit problematically, for many years.[215] Given this variety of Stafford connections, it has been suggested that the conflict formed part of a wider rivalry for the rule of the midlands between Buckingham and Richard Neville.[216] Susan Wright suggests that 'the frontier between the respective spheres of influence of Warwick and Buckingham shifted northwards and Derbyshire became part of the broad arena of "national" or "court" conflict identifiable in

[211] KB9/12/1 m. 13. Nicholas Fitzherbert's name was also struck out from this part of the indictment. All those present during the attack were said to have pledged to stand together in all things against Blount, his kinsmen, friends, servants, and tenants. For Foljambe's marriage to Margery Longford, see NA DDFJ 4/5/1–2.

[212] Griffiths, *Henry VI*, 765.

[213] In 1912 it was suggested that the raid on Elvaston constituted a gathering of 'practically the whole of the militant Lancastrian party in and around the county', for whom Blount 'was merely a side issue upon a march southward, probably to join the Queen'; cf. Morgan's not dissimilar conclusion that 'in 1453–4 [Blount] became a retainer of Richard of York, and as a result in May 1454 his house at Elvaston was sacked by a vengeful posse of the neighbouring gentry of Staffordshire and Derbyshire': Carrington and Andrew, 'A Lancastrian Raid', 33, 35; Morgan, 'The House of Policy', 50.

[214] Storey, *End of the House of Lancaster*, 150.

[215] See Ch. 7.2 at n. 54, and above, at n. 31. Hugh Egerton had been granted the annuity formerly received by his father Ralph, who had recently died: Wedgwood, *Staffordshire Parliamentary History*, 214; SRO D641/1/2/59 (cf. NLW Peniarth MS 280, fo. 54); C146/9559.

[216] Rowney, 'Staffordshire Political Community', 22–3, 40; Wright, *The Derbyshire Gentry*, 73–4, 136–7.

the 1450s'; she argues that their antagonism 'found a focal point in south Derbyshire in Blount'. Although in the course of a detailed and nuanced account she warns that 'this was no simple case . . . of one group of retainers versus another', she concludes that 'with Buckingham's approval and probable encouragement, current divisions in gentry society were exploited for wider political ends'.[217] There are, however, significant problems with this analysis.

First, there is no conclusive evidence to link Blount specifically with Warwick before the attack on Elvaston took place.[218] Richard Neville's attempts to rebuild the Beauchamp sphere of interest in Warwickshire since 1450 had certainly brought him into conflict with Buckingham in the north of that county.[219] However, even if an association with Blount by 1454 could be proved, there would be little reason to interpret this as evidence that Warwick was challenging Buckingham in Derbyshire, where Neville held no lands and where the Beauchamps had never wielded any authority, or even in Staffordshire, where Beauchamp interests in the 1420s and 1430s had depended on a coalition with the Staffords and the Ferrers of Chartley.[220] Moreover, Blount's very isolation in 1454 would suggest that any possible association with Warwick could not adequately be interpreted as an extension of the latter's 'sphere of influence'. Indeed, far from Derbyshire being the scene of rivalry between Warwick and Buckingham, there must also be some hesitation over the latter's local role. While the region was undoubtedly in many senses within Buckingham's sphere of influence, it has already been argued that the duke's control over his retainers and over local affairs was limited. There is little evidence that Buckingham's lordship played even a tacit role in orchestrating the conflict.[221] John Gresley, the sheriff whose authority was so forcefully challenged, was one of the duke's most recent retainers, while among Blount's opponents the regional concerns of the Vernons and the Cokayns had left their relationship with Buckingham ambiguous.[222] Rather, the violence

---

[217] Wright, *The Derbyshire Gentry*, 137, 74.

[218] See above, pp. 287–8.

[219] Carpenter, *Locality and Polity*, 452–8.

[220] Ibid. 449 (map of the Warwick inheritance). There is little evidence that Richard Neville, who did not even hold the Beauchamp estate in its entirety, showed any significant interest in Staffordshire in the 1450s, preoccupied as he was with Warwickshire and, increasingly, with national politics.

[221] Susan Wright's argument for 'Buckingham's approval and probable encouragement' of the attack on Blount rests on the fact that he 'did nothing to stop the assaults on this retainer of Warwick' (*The Derbyshire Gentry*, 74, 136). However, while this is undoubtedly true (with the proviso that there is no evidence that Blount *was* a retainer of Warwick at this point), he had also done nothing to stop repeated assaults on his own retainer Ralph Basset throughout the 1440s, which makes any attempt to draw conclusions from such inactivity extremely difficult.

[222] See above, at nn. 117, 159.

reflected the political vacuum which Buckingham's deficient management had left in the 'Duchy' areas of eastern Staffordshire and western Derbyshire; the impression created by these attacks on Blount, the steward of the Peak, by men associated with Buckingham, the steward of Tutbury, is one of extreme confusion.

Yet even if Buckingham's involvement before the event in the attack on Blount was limited, it does seem that the duke actively *responded* to the conflict, and that this response may have owed something to his wider political concerns. In the months after the assault on Elvaston, Buckingham chose overtly to demonstrate his support for those responsible. Longford and Curson had already received annuities from the duke for more than a decade.[223] As has already been suggested, the actual significance of these formal links in shaping the events of May 1454 is called into question by the fact that Buckingham had failed during that decade to establish his lordship as a controlling force in the region. However, in August 1454 the duke granted John Cokayn an annuity of 10 marks and, in the same month, awarded William Vernon a fee of £10.[224] The decision to retain two of the leading figures responsible for the attack on Blount's property only three months after it took place seems unlikely to have been coincidental, particularly since the grants made no political sense within the context of Buckingham's existing retinue. Vernon was at loggerheads with the duke's recent recruit John Gresley, while Cokayn's inheritance was still in the hands of his stepfather, Buckingham's Warwickshire retainer Thomas Bate. Both Vernon and Cokayn, moreover, had been closely involved in Sampson Meverell's continuing campaign against the Stafford annuitant Ralph Basset.[225] It is possible that the duke's decision to offer such overt backing to Blount's opponents was prompted by his rivalry elsewhere in the midlands with the earl of Warwick. However, given the fact that Warwick had no political stake in Derbyshire, and that it is unclear whether Blount was now developing links specifically with Warwick or with York himself, an equally important role in shaping Buckingham's actions may well have been played by his opposition to the Yorkist regime as a whole.[226]

Buckingham's willingness to offer partisan support in the aftermath of the violence is perhaps reflected by the fact that he was not among the justices who heard the indictments when a commission of *oyer* and *terminer* sat at Derby in July 1454.[227] The events of May, and especially

[223] So had Hugh Egerton's father: see above, at n. 31.

[224] SRO D641/1/2/59; SC6/1040/15 (Vernon retained for life to serve both Buckingham and his heir Humphrey, Lord Stafford).

[225] See above, pp. 271–2, 276, 283.

[226] Cf. Carpenter, *Locality and Polity*, 466–7.

[227] KB9/12/1 m. 12v.

Longford's explicit challenge to the legitimacy of York's authority as protector, had made it even more essential for the duke to demonstrate rapidly that his regime could offer credible, impartial justice, which, if Buckingham were to some degree implicated in the dispute after the Elvaston raid, would have provided a compelling reason for excluding him from a judicial role at the sessions. The fact that Warwick too was absent from the commission may lend support to the suggestion that the tensions between the earl and Buckingham in Warwickshire had influenced the repercussions of the dispute. Alternatively, his absence may reflect the fact that Warwick—unlike the earl of Shrewsbury who did appear on the commission, and unlike Buckingham—had neither estates nor significant political interests in Derbyshire.[228] In fact, since there is no evidence that Warwick, unlike Buckingham, made a show of partisan commitment even after the raid,[229] the earl cannot be demonstrated to have taken any action at all in relation to the dispute; he had no lands in the area in which it occurred, and no demonstrable connections with any of the protagonists at the time of the conflict. It seems that the events of 1454 may best be understood in terms both of the power structures of a region which was nominally under Buckingham's authority, and of the relationship between the latter and the dominant interests in national government, rather than as a manifestation of regional rivalry between Buckingham and Warwick.

Both Longford and Blount were on 3 June again ordered to appear before the council and charged on pain of £1,000 to 'attempte noo thing ayens oure pees in the meane tyme', and on 1 July York himself arrived at Derby with the earl of Shrewsbury to hear the indictments.[230] The government's concern to manifest its impartiality is evident in the fact that efforts seem to have been made to select juries unconnected with either side.[231] Nevertheless, the commission failed to compel the attendance of Longford, Cokayn, or Vernon, and York could not stay long in Derby, so that many of the accused were bailed until September.[232]

Despite York's presence, the government's intervention had failed to

[228] Warwick had been appointed to the commission of the peace in Derbyshire in 1454, but then so had York, who had no claims to regional lordship in the north midlands: see above, at n. 189.

[229] Indeed, as a central figure in the Yorkist regime, Warwick too had every incentive to demonstrate his commitment to impartial justice. In Warwickshire, for example, his local ascendancy between 1453 and 1456 seems to have been characterized by conciliation and compromise: Carpenter, *Locality and Polity*, 467–75.

[230] *POPC*, vi. 192; KB9/12/1 m. 12v.

[231] Among the names empanelled but not selected for the jury of Appletree and Wirksworth, for example, were Thomas Blount, and William Basset and Thomas Okeover, who presumably had common cause with the Blounts because of their mutual enemies: KB9/12/2 m. 5; Wright, *The Derbyshire Gentry*, 135 n. 112.

[232] Wright, *The Derbyshire Gentry*, 136; Storey, *End of the House of Lancaster*, 155.

secure the co-operation of the bulk of local society with the judicial proceedings of July 1454. Blount and Shirley were virtually the only gentlemen to present complaints, and their opponents stayed away from the hearings.[233] It has been suggested that 'in the short term the gentry were not deterred from pursuing their private quarrels and the assaults were continued for a little while after the sessions',[234] but this general conclusion obscures two significant aspects of the continuing conflict. First, the display of royal authority by the Yorkist regime does seem to have been enough to prevent further hostilities in the months that followed.[235] Secondly, when the violence was eventually renewed, it correlated closely with changes in national government, which suggests that the disputants acted when they believed the wider political climate might be favourable to their cause.

The region seems to have remained relatively quiet throughout the period of York's rule, but less than two months after the end of the first protectorate and the political eclipse of the Yorkist lords there was a renewal of hostilities against the Blounts. Their enemies may well have been encouraged to strike by the fact that Buckingham, who had demonstrated his support for Blount's opponents in the summer of 1454, had been instrumental in securing Somerset's restoration to power.[236] On 11 April 1455 Roland Blount was murdered at Derby by a group of men led by Henry Curson of Kedleston, allegedly acting on the orders of his father John, who had earlier been accused of supporting the raid on Elvaston.[237] In the following month, York's victory at St Albans over a royal army commanded by Buckingham re-established the Yorkist regime,[238] thus restoring the upper hand at a local level to the Blounts. Walter Blount, for example, represented Derbyshire in the parliament of July 1455.[239] In the unsettled political climate immediately after the battle, the Blounts may have hoped that York would be prepared to give them the partisan support which he had

---

[233] The earl of Shrewsbury also presented charges against John Cokayn for incursions into property he owned at Ashbourne between Jan. and Mar. 1454: KB9/12/1 mm. 16, 20–1.

[234] Wright, *The Derbyshire Gentry*, 137.

[235] The records of King's Bench in the Michaelmas term of 1454 make no mention of conflict between Blount and Longford. The only indication of trouble in the region was the continued appearance of charges relating to the Meverell–Basset dispute: KB9/275 mm. 31–2; KB27/774 Coram Rege roti. 14–14v, 15v.

[236] Buckingham, with Wiltshire and Roos, stood bail for Somerset on 5 Feb. 1455. Bale's Chronicle alleges that Somerset had ten days earlier been 'straungely conveied out of the Tour' by the three lords: *CCR 1454–61*, 44; *CPR 1452–61*, 226; R. Flenley (ed.), *Six Town Chronicles of England* (Oxford, 1911), 141. For the end of the protectorate, see Griffiths, *Henry VI*, 739–41; Watts, *Henry VI*, 312–14.

[237] KB9/280 m. 67. For the Curson family, see Rowney, 'The Cursons', 108.

[238] *PL* Gairdner, iii. 25–30; Griffiths, *Henry VI*, 741–6; Watts, *Henry VI*, 314–17. By June Buckingham had bound himself to co-operate with York's restored government: *PL* Gairdner, iii. 32.

[239] *Return of the Name*, 350.

withheld the previous year. Certainly, they felt able to adopt a newly aggressive strategy: six weeks after the Yorkist victory, Thomas Blount led an assault on John Cokayn, Roger Vernon, and Nicholas Montgomery, allegedly intending to kill them.[240] However, York's renewed authority in 1455 depended, just as it had in 1453, on the maintenance of consensus among the lords and on the duke's public commitment to non-partisan government.[241] In this context, a demonstration of active support for the Blounts was no more possible than it had been during the first protectorate. In August 1455, therefore, Nicholas Longford was granted a royal pardon. Sir Thomas Blount, presumably realizing that support would not be forthcoming, took the precaution of securing a general pardon later in the year, as did his son Thomas in February 1456.[242]

The regime's concern to impose order on the localities also resulted in an attempt to deal with another dispute which had been festering for several years. In July 1455 Roger Vernon and John and Nicholas Gresley were summoned before the council, which had been informed 'to oure gret displesour' that they had 'now late riottously assembled oure people ayenst our pees'.[243] Significantly, it was only as a result of this government initiative that Buckingham made any attempt to intervene in this longstanding dispute between two families who were both closely connected with Stafford lordship. The council referred the conflict to the duke for arbitration, and judgment was given on 12 September. In the light of Buckingham's apparent indifference to the dispute for the past decade, his instruction that William Vernon and John Gresley 'shalbe full frendes', and his assertion that he would immediately deal with any future 'cause of gruggyng', if 'we ben in countrey', sound remarkably optimistic.[244]

For much of the next year, Buckingham does not in fact seem to have been 'in countrey'. By the spring of 1456 York had been removed from the protectorate, although the noble consensus on which his authority had rested since his victory at St Albans seems to have survived as the basis of government.[245] The one exception to this political co-operation was the queen, who seems actively to have sought the end of the protectorate, but who was apparently unwilling subsequently to accept the continued participation of the Yorkist lords in government. Her hostility to the broadly based regime which emerged in February and March 1456 was manifested in her withdrawal to Tutbury, in the heart

---

[240] KB9/280 mm. 26–7.
[241] Griffiths, *Henry VI*, 746–8; Watts, *Henry VI*, 317–22.
[242] Storey, *End of the House of Lancaster*, 155.
[243] *POPC*, vi. 250–1.
[244] Jeayes (ed.), 'Charters and Muniments of the Gresley Family', 96–7.
[245] Watts, *Henry VI*, 332–4.

of her dower lands, by the beginning of May.[246] Buckingham, on the other hand, seems characteristically to have based himself during this period at Writtle in Kent.[247] His absence from the north midlands may have prompted the addition during April and May of his son Humphrey, Lord Stafford, and his kinsman Humphrey Bourchier to local commissions of the peace, the latter in Derbyshire and the former in both Derbyshire and Staffordshire, in an attempt to reinforce Stafford influence in the region.[248] The regime's concern for the maintenance of order may also be reflected in the omission of the controversial figures of Walter Blount and William Vernon, who had both been named as JPs in February 1455, from the Derbyshire commission of the peace in May 1456.[249]

The queen's seizure of the political initiative in the autumn of 1456 was a key moment in the development of the more overtly confrontational politics which characterized the rest of the decade.[250] Nevertheless, now that the person of the king provided not even a semblance of a viable national authority, power and whatever legitimacy was possible in such circumstances accrued to the government only in so far as it represented the public authority of the crown as constituted by the unity of the lords.[251] Since power could effectively be achieved only through noble consensus, neither the queen nor York could exclude their opponents without undermining the basis of their own authority. This is reflected in the continued appointment of a broad group of magnates to the commissions of the peace in the north midlands. The Derbyshire bench included York, Warwick, Buckingham and his son Stafford, Shrewsbury, and Audley; the same group also sat on the Staffordshire commission, with the addition of Lord Dudley.[252] William Vernon was restored to the bench in Derbyshire in May 1457, and, although Walter Blount was not, his father Thomas was consistently appointed. The fact that in 1458, after Thomas Blount's death, Vernon again lost his place may reflect concern to maintain the balance of the commission.[253]

While this accommodation of a broad range of interests represented the theory of noble involvement in Staffordshire and Derbyshire

---

[246] *PL* Gairdner, iii. 75; *PL* Davis, ii. 143 (Gairdner, iii. 86–7); Flenley (ed.), *Six Town Chronicles*, 110.   [247] *PL* Davis, ii. 143, 148 (Gairdner iii. 86, 92).

[248] *CPR 1452–61*, 663–4, 677.

[249] Walter's father, Sir Thomas Blount, retained his place on the bench: *CPR 1452–61*, 663–4.

[250] Griffiths, *Henry VI*, 773–5; Watts, *Henry VI*, 335–7.

[251] For discussion of the constitutional issues on which this assertion is based, see Watts, *Henry VI*, 335–41.

[252] The bishop of Coventry and Lichfield was also named to the bench in both counties, and the archbishop of York in Derbyshire: *CPR 1452–61*, 663–4, 677.

[253] *CPR 1452–61*, 663–4. John Gresley was also omitted from this commission.

between 1456 and 1459, the reality was somewhat different. In practice, the Yorkist lords were based in London, while the queen set about creating a power base for herself in the north midlands.[254] In her own right, Margaret held the Duchy honours of Tutbury and Leicester, as well as Kenilworth Castle in Warwickshire.[255] To the north-west lay her son's earldom of Chester, where she seems to have been actively recruiting support by distributing the livery of the white swan from 1455.[256] Many of the lords associated with her during these years also held estates in the region. Among the most important of these lords was Buckingham, the steward of the queen's estates at Tutbury, who, despite initial differences of opinion with Margaret, became one of her leading supporters.[257] Others included the earl of Shrewsbury, a close ally of Buckingham, whose estates lay in Shropshire, Derbyshire, and south Yorkshire, as well as Viscount Beaumont and the earl of Wiltshire, who were influential in Leicestershire and Warwickshire respectively, and Lord Dudley, who held lands in southern Stafford-shire.[258]

It has been suggested that Margaret's construction of this regional power base constituted an attempt to revive the Lancastrian retinue in the traditional Duchy heartlands.[259] Analysis of this proposition is hampered by the fact that almost no records survive of the queen's estate management; the only extant account relating to her administration dates from 1452–3, before she had become a significant political player in her own right.[260] Some comments can nevertheless be made.

---

[254] Griffiths, *Henry VI*, 777–8; Watts, *Henry VI*, 330–1. For Margaret and Henry at Coventry and Kenilworth, see, for example, Harris (ed.), *The Coventry Leet Book*, 285–92, 297–301.

[255] Somerville, *History of the Duchy*, 208.

[256] J. S. Davies (ed.), *An English Chronicle of the Reigns of Richard II, Henry IV, Henry V, and Henry VI*, Camden Society, 1st series, 64 (1856), 79; J. L. Gillespie, 'Cheshiremen at Blore Heath: A Swan Dive', in J. Rosenthal and C. Richmond (eds.), *People, Politics and Community in the Later Middle Ages* (Gloucester, 1987), 79.

[257] In Oct. 1456 it was reported that Buckingham 'taketh rught straungely that bothe his brethren [the Bourchiers] arn so sodeynly discharged from ther offices of Chauncellerie and Tresoryship; and that among other causeth hym that his opynyon is contrary to the Whenes entent'. By the spring of 1457, however, Buckingham was in close attendance on the king and queen, and his son had been appointed to Prince Edward's council: *PL* Davis, ii. 164–5, 172 (Gairdner, iii. 108, 118); *PL* Gairdner, iii. 127; *CPR 1452–61*, 359.

[258] Shrewsbury, who acquired several manors in Derbyshire during the 1450s, was one of Cromwell's closest associates until the latter's death in 1456. He subsequently seems to have developed particular links with Buckingham: Pollard, 'The Family of Talbot', 65, 71, 82–3, 411–13; Griffiths, *Henry VI*, 784; Rowney, 'Staffordshire Political Community', 12–16; Watts, *Henry VI*, 338–9.

[259] See references and discussion in Carpenter, *Locality and Polity*, 475–6; also Morgan, 'The House of Policy', 51–2; Payling, *Political Society*, 147–8.

[260] DL28/5/8; see A. R. Myers, 'The Household of Queen Margaret of Anjou, 1452–3', in A. R. Myers, *Crown, Household and Parliament in Fifteenth-Century England* (London, 1985), 135–209.

The Duchy retinue in Staffordshire and Derbyshire had in its heyday been a broad network encompassing most of the gentry families of the Tutbury region under Lancastrian lordship, which, after 1399, meant the person of the king and the power of the crown. The lack of noble contenders for local rule during the first two decades of the century strengthened these direct links between the region's gentry and royal authority.[261] When Margaret came to establish herself in the north midlands, however, the region had experienced three decades without personal royal lordship. For the last twenty years of this period, control of the Duchy estates had been delegated to Buckingham, who had failed to reconstitute local Lancastrian networks to such an extent that violent conflict had broken out among former Duchy families, and that Walter Blount, the steward of the Peak, was now the one committed Yorkist in the region. It is true that several leading magnates now had territorial interests in the area,[262] and it was with these magnates that the queen surrounded herself as she established her court at Coventry in the later 1450s. However, during the previous three decades it had become apparent that, certainly in the case of Buckingham, territorial interests were not in themselves sufficient to secure effective regional lordship. The duke's presence at the queen's side by no means guaranteed that, should political crisis lead to war, the local gentry would be with them.

It has been suggested that in Warwickshire the increasingly confrontational and partisan politics of these years produced a divergence between the interests of the gentry and those of the magnates, who had previously played a significant part in directing local affairs. Increasingly, 'neutrality was not an option that was open to the nobility'; for the gentry, however, it was almost their only safeguard against protracted disorder and political uncertainty. It seems that, as the magnates' demands for support began to magnify the strains in local society (where once their lordship had helped to contain conflict), the gentry began to turn instead to co-operation through 'horizontal' networks as the primary source of regional stability.[263] In Staffordshire and Derbyshire, the background against which the events of 1456–9 unfolded was somewhat different, in that the local gentry had had to navigate the political waters of the previous two decades with little help from magnate lordship. Indeed, some gentry families had apparently thought that partisan support would be available to them earlier in the decade, and had largely been disappointed. Crucially, their attempts to secure such lordship in 1454 and 1456 had taken place when at least the

---

[261] See above, Chs. 6, 7.1.

[262] See above, at nn. 257–8.

[263] Carpenter, *Locality and Polity*, 478–83 (quotation from 478).

semblance of a unified royal authority still existed. Now, however, the queen was seeking to turn the region into a bastion of factional rule—in a sense, to turn the clock back, so that the Duchy estates once more supported a partisan interest rather than a universally representative authority. For the gentry to secure partisan backing in their own affairs therefore meant committing themselves irrevocably to one of the competing poles of authority which were dividing the polity at a national level.[264] Confronted with these raised stakes, they seem to have returned to the mode of self-regulation which had been forced on them in the 1440s by Buckingham's absenteeism. In the process, as was the case in Warwickshire, bridges were built across some of the enmities which had divided local society earlier in the 1450s.

Walter Blount seems initially to have been active in the attempt to secure legal redress for the death of Roland Blount, inundating King's Bench in November 1456 with bills against the alleged murderer, Henry Curson.[265] Nevertheless, the Blounts' isolation, which had resulted from the events of 1453–4, seems gradually to have lessened. In August 1456 Thomas Blount witnessed a local grant in which one of the feoffees was Nicholas Fitzherbert, whose family had been involved in the Elvaston raid two years earlier.[266] Between 1456 and 1458 Edward Longford, the brother of the leader of the raid, was active in his capacity as feoffee for Ralph Shirley in co-operation with his fellow trustees, Shirley's father-in-law Sir Thomas Blount and the latter's sons Walter and Thomas.[267] Remarkably, in view of the murder of Roland Blount, in October 1457 Walter Blount was acting as a co-feoffee with Thomas and John Curson.[268]

The death of Ralph Basset by the end of 1455 also seems to have facilitated some degree of *rapprochement* between his family and the Meverells.[269] In 1456–7 his heir William and Sampson Meverell's son Thomas acted together as witnesses of a lease granted by Nicholas

---

[264] Watts, *Henry VI*, 331–50.

[265] For the murder, see above, at n. 237. Although the accused did appear in court that term, pleading self-defence, the case had still not been tried a year later: KB27/782 Coram Rege roti. 52–52v, 85–85v, 86–86v, 90–90v, 95; Rex rot. 8; KB27/786 Coram Rege roti. 83v, 109; Rex roti. 27, 28v.

[266] The grant was made by John Sacheverell: DRO D518M/T73; see above, at nn. 203, 211.

[267] W. W. Longford, 'Some Notes on the Family History of Nicholas Longford', *Transactions of the Historic Society of Lancashire and Cheshire*, 86 (1934), 63; LRO 26D53/192, 503; LRO 72'30 vol. i unnumbered deed (31 Dec. 36 Henry VI); see above, n. 176.

[268] Blount and the Cursons were trustees for Thomas Okeover. It is possible that these were Thomas and John Curson of Croxall rather than of Kedleston, the branch of the family responsible for the attack on Roland Blount. However, the identification of these Cursons with the Kedleston family seems plausible, since John Curson of Kedleston was connected by marriage with Okeover, and had witnessed a deed for him as recently as Dec. 1455. DRO D231M/E482 (printed in Jeayes (ed.), *Derbyshire Charters*, 21 [161]); D231M/E480 (*Derbyshire Charters*, 271 [2137]); Rowney, 'The Cursons', 108, 113.

[269] Jeayes (ed.), *Derbyshire Charters*, 270 [2136].

Longford to Thomas Foljambe.[270] William Vernon and John Gresley were also apparently able to lay aside their differences during these years, witnessing deeds together, for example, in 1457, 1459, and 1460.[271] It may be, of course, that this latter case indicates that Buckingham's arbitration of 1455 had been successful,[272] but in the light of the duke's record it seems appropriate to take into account the indications that the region's gentry were turning to increased co-operation in the attempt to preserve local stability. This self-reliance was, in one case at least, expressed in terms which explicitly recognized the fact that mutual support was a necessity when sources of national authority were neither unified nor dependable. In the deed of 1456–7 mentioned above, when Nicholas Longford leased lands to his son-in-law Thomas Foljambe, he added a clause specifying that if Thomas 'should be troubled or hindered by the lord king, Richard, duke of York or whomever else', he was to receive compensation.[273]

This co-operation undoubtedly had its limits. Conflict was renewed between the Bassets and Meverells at the end of 1457, possibly over the fact that William Basset seems to have claimed some of the Meverell estates.[274] According to Basset, he was assaulted in November 1457 by Thomas Meverell and the latter's father-in-law Nicholas Montgomery, and Meverell in turn brought counter-charges against Basset.[275] However, even where, as in this instance, disputes did persist into the later 1450s, there were no incidents on anything like the scale of the early years of the decade, or even of the 1440s.[276] The spectre of national civil war was apparently looming so large that the gentry realized the benefits of at least some degree of regional co-operation.

In 1459 political division became armed opposition, as the queen seized control of government and the Yorkists withdrew to prepare for

[270] NA DDFJ 4/5/2 (printed in Jeayes (ed.), *Derbyshire Charters*, 187 [1512]). In 1457 Thomas Meverell was able to secure the reversal of an outlawry which had been passed against him in the course of the feud in 1450: KB27/786 Rex rot. 7.

[271] DRO D156M/150; DRO D410M Box 2/87; Jeayes (ed.), *Derbyshire Charters*, 198 [1596] (cf. Wright, *The Derbyshire Gentry*, 215–16).

[272] For which, see above, at n. 244.

[273] 'vexetur aut impediatur per dominum Regem, Ricardum Ducem Eboracensium aut alios quoscumque': NA DDFJ 4/5/2 (this clause is not included in Jeayes's calendar: see above, n. 270).

[274] Basset had apparently acquired a title to these lands through his family's connection with Richard Meverell, who had not supported his brother Sampson in the course of the conflict: BL Add. Ch. 57231; cf. L. Morsbach, 'Eine englische Urkunde aus dem Jahre 1470', in K. Malone and M. B. Ruud (eds.), *Studies in English Philology* (Minneapolis, 1929), 378–9; Rowney, 'Staffordshire Political Community', 311.

[275] KB27/790 Coram Rege roti. 42, 48, 54–54v, 86, 96; G. Wrottesley (ed.), 'Extracts from the Plea Rolls, 34 Henry VI–14 Edward IV', *Collections for a History of Staffordshire*, William Salt Archaeological Society, new series, 4 (1901), 110; cf. KB29/88 m. 33.

[276] Cf. Wright, *The Derbyshire Gentry*, 137–8, and similar conclusions for Warwickshire in Carpenter, *Locality and Polity*, 613–14.

confrontation.[277] At the end of May the king and queen arrived at Coventry, where a council of the lords, excluding York, Warwick, and Salisbury, was held in June.[278] The opportunity seems to have been taken at this point to demonstrate the regional authority wielded by the lords about the queen; there is little else to explain the fact that, after seventeen years of conflict, Buckingham, accompanied by the earl of Shrewsbury, finally sought to arbitrate between the Meverells and the Bassets on 10 June.[279] The commissions of the peace issued for Staffordshire and Derbyshire in March 1460 were little changed, apart from the omission of the Yorkist lords.[280]

Despite the fact that the gentry of the two shires were co-operating as they always had with the regional hierarchy in the processes of government, it became clear during 1459 and 1460 that they were not prepared to fight. The greatest representation of local men on the battlefield, unsurprisingly, was at Blore Heath, the one battle to take place within Staffordshire. Lord Audley, who had only ever been a nominal presence in the shire, was killed fighting for the king, as was John Egerton. With them in the Lancastrian army were John, Lord Dudley, and John Gresley.[281] The only local gentleman known to have been present at Ludford in October 1459 was Walter Blount, who was fighting for the Yorkists.[282] The backbone of what Lancastrian support there was in the region was all but destroyed by the battle of Northampton in July 1460, when Buckingham and Shrewsbury were killed.[283] Audley's son and heir had already joined the Yorkists by the time of the battle; Dudley was a member of Warwick's retinue by

---

[277] Griffiths, *Henry VI*, 807–8, 817–19; Watts, *Henry VI*, 348–50.

[278] Griffiths, *Henry VI*, 777, 817; B. P. Wolffe, *Henry VI* (London, 1981), 317; Watts, *Henry VI*, 350.

[279] Award printed in Morsbach, *Mittelenglische Originalurkunden*, 50–2. Both sides were to abandon all actions against the other, and William Basset was to pay Thomas Meverell £20. Unsurprisingly, the settlement did not last. Henry Grey of Codnor made another award between the two in 1469 (printed in Morsbach, 'Eine englische Urkunde', 378–9).

[280] William Vernon was given a place for the first time on the Staffordshire bench, while John Gresley was briefly restored to the commission in Derbyshire. Gresley was omitted again when a new commission was issued in May. John Curson in Derbyshire and the Stafford servants Harper, Comberford, Hampton, and Arblaster in Staffordshire all kept their places. Vernon, Curson, and Gresley had also been appointed to the anti-Yorkist commission of array in Derbyshire the previous December, as had Harper, Hampton, and Arblaster with the veteran Sampson Meverell in Staffordshire; Buckingham and Shrewsbury led the commissions in both shires, with the addition of Dudley in Staffordshire and of Beaumont in Derbyshire: *CPR 1452–61*, 558–9, 663–4, 677.

[281] Rowney, 'Staffordshire Political Community', 443. Most of the gentlemen known to have taken part in the battle seem to have been from Cheshire, the queen's recent recruiting-ground, rather than Staffordshire: Davies (ed.), *An English Chronicle*, 80; Gillespie, 'Cheshire-men at Blore Heath', 79–85; Griffiths, *Henry VI*, 820–1.

[282] Rowney, 'Staffordshire Political Community', 443. Blount secured a general pardon two months later: *CPR 1452–61*, 568.

[283] *Complete Peerage*, ii. 389; xi. 705.

November; and, of the few local gentry who had earlier been prepared to take up arms with Buckingham and the queen, John Gresley was a member of the Yorkist commission of the peace appointed in Derbyshire in December 1460.[284]

The north midlands had once been among the heartlands of Lancastrian power, and had provided the backbone of the army which established the Lancastrian monarchy in 1399.[285] Henry IV had displayed his complete commitment to the powerful Duchy network in the region, a network which his son succeeded in assimilating into a unified structure of local authority under royal control. Four decades after the latter's death, the region's gentry, worn down by the strain placed on local society by the vacuity of the king and the ineptitude of the duke to whom regional rule had been delegated in his stead, were no longer prepared to fight in defence of the Lancastrian crown. The death of Buckingham, leaving his 5-year-old grandson as his heir, and the abrupt separation of the Duchy from the dynasty whose personal inheritance it was, paved the way for sweeping changes in local hierarchies during the following years, with the expansion of the sphere of interest of Richard, earl of Warwick, and the arrival in the region of George, duke of Clarence, and William, Lord Hastings.[286] It is symptomatic of the profound dislocation in regional society which occurred under the disastrous rule of Henry VI that the only local gentleman to declare unequivocally for York in the later 1450s—a man who, elevated to the peerage as Lord Mountjoy and married to the widowed duchess of Buckingham, was to become a major player in the region under the new regime—was Walter Blount, the grandson and namesake of one of Henry IV's leading Lancastrian retainers.[287]

---

[284] Rowney, 'Staffordshire Political Community', 443–4; *DKR* 48, 'Calendar of French Rolls, Henry VI', 444; *CPR 1452–61*, 663–4.

[285] See above, Ch. 6.

[286] *Complete Peerage*, ii. 389; Somerville, *History of the Duchy*, 230–1, 233, 540; Carpenter, *Locality and Polity*, 487–527; C. Carpenter, 'The Duke of Clarence and the Midlands', *Midland History*, 11 (1986); I. Rowney, 'Resources and Retaining in Yorkist England: William, Lord Hastings and the Honour of Tutbury', in A. J. Pollard (ed.), *Property and Politics* (Gloucester, 1984); I. Rowney, 'The Hastings Affinity in Staffordshire and the Honour of Tutbury', *BIHR* 57 (1984); Wright, *The Derbyshire Gentry*, 75–82, 87–9, 102–7, 116–17.

[287] See above, Ch. 6.1 at n. 12; *Complete Peerage*, ix. 334–6.

9
Conclusion

Possession of 'incomparably the greatest of all affinities'[1] allowed Henry IV to seize the throne in 1399, but in the context of the attempt to establish a new Lancastrian monarchy this formidable political resource was a double-edged sword. In a society where the hierarchies of government, both formal and informal, depended fundamentally on the universal and universally representative authority of the crown, the king's leadership of a private, regional affinity threatened to compromise the credibility of his claim to the public power of the monarchy. The reigns of the three Lancastrian kings reveal a variety of responses to the task of combining private, regional Lancastrian lordship with public, national Lancastrian kingship.

One such response was an attempt to preserve the private power of the Duchy intact by maintaining the Lancastrian affinity in its existing form—in effect, an attempt to tackle the tensions between the king's two roles head on. This, in general, was the approach adopted by Henry IV. It was the Duchy retinue which had secured Henry the crown, and his dependence on their loyalty meant that he was not prepared to compromise his commitment to his Lancastrian retainers because of his new public responsibilities to the realm as a whole. Indeed, he could not afford to do so, since, in the turbulent years after 1399, the support of the Duchy affinity was crucial to the survival of the regime and to the establishment of his authority as king. The double bind in which Henry found himself was evident at a national level in the financial turmoil which beset his government in the early years of the reign. His possession of the valuable lands of the Duchy inspired the demand that the king should 'live of his own', a chorus which Henry himself had encouraged with a rash promise in 1399, but the cost of rewarding the men who had won him the throne meant that it was a promise he could not keep. In this case, though the Duchy appeared to contemporaries to be a substantial asset to the Lancastrian crown, it seems rather to have provoked demands it could not satisfy.

However, the tensions inherent in Henry's position were most significant at the level of local government. Here, it seems to have been demands made by Henry himself which the Duchy could not entirely

---

[1] S. J. Payling, *Political Society in Lancastrian England* (Oxford, 1991), 219.

fulfil. He seems to have assumed—or, in the throes of securing his hold on the throne, perhaps had no alternative but to assume—that the Lancastrian affinity which had served him and his father so well could be used to maintain direct control of those areas where the Duchy connection had a substantial stake in regional affairs. The risk he ran in deciding to use his personal retinue as an agent of local control was that this would exacerbate the tensions which already existed between the public and private aspects of his authority. In the short term, these tensions were likely to prove containable, since the vast powers with which the king could reinforce his private regional authority allowed him a greater latitude in the exercise of his rule than a noble could hope for. Nevertheless, the potential repercussions of using royal power to push those tensions to the limit were far more serious than any stemming from merely noble misrule.

The effects of Henry's delegation of local authority to the Lancastrian retinue were shaped by the differing political circumstances of the areas involved, and the problems of combining the roles of king and magnate varied accordingly. Perhaps the most manageable situation was that which Henry encountered in Derbyshire, where there were few other sources of local lordship, and where the extensive and broadly representative Lancastrian affinity had already dominated the county for several decades. In the absence of competing local interests, there was little incompatibility between Henry's role as king and as lord of the Lancastrians, whose regional dominance was legitimate and uncontroversial. However, the neighbouring county of Staffordshire offers an example of another, more problematic configuration of authority in an area where the king's private influence was strong. There, the Duchy retinue was based only around the Tutbury lands in the east of the shire. Comprehensive local representation was achieved during the early years of the reign through power-sharing with the earl of Stafford in the west of the county, but after his death in 1403 this political balance was lost. Henry's response was to hand over the rule of the shire almost exclusively to his Lancastrian retainers, whether out of political conviction or because, buffeted by ill health and repeated rebellion, he had little opportunity to formulate a more sophisticated policy. The fact that the Duchy retinue to which local government had been delegated was too restricted in terms of both territory and personnel to represent the shire as a whole meant that royal authority no longer appeared to be a universal and public force, but was instead apparently being manipulated in the interests of partisan lordship. The exercise of his private Lancastrian authority was compromising Henry's status as king, and violence on the part of those excluded from local political structures was the result. The events of these years clearly demonstrated that the exploitation of royal authority to buttress the power of a private affinity which did not otherwise have the resources to control a region was not a viable form of local rule.

The attempt to preserve the Duchy as a private interest in local affairs after its lord became king therefore seems to have been problematic, and sometimes untenable. A different approach was, however, possible. The private power of the Duchy could be assimilated into a wider public authority—a strategy which, although it compromised the degree of direct control which the Lancastrian establishment afforded its lord, correspondingly dissolved the tensions between the roles of magnate and king, incorporating the one within the overarching authority of the other. This approach is evident from the beginning of the reign of Henry V. Although he confirmed the legal status of the Duchy as the king's private possession, he immediately began to broaden the Lancastrian connection and to open up the Duchy establishment. In central government, the Duchy's privileged financial position was removed. Its previously self-regulating administration was subjected to stringent royal control, and the decision to give priority to the financial value of the Duchy, rather than to its role as a source of loyal service, meant that for the first time Lancastrian revenues made a significant contribution to royal finances.

At a regional level, Henry broadened the range of his local associates, taking care to retain the support of his father's retainers, but also welcoming the service of men who had previously been excluded from Duchy circles. In Staffordshire, he included in local administration for the first time those who had led the attacks on the local Lancastrians during his father's reign. The new king's willingness to allow the Duchy affinity to be assimilated fully into regional society enabled him to control a broad sphere of influence stretching from Staffordshire into Derbyshire and across into Duchy-dominated Nottinghamshire, a power bloc based on his possession of the Lancastrian estates but subject to an authority that was unequivocally royal and fully representative. In other words, Henry's acceptance that the maintenance of direct control of the Lancastrian affinity as a private resource belonging to the person of the king was not fully compatible with the preservation of universal royal authority allowed him to assimilate the Duchy into a public hierarchy of power in which the king was able to exploit all the resources at his disposal to the benefit of the crown.

Perhaps the most interesting example of this adaptation of private interests to serve the public power of the king can be found in East Anglia under both Henry IV and Henry V. John of Gaunt had made no attempt to establish his lordship as a controlling force in Norfolk, but this allowed his son to build up from scratch a local affinity which owed its allegiance to the Lancastrian lordship of Henry as king, rather than having to negotiate an uneasy compromise between the demands of private, partisan lordship and his new royal authority over the realm as a whole. Because virtually all the noble interests in Suffolk were in abeyance during the early years of the century, this affinity was able to extend its influence across the region under a powerful hierarchy—including the eminent local knight Thomas Erpingham, the 'royal' magnate Thomas Beaufort, and the prince of Wales—through which the authority of the crown was delegated. By the end of the reign of Henry V, the territorial interests of the Duchy formed one element in the complex web of public and private authority which formed the crown–Duchy connection in East Anglia, an extraordinarily broad and cohesive network which had peacefully ruled and represented the region for two decades.

The 'royal affinity' which developed in East Anglia during the early years of the century formed a stable and successful structure of local control and posed no threat to the central role in the polity played by the crown. However, it is important to recognize the crucial differences which distinguished the crown–Duchy connection in East Anglia from private magnate affinities or from the Duchy affinity in areas such as the north midlands. In the latter cases, local influence was secured primarily by territorial power, and the cohesion of the affinity which developed around that territorial power was underpinned by the personal and essentially private authority of a single lord. By contrast, although the Duchy lands in northern Norfolk were an essential pre-requisite of the development of the crown–Duchy connection in East Anglia, it was the ubiquitous public authority of the crown which enabled this network to expand until it dominated political society in both Norfolk and Suffolk. Moreover, the universality of royal authority was protected from the taint of partisanship not only by the fact that the connection was so broadly representative of local society, but also because the delegation of regional lordship to eminent local representatives of the crown meant that the king could avoid any necessity for involvement in the minutiae of local affairs, and thus preserve his role as guarantor of justice to all his subjects.

The problem of the relationship between the public and private aspects of the king's authority reasserted itself strongly during the crises of Henry VI's reign, since the two elements could only be combined into a workable unity through the active participation of the king. Because of the almost complete passivity of Henry VI, the polity had to find ways of directing itself, and the public authority of the crown was therefore managed by a succession of private interests. This situation produced a redoubling of the original problem. Whereas previously it had been the king who had to maintain his public authority while simultaneously controlling his own private resources, now private individuals were attempting to embody the authority of the crown in order to carry out the same task in place of a king who was failing to assert his own will. The tensions produced by this hybrid authority, formed from a compound of public and private, royal and non-royal interests, played an important role in the disorder which developed during the late 1440s and 1450s in regions where the king was a substantial landowner.

East Anglia provides a particularly interesting example, since the duke of Suffolk was attempting to embody a threefold authority there during the 1440s. His pre-eminence in the royal administration was matched by his control of the Duchy lands in northern Norfolk, and both in turn bolstered his substantial territorial power as one of the foremost landowners in Suffolk. His control of East Anglia in the absence of effective royal direction for more than a decade was remarkable, and owed much to the support and continued vitality of the crown–Duchy connection, which remained highly representative of local society. However, the attempt in central and regional government to circumvent the king's incapacity through the management of royal power by the nobility could not adequately reproduce the public and universally representative authority of the crown.[2] Thus, Suffolk was unable to formulate an adequate response to the ill-managed regional challenge of the duke of Norfolk or to the aggressive opportunism of Thomas Daniel, since the responsibility of the crown (represented locally by Suffolk) to arbitrate and enforce a representative division of power conflicted with the needs of his personal local lordship. The contradictions inherent in Suffolk's position contributed to the increasing stresses apparent in East Anglian society in the later 1440s. Nevertheless, the abnormalities of Henry VI's rule were not explicitly apparent to the nobility for much of the reign. The duke of Norfolk seems to have assumed that he himself should inherit the rule of the entire region after his rival's fall, despite the fact that control of the shire of Norfolk was not, and had never been, a viable prospect on the basis of the Mowbray lands alone. The conflict between Norfolk's ambitions and the surviving power of the de la Pole affinity, now cut off from much of the direct access to royal authority which it had enjoyed during the 1440s but still in control of both the de la Pole estates in Suffolk and the Duchy interest in Norfolk, lay behind much of the instability evident in East Anglian politics during the 1450s. The local power of the Lancastrian crown was such that, without the royal direction which could combine private and public interests into a workable

[2] J. L. Watts, *Henry VI and the Politics of Kingship* (Cambridge, 1996), 195–9 and *passim*.

system of regional government, political consensus in this most competitive of local societies could not be secured.

In the north midlands, the structure of local government created by Henry V, which harnessed the king's private territorial interests in support of the public power of the crown in the region, could not be maintained without constant royal supervision. During the 1420s and 1430s, therefore, noble interests began to play an increasingly influential role in local politics, filling the vacuum left by the loss of Henry V's personal authority. Since there appeared to be no prospect that royal control of the north midlands would be reconstituted under Henry VI's adult rule, the region was included in the attempt made in 1437 to 'manage' the localities on the king's behalf by creating a series of power blocs under magnate control. The king's private estates were used to supplement the regional influence of the territorial nobility, who were having to act together to constitute the crown's public authority at both a national and a local level, and the rule of the Duchy-dominated areas of the north midlands was delegated to the duke of Buckingham. Though undoubtedly a means by which the devastating effects of the king's incapacity could be contained, at least in the short term, this strategy for managing regional rule placed enormous strain upon local society. Under normal circumstances, regional lordship which was less than competent could be supported or corrected by the universal authority of the crown. If regional lordship simultaneously represented the universal authority of the crown, however, no safety-valve remained to deal with tensions in local society should that lordship prove inadequate. Unlike the duke of Suffolk in East Anglia, Buckingham faced no rival for local rule in Staffordshire and western Derbyshire, but the inadequacies of his lordship nevertheless had profound consequences for regional society. The duke dominated local power structures through his own territorial interests and his Duchy office to such an extent that no one else could intervene. His failure, despite these advantages, to secure the rule of the region meant that the local gentry were left without access to any effective authority. The fact that Buckingham was forced to attempt to represent the king's authority in the region as well as his own, and in the event failed to establish even the latter, played a significant part both in distancing local society from traditions of service to the Lancastrian monarchy in both its public and private capacities, and in estranging the gentry from 'vertical' hierarchies of magnate lordship, since co-operation through 'horizontal' networks increasingly appeared to offer the only reliable chance of maintaining regional stability.

It was in these circumstances that a genuinely 'royal' affinity seems to have developed in the later fifteenth century. The increasing disparity between the interests of the nobility and gentry meant that for the first time there were disjunctions in the informal hierarchies which connected centre and locality—disjunctions which offered opportunities for a king who wished to establish a closer relationship with members of the local gentry. Since the gentry had been forced during the mid-century crisis to manage their affairs without consistent noble direction, they were experienced enough under Edward IV and his successors to adopt this state as a permanent one and to operate instead under the necessarily looser direction of the crown.[3] Under Edward, membership of the royal household increasingly became a means by which direct connections could be established and maintained between lesser landowners in the localities and the king. Though significant areas of the country continued to be managed by members of the nobility, the power of the individuals concerned—Hastings, a nobleman newly created by the king, for example, in the midlands, or Gloucester, the king's brother, in the north—remained intrinsically connected to the authority of the crown.[4]

This change in the polity must be seen for what it was—not as part of a gradually evolving 'bastard feudal policy' which had become the basis of royal power with the accession of Henry IV at the head of his own affinity, but as the result of a prolonged period of political crisis which resulted in a realignment of the relationship between the public authority of the crown and its subjects in the localities. The estates of the Duchy of Lancaster and the retinue they supported were unquestionably a powerful resource in the hands of the Lancastrian kings, but it was only when they were assimilated into an incontrovertibly public, national authority that their value was fully realized. It is perhaps no accident that a national 'royal affinity' developed only after 1461, when the Duchy had finally been separated from the Lancastrian dynasty. Edward IV, unlike his predecessors, held the Duchy not as a private possession but in right of the crown.[5] To the new king, therefore, the Lancastrian estates formed merely one part of his royal inheritance, and Lancastrian lordship one aspect of his royal authority. The Duchy was no longer a personal power base held by the king in his 'body natural'; its incorporation into the 'body politic' of the crown was complete.

[3] C. Carpenter, *Locality and Polity* (Cambridge, 1992), 609–10, 634–7

[4] R. Horrox, *Richard III* (Cambridge, 1989), 14–17; D. A. L. Morgan, 'The King's Affinity in the Polity of Yorkist England', *TRHS* 5th series, 23 (1973), 9–11, 18–21, 24; for Hastings, see references given above, Ch. 8 n. 286. That this was a general development within the public processes of government is demonstrated by the fact that it took place not only in regions where the king was a substantial landowner, but also in areas such as Kent and the north-east where there was no local abundance of crown estates: Carpenter, *Locality and Polity*, 635.

[5] E. H. Kantorowicz, *The King's Two Bodies* (Princeton, 1957), 9–10, 403–4.

Bibliography

UNPRINTED PRIMARY SOURCES

London: British Library

Additional MSS
Additional Charters
Cotton
Egerton
Harley
Stowe

London: Public Record Office

C1	Early Chancery Proceedings
C81	Chancery, Warrants for the Great Seal, series I
C139	Chancery, Inquisitions *Post Mortem*, Henry VI
C146	Chancery, Deeds, series C
C219	Chancery, Election Indentures
CHES3	Palatinate of Chester, Inquisitions *Post Mortem*
CP40	Common Pleas, Plea Rolls
DL28	Duchy of Lancaster, Various Accounts
DL29	Duchy of Lancaster, Ministers' Accounts
DL37	Duchy of Lancaster, Chancery Rolls
DL42	Duchy of Lancaster, Registers
DL43	Duchy of Lancaster, Rentals and Surveys
E28	Exchequer, Council and Privy Seal
E101	Exchequer, Various Accounts
E163	Exchequer, Miscellanea
E179	Exchequer, Subsidy Rolls
E210	Exchequer, Deeds, series D
E403	Exchequer, Enrolments and Registers of Issues
E404	Exchequer, Warrants for Issue
JUST1	Assize Rolls
KB9	King's Bench, Ancient Indictments
KB27	King's Bench, *Coram Rege* Rolls
KB29	King's Bench, Controlment Rolls
SC6	Special Collections, Ministers' and Receivers' Accounts
SC8	Special Collections, Ancient Petitions

Aberystwyth: National Library of Wales

Peniarth MS 280

Derby: Derby Central Library

Every
Jeayes, I. H. (ed.), 'Descriptive Catalogue of the Charters and Muniments in the possession of R. W. Chandos-Pole esq. at Radbourne Hall' (MS copy)

Ipswich: Suffolk Record Office

T1 and V5   Miscellaneous manorial MSS (Redstone catalogue)

Leicester: Leicestershire Record Office

26D53	Ferrers of Staunton Harold
72'30	Charters and deeds
DE40	Collections formerly of the City of Leicester Museum
DE170	Fisher
DE2242/3	Additional Ferrers MSS

Matlock: Derbyshire Record Office

D37	Turbutt and Revell
D77	Gresley
D156	Burdet of Foremark
D158	Beresford of Fenny Bentley
D231	Okeover
D258	Chandos Pole Gell
D410	Vernon of Sudbury
D518	Harrington
D779	Moody and Woolley

Norwich: Norfolk Record Office

Le Strange
NCC	Norwich Consistory Court, Register of Wills
NRS	Norfolk Record Society
WKC	Ketton-Cremer
Phi	Phillips

Nottingham: Nottingham University Library

Mi   Middleton

Nottingham: Nottinghamshire Archives

DDFJ   Foljambe of Osberton
DDP   Portland

Oxford: Magdalen College

Fastolf MSS
Guton deeds
Hickling MSS

San Marino, California: Huntington Library

HAM   Hastings manorial MSS
HAP   Hastings personal and family papers

Stafford: Staffordshire Record Office

D260   Hatherton
D641   Stafford
D1721   Bagot

Stafford: William Salt Library

HM Chetwynd

PRINTED PRIMARY SOURCES

Annales Ricardi Secundi et Henrici Quarti, J. de Trokelowe et Anon., *Chronica et Annales*, ed. H. T. Riley (Rolls Series, 1866).
ARMITAGE-SMITH, S. (ed.), *John of Gaunt's Register, 1372–6*, 2 vols., Camden Society, 3rd series, 20–1 (1911).
ANSTIS, J., *The Register of the Most Noble Order of the Garter*, 2 vols. (London, 1724).
BARR, H. (ed.), *The Piers Plowman Tradition* (London, 1993).
Calendar of the Charter Rolls, 6 vols. (London, 1903–27).
Calendar of the Close Rolls, 61 vols. (London, 1892–1963).
Calendar of the Fine Rolls, 22 vols. (London, 1911–62).
Calendar of the Patent Rolls, 55 vols. (London, 1891–1916).
Calendarium Inquisitionum Post Mortem, 4 vols. (London, 1806–28).
CARRINGTON, A., and ANDREW, W. J., 'A Lancastrian Raid in the Wars of the Roses', *Journal of the Derbyshire Archaeological and Natural History Society*, 34 (1912), 33–49.
——and POYNTON, E. M., 'A Lancastrian Raid in the Wars of the Roses', *Journal of the Derbyshire Archaeological and Natural History Society*, 35 (1913), 207–44.

DAVIES, J. S. (ed.), *An English Chronicle of the Reigns of Richard II, Henry IV, Henry V, and Henry VI*, Camden Society, 1st series, 64 (1856).

DAVIS, N. (ed.), *Paston Letters and Papers of the Fifteenth Century*, 2 vols. (Oxford, 1971–6).

A Descriptive Catalogue of Ancient Deeds . . ., 6 vols. (London, 1890–1915).

DU BOULAY, F. R. H. (ed.), *Documents Illustrative of Medieval Kentish Society*, Kent Archaeological Society, 18 (1964).

ELLIS, H. (ed.), *Original Letters Illustrative of English History*, 2nd series, i (reprint, London, 1969).

FLENLEY, R. (ed.), *Six Town Chronicles of England* (Oxford, 1911).

GAIRDNER, J. (ed.), *Three Fifteenth-Century Chronicles*, Camden Society, new series, 28 (1880).

—— (ed.), *The Paston Letters*, 6 vols. (London, 1904).

GARRATT, H. J. H. (ed.), *Derbyshire Feet of Fines 1323–1546*, Derbyshire Record Society, 11 (1985).

GIVEN-WILSON, C. (trans. and ed.), *Chronicles of the Revolution, 1397–1400* (Manchester, 1993).

—— (trans. and ed.), *The Chronicle of Adam Usk, 1377–1421* (Oxford, 1997).

HARDY, W. (trans. and ed.), *The Charters of the Duchy of Lancaster* (London, 1845).

HARRIS, M. (ed.), 'The Account of the Great Household of Humphrey, First Duke of Buckingham, for the year 1452–3', Camden Miscellany, 28, 4th series, 29 (1984), 1–57.

HARRIS, M. D. (ed.), *The Coventry Leet Book*, Early English Text Society (London, 1907–13).

HARVEY, J. H. (ed.), *William Worcestre: Itineraries* (Oxford, 1969).

Historical Manuscripts Commission, *Report on the Manuscripts of the Duke of Rutland*, i and iv (London, 1888 and 1905).

—— *Report on the Manuscripts of the Marquis of Lothian* (London, 1905).

—— *Report on the Manuscripts of Lord de L'Isle and Dudley*, i (London, 1925).

HUDSON, W., and TINGEY, J. C. (eds.), *The Records of the City of Norwich*, 2 vols. (Norwich, 1906–10).

JACOB, E. F. (ed.), *The Register of Henry Chichele*, 4 vols. (Oxford, 1938–47).

JEAYES, I. H. (ed.), *Descriptive Catalogue of the Charters and Muniments of the Gresley Family* (London, 1895).

—— (ed.), *Descriptive Catalogue of Derbyshire Charters* (London, 1906).

KIRBY, J. L. (ed.), *Calendar of Signet Letters of Henry IV and Henry V (1399–1422)* (London, 1978).

—— (ed.), *Calendar of Inquisitions Post Mortem*, xix (London, 1992).

—— (ed.), *Calendar of Inquisitions Post Mortem*, xx (London, 1995).

List of Escheators for England and Wales, PRO Lists and Indexes, 72 (1971).

List of Sheriffs for England and Wales, PRO Lists and Indexes, 9 (1898).

LODGE, E. C., and SOMERVILLE, R. (eds.), *John of Gaunt's Register, 1379–83*, Camden Society, 3rd series, 56–7 (1937).

MONRO, C. (ed.), *The Letters of Queen Margaret of Anjou . . .*, Camden Society, old series, 86 (London, 1863).

MORSBACH, L. (ed.), *Mittelenglische Originalurkunden von der Chaucer-zeit bis zur Mitte des XV Jahrhunderts* (Heidelberg, 1923).

—— 'Eine englische Urkunde aus dem Jahre 1470', in K. Malone and M. B. Ruud (eds.), *Studies in English Philology* (Minneapolis, 1929), 375–9.

MYERS, A. R., 'The Household of Queen Margaret of Anjou, 1452–3', in A. R. Myers, *Crown, Household and Parliament in Fifteenth-Century England* (London, 1985), 135–209.

NICHOLS, J. (ed.), *A Collection of all the Wills . . . of the Kings and Queens of England* (London, 1780).

NICOLAS, N. H. (ed.), *Testamenta Vetusta*, 2 vols. (London, 1826).

—— (ed.), *Proceedings and Ordinances of the Privy Council of England*, 7 vols. (London, 1834–7).

PLOWDEN, E., *Commentaries or Reports*, 2 vols. (London, 1816).

PRO Lists and Indexes, Suppl. Ser. ix, pt. 2, 'Warrants for Issues, 1399–1485' (New York, 1964).

PUTNAM, B. H. (ed.), *Proceedings Before the Justices of the Peace in the Fourteenth and Fifteenth Centuries*, Ames Foundation (London, 1938).

Reports of the Deputy Keeper of the Public Records, No. 41, 'Calendar of Norman Rolls, Henry V', 671–810 (London, 1880).

—— No. 44, 'Calendar of French Rolls, 1–10 Henry V', 543–638 (London, 1883).

—— No. 48, 'Calendar of French Rolls, Henry VI', 217–450 (London, 1887).

Return of the Name of Every Member of the Lower House of the Parliament of England, 1213–1874, Parliamentary Papers, lxii pts. i–iii (London, 1878).

Rotuli Parliamentorum, 6 vols., Record Commission.

ROUS, J., *The Rous Roll* (reprint, Gloucester, 1980).

RYE, W. (ed.), *A Calendar of the Feet of Fines for Suffolk* (Ipswich, 1900).

SHIRLEY, E. P. (ed.), *Stemmata Shirleiana* (London, 1873).

SMITH, L. T. (ed.), *Expeditions to Prussia and the Holy Land made by Henry, Earl of Derby*, Camden Society, new series, 52 (London, 1894).

STAPLETON, T. (ed.), *The Plumpton Correspondence* (reprint, Gloucester, 1990).

VIRGOE, R. (ed.), 'Some Ancient Indictments in the King's Bench referring to Kent 1450–2', in F. R. H. Du Boulay (ed.), *Documents Illustrative of Medieval Kentish Society* (1964), 214–65.

WRIGHT, T. (ed.), *Political Poems and Songs*, 2 vols., Rolls Series (London, 1859–61).

WROTTESLEY, G. (ed.), 'The Chetwynd Cartulary', *Collections for a History of Staffordshire*, William Salt Archaeological Society, 12 (1891).

—— (ed.), 'Extracts from the Plea Rolls of the Reigns of Richard II and Henry IV', *Collections for a History of Staffordshire*, William Salt Archaeological Society, 15 (1894).

—— (ed.), 'Extracts from the Cheshire Plea Rolls of the Reigns of Edward III, Richard II and Henry IV, and from the De Banco and Coram Rege Rolls of Richard II and Henry IV', *Collections for a History of Staffordshire*, William Salt Archaeological Society, 16 (1895).

—— (ed.), 'Extracts from the Plea Rolls of the Reigns of Henry V and Henry VI', *Collections for a History of Staffordshire*, William Salt Archaeological Society, 17 (1896).

WROTTESLEY, G. (ed.), 'Extracts from the Plea Rolls of the Reign of Henry VI', *Collections for a History of Staffordshire*, William Salt Archaeological Society, new series, 3 (1900).

—— (ed.), 'Extracts from the Plea Rolls, 34 Henry VI—14 Edward IV', *Collections for a History of Staffordshire*, William Salt Archaeological Society, new series, 4 (1901).

PRINTED SECONDARY SOURCES

ACHESON, E., *A Gentry Community: Leicestershire in the Fifteenth Century, c.1422–c.1485* (Cambridge, 1992).

ARCHER, R. E., 'Rich Old Ladies: The Problem of Late Medieval Dowagers', in A. J. Pollard (ed.), *Property and Politics* (Gloucester, 1984), 15–35.

—— 'Parliamentary Restoration: John Mowbray and the Dukedom of Norfolk in 1425', in R. E. Archer and S. Walker (eds.), *Rulers and Ruled in Late Medieval England* (London, 1995), 99–116.

—— (ed.), *Crown, Government and People in the Fifteenth Century* (Stroud, 1995).

—— and Walker, S. (eds.), *Rulers and Ruled in Late Medieval England* (London, 1995).

BARBER, M., 'John Norbury (*c.*1350–1414): An Esquire of Henry IV', *EHR* 68 (1953), 66–76.

BARRON, C. M., 'The Tyranny of Richard II', *BIHR* 41 (1968), 1–18.

—— 'The Quarrel of Richard II with London 1392–7', in F. R. H. Du Boulay and C. M. Barron (eds.), *The Reign of Richard II* (London, 1971), 173–201.

BEAN, J. M. W., *From Lord to Patron: Lordship in Late Medieval England* (Manchester, 1989).

BENNETT, M. J., *Community, Class and Careerism: Cheshire and Lancashire Society in the Age of 'Sir Gawain and the Green Knight'* (Cambridge, 1983).

BLAKE, W. J., 'Fuller's List of Norfolk Gentry', *Norfolk Archaeology*, 32 (1961), 261–91.

BLOMEFIELD, F., *An Essay towards a Topographical History of the County of Norfolk*, 11 vols. (London, 1805–10).

BRIDGEMAN, the Hon. and Rev. Canon, 'A History of the Family of Swynnerton of Swynnerton', *Collections for a History of Staffordshire*, William Salt Archaeological Society, 7 pt. II (1886).

BRITNELL, R. H., and POLLARD, A. J., *The McFarlane Legacy* (Stroud, 1995).

BROWN, A. L., 'The Reign of Henry IV: The Establishment of the Lancastrian Regime', in S. B. Chrimes *et al.* (eds.), *Fifteenth-Century England* (Manchester, 1972), 1–28.

—— 'The English Campaign in Scotland, 1400', in H. Hearder and H. R. Loyn (eds.), *British Government and Administration* (Cardiff, 1974), 40–54.

CAMPBELL, B. M. S., 'The Complexity of Manorial Structure in Medieval Norfolk: A Case Study', *Norfolk Archaeology*, 39 (1986), 225–61.

CARPENTER, C., 'The Beauchamp Affinity: A Study of Bastard Feudalism at Work', *EHR* 95 (1980), 514–32.

—— 'The Duke of Clarence and the Midlands: A Study in the Interplay of Local and National Politics', *Midland History*, 11 (1986), 23–48.

—— *Locality and Polity: A Study of Warwickshire Landed Society, 1401–1499* (Cambridge, 1992).

—— 'Gentry and Community in Medieval England', *Journal of British Studies*, 33 (1994), 340–80.

—— 'Who Ruled the Midlands in the Later Middle Ages?', *Midland History*, 19 (1994), 1–20.

—— 'Political and Constitutional History: Before and After McFarlane', in R. H. Britnell and A. J. Pollard (eds.), *The McFarlane Legacy* (Stroud, 1995), 175–206.

—— *The Wars of the Roses: Politics and the Constitution in England, c.1437–1509* (Cambridge, 1997).

CASTOR, H. R., ' "Walter Blount is gone to serve Traytours": The Sack of Elvaston and the Politics of the North Midlands in 1454', *Midland History*, 19 (1994), 21–39.

—— 'New Evidence on the Grant of Duchy of Lancaster Office to Henry Beauchamp, Earl of Warwick, in 1444', *Historical Research*, 68 (1995), 225–8.

—— 'The Duchy of Lancaster and the Rule of East Anglia, 1399–1440: A Prologue to the Paston Letters', in R. E. Archer (ed.), *Crown, Government and People in the Fifteenth Century* (Stroud, 1995), 53–78.

CATTO, J., 'The King's Servants', in G. L. Harriss (ed.), *Henry V: The Practice of Kingship* (Oxford, 1985), 75–95.

CHENEY, C. R. (ed.), *Handbook of Dates For Students of English History* (reprint, London, 1991).

CHRIMES, S. B., *English Constitutional Ideas in the Fifteenth Century* (Cambridge, 1936).

—— Ross, C. D., and GRIFFITHS, R. A. (eds.), *Fifteenth-Century England 1399–1509* (Manchester, 1972).

CLAYTON, D. J., DAVIES, R. G., and McNIVEN, P. (eds.), *Trade, Devotion and Governance* (Stroud, 1994).

COKAYNE, A. E., *Cokayne Memoranda* (Congleton, 1873).

COKAYNE, G. E., *The Complete Peerage*, ed. H. V. Gibbs *et al.*, 13 vols. (London, 1910–59).

COMPTON REEVES, A., 'Some of Humphrey Stafford's Military Indentures', *Nottingham Medieval Studies*, 16 (1972), 80–91.

CROKE, A., *The Genealogical History of the Croke Family*, 2 vols. (Oxford, 1823).

CROW, M. M., and OLSON, C. C., *Chaucer Life-Records* (Oxford, 1966).

DAVIES, R. R., 'Richard II and the Principality of Chester', in F. R. H. Du Boulay and C. M. Barron (eds.), *The Reign of Richard II* (London, 1971), 256–79.

DU BOULAY, F. R. H., and BARRON, C. M. (eds.), *The Reign of Richard II* (London, 1971).

FLETCHER, J. M. J., 'Sir Sampson Meverill of Tideswell, 1388–1462', *Journal of the Derbyshire Archaeological and Natural History Society*, 30 (1908), 1–22.

FRIEDRICHS, R. L., 'Ralph, Lord Cromwell and the Politics of Fifteenth-Century England', *Nottingham Medieval Studies*, 32 (1988), 207–27.

FRYDE, E. B., GREENWAY, D. E., PORTER, S., and ROY, I. (eds.), *Handbook of British Chronology*, 3rd edn. (London, 1986).

GILLESPIE, J. L., 'Cheshiremen at Blore Heath: A Swan Dive', in J. Rosenthal and C. Richmond (eds.), *People, Politics and Community in the Later Middle Ages* (Gloucester, 1987), 77–89.

GILLINGHAM, J. B., 'Crisis or Continuity? The Structure of Royal Authority in England 1369–1422', in R. Schneider (ed.), *Das Spätmittelalterliche Königtum Im Europäischen Vergleich* (Sigmaringen, 1987), 59–80.

GIVEN-WILSON, C., *The Royal Household and the King's Affinity: Service, Politics and Finance in England, 1360–1413* (New Haven, 1986).

—— 'The King and the Gentry in Fourteenth-Century England', *TRHS* 5th series, 37 (1987), 87–102.

GRAZEBROOK, H. S., 'The Barons of Dudley', *Collections for a History of Staffordshire*, William Salt Archaeological Society, 9 (1888).

GRIFFITHS, R. A., 'Patronage, Politics and the Principality of Wales, 1413–61', in H. Hearder and H. R. Loyn (eds.), *British Government and Administration* (Cardiff, 1974), 69–86.

—— *The Reign of King Henry VI* (London, 1981).

—— (ed.), *Patronage, the Crown and the Provinces* (Gloucester, 1981).

GUNN, S. J., *Charles Brandon, Duke of Suffolk, c.1484–1545* (Oxford, 1988).

GUY, J., *Tudor England* (Oxford, 1988).

HARRISS, G. L., 'The Struggle for Calais: An Aspect of the Rivalry between Lancaster and York', *EHR* 75 (1960), 30–53.

—— *King, Parliament, and Public Finance in Medieval England to 1369* (Oxford, 1975).

—— introduction to K. B. McFarlane, *England in the Fifteenth Century* (London, 1981).

—— 'Financial Policy', in G. L. Harriss (ed.), *Henry V: The Practice of Kingship* (Oxford, 1985), 159–79.

—— 'The King and His Magnates', in G. L. Harriss (ed.), *Henry V: The Practice of Kingship* (Oxford, 1985), 31–51.

—— *Cardinal Beaufort: A Study of Lancastrian Ascendancy and Decline* (Oxford, 1988).

—— (ed.), *Henry V: The Practice of Kingship* (Oxford, 1985).

HARVEY, J. H., 'Richard II and York', in F. R. H. Du Boulay and C. M. Barron (eds.), *The Reign of Richard II* (London, 1971), 202–17.

HAWES, R., and LODER, R., *The History of Framlingham* (Woodbridge, 1798).

HEARDER, H., and LOYN, H. R. (eds.), *British Government and Administration: Studies presented to S. B. Chrimes* (Cardiff, 1974).

HIGHFIELD, J. R. L., and JEFFS, R. (eds.), *The Crown and the Local Communities* (Gloucester, 1981).

HORROX, R., *Richard III: A Study of Service* (Cambridge, 1989).

IVES, E. W., *The Common Lawyers of Pre-Reformation England* (Cambridge, 1983).

JACOB, E. F., *The Fifteenth Century* (Oxford, 1961).

JOHN, E. L. T., 'Sir Thomas Erpingham, East Anglian Society and the Dynastic Revolution of 1399', *Norfolk Archaeology*, 35 (1970), 96–108.

JOHNSON, P. A., *Duke Richard of York 1411–1460* (Oxford, 1988).

JOHNSTON, C. E., 'Sir William Oldhall', *EHR* 25 (1910), 715–22.

KANTOROWICZ, E. H., *The King's Two Bodies: A Study in Medieval Political Theology* (Princeton, 1957).

KINGSFORD, C. L., *Prejudice and Promise in Fifteenth-Century England* (Oxford, 1925).

KIRBY, J. L., *Henry IV of England* (London, 1970).

LANDER, J. R., *Conflict and Stability in Fifteenth-Century England* (London, 1969).

LEWIS, P. S., 'Sir John Fastolf's Lawsuit over Titchwell 1448–55', *Historical Journal*, 1 (1958), 1–20.

LONGFORD, W. W., 'Some Notes on the Family History of Nicholas Longford, Sheriff of Lancashire in 1413', *Transactions of the Historic Society of Lancashire and Cheshire*, 86 (1934), 47–71.

MACCULLOCH, D., *Suffolk and the Tudors: Politics and Religion in an English County 1500–1600* (Oxford, 1986).

MCFARLANE, K. B., *Lancastrian Kings and Lollard Knights* (Oxford, 1972).

—— *The Nobility of Later Medieval England* (Oxford, 1973).

—— *England in the Fifteenth Century: Collected Essays* (London, 1981).

—— '"Bastard Feudalism"', in K. B. McFarlane, *England in the Fifteenth Century* (London, 1981), 23–43.

—— 'Henry V, Bishop Beaufort and the Red Hat, 1417–1421', in K. B. McFarlane, *England in the Fifteenth Century* (London, 1981), 79–113.

—— 'The Investment of Sir John Fastolf's Profits of War', in K. B. McFarlane, *England in the Fifteenth Century* (London, 1981), 175–97.

MCKISACK, M., *The Fourteenth Century* (Oxford, 1959).

MCNIVEN, P., 'Prince Henry and the English Political Crisis of 1412', *History*, 65 (1980), 1–16.

—— 'The Problem of Henry IV's Health 1405–13', *EHR* 100 (1985), 747–72.

MADAN, F., 'The Gresleys of Drakelow', *Collections for a History of Staffordshire*, William Salt Archaeological Society, new series, 1 (London, 1898).

MADDERN, P. C., *Violence and Social Order: East Anglia 1422–1442* (Oxford, 1992).

MADDICOTT, J. R., *Thomas of Lancaster* (Oxford, 1970).

MALONE, K., and RUUD, M. B. (eds.), *Studies in English Philology* (Minneapolis, 1929).

MEDCALF, S. (ed.), *The Context of English Literature: The Later Middle Ages* (London, 1981).

MILNER, J. D., 'Sir Simon Felbrigg KG: The Lancastrian Revolution and Personal Fortune', *Norfolk Archaeology*, 37 (1978), 84–91.

MORGAN, D. A. L., 'The King's Affinity in the Polity of Yorkist England', *TRHS* 5th series, 23 (1973), 1–25.

—— 'The House of Policy: The Political Role of the Late Plantagenet Household, 1422–1485', in D. Starkey (ed.), *The English Court* (London, 1987), 25–70.

MYERS, A. R., *Crown, Household and Parliament in Fifteenth-Century England* (London, 1985).

NICOLAS, H., *History of the Battle of Agincourt* (London, 1833).

PAYLING, S. J., 'Inheritance and Local Politics in the Later Middle Ages: The Case of Ralph, Lord Cromwell, and the Heriz Inheritance', *Nottingham Medieval Studies*, 30 (1986), 67–96.

—— 'Law and Arbitration in Nottinghamshire 1399–1461', in J. Rosenthal and C. Richmond (eds.), *People, Politics and Community in the Later Middle Ages* (Gloucester, 1987), 140–60.

—— *Political Society in Lancastrian England: The Greater Gentry of Nottinghamshire* (Oxford, 1991).

POLLARD, A. J., *North-Eastern England during the Wars of the Roses* (Oxford, 1990).

—— (ed.), *Property and Politics: Essays in Later Medieval English History* (Gloucester, 1984).

—— (ed.), *The Wars of the Roses* (London, 1995).

POWELL, E., 'The Restoration of Law and Order', in G. L. Harriss (ed.), *Henry V: The Practice of Kingship* (Oxford, 1985), 53–74.

—— *Kingship, Law, and Society: Criminal Justice in the Reign of Henry V* (Oxford, 1989).

—— 'After "After McFarlane": The Poverty of Patronage and the Case for Constitutional History', in D. J. Clayton, R. G. Davies, and P. McNiven (eds.), *Trade, Devotion and Governance* (Stroud, 1994), 1–16.

PUGH, T. B., *The Marcher Lordships of South Wales 1415–1536* (Cardiff, 1963).

—— 'The Magnates, Knights and Gentry', in S. B. Chrimes *et al.* (eds.), *Fifteenth-Century England* (Manchester, 1972), 86–128.

RAIMES, A. L., 'Reymes of Overstrand', *Norfolk Archaeology*, 30 (1952), 15–64.

RAWCLIFFE, C., *The Staffords, Earls of Stafford and Dukes of Buckingham, 1394–1521* (Cambridge, 1978).

RICHMOND, C., *John Hopton: A Fifteenth-Century Suffolk Gentleman* (Cambridge, 1981).

—— *The Paston Family in the Fifteenth Century: The First Phase* (Cambridge, 1990).

—— *The Paston Family in the Fifteenth Century: Fastolf's Will* (Cambridge, 1996).

ROGERS, A., 'The Political Crisis of 1401', *Nottingham Medieval Studies*, 12 (1968), 85–96.

ROSENTHAL, J., and RICHMOND, C. (eds.), *People, Politics and Community in the Later Middle Ages* (Gloucester, 1987).

ROSKELL, J. S., 'Sir Richard Vernon of Haddon, Speaker in the Parliament of Leicester, 1426', *Derbyshire Archaeological Journal*, 82 (1962), 43–53.

—— *Parliament and Politics in Late Medieval England*, 3 vols. (London, 1981–3).

ROSS, C. D., *Edward IV* (London, 1974).

—— (ed.), *Patronage, Pedigree and Power* (Gloucester, 1979).

ROWLING, M. A., 'New Evidence on the Disseisin of the Pastons from their Norfolk Manor of Gresham, 1448–1451', *Norfolk Archaeology*, 40 (1989), 302–8.

ROWNEY, I., 'The Cursons of Fifteenth-Century Derbyshire', *Derbyshire Archaeological Journal*, 103 (1983), 107–17.

—— 'Government and Patronage in the Fifteenth Century: Staffordshire 1439–59', *Midland History*, 8 (1983), 49–69.

—— 'The Hastings Affinity in Staffordshire and the Honour of Tutbury', *BIHR* 57 (1984), 35–45.

—— 'Resources and Retaining in Yorkist England: William, Lord Hastings and the Honour of Tutbury', in A. J. Pollard (ed.), *Property and Politics* (Gloucester, 1984), 139–55.

SAUL, N., 'The Commons and the Abolition of Badges', *Parliamentary History*, 9 (1990), 302–15.

—— *Richard II* (New Haven and London, 1997).

SCHNEIDER, R. (ed.), *Das Spätmittelalterliche Königtum Im Europäischen Vergleich* (Sigmaringen, 1987).

SMITH, A. H., *County and Court: Government and Politics in Norfolk 1558–1603* (Oxford, 1974).

SMITH, A. R., 'Litigation and Politics: Sir John Fastolf's Defence of his English Property', in A. J. Pollard (ed.), *Property and Politics* (Gloucester, 1984), 59–75.

—— ' "The Greatest Man of That Age": The Acquisition of Sir John Fastolf's East Anglian Estates', in R. E. Archer and S. Walker (eds.), *Rulers and Ruled in Late Medieval England* (London, 1995), 137–54.

SOMERVILLE, R., *History of the Duchy of Lancaster*, i (London, 1953).

STARKEY, D., 'The Age of the Household: Politics, Society and the Arts *c.*1350–*c.*1550', in S. Medcalf (ed.), *The Context of English Literature* (London, 1981), 225–90.

—— (ed.), *The English Court: From the Wars of the Roses to the Civil War* (London, 1987).

STEEL, A., *Richard II* (Cambridge, 1941).

—— *The Receipt of the Exchequer 1377–1485* (Cambridge, 1954).

STEPHEN, L., and LEE, S. (eds.), *Dictionary of National Biography*, 63 vols. (London, 1885–1900).

STOREY, R. L., *The End of the House of Lancaster* (London, 1966).

STUDD, J. R., 'The Lord Edward and King Henry III', *BIHR* 50 (1977), 4–19.

THOMSON, J. A. F., 'John de la Pole, Duke of Suffolk', *Speculum*, 54 (1979), 528–42.

THURGOOD, J. M., introduction to M. Harris (ed.), 'The Account of the Great Household of Humphrey, First Duke of Buckingham, for the year 1452–3', Camden Miscellany, 28, 4th series, 29 (1984).

TOUT, T. F., 'The Earldoms under Edward I', *TRHS*, new series, 8 (1894), 129–55.

TUCK, J. A., *Richard II and the English Nobility* (London, 1973).

VIRGOE, R., *East Anglian Society and the Political Community of Late Medieval England* (Norwich, 1997).

—— 'Three Suffolk Parliamentary Elections of the Mid-Fifteenth Century', in R. Virgoe, *East Anglian Society* (Norwich, 1997), 53–64 (first printed in *BIHR* 39 (1966), 185–96).

—— 'The Divorce of Sir Thomas Tuddenham', in R. Virgoe, *East Anglian*

Society (Norwich, 1997), 117–31 (first printed in *Norfolk Archaeology*, 34 (1969), 406–18).

VIRGOE, R., 'The Crown and Local Government: East Anglia under Richard II', in R. Virgoe, *East Anglian Society* (Norwich, 1997), 25–43 (first printed in F. R. H. Du Boulay and C. M. Barron (eds.), *The Reign of Richard II* (London, 1971), 218–41).

—— 'The Murder of James Andrew: Suffolk Faction in the 1430s', in R. Virgoe, *East Anglian Society* (Norwich, 1997), 109–15 (first printed in *Proceedings of the Suffolk Institute of Archaeology and History*, 34 (1980), 263–8).

—— 'The Crown, Magnates and Local Government in Fifteenth-Century East Anglia', in R. Virgoe, *East Anglian Society* (Norwich, 1997), 79–93 (first printed in J. R. L. Highfield and R. Jeffs (eds.), *The Crown and the Local Communities* (Gloucester, 1981), 72–87).

—— 'The Earlier Knyvetts: The Rise of a Norfolk Gentry Family', Part I, in R. Virgoe, *East Anglian Society* (Norwich, 1997), 159–77 (first printed in *Norfolk Archaeology*, 41 (1990), 1–14).

—— 'Inheritance and Litigation in the Fifteenth Century: The Buckenham Disputes', in R. Virgoe, *East Anglian Society* (Norwich, 1997), 133–50 (first printed in *Journal of Legal History*, 15 (1994), 23–40).

WALKER, S., *The Lancastrian Affinity 1361–99* (Oxford, 1990).

—— 'Richard II's Views on Kingship', in R. E. Archer and S. Walker (eds.), *Rulers and Ruled in Late Medieval England* (London, 1995), 49–64.

WATTS, J. L., 'The Counsels of King Henry VI *c.*1435–1445', *EHR* 106 (1991), 279–98.

—— 'Ideas, Principles and Politics', in A. J. Pollard (ed.), *The Wars of the Roses* (London, 1995), 110–33.

—— *Henry VI and the Politics of Kingship* (Cambridge, 1996).

WEDGWOOD, J. C., *Staffordshire Parliamentary History*, William Salt Archaeological Society (London, 1917–18).

—— *History of Parliament: Biographies of the Members of the Commons House 1439–1509* (London, 1936).

WOLFFE, B. P., *The Royal Demesne in English History* (London, 1971).

—— 'The Personal Rule of Henry VI', in S. B. Chrimes *et al.* (eds.), *Fifteenth-Century England* (Manchester, 1972), 29–48.

—— *Henry VI* (London, 1981).

WRIGHT, S. M., *The Derbyshire Gentry in the Fifteenth Century*, Derbyshire Record Society, 8 (Chesterfield, 1983).

WROTTESLEY, G., 'An Account of the Family of Okeover of Okeover', *Collections for a History of Staffordshire*, William Salt Archaeological Society, new series, 7 (1904).

—— 'A History of the Bagot Family', *Collections for a History of Staffordshire*, William Salt Archaeological Society, new series, 11 (1908).

WYLIE, J. H., *History of England under Henry the Fourth*, 4 vols. (London, 1884–98).

—— and WAUGH, W. T., *The Reign of Henry the Fifth*, 3 vols. (Cambridge, 1914–29).

UNPUBLISHED DISSERTATIONS

ARCHER, R. E., 'The Mowbrays: Earls of Nottingham and Dukes of Norfolk, to 1432', D.Phil., Oxford, 1984.

AYRES, E. A., 'Parliamentary Representation in Derbyshire and Nottinghamshire in the Fifteenth Century', MA, Nottingham, 1956.

BELLAMY, J. G., 'The Parliamentary Representation of Nottinghamshire, Derbyshire and Staffordshire in the reign of Richard II', MA, Nottingham, 1961.

BIRRELL, J. R., 'The Honour of Tutbury in the Fourteenth and Fifteenth Centuries', MA, Birmingham, 1962.

CASTOR, H. R., 'The Duchy of Lancaster in the Lancastrian Polity, 1399–1461', Ph.D., Cambridge, 1993.

CRAWFORD, A., 'The Career of John Howard, Duke of Norfolk, c.1420–85', M.Phil., London, 1975.

DAVIES, R. R., 'The Bohun and Lancaster Lordships in Wales in the Fourteenth and Early Fifteenth Centuries', D.Phil., Oxford, 1965.

ELDER, A. J., 'A Study of the Beauforts and their Estates, 1399–1450', Ph.D., Bryn Mawr, 1964.

EVANS, S., 'The Earl of Arundel, Richard II and the March of Wales', BA, Cambridge, 1979.

FAGAN, E. de L., 'Some Aspects of the King's Household in the Reign of Henry V', MA, London, 1935.

FRIEDRICHS, R. L., 'The Career and Influence of Ralph, Lord Cromwell, 1393–1456', Ph.D., Columbia, 1974.

GRIFFITHS, W. R. M., 'The Military Career and Affinity of Henry, Prince of Wales 1399–1413', M.Litt., Oxford, 1980.

HARRISS, G. L., 'The Finance of the Royal Household, 1437–60', D.Phil., Oxford, 1953.

HOLMES, C., 'East Anglia and the Royal Court, 1440–1450', BA, Cambridge, 1993.

JAMES, L. E., 'The Career and Political Influence of William de la Pole, First Duke of Suffolk, 1437–50', B.Litt., Oxford, 1979.

MOREY, G. E., 'The Administration of the Counties of Norfolk and Suffolk in the Reign of Henry IV', MA, London, 1941.

—— 'East Anglian Society in the Fifteenth Century: An Historico-regional Survey', Ph.D., London, 1951.

POLLARD, A. J., 'The Family of Talbot, Lords Talbot and Earls of Shrewsbury in the Fifteenth Century', Ph.D., Bristol, 1968.

ROGERS, A., 'The Royal Household of Henry IV', Ph.D., Nottingham, 1966.

ROWNEY, I. D., 'The Staffordshire Political Community, 1440–1500', Ph.D., Keele, 1981.

SMITH, A. R., 'Aspects of the Career of Sir John Fastolf (1380–1459)', D.Phil., Oxford, 1982.

WALKER, S. K., 'John of Gaunt and his Retainers, 1361–99', D.Phil., Oxford, 1986.

WATTS, J. L., 'Domestic Politics and the Constitution in the Reign of Henry VI, c.1435–61', Ph.D., Cambridge, 1990.

Index

Adam of Usk 13
Agardsley (Staffs.) 193 n.
Agincourt, battle of (1415) 75, 84, 222, 236 n.
Alred, Richard 43 n.
Alton (Staffs.) 200, 239 n.
Andrew, James 108, 111 n.
Andrew, John 96 n., 109 n., 159 n., 162, 184 n., 185 n., 186, 187
Andrew, Richard 43 n.
Apedale (Staffs.) 215
Appletree hundred (Derbys.) 193 n., 196 n., 296 n.
Arblaster, Thomas 235–8, 255, 256, 258, 274, 304 n.
  Thomas, father of 236
Archer, Richard 262
Ardern, Sir John 215 n.
  Maud, daughter of 215 n.
Arundel, earls of, see Fitzalan
Ashbourne (Derbys.) 195 n., 196, 204, 223, 297 n.
Ashover (Derbys.) 243
Ashton, Hugh 177
Ashton, Sir William 177, 178–9
Aslak, Walter 77, 107
Aston, family of 274
Aston, Sir Roger 239, 274
Aston, Sir Thomas 198, 200, 202 n., 207, 208, 209 n., 210, 215 n.
Atherstone (Warwicks.) 254 n.
Audley, family of, Lords Audley 200, 201
  see also Tochet
Audley, Nicholas, Lord Audley 200
Axholme, Isle of (Lincs.) 102, 104, 105
Aylsham (Norf.) 55

Babingley (Norf.) 112 n., 116 n.
Bache, Simon 25 n.
Baconsthorpe (Norf.) 96, 135, 136, 138
Badingham (Suff.) 108, 109, 165, 166 n.
Bagot, Sir John 197–8, 207, 208, 210, 211, 220, 221, 230 n., 231, 239
  Joan, daughter of, see Curson, John II (of Kedleston)
  Margaret, daughter of, see Bradbourne, Henry
Bagot, Richard 279, 280 n.
Bale's Chronicle 297 n.

Bardolf, Joan, Lady Bardolf 69, 81, 88–9, 92 n., 150, 152
  Anne, sister of 150
Bardolf, Thomas, Lord Bardolf 60, 68
  see also Beaumont, William; Phelip, William
Baroun, Margaret 78
Barry, Sir Edmund 59, 76 n., 80, 129
  Agnes, daughter of, see Paston, William
Barton (Staffs.) 193 n.
Barton Blount (Derbys.) 196, 216, 291
Basset, family of, Lords Basset of Drayton 200, 286
Basset, Ralph, Lord Basset of Drayton 200
Basset (of Blore), family of 263, 264 n., 302–4
Basset, Edmund (of Blore) 220, 263
Basset, Ralph (of Blore) 263–6, 270–3, 275, 278, 279–84, 294 n., 295, 297 n., 302
  Thomasine, daughter of, see Okeover, Philip
  William, son of 296 n., 302–3, 304 n.
Basset, Ralph (of Cheadle) 220
Bate, Thomas 273 n., 276, 295
  Isabel Cokayn (née Shirley), wife of, see Cokayn, Sir John I:
Bath and Wells, bishop of:
  Beckington, Thomas (1443–65) 43 n.
Baylham (Suff.) 108 n.
Beauchamp, family of, earls of Warwick 201, 268 n., 287 n., 294
Beauchamp, Henry, earl and duke of Warwick (d. 1446) 255, 262 n., 266–70, 272, 276, 277, 285
  Anne, daughter of 269
Beauchamp, Joan, Lady Bergavenny 35 n., 237–8, 239 n., 245 n.
Beauchamp, John, Lord Beauchamp of Powick 43 n., 269, 277 n.
Beauchamp, Richard, earl of Warwick (d. 1439) 231 n., 233–5, 237–40, 242, 253–5, 259, 261–2, 269 n., 275, 276, 277 n.
  Anne, daughter of, see Neville, Richard, earl of Warwick
  Eleanor, daughter of, see Beaufort, Edmund, duke of Somerset
  Elizabeth, daughter of, see Neville, George, Lord Latimer

Beauchamp, Richard (*cont.*):
  Margaret, daughter of, *see* Talbot, John,
    earl of Shrewsbury
Beauchamp, Thomas, earl of Warwick (d.
    1401) 11
Beaufort, family of 277 n.
Beaufort, Edmund, duke of Somerset 41,
    114 n., 156, 161, 162 n., 167, 172,
    176–8, 180, 182, 281, 285 n., 287,
    288 n., 289, 297
  Eleanor Beauchamp, wife of 285 n.
Beaufort, Henry, bishop of Winchester,
    cardinal of England 38 n., 39 n., 40 n.,
    42, 92, 240, 250
Beaufort, Thomas, earl of Dorset, duke of
    Exeter 38 n., 39 n., 62, 68–70, 71,
    74–5, 76 n., 77–9, 80–1, 82, 83, 84,
    86–7, 90, 91, 93, 94, 107, 112, 130, 158,
    165–6, 226, 229, 230, 240, 309
  Margaret Neville, wife of 68 n.
Beaumont, John, Viscount Beaumont 43 n.,
    46, 47 n., 92 n., 187, 252, 259 n., 262,
    300, 304 n.
  Elizabeth Phelip, wife of 92 n., 130 n.
  Henry, son of 92 n.
  William, Viscount Beaumont and Lord
    Bardolf, son of 92 n.
Bedford, John, duke of 40 n., 89 n., 107,
    244, 248, 249
Bedfordshire 75 n.
Beek, Sir Thomas 26, 198, 202 n., 211
Beeston Regis (Norf.) 55, 96, 136
Beighton (Norf.) 150, 159 n.
Bekyswell, John 98
Belsham, John 117
Bergavenny, Lady, *see* Beauchamp, Joan
Berkshire 75 n., 90 n.
Bermingham, William 261
Berney, John 154, 165
Berney, Philip 185 n.
Berney, Sir Robert 63, 64, 66
Berney (of Reedham), family of 167 n.
Berney, John (of Reedham) 77 n., 111 n.,
    166
Berney, Thomas (of Reedham) 166
  Elizabeth, wife of 166 n.
  John, son of 166, 168 n.
Berwick (Northumb.) 109 n.
Bessingham (Norf.) 136, 138
Bigod, family of, earls of Norfolk 60, 101,
    110 n.
Bigot, family of 179 n.
Bigot, Elizabeth 110 n.
Bigot, John 110 n.
  Elizabeth, granddaughter of, *see* Garneys,
    William
Bingham, Richard 274 n.

Birmingham (Warwicks.) 237, 261–2
Blackburn (Lancs.) 46
Blake, Edmund 186, 187
Blore (Staffs.) 220, 263, 271, 279, 283
Blore Heath, battle of (1459) 304
Blount, family of 196, 197 n., 227, 241 n.,
    260, 274, 286–8, 290–1, 296 n., 297,
    302
Blount, Sir John 206, 207, 210 n., 211–12,
    213–14, 216, 217 n., 221, 226, 229, 231,
    292 n.
Blount, Roland 297, 302
Blount, Sir Thomas 221, 227 n., 260,
    261 n., 268, 271, 274 n., 284, 291,
    292 n., 296 n., 298, 299, 302
  Margaret Gresley, wife of 221, 227 n.
Blount, Sir Walter 26, 196, 202 n., 206 n.,
    210, 211, 224, 226, 305
  Constance, daughter of, *see* Sutton, John,
    of Dudley
  Sanchia de Ayala, wife of 196, 210 n.,
    211, 216
Blount, Walter 274 n., 282 n., 284–97, 299,
    301, 302, 304–5
  Anne Neville, dowager duchess of
    Buckingham, second wife of, *see*
    Stafford, Humphrey, earl of Stafford
    and duke of Buckingham
  Elizabeth, sister of, *see* Shirley, Ralph II
  Thomas, brother of 286, 289, 298, 302
  William, son of 292 n.
Bocking, John 162 n.
body politic 3–5, 38, 50, 232, 312
Bohun inheritance 22, 26, 27, 73 n., 235 n.
  see also Hereford heritage
Bolingbroke (Lincs.) 36, 39 n., 55, 57, 73 n.
Bolsover (Derbys.) 201, 226, 242, 249
Bolton, Robert 85 n.
Bonington, John 28 n.
Botetourt inheritance 238
Bothe, Henry 202 n., 206, 264 n.
Botiller, Sir Andrew 64, 66, 67
Bourchier, Henry 168 n.
Bourchier, Henry, Viscount Bourchier
    179 n., 300 n.
Bourchier, Humphrey 299
Boure, Thurstan del 202 n.
Boys, Thomas 74 n.
Brackley, Friar John 184 n., 185 n.
Bradbourne, family of 263 n.
Bradbourne, Henry 245, 257, 259 n., 262,
    271, 279, 280 n.
  Margaret Bagot, wife of 280 n.
Bradbourne, Roger 202 n., 206 n.
Bradeston (Norf.) 111 n., 122, 157, 165–8,
    173–4, 184 n.
Bradshaw, William 243 n.

Bradshawe, Nicholas 208
Bradshawe, Roger 206 n., 211
Brailsford (Derbys.) 286
Bramshall (Staffs.) 212–13
Brandon, William 110 n., 113 n., 114–15, 116, 180
  Elizabeth Wingfield, wife of 113 n.
Bradwell (Suff.) 147, 150–1
Breadsall (Derbys.) 264 n.
Bressingham (Norf.) 105
Brewes, Thomas 99, 111 n., 159–60, 162, 166, 182 n., 188
Bromholm priory (Norf.) 97
Brothercross hundred (Norf.) 55
Brown, Richard 246 n.
Bruisyard convent (Suff.) 84 n.
Buckingham, duke of, *see* Stafford, Humphrey
Buckinghamshire 75 n., 90 n.
Bukton, Sir Peter 26 n.
Bungay (Suff.) 103, 110
Burgeys, William 112
Burgoyne, William 28 n.
Burnell, Hugh, Lord Burnell 211
Burton on Trent abbey (Staffs.) 212 n., 222, 283 n.
Bury St Edmunds (Suff.) 117
Butler, James, earl of Wiltshire 269, 297 n., 300
Butler, Ralph, Lord Sudeley 43 n., 269, 277 n., 281 n.

Cade's rebellion (1450) 177, 281
Caen 85 n.
Caister (Norf.) 145, 147, 153, 185 n.
Caister Bardolf (Norf.) 150
Calais 36 n., 168, 266, 287
Caldicot Castle 236 n.
Calthorp, William 74 n., 99, 186, 188
Cambridge 65
Cambridgeshire 60, 65, 124, 188 n.
Canterbury, archbishops of:
  Bourchier, Thomas (1454–86) 179 n., 300 n.
  Chichele, Henry (1414–43) 38 n., 39 n., 42 n.
  Stafford, John (1443–52) 43 n., 263–4, 281 n.
Carbonell, family of 165
Carbonell, Sir John 74 n., 77, 165–6
Carbonell, Sir Richard 74 n., 108, 165 n., 166
  son of 166
  wife of 166 n.
Carbonell, Sir William 108, 109
Castile 23, 196
Castle Acre (Norf.) 68

Castle Donington (Leics.) 28, 46, 195 n., 204, 206 n., 210
Castle Rising (Norf.) 70, 71, 121, 167, 168
Caston, family of 165–6
Catherine de Valois, queen of England 39, 40, 42, 44, 76, 88, 90, 260 n.
Chamberleyn, Roger 180, 188
Chambre, Thomas 174 n., 177 n.
Chartley (Staffs.) 200, 219, 220, 222
Chartres 85 n.
Chatsworth (Derbys.) 204, 228, 240
Chaucer, Alice, duchess of Suffolk 75, 86, 88, 94, 112 n., 114 n., 116 n., 117, 147, 148 n., 156, 161–2, 174 n., 176, 179 n., 185 n., 188–9
Chaucer, Thomas 75, 76 n., 86, 88
  Philippa, mother of 76 n.
Chaworth, Sir Thomas 246–7, 274
Cheadle (Staffs.) 220
Cheshire 26 n., 29 n., 39 n., 46, 120 n., 198 n., 201, 215, 217, 222, 228, 240, 254, 290, 291 n., 304 n.
  Cheshire retinue, *see* Richard II
Chester, earldom of 17, 32, 217, 300
Chester, principality of 11–13, 23, 201
Chesterfield (Derbys.) 197, 242–3, 246, 247, 249, 251 n.
Chetwynd, family of 236
Chetwynd, Philip 236–7, 238–9, 254, 256, 261–2
  Ellen, Lady Ferrers, wife of, *see* Ferrers, Edmund, Lord Ferrers of Chartley
  John, uncle of 239
Chirche, Roger 173 n., 174 n., 175, 182 n.
Cinque Ports 71 n., 281 n.
Clare, honour of 56, 65, 187
Clarence, George, duke of (d. 1478) 305
Clarence, Thomas, duke of (d. 1421) 223 n.
  Margaret, wife of 35 n.
Clere, Robert 111 n.
Clifton, family of 290 n.
Clifton, Sir John 84, 97 n., 99, 111, 121 n., 145, 147
Clifton, Sir Nicholas 201
Clifton, Sir Robert 74 n., 77
Clinton, John, Lord (d. 1464) 237 n., 254
  Joan Ferrers, wife of 237 n.
Clinton, William, Lord (d. 1431) 237 n.
Clippesby, Edmund 58 n.
Clippesby, John 180 n.
Clitheroe (Lancs.) 39 n.
Clopton, John 175
Codnor (Derbys.) 199, 211 n., 250
Cokayn, family of 231, 241 n., 246, 259, 263 n., 287, 292, 293, 294
Cokayn, Edward 290–1
Cokayn, John 26, 197

Cokayn, Sir John I 197, 202 n., 204, 206, 221, 223, 242 n., 244–7, 248 n., 253 n., 258 n., 270–1 n., 276
Isabel Shirley, wife of 197, 273 n., 276
Cokayn, Sir John II 197
Joan Dabridgecourt, wife of 197
Cokayn, John III 257–8, 262, 270 n., 271, 272, 273, 275, 276, 279, 282, 286, 288 n., 290–1, 295, 296, 297 n., 298
Agnes Vernon, wife of 271 n.
William, brother of 279–80, 282
Cokefield, Thomas 202 n.
Comberford, William 258, 274, 282 n., 304 n.
commissions:
of *oyer* and *terminer* 111, 113 n., 115, 156–7, 158 n., 160, 163–4, 169 n., 173 n., 174, 177, 212 n., 244, 248, 250, 295–6
of the peace 63–4, 65, 67–8, 69, 74, 76, 83, 87, 97–8, 99 n., 104, 112, 120, 124, 136, 145, 154 n., 157, 159, 173, 181, 186–7, 188–9, 204 n., 205–6, 207–8, 216 n., 219, 225 n., 226, 228, 230–1, 233 n., 235, 239–40, 242, 245, 255, 256, 258, 262, 274, 282, 284, 285 n., 288, 291, 299, 304, 305
Common Pleas, court of 129, 178
common weal 4, 6, 17–18, 48, 118, 163–4, 171
Congham (Norf.) 120–1, 140 n.
Constable, Robert 150
constitution 5–7, 16–18, 48, 127
see also crown
Conyers, Sir Robert 113 n.
Cornwall, duchy of 17, 32, 39 n., 70, 71, 88, 121, 217
Costessey (Norf.) 87 n., 148
Cotentin 85 n.
Cotes, Humphrey 235–7
Cotton (Suff.) 145, 147–8, 149
Cotton, William 97 n., 162 n.
council, *see* king
Coventry 257 n., 283, 285, 300 n., 301, 304
Coventry and Lichfield, bishops of:
Booth, William (1447–52) 274 n.
Boulers, Reginald (1453–9) 299 n.
Craneworth (Norf.) 76 n.
Creting St Peter (Suff.) 108
Cromer (Norf.) 132, 136
Cromwell, Ralph, Lord Cromwell 43 n., 46, 47 n., 121 n., 158 n., 168 n., 242, 245 n., 247–52, 255–6, 259, 273–4, 278 nn., 282 n., 300 n.
crown 24, 27, 68, 70, 78, 80, 82, 86, 120, 161, 171, 177, 183, 241, 259
finances of 17, 27, 29–32, 33 n., 34–5,

37–8, 40, 41–4, 72, 185, 306, 308
judicial powers of 5–6, 12, 17–18, 38 n., 49, 177 n., 205, 222, 288–90, 296
public authority of 3–7, 10, 12, 16–21, 37, 40, 44, 45, 47, 48–9, 53, 60, 61, 64, 73, 79, 81, 93–5, 100–1, 118–19, 123, 126–7, 141, 181–2, 193, 198, 202, 205, 219, 224, 225–8, 232, 252, 260, 265, 267, 289, 291–2, 297–9, 301–3, 305, 306–12
Cubley (Derbys.) 196, 214, 261
Curson, Sir John 74 n.
Curson (of Croxall), family of 302 n.
Curson (of Kedleston), family of 196, 241 n., 246, 259, 263 n.
Curson, John I (of Kedleston) 26, 197, 202 n., 204, 206–7, 211, 226
Margaret, daughter of, *see* Okeover, Thomas II
Margaret Montgomery, wife of 197
Curson, John II (of Kedleston) 197, 242, 244, 245, 248 n., 249, 257–8, 259, 260, 270 n., 274, 279, 280 n., 283 n., 286 n., 290 n., 292–3, 295, 297, 302, 304 n.
Henry, son of 297, 302
Joan Bagot, wife of 197, 280 n.
Curson, Thomas (of Kedleston) 302

Dabridgecourt, Sir John 26, 196, 197, 201, 202 n., 206, 207, 211 n., 231, 292 n.
Joan and Joan, daughters of, *see* Cokayn, Sir John II; Willoughby, Hugh II
Maud Willoughby, wife of, *see* Willoughby, Sir Richard
Dallinghoo (Suff.) 108
Dallyng, William 76 n.
Daniel, Thomas 94 n., 114 n., 120–3, 126, 140–3, 150, 152, 157, 165–8, 169 n., 170 n., 172–4, 176 n., 177–8, 182, 183–5, 188, 288 n., 310
Elizabeth, sister of 121, 140 n.
Margaret Howard, wife of 172
Daniel, Thomas (of Walsoken) 184 n.
Davenport, Hugh 283 n.
Davenport, John 291 n.
Daventry (Northants.) 226 n.
de la Bere, John 43 n.
de la Pole, family of, earls of Suffolk 56, 57, 82, 96 n.
de la Pole, Isabella, Lady Morley 148
de la Pole, John, duke of Suffolk (d. 1491/2) 148 n., 156, 161, 185 n., 187, 188, 189
Elizabeth of York, wife of 185 n.
de la Pole, Michael, earl of Suffolk (d. 1389) 60, 83, 152
Katherine Wingfield, wife of 83
de la Pole, Michael, earl of Suffolk (d. Sept.

1415) 60, 64, 69, 75, 79, 83–4, 85
Katherine Stafford, wife of 75, 84, 85 n., 110
de la Pole, Michael, earl of Suffolk (d. Oct. 1415) 75, 84
  Elizabeth Mowbray, wife of 84–5
  Katherine, Elizabeth, and Isabel, daughters of 84
de la Pole, William, earl and duke of Suffolk (d. 1450) 43 n., 79, 81, 103 n., 107, 166, 244, 248, 274 n.
  affinity in East Anglia 86–7, 91, 93, 94, 95–7, 98–100, 105, 108, 109–12, 115–17, 119, 120, 121–9, 134, 137, 141, 144, 151–4, 156–74, 177–8, 180–1, 182–9, 310
  establishment of local power in East Anglia 82–93, 105, 108, 260 n., 273 n.
  fall from power 129, 156, 158, 160–1, 165, 168, 171, 176–7, 281
  niece of 99
  role in East Anglia 1437–50 93–5, 96 n., 97–101, 108–17, 118–27, 128–9, 133, 134, 136–7, 139–49, 151–4, 158, 169–70, 189, 278 n., 279, 310–11
  role in royal government 41, 42, 45–7, 48 n., 49, 85–6, 92–3, 94, 95, 98, 100–1, 118–20, 122–7, 129, 141, 149, 152–3, 160–1, 176–7, 182, 277 n., 279, 280–1, 289, 310–11
  wife of, *see* Chaucer, Alice
de Vere, family of, earls of Oxford 56
de Vere, Aubrey, earl of Oxford (d. 1400) 60
de Vere, John, earl of Oxford (d. 1462) 74, 82, 122 n., 125 nn., 157, 158 n., 159 n., 160, 163 n., 167, 179 n., 182
de Vere, Richard, earl of Oxford (d. 1417) 74
Debenham, Gilbert 74 n., 108, 110 n., 112, 148–9, 173, 178, 182
Dedham (Essex) 151–2
Delves, John 201 n., 208, 209, 215–16, 218 n., 231
Dennington (Suff.) 69 n., 75, 90, 166 n.
Denys, Thomas 122, 140
Derby 207, 244, 245, 286, 291, 295–6, 297
Derby, earldom of, *see* Ferrers; Henry IV
Derbyshire:
  Duchy affinity in 27, 32, 36 n., 197–8, 202, 208, 210–11, 222–4, 230, 241, 246, 247–8, 249
  officeholding in 199, 200 n., 204–7, 226, 227–30, 240, 242, 250, 255–6, 258, 270, 273–4, 284, 285 n., 289–91, 297, 299, 304

political society in 198–9, 233, 239–41, 242, 245–8, 249, 251–3, 255, 257, 259–61, 269, 270–1, 272–3, 274–5, 277–8, 281, 289–91, 292–5, 299–305, 307–8, 311
  see also north midlands
Derham, Thomas 77, 98
Dethick, Thomas 216 n.
Devereux, Sir Walter 281 n.
  Anne Ferrers, wife of 281
Dieulacres chronicle 13–14
Dorset 75 n.
Dorset, earl of, *see* Beaufort, Thomas
Dove river 196 n.
Dover Castle 66, 71 n., 281 n.
Dowebyggyng, John 167 n., 174 n., 176 n.
Drakelow (Derbys.) 203, 212 n.
Drayton (Norf.) 148
Drayton Basset (Staffs.) 200
Drury, Sir William 74 n.
Dudley (Staffs.) 200
Dudley, Lords, *see* Sutton
Duffield (Derbys.) 26, 46, 193, 196–7, 204, 211 n., 226, 228, 242, 243, 244, 253, 258 n., 267
Dunstanburgh (Northumb.) 26 n.
Dunwich (Suff.) 69
Durham, bishop of:
  Langley, Thomas (1406–37) 38 n., 39 n.

earls' rebellion (1400) 26 n., 30, 62
Earsham (Norf.) 104 n.
East Anglia 278 n., 279, 288 n.
  conflict in 76–8, 100–1, 105, 108–11, 113–16, 118–24, 125–7, 129, 131–45, 146–55, 156–60, 162–8, 171–81, 182–5, 310–11
  crown-Duchy connection in 64–83, 85–8, 90–5, 98–100, 106, 108, 127, 129–30, 141, 145, 152, 158, 166, 226–7, 229–30, 232–3, 273 n., 308–9, 310
  Duchy offices in 46–7, 58, 62–3, 66, 90–1, 95–7, 136, 158, 181, 188, 196 n.
  Duchy retinue in 30 n., 36, 41, 57–9, 61–2, 64–5, 72–3
  see also de la Pole, William, earl and duke of Suffolk; Henry IV; Henry V; Henry VI; Mowbray, John, duke of Norfolk (d. 1461)
East Beckham (Norf.) 131–6, 138–9, 141
Edward I 9 n.
Edward II 101
Edward III 8–10, 11, 197 n., 259
  Philippa of Hainault, wife of 197 n.
Edward IV 19, 20 n., 188–9, 312
  as earl of March 185 n., 187
Edward VI 3

Edward, prince of Wales, the Black Prince (d. 1376) 11
Edward, prince of Wales (d. 1471) 185, 300
Egerton, family of 292
Egerton, John 304
Egerton, Ralph 257–8, 293 n., 295 n.
  Hugh, son of 291, 293, 295 n.
Egmere (Norf.) 132 n.
Elford (Staffs.) 215 n.
Elizabeth I 3
Elmham, Sir William 59, 105
Elmsett (Suff.) 73 n., 96
Elvaston (Derbys.) 197 n., 291–7, 302
Epworth (Lincs.) 102, 104
Erdeswick, family of 212
Erdeswick, Hugh 213–22, 227, 229, 230–1, 232, 233, 236–7, 238–9, 256–8, 281–2 n., 291
  Robert, brother of 213 n., 218 n., 220, 222 n.
  Roger, brother of 222 n.
  Sampson, brother of 213 n., 218 n., 221, 257 n.
Erdeswick, Thomas 212–13
  Margaret Stafford, mother of 212
Eriswell (Suff.) 80, 98 n.
Erpingham (Norf.) 64, 67
Erpingham hundred (Norf.) 55, 65, 81, 130–2, 135–8, 158
Erpingham, Sir Thomas 26 n., 58, 59, 64–8, 69, 70–3, 75, 76 n., 77, 78 n., 79–80, 82, 84, 85, 86, 87, 88, 91 n., 92 n., 102, 107, 130, 226, 229, 230, 309
  Juliana, sister of, see Phelip, Sir William
Essex 56, 60, 65, 76 n., 145, 151, 186, 187, 277, 299
Evesham, Monk of 13
Ewelme (Oxfs.) 94 n., 162
Exeter, duke of, see Beaufort, Thomas; Holand, John
Eyke (Suff.) 112 n.

Fakenham (Norf.) 55
Fastolf, Sir Hugh 150
  Thomas, son of 150
Fastolf, Sir John 126, 144–55, 156–7, 158 n., 159 n., 160, 161 n., 162–5, 167 n., 168, 174 n., 182, 183 n., 184 n.
Fastolf, Sir Thomas 121 n.
Felbrigg (Norf.) 67
Felbrigg, Sir George 105
Felbrigg, Sir Simon 67, 72, 76 n., 77, 80, 87, 96, 97, 105 n., 106, 116 n., 130 n.
Felthorpe (Norf.) 148
Ferrers, family of, earls of Derby 39 n.
Ferrers, Robert, earl of Derby 195

Ferrers of Chartley, family of 200, 263, 264 n., 278, 294
Ferrers, Edmund, Lord Ferrers of Chartley (d. 1435) 219–22, 231, 233, 234, 237–9, 242, 253, 254, 255, 256, 258, 261–3
  Ellen, wife of 239, 254, 256, 261–2
  Joan, daughter of, see Clinton, John, Lord Clinton
Ferrers, Robert, Lord Ferrers of Chartley (d. 1413) 219–20
Ferrers, William, Lord Ferrers of Chartley (d. 1450) 238 n., 254, 261–2, 264 n., 266, 269, 272, 274 n., 279, 281, 283 n.
  Anne, daughter of, see Devereux, Sir Walter
  Elizabeth, wife of 281 n.
Ferrers, Thomas (of Tamworth) 278 n.
Fiennes, James 43 n.
Fitzalan, family of, earls of Arundel 68
Fitzalan, Elizabeth, duchess of Norfolk 103, 104, 106, 107
  Elizabeth Goushill, daughter of, see Wingfield, Sir Robert
  Robert Goushill, second husband of 106
Fitzalan, Richard, earl of Arundel (d. 1397) 10, 11
Fitzalan, Thomas, earl of Arundel (d. 1415) 38 n., 103 n.
Fitzherbert, family of 263 n., 292
Fitzherbert, Nicholas 264–5, 270–1, 274, 275, 288 n., 290, 293 n., 302
Fitzherbert, Ralph 290
Fitzhugh, Sir Henry 38 n., 39 n., 79 n.
FitzRalph, Sir John 78, 99
  son of 99
FitzRalph, Robert 78
Fitzwilliam, Edmund 110 n., 115, 174 n., 177 n., 179 n.
Flegg hundred (Norf.) 147
Flintshire 17 n.
Foljambe, John 207, 243
Foljambe (of Hassop), family of 244 n.
Foljambe, Sir Godfrey I (of Hassop) 206 n., 244 n.
Foljambe, Sir Godfrey II (of Hassop) 206 n., 244 n.
  Alice, daughter of, see Plumpton, Sir William
  Margaret Leek, wife of, see Rempston, Sir Thomas
Foljambe (of Walton), family of 27, 197, 231, 241 n., 242–9
Foljambe, Thomas I (of Walton) 201, 202 n., 206, 242 n., 243, 244 n.
  Margaret Loudham, wife of 242 n.
Foljambe, Thomas II (of Walton) 243–50

Foljambe, Thomas III (of Walton) 249 n., 293, 303
  Margery Longford, wife of 249 n., 293 n.
Foremark (Derbys.) 203
Forncett (Norf.) 104 n., 110 n., 179 n.
Forster, Humphrey 162
Fortescue, Sir John 113
Framingham (Norf.) 65 n., 104 n.
Framlingham (Suff.) 65, 67 n., 70, 71, 101, 102, 103, 105, 106, 108, 113 n., 115, 117, 172, 174–5, 184 n.
Framlyngham, John 174 n., 177
Frampton, Thomas 85 n.
France 9 n., 16, 25 n., 29 n., 36, 38, 44, 45, 48 n., 74, 83, 84, 85, 86, 99, 104, 106 n., 107 n., 139 n., 145, 146, 149 n., 150 n., 151, 153, 154, 160, 183 n., 225, 227, 230, 231, 237, 239 n., 241 n., 264, 277 n.
Fraunceys, family of 203
Fraunceys, Sir Robert 203, 206, 207–8, 209–11, 214, 225, 226, 246 n.
  Isabella, wife of 210
  Robert, son of 246 n.
Fraunceys, Simon 202 n., 203
Fritton (Suff.) 147, 148–9
Fulmerston (Norf.) 73 n.
Furnival, Lords 200
  see also Neville, Thomas; Talbot, John

Gallow hundred (Norf.) 55, 135
Garneys, family of 179 n.
Garneys, Ralph 110–11, 152
Garneys, William 110
  Elizabeth Bigot, wife of 110 n.
Gascoigne, Richard 211 n.
Gascony 203 n.
Gayton (Norf.) 120–1, 122 n., 140 n.
Geldeston (Norf.) 110–11, 152, 179
Giffard, Thomas 216 n., 220 n., 222 n.
Gimingham (Norf.) 55, 63, 96 n., 130
Gloucester, Humphrey, duke of (d. 1447) 40 n., 43 n., 86, 92, 97, 104, 107, 183 n.
Gloucester, Richard, duke of (d. 1485) 312
Gloucester, Thomas, duke of (d. 1397) 10, 11, 259
Gloucestershire 75 n.
Gloys, James 142 n.
Glyn Dŵr, Owain, rebellion of 29 n., 30
Gorleston (Suff.) 147
Gournay, Edmund 58 n., 63
Gournay, John 63, 66, 69, 72
Great Yarmouth (Norf.) 56, 63 n., 154 n.
Greenhoe hundred (Norf.) 135
Grendon (Warwicks.) 238

Gresham (Norf.) 125, 126 n., 132 n., 136, 137–40, 143, 144 n., 151 n., 168, 170 n.
Gresley, family of 203, 241 n., 260, 262 n., 274, 283
Gresley, Sir John I 228, 231, 243 n., 260 n., 283 n.
Gresley, Sir John II 272, 274 n., 283, 289–91, 294–5, 298, 299 n., 303, 304–5
  brothers of 283 n.
  Nicholas, brother of 289–90, 298
  Thomas, son of 283 n.
Gresley, Sir Thomas 202 n., 203, 206 n., 212 n., 214, 221, 222, 227–8, 231, 292 n.
  Margaret, daughter of, *see* Blount, Sir Thomas
Gresley hundred (Derbys.) 203 n.
Grey of Codnor, family of 199, 241
Grey, Henry, Lord Grey of Codnor (d. 1444) 242, 245–8, 250–1, 259, 278 n.
Grey, Henry, Lord Grey of Codnor (d. 1496) 251, 304 n.
Grey, John, Lord Grey of Codnor (d. 1392) 199 n.
Grey, John, Lord Grey of Codnor (d. 1430) 231, 241–2
Grey, Richard, Lord Grey of Codnor (d. 1418) 205, 206, 211 n., 231, 241 n.
  Elizabeth, wife of 242 n.
Grey, Edward, Lord Grey of Groby 280 n.
Grimston (Norf.) 120–1, 140 n.
Groos, Oliver 76 n., 77, 78, 83–4, 87, 97, 121 n.
Gunnor, Simon 133, 138
Guton (Norf.) 148

Haddon (Derbys.) 207 n., 223, 228, 240
Hadilsay, Richard 114–15
Hadleigh (Suff.) 117
Hainford (Norf.) 148
Halton (Chesh.) 29 n., 35 n., 39 n., 46, 198 n., 202 n., 215, 254
Hampton, John 43 n., 257–8, 274, 278 n., 304 n.
  John, father of 257
Hanworth (Norf.) 65 n., 104 n.
Harecourt, Robert 285
Harfleur 36 n., 74 n., 75, 79 n., 84
Harlaston (Staffs.) 228
Harleston, John 99, 159–60
Harleston, William 99, 162
Harling, Sir Robert 146, 147 n.
  Anne, daughter of 146–7, 148, 149
  Margaret, sister of, *see* Tuddenham, Sir Thomas

Harper, John 235–8, 255, 256, 258, 274, 282 n., 304 n.
Hartington (Derbys.) 193 n., 196, 210 n., 263 n., 274 n.
Hartismere hundred (Suff.) 85 n.
Hastings, William, Lord Hastings 305, 312
Hauteyn, John 134 n.
Heighley (Staffs.) 200
Hellesdon (Norf.) 148
Henry III 195
Henry IV 14, 41 n., 83, 102, 103, 105, 199 n., 213 n., 220, 231
  as earl of Derby 25, 28, 32
  as heir to the Duchy of Lancaster 22, 23, 24, 25–6, 32, 58–9
  Joan of Navarre, second wife of 39 n., 41 n., 203 n., 209
  management of the Duchy 3–4, 8, 18–20, 27–32, 34, 35, 36, 37–8, 39, 40, 44, 50, 95, 306–7; in East Anglia 53, 55, 59–73, 78–9, 95, 127, 308–9; in the north midlands 53, 118–19, 127, 193, 202–12, 214–15, 216–19, 221, 222–4, 225, 226, 227, 229, 230, 232, 233 n., 234, 237, 241, 249, 252, 255, 259–60, 305, 307–8
  management of royal authority 18–20, 27, 29, 30–32, 37–8, 64, 70, 73, 78–9, 95, 202, 204–5, 209–10, 214–15, 216–18, 259–60, 306–8
  Mary de Bohun, first wife of 22
  usurpation of 12, 26–7, 31, 53, 39, 201–2, 203, 312
Henry V 42, 82, 84, 102, 106, 199 n., 213 n., 220, 240, 246
  management of the Duchy 29 n., 33–39, 40, 41, 44, 50, 308; in East Anglia 72–9, 308–9; in the north midlands 219, 224, 225–35, 237, 241, 249, 252, 255, 259–60, 305, 308, 311
  management of royal authority 37–8, 50, 73–4, 78–9, 222, 224, 225–6, 232–5, 259–60, 308–9
  as prince of Wales 31, 32, 33 n., 37, 70–2, 206 n., 217–8, 221 n., 223–4, 225, 309
  wife of, *see* Catherine de Valois
Henry VI 21, 85, 106 n., 121, 128, 145, 167, 169, 175, 283
  deposition of 187–8, 304–5
  failings as king 41, 45, 47–50, 119–20, 123, 127, 250, 252, 309–10
  foundations at Eton and Cambridge 43, 44 n.
  management of the Duchy in the reign of 38–40, 41–7, 49–50, 267–8; in East Anglia 74–9, 85–7, 89–97, 98, 99–101, 108, 118–19, 127, 141, 152, 158–9, 181, 310–11; in the north midlands 234–5,

240–2, 243, 246, 247–8, 249, 251–2, 253–7, 259–63, 264–5, 266–73, 275, 284–5, 286–7, 300–1, 305, 311
  management of royal authority in the reign of 45, 47–50, 92–5, 100–1, 118–20, 123–5, 126–7, 134, 141, 149, 152–3, 156–8, 160–1, 171, 176–7, 180–2, 183–4, 185–6, 250–2, 255, 259–60, 264–5, 267–9, 277–81, 287–93, 295–302, 303–5, 309–11
  minority of 39–41, 45, 47, 85–6, 186 n., 249–50
  role of the court in the reign of 45–6, 47, 49, 93, 98, 100, 105, 114 n., 120, 121, 126, 128, 134, 137, 139, 141, 143, 158, 189, 239 n., 265, 266, 267–8, 269, 277, 280, 284–5, 288, 293
  role of the nobility in the reign of 40–1, 45–9, 92–4, 123, 125, 126–7, 160–1, 176–7, 180–2, 250–2, 259, 267–9, 277–81, 299–302, 304–5, 309–12
  wife of, *see* Margaret of Anjou
Henry VII 19
Hereford, earldom and dukedom of 22, 23 n.
Hereford heritage 32, 33 n., 38–9, 73 n., 90, 91, 96
Hereford, Joan, countess of 102 n.
Herefordshire 281 n.
Heriz inheritance 247, 249–50, 251 n.
Hertford 39
Hertfordshire 113, 124, 186 n.
Heveningham, Sir John I 99, 106, 111, 166
  wife of 116
Heveningham, Sir John II 111, 112 n., 115, 159–60
Heydon, John 56 n., 80, 90 n., 91–2, 95–8, 99 nn., 109–10, 111 n., 112 n., 115, 116, 122, 126, 134–43, 144 n., 151–2, 156–67, 169, 171–2, 181, 183–4, 185 nn., 186, 187–8, 280 n.
  Eleanor Winter, wife of 135, 137 n.
Hickling Priory, Norfolk 148–9, 151
High Peak (Derbys.) 26, 32, 37, 43, 193 n., 195, 204, 210 n., 211 n., 219 n., 223, 226, 228, 232, 240–1, 242, 246, 248 n., 257, 263, 267, 271, 272, 277, 282, 284–5, 286, 295, 301
Higham Ferrers (Northants.) 25 n., 35 n., 39 n., 73 n.
Hinkley (Leics.) 226 n.
Hintlesham (Suff.) 122 n.
Hobland (Suff.) 147
Holand, Joan, countess of Kent 243
Holand, John, earl of Huntingdon, duke of Exeter 58, 61, 103 n., 202
  Constance, daughter of, *see* Mowbray,

Thomas, earl of Norfolk (d. 1405)
  Elizabeth of Lancaster, wife of 103 n.
Holand, Thomas, earl of Kent, duke of
  Surrey 201–2
Holford, Thomas 23
Holt hundred (Norf.) 135
Holy Land 59 n.
Hoo (Suff.) 107, 113, 114 n., 116, 117
Hoo, Thomas 87, 91
Hopton, John 182 n.
Horstead (Norf.) 72
Horston Castle (Derbys.) 207, 211 n., 250
Hough (Lancs.) 290
household, *see* king
Howard, family of 107, 189
Howard, Sir John 107, 174 nn., 176 n., 178,
  180
Howard, Sir Robert 107
  Margaret, daughter of, *see* Daniel,
    Thomas
  Margaret Mowbray, wife of 107
Howes, Thomas 154, 157, 158–9, 160,
  184 n.
Hull, Sir Edward 43 n., 126, 149 n., 150–1
  Margery, wife of 150
Hungerford, Sir Edmund 43 n.
Hungerford, Robert, Lord Moleyns 125–6,
  137–9, 141, 143, 144 n., 170 n.
  Eleanor Moleyns, wife of 125 n., 138
Hungerford, Walter, Lord Hungerford
  38–9 nn., 42 n., 43 n.
Huntingdon, earl of, *see* Holand, John
Huntingdonshire 122 n.

Ilam (Staffs.) 263
Ingestre (Staffs.) 236, 238
Inglesthorpe, Sir John 69 n., 105
Inglose, Sir Henry 77 n., 97, 145
Ipstones, Sir John 198, 200, 207, 213
Ipstones, William 207 n.
Ipswich (Suff.) 122 n., 178
Ireland 12, 239 n., 241 n.
Italy 25 n., 101

Jenney, William 154, 165, 180
Jermy, Sir John 106, 107 n.

Kedleston (Derbys.) 196, 197, 204, 263 n.,
  297, 302 n.
Kelsale (Suff.) 65 n.
Kenilworth (Warwicks.) 26 n., 43, 44,
  202 n., 283, 300
Kent 75 n., 157, 277, 281, 312 n.
Kent, earldom of, *see* Holand
Kettlebaston (Suff.) 86 n.
Kimberley (Norf.) 121 n.
Kinderton (Chesh.) 215

king:
  as duke of Lancaster 3–4, 19–20, 25, 33,
    34, 37, 44, 47, 53, 60, 61, 64, 72, 73,
    78, 82, 95, 100, 119, 127, 141, 193, 205,
    215, 217, 218, 219, 224, 226–8, 232,
    234, 237, 241, 247, 249, 252, 255, 260,
    264–5, 267, 279, 285, 288, 302, 306–12
  king's council 40–1, 48, 75, 85, 88, 91–2,
    109, 113, 116, 178, 180, 182 n., 213,
    214, 218, 250, 264, 280, 296, 298, 304
  king's household 8–9, 10, 11, 27, 30,
    41–4, 45–6, 47, 49, 64, 65, 71, 75 n.,
    88, 91–2, 97, 100, 110, 115 n., 119, 120,
    122, 123, 124–6, 149–50, 152, 160 n.,
    161, 182, 184, 185, 223, 259, 266, 277,
    281 n., 284, 312
  personal authority of 3, 5–6, 7–8, 10, 12,
    16–20, 40–1, 45, 47–9, 53, 73, 81,
    119–20, 127, 181–2, 184, 215, 217, 226,
    234, 237, 241, 247, 252, 255, 267,
    288–9, 291, 299, 301, 306–12
  see also crown; Henry IV; Henry V; Henry
    VI; royal affinity
King's Bench, court of 76–7, 111, 114, 115,
  116 n., 125 n., 166 n., 168 n., 173, 179,
  183, 212 n., 216, 222, 282, 297 n., 302
King's Lynn (Norf.) 56, 65, 69, 70, 78,
  157 nn., 162 n., 164, 183
Kingsley, John 217 n., 222 n.
Knaresborough (Yorks.) 26 n., 29, 39, 43 n.
Knightley, John 208, 211
Kniveton, Henry 245
Knowsley (Chesh.) 215 n.
Knyvet, Sir John 87 n.

Lacy, family of, earls of Lincoln 39 n., 195 n.
Lancashire 23 n., 30 n., 39 n., 41, 46, 290,
  291 n.
Lancaster, Duchy of:
  administration and office-holding 25,
    27–30, 32–5, 37–40, 41, 43–5, 46–7,
    49–50, 89–90, 195–6, 226, 252–4, 308
  administrative reorganization in 1437
    44–5, 46–7, 49–50, 89–91, 251–4, 311
  affinity 8, 18–21, 22–31, 32–7, 40–1, 43,
    44, 50, 58, 61, 306–9, 312
  annuities 22 n., 24, 28–31, 33 n., 34–6,
    38, 41, 61–2, 72–3, 96, 195, 201, 202–3,
    225, 232
  estates 22, 25, 28–9, 38–9, 43, 68
  feoffments 38–40, 41–4, 74, 89–90
  legal status 3–4, 27, 33, 308, 312
  military resources 24, 26–7, 29–30, 36,
    58, 59, 193, 198, 201–2, 231, 305
  North Parts 28, 35 n., 36, 37, 39, 46, 89,
    90 n., 95, 158 n., 186 n., 197, 211 n.,
    214, 226

Lancaster, Duchy of (*cont.*):
  palatinate and honour of Lancaster 22–4,
    25, 27, 28, 29, 35 n., 36 n., 55, 57,
    73 n., 195, 202 n.
  revenues 29, 33–5, 37–8, 40, 41–2, 43,
    44, 50, 72–3, 306, 308
  'south parts' 30 n., 35 n., 36, 55, 73 n.
  South Parts 28, 35 n., 36, 39, 89, 90 n.,
    91, 95
  see also Derbyshire; East Anglia; Henry
    IV; Henry V; Henry VI; Norfolk; north
    midlands; Staffordshire; Suffolk
Lancaster, Edmund, earl of (d. 1296) 195
Lancaster, Henry of Grosmont, duke of
    (d. 1361) 22, 55 n., 195 n.
Lancaster, John of Gaunt, duke of (d. 1399)
    10, 22–7, 28 n., 30, 32, 35 n., 55,
    57–62, 65, 67, 68, 106, 193, 195–201,
    203–4, 206 n., 207, 229, 277 n., 307,
    308
  Blanche of Lancaster, first wife of 22, 55
  Constance of Castile, second wife of
    76 n., 196
  Elizabeth, daughter of, *see* Holand, John,
    earl of Huntingdon, duke of Exeter
  Katherine Swynford, third wife of 76 n.,
    203
Lancaster, Thomas, earl of (d. 1322) 23 n.,
    55, 195 n., 213
  Alice Lacy, wife of 195 n.
Lancaster, John 105–6
Langton, Christopher 290
Langton, Henry 115 n.
Langton, John 43 n.
Lathbury, family of 292 n.
Latimer, Lord, *see* Neville, George
Leche, Sir Roger 32, 37, 38 n., 204, 206–7,
    211, 218 n., 222–4, 225–7, 228–30, 231,
    232, 240, 263 n.
  Anne and Dionysia, daughters of 227,
    263 n.
  Isabella, daughter of, *see* Meverell,
    Sampson
  Philip, son of 226, 227, 229, 231, 263 n.
Legbourne, John 27
Leicester 140, 167 n., 207, 222
Leicester, honour and castle of 26 n., 28,
    30 n., 35 n., 39, 43, 44, 46, 73 n., 206
    n., 260 n., 300
Leicestershire 43 n., 46, 104 n., 195 n.,
    199 n., 206, 207 n., 208, 224, 226 n.,
    241, 249, 252, 259 n., 286, 300
Lescrope, Sir Hugh 38 n.
Lestrange, Richard, Lord Strange 244 n.
Letheringham (Suff.) 106–7, 108, 113, 115
Lethum, Robert 166 n., 173–4, 177, 182–3,
    184 n.

Leventhorp, John 26 n., 28 n., 39 nn.
Lichfield (Staffs.) 214, 222
Lincoln, earls of, *see* Lacy
Lincolnshire 28, 32, 39 n., 47 n., 68 n.,
    71 n., 73, 92 n., 101, 102, 104, 209 n.,
    259 n.
Liverpool 202 n.
Lodyngton, William 69 n.
Loes hundred (Suff.) 65 n.
London 12 n., 56, 81 n., 94, 104, 122 n.,
    153, 154, 186, 187, 188 n., 244 n., 251,
    277, 278, 285 n., 300
  Tower of London 109–10, 116, 223 n.,
    251, 297 n.
London, bishop of:
  Gilbert, Robert (1436–48) 43 n.
Longford (Derbys.) 196, 286, 289, 290
Longford, family of 196, 241 n., 245 n.,
    246, 248 n., 259, 263 n., 287, 290, 292
Longford, Henry 243–4, 249
Longford, John 290
Longford, Sir Nicholas I 197, 206, 210 n.,
    226 n., 243 n.
  Ellen, daughter of, *see* Pierpoint, Sir
    Henry
  Joan, daughter of, *see* Montgomery, Sir
    Nicholas II
Longford, Sir Nicholas II 231, 249 n., 257,
    260, 283 n., 286–91, 293, 295–6, 298,
    302–3
  Edward, brother of 290, 302
  Margery, daughter of, *see* Foljambe,
    Thomas III (of Walton)
Longford, Richard 290
Lopham (Norf.) 104 n.
lordship 6–7, 8, 17–20, 24, 34, 57, 73, 78–9,
    94, 95, 97, 100, 104, 118, 130–1, 141,
    143, 146, 169–72, 175–6, 181, 209,
    226–7, 260, 264–5, 274–5, 276, 278–9,
    301–3, 304, 309, 311–12
Lothingland hundred (Suff.) 147, 148
Loudham, Sir John 242 n.
  Margaret, daughter of, *see* Foljambe,
    Thomas I (of Walton)
Lowell, Alice 117
Lowestoft (Suff.) 147
Ludford, battle of (1459) 304
Lyston, Robert 91 n., 108–9, 113 n., 114,
    116 n.

Macclesfield (Chesh.) 217
Maine 123, 153, 279
Mainwaring, Sir John 290–1 n.
March, earls of, *see* Edward IV; Mortimer
Marchington (Staffs.) 193 n.
Margaret of Anjou, queen of England 41,
    43, 44, 114, 150, 181–2, 183 n., 184–7,

277, 284, 293 n., 298–302, 304–5
Mariot, John 133–4, 136–7, 138–9
Mariot, William 132, 136
 Joan, wife of 132–3, 139 n.
Markham, John 111 n.
Matlask (Norf.) 136, 138
Matlock (Derbys.) 193 n.
Mautby, Edward 136 n.
Mautby, Margaret, *see* Paston, John
Mauveisin, family of 221
Mauveisin, Joan 220, 221 n.
Mauveisin, Robert 208
Mauveisin Ridware (Staffs.) 221 n.
Maxstoke (Warwicks.) 254, 275, 277 n.
Melbourne (Derbys.) 39, 195, 196, 204
Melbourne, Peter 196, 204, 206
Melton (Suff.) 115
Methwold (Norf.) 55
Methwold, John 58 n.
Mettingham (Suff.) 111
Meverell, family of 263, 264 n., 302–4
Meverell, John 220, 231, 263
Meverell, Sampson 263, 264–5, 266 n.,
 270–2, 274, 275, 278–9, 282–3, 295,
 297 n., 302, 303 n., 304 n.
 Isabella Leche, wife of 227, 263 n.
 Richard, brother of 303 n.
Meverell, Thomas 271, 279, 283–4, 302–3,
 304 n.
 Elizabeth Montgomery, wife of 271
Middlesex 186 n.
Moleyns, Adam 43 n.
Moleyns, Lord, *see* Hungerford, Robert
Moleyns, William 138
 Margery Bacon, wife of 138
Montague, Lord, *see* Neville, John
Montague, Thomas, earl of Salisbury 86
 wife of, *see* Chaucer, Alice, duchess of
 Suffolk
Montfort, Simon de 195 n.
Montgomery, family of 27, 196, 229, 241
 n., 261, 263 n., 287, 292
Montgomery, Sir Nicholas I 197, 202 n.,
 206, 211, 212 n., 214, 229–30, 231,
 253 n.
 Margaret, daughter of, *see* Curson, John I
 (of Kedleston)
Montgomery, Sir Nicholas II 197, 229–30,
 231, 244, 253
 Joan Longford, wife of 197
Montgomery, Nicholas III 271, 284, 286,
 298, 303
 Elizabeth, daughter of, *see* Meverell,
 Thomas
Montgomery, Nicholas IV 290 nn., 291
Morieux, Sir Thomas 58
Morley (Derbys.) 250

Morley, Lady, *see* de la Pole, Isabella
Morley, Thomas, Lord Morley 105
Mortimer, family of, earls of March 56, 65,
 68, 70, 74
Mortimer, Edmund, earl of March
 (d. 1425) 65, 79 n., 82
Mortimer, Roger, earl of March (d. 1398)
 60
Mortimer, Hugh 37, 39 n.
Mountford, William 261 n., 278 n.
Mowbray, family of, earls and dukes of
 Norfolk 56, 57, 65, 68, 71, 82, 92, 102,
 105–7, 158, 169
Mowbray, John, duke of Norfolk (d. 1432)
 79, 102, 103–4, 105 n., 106–7, 113,
 179 n.
 Katherine Neville, wife of 104, 105, 172,
 181 n.
Mowbray, John, duke of Norfolk (d. 1461)
 91, 107, 152, 158 n., 163, 187, 188, 189,
 257
 association with Thomas Daniel 120,
 122–3, 172–4, 184
 attempts to assert himself in East Anglia
 100–1, 104–5, 108–19, 126, 141, 156–7,
 160, 164, 168, 170–1, 174–5, 177–82,
 184–5, 310
 Eleanor Bourchier, wife of 180 n.
 limitations of his lordship 109–10,
 111–17, 143, 159–60, 168–76, 177, 181,
 250 n.
Mowbray, John, duke of Norfolk (d. 1476)
 189
Mowbray, John, Lord Mowbray 101
Mowbray, Thomas, earl and duke of
 Norfolk (d. 1399) 60, 101, 103, 105
 wife of, *see* Fitzalan, Elizabeth
Mowbray, Thomas, earl of Norfolk
 (d. 1405) 60, 61, 70, 101–2, 103,
 105 n., 207 n.
 Constance Holand, wife of 103, 104
Mulso, Sir Edmund 287 n.
Mundford, Osbert 122, 157, 166–8, 170 n.,
 173–4
Mynors, John 213–15, 218–19, 220, 238
Mynors, Robert 218
Mynors, Thomas 213–15, 218, 220
Mynors, William 213–15, 218, 219 n., 220

Nedding (Suff.) 86 n.
Needwood (Staffs.) 46, 193 n., 196, 211,
 229, 253, 267
Neville, George, Lord Latimer 285 n.
 Elizabeth Beauchamp, wife of 285 n.
Neville, John, Lord Montague 188 n.
Neville, Ralph, earl of Westmorland 38 n.,
 39 n., 102, 104 n., 205, 209 n.

Neville, Ralph (*cont.*):
  Anne, daughter of, *see* Stafford,
    Humphrey, earl of Stafford and duke of
    Buckingham
  Katherine, daughter of, *see* Mowbray,
    John, duke of Norfolk (d. 1432)
Neville, Richard, earl of Salisbury 46, 185,
  187–8, 280, 304
Neville, Richard, earl of Warwick 47 n.,
  185, 187–8, 285, 287–9, 293–6,
  299–300, 304–5
  Anne Beauchamp, wife of 285
Neville, Thomas, Lord Furnival 205,
  209 n., 211
  Joan Furnival, wife of 205
  Maud Neville, daughter of, *see* Talbot,
    John, Lord Furnival, earl of
    Shrewsbury (d. 1453)
Newcastle-under-Lyme (Staffs.) 26, 43 n.,
  195 n., 198 n., 200, 211, 212, 213–14,
  215, 216 n., 256
Newport (Shrops.) 220 n.
Newport (Wales) 236
Newport, Sir William 198, 204, 207–8,
  209–10, 214, 217, 218 n., 221
Norbury (Derbys.) 264
Norbury, John 24 n., 26 n.
Noreys, John 43 n.
Norfolk 280 n.
  Duchy estates in 42 n., 43 n., 53–5, 56,
    57, 130, 181, 193, 309, 310
  officeholding in 55, 63, 65–6, 69, 74–6,
    83, 87, 97–8, 104, 112, 120, 124, 136,
    157–8, 159–60, 180–1, 182, 186–9
  political society in 55–7, 59–61, 63–4, 68,
    79, 82, 93, 126–9, 130–1, 138–9, 146,
    149, 151, 153–6, 158–60, 164–5, 170–2,
    174 n., 177, 198, 274
  see also East Anglia
Norfolk, earldom and dukedom of 68, 104,
  107
  see also Bigod; Mowbray
Norfolk, Thomas of Brotherton, earl of (d.
  1338) 60, 101
Norfolk, Margaret of Brotherton, duchess of
  (d. 1399) 60, 101, 102–3, 110 n.
  Alice, sister of 101
Normandy 85 n., 254
Normanton, John 202 n.
North Greenhoe hundred (Norf.) 55
north midlands 20–1, 24
  conflict in 201, 212–16, 218–23, 233, 237,
    242–51, 261–2, 263–6, 269–73, 275–6,
    278–82, 283–98, 301–2, 303
  Duchy affinity in 36 n., 193, 196–8,
    202–4, 225–8, 232–4, 252, 255, 259–61,
    262–3, 270–1, 286–7, 300–1, 307–8, 309

Duchy estates in 43, 193–6, 199–200, 254
Duchy offices in 195–7, 210–11, 213–14,
  219, 226, 228, 229, 235, 240–1, 253–4,
  256, 257, 258 n., 267–8, 272, 275, 277,
  281, 282, 284–5, 286, 300, 301, 311
  see also Henry IV; Henry V; Henry VI;
    Stafford, Humphrey, earl of Stafford
    and duke of Buckingham
Northampton, battle of (1460) 187, 304
Northampton, earldom of 22
Northamptonshire 28, 39 n., 43 n., 46,
  226 n.
Northumberland, earls of, *see* Percy
Norwich (Norf.) 56, 62, 65, 74 n., 97,
  116 n., 148, 157 nn., 158, 159 nn., 160,
  163–4, 183 n., 188 n.
Norwich, bishopric of 69, 72, 74 n.
Norwich, bishops of:
  Alnwick, William (1426–36) 43 n., 75
  Brown, Thomas (1436–45) 113, 166
  Courtenay, Richard (1413–15) 38 n., 78
  Despenser, Henry (1370–1406) 59, 65
  Lyhert, Walter (1445–72) 43 n., 142 n.,
    168 n., 172, 175 n.
  Tottington, Alexander (1406–13) 69, 75
Norwich, Holy Trinity Priory 97, 159 n.
  John Heverlond, prior of 159 n.
Nottingham 203 n., 206 n., 207
Nottinghamshire 46, 106, 108, 195 n., 199,
  200 n., 204 n., 205, 206, 208, 209 n.,
  212 n., 224, 229, 241–50, 252, 255–6,
  273, 274, 280 n., 286, 290 n., 308
Nowell, Arthur 174 n.
Nowell, Charles 173–7, 182, 185 n.
Nowell, Otwell 174 n., 177 n.

Offton (Suff.) 73 n., 96
Ogard, Sir Andrew 99, 145, 160
Okeover (Staffs.) 196, 263, 271, 280
Okeover, family of 196, 241 n., 263
Okeover, Philip 263, 270 n., 280, 281, 282
  Thomasine Basset, wife of 263
Okeover, Thomas I 206 n., 244, 263–5,
  270, 271 n., 275, 280 n., 296 n., 302 n.
  Thomasine Sallow, second wife of 280 n.
Okeover, Thomas II 197, 270 n.
  Margaret Curson, wife of 197, 270 n.
Oldhall, Edmund 63, 66, 69, 72, 76 n., 79
Oldhall, Sir William 74 n., 76 n., 145, 157,
  177 n.
Osbern, John 175 n.
Oxburgh (Norf.) 87, 97, 98, 122, 168 n.
Oxford, earls of, *see* de Vere
Oxfordshire 90 n., 94 n.
Oxnead (Norf.) 132 n., 134 n.

Parker, Henry 122 n.

parliament 6, 16, 32 n.
  acts of 27, 32 n., 42
  Commons in 42, 114 n., 161, 281 n.
  members of 63–4, 76, 97–8, 176 n.,
    178–9, 180, 186, 200 n., 206, 207–8,
    210, 216 n., 219, 226, 227 n., 230–1,
    235–6, 240, 258, 284, 285 n.
  petitions to 16, 114 n., 122 n., 216, 280–2
Pasmere, John 214 n.
Paston (Norf.) 129, 130
Paston, family of 128–9, 144–5, 150, 151,
  154–5
  letters of 20–1, 128–9, 154–5, 163, 169,
    173–4, 184
Paston, Clement 129
Paston, Edmund 120
Paston, John 109 n., 116 n., 121 n., 125,
  126 n., 134–44, 154, 155, 156–7, 159,
  163–5, 167 n., 168 n., 172–5, 180 n.,
  182–3, 184, 187–8, 281 n.
  Margaret Mautby, wife of 123 n., 125–6,
    135, 136 n., 137 n., 138, 140, 142–4,
    151 n., 156, 187
Paston, William 56 n., 77, 107, 112, 125 n.,
  129–36, 138–41, 144 n., 145
  Agnes Barry, wife of 129
Paunfield (Essex) 76 n.
Payn, John 59, 62–3, 66
Payn, John (of Helhoughton) 59 n.
Pelham, Sir John 26 n.
Pembrigge, Sir Fulk 240 n., 271 n.
Percy, family of, earls of Northumberland
  30
Percy, Henry, earl of Northumberland (d.
  1408) 29 n., 65
  Henry 'Hotspur', Lord Percy, son of 215,
    217 n.
Percy, Henry, earl of Northumberland (d.
  1455) 43 n., 97
Percy, Thomas, earl of Worcester 65
Peshale, family of 207 n.
Peshale, Nicholas 220 n.
Peshale, Richard 220 n.
Peterborough 59
Phelip, Sir John 39 n., 71–2, 75, 86
  wife of, *see* Chaucer, Alice, duchess of
    Suffolk
Phelip, Sir William, Lord Bardolf 47, 69,
  71–2, 74, 75, 76, 79 n., 80–1, 85, 88–
  92, 96 n., 109 n., 110, 130 n., 136, 150,
  151 n., 165 n., 166
  Elizabeth, daughter of, *see* Beaumont,
    John, Viscount Beaumont
  Juliana Erpingham, mother of 69 n.
  wife of, *see* Bardolf, Joan
  Sir William Phelip, father of, 69 n.
Pickering (Yorks.) 26 n., 29, 43 n., 46

Pierpoint, Sir Henry 242–50, 251 n.
  Ellen Longford, wife of 243 n.
  Henry, son of 243, 245
Plays, Sir John 58
Pleshey (Essex) 39
Plumpton, family of 290 n.
Plumpton, Sir William 244
  Alice Foljambe, mother of 244 n.
Pole, family of 196, 241 n., 246, 259, 263 n.
Pole, John de la 244, 245 n., 248 n., 249,
  274, 288 n.
Pole, Peter de la 206
Pole, Ralph de la 242, 258–9, 260, 262,
  274, 288 n.
Polesworth (Warwicks.) 276
Pontefract (Yorks.) 26, 28–9, 30 n., 46,
  73 n.
Poynton (Chesh.) 290
Prentys, John 116 n., 163
Prisot, John 97 n., 115, 158–9
private power 4–5, 6–7, 9, 16–18, 20–1, 47,
  49, 53, 60, 73, 79, 81, 93–4, 95, 100–1,
  118, 119, 126–7, 141, 193, 198, 202,
  225, 252, 260, 264, 267, 279, 306–12
  see also lordship
Prussia 59 n.
public authority, *see* crown
Puttok, John 90, 111 n.

Radcliff, John 174, 177 n., 179 n.
Radcot Bridge, battle of (1387) 11
Ramsey Abbey 185 n.
Ramsey, Ralph 63 n., 64
Rempston, Sir Thomas 26 n., 206–7
  Margaret Foljambe (née Leek), wife of
    206 n.
Repingdon, Holy Trinity Priory 283 n.
Repton hundred (Derbys.) 193 n.
Reymerston (Norf.) 76 n.
Reymes, John 59, 62–3, 66, 79
Richard II 22–3, 30, 67, 68, 83, 152, 200 n.,
  201–2, 215, 217, 223
  Cheshire retinue 11–15, 23, 79
  retaining policy of 8–20, 23–26, 79, 201
Richard the Redeless 14–15, 18
Richmond, earldom of 22, 55, 57, 89 n., 195
Rocester (Staffs) 216
Rodmere (Norf.) 55
Rolleston (Staffs.) 193 n., 212 n.
Roos, Thomas, Lord Roos (d. 1464) 297 n.
Roos, William, Lord Roos (d. 1414) 209 n.
Rous, John 268 n.
Rous, Reginald 90, 91, 96, 98, 109, 111 n.,
  112, 115, 160, 162, 173, 186, 188
Rous, William 96 n.
royal affinity 7–20, 79, 309, 311–12
  see also Richard II

Rutland, Edmund, earl of 185 n.
Rydon (Norf.) 120–2, 140 n., 165, 172, 174 n., 184 n.
Ryplay, John 77

Sacheverell, John 302 n.
St Albans, first battle of (1455) 44, 179, 297, 298
St Lo, Giles 124
St Lo, John 43 n., 124 n.
Salisbury, bishop of:
Aiscough, William (1438–50) 43 n.
Salisbury, earl of, *see* Montague, Thomas; Neville, Richard
Sandon (Staffs.) 212, 220, 236
Savage, John 221
Saxthorpe (Norf.) 148
Say, John 124
Scales, Robert, Lord Scales (d. 1402) 60
Scales, Thomas, Lord Scales (d. 1460) 98–9, 110 n., 112 n., 116, 148–9 n., 159–60, 161–2, 164, 167–8, 169–72, 173, 177, 180, 182, 183, 184, 185–6, 187
Scarle, John 27, 30 n.
Scrope, Richard, archbishop of York, rebellion of (1405) 60, 61, 102
Scropton (Derbys.) 193 n.
Segrave, John, Lord 101
wife of, *see* Norfolk, Margaret of
· Brotherton, duchess of
Shardelowe, Sir John 74 n., 87
Sharneburne, Thomas 168 n., 178–9, 184 n.
sheriffs 64, 97, 99 n., 112, 120, 124, 157, 178, 180, 185 n., 186, 199, 204 n., 206, 208, 209, 215 n., 216, 217 n., 228, 229, 231, 235, 240, 249, 255, 258, 262, 270, 273, 274, 278 n., 285 n., 289, 291, 294
Sherrington, Walter 43 n.
Sherwood Forest 206 n.
Shirley (Derbys.) 196, 286, 290 n.
Shirley, family of 196, 241 n., 286–7, 288
Shirley, Sir Hugh 196, 197, 200 n., 204, 206, 210, 211 n., 224, 226, 229 n., 286
Beatrice, wife of 196, 210 n., 229 n.
Isabel, daughter of, *see* Cokayn, Sir John I
Shirley, Sir Ralph I 38 n., 210 n., 229 n., 231, 286
Shirley, Ralph II 244, 245, 264 n., 286, 290 n., 297, 302
Elizabeth Blount, second wife of 286 n.
Margaret Staunton, first wife of 286
Shirley, Richard 246 n.
Shirley, William 212 n.
Shrewsbury, battle of (1403) 30, 208, 210, 211 nn.
Shropshire 11, 199, 200, 217, 220 n., 228,

239 n., 240, 254 n., 300
Shuldham, Thomas 97 n., 98, 116 n., 184 n.
Smithdon hundred (Norf.) 55
Snelston (Derbys.) 264
Snettisham (Norf.) 55
Soham (Cambs.) 65, 73 n.
Soham (Suff.) 65 n., 115
Somercotes, Thomas 28 n.
Somerset 124 n., 125
Somerset, duke of, *see* Beaufort, Edmund
Somerset, John 43 n.
Somersham (Suff.) 73 n., 96
South Wingfield (Derbys.) 247, 251 n.
Southampton 75 n., 79 n.
Southwark (London) 153
Southwell (Notts.) 106
Southwell, John 179 n.
Southwell, Richard 106 n., 167 n., 173, 179 n., 180
Southwell, Robert 106
Southworth, John 263–4, 265 n., 270, 271, 282
Spain 25 n., 196, 198
Spenser, John 71–2
Stafford (Staffs.) 201, 236, 254, 275
Stafford, James 212
Margaret, daughter of, *see* Erdeswick, Thomas
Stafford, Ralph 210 n.
Stafford, Richard 285
Stafford, family of, earls of Stafford 30, 62, 200, 208–9, 233–4, 236, 274, 294
Stafford, Anne, countess of 104 n., 235, 236, 254
William Bourchier, third husband of 236 n.
Stafford, Edmund, earl of Stafford (d. 1403) 200, 207–8, 210, 211, 214–15, 219, 234, 235 n., 236, 307
Stafford, Hugh, earl of Stafford (d. 1386) 200, 202 n.
Ralph, eldest son of 202
Stafford, Humphrey, earl of Stafford and duke of Buckingham (d. 1460) 98 n., 208–9
activities at court 277–8, 280–1
Anne Neville, wife of 209 n., 305
delegation of Duchy authority in the north midlands to 46, 94 n., 252, 253–7, 259–61, 262–3, 264–5, 267–9, 270–1, 272, 273, 275, 277–9, 281, 285, 286, 294–5, 300–1, 311
Henry, duke of Buckingham, grandson of 305
Humphrey, Lord Stafford, son of 295 n., 299, 300 n.
involvement in the north midlands before

1437 234–9, 242, 244, 248, 249
involvement in the north midlands from
1437 253–90, 293–305, 311
limitations of his lordship in the north
midlands 260–3, 264–6, 269–70,
271–82, 283, 285, 294–5, 298–9, 301–2,
304, 311
Stafford, Thomas, earl of Stafford (d. 1392)
200, 201, 235 n.
Stafford, William, earl of Stafford (d. 1395)
200, 235 n.
Stafford, Sir Humphrey (of Southwick)
209–10, 213, 217 n., 221
Sir Humphrey, father of 212–13
Staffordshire:
Duchy affinity in 36 n., 118–19, 197–8,
201–2, 208–10, 213–19, 221–2, 224,
230–1
officeholding in 199, 201, 204–5, 207–12,
216, 219, 226, 227–31, 235–6, 239, 255,
258, 262, 274, 282 n., 284, 285 n., 299,
304, 308
political society in 198–200, 233–4,
234–5, 237–40, 242, 253, 255, 259–60,
269, 270–1, 272–3, 274–5, 277–9, 281,
292–3, 294–5, 299–305, 307–8, 311
see also north midlands
Stanhoe (Norf.) 184 n.
Stanley, Sir John 46
Stanley, Sir Thomas 257
Stanley, Sir John (of Knowsley) 215 n.
Thomas, son of 215 n., 216 n.
Stapleton, Sir Brian 77 n., 79 n., 87, 99 n.
Stapleton, Sir Miles 76 n., 87, 97, 99,
111 n., 159–60, 162, 163, 166, 169,
171–2, 173, 182, 188
wife of 99
Stathum, John 250
Staunton, family of 290 n.
Staunton Harold (Leics.) 286
Staveley, family of 231
Staveley, Ralph 211 n., 223
Steresacre, Richard 106, 108
Stockton (Norf.) 110–11, 112 n., 116 n.,
152, 162 n., 179
Stoke-by-Nayland (Suff.) 107
Stourton (Staffs.) 257
Stow hundred (Suff.) 85 n.
Strange, Sir John 64, 66, 72
Strange, Lord, *see* Lestrange, Richard
Streche, Joan 87 n.
Strelley, family of 290 n.
Strelley, John 206 n.
Strelley, Sir Robert 244 n.
Sudeley, Lord, *see* Butler, Ralph
Suer, Henry 43 n.
Suffield (Norf.) 65 n., 104 n.

Suffolk:
Duchy estates in 73 n., 96
officeholding in 55, 64, 69, 74–5, 83, 87,
98, 104, 112, 120, 124, 157, 159–60,
178–81, 182 n., 186–9
political society in 56–7, 60–1, 64, 68, 79,
82, 93, 126–9, 146, 149, 151, 153–6,
158–60, 164–5, 170–2, 174 n., 177, 198
see also East Anglia
Suffolk, earldom of 68
see also de la Pole; Ufford, William
Surrey 122 n., 153 n., 186 n.
Surrey, earl of, *see* Warenne, John de; duke
of, *see* Holand, Thomas
Sussex 30 n., 36, 43 n., 75 n., 122 n.
Sustead (Norf.) 125 n.
Sutton (Derbys.) 290
Sutton, family of, Lords Dudley 200, 212,
234
Sutton, John, of Dudley 211
Constance Blount, wife of 211
Sutton, John, Lord Dudley 200 n., 211,
237, 239 n., 262, 265, 274 n., 278 n.,
279, 284, 299–300, 304
Swaffham (Norf.) 89–90, 97, 157 n., 163,
164, 165, 183
Swathyng, Edmund 76 n.
Swillington, family of 27
Swynnerton, family of 207 n.
Swynnerton, Thomas 213, 214, 215, 216 n.,
218 n.

Talbot, John, Lord Furnival, earl of
Shrewsbury (d. 1453) 205 n., 209 n.,
239 n., 256 n., 282 n., 285 n., 288 n.
Margaret Beauchamp, second wife of
239 n., 285 n., 288 n.
Maud Neville, first wife of 205 n., 209 n.
Talbot, John, earl of Shrewsbury (d. 1460)
288, 296, 297 n., 299–300, 304
Tamworth (Staffs.) 278 n.
Thames Valley 88, 90 n., 91, 94, 153,
278 n.
Thetford (Norf.) 55
Thetford, William 115 n.
Throwley (Staffs.) 220, 263, 266 n.
Thweyt (Norf.) 90 n.
Tibshelf (Derbys.) 247
Tickhill (Yorks.) 29 n., 30 n., 39 n., 46,
199 n.
Titchwell (Norf.) 149 n., 150–1
Tochet, James, Lord Audley (d. 1459) 209,
239, 274, 299, 304
Tochet, John, Lord Audley (d. 1408)
200 n., 205, 206, 209, 211
Tochet, John, Lord Audley (d. 1490) 304
Tofts (Norf.) 65

Tonbridge (Kent) 277
Town Barningham (Norf.) 62, 66, 131, 135
Tresham, William 43 n.
Trevilian, John 115 n.
Trussell, Sir John 244 n.
Trussell, Sir William 271 n.
Tuddenham, Henry 122, 168 n.
Tuddenham, Sir Thomas 41 n., 80, 87, 90,
    91–2, 95–8, 99 nn., 109 n., 112 nn.,
    116, 121–2, 124, 134 n., 136, 137 n.,
    140–2, 146 n., 156–67, 169, 171–3,
    180 n., 181, 182–5, 187–8
  Alice Wodehous, wife of 80, 121, 122 n.,
    137 n., 166 n.
  Margaret Harling, mother of 146 n.
Tunstead (Norf.) 55
Tutbury, honour and castle of
    (Staffs./Derbys.) 28, 41, 43, 44, 55, 57,
    73 n., 193, 195–9, 201–3, 210 n., 219 n.,
    225, 228, 230, 232, 234, 240–1, 242,
    246, 248 n., 249, 255, 260–1, 267, 298,
    300–1, 307
  offices at 26, 32, 37, 46, 195–6, 197, 204,
    206 n., 211, 226, 229–30, 235, 240,
    253–4, 255–6, 258 n., 259–61, 267–9,
    272, 275, 277, 281, 284, 285, 287, 288,
    295
Tutbury priory 207
Tutbury, Thomas 27
Twyford, Ralph 286
Tymperley, John 110 n., 112, 116 n.
Tyrell, Sir John 89, 186 n.
Tyrell, William 186

Ufford, William, earl of Suffolk 60, 83, 101,
    152
  Joan, first wife of 101
  Isabel, second wife of 84 n.
Ulveston, John 98, 157, 159, 162, 176 n.
Usflete, family of 27
Uttoxeter (Staffs.) 193 n., 212, 213, 214

Vale Royal, abbey of 254 n.
Vampage, John 43 n.
Venables, Hugh 217 n., 222 n.
Venables, Ralph 222 n.
Venables, Sir Richard 215
Venables, William 215–16, 217, 221–2
Vergeons, John 76 n.
Vernon, family of 246, 283, 292–4
Vernon, Edmund 290–1
Vernon, Sir Richard 207 n., 219 n., 223,
    228–9, 231, 236–8, 239–41, 242, 244–9,
    251, 256–8, 271–5, 278–9, 282–3, 284,
    285
  Agnes, daughter of, see Cokayn, John III
  Fulk, son of 240, 257 n., 271, 282 n., 284

  Sir Richard, father of 223
  Richard, son of 240, 282 n.
  Thurstan, son of 279–80
  William, brother of 223 n., 246 n.
Vernon, Roger 290–1, 298
Vernon, William 272, 282, 283 n., 285,
    288 n., 290–1, 295, 296, 298–9, 303,
    304 n.
Vita Ricardi Secundi, see Evesham, Monk of

Wales 11, 17, 43 n., 70, 71, 89, 217, 236,
    239 n., 241 n., 277 n.
Wallingford (Oxfs.) 88–9, 90 n., 91
Walsall, William 201, 208, 209 n., 210 n.,
    217 n.
Walsingham (Norf.) 132 n., 158–9, 160
Walsingham, Thomas 13
Walton (Derbys.) 197, 242 n., 244 n.
Warenne, John de, earl of Surrey 55
Warwick, earls of, see Beauchamp; Neville
Warwickshire 104 n., 198, 199 n., 204–5 n.,
    206 n., 207 n., 220 n., 231 n., 233 n.,
    234–5, 237–9, 253, 254, 261, 262, 267,
    269, 275–6, 277 n., 278, 280 n., 281 n.,
    294, 295–6, 300, 301–2, 303 n.
Waterton, Sir Hugh 26 n.
Waterton, Robert 26, 37, 214
Wayte, William 116 n., 144 n., 163, 164, 167
Welles (Norf.) 76 n.
Wendesley, family of 197
Wendesley, Sir Thomas 26, 201, 202 n.,
    204 n., 206, 211 n., 217, 223 n.
Wentworth, Philip 124, 126, 150–1, 160,
    162, 178, 179 n., 182 n., 184, 185 n.,
    186–8
West Beckham (Norf.) 135–6
Westmorland, earl of, see Neville, Ralph
Weston by Baldock (Herts.) 113, 114 n.,
    116
Weyland, Sir John 87 n.
Whitgreve, Robert 235–8, 255, 256, 258, 274
Wichingham, Edmund 99, 188
Wichingham, Nicholas 66
Wickham Market (Suff.) 115 n.
Wicklewood (Norf.) 116 n.
Wighton (Norf.) 55
Willoughby, family of 197 n., 290 n.,
    291–2 n.
Willoughby, Edmund 291–2 n.
Willoughby, Hugh I 291–2 n.
Willoughby, Hugh II 197 n., 292 n.
  Joan Dabridgecourt, wife of 197 n.,
    292 n.
Willoughby, Sir Hugh III 244 n., 292 n.
  Robert, son of 292 n.
Willoughby, Sir Richard 197 n., 291–2 n.
  Maud, wife of 197 n., 292 n.

Wilton-by-Blofield (Norf.) 166 n.

Wiltshire 125, 137

Wiltshire, earl of, *see* Butler, James

Wingerworth (Derbys.) 197

Wingfield (Suff.) 83 n.

Wingfield, Sir John 83
  Katherine, daughter of, *see* de la Pole,
    Michael, earl of Suffolk (d. 1389)

Wingfield, Sir Robert 91 n., 106–7, 108–10,
  112–16, 180
  Elizabeth, daughter of, *see* Brandon,
    William
  Elizabeth Goushill, wife of 106
  John, son of 116 n., 178, 180, 182 n.
  Robert, son of 114–15, 116 n., 180
  Thomas, son of 116 n.

Winter, Edmund 79–80, 106, 131–6, 137 n.,
  138, 139 n., 141
  Eleanor, daughter of, *see* Heydon, John
  John, son of 138, 139 n.

Winter, John 58 n., 62–3, 66, 67, 69, 71–2,
  79–80, 130, 131

Winter, William 56 n., 66, 131

Wirksworth (Derbys.) 193 n., 195 n., 196
  n., 296 n.

Wodehous, Henry 121–2, 140, 165, 168,
  173, 174 n., 184 n.

Wodehous, Jerome 122 n.

Wodehous, John I 39 nn., 71, 72, 75–6, 80,
  90, 121–2, 130, 141 n., 158
  Alice, daughter of, *see* Tuddenham, Sir
    Thomas
  Alice, wife of 80, 141

Wodehous, John II 122

Wolf, Sir William 74 n.

Wollaton (Notts.) 197 n., 291 n.

Wolverhampton (Staffs.) 218, 219 n.

Worcester, bishop of:
  Carpenter, John (1443–76) 43 n.

Worcester, earl of, *see* Percy, Thomas

Worcestre, William 74, 140 n., 172

Wormegay (Norf.) 60, 68–9, 70, 77, 81, 86,
  88–90

Writtle (Essex) 277, 299

Wyndham, John 112 n., 116–17, 173, 184 n.,
  185 n., 186, 187

Yelverton, William 111 n., 142 n., 157,
  159 n., 162–5, 168, 274 n.

York 12 n.

York, archbishops of:
  Booth, William (1452–64) 299 n.
  Kemp, John (1425–52) 43 n., 249, 281 n.
  see also Scrope, Richard

York, Edward, duke of (d. 1415) 38 n., 69,
  70 n.

York, Richard, duke of (d. 1460) 41, 56,
  74, 82, 99, 157, 160, 163, 167, 177–83,
  184 n., 185, 187–8, 280, 287–93,
  295–300, 303–5
  Elizabeth, daughter of, *see* de la Pole,
    John, duke of Suffolk

Yorkshire 26 n., 27, 29 n., 39 n., 43 n., 46,
  68 n., 124, 150, 195 n., 199 n., 209 n.,
  256 n., 300

Zouche, Sir John 244 n.